BRADFORD'S
CROSSWORD
SOLVER'S
LISTS

HarperCollins Publishers
Westerhill Road
Bishopbriggs
Glasgow
G64 2QT
Great Britain

Third Edition 2011

Reprint 10 9 8 7 6 5 4 3 2 1 0

© HarperCollins Publishers 2004, 2008, 2011

ISBN 978-0-00-744136-5

Collins® is a registered trademark of HarperCollins Publishers Limited

www.collinslanguage.com

A catalogue record for this book is available from the British Library

Technical Production Coordination by Thomas Callan
Typeset by Aptara in India

Printed by LEGO Spa,
Lavis (Trento), Italy

EDITORS
Gerry Breslin
Freddy Chick

CONSULTANT EDITOR
Anne R. Bradford

FOR THE PUBLISHER
Lucy Cooper
Kerry Ferguson
Elaine Higgleton

Note

Preface

Since the *Bradford's Crossword Solver's Dictionary* was first published in 1986, it has proved to be an invaluable aid for countless cruciverbalists. Compiled as a daily task since 1957 by Anne R. Bradford, a true crossword lover and an active member of the Crossword Club who still solves around 20 crosswords a week, the book has gone from strength to strength over a number of editions, offering the user over 200,000 crossword solutions as well as advice on solving cryptic clues. The latest edition has proved to be the most successful and popular yet.

The *Bradford's Crossword Solver's Lists* offers all crossword solvers the essential companion to the *Bradford's Crossword Solver's Dictionary*. It provides hundreds of word lists covering a wide range of subjects, to help with solving tricky crossword clues.

This brand-new addition to the Bradford's crossword series has been compiled from the Collins thesaurus database, with additional material and advice from Anne Bradford, and gives useful word lists on hundreds of subjects, from **Artists**, **Birds**, and **Collectors** to **Winds**, **Worms**, and **Zoology**. Where the entry consists of a straight list of vocabulary on a given subject – for example at **Fish** – the lists are arranged by number of letters and then alphabetically, so that you can spot the word you need to complete your grid quickly. Where an entry includes additional useful information – for example, at **Capitals**, where both the capital and its country are shown – the list is arranged in columns to allow you to find the relevant material which will help you to solve your clue. The book therefore provides both vocabulary lists and encyclopedic information – both of which are invaluable for crossword solving.

Solving Crossword Clues

Crossword puzzles tend to be basically 'quick' or 'cryptic'. A 'quick' crossword usually relies on a one or two-word clue which is a simple definition of the answer required. As has been stated, many words have different meanings, so that the clue 'ball' could equally well lead to the answer 'sphere', 'orb' or 'dance'. The way to solve 'quick' crosswords is to press on until probable answers begin to interlink, which is a good sign that you are on the right track.

'Cryptic' crosswords are another matter. Here the clue usually consists of a basic definition, given at either the beginning or end of the clue, together with one or more definitions of parts of the answer. Here are some examples taken from alltime favourites recorded over the years:

1. *'Tradesman who bursts into tears'* (**Stationer**)

   Tradesman is a definition of stationer. Bursts is cleverly used as an indication of an anagram, which into tears is of stationer.

2. *'Sunday school tune'* (**Strain**)

   Here Sunday is used to define its abbreviation S, school is a synonym for train, and put together they give strain, which is a synonym of tune.

3. *'Result for everyone when head gets at bottom'* (**Ache**) (used as a 'down' clue)

   This is what is known as an '& lit' clue, meaning that the setter has hit on a happy composition which could literally be true. Everyone here is a synonym for each, move the head (first letter) of the word to the bottom, and the answer is revealed, the whole clue being the definition of the answer in this case.

4. *'Tin out East'* (**Sen**)

   In this example, tin, implying 'money', requires its chemical symbol Sn to go out(side) East, or its abbreviation, E, the whole clue being a definition of a currency (sen) used in the East.

5. *'Information given to communist in return for sex'* (**Gender**)

Information can be defined as gen; communist is almost always red, in return indicates 'reversed', leading to gen-der, a synonym for sex.

6. *'Row about no enclosure of this with sardines'* (**Tin-opener**)

Row is a synonym for tier, about indicates 'surrounding', no enclosure can be no pen, leading to ti-no pen-er, and another '& lit' clue.

7. *'Cake-sandwiches-meat, at Uncle Sam's party'* (**Clambake**)

Meat here is lamb, sandwiches is used as a verb, so we have C-lamb-ake, which is a kind of party in America. Uncle Sam or US is often used to indicate America.

8. *'Initially passionate meeting of boy and girl could result in it'* (**Pregnancy**)

Initially is usually a sign of a first letter, in this case 'p' for passionate + Reg (a boy) and Nancy (a girl), and another clever '& lit'.

With 'cryptic' clues the solver needs to try to analyse the parts to see what he or she is looking for – which word or words can be the straight definition, and which refer to the parts or hint at anagrams or other subterfuges. Whilst it would be unrealistic to claim total infallibility, practice has shown that in most crosswords some 90% of the answers are to be found in the *Bradford's Crossword Solver's Dictionary* and the *Bradford's Crossword Solver's Lists*.

Anne R. Bradford

How to Use the Book

This book gives useful vocabulary lists and information on hundreds of subjects which are likely to come up as part of crossword clues. The lists are arranged alphabetically by subject, so finding the one you want is as quick and easy as looking up a dictionary. A full table of subjects that appear under multiple headings or are integrated into other lists is given in **Finding the Right List**.

Where the entry consists of a straightforward list of words relevant to a given subject, such as **Pigs**, **Pasta**, or **Birds**, the words are arranged by length, with all three-letter words grouped together in alphabetical order, then all four-letter words, then all five-letter words, and so on.

Where an entry includes additional useful information – for example at **US States**, where not only the name of each state is shown, but also its **abbreviation**, **zip code**, **nickname**, and **capital** – the list is arranged in columns to allow you to find the relevant information you need to solve your clue. The book thus provides both vocabulary and encyclopaedic information, set out in whichever way will be most helpful to the user.

Lists such as **Artists** and **Composers**, which consist of people's names, are arranged by length of the surname, or whichever part of the name the person is best known by, and then alphabetically within each length group. First names and other more 'optional' elements, such as nicknames and initials, are shown after the main part of the name, in italics. You can therefore find the person you are looking for straight away, and then choose the part of their name which is relevant to your crossword solution.

Cross-references are also included wherever appropriate at the ends of entries, so that if you happen to be looking up, for example, the entry for **Animals**, you can see straight away that there are also related lists at **Amphibians**, **Birds**, **Insects**, and so on, which may provide further useful information to help you solve your clue. The cross-references are introduced by the line 'See also:' and each is preceded by the symbol ➤ with the cross-referenced list's title shown in bold type.

About the Author

Anne Bradford's love of words began to make itself evident even in her schooldays, when, as Head Girl of her school, she instituted a novel punishment – instead of making rulebreakers write lines, she had them write out pages from a dictionary, on the grounds that this was a more useful exercise. Little did she know this was soon to be her own daily routine!

In time, crosswords became a magnificent obsession for Anne. All lovers of crosswords can understand the irresistible lure of solving them, but Anne's interest went much deeper than most people's, and when she stopped work in 1957 to have her first child, she found herself starting to note down answers to particularly tricky clues as an aid to memory, in case she should come across them again in another puzzle. It was from this simple beginning that this crossword dictionary evolved.

Over the space of 25 years, Anne continued to build on her collection of solutions, analysing every crossword clue as she solved it and adding it to her steadily growing bank of entries. This unique body of material eventually reached such proportions that she had the idea of offering it to her fellow crossword-solvers as a reference book, and since then, the book has gone from strength to strength, providing valuable help to countless cruciverbalists over a number of editions.

Anne Bradford continues to devote time each day to solving crosswords, averaging some 20 a week – both quick and cryptic – and still avidly collects new solutions for her Crossword Solver's Dictionaries at a rate of around 150 a week, compiling each solution by hand (without the use of a computer!) This latest edition therefore includes much new material.

The Crossword Club

If you are interested in crosswords, you might like to consider joining the Crossword Club. Membership is open to all who enjoy tackling challenging crosswords and who appreciate the finer points of clue-writing and grid construction. The Club's magazine, Crossword, contains two prize puzzles each month. A sample issue and full details are available on request.

The Crossword Club
Coombe Farm
Awbridge
Romsey, Hants.
SO51 0HN
UK

email: bh@thecrosswordclub.co.uk
website address: www.thecrosswordclub.co.uk

Contents

Bradford's Crossword Solver's Lists contains hundreds of lists and thousands upon thousands of possible solutions. No matter what corner of human knowledge or nomenclature a clue is directing you towards, this book will have an answer.

The lists are arranged alphabetically by subject. A catalogue of all the subject headings is provided below so that you can survey them at a glance and quickly find the list for you.

D

J

K

L

M

Q

R

S

T

U

Finding the Right List

We have tried to list every subject under the most logical heading but, inevitably, some items will not appear under the heading you first look for. The following shows where subjects that are covered by this book but which do not appear under eponymous headings can be found.

A

abuse *see* Insults and terms of abuse

academia *see* Colleges ➜Degrees ➜Education terms ➜Ivy League universities

accommodation *see* Homes

accountancy *see* Economics ➜Trade terms

aeronautics *see* Aircraft ➜Aviation terms

aeroplane *see* Aircraft ➜Airline Flight Codes ➜Aviation terms

afflictions *see* Diseases ➜Skin, afflictions of

agronomy *see* Agriculturalists ➜Agricultural terms

air *see* Atmosphere, layers of

alliances *see* European Union

American football *see* Football: Terms used in American football

American universities *see* Ivy League universities

amusements *see* Entertainment

anatomy *see* Blood cells ➜Body, parts of ➜Bones ➜Brain, parts of ➜Ear, parts of ➜Eye ➜Glands ➜Heart, parts of ➜Humours of the body ➜Membranes ➜Muscles ➜Nerves ➜Organs ➜Teeth ➜Veins

Ancient Greece *see* Gods and Goddesses ➜Gorgons ➜Graces ➜Greeks ➜Harpies ➜Hercules, Labours of ➜Muses

ancient languages *see* Languages

Ancient Rome *see* Emperors ➜Festivals ➜Furies ➜Gods and Goddesses ➜Muses

animal years *see* Zodiac: Chinese animal years

animation *see* Cartoon characters ➜Dwarfs

anthropology *see* Inhabitants ➜Peoples

antiques *see* Chinaware ➜Furniture

Apocrypha *see* Bible

apparel *see* Caps →Clothing →Coats and cloaks →Dresses →Hats →Hoods →Jackets →Scarves →Shirts →Shoes and Boots →Skirts →Socks and Tights →Suits →Sweaters →Ties and cravats →Trousers and shorts →Underwear

apparitions *see* Supernatural

arachnids *see* Spiders and other arachnids

aristocracy *see* Nobility

arithmetic *see* Mathematics

army *see* Aircraft →British Forces →Crosses →History →Military ranks →Regimental nicknames

aromatherapy *see* Medicine: Branches of alternative medicine →Oils

artillery *see* Guns →Warfare terms →Weapons

Association football *see* Football: Terms used in (association) football

astrophysicists *see* Astronomy

attire *see* Caps →Clothing →Coats and cloaks →Dresses →Hats →Hoods →Jackets →Scarves →Shirts →Shoes and boots →Skirts →Socks and tights →Suits →Sweaters →Ties and cravats →Trousers and shorts →Underwear

Australia *see* Marsupials →Prime Ministers: Australian Prime Ministers

Australian football *see* Football: Terms used in Australian Rules Football

authors *see* Novelists →Poetry: Poets →Writers

automobiles *see* Cars

awards *see* Cups →Film and television →Medals

Aztec *see* Emperors →Gods and Goddesses

B

bathroom *see* Household items

battle *see* Armour →Battles →Guns →Warfare terms →Weapons

beasts *see* →Giants and giantesses →Gorgons →Harpies →Hercules, labours of →Monsters →Mythology: Characters in classical mythology, Mythological creatures

bedroom *see* Beds →Household items

beliefs *see* Religion: Religions, Religious books

beverages *see* Alcohols →Drinks →Wines

Biblical figures *see* Angels →Apocalypse, Four Horsemen of →Giants and giantesses →Lovers

billiards *see* Snooker and billiards terms

biography *see* Diarists

birds of prey *see* Prey, birds of
birthstones *see* Birthstones →Gemstones →Stones
board games *see* Games
boas *see* Snakes
boats *see* Boats and ships →Ships, parts of
boiled sweets *see* Confectionery
bombs *see* Explosives
books *see* Books →Religion: Religious books →Works of literature and
music
boots *see* Shoes and boots
boroughs *see* London, boroughs of
bovine *see* Cattle, breeds of →Cows
breeds *see* Cats →Cattle, breeds of →Dogs →Horses →Pigs →Rabbits and
hares →Sheep
Britain *see* Counties →Prime Ministers: British Prime Ministers
British Empire, former colonies *see* Commonwealth members
broadcasting *see* Cinema and television →Film and television
Broadway *see* Theatre terms
Buddhism *see* Buddhism →Monastic orders →Monks →Religion
buildings *see* Arches →Architecture →Castles →Cathedrals
→Entertainment: Places of entertainment →Homes →Religion: Religious
buildings →Roofing
business *see* Business people →Economics

C

cabins *see* Huts
calculus *see* Mathematics
Cambridge *see* Oxbridge Colleges
Canada *see* Prime Ministers: Canadian Prime Ministers →Provinces:
Provinces of Canada
cancers *see* Tumours
canine *see* Dogs
cantons *see* Swiss cantons
Capitoline *see* Rome, the seven hills of
cash *see* Coins →Currencies
catalysts *see* Enzymes

combat *see* Clubs and bats ➜Fencing terms ➜Martial arts ➜Military ranks ➜Missiles ➜Warfare terms ➜Weapons

commerce *see* Economics ➜Trade terms

Communism *see* Political parties

composition *see* Music: types of composition

compounds *see* Alcohols ➜Alloys ➜Compounds

conditions *see* Diseases ➜Skin, afflictions of

constellations *see* Galaxies ➜Stars and constellations

constituencies *see* London, boroughs of

constrictors *see* Snakes

construction *see* Bridges ➜Engineering

contact sports *see* American football teams ➜Ball games ➜Boxing weights ➜Fencing terms ➜Football ➜Football: Football clubs ➜Football: Footballers ➜Martial arts ➜Rugby terms ➜Winter sports

contagions *see* Diseases ➜Skin, afflictions of

containers *see* Bottles ➜Cases ➜Champagne bottles ➜Containers for liquids

cosmology *see* Astronomy: Astronomy terms ➜Comets ➜Galaxies ➜Meteor showers ➜Planets ➜Satellites ➜Stars and constellations

costume *see* Caps ➜Clothing ➜Coats and cloaks ➜Dresses ➜Hats ➜Hoods ➜Jackets ➜Scarves ➜Shirts ➜Shoes and boots ➜Skirts ➜Socks and tights ➜Suits ➜Sweaters ➜Ties and cravats ➜Trousers and shorts ➜Underwear

couples *see* Lovers

court *see* Crime terms ➜Law

crabs *see* Crustaceans

criminology *see* Crime terms

crockery *see* Household items ➜Pottery

crops *see* Rice and other cereals

cuisine *see* Apples ➜Beans and other pulses ➜Cakes and pastries ➜Cheeses ➜Chefs ➜Confectionery ➜Cookery ➜Curries ➜Desserts ➜Dishes ➜Herbs ➜Meals ➜Meats ➜Mushrooms and other edible fungi ➜Nuts ➜Oils ➜Pasta ➜Pastry ➜Potatoes ➜Sauces ➜Seafood ➜Shellfish

cultivation *see* Agriculturalists ➜Agricultural terms

culture *see* Alphabets ➜American and British Equivalents ➜Dialects

cured meats *see* Meats ➜Sausages

cutlery *see* Household items

D

dairy *see* Agricultural terms ➜Cattle and other artiodactyls ➜Cattle, breeds of ➜Cheeses ➜Cows

dates *see* Calendars

decorating *see* Household items

deer *see* Cattle and other artiodactyls

deity *see* Actaeon's Hounds ➜Gods and Goddesses

democracy *see* Governments ➜Political parties ➜Presidents ➜Prime Ministers

denominations *see* Christian denominations and sects ➜Hindu denominations and sects ➜Muslim denominations and sects

dentistry *see* Teeth

départements *see* Regions, administrative

derogatory terms *see* Insults

design *see* Art ➜Engineering ➜Furniture

desks *see* Tables and desks

digital *see* Communications ➜Computer games ➜Computers ➜Internet domain names ➜Programming languages

dignitaries *see* Officials

directions *see* Compass and cardinal points

disinfectant *see* Alcohols

Disney *see* Cartoon characters ➜Cats: Famous cats ➜Dwarfs

distillation *see* Alcohols ➜Whiskies

doctors *see* Medicine: Medical practitioners and specialists

doctrines *see* Philosophy

dogs *see* Carnivores ➜Dogs

double-acts *see* Comedians

drama *see* Actors ➜Shakespeare

drawing *see* Art

dressings *see* Sauces

dwellers *see* Inhabitants ➜Peoples

dyes *see* Colours ➜Dyes ➜Pigments

E

earthenware *see* Pottery

educational establishments *see* Colleges ➜Oxbridge Colleges

eels *see* Fish
Egyptian *see* Gods and Goddesses
elected officials *see* Officials →Parliaments
epochs *see* Geology
equations *see* Mathematics
equipment *see* Apparatus →Cutting tools
equitation *see* Equestrianism →Horses
energy *see* Electronics terms
England *see* Counties
entertainers *see* Comedians →Jazz: Jazz musicians
eras *see* Geology
ethereal *see* Supernatural
ethnic minorities *see* Inhabitants →Peoples
events *see* Festivals →History
Everest *see* Mountains
executive *see* Officials

F

fanatics *see* Collectors and enthusiasts →Mania
farm(ing) *see* Agriculturalists →Agricultural terms →Cattle and other
artiodactyls →Cattle, breeds of →Cheeses →Pigs
fashion *see* Caps →Clothing →Coats and cloaks →Dresses →Hats →Hoods
→Jackets →Scarves →Shirts →Shoes and boots →Skirts →Socks and tights
→Suits →Sweaters →Ties and cravats →Trousers and shorts →Underwear
fears *see* Phobias
feast days *see* Religion: Religious festivals
federal republics of Russia *see* Russian federal republics
feline *see* Cats
felonies *see* Crime terms
fences *see* Agricultural terms
fermentation *see* Alcohols
fiction *see* Diarists →Dramatists →Musketeers →Novelists →Poetry
→Shakespeare →Works of literature and music →Writers
films *see* Actors →Cats: Famous cats →Cinema and television →Directors
→Dwarfs
finance *see* Economics →Trade terms

fireworks *see* Explosives

flight *see* Aircraft →Airline Flight Codes →Aviation terms

folklore *see* Heroes →Monsters

fonts *see* Typefaces

food *see* Apples →Beans and other pulses →Cakes and Pastries →Cheese →Chefs →Confectionery →Cookery →Curries →Desserts →Dishes →Eating habits →Fruits →Herbs →Meals →Meats →Mushrooms and other edible fungi →Nuts →Pasta →Pastry →Potatoes →Rice and other cereals →Sauces →Sausages →Seafood →Shellfish

footwear *see* Shoes and boots →Socks and tights

foresight *see* Divination

formal dress *see* Coats and cloaks →Dresses →Hats →Jackets →Ties and cravats

forms *see* Poetry →Verse forms →Literature

formulae *see* Mathematics

fort(ress) *see* Castles

fortune telling *see* Divination

fossil fuels *see* Hydrocarbons

France *see* Regions, administrative →Time: French Revolutionary calendar

fraternities *see* Clubs

French *see* Foreign words and phrases

fuel *see* Hydrocarbons →Oils

furnishings *see* Carpets and rugs

future *see* Divination

G

gambling *see* Bets and betting systems →Cards →Games →Races

game *see* Fowl

garments *see* Caps →Clothing →Coats and cloaks →Dresses →Hats →Hoods →Jackets →Scarves →Shirts →Shoes and boots →Skirts →Socks and tights →Suits →Sweaters →Ties and cravats →Trousers and shorts →Underwear

gastropods *see* Snails, slugs and other gastropods

gateau *see* Cakes and Pastries

gates *see* Agricultural terms

genres *see* Music: Classical music genres

gentry *see* Nobility

geographical features *see* Bays →Canals →Capes →Capitals →Channels →Cities →Continents →Countries →Deserts →Earth's crust →Hills →Islands and island groups →Lakes, lochs and loughs →Peninsulas →Ports →Rivers →Seas and oceans →Sounds →Straits →Towns →Volcanoes →Waterfalls

German(y) *see* Foreign words and phrases →Regions, administrative

germs *see* Parasites

glands *see* Glands →Hormones

glasses *see* Cups and other drinking vessels →Glasses

glues *see* Resins

goddesses *see* Fates →Furies →Gods and Goddesses →Graces

grammar *see* Figures of speech →Grammatical cases

Great Britain *see* Counties

Greek *see* Alphabets →Ancient cities →Foreign words and phrases →Gods and Goddesses →Gorgons →Graces →Greek figures →Harpies →Hercules, Labours of →Muses

Gregorian *see* Time: Gregorian calendar

groups *see* Collective nouns

growths *see* Skin, afflictions of →Tumours

guilds *see* Clubs

gulls *see* Sea birds

gums *see* Resins

H

habits *see* Eating habits

Hades *see* Rivers of Hell

handiwork *see* Crafts

hardware *see* Communications →Computers: Computer parts, Computer terms →Cutting tools

hares *see* Rabbits and hares

headwear *see* Caps →Hats →Hoods

hearing *see* Ear, parts of

Heaven *see* Angels

Hell *see* Rivers of Hell

Hellenism *see* Actaeon's Hounds

herbivores *see* Cattle →Dinosaurs

hide *see* Leather
Hinduism *see* Gods and Goddesses →Religion
hobbies *see* Crafts →Embroidery stitches →Knitting stitches
holidays *see* Airline flight codes →Airports →Festivals
Hollywood *see* Actors →Film and television
homeware *see* Carpets and rugs →Chinaware →Cupboards and cabinets
→Furniture →Household items
hominids *see* Mammals, extinct
honour *see* Medals
horoscope *see* Astrology →Zodiac
horse racing *see* Racing
horticulture *see* Flowers →Plants
hosiery *see* Underwear
houses *see* Homes →Huts

I

ideology *see* Philosophy
idioms *see* American and British Equivalents
Iliad *see* Graces
illnesses *see* Diseases →Parasites
Incan *see* Gods and Goddesses
industry *see* Electronics terms →Engineering →Fabrics
infantry *see* Regimental nicknames
infections *see* Diseases
information *see* Newspapers and magazines
Information Technology *see* Communications →Computers →Internet
domain names →Programming languages
institutions *see* Schools
instruments, musical *see* Music: Musical instruments →Orchestral
instruments
Internet *see* Communications →Internet domain names
Islam *see* Festivals →Muslim denominations and sects →Time: Muslim
calendar
isles *see* Islands and island groups
Italian *see* Foreign words and phrases
Italy *see* Regions, administrative

J

jewellery *see* Gemstones
jobs *see* Occupations
Judaism *see* Festivals →Religion →Time: Jewish calendar

K

Kilimanjaro *see* Mountains
killers *see* Murderers
King Arthur *see* Arthurian legend →Knights
kitchen *see* Household items
knives *see* Household items →Swords and other weapons with blades

L

landscape *see* Deserts →Geography →Hills →Mountains →Peninsulas
→Volcanoes
language *see* Alphabets →American and British Equivalents →Dialects
→Figures of speech →Foreign words and phrases →Grammatical cases
→Homophones
Latin *see* Foreign words and phrases
leaders *see* Generals →Presidents →Prime Ministers
leagues *see* American football teams
leaves *see* Palms →Plants
legend *see* Actaeon's Hounds →Ancient cities →Arthurian legend →Fates
→Furies →Giants and giantesses →Gods and Goddesses →Gorgons
→Graces →Greeks →Harpies →Hercules, Labours of →Heroes →Monsters
→Muses →Rivers of Hell →Seven against Thebes →Wonders of the
ancient world
legislation *see* Law
leisure *see* Entertainment
letters *see* Alphabets
lexicography *see* Alphabets
lingerie *see* Underwear
lochs *see* Lakes, lochs and loughs
loughs *see* Lakes, lochs and loughs
love *see* Affection, terms of

M

machinery *see* Agricultural terms →Aircraft parts →Apparatus →Cutting tools

mammals *see* Animals →Anteaters →Antelopes →Carnivores →Cats →Cattle →Cows →Dinosaurs →Dogs →Horses →Mammals, extinct →Marsupials →Rabbits and hares →Rodents →Shrews and other insectivores →Seals

mapping *see* Compass →Continents →Counties →Countries →Geography

marinade *see* Cookery →Sauces

marine life *see* Algae →Crustaceans →Fish →Seals →Sea mammals →Seaweeds →Sharks →Shellfish →Whales and dolphins

marriage *see* Anniversaries

masonry *see* Arches →Architecture →Stone

maths *see* Mathematics →Units

Mayan *see* Gods and Goddesses

meals *see* Cookery →Dishes →Meals

measurements *see* Units →Weather: weather measuring instruments →Weights and measures

mechanics *see* Aircraft parts →Engineering

media *see* Communications →Newspapers and magazines

medication *see* Drugs and drug terms

medieval *see* Armour →Arthurian legend →Heraldry terms →Knights

menswear *see* Ties and cravats

mental health *see* Mania →Phobias →Psychology

mental illness *see* Mania →Phobias →Psychology

Mesopotamia *see* Ancient Cities

metamorphoses *see* Actaeon's Hounds →Artemis

meteorology *see* Weather: Meteorological terms

metric *see* Weights and measures: Metric system

mice *see* Rodents

military *see* Aircraft →British Forces →Crosses →History →Military ranks →Regimental nicknames

modes *see* Music: Musical modes

monarchy *see* Castles →Emperors →History →Kings →Queens

money *see* Coins →Currencies →Economics

moons *see* Satellites

motor racing *see* Grand Prix circuits →Racing

movements *see* Poetry: Poetry movements and groupings ➔Religion: Religious buildings

movies *see* Actors ➔Cinema and television ➔Directors ➔Dwarfs ➔Film and television

mugs *see* Cups and other drinking vessels

mushrooms *see* Fungi ➔Mushrooms and other edible fungi

music(ians) *see* Composers ➔Jazz: Jazz Musicians ➔Jazz: Jazz terms ➔Works of literature and music

N

names *see* First names

nations *see* Countries ➔Flags ➔Republics

natural history *see* Fossils ➔Mammals, extinct ➔Time

nature *see* Flowers

nautical terms *see* Ropes ➔Ships, parts of

navy *see* Military ranks ➔Regimental nicknames

nebula *see* Galaxies ➔Stars and constellations

New Testament *see* Bible

New Zealand *see* Prime Ministers: New Zealand Prime Ministers ➔States and Territories: Territories of New Zealand

nicknames *see* Places and their nicknames ➔Regimental nicknames

nobility *see* Emperors ➔Kings ➔Nobility ➔Queens ➔Rulers

non-contact sports *see* Sports

norse *see* Gods and Goddesses

Northern Ireland *see* Counties

notes *see* Notes and rests

novels *see* Literature ➔Works of literature and music

numbers *see* Roman numerals

numerals *see* Roman numerals

O

ocean *see* Algae ➔Channels ➔Crustaceans ➔Fish

offences *see* Crime terms

offensive *see* Insults

ointments *see* Resins

Old Testament *see* Bible
Olympics *see* Athletic events
operations *see* Surgical operations
orchestra *see* Composers →Orchestral instruments
organs *see* Heart, parts of
orienteering *see* Compass
ornaments *see* Chinaware
outfits *see* Clothing
outhouses *see* Huts
Ovid *see* Actaeon's Hounds
ovine *see* Sheep
Oxford *see* Oxbridge Colleges

P

Pagan *see* Festivals
painters *see* Artists
painting *see* Art →Colours →Pigments
palaeontology *see* Mammals, extinct
Palatine *see* Rome, the seven hills of
pants *see* Underwear
Paradise *see* Angels
particles *see* Subatomic particles
party games *see* Games
pastimes *see* Crafts →Embroidery stitches
people *see* Inhabitants →Peoples
periodicals *see* Newspapers and magazines
periods *see* Geology →Time
pharmaceuticals *see* Alcohols →Drugs and drug terms
phenomena *see* Weather: Weather phenomena
philosophers *see* Greeks →Philosophy
phonetics *see* Homophones
photography *see* Cameras →Photography
phrases *see* Foreign words and phrases
physicists *see* Astronomy: Astronomers →Physics: Physicists
physics *see* Astronomy →Comets →Electronics terms →Engineering
pictures *see* Photography

pigments *see* Colours →Dyes

pills *see* Drugs and drug terms

piscine *see* Fish

place names *see* Capes →Capitals →Cities →Places and their nicknames

plankton *see* Algae →Plants

plays *see* Shakespeare: Plays of Shakespeare →Theatre terms

pleasure *see* Entertainment

poems *see* Poetry →Shakespeare: Poems of Shakespeare

police *see* Crime terms

politics *see* European Union →Government →Parliaments →Political parties →Presidents →Prime Ministers →Swiss cantons

popular music *see* Music: Popular music types

ports *see* Capes

poultry *see* Fowl

power *see* Electronics terms →Emperors →Kings →Political parties →Presidents →Prime Ministers →Queens →Rulers

precious stones *see* Gemstones →Stones

prehistoric *see* Dinosaurs →Fossils →Mammals, extinct

print *see* Newspapers and magazines →Papers →Typefaces

production *see* Drama →Theatre terms

profession *see* Occupations

programmes *see* Cinema and television

programs see Computers →Programming languages

prosody *see* Poetry: Poetry and prosody terms

Protestantism *see* Christian denominations and sects

psychiatry *see* Mania →Medicine →Phobias →Psychology

publishing *see* Newspapers and magazines →Typefaces

puddings *see* Cakes and Pastries →Desserts

puzzles *see* Games

pythons *see* Snakes

Q

qualifications *see* Degrees

R

racing *see* Bets and betting systems → Equestrianism → Racing

ranks *see* British Forces → Military ranks

rashes *see* Skin, afflictions of the

rats *see* Rodents

rays *see* Fish

reconstructive surgery *see* Surgical operations

recreation *see* Entertainment

Regents *see* Rulers

regions *see* Places and their nicknames → Provinces → Regions, administrative → Wine: Wine-producing areas

republics of Russia *see* Russian federal republics

Republic of Ireland *see* Counties

revolution *see* History → Time: French Revolutionary calendar

rigging *see* Knots → Ropes

Roman *see* Emperors → Festivals → Furies → Gods and Goddesses

rope *see* Knots → Ropes

Round Table *see* Arthurian legend → Knights

rowing *see* Racing

royalty *see* History

rulers *see* Government → Kings → Queens → Rulers

rules *see* Law

S

sailing *see* Knots → Pirates → Ports → Ships, parts of

schools *see* Colleges → Degrees → Education terms → Ivy League universities → Oxbridge colleges

science *see* Archaeology → Asteroids → Astronomy → Biology → Botany → Geography → Geology → Mathematics → Medicine → Physics → Psychology → Zoology

Scotland *see* Counties

Scottish law *see* Law: Scots law terms

scriptures *see* Ecclesiastical terms

sculptors *see* Artists

sculpture *see* Art

seating *see* Chairs ➔Furniture ➔Household items

sects *see* Christian denominations and sects ➔Hindu denominations and sects ➔Muslim denominations and sects

serial killers *see* Murderers

serials *see* Detectives

seven hills of Rome *see* Rome, the seven hills of

seven wonders of the world *see* Wonders of the ancient world

sewing *see* Embroidery stitches

shades *see* Blue, shades of ➔Brown, shades of ➔Colours ➔Green, shades of ➔Orange, shades of ➔Purple, shades of ➔Red, shades of ➔Yellow, shades of

shooting stars *see* Meteor showers

shows *see* Entertainment: Types of entertainment

Siberia *see* Russian federal republics

sight *see* Eye: Afflictions of the eye ➔Eye: Parts of the eye

Sikhism *see* Religion

simian *see* Monkeys, apes and other primates

skins *see* Leather ➔Skin, afflictions of

slander *see* Insults

slugs *see* Snails, slugs and other gastropods

snacks *see* Confectionery

Socialism *see* Political parties

societies *see* Clubs

software *see* Communications ➔Computer games ➔Computers: Computer terms

soldiers *see* Military ranks

South Africa *see* Provinces: Provinces of South Africa

space *see* Asteroids ➔Astronomy ➔Comets ➔Galaxies ➔Meteor showers

Spain *see* Regions, administrative

Spanish *see* Foreign words and phrases

speech *see* Dialects

spirits *see* Supernatural

sportsmen and women *see* Cricket: Cricketers ➔Football: Footballers ➔Golfers ➔Mountaineers ➔Tennis players

stage *see* Entertainment ➔Theatre terms

staples *see* Rice and other cereals

star signs *see* Astrology

states *see* Regions, administrative ➔Republics

stimulants *see* Drugs and drug terms

stingrays *see* Fish

stockings *see* Socks and tights

stock market *see* Economics ➔Trade terms

storage *see* Cupboards and cabinets ➔Furniture ➔Household items

straits *see* Channels

string *see* Knots

structures *see* Dams

Styx *see* Rivers of Hell

substances *see* Acids ➔Alkalis ➔Drugs and drug terms ➔Poisons: Poisonous substances and gases

superstition *see* Humours of the body ➔Supernatural

surgery *see* Medicine ➔Surgical operations

sweets and sweet dishes *see* Cakes and pastries ➔Confectionery ➔Desserts

Switzerland *see* Swiss cantons

sword fighting *see* Fencing terms ➔Swords and other weapons with blades

symbols *see* Alphabets ➔Chemical elements ➔Crosses ➔Roman numerals

syndromes *see* Diseases

T

tablets *see* Drugs

tack *see* Horses: Tack and equipment and their parts

tarts *see* Cakes and pastries

tax *see* Economics ➔Law: Law terms

taxonomy *see* Algae ➔Amphibians ➔Animals ➔Birds ➔Botany ➔Cats ➔Dinosaurs ➔Dogs ➔Ferns ➔Fish ➔Flowers ➔Fungi ➔Grasses ➔Insects ➔Invertebrates ➔Lilies ➔Mammals ➔Mosses ➔Palms ➔Parasites ➔Plants ➔Rabbits and hares ➔Reptiles ➔Seaweeds ➔Shrubs ➔Trees ➔Weeds

teaching *see* Education terms

technology *see* Communications →Computers →Computer games

television *see* Actors →Cartoon characters →Cats: Famous cats →Cinema and television →Comedians →Detectives →Drama →Film and television

tempo *see* Music: Musical expressions and tempo instructions

term *see* Education terms →Seasons →Time

terminology *see* American and British Equivalents

theatre *see* Actors →Cats: Famous cats →Drama →Dramatists →Entertainment →Theatre terms

Thebes *see* Seven against Thebes

tights *see* Socks and tights

titles *see* Degrees →Military ranks →Nobility

toadstools *see* Fungi

tools *see* Cutting tools

trains *see* Locomotives

transport *see* Aircraft →Canals →Carriages and carts →Locomotives

treatment *see* Medicine →Psychology

tribes *see* Peoples

tyrants *see* Emperors →Rulers

U

uniform *see* Jackets

United Kingdom *see* Counties

universe *see* Astronomy →Galaxies →Stars and constellations

universities *see* Colleges →Degrees →Education terms →Ivy league universities →Oxbridge Colleges

V

valves *see* Heart, parts of

vegetation *see* Flowers →Plants →Shrubs

vehicles *see* Aircraft →Carriages and carts →Cars →Locomotives →Vehicles

vermin *see* Insects →Rodents →Shrews and other insectivores

vernacular *see* Alphabets →Dialects →Languages

vertebrates *see* Amphibians →Animals →Anteaters and other edentates →Antelopes →Bats →Birds →Carnivores →Cats →Cattle and other artiodactyls →Cattle, breeds of →Dinosaurs →Dogs →Ducks →Hawks

→Horses →Lizards →Mammals, extinct →Marsupials →Monkeys, apes and other primates →Pigs →Prey, birds of →Rabbits and hares →Reptiles →Rodents →Sea birds →Seals →Sea mammals →Sharks →Sheep →Shrews and other insectivores →Snakes →Whales and dolphins

vessels *see* Cases →Containers for liquids →Ships, parts of

vipers *see* Snakes

virology *see* Diseases →Eye: Afflictions of the eye

vocations *see* Occupations

Volga *see* Russian federal republics

volume *see* Units

W

Wales *see* Counties

war *see* Aircraft →Apocalypse, Four Horsemen of →Armour →Battles →Clubs and bats →Generals →Heroes →History →Knights →Martial arts →Military ranks →Missiles →Models →Seven against Thebes →Swords and other weapons with blades →Warfare terms →Weapons

Warner Brothers *see* Cartoon characters

water *see* Lakes, lochs and loughs →Sounds →Straits

waterways *see* Canals →Dams →Rivers

weapons *see* Clubs and bats →Guns →Missiles →Swords and other weapons with blades

witches *see* Supernatural

wizards *see* Supernatural

work *see* Occupations

writing *see* Alphabets →Crime writers →Critics →Diarists →Dramatists →Greek figures →Novelists →Papers →Poets →Shakespeare →Works of literature and music

Z

zip codes *see* States

zones *see* Time: Time zones

Aa

Abbreviations

CLASSIFIED ADVERTISEMENTS

Abbreviation	Meaning
AMC *or* amc	All mod cons
Deps	Deposit
Exc *or* excl	Excluding
F/f	Furnished flat
GCH	Gas central heating
Inc *or* incl	Including
Pcm	Per calendar month
Pw	Per week

LONELY HEARTS COLUMN ABBREVIATIONS

Abbreviation	Meaning
ACA	All calls answered
ALAWP	All letters answered with a photo
BF	Boyfriend/Black woman
GL	Good looking
GSOH	Good sense of humour
GWM	Gay white male
LTR	Long term relationship
NS *or* N/S	Non-smoker
OHAC	Own house and car
SA or S/A	Straight-acting
SOH	Sense of humour
SWF	Single white female
VGSOH	Very good sense of humour
WLTM	Would like to meet
WSOH	Weird *or* wicked sense of humour

SMS, CHATROOM ABBREVIATIONS

AAF	As a friend	COZ	Because
AAR	At any rate	CU	See you
ATM	At the moment	DL	Download
B	Be	EG	Evil grin
BRB	Be right back	EM	Excuse me?

EZ	Easy	OOC	Out of character
FRM	From	OT	Off topic
GL	Good luck	OTT	Over the top
HUGZ	Hugs	PM	Personal message
IC	I see	PTB	Please text back
IMNSHO	In my not-so-humble opinion	PWNED	Owned (beaten)
		R	Are
IMO	In my opinion	RL	Real life
IMS	I am sorry	RN	Right now
INMP	It's not my problem	ROFL	Rolling on the floor laughing
IRL	In real life		
IYKWIMAITYD	If you know what I mean and I think you do	RU	Are you
		SOZ	Sorry
		THX	Thank you
JK	Just kidding	TTTT	To tell the truth
K	Okay	WE	Whatever
LMAO	Laugh my ass off	WKND	Weekend
LOL	Laugh out loud	WO	Without
MYOB	Mind your own business	WRK	Work
		WTH	What the hell
NALOPKT	Not a lot of people know that	WUD	What are you doing?
		XLNT	Excellent
NE	Any	Y	Why
NOOB	New person	YA	Yet another
NW	No way!	YR	Why are
OMG	Oh my god	YW	You're welcome
OMIK	Open mouth, insert keyboard	ZZ	Sleeping/bored/tired

OTHER ABBREVIATIONS

1 letter:	P	AB	A/M	AV	BJ
A	Q	A/C	AM	Av	Bk
B	R	AC	Am	A-v	B/L
C	S	A/c	AN	AZ	BL
D	T	Ac	A/O	Az	Bl
E	U	AD	AO	BA	BM
F	V	Ae	AP	BB	Bm
G	W	A/F	AQ	BC	Bn
H	X	AF	Aq	B/D	B/O
I	Y	Af	AR	BD	BO
K	Z	AG	Ar	Bd	Bo
L		AH	AS	B/E	Bp
M	2 letters:	AI	At	BE	B/R
N	AA	AK	AU	Bé	BR
O	Aa	AL			Br

B/S	CW	FA	Hg	JJ
BS	D/A	Fa	HH	JP
BT	DA	FC	HI	Jr
Bt	DB	Fc	HJ	Jt
BV	DC	FD	HK	KB
B/W	DD	FI	HL	Kb
BW	DE	FL	HM	KC
Bx	D/F	Fl	HO	Kc
Bz	DF	FM	Ho	KD
C/A	DG	Fm	HP	KE
CA	Dg	FO	HQ	KG
Ca	DI	Fo	HR	Kg
CB	DJ	FP	Hr	Kn
Cb	DM	Fp	HS	KP
CC	D/O	Fr	HT	Kr
Cc	DO	Fs	Ht	KS
CD	Do	FT	HV	KT
C/d	D/P	Ft	HW	Kt
Cd	DP	Fv	Ia	KV
CE	DR	FX	IC	KW
CF	Dr	GA	I/c	Ky
C/f	DS	Ga	ID	LA
Cf	DU	GB	Id	La
CG	Du	Gb	IE	Lb
Cg	DV	GC	Ie	L/C
CH	D/W	GG	IF	LC
Ch	Ea	GI	IG	Lc
CI	EC	Gi	IL	LD
CJ	Ed	Gk	IM	Ld
CM	EE	GM	IN	LE
C/N	Ee	GO	In	LF
CO	Eg	GP	I/O	LG
C/o	EI	GQ	IP	Lg
Co	EN	Gr	IQ	LH
CP	Eo	GS	Iq	Lh
Cp	EP	GT	IR	LI
CQ	Ep	Gu	Ir	LJ
CR	EQ	Gv	Is	LL
Cr	Eq	Ha	IT	Ll
CS	ER	HC	It	Ln
CT	ET	Hd	IU	LO
Ct	EU	HE	Iv	L/P
CU	EV	HF	JA	LP
Cu	Ex	Hf	JC	LT
CV	Ez	HG	JD	Lt

LU	NF	PC	RA	SP
LV	NG	Pc	RC	Sp
Lv	NH	PD	Rc	Sq
LW	NI	Pd	RD	Sr
MA	NJ	PE	Rd	SS
MB	NL	Pf	RE	St
Mb	Nl	PG	RF	SU
MC	NM	Pg	Rf	SV
MD	Nm	Ph	RH	Sv
Md	No	PI	Rh	SW
ME	NP	PK	RI	Sw
Me	Np	Pk	RL	TA
MF	Nr	PL	RM	TB
Mf	NS	Pl	Rm	Tb
MG	Ns	PM	RN	TC
MI	NT	Pm	RP	TD
Mi	NV	PN	RQ	TG
Mk	NY	PO	RR	Tg
ML	NZ	PP	RS	TM
MM	OB	Pp	RT	TN
Mm	Ob	PQ	Rt	Tr
MN	OC	Pq	RU	TT
MO	O/c	PR	RV	TU
Mo	OD	Pr	Rv	TV
MP	OE	PS	RW	TX
Mp	Oe	Ps	SA	UA
MR	OF	PT	Sa	UC
MS	OG	Pt	Sb	Uc
MT	Og	PW	SC	UK
Mt	OH	PX	Sc	UN
MU	OJ	QB	SD	UP
MV	OK	QC	Sd	UR
Mv	OM	Qe	SF	U/S
MW	ON	QF	Sf	US
MX	OP	Ql	SG	Us
MY	Op	QM	Sg	UT
NA	OR	Qm	SI	UU
N/a	OS	Qn	SJ	UV
NB	OT	QR	SK	VA
Nb	OU	Qr	Sk	Va
NC	Oz	QS	S/L	VB
ND	PA	Qs	SL	Vb
Nd	Pa	Qt	Sl	VD
NE	PB	Qv	SM	Vd
N/F	P/C	Qy	SO	VF

VG	**3 letters:**	AIA	Arr	BCG
Vg	AAA	AID	ART	BCh
VI	AAM	AIF	ARV	BCL
Vi	AAP	AIH	ASA	BCS
VJ	ABA	AIM	ASB	BDA
VL	ABC	AIR	ASL	Bde
Vl	ABH	AIS	Asl	Bdl
VO	Abl	AJA	ASM	BDS
Vo	ABM	AJC	AST	Bds
VP	Abp	Aka	ASW	BEA
VR	ABS	Ala	ATB	BEd
VS	ABV	Alb	ATC	BEF
Vs	ACA	Ald	ATK	BEM
Vt	ACC	ALF	ATM	BeV
Vv	Acc	Alg	Atm	BFA
VW	ACM	Alk	ATN	BFI
WA	ACT	ALP	ATP	BFN
WB	ACW	ALS	ATV	BHP
Wb	ADC	ALU	AUC	Bhp
WC	ADD	AMA	Aug	Bid
Wc	ADH	AMF	AUS	BIM
WD	Adj	AMM	Aus	BIS
Wd	Adm	AMP	AUT	Bkg
Wf	ADO	Amp	AVC	Bks
Wg	Adv	Amt	Ave	BLL
WI	AEA	AMU	AVM	BMA
WK	AEC	Amu	Avn	BMI
Wk	Aet	ANA	AWA	BMJ
WO	AEW	ANC	AWS	BMR
W/o	AFB	ANU	AWU	BMX
WP	AFC	ANZ	AZT	BNA
WR	Afg	AOB	BAF	BNP
Wt	AFK	AOC	BAK	BOD
WV	AFL	AOH	BAL	Bol
WY	AFM	AOR	BAR	BOT
Xn	AFN	APB	Bar	Bot
XO	Afp	APR	BBC	BPC
Xt	AFV	Apr	BBL	BPE
YC	AGC	APT	BBQ	Bpi
Yd	AGM	Apt	BBS	BPR
Yr	AGN	ARA	BCA	Bps
YT	AGR	ARC	BCC	Bpt
ZB	Agr	Arg	BCD	BRB
	Agt	Ark	BCE	BRE
	AHQ	Arm	BCF	Bro

DOM	EFL	ESR	FMS	GLA
Dom	EGM	EST	Fob	GLC
Doz	EHF	Est	FoC	Gld
DPB	EHO	Esu	FoE	GMB
DPH	EHV	ETA	Fol	GMC
Dpi	EIA	Etc	For	Gmc
DPM	EIB	ETD	FPA	GMO
DPP	EKG	ETF	FPO	GMT
Dpt	ELF	Eth	Fps	GNC
DPW	ELT	Ety	FRG	GNP
DSC	Emf	EVA	Fri	Gns
DSc	EMS	EWO	Frl	GOC
DSM	EMU	Exc	FRS	GOM
DSO	Emu	Exr	Frt	GOP
Dsp	EMV	Ext	FSA	Gov
DSS	Enc	FAA	FSB	GPI
DST	ENG	FAB	FSH	GPO
DTI	Eng	FAI	Fth	GPS
DTL	ENO	FAO	Ft-l	GPU
DTP	Ens	FAQ	Fur	GRF
DT's	ENT	Faq	FWD	Gro
DTT	EOC	FAS	Fwd	GSM
Dur	Eom	FBA	FYI	Gsm
DVD	EPA	FBI	FZS	GSR
DVM	EPG	FBL	GAA	GST
DVT	Eph	FBW	GAI	GTC
DWP	EPO	FCA	GAL	Gtd
Dwt	EPP	FCC	Gal	GUM
EAS	EPR	FCO	GBE	Gyn
EBS	Eps	FDA	GBH	HAA
EBU	EPZ	Fdm	GBS	Hab
EBV	EQC	FDP	GCA	HAC
ECB	ERA	FDR	GCB	Hag
ECG	Erf	Feb	GCE	HBC
ECR	ERM	Fec	GCF	HBM
ECS	ERO	Fed	GDP	HCF
ECT	ERS	Fem	GDR	HCG
EDC	ESA	FET	Gds	Hcp
EDI	ESB	Ffa	Gen	HDL
EDM	Esd	FIA	Ger	Heb
EDT	ESL	Fig	GeT	Her
EEA	ESN	Fin	GeV	HEU
EEC	ESO	Fla	GHB	HEW
EEG	ESP	Fld	GHQ	HGH
EFA	Esq	FMD	GIS	Hgt

HGV	IDD	IRW	Kčs	Loq
Hhd	IDN	ISA	Ken	LPG
HIE	IDP	ISD	KeV	LPO
HIH	IEA	Isl	KIT	LPS
HIM	IEE	ISM	KKK	LRT
HIV	IFA	ISP	Knt	LSD
HJS	IFC	ITA	Kph	LSE
HMG	IFF	Ita	KRL	LSI
HMI	IFP	ITC	KWh	LSO
HMS	IFR	ITN	KZN	LSZ
HNC	IFS	ITO	Lab	LTA
HND	IGC	ITU	LAC	Ltd
Hon	IGM	ITV	Lam	LTR
Hos	IGY	IUD	LAN	LUV
HPV	IHC	IUS	Lat	Lux
HRE	Iid	IVF	LBD	LVP
HRH	IJC	IVR	Lbf	Lwl
HRT	Ill	IWC	LBJ	LWM
HSE	ILO	IWW	LBO	MAC
HSH	ILR	JAG	LBV	Mac
HSM	ILS	Jam	Lbw	Mag
HST	ILU	Jan	LCD	Maj
Hts	IMF	JAP	Lcd	Mal
HUD	IMO	Jap	LCJ	Mar
HWM	Imp	Jas	LCL	Mat
Hyp	IMS	JCD	Lcm	Max
IAA	Inc	JCL	Ldg	MBA
IAF	IND	JCR	LDL	MBE
IAP	Ind	JCS	LDR	MBO
IAS	INF	Jer	LDS	MCB
IBA	INS	JFK	LEA	MCC
IBF	Ins	JIT	LED	MCG
ICA	IOC	Jnd	LEO	MCh
ICC	IOM	Jnr	Lev	MCP
ICE	IOW	Jon	LGV	MCS
Ice	IPA	JSA	Lhd	MDF
ICI	IPO	JSD	Lib	MDR
ICJ	IRA	JUD	Liq	MDS
ICS	IRC	Jud	Lit	MEC
ICT	IRD	Jul	LLB	MEd
ICU	Ire	Jun	LLD	Med
IDA	IRL	JWV	LLM	MEP
Ida	IRM	Kan	LMS	Mer
IDB	IRO	KBE	LNG	Met
IDC	IRS	KCB	LOL	Mex

MEZ	MPC	NDP	NRN	OLG
MFA	MPG	NDT	NRT	OMM
Mfd	Mpg	NEB	NRV	OMS
Mfg	Mph	NEC	NSB	ONC
MFH	MPP	NEG	NSF	OND
Mfr	MPS	Neg	NSG	Ono
MGB	MPV	Neh	NSU	ONS
Mgr	MRA	NEP	NSW	Ont
MHA	MRC	Nev	Nth	ONZ
MHC	MRE	NFA	NTO	OPC
MHD	MRI	NFB	NTP	Ops
MHG	MRM	NFL	NTS	Org
MHR	MRP	NFS	NUJ	OSA
MIA	Msb	NFT	NUM	OSB
Mic	MSC	NFU	Num	OSD
Mid	MSc	NGA	NUR	OSF
Mil	MSD	NGC	NUS	OSI
Min	MSF	NGF	NUT	OST
MIP	MSG	NGk	NVQ	OTC
MIT	MSI	NGL	NWT	OTE
Mkt	Msl	NGO	NYC	OTT
MLA	MSM	NHI	NZC	Ozs
MLC	MSP	NHL	NZE	PAC
MLD	MSS	NHS	NZR	Pac
MLF	MST	NIC	OAP	Pal
MLG	Mtg	NII	OAS	Pan
MLR	MTV	NLC	OAU	Par
MMC	Mus	NLF	Obb	PAU
Mmf	MVD	NLS	OBE	PAX
MMM	MVO	NLW	Obj	PBX
MMP	MVP	NMR	Obs	PCB
MMV	MVS	NNP	OCD	PCC
MNA	Nah	NOI	OCR	Pcm
MOB	NAI	Nom	OCS	PCP
MoC	NAS	Nos	Oct	PCR
MOD	Nat	Nov	ODA	Pct
Mod	NAV	NPA	ODI	PCV
MOH	NBA	NPC	OED	PDA
MOI	NBC	NPD	OEM	Pdl
Mol	NBG	NPL	OFM	Pdq
Mon	NCC	NPV	OFS	PDR
MOR	NCM	NQA	OFT	PEI
Mor	NCO	NRA	OHG	Pen
MOS	NCP	NRC	Ohv	PEP
MOT	NDE	NRL	OIC	PER

PET	PRO	Que	Rit	Sam
Pet	PRP	RAC	Rly	SAR
Pfa	Prs	Rad	RMA	SAS
PFI	PRT	RAE	RME	SAT
PGA	PRW	RAF	Rmm	SAW
PGD	Psf	RAM	RMS	SBA
PGR	PSG	Ram	Rms	SBE
PHC	Psi	RAN	RMT	SBS
PhD	PSK	RAR	RNR	SBU
PHS	PSL	RAS	RNZ	ScD
PID	PSS	RBE	ROC	SCE
P-i-n	PST	RCA	Rom	SCG
Pkg	PSV	RCD	Rot	Sch
Pkt	PTA	Rcd	RPC	Sci
PKU	Pte	RCL	RPG	SCM
PLA	Ptg	RCM	RPI	SCP
Plc	PTN	RCN	Rpm	SCR
PLO	PTO	RCO	RPS	Scr
PLP	Pts	RCP	Rps	SDI
PLR	Pty	RCS	Rpt	SDP
PLU	Pub	RCT	RPV	SEC
PMG	PVA	Rct	RRP	Sec
PMI	PVC	RDA	RSA	SEN
PMS	PVR	RDC	RSC	Sen
PMT	PVS	RDS	RSG	Seq
PNI	Pvt	RDX	RSI	SFA
POB	PWA	Ref	RSJ	SFO
POD	PWR	Reg	RSL	SFW
POE	Pwt	Rel	RSM	Sgd
POL	QCA	REM	RSV	Sgt
Pol	QCD	Rep	RTA	SHA
POM	QED	Res	RTC	SHF
POP	QEF	Rev	RTE	SHM
Pop	QFD	RFC	RTF	SIB
POS	Qld	RGB	RTR	Sig
Pos	QMC	RGN	RTT	SIN
POW	QMG	RGS	RUC	Sin
Ppd	QMS	Rgt	RUG	SIS
PPE	QMV	RHA	Rwd	SIT
Ppm	Qqv	Rhd	Rwy	SJA
PPP	QSM	RHG	SAC	SJC
Ppr	QSO	RHS	SAD	SJD
PPS	Qto	RIA	SAE	Skt
PRB	QTS	RIC	Sae	SLD
Prn	Qty	RIP	SAm	Sld

SLR	Sth	Tox	USA	WBC
SMD	Stk	TPI	USB	WBO
SMP	STP	Tpr	USM	WBU
SMS	Str	TQM	USN	WCC
SMV	STV	TRC	USO	WDA
SNG	Sub	TRH	USP	WDM
SNP	Suf	Trs	USS	WEA
Snr	Sun	TSB	USW	Wed
Sob	Sup	TSE	UTC	Wef
Soc	SUV	TSH	UV-A	WEU
SOE	SVQ	TSO	UV-B	WFF
Sol	Syn	Tsp	UVF	Whf
Som	Syr	TTA	UWT	WHO
SOP	TAB	TTL	VAD	Whr
Sop	Tab	TUC	VAR	Wig
SPA	TAC	TUF	Var	Wis
SpA	TAI	TVM	VAT	WLM
SPD	Tan	TVP	Vat	WMD
SPF	Tbc	TVR	VCR	Wmk
Spp	Tbs	TXT	VDC	WMO
SPR	TBT	Typ	VDT	WOF
Spt	TCM	UAE	VDU	WOW
SQA	Tdc	UAM	Ven	WPA
SQL	Tdm	UAR	Vet	WPB
Sqn	TES	UAV	VGA	WPC
Sqq	Tex	UBR	VHF	Wpm
SRA	TGV	UCL	VHS	WST
Sra	ThB	UCT	VIP	WTC
SRN	ThD	UDA	VIR	WTG
SRO	THI	UDC	Vis	WTO
SSB	THX	UDI	Viz	W Va
SSC	TIA	UDR	VLA	WVS
SSD	Tid	UFO	VLF	WWF
SSM	Tim	UGC	VMD	WWI
SSN	TIR	UHF	VMI	WWW
SSP	Tit	UHT	Voc	Wyo
Ssp	TKO	Ukr	Vol	XUV
SSR	TLA	Ult	VPL	YBA
SST	TLC	UNA	VRI	YHA
Sta	TLS	UNO	Vsb	Yrs
STC	TMI	UPC	VSO	YTS
STD	TMT	UPI	VTR	ZCC
Std	TMV	URC	WAN	ZPG
Ste	Tng	URL	War	
Stg	Tob	Uru	WBA	

4 letters:	Atty	CBSO	CSCE	Et al
ACCA	At wt	CCEA	CSYS	Exec
ACCC	AUEW	CCMA	DATV	Exod
ACER	Aust	CCRC	DBib	Exor
ACGI	Avdp	CCTA	DBMS	Ezek
ACII	AWRE	CCTV	DCMG	FACE
ACLU	BAOR	CDNA	DCMS	FAHA
Actg	Bapt	Cdre	DCVO	Fath
ACTT	Bart	CEGB	DDSc	Fcap
ACTU	BBBC	CEng	Decd	FCCA
ADFA	BBFC	CGBR	DEng	FCII
ADHD	BCAR	Chap	Dent	F Eng
Advt	BCNU	Chem	Dept	FIDE
AECL	BCNZ	Ches	DETR	Fl dr
AFTN	BCom	Chin	Deut	Flem
AICC	Beds	CICA	DfEE	Fl oz
Alas	Belg	CIFE	DFID	FMCG
ALCM	BEng	CIGS	DHSS	FMRI
Alta	BFPO	C in C	Diag	Foll
AMDG	Biog	Cllr	Dial	FONE
Amer	Biol	Cmdr	Diam	FRCM
Anat	Bkcy	CMEA	DMAC	FRCO
Anim	Bkpt	CNAA	DMSO	FRCP
Anon	Bldg	CNAR	DMus	FRCS
ANSI	BLit	C of E	DOCG	FRGS
AOCB	Blvd	C of I	DTLR	FRPS
AONB	BMus	C of S	DVLA	FRSC
Apoc	BNFL	Colo	Ebor	Ft-lb
APRA	BOAC	Comr	EBRD	FWIW
Arch	Braz	Cong	Eccl	GAIN
ARCM	BRCS	Conj	Ecol	Gall
ARCS	Brig	Conn	Econ	GCHQ
Ariz	Brit	Cons	ECSC	GCMG
ARSM	Bros	Coop	Ecua	GCSE
Asap	BSSc	Corp	EFIS	GCVO
ASDE	Bulg	CPAG	EFTS	Gdns
ASIO	BYOB	CPRE	Encl	Genl
Assn	CABE	CPSA	ENEA	Geod
ASSR	Camb	CPSU	Engr	Geog
Asst	Cant	CPVE	Epis	Geol
ASTM	Caps	CQSW	EPNS	Geom
Astr	Capt	CRAC	ERCP	Glos
At no	Card	Cres	ERDF	GmbH
A to J	CART	Crim	ESRC	GMTA
Attn	CATV	Crit	Esth	GnRH

GNVQ	INRI	Math	NFWI	Phon
Govt	Inst	Matt	NIHE	PHSE
GPMU	Intl	MCom	NKGB	Phys
GPRS	Intr	MCPS	NKVD	Pizz
Grad	IOOF	MDMA	Norm	Plur
Gram	IPCC	Meth	Norw	PNdB
Gr wt	IRAS	Mich	NRMA	Port
GSOH	IRBM	MICR	Nt wt	Poss
GSVQ	ISBN	MIHL	NYSE	POST
Guat	ISDN	Minn	NZEF	PPTA
Guin	ISSN	Misc	NZEI	Pred
HAND	ISSP	Miss	NZLR	Pref
Hdbk	Isth	MMDS	NZMA	Prem
HDTV	Ital	MmHg	NZOM	Prep
HFEA	IUCD	MMus	NZPA	Pres
HFMD	Josh	Mont	NZRN	Priv
Hind	Junc	MPLA	NZSE	Prob
HMAS	Junr	MRBM	NZSO	Proc
HMCS	JurD	MRCA	Obad	Prod
HMSO	Kcal	MRIA	Obdt	Prof
Hond	KCMG	MRNA	OCAM	Prog
HSRC	KCVO	MRSA	OECD	Pron
HTLV	KISS	MRSC	OEEC	Prot
HTML	KStJ	Msgr	OHMS	Prov
HTTP	LACW	MTBE	Okla	Prox
Hung	LAIA	MTBF	Oreg	PSBR
IAAF	Lb tr	MTNG	Orig	Psia
IAEA	L/Cpl	MusB	Orth	Psid
IARU	Lgth	MusD	OSCE	Psig
Ibid	LH-RH	MusM	Oxon	PSIS
IBRD	Ling	MVDI	PABX	PSNI
ICAO	Lith	MVSc	Part	PSTN
ICBM	LMVD	Myth	Pass	PTFE
ICSH	Long	NAHT	Patd	PTSD
ICTZ	LRSC	NAIC	Path	Quad
IDDM	LTNS	Natl	PAYE	Quot
IFAD	LTSA	NCCL	Payt	RAAF
IGBP	Luth	NCEA	PCOS	RACQ
IKBS	LVAD	NCIS	PDSA	RAEC
ILEA	Macc	NCVO	Penn	Rall
IMCO	MAgr	Nebr	Perf	RAMC
IMHO	MAOI	NEDC	Peta	RAOC
Inbd	Marq	NERC	Phar	RASC
Incl	Masc	Neth	Phil	RAVC
INLA	Mass	Neut	PHLS	RCAF

RCMP	SDLP	TCAS	WRNS	Const
Rcpt	SDRs	Tech	Wrnt	Contd
RCVS	Secy	Temp	WRVS	Cosec
Recd	SEED	Tenn	WSSD	Cotan
Rect	SEPA	Terr	WWII	Cryst
Regd	Sept	TGWU	XLNT	CSIRO
Regt	Seqq	TIGR	Xnty	Cwlth
Rept	SGML	TPWS	YMCA	Denom
Retd	Shpt	Trig	YMHA	DipAD
Revd	SIDS	T-RNA	Yugo	DipEd
RFID	Sing	TTFN	YWCA	DLitt
RFLP	SIPS	TTYL	YWHA	DPhil
RIBA	SLBM	Tues	ZAMS	Epiph
RICS	SLCM	Turk	Zech	Epist
RNAS	SLSC	TVEI	Zeph	Equiv
RNIB	SNCF	TVNZ	Zool	Et seq
RNID	SOHF	TVRO		Ex div
RNLI	Span	UKCC	**5 letters:**	Ex lib
RNVR	SPCK	ULCC	A'asia	Ex off
RNZN	Spec	Unit	Accel	Exptl
ROFL	Sp gr	Univ	Aeron	FASSA
Ronz	Sp ht	UPVC	AFAIK	FRACP
RRNA	SPQR	USAF	AFNOR	FRACS
RRSP	Srta	USSR	AMICE	FRCVS
RSGB	SSHA	V aux	AMIEE	FRICS
RSNO	SSRI	VCJD	Archd	Front
RSNZ	SSSI	VDQS	Assoc	FRSNZ
RSPB	SSTA	Vers	BArch	FYROM
RSVP	Stat	Vert	Barit	Genit
RUOK	Stbd	Visc	BBSRC	Gloss
Russ	Stge	VLBI	BECTU	GMDSS
SABC	Stir	VLCC	Berks	H and c
SABS	STUC	VLSI	BLitt	Hants
SACC	Subj	Vols	BPhil	Hdqrs
SACP	Suff	V Rev	Bucks	Herts
SAfr	Supt	VSOP	Calif	Horol
Sans	Surg	Vulg	Cambs	ICFTU
SARS	Surv	Wash	CCANZ	Ichth
Sask	Suth	WFTU	Chron	IMarE
SATB	SVGA	Wisd	Cifci	IMinE
SAYE	SWFF	Wkly	CITES	IMunE
SCID	SWOT	WKND	CMIIW	Incog
Scot	SYHA	WLTM	Comdg	Indef
SCQF	TATT	WRAC	Comdr	Indic
S Dak	TAVR	WRAF	Comdt	Indiv

Infin
In mem
Inorg
Inter
Intro
Irreg
Kbyte
Lancs
Leics
Lieut
Lincs
LittB
LittD
L'pool
Lt Cdr
Lt Col
Lt Gen
Lt Gov
Maced
Madag
Manuf
MArch
March
Maths
Mbyte
MEcon
Metal
Middx
MLitt
Moham
Mol wt
Morph
MPhil
MTech
Mt Rev
Mycol
NAACP
Navig
NIDDM
NLLST
Nottm
Notts
NSAID
NSPCC
NZCER

NZRFU
OFris
Op cit
PAGAD
Paren
PPARC
Presb
Propr
Pseud
RAFVR
R and R
Réaum
Ref Ch
Repub
RNWMP
RNZAF
RSFSR
RSPCA
Rt Hon
SAARC
SARFU
Sergt
SGHWR
SHEEP
SMATV
SQUID
Stacc
Subst
Suffr
Switz
Synop
Theol
Theos
Thess
Thurs
Topog
TRALI
Trans
Treas
UKAEA
UNHCR
V and A
Venez
Visct
WAAAF

Warks
Westm
Whsle
Wilts
Worcs
WRAAC
WRAAF
WRANS
Yorks

6 letters:
AARNet
Abbrev
AFL-CIO
AFRAeS
A into G
Am-dram
Approx
Arccos
Archbp
Archit
Arcsin
Arctan
Astrol
Att Gen
Attrib
BPharm
Cantab
CertEd
Colloq
Com Ver
Confed
Covers
DipCom
DipMet
EBITDA
Eccles
Ecclus
Geneal
GOC-in-C
Hon Sec
IChemE
Illust
IMechE
Imperf

Imp gal
Interj
IONARC
Lib Dem
Loc cit
Maj Gen
MIMinE
MIMunE
NATFHE
Nem con
Neurol
Non seq
Northd
NZEFIP
Obstet
Pat Off
Petrog
Petrol
Philem
Philol
Philos
Photog
Prelim
QARANC
Rev Ver
ROFLOL
Rt Revd
Sgt Maj
Sociol
S of Sol
Sqn Ldr
Staffs
UNCTAD
Ut dict

7 letters:
AFSLAET
Anthrop
Austral
Auth Ver
Bibliog
Brig Gen
Cantuar
Co Derry
Contrib

Decresc
Embryol
Entomol
E Sussex
Intrans
Lexicog
Mineral
New Test
Nol pros
Non pros
Oceanog

Old Test
OTPOTSS
Pat pend
P/E ratio
Physiol
Psychol
Reg prof
Rom Cath
Technol
TE score
Verb sap

8 letters:
AMIChemE
AMIMechE
Archaeol
Co Durham
In loc cit
Meteorol
Ornithol
TCA cycle

9 letters:
Bacteriol
Northants
Pharmacol

10 letters:
Cur adv vult
DipChemEng
Ophthalmol
Palaeontol
Psychoanal

Acids

SPECIFIC ACIDS

2 letters:
PH

3 letters:
DNA
HCL
RNA

4 letters:
Dopa
Uric

5 letters:
Auric
Boric
Caro's
L-dopa
Malic
Mucic
Oleic
Orcin
Trona

6 letters:
Acetic
Adipic
Bromic
Capric
Cholic

Citric
Cyanic
Erucic
Formic
Gallic
Lactic
Lauric
Leucin
Lipoic
Maleic
Niacin
Nitric
Oxalic
Pectic
Phenol
Picric
Quinic
Sialic
Sorbic
Tannic
Tiglic
Toluic
Valine

7 letters:
Abietic
Alginic
Benzoic
Butyric

Caproic
Cerotic
Chloric
Chromic
Creatin
Ellagic
Euginic
Ferulic
Folacin
Fumaric
Fusidic
Guanine
Malonic
Meconic
Muramic
Nitrous
Orcinol
Prussic
Pteroic
Pyruvic
Racemic
Sebacic
Selenic
Silicic
Stannic
Stearic
Suberic
Terebic
Titanic

Valeric
Xanthic
Xylonic

8 letters:
Abscisic
Adeninic
Ascorbic
Aspartic
Butanoic
Caprylic
Carbamic
Carbolic
Carbonic
Chlorous
Cinnamic
Creatine
Cresylic
Crotonic
Cyclamic
Decanoic
Ethanoic
Fulminic
Glutamic
Glyceric
Glycolic
Guanylic
Hexanoic
Hippuric

Itaconic
Linoleic
Lysergic
Manganic
Molybdic
Muriatic
Myristic
Nonanoic
Palmitic
Phthalic
Retinoic
Rhodanic
Succinic
Sulfonic
Tantalic
Tartaric
Telluric
Tungstic
Tyrosine
Valproic

9 letters:
Aqua-regia
Cevitamic
Citydylic
Dichromic
Hydrazoic
Hydriodic
Isocyanic

Linolenic
Methanoic
Nalidixic
Nicotinic
Panthenic
Pentanoic
Propanoic
Propenoic
Pyroboric
Saccharic
Salicylic
Sassolite
Selenious
Sulphonic
Sulphuric
Tellurous

10 letters:
Aquafortis
Asparagine
Barbituric
Citrulline
Dithionous
Dodecanoic
Glucuronic
Glutaminic
Hyaluronic

Methionine
Neuraminic
Pelargonic
Perchloric
Phosphonic
Phosphoric
Proprionic
Pyrogallic
Ricinoleic
Sulphurous
Thiocyanic
Tryptophan

11 letters:
Arachidonic
Decanedioic
Ethanedioic
Ferricyanic
Ferrocyanic
Gibberellic
Hydnocarpic
Hydrobromic
Hydrocyanic
Hyponitrous
Methacrylic
Octanedioic
Pantothenic

Permanganic
Phosphorous
Ribonucleic
Sarcolactic
Taurocholic
Typonitrous

12 letters:
Aminobenzoic
Chloroacetic
Hydrochloric
Hydrofluoric
Hypochlorous
Indoleacetic
Orthosilicic
Persulphuric
Phenylalanin
Polyadenalic
Prostacyclin
Pyroligneous
Spiraeic acid
Terephthalic

13 letters:
Galactosamine
Glacial acetic
Heptadecanoic

Indolebutyric
Phenylalanine
Platinocyanic
Prostaglandin
Pyrosulphuric
Thiosulphuric

14 letters:
Hypophosphoric
Metaphosphoric
Polyphosphoric
Pyrophosphoric

15 letters:
Hypophosphorous
Orthophosphoric
Transbutanedoic
Trichloroacetic

16 letters:
Deoxyribonucleic
Para-
  aminobenzoic

TYPES OF ACID

4 letters:
Acyl
Pyro

5 letters:
Amide
Amino
Eisel
Fatty
Folic
Iodic
Lewis

Osmic

6 letters:
Marine

7 letters:
Dibasic
Melanic
Mineral
Nucleic
Peracid

8 letters:
Hydracid
Margaric
Periodic

9 letters:
Carnitine
Mefenamic
Polybasic
Propionic

10 letters:
Carboxylic
Margaritic
Transfatty

12 letters:
Dicarboxylic

14 letters:
Polycarboxylic

AMINO ACIDS

4 letters:
PABA

6 letters:
Domoic

Lysine
Serine

7 letters:
Alanine

Cystine
Glycine
Leucine
Proline

8 letters:
Arginine
Cysteine

9 letters:
Ethionine
Glutamine
Histidine
Ornithine
Threonine

10 letters:
Citrulline

Isoleucine

11 letters:
Tryptophane

16 letters:
Para-aminobenzoic
Triiodothyronine

Actaeon's hounds

4 letters:
Agre
Alce
Nape

5 letters:
Aello
Arcas
Lacon
Ladon
Thous

6 letters:
Canace
Dromas
Lachne
Lebros
Leucon
Sticte

Theron
Tigris

7 letters:
Asbolus
Cyprius
Dorceus
Harpyia
Hylaeus
Laelaps
Lycisce

8 letters:
Agriodus
Arethusa
Harpalus
Hylactor
Melampus
Melaneus

Oribasus
Poemenis
Pterelas

9 letters:
Pamphagus

10 letters:
Ichnobates
Theridamas

11 letters:
Nebrophonus

12 letters:
Melanchaetes

13 letters:
Oresistrophus

Actors

MALE

3 letters:
Lee, *Bruce*
Lee, *Christopher*
Rey, *Fernando*

4 letters:
Cook, *Peter*
Dean, *James*
Depp, *Johnny*
Ford, *Harrison*

Hope, *Bob*
Hurt, *John*
Kean, *Edmund*
Peck, *Gregory*
Penn, *Sean*
Roth, *Tim*
Shaw, *Glen Byam*
Tati, *Jacques*
Wood, *Elijah*

5 letters:
Allen, *Woody*
Bates, *Alan*
Boyer, *Charles*
Brody, *Adrien*
Caine, *Michael*
Firth, *Colin*
Flynn, *Errol*
Fonda, *Henry*
Gabin, *Jean*

Gable, *Clark*
Grant, *Cary*
Hanks, *Tom*
Hardy, *Oliver*
Irons, *Jeremy*
Jones, *Tommy Lee*
Kelly, *Gene*
Lloyd, *Harold*
Mason, *James*
Miles, *Bernard*
Mills, *John*
Moore, *Dudley*
Neill, *Sam*
Niven, *David*
Quinn, *Anthony*
Tracy, *Spencer*
Wayne, *John*

6 letters:
Bardem, *Javier*
Beatty, *Warren*
Bogart, *Humphrey*
Brando, *Marlon*
Brooks, *Mel*
Burton, *Richard*
Cagney, *James*
Callow, *Simon*
Carrey, *Jim*
Cleese, *John*
Cooper, *Chris*
Cooper, *Gary*
Coward, *Noel*
Cruise, *Tom*
De Niro, *Robert*
De Sica, *Vittorio*
Dexter, *John*
Fields, *WC*
Finney, *Albert*
Gibson, *Mel*
Howard, *Leslie*
Howard, *Trevor*
Hudson, *Rock*
Irving, *Henry*
Jacobi, *Derek*
Jolson, *Al*

Keaton, *Buster*
Keitel, *Harvey*
Kemble, *John*
Laurel, *Stan*
Ledger, *Heath*
Lugosi, *Bela*
Massey, *Raymond*
Morley, *Robert*
Neeson, *Liam*
Newman, *Paul*
Oldman, *Gary*
O'Toole, *Peter*
Pacino, *Al*
Quayle, *Anthony*
Reagan, *Ronald*
Rourke, *Mickey*
Spacey, *Kevin*
Welles, *Orson*
Willis, *Bruce*

7 letters:
Astaire, *Fred*
Bennett, *Alan*
Bogarde, *Dirk*
Branagh, *Kenneth*
Bridges, *Jeff*
Burbage, *Richard*
Carlyle, *Robert*
Chaplin, *Charlie*
Clooney, *George*
Connery, *Sean*
Costner, *Kevin*
Douglas, *Kirk*
Douglas, *Michael*
Fiennes, *Ralph*
Freeman, *Morgan*
Garrick, *David*
Gielgud, *John*
Hackman, *Gene*
Hoffman, *Dustin*
Hoffman, *Phillip Seymour*
Hopkins, *Anthony*
Hordern, *Michael*
Karloff, *Boris*

Maguire, *Toby*
McQueen, *Steve*
Mitchum, *Robert*
Olivier, *Laurence*
Phoenix, *Joaquin*
Redford, *Robert*
Robbins, *Tim*
Robeson, *Paul*
Sellers, *Peter*
Shepard, *Sam*
Stewart, *James*
Ustinov, *Peter*

8 letters:
Barrault, *Jean-Louis*
Belmondo, *Jean-Paul*
Crawford, *Michael*
Day-Lewis, *Daniel*
DiCaprio, *Leonardo*
Eastwood, *Clint*
Guinness, *Alec*
Harrison, *Rex*
Kingsley, *Ben*
Laughton, *Charles*
Macready, *William*
McGregor, *Ewan*
McKellen, *Ian*
Redgrave, *Michael*
Robinson, *Edward G*
Scofield, *Paul*
Stallone, *Sylvester*
Travolta, *John*
Von Sydow, *Max*

9 letters:
Barrymore, *John*
Chevalier, *Maurice*
Depardieu, *Gerard*
Fairbanks, *Douglas Jr*
Fairbanks, *Douglas Snr*
Humphries, *Barry*
Lancaster, *Burt*
Mortensen, *Viggo*

Nicholson, *Jack*
Pleasence, *Donald*
Radcliffe, *Daniel*
Valentino, *Rudolph*

10 letters:
Richardson, *Ralph*

Sutherland, *Donald*

11 letters:
Mastroianni, *Marcello*
Weissmuller, *Johnny*

12 letters:
Attenborough, *Richard*
Stanislavsky, *Konstantin*

14 letters:
Schwarzenegger,
  Arnold

FEMALE

3 letters:
Bow, *Clara*

4 letters:
Cruz, *Penelope*
Gish, *Lillian*
Hawn, *Goldie*
Page, *Ellen*
Qing, *Jian*
West, *Mae*

5 letters:
Brice, *Fanny*
Close, *Glenn*
Davis, *Bette*
Davis, *Geena*
Davis, *Judy*
Dench, *Judi*
Evans, *Edith*
Fonda, *Jane*
Garbo, *Greta*
Jolie, *Angelina*
Kelly, *Grace*
Lange, *Jessica*
Leigh, *Vivien*
Lenya, *Lotte*
Lopez, *Jennifer*
Loren, *Sophia*
Smith, *Maggie*
Stone, *Sharon*
Swank, *Hilary*
Terry, *Ellen*
Weisz, *Rachel*
Welch, *Raquel*

6 letters:
Arnaud, *Yvonne*
Bardot, *Brigitte*
Bening, *Annette*
Foster, *Jodie*
Harlow, *Jean*
Hiller, *Wendy*
Hunter, *Holly*
Keaton, *Diane*
Kemble, *Fanny*
Kidman, *Nicole*
Mirren, *Helen*
Monroe, *Marilyn*
Moreau, *Jeanne*
Robson, *Flora*
Rogers, *Ginger*
Seyrig, *Delphine*
Spacek, *Sissy*
Streep, *Meryl*
Suzman, *Janet*
Tautou, *Audrey*
Taylor, *Elizabeth*
Temple, *Shirley*
Theron, *Charlize*
Weaver, *Sigourney*

7 letters:
Andrews, *Julie*
Bergman, *Ingrid*
Binoche, *Juliette*
Bullock, *Sandra*
Colbert, *Claudette*
Deneuve, *Catherine*
Dunaway, *Faye*

Gardner, *Ava*
Garland, *Judy*
Hepburn, *Audrey*
Hepburn, *Katharine*
Huppert, *Isabelle*
Jackson, *Glenda*
McKenna, *Siobhan*
Portman, *Natalie*
Roberts, *Julia*
Siddons, *Sarah*
Walters, *Julie*
Winslet, *Kate*

8 letters:
Ashcroft, *Peggy*
Bankhead, *Tallulah*
Christie, *Julie*
Crawford, *Joan*
Dietrich, *Marlene*
Grenfell, *Joyce*
Hathaway, *Anne*
Lawrence, *Gertrude*
Lockwood, *Margaret*
MacLaine, *Shirley*
Mercouri, *Melina*
Minnelli, *Liza*
Pfeiffer, *Michelle*
Pickford, *Mary*
Redgrave, *Vanessa*
Sarandon, *Susan*
Signoret, *Simone*
Staunton, *Imelda*
Thompson, *Emma*
Whitelaw, *Billie*

9 letters:
Bernhardt, *Sarah*
Blanchett, *Cate*
Cotillard, *Marion*
Knightley, *Keira*
Plowright, *Joan*
Streisand, *Barbra*

Thorndike, *Sybil*
Zellweger, *Renée*
Zeta-Jones, *Catherine*

10 letters:
Rutherford, *Margaret*
Woffington, *Peg*

11 letters:
Scott Thomas, *Kristin*
Witherspoon, *Reese*

12 letters:
Bonham Carter, *Helena*

Affection, terms of

3 letters:
Pet

4 letters:
Babe
Baby
Bean
Dear
Doll
Lamb
Love
Star

5 letters:
Angel
Babes
Goose
Honey

Kitty
Lover
Petal
Puppy
Sugar
Tiger
Toots

6 letters:
Flower
Kitten
Muppet
Poppet
Sweets
Weasel

7 letters:
Beloved

Chicken
Darling
Dearest
Dear one
Pet lamb
Pumpkin
Treacle

8 letters:
Kitty cat
Little 'un
Loved one
Munchkin
Precious
Princess
Pussycat
Treasure
Truelove

9 letters:
Bunnykins
Dearheart
Little one
Pepperpot

10 letters:
Honey bunny
Sweetheart
Sweetie pie

11 letters:
Fluffy bunny

12 letters:
Chicken bunny

Agriculturalists

4 letters:
Coke, *Thomas William*
Tull, *Jethro*

5 letters:
Lawes, *Sir John Bennet*
Young, *Arthur*

6 letters:
Carver, *George Washington*

7 letters:
Borlaug, *Norman Ernest*
Burbank, *Luther*

8 letters:
Bakewell, *Robert*

9 letters:
McCormick, *Cyrus Hall*

12 letters:
Boussingault, *Jean-Baptiste Joseph*

Agricultural terms

2 letters:
EE

3 letters:
Agr
Bed
Box
BST
CAP
Cot
Cow
Cut
Dag
Dip
Dry
End
Ewe
Fan
Hay
Hoe
Hog
Hut
Kye
Lea
Ley
Mob
Mow
NFU
Pen
Pig
Pug
Ram
RAS
Rig
Run
Rye
Set
Sow
Sty
Tag
Ted
Teg
Tup

Van
Win

4 letters:
Bail
Bale
Balk
Barn
Beam
Bone
Boss
Bull
Byre
Calf
Chip
Clip
Cock
Comb
Come
Coop
Corn
Cote
Crib
Crop
Cull
Disc
Dogy
Drag
Dump
Dung
Duty
Fall
Farm
Feed
Fire
Foal
Fold
Frib
Gang
Grow
Hack
Ha-ha
Hame

Heel
Herd
Hind
Hops
IFAD
Lair
Lamb
Land
Leaf
Lime
List
Loan
Mare
Marl
Mash
Meal
Milk
Muck
Oast
Oats
Pest
Plow
Poll
Pook
Rabi
Rape
Raze
Rean
Reap
Rear
Reen
Rich
Rick
Ring
Salt
Seed
Shaw
Shed
Show
Sick
Silo
Slop
Soil

Sole
Sour
Span
Spit
Spud
Stub
Till
Toun
Turn
Unit
Wain
Walk
Wisp
Yard
Yeld
Yoke

5 letters:
Baler
Bench
Board
Bogle
Brake
Cadet
Calve
Capon
Carry
Cavie
Chaff
Chalk
Check
Churn
Chute
Clamp
Clear
Cling
Close
Cocky
Colon
Cover
Crawl
Croft
Dairy

Daych
Dogie
Dress
Drift
Drill
Drove
Field
Flail
Flake
Flush
Force
Frame
Frost
Fruit
Glean
Grain
Grass
Graze
Grist
Haunt
Heart
Hedge
Hodge
Horse
Hough
Hovel
Jembe
Kraal
Lands
Lease
Levee
Lodge
Milch
Mulch
Oxbow
Paddy
Plaas
Plant
Poley
Punch
Quern
Quick
Raise

Ranch
Range
Rodeo
Rogue
Rural
Share
Sheaf
Shear
Sheep
Shoat
Shock
Shook
Shote
Singe
Sloot
Spell
Stack
Stale
Stall
Stand
Stile
Stirk
Stock
Stook
Store
Straw
Strip
Swath
Swede
Sweep
Swill
Tally
Tilth
Tolly
Trash
Tribe
Truck
Wheat

6 letters:
Animal
Apiary
Arable
Bail up
Barley

Barren
Barrow
Barton
Binder
Candle
Cattle
Cereal
Cheque
Clutch
Colter
Corral
Cotton
Cowboy
Cowman
Cowpat
Cradle
Cratch
Crutch
Culler
Cut out
Dobbin
Drover
Duster
Eatage
Enrich
Ensile
Fallow
Farmed
Farmer
Farrow
Fatten
Feeder
Fleece
Fodder
Foison
Forage
Furrow
Garner
Gavage
Grange
Grease
Greasy
Grieve
Harrow
Haw-haw

Haymow
Heeler
Heifer
Hen run
Herder
Hockey
Hogget
Hopper
Hummel
Hurdle
Incult
Kharif
Lea-rig
Linhay
Lister
Litter
Manger
Manure
Meadow
Mealie
Mellow
Middle
Mielie
Milker
Mistal
Moshav
Muster
Pakahi
Parity
Pastor
Pigpen
Pigsty
Pleugh
Plough
Porker
Rancho
Ratoon
Reaper
Reddle
Ringer
Ripple
Roller
Ruddle
Run off
Runway

Scythe
Seeder
Shamba
Shears
Shed up
Sheepo
Sheuch
Shorts
Sickle
Silage
Smudge
Spider
Spread
Stable
Stitch
Stover
Summer
Swathe
Take up
Tar boy
Tedder
Thrash
Thresh
Titman
Vinery
Winnow
Winter
Zoo doo

7 letters:
Breaker
Break in
Breeder
Bucolic
Calving
Chamber
Combine
Compost
Conacre
Contact
Coulter
Cowbell
Cowherd
Cowshed
Crofter

Cropper
Culture
Daglock
Dockage
Drummer
Earmark
Exhaust
Farming
Fatling
Feedbag
Feedlot
Fertile
Florist
Foaling
Freshen
Fruiter
Granary
Grazier
Grazing
Grow bag
Haggard
Harvest
Haycock
Hayfork
Hayrick
Hayseed
Hencoop
Hennery
Herbage
Hogwash
Infield
Kolkhoz
Lairage
Lambing
Lay down
Lazy bed
Machair
Milkman
Milling
Multure
Nest box
Nest egg
Nitrate
Nitrify
Oil cake

Orchard
Organic
Paddock
Pannage
Parlour
Pasture
Piggery
Pinfold
Planter
Pork pig
Poultry
Poverty
Prairie
Predial
Produce
Pruning
Rattoon
Reaping
Rearing
Reclaim
Round up
Scarify
Shedder
Shed out
Show day
Skirter
Sleeper
Soilage
Sovkhoz
Sprayer
Staddle
Station
Stubble
Subsoil
Swidden
Swipple
Tankage
Tillage
Topsoil
Tractor
Tumbrel
Turbary
Upgrade
Vintage
Wigging

Windrow
Wrangle
Wrestle
Yarding

8 letters:
Abattoir
Agrarian
Agrestal
Agrology
Agronomy
Apiarian
Apiarist
Barnyard
Bone meal
Butchery
Caponize
Cash crop
Checkrow
Chin ball
Churning
Cockatoo
Cockerel
Corncrib
Cornhusk
Cow cocky
Creamery
Crofting
Dairying
Dairyman
Dieldrin
Ditching
Domestic
Drainage
Dressing
Elevator
Empty cow
Ensilage
Farm hand
Farmland
Farmyard
Fishmeal
Flushing
Foremilk
Forestry

Fruitage
Fumatory
Generous
Geoponic
Goatherd
Hacienda
Handfeed
Hatchery
Haymaker
Haystack
Haywagon
Headland
Henhouse
Herdsman
Home farm
Hot fence
Huntaway
Irrigate
Lamb down
Land girl
Land-poor
Landside
Loosebox
Marginal
Maverick
Milkmaid
Moorburn
Mowburnt
Muckrake
Muirburn
Muleteer
Outfield
Overcrop
Pastoral
Perchery
Pharming
Pigswill
Plant out
Plougher
Poundage
Praedial
Preserve
Property
Quickset
Richness

Root crop
Rotation
Seed corn
Seminary
Set-aside
Shambles
Shed hand
Sheep-dip
Shepherd
Shieling
Soil bank
Spreader
Stabling
Stampede
Steading
Stockman
Stubbled
Swanherd
Sweatbox
Systemic
Thresher
Top-dress
Town milk
Two-tooth
Unbolted
Vineyard
Vintager
Voorskot
Watering
Wayleggo
Wool clip
Woolshed
Workfolk
Wrangler
Zamindar
Zemindar

9 letters:
Aftermath
Agterskot
Beastings
Beestings
Bell sheep
Bellyband
Biestings

Biosafety
Breakaway
Broadcast
Bunkhouse
Butterfat
Canebrake
Cane piece
Catalogue
Catch crop
Cattleman
Cleanskin
Cornfield
Corn shock
Corn shuck
Cornstalk
Cover crop
Cultivate
Dairymaid
Dead stock
Depasture
Dog tucker
Enclosure
Expellers
Extensive
Farmstead
Fertilize
Field corn
Field tile
Flystrike
Free-range
Geoponics
Gleanings
Grassland
Hand glass
Hand-piece
Hard wheat
Harvester
Haymaking
Home-grown
Homestead
Hop-picker
Husbandry
Intensive
Intercrop
Livestock

Moldboard
Mole drain
No-tillage
Overgraze
Overstock
Pasturage
Pesticide
Phosphate
Pitchfork
Ploughboy
Ploughing
Ploughman
Poulterer
Provender
Rangeland
Rice field
Rotary hoe
Rotovator
Scarifier
Scourings
Seed drill
Sharecrop
Shearling
Sheepcote
Sheepfold
Sheep race
Sheepwalk
Shrinkage
Side-dress
Slaughter
Soft wheat
Stall-feed
Stock unit
Stock whip
Stockyard
Sundowner
Sunk fence
Swineherd
Tea garden
Thrashing
Threshing
Ventilate
Vernalize
Water-sick
Winnowing

Wool table
Zamindari

10 letters:
Apiculture
Aviculture
Battery hen
Bull tongue
Cattle-cake
Cattle-grid
Cattle prod
Cattle-stop
Corn circle
Corn-picker
Cotton belt
Cotton cake
Cottonseed
Cowfeteria
Crop circle
Crutchings
Cultivable
Cultivated
Cultivator
Deep-litter
Disc harrow
Disc plough
Dry farming
Energy crop
Fertilizer
Fire blight
Fumatorium
Gang plough
Hamshackle
Harvesting
Harvestman
Heading dog
Herd tester
Husbandman
Impregnate
Irrigation
Land reform
Ley farming
Mouldboard
Nitro-chalk
Plantation

Poultryman
Quernstone
Rouseabout
Roustabout
Seed potato
Self-feeder
Semination
Showground
Stockhorse
Stockroute
Stump ranch
Turkey nest
Underdrain
Ungrateful
Unimproved
Virgin soil
Wine grower
Winterfeed
Wool cheque
Woolgrower

11 letters:
Agriculture
Agrobiology
Aquaculture
Aquiculture
Catching pen
Chamberhand
Compostable
Crop-dusting
Cultivation
Dogleg fence
Estate agent
Extractions
Factory farm
Full-mouthed
Green manure
Harvest home
Head station
Hedge laying
Hobby farmer
Hydroponics
Insecticide
Latifundium
Mariculture

Milking shed
Monoculture
Mule skinner
Pastoralist
Ploughshare
Ploughstaff
Pomiculture
Reclamation
Sericulture
Sharefarmer
Share-milker
Stock saddle
Subirrigate
Submarginal
Tank farming
Tattie-bogle
Top dressing
Vinedresser
Viniculture
Viticulture
Water meadow
Windlestraw
Winter wheat
Zero grazing

12 letters:
Agribusiness
Agricultural
Agrochemical
Agroforestry
Break feeding
Broiler house
Citriculture
Cotton picker
Crop rotation
Cutting horse
Double-dumped
Forcing house
Furfuraceous
Market garden
Mixed farming
Muck spreader
Rotary plough
Sharecropper
Shearing gang

Shearing shed
Sheep station
Slash-and-burn
Slaughterman
Smallholding
Staddlestone
Strong-eye dog
Taranaki gate
Ten-acre block
Tenant farmer
Transhumance
Trash farming
Uncultivated

13 letters:
Anthropophyte
Double digging
Freezing works
Middlebreaker
Pumice country
Sheepshearing
Strip cropping
Stubble-jumper
Thremmatology

14 letters:
Cottonseed meal
Holding paddock
Milking machine
Slaughterhouse
Terminator seed

15 letters:
Animal husbandry
Butterfat cheque
Cooperative farm
Gentleman-farmer
Green revolution
Market gardening
Nonagricultural
Stump-jump plough

16 letters:
Combine harvester
Contour ploughing
Rabbit-proof fence
Sacrifice paddock
Soil conservation
Threshing machine

17 letters:
Aerial top
 dressing
Potassium chloride
Soldier settlement

18 letters:
Subsistence farming

19 letters:
Bovine
 somatotrophin
Shifting cultivation

20 letters:
Stock and station agent

24 letters:
Common Agricultural
 Policy

Aircraft

TYPES OF AIRCRAFT

3 letters:
Jet
MIG
SST

4 letters:
Kite
Moth
STOL
VTOL
Wing

5 letters:
Avion
Blimp
Camel
Comet

Drone
Gotha
Jumbo
Rigid
Scout
Stuka
Taube

6 letters:
Airbus
Auster
Bomber
Canard
Chaser
Fokker
Galaxy
Glider

Hunter
Mirage
Ramjet
Tanker
Tri-jet

7 letters:
Airship
Aviette
Balloon
Biplane
Chopper
Clipper
Fighter
Harrier
Heinkel
Jump jet

Parasol
Penguin
Phantom
Propjet
Shuttle
Sopwith
Trident
Warbird

8 letters:
Aerodyne
Aerostat
Airliner
Autogiro
Autogyro
Brabazon
Concorde

Gyrodyne
Jetliner
Jet plane
Jumbo jet
Lysander
Microjet
Mosquito
Oerlikon
Rotodyne
Scramjet
Seaplane
Skiplane
Spitfire
Tiltwing
Triplane
Turbofan
Turbojet
Viscount
Warplane
Widebody
Zeppelin

9 letters:
Amphibian

Autoflare
Coleopter
Cyclogiro
Delta-wing
Dirigible
Doodlebug
Fixed-wing
Freighter
Hurricane
Lancaster
Liberator
Microlite
Monoplane
Orthopter
Rotaplane
Sailplane
Semi-rigid
Swept-wing
Swing-wing
Taxiplane
Tiltrotor
Turboprop

10 letters:
Dive bomber
Flying boat
Flying wing
Hang-glider
Helicopter
Hydroplane
Microlight
Multiplane
Paraglider
Super sabre
Tankbuster
Wild weasel

11 letters:
Eurofighter
Intercepter
Interceptor
Lifting body
Ornithopter
Starfighter
Turboramjet

12 letters:
Night fighter
Sopwith Camel
Stealth plane
Stratotanker
Troop carrier

13 letters:
Convertaplane
Convertiplane
Convertoplane
Fighter-bomber
Hot-air balloon
Light aircraft
Messerschmitt
Stealth bomber
Stratocruiser
Torpedo bomber

16 letters:
Gas-filled balloon

17 letters:
Helicopter gunship

AIRCRAFT PARTS

3 letters:
Fin
Pod
Tab

4 letters:
Body
Cowl
Flap
Hold
Horn
Keel
Nose
Slat
Tail
Wing

5 letters:
Cabin
Pylon
Rotor
Waist

6 letters:
Basket
Canopy
Elevon
Engine
Galley
Pusher
Ramjet
Rudder
Turret

7 letters:
Aileron
Airlock
Athodyd
Blister
Bomb bay
Capsule
Chassis
Cockpit
Cowling
Fairing
Gondola
Jet pipe
Nacelle
Spinner
Spoiler
Trim tab
Winglet

Wing tip

8 letters:
Aerofoil
Airframe
Air scoop
Airscrew
Anti-icer
Arrester
Black box
Bulkhead
Drop tank
Elevator
Fuel tank
Fuselage
Heat sink
Joystick
Longeron

Pulsejet	Pitot tube	Landing gear	Undercarriage
Tailskid	Propeller	Slinger ring	
	Tailplane		**14 letters:**
9 letters:	Tail wheel	**12 letters:**	Flight recorder
Air-intake		Control stick	
Altimeter	**10 letters:**	Ejection seat	**15 letters:**
Astrodome	Astrohatch	Inclinometer	Instrument panel
Autopilot	Cantilever	Landing light	
Bombsight	Flight deck	Ramjet engine	**16 letters:**
Clamshell	Hydroplane	Trailing edge	Aerometeorograph
Dashboard	Launch shoe		
Empennage	Stabilizer	**13 letters:**	**17 letters:**
Engine pod		Aerostructure	Artificial horizon
Jet engine	**11 letters:**	All-flying tail	
Main plane	Afterburner	Control column	**18 letters:**
Nose wheel	Horn balance	Launching shoe	Auxiliary power unit

Airline flight codes

Code	Airline	Code	Airline
AA	American Airlines	EI	Aer Lingus
AC	Air Canada	EK	Emirates
AF	Air France	FE	Royal Khmer
AH	Air Algerie		Airlines
AI	Air India	FI	Icelandair
AJ	Air Belgium	FR	Ryanair
AM	Aeromexico	GF	Gulf Air
AQ	Aloha Airlines (Hawaii)	GH	Ghana Airways
AR	Aerolineas Argentinas	GM	Air Slovakia
AY	Finnair	HA	Hawaiian Airlines
AZ	Alitalia	IB	Iberia
BA	British Airways	IC	Indian Airlines
BD	British Midland	IL	Istanbul Airways
BY	Britannia Airways	IR	Iran Air
CA	Air China	JA	Air Bosnia
CO	Continental Airlines	JE	Manx Airlines
CP	Canadian Airlines	JG	Air Greece
	International	JL	Japan Airlines
CT	Air Sofia	JM	Air Jamaica
CU	Cubana	JU	JAT (Yugoslavia)
CY	Cyprus Airways	KL	KLM
DA	Air Georgia	KQ	Kenya Airways
DI	Deutsche BA	KU	Kuwait Airways
DL	Delta Airlines	LG	Luxair
DX	Danish Air Transport	LH	Lufthansa

Code	Airline	Code	Airline
LV	Albanian Airlines	RM	Air Moldova
LY	El Al	RO	Tarom (Romania)
MA	Malev (Hungary)	RR	Royal Air Force
MS	Egyptair	SA	South African Airways
NG	Lauda Air (Austria)	SK	SAS (Scandinavian Airlines, Sweden)
NH	All Nippon Airlines		
NV	Northwest Territorial Airways (Canada)	SN	Sabena Belgian World Airlines
NW	Northwest Airlines (USA)	SQ	Singapore Airlines
NY	Air Iceland	SR	Swissair
NZ	Air New Zealand	SU	Aeroflot (Russia)
OA	Olympic Airlines (Greece)	TE	Lithuanian Airlines
OG	Go	TK	Turkish Airlines
OK	Czech Airlines	TP	TAP Air Portugal
OS	Austrian Airlines	TT	Air Lithuania
OU	Croatia Airlines	TW	TWA (USA)
OV	Estonian Air	U2	Easyjet
PC	Fiji Air	UA	United Airlines (USA)
PK	Pakistan International Airlines	UK	KLM UK
		UL	Sri Lankan Airlines
PS	Ukraine International Airlines	UM	Air Zimbabwe
		US	USAir
QF	Qantas	VS	Virgin Atlantic Airways
QR	Qatar Airways	WN	Southwest Airlines (USA)
QS	Tatra Air (Slovakia)	WT	Nigeria Airways
QU	Uganda Airlines	WX	Cityjet (Ireland)
QZ	Zambia Airways	ZB	Monarch Airlines (UK)
RG	Varig (Brazil)		

Airports

3 letters:
JFK
Lod

4 letters:
City
Dyce
Faro
Lydd
Orly
Sfax
Wick

5 letters:
Kimpo
Logan
Luton
Lydda
McCoy
O'Hare
Tegel

6 letters:
Changi
Dorval
Dulles

Findel
Gander
Gerona
Linate
Lympne
Narita
Okecie
St Paul
Subang

7 letters:
Arlanda
Ataturk

Barajas
Dalaman
Douglas
Entebbe
Fornebu
Gatwick
Hopkins
Kennedy
Kerkyra
Lincoln
Mirabel
Pearson
Shannon

8 letters:
Beauvais
Ciampino
Cointrin
G Marconi
Heathrow
Hongqiao
Idlewild
Keflavik
McCarran
Mohamed V
Schiphol
Stansted

9 letters:
Ben Gurion

Charleroi
Fiumicino
Jose Marti
La Guardia
Marco Polo
Peninsula
Prestwick
Queen Alia
Sky Harbor
Turnhouse

10 letters:
Hartsfield
Hellenikon
King Khaled
Louis Botha
Reina Sofia
Will Rogers

11 letters:
Ninoy Aquino
Tullamarine
Wayne County

12 letters:
Benito Juarez
Chiang Kai She
Echterdingen
Indira Gandhi
Jomo Kenyatta

Norman Manley
Papola Casale
Queen Beatrix
Santos Dumont
Sherenetyevo
Simon Bolivar

13 letters:
Grantley Adams
King Abdul Aziz
Soekarno Hatta

14 letters:
Galileo Galilei
Kingsford Smith
Lester B Pearson
Lindbergh Field
Luis Munoz Marin

15 letters:
Charles De Gaulle
General Mitchell
Leonardo da Vinci
Murtala Muhammed
Sir Seretse Khama

17 letters:
Cristoforo Colombo
Houari Boumedienne

Alcohols

4 letters:
Diol

5 letters:
Cetyl
Ethal
Ethyl
Meths
Nerol
Pisco
Thiol

6 letters:
Cresol
Lauryl
Mescal
Phytol
Polyol
Propyl
Sterol

7 letters:
Borneol
Choline

Ethanol
Mannite
Xylitol

8 letters:
Acrolein
Aldehyde
Catechol
Farnesol
Fusel-oil
Geraniol
Glycerin

Inositol
Linalool
Mannitol
Methanol
Sorbitol

9 letters:
Glycerine
Isopropyl
Mercaptan

11 letters:	Citronellol	12 letters:	14 letters:
Cholesterol	Sphingosine	Potato spirit	White lightning

Algae

3 letters:	Nostoc	9 letters:	12 letters:
Red	Volvox	Carrageen	Bladderwrack
		Chlorella	Heterocontae
		Irish moss	Reindeer moss
4 letters:	7 letters:	Prokaryon	Ulotrichales
Kelp	Euglena	Sargassum	Zooxanthella
	Isokont	Sea tangle	
	Oarweed	Spirogyra	13 letters:
5 letters:	Seaweed	Star-jelly	Blackfish weed
Brown	Valonia	Stonewort	Phytoplankton
Dulse			
Fucus	8 letters:	10 letters:	14 letters:
Green	Anabaena	Carragheen	Dinoflagellate
Jelly	Carageen	Rhodophyte	
Laver	Conferva	Sea lettuce	16 letters:
Wrack	Gulfweed		Neptune's
	Plankton	11 letters:	necklace
6 letters:	Pleuston	Blanketweed	
Desmid	Rockweed	Chlorophyte	
Diatom	Sargasso	Iceland moss	
Fucoid	Sea wrack	Protococcus	
Lichen	Ulothrix	Yellow-green	

Alkalis

5 letters:	Narceen	9 letters:
Borax	Quinine	Bebeerine
White	Tropine	Berberine
		Capsaicin
6 letters:	8 letters:	Ephedrine
Betane	Harmalin	Gelsemine
Emetin	Hyoscine	Guanidine
Harmin	Lobeline	Harmaline
Potash	Narceine	Limewater
	Nicotine	Reserpine
7 letters:	Piperine	Rhoeadine
Brucine	Thebaine	Sparteine
Codeine	Veratrin	Veratrine
Emetine		Yohimbine
Harmine		

10 letters:
Colchicine
Papaverine
Stramonium

11 letters:
Apomorphine
Gelseminine
Scopolamine
Theobromine
Vinblastine

Vincristine

12 letters:
Theophylline
Tubocurarine

Alloys

1 letter:
Y

4 letters:
Alni
Beta

5 letters:
Alpha
Brass
Invar®
Mazac
Monel
Potin
Steel
Terne

6 letters:
Albata
Alnico®
Billon
Bronze
Cermet
Chrome
Cunico
Cunife
Feroba
Latten
Magnox
Marmem
Occamy
Oreide
Ormolu
Oroide
Pewter
Solder

Tambac
Tombac
Tombak

7 letters:
Alcomax
Alumnel
Amalgam
Babbitt
Chromel
Columen
Elinvar
Inconel
Kanthal
Mumetal
Nimonic
Nitinol
Paktong
Platina
Shakudo
Similor
Spelter
Tutenag

8 letters:
Cast iron
Dowmetal
Electron
Electrum
Gunmetal
Hipernik
Kamacite
Kirksite
Manganin®
Nichrome®
Orichalc

Stellite®
Vicalloy
Zircaloy
Zircoloy

9 letters:
Bell metal
Duralumin®
Hastelloy
Magnalium
Permalloy
Perminvar
Pinchbeck
Platinoid
Shibuichi
Type metal
White gold
Zircalloy

10 letters:
Bell bronze
Constantan
Misch metal
Muntz metal
Nicrosilal
Osmiridium
Rose's metal
Soft solder
Superalloy
White metal
Wood's metal

11 letters:
Babbit metal
Cupronickel
Electrotype

Ferronickel
Monell metal
Supermalloy
Supermendur

12 letters:
Ferrosilicon
German silver
Nickel silver
Nimonic alloy
Silver solder

13 letters:
Brazing solder
Fernotungsten
Ferrochromium
Ferrovanadium
Magnolia metal
Platiniridium
Speculum metal

14 letters:
Admiralty metal
Britannia metal
Ferromanganese
Phosphor bronze
Stainless steel
Sterling silver

15 letters:
Ferromolybdenum

24 letters:
Austenitic
   stainless steel

Alphabets

RELATED VOCABULARY

3 letters:
ITA

4 letters:
Kana
Ogam

5 letters:
Cufic
Kanji
Kufic
Latin
Ogham
Roman

6 letters:
Brahmi
Finger
Glagol
Hangul
Nagari
Pinyin
Romaji

7 letters:
Braille
Futhark
Futhorc
Futhork

Glossic
Grantha
Linear A
Linear B
Pangram

8 letters:
Cyrillic
Hiragana
Katakana
Logogram
Phonetic

9 letters:
Logograph
Syllabary

10 letters:
Devanagari
Estrangelo
Glagolitic
Lexigraphy

11 letters:
Estranghelo

ARABIC ALPHABET

Alif	Khā	Shīn	Ghain	Nūn
Bā	Dāl	Ṣād	Fā	Hā
Tā	Dhāl	Ḍād	Qāf	Wāw
Thā	Rā	Ṭā	Kāf	Yā
Jīm	Zā	Ẓā	Lām	
Ḥā	Sīn	'Ain	Mīm	

GREEK ALPHABET

Alpha	Gamma	Omega	Sigma
Beta	Iota	Omicron	Tau
Chi	Kappa	Phi	Theta
Delta	Lambda	Pi	Upsilon
Epsilon	Mu	Psi	Xi
Eta	Nu	Rho	Zeta

HEBREW ALPHABET

Aleph	Kaph	Sade	Yod
Ayin	Koph	Tsade	Yodh
Ain	Qoph	Samekh	Zayin
Beth	Lamed	Shin	
Daleth	Lamedh	Sin	
Daled	Mem	Tav	
Gimel	Nun	Taw	
He	Pe	Teth	
Heth	Resh	Vav	
Cheth	Sadhe	Waw	

COMMUNICATIONS CODE WORDS FOR THE ALPHABET

Alpha	Hotel	Oscar	Victor
Bravo	India	Papa	Whiskey
Charlie	Juliet	Quebec	X-Ray
Delta	Kilo	Romeo	Yankee
Echo	Lima	Sierra	Zulu
Foxtrot	Mike	Tango	
Golf	November	Uniform	

American and British equivalences

British	American
Aeroplane	Airplane
American football	Football
Antenatal	Prenatal
Aubergine	Egg plant
Autumn	Fall
Bad-tempered	Mean
Banknote	Bill
Bat	Paddle
Benefit	Welfare
Bin *or* dustbin	Trashcan
Biscuit	Cookie
Black pudding	Blood sausage
Blinds	Shades
Bonnet	Hood
Boot	Trunk
Braces	Retainer
Braces	Suspenders
Breve	Double whole note
Broad bean	Fava bean
Building society	Savings and loan
Burgle	Burglarize
Candy floss	Cotton candy
Car	Automobile
Car park	Parking lot
Chemist	Drug store
Chips	French fries
Clothes peg	Clothes pin
Coffin	Casket
Condom	Rubber
Cornflour	Corn starch
Courgette	Zucchini
Crisps	Chips *or* potato chips

British	American
Crossroads	Intersection
Crotchet	Quarter note
Current account	Checking account
Curtains	Drapes
Cutlery	Flatware *or* silverware
CV	Résumé
Dialling code	Area code
Dinner jacket	Tuxedo
Double cream	Heavy cream
Drapery	Dry goods
Draughts	Checkers
Drawing pin	Thumb tack
Dressing gown	Robe
Dummy	Pacifier *or* soother
Engaged tone	Busy signal
Estate agent	Realtor
Estate car	Station wagon
Fire lighter	Fire starter
First floor	Second floor
Flat	Apartment
Flick knife	Switch blade
Football	Soccer
Foyer	Lobby
Fringe	Bangs
Garden	Yard
Gear lever	Stick shift
Goose pimples	Goose bumps
Ground floor	First floor
Hair grip	Bobby pin
Hairpin bend	Switchback
Handbag	Purse
Hessian	Burlap
High street	Main street
Holiday	Vacation
Indicator	Blinker
Invigilator	Proctor
Ironmonger	Hardware store
Jam	Jelly
Janitor	Caretaker
Lawyer	Attorney
Lift	Elevator
Mangetout	Snowpea
Mate	Friend
Merry-go-round	Carousel

British	American
Methylated spirits	Denatured alcohol
Mince	Ground beef
Minim	Half note
Nappy	Diaper
Neat	Straight
Noughts and crosses	Tick-tack-toe
Nursery	Kindergarten
Off-licence	Liquor store
Paraffin	Kerosene
Pavement	Sidewalk
Pepper	Bell pepper
Petrol	Gas *or* gasoline
Pissed	Drunk
Plait	Braid
Plasterboard	Dry lining
Plot	Lot
Porridge	Oatmeal
Postcode	Zip code
Postman	Mail man
Pub *or* public house	Bar
Public school	Private school
Purse	Pocketbook
Pushchair	Stroller
Quaver	Eighth note
Quilt *or* eiderdown	Comforter
Railway	Railroad
Receptionist	Desk clerk
Reverse charge	Collect
Ring road	Beltway
Roll *or* bap	Bun
Rubber	Eraser
Rubbish	Trash *or* garbage
Semibreve	Whole note
Semi-detached	Duplex
Semiquaver	Sixteenth note
Shop	Store
Silencer	Muffler
Skip	Dumpster
Skirting board	Baseboard
Sleeper	Tie
Slowcoach	Slowpoke
Soft drink	Soda
Spanner	Wrench
Spring onion *or* salad onion	Scallion

British	American
State school	Public school
Stream	Creek
Surgical spirit	Rubbing alcohol
Sweet	Candy
Tap	Faucet
Tarmac	Asphalt
Telegram	Wire
Thread	Cotton
Tights	Pantyhose
Timber	Lumber
Torch	Flashlight
Town centre	Downtown
Trainers	Sneakers
Tram	Streetcar
Trousers	Pants
Turn up	Cuff
VAT	Sales tax
Vest	Undershirt
Waistcoat	Vest
Windscreen	Windshield

American football teams

11 letters:
New York Jets
St Louis Rams

12 letters:
Buffalo Bills
Chicago Bears
Detroit Lions

13 letters:
Dallas Cowboys
Denver Broncos
Houston Texans
Miami Dolphins
New York Giants

14 letters:
Atlanta Falcons
Oakland Raiders

15 letters:
Baltimore Ravens
Cleveland Browns
Green Bay Packers
Seattle Seahawks
Tennessee Titans

16 letters:
Arizona Cardinals
Carolina Panthers
Kansas City Chiefs
Minnesota Vikings
New Orleans Saints
San Diego Chargers

17 letters:
Cincinnati Bengals
Indianapolis Colts

18 letters:
New England Patriots
Philadelphia Eagles
Pittsburgh Steelers
Tampa Bay Buccaneers
Washington Redskins

19 letters:
Jacksonville Jaguars

23 letters:
San Francisco
 Forty-niners

Amphibians

3 letters:
Eft
Olm

4 letters:
Frog
Hyla
Newt
Pipa
Rana
Toad

5 letters:
Anura
Guana
Siren

Snake

6 letters:
Desman
Hassar

7 letters:
Axolotl
Crapaud
Proteus
Tadpole
Urodela
Urodele

8 letters:
Bullfrog

Caecilia
Cane toad
Congo eel
Mud puppy
Tree frog
Urodelan

9 letters:
Ambystoma
Caecilian
Hairy frog
Salientia

10 letters:
Amblystoma
Batrachian

Hellbender
Natterjack
Salamander

11 letters:
Goliath frog
Midwife toad
Surinam toad

16 letters:
Brown-striped frog

18 letters:
Queensland cane
toad

Ancient cities

2 letters:
Ur

3 letters:
Bam

4 letters:
Coba
Rome
Susa
Troy
Tula
Tyre
Uruk

5 letters:
Aksum
Argos
Bosra
Copán
Hatra
Huari
Kabah
Khiva

Labna
Mitla
Moche
Nemea
Petra
Sayil
Shloh
Tegea
Tikal
Tultm
Uxmal

6 letters:
Athens
Byblos
Delphi
Jabneh
Jamnia
Megara
Napata
Nippur
Sardis
Sikyon
Sparta

Thebes
Ugarit
Xlapak

7 letters:
Antioch
Babylon
Bukhara
Cahokia
Corinth
Eleusis
El Tajin
Ephesos
Ephesus
Mayapan
Miletus
Mycenae
Mykenae
Nineveh
Olympia
Pompeii
Samaria
Sybaris

8 letters:
Carthage
Cihuatán
Damascus
Palenque
Pergamon
Pergamum
Sigiriya
Tashkent
Thysdrus

9 letters:
Byzantium
Perepolis
Samarkand
Sukhothai

10 letters:
Alexandria
Carchemish
Heliopolis
Hierapolis

11 letters:	**12 letters:**	**14 letters:**
Chichén Itzá	Anuradhapura	Constantinople
Machu Picchu		
Polonnaruwa	**13 letters:**	
	Halicarnassus	

Angels

SPECIFIC ANGELS

5 letters:	Belial	Lucifer	Ithuriel
Ariel	Rimmon	Michael	
Uriel	Uzziel	Raphael	**9 letters:**
		Zadkiel	Beelzebub
6 letters:	**7 letters:**	Zephiel	
Abdiel	Asmadai		**10 letters:**
Arioch	Gabriel	**8 letters:**	Adramelech
Azrael	Israfel	Apollyon	

ANGELIC ORDERS

6 letters:	Virtues	**9 letters:**	**11 letters:**
Angels		Dominions	Dominations
Powers			
	8 letters:	**10 letters:**	**14 letters:**
7 letters:	Cherubim	Archangels	Principalities
Thrones	Seraphim	Princedoms	

Animals

RELATED WORDS

Animal	Related adjective	Animal	Related adjective
Ant	Formic	Fish	Piscine or ichthyoid
Ass	Asinine	Fowl	Gallinaceous
Bear	Ursine	Fox	Vulpine
Bee	Apian	Goat	Caprine or hircine
Bird	Avian or ornithic	Goose	Anserine or
Bull	Taurine		anserous
Cat	Feline	Gull	Larine
Crab	Cancroid	Hare	Leporine
Crow	Corvine	Hawk	Accipitrine
Deer	Cervine	Horse	Equine
Dog	Canine	Lion	Leonine
Dove	Columbine	Lynx	Lyncean
Eagle	Aquiline	Mite or tick	Acaroid
Elephant	Elephantine	Monkey	Simian
Falcon	Falconine	Ox	Bovine

Animal	Related adjective	Animal	Related adjective
Parrot	Psittacine	Snake	Serpentine, anguine, ophidian, *or* colubrine
Peacock	Pavonine		
Pig	Porcine		
Puffin	Alcidine	Swallow	Hirundine
Seal	Phocine	Wasp	Vespine
Sheep	Ovine	Wolf	Lupine

COLLECTIVE ANIMALS

Animal	Collective noun	Animal	Collective noun
Antelopes	Herd	Gnats	Swarm *or* cloud
Apes	Shrewdness	Goats	Herd *or* tribe
Asses	Pace *or* herd	Goldfinches	Charm
Badgers	Cete	Grouse	Brood, covey, *or* pack
Bears	Sloth		
Bees	Swarm *or* grist	Gulls	Colony
Birds	Flock, congregation, flight, *or* volery	Hares	Down *or* husk
		Hawks	Cast
Bitterns	Sedge *or* siege	Hens	Brood
Boars	Sounder	Herons	Sedge *or* siege
Bucks	Brace *or* lease	Herrings	Shoal *or* glean
Buffaloes	Herd	Hounds	Pack, mute, *or* cry
Capercailzies	Tok	Insects	Swarm
Cats	Clowder	Kangaroos	Troop
Cattle	Drove *or* herd	Kittens	Kindle
Choughs	Chattering	Lapwings	Desert
Colts	Rag	Larks	Exaltation
Coots	Covert	Leopards	Leap
Cranes	Herd, sedge, *or* siege	Lions	Pride *or* troop
Crows	Murder	Mallards	Sord *or* sute
Cubs	Litter	Mares	Stud
Curlews	Herd	Martens	Richesse
Curs	Cowardice	Moles	Labour
Deer	Herd	Monkeys	Troop
Dolphins	School	Mules	Barren
Doves	Flight *or* dule	Nightingales	Watch
Ducks	Paddling *or* team	Owls	Parliament
Dunlins	Flight	Oxen	Yoke, drove, team, span, *or* herd
Elk	Gang		
Fish	Shoal, draught, haul, run, *or* catch	Partridges	Covey
		Peacocks	Muster
Flies	Swarm *or* grist	Pheasants	Nye *or* nide
Foxes	Skulk	Pigeons	Flock *or* flight
Geese	Gaggle *or* skein	Pigs	Litter
Giraffes	Herd	Plovers	Stand *or* wing

Animal	Collective noun	Animal	Collective noun
Pochards	Flight, rush, bunch, or knob	Sparrows	Host
		Starlings	Murmuration
Ponies	Herd	Swallows	Flight
Porpoises	School or gam	Swans	Herd or bevy
Poultry	Run	Swifts	Flock
Pups	Litter	Swine	Herd, sounder, or dryft
Quails	Bevy		
Rabbits	Nest	Teal	Bunch, knob, or spring
Racehorses	Field or string		
Ravens	Unkindness	Whales	School, gam, or run
Roes	Bevy	Whelps	Litter
Rooks	Building or clamour	Whiting	Pod
Ruffs	Hill	Wigeon	Bunch, company, knob, or flight
Seals	Herd or pod		
Sheep	Flock	Wildfowl	Plump, sord, or sute
Sheldrakes	Dopping	Wolves	Pack, rout, or herd
Snipe	Walk or wisp	Woodcocks	Fall

HABITATIONS

Animal	Habitation	Animal	Habitation
Ant	Ant hill or formicary	Pig	Sty
Badger	Set or sett	Puffin	Puffinry
Beaver	Lodge	Rabbit	Warren
Bee	Hive or apiary	Rook	Rookery
Bird	Nest	Seal	Sealery
Eagle	Aerie or eyrie	Squirrel	Drey or dray
Fish	Redd	Termite	Termitarium
Fox	Earth	Wasp	Vespiary or bike
Otter	Holt		

MALE ANIMALS

Animal	Male	Animal	Male
Ass	Jack	Goose	Gander
Bird	Cock	Hare	Buck
Cat	Tom	Horse	Stallion
Deer	Hart or stag	Kangaroo	Buck or old man
Donkey	Jack	Lobster	Cock
Duck	Drake	Ox	Bull
Elephant	Bull	Peafowl	Peacock
Falcon	Tercel or tiercel	Pig	Boar
Ferret	Hob	Rabbit	Buck
Fowl	Cock	Reindeer	Buck
Fox	Dog	Ruff	Ruff
Goat	Billy or buck	Sheep	Ram or tup

Animal	Male	Animal	Male
Swan	Cob	Whale	Bull
Weasel	Whittret		

FEMALE ANIMALS

Animal	Female	Animal	Female
Ass	Jenny	Lion	Lioness
Bird	Hen	Lobster	Hen
Cat	Queen	Mink	Sow
Deer	Doe *or* hind	Ox	Cow
Dog	Bitch	Peafowl	Peahen
Donkey	Jenny	Pig	Sow
Elephant	Cow	Rabbit	Doe
Ferret	Gill *or* jill	Ruff	Reeve
Fowl	Hen	Sheep	Ewe
Fox	Vixen	Swan	Pen
Goat	Nanny	Tiger	Tigress
Hare	Doe	Whale	Cow
Horse	Mare	Wolf	Bitch
Leopard	Leopardess	Wren	Jenny

YOUNG ANIMALS

Animal	Young	Animal	Young
Bear	Cub	Hare	Leveret
Bird	Chick, fledgling, fledgeling, *or* nestling	Herring	Alevin, brit, *or* sparling
		Horse	Foal, colt, *or* filly
Butterfly	Caterpillar, chrysalis, *or* chrysalid	Kangaroo	Joey
		Lion	Cub
		Moth	Caterpillar
Cat	Kitten	Owl	Owlet
Cod	Codling	Ox	Calf
Deer	Fawn	Pig	Piglet
Dog	Pup *or* puppy	Pigeon	Squab
Duck	Duckling	Salmon	Alevin, grilse, parr, *or* smolt
Eagle	Eaglet		
Eel	Elver *or* grig	Seal	Pup
Elephant	Calf	Sheep	Lamb *or* yeanling
Falcon	Eyas	Sprat	Brit
Ferret	Kit	Swan	Cygnet
Fish	Fry *or* fingerling	Tiger	Cub
Fox	Kit *or* cub	Toad	Tadpole
Frog	Tadpole	Whale	Calf
Goat	Kid *or* yeanling	Wolf	Cub *or* whelp
Goose	Gosling		

See also:
- ➤ **Amphibians** ➤ **Anteaters and other edentates**
- ➤ **Antelopes** ➤ **Birds** ➤ **Dinosaurs** ➤ **Fish** ➤ **Insects**
- ➤ **Invertebrates** ➤ **Mammals, extinct** ➤ **Parasites** ➤ **Reptiles**

Anniversaries

Year	Traditional	Modern
1st	Paper	Clocks
2nd	Cotton	China
3rd	Leather	Crystal or glass
4th	Linen or silk	Electrical appliances
5th	Wood	Silverware
6th	Iron	Wood
7th	Wool or copper	Desk sets
8th	Bronze	Linen or lace
9th	Pottery or china	Leather
10th	Tin or aluminium	Diamond jewellery
11th	Steel	Fashion jewellery or accessories
12th	Silk	Pearls or coloured gems
13th	Lace	Textile or furs
14th	Ivory	Gold jewellery
15th	Crystal	Watches
20th	China	Platinum
25th	Silver	Sterling silver
30th	Pearl	Diamond
35th	Coral or jade	Jade
40th	Ruby	Ruby
45th	Sapphire	Sapphire
50th	Gold	Gold
55th	Emerald	Emerald
60th	Diamond	Diamond

Anteaters and other edentates

2 letters:
Ai

5 letters:
Sloth

6 letters:
Numbat

7 letters:
Echidna
Tamandu

8 letters:
Aardvark
Anteater
Pangolin

Tamandua

9 letters:
Armadillo

13 letters:
Scaly anteater
Spiny anteater

14 letters:
Banded anteater
Lesser anteater

Antelopes

3 letters:
Elk
Gnu
Kob

4 letters:
Kudu
Oryx
Puku
Suni
Thar
Topi

5 letters:
Addax
Bongo
Bubal
Eland
Goral
Kaama
Nagor
Nyala
Oribi

Sable
Saiga
Sasin
Serow
Takin

6 letters:
Dikdik
Duiker
Duyker
Dzeren
Impala
Inyala
Koodoo
Lechwe
Nilgai
Nilgau
Ourebi
Pallah
Pygarg
Reebok
Rhebok

7 letters:
Blaubok
Blesbok
Bloubok
Bubalis
Chamois
Chikara
Gazelle
Gemsbok
Gerenuk
Grysbok
Kongoni
Madoqua
Nylghau
Sassaby
Stembok

8 letters:
Bluebuck
Bontebok
Bushbuck
Hartbees
Pale-buck

Reedbuck
Steenbok
Stemback
Tsessebe

9 letters:
Blackbuck
Prongbuck
Pronghorn
Sitatunga
Situtunga
Steinbock
Tragelaph
Waterbuck

10 letters:
Hartebeest
Wildebeest

12 letters:
Klipspringer

Antibiotics

7 letters:
Opsonin

8 letters:
Colistin
Neomycin
Nystatin

9 letters:
Kanamycin
Linezolid
Mitomycin
Oxacillin
Polymyxin
Puromycin
Rifamycin

10 letters:
Bacitracin
Daptomycin
Gentamicin
Gramicidin
Lincomycin
Rifampicin
Terramycin®
Tyrocidine

11 letters:
Aclarubicin
Actinomycin
Cloxacillin
Doxorubicin

Doxycycline
Interleukin
Methicillin
Tigecycline
Tyrothricin

12 letters:
Erythromycin
Griseofulvin
Streptomycin
Tetracycline

13 letters:
Carbenicillin
Cephalosporin

Spectinomycin
Streptokinase

14 letters:
Streptothricin

15 letters:
Oxytetracycline

Antiques

3 letters:
Bow
FSA

4 letters:
Adam
Buhl

5 letters:
Bulla
Curio
Inlay
Relic
Resto
Spode
Style
Tudor

6 letters:
Boulle
Branks
Bureau
Bygone
Flacon
Gothic
Period
Rococo

Sconce
Settle

7 letters:
Antique
Baroque
Charger
Curiosa
Diptych
Dresser
Gadroon
Godroon
Kiwiana
Netsuke
Regency
Snuffer
Tallboy

8 letters:
Baluster
Coalport
Ephemera
Jacobean
Snuffbox

9 letters:
Antiquary

Antiquate
Bed warmer
Davenport
Fleurette
George III
Marquetry
Porcelain
Queen Anne
Washstand

10 letters:
Art Nouveau
Bellarmine
Blue willow
Escritoire
Escutcheon
Four-poster
Secretaire
Victoriana

11 letters:
Antiquarian
Antiquities
Chinoiserie
Chippendale
Collectible
Cromwellian

Hepplewhite
Museum piece
Period piece
Renaissance

12 letters:
Apostle spoon
Elgin marbles
Gateleg table
Sanction mark
Welsh dresser

13 letters:
Drop-leaf table
Early Georgian
Fiddle pattern
Neo-classicism

14 letters:
Collector's item
William and Mary

15 letters:
English Heritage

Ants, bees, and wasps

3 letters:
Ant
Bee

4 letters:
Wasp

5 letters:
Emmet
Minga

7 letters:
Army ant
Blue ant
Bull ant
Bull Joe
Hive bee
Termite
Wood ant

8 letters:
Gall wasp
Honey ant
Honeybee

Horntail
Kootchar
Mason bee
Sand wasp
Slave ant
White ant
Wood wasp

9 letters:
Amazon ant
Bumblebee
Cuckoo bee
Driver ant

Humblebee
Killer bee
Mason wasp
Mining bee
Mud dauber
Native bee
Sirex wasp
Velvet ant

10 letters:
Bulldog ant
Digger wasp

Flower wasp
Pharaoh ant

11 letters:
Honeypot ant
Sugarbag fly

12 letters:
Carpenter bee
Cicada hunter
Ichneumon fly
Legionary ant
Policeman fly
Ruby-tail wasp
Yellow jacket

13 letters:
Ichneumon wasp
Leafcutter ant
Leafcutter bee

17 letters:
Spider-hunting wasp

Apocalypse, Four Horsemen of

Colour	Represents	Colour	Represents
White	Christ	Black	Famine
Red	War	Pale	Death

Apostles

4 letters:
John
Jude

5 letters:
James (the Great)
James (the Less)
Peter

Simon

6 letters:
Andrew
Philip
Thomas

7 letters:
Matthew

8 letters:
Matthias

11 letters:
Bartholomew

Apparatus

4 letters:
Loom

5 letters:
Churn
Davis
Golgi
Kipp's
Proto®
Snake
Still
Tromp
Tuner

6 letters:
Graith
Retort

Rounce
Tackle
Trompe

7 letters:
Alembic
Caisson
Coherer
Exciter
Skimmer
Sniffer
Snorkel
Tokamak

8 letters:
Critical
Cryostat

Digester
Gasogene
Gazogene
Injector
Jacquard
Lease-rod
Multi-gym
Pulmotor®
Push-pull
Resistor
Scrubber
Substage
Tackling
Telecine
Teleseme
Ventouse

9 letters:
Appliance
Aspirator
Autoclave
Chemostat
Clinostat
Condenser
Cosmotron
Equipment
Gyroscope
Hodoscope
Holophote
Hygrostat
Incubator
Kymograph
Phonmeter
Photostat®

Phytotron
Potometer
Projector
Rattlebag
Slide rest
Tellurian
Tellurion

10 letters:
Commutator
Eprouvette
Eudiometer
Heliograph
Helioscope
Hydrophone
Inspirator
Mimeograph
Nephoscope
Nitrometer
Oxygenator
Peatseeker
Percolator
Phonometer
Photophone
Radiosonde
Respirator

Rotisserie
Soundboard
Spirophore
Steriliser
Switchgear
Thermopile

11 letters:
Alkalimeter
Calorimeter
Colorimeter
Microreader
Pasteuriser
Plate-warmer
Pommel horse
Replenisher
Searchlight
Stellarator
Teleprinter
Transformer
Transmitter

12 letters:
Ebullioscope
Effusiometer
Electrograph

Electroscope
Installation
Oscillograph
Respirometer
Resuscitator
Sphygmograph
Whip-and-derry

13 letters:
Defibrillator
Electrophorus
Hemocytometer
Kipp generator
Life-preserver
Plumber's snake
Scintiscanner

14 letters:
Plethysmograph

16 letters:
Wheatstone bridge

17 letters:
Wheatstone's bridge

Apples

4 letters:
Crab
Fuji
John
Lobo
Love
Pome
Snow

5 letters:
Pyrus
Sugar
Thorn

6 letters:
Balsam

Biffin
Codlin
Elstar
Empire
Idared
Mammee
Medlar
Pippin
Pomace
Pomroy
Rennet
Russet
Sunset

7 letters:
Baldwin

Bramley
Codling
Costard
Custard
Pomeroy
Ribston
Ruddock
Spartan
Sturmer
Winesap

8 letters:
Braeburn
Greening
Jonagold

Jonathan
Jonathon
Pearmain
Pink Lady
Reinette
Ribstone
Sweeting

9 letters:
Alligator
Charlotte
Crab apple
Discovery
Grenadier
Jenneting
Nonpareil

Quarenden
Quarender
Redstreak
Royal Gala

James Grieve
Leather-coat
Quarrington

14 letters:
Blenheim Orange
Egremont Russet
Rosemary Russet

10 letters:
Quarantine
Quarrender
Red Ellison
Sops-in-wine

12 letters:
Greensleeves
Laxton Superb
Prince Albert
Red Delicious

15 letters:
Golden Delicious

16 letters:
Cox's orange pippin

11 letters:
Charles Ross
Granny Smith

13 letters:
Lord Lambourne
Seek-no-further

17 letters:
Worcester Pearmain

Archaeology

ARCHAEOLOGICAL PERIODS

6 letters:
Ice Age
La Tène
Minoan

Acheulian
Bronze Age
Levallois
Mycenaean
Neolithic
Solutrean

Magdalenian
New Stone Age
Old Stone Age

12 letters:
Chalcolithic
Levalloisian
Palaeolithic

7 letters:
Azilian
Iron Age

10 letters:
Eneolithic
Gravettian
Mesolithic
Mousterian

8 letters:
Asturian
Helladic

13 letters:
Neo-Babylonian
Old Babylonian

9 letters:
Acheulean

11 letters:
Aurignacian

15 letters:
Châtelperronian

ARCHAEOLOGICAL TERMS

4 letters:
Celt
Cist
Core
Kist

Cairn
Flake
Flint
Henge
Mound
Pylon
Stela
Stele

6 letters:
Arcade
Barrow
Bogman
Cirque
Dolmen
Eolith
Larnax
Vallum

5 letters:
Baulk
Blade
Burin

7 letters:
Callais
Caveman
Hogback
Ley line
Neolith
Obelisk
Patella
Retouch
Sondage
Tumulus

8 letters:
Bifacial
Cartouch
Cromlech
Graffito

Hillfort
Megalith
Palmette
Palstave
Tribrach

9 letters:
Acropolis
Alignment
Bracteate
Cartouche
Earthwork
Hut circle
Microlith

10 letters:
Souterrain

11 letters:
Clovis point
Cross-dating
Stone circle

12 letters:
Robber trench
Stratigraphy

15 letters:
Archeomagnetism

16 letters:
Archaeomagnetism

17 letters:
Radiocarbon dating

ARCHAEOLOGISTS

4 letters:
Bell, *Gertrude*

6 letters:
Childe, *V. Gordon*

8 letters:
Mallowan, *Max*

11 letters:
Winckelmann, *Johann*

Archbishops of Canterbury

3 letters:
Oda

4 letters:
Lang, *Cosmo*
Laud, *William*
Pole, *Reginald*
Rich, *Edmund*
Tait, *Archibald*
Wake, *William*

5 letters:
Abbot, *George*
Carey, *George*
Deane, *Henry*
Islip, *Simon*
Juxon, *William*
Kempe, *John*

Moore, *John*
Serio, *Sigeric*

6 letters:
Anselm
Becket, *Thomas à*
Benson, *Edward*
Coggan, *Frederick*
Fisher, *Geoffrey*
Howley, *William*
Hutton, *Matthew*
Justus
Lyfing
Mepham, *Simon*
Morton, *John*
Offord, *John*
Parker, *Matthew*
Pecham, *John*

Potter, *John*
Ramsey, *Arthur*
Robert *of Jumieges*
Runcie, *Robert*
Secker, *Thomas*
Sumner, *John*
Sutton, *Charles*
Temple, *Frederick*
Temple, *William*
Walden, *Roger*
Walter, *Hubert*
Warham, *William*

7 letters:
Aelfric
Arundel, *Thomas*
Baldwin
Cranmer, *Thomas*

Dunstan
Eadsige
Grindal, *Edmund*
Herring, *Thomas*
Langham, *Simon*
Langton, *Stephen*
Le Grant, *Richard*
Longley, *Charles*
Nothelm
Richard *of Dover*
Sheldon, *Gilbert*
Stigand
Sudbury, *Simon*
Tatwine
Tenison, *Thomas*
William *of Corbeil*
Wulfred

8 letters:
Aelfheah
Aelfsige
Bancroft, *Richard*
Boniface *of Savoy*

Ceolnoth
Chichele, *Henry*
Davidson, *Randall*
D'Escures, *Ralph*
Honorius
Lanfranc
Mellitus
Plegmund
Reynolds, *Walter*
Sancroft, *William*
Stafford, *John*
Theobald *of Bec*
Whitgift, *John*
Williams, *Rowan*
Wulfhelm

9 letters:
Aethelgar
Aethelred
Augustine
Breguwine
Courtenay, *William*
Deusdedit

Feologild
Kilwardby, *Robert*
Stratford, *John*
Theodorus
Tillotson, *John*

10 letters:
Aethelhelm
Aethelnoth
Beorhthelm
Bourgchier, *Thomas*
Cornwallis, *Frederick*
Cuthbeorht
Jaenbeorht
Laurentius
Whittlesey, *William*
Winchelsey, *Robert*

11 letters:
Aethelheard
Beorhtweald
Bradwardine

Arches

3 letters:
Gee

4 letters:
Keel
Ogee
Skew

5 letters:
Acute
Hance
Ogive
Roman

Vault

6 letters:
Gothic
Haunch
Lancet
Lierne
Marble
Norman
Portal
Soffit
Trajan

7 letters:
Plantar
Pointed
Squinch

8 letters:
Cross-rib
Intrados

9 letters:
Admiralty
Arblaster

Archivolt
Ctesiphon
Horseshoe
Triumphal

10 letters:
Proscenium

11 letters:
Counterfort

Architecture

ARCHITECTURAL STYLES

5 letters:			**6 letters:**
Doric	Ionic	Saxon	Empire
	Roman	Tudor	

Gothic
Norman
Rococo
Tuscan

7 letters:
Art Deco
Baroque
Bauhaus
Moderne
Moorish
Morisco
Mudéjar
Regency
Saracen

8 letters:
Colonial
Georgian
Jacobean

9 letters:
Brutalist
Byzantine
Classical

Composite
Decorated
Edwardian
Mannerist
Modernist
Palladian
Queen-Anne
Victorian

10 letters:
Art Nouveau
Corinthian
Federation
Louis Seize
Pycnostyle
Romanesque
Transition

11 letters:
Elizabethan
Louis Quinze
Louis Treize
Renaissance

12 letters:
Early English
Greek Revival
New brutalist
Transitional

13 letters:
Functionalism
Gothic Revival
Louis Quatorze
Neoclassicist
Perpendicular
Postmodernist

14 letters:
Churrigueresco
Early Christian

15 letters:
Churrigueresque

18 letters:
International Style

ARCHITECTURAL TERMS

3 letters:
Hip

4 letters:
Drum
Naos
Rise

5 letters:
Giant
Order
Shaft
Shell
Stria

6 letters:
Filler
Florid

Fluted
Hipped
Invert
Lierne
Lintel
Listed
Loggia
Member
Module
Return
Rhythm
Soffit
Spring
Storey
String
Summer

7 letters:
Abuttal
Astylar
Bolster
Bracket
Castled
Engaged
Galilee
Profile
Rampant
Respond
Stilted
Subbase
Surbase

8 letters:
Abutment
Colossal

Cradling
Diastyle
Diminish
Dipteral
Foliated
Galleria
King post
Lanceted
Moresque
Postiche
Prostyle
Shafting
Stringer
Tail beam
Trabeate
Tympanic

9 letters:
Composite
Crenelate
Discharge
Elevation
Eurhythmy
Floor plan
Floreated
Floriated
Foliation
Hexastyle
Hypostyle
Imbricate
Pulvinate
Queen post
Rendering
Rusticate
Springing
Stylobate
Tailpiece
Trabeated

10 letters:
Cloistered
Crenellate
Flamboyant
Ground plan
Imbricated
Joggle post
Polychromy
Pulvinated
Sexpartite
Summer tree

11 letters:
Castellated
Cinquecento
Denticulate
Fenestrated
High-pitched
Orientation

12 letters:
String course

13 letters:
Architectonic
Architectural
Springing line
Supercolumnar

14 letters:
Architectonics
Springing point

15 letters:
Underpitch vault

17 letters:
Intercolumniation
Ribbon development

ARCHITECTURAL FEATURES

3 letters:
Bow
Cap
Die
Ell
Fan
Rib
Web

4 letters:
Anta
Apse
Arch
Balk
Band
Base
Bead
Beak
Case
Cove
Cusp
Cyma

Dado
Drip
Foil
Jube
Naos
Neck
Ogee
Pace
Pier
Quad
Reed
Sill
Stoa
Term
Tore
Xyst

5 letters:
Aisle
Ancon
Apsis
Arris

Atlas
Attic
Cella
Cheek
Choir
Coign
Conch
Congé
Crown
Doors
Facet
Facia
Gable
Garth
Glyph
Groin
Gutta
Hance
Helix
Label
Newel
Niche

Ogive
Oriel
Ovolo
Patio
Porch
Pylon
Quirk
Quoin
Ridge
Shaft
Spire
Splay
Stela
Stele
Stria
Table
Talon
Tenia
Thumb
Torus
Truss
Vault

Verge

6 letters:
Abacus
Ancone
Arcade
Atrium
Baguet
Belfry
Bezant
Billet
Binder
Breast
Broach
Byzant
Canopy
Casing
Cellar
Coffer
Coigne
Column
Concha
Corbel
Cordon
Corona
Coving
Crenel
Cullis
Cupola
Dentil
Ectype
Exedra
Facade
Facial
Fascia
Fillet
Finial
Flèche
Frieze
Garret
Gazebo
Gradin
Griffe
Grotto
Haunch

Hipped
Impost
Lacuna
Leaded
Listel
Loggia
Louvre
Metope
Mutule
Offset
Perron
Piazza
Pillar
Plinth
Podium
Portal
Reglet
Relief
Return
Reveal
Rosace
Scotia
Screen
Soffit
Squint
Summer
Taenia
Trophy
Turret
Tympan
Volute

7 letters:
Acroter
Annulet
Antefix
Apteral
Balcony
Bezzant
Bracket
Caisson
Calotte
Capital
Cavetto
Ceiling

Channel
Chaplet
Chevron
Corbeil
Cornice
Crochet
Crocket
Cushion
Echinus
Entasis
Fantail
Fascial
Festoon
Fluting
Footing
Frustum
Gadroon
Gallery
Gambrel
Godroon
Hip roof
Landing
Lantern
Lucarne
Mansard
Meander
Minaret
Mullion
Narthex
Necking
Obelisk
Parapet
Pendant
Perpend
Portico
Postern
Reeding
Respond
Rosette
Rotunda
Roundel
Squinch
Steeple
Strigil
Tambour

Telamon
Tracery
Trefoil
Tribune
Trumeau
Veranda

8 letters:
Acanthus
Accolade
Apophyge
Arcature
Astragal
Atlantes
Baguette
Baluster
Banderol
Bannerol
Basement
Buttress
Caryatid
Casement
Chapiter
Cloister
Crenelle
Cresting
Crossing
Crow step
Curb roof
Cymatium
Dancette
Dogtooth
Extrados
Fanlight
Fenestra
Gable end
Gargoyle
Gorgerin
Headwork
Imperial
Intrados
Keystone
Moulding
Ogee arch
Pedestal

Pediment
Pinnacle
Platform
Predella
Semidome
Shafting
Skew arch
Skylight
Spandrel
Spandril
Springer
Tellamon
Terminal
Terminus
Transept
Traverse
Triglyph
Tympanum
Verandah
Vignette

9 letters:
Anthemion
Archivolt
Arcuation
Baldachin
Banderole
Bay window
Bilection
Bolection
Bow window
Cartouche
Choir loft
Colonnade
Corbeille
Decastyle
Dripstone
Embrasure
Footstall
Gatehouse
Headstone
Helicline
Hood mould
Hypophyge
Medallion

Modillion
Onion dome
Penthouse
Peristyle
Poppyhead
Roman arch
Strap work
Stylobate
Triforium

10 letters:
Ambulatory
Arc-boutant
Architrave
Ballflower
Belt course
Cantilever
Cinquefoil
Clerestory
Corbel step
Corbie-step
Egg and dart
Fan tracery
Fenestella
Gothic arch
Hagioscope
Lancet arch
Norman arch
Propylaeum
Quadrangle
Quatrefoil
Rose window
Saddleback
Saddle roof
Sash window
Scrollwork
Stereobate
Wagon vault
Water table

11 letters:
Amphistylar
Barge couple
Barge course
Barrel vault

Bed moulding
Bottom house
Brattishing
Columbarium
Corbie gable
Curtail step
Curtain wall
Cuspidation
Entablature
Gable window
Half landing
Oeil-de-boeuf
Oriel window
Tunnel vault

12 letters:
Articulation
Columniation
Egg and anchor
Egg and tongue
Frontispiece
Lancet window
Palm vaulting
Porte-cochere
Quarter round
String course

13 letters:
Amphiprostyle
Compass window
French windows
Machicolation

14 letters:
Catherine wheel
Flying buttress
Straining piece

15 letters:
Underpitch vault

16 letters:
Long-and-short work

17 letters:
Whispering gallery

ARCHITECTS

3 letters:
Cox, *David*
Oud, *Jacobus Johann Pieter*
Pei, *I(eoh) M(ing)*

4 letters:
Adam, *James*
Adam, *Robert*
Adam, *William*
Kahn, *Louis I(sadore)*
Kent, *William*
Loos, *Adolf*
Nash, *John*
Shaw, *Richard Norman*
Webb, *Aston*
Webb, *Philip*
Wood, *John*
Wren, *Christopher*

5 letters:
Aalto, *Alvar*
Baker, *Herbert*
Barry, *Charles*
Bryce, *David*
Dance, *George*
Doshi, *Balkrishna Vithaldas*
Dudok, *Willem Marinus*
Engel, *Johann Carl Ludwig*
Gaudí, *Antonio*
Gibbs, *James*
Gilly, *Friedrich*
Hooke, *Robert*
Horta, *Victor*
Jones, *Inigo*
Levau, *Louis*
Moore, *Charles Willard*
Nervi, *Pier Luigi*
Pugin, *Augustus (Welby Northmore)*
Scott, *George Gilbert*
Scott, *Giles Gilbert*
Soane, *John*
Tange, *Kenzo*
Terry, *(John) Quinlan*

Utzon, *Jorn*
Wyatt, *James*

6 letters:
Boulle, *Etienne-Louis*
Breuer, *Marcel Lajos*
Burton, *Decimus*
Casson, *Hugh (Maxwell)*
Coates, *Wells Wintemute*
Foster, *Norman*
Fuller, *(Richard) Buckminster*
Geddes, *Patrick*
Giotto *(di Bondone)*
Howard, *Ebenezer*
Lasdun, *Denys*
Ledoux, *Claude Nicolas*
Lescot, *Pierre*
Nissen, *Godber*
Paxton, *Joseph*
Perret, *Auguste*
Pisano, *Andrea*
Pisano, *Nicola*
Pollio, *Marcus Vitruvius*
Repton, *Humphrey*
Rogers, *Richard*
Romano, *Giulio*
Scopas
Serlio, *Sebastiano*
Smirke, *Robert*
Spence, *Basil (Unwin)*
Street, *George Edmund*
Stuart, *James*
Vasari, *Giorgio*
Voysey, *Charles (Francis Annesley)*
Wagner, *Otto*
Wright, *Frank Lloyd*

7 letters:
Alberti, *Leon Battista*
Asplund, *Erik Gunnar*
Behrens, *Peter*
Berlage, *Hendrick Petrus*
Bernini, *Gian Lorenzo*

Blacket, *Edmund*
Burnham, *David Hudson*
Candela, *Felix*
Columbo, *David*
Da Vinci, *Leonardo*
De l'Orme, *Philibert*
Erskine, *Ralph*
Gabriel, *Ange-Jacques*
Garnier, *Tony (Antoine)*
Gibberd, *Frederick*
Gilbert, *Cass*
Griffin, *Walter*
Gropius, *Walter*
Guarini, *Guarino*
Holland, *Henry*
Ictinus
Imhotep
Johnson, *Philip Cortelyou*
Lethaby, *William Richard*
Lorimer, *Robert Stodart*
Lutyens, *Edwin*
Maderna, *Carlo*
Maderno, *Carlo*
Mansart, *François*
Mansart, *Jules Hardouin*
Neumann, *Johann Balthasar*
Orcagna *(Andrea di Cionne)*
Percier, *Charles*
Peruzzi, *Baldassare Tommaso*
Poelzig, *Hans*
Raphael
Renwick, *James*
Seidler, *Harry*
Thomson, *Alexander (Greek)*
Venturi, *Robert*
Vignola, *Giacomo*

8 letters:
Bramante, *Donato*
Chalgrin, *Jean*
Chambers, *William*
Daedalus
De Brosse, *Salomon*
Di Cambio, *Arnolfo*
Erickson, *Arthur Charles*

Fontaine, *Pierre*
Greenway, *Francis*
Hamilton, *Thomas*
Hoffmann, *Josef*
Jacobsen, *Arne*
Niemeyer, *Oscar*
Palladio, *Andrea*
Piranesi, *Giambattista*
Playfair, *William Henry*
Rietveld, *Gerrit Thomas*
Saarinen, *Eero*
Schinkel, *Karl Friederich*
Smythson, *Robert*
Sottsass, *Ettore Jr*
Soufflot, *Jacques Germain*
Stirling, *James*
Sullivan, *Louis (Henri)*
Vanbrugh, *John*
Yamasaki, *Minoru*

9 letters:
Anthemias *of Tralles*
Bartholdi, *Frédéric August*
Borromini, *Francesco*
Cockerell, *Charles Robert*
Da Cortona, *Pietro Berrettini*
Da Vignola, *Giacomo Barozzi*
Di Giorgio, *Francesco*
Haussmann, *Georges Eugene*
Hawksmoor, *Nicholas*
Labrouste, *(Pierre Francois) Henri*
Mackmurdo, *Arthur Heygate*
Macquarie, *Lachlan*
Sansovino, *Jacopo*
Van Campen, *Jacob*
Vitruvius
Von Erlach, *Johann Bernhard Fischer*

10 letters:
Chermayeff, *Serge*
Mackintosh, *Charles Rennie*
Mendelsohn, *Eric*
Michelozzo
Sanmicheli, *Michele*
Tange Kenzo

Trophonius
Van der Rohe, *Ludwig Mies*
Van de Velde, *Henry*
Waterhouse, *Alfred*

11 letters:
Abercrombie, *(Leslie) Patrick*
Butterfield, *William*
Callicrates
Churriguera, *Don Jose*
De Cuvillies, *Francois*

Le Corbusier
Van Doesburg, *Theo*

12 letters:
Brunelleschi, *Filippo*
Michelangelo
Viollet-le-Duc, *Eugène Emmanuel*

14 letters:
Von Hildebrandt, *Johann Lukas*

Armour

4 letters:
Cush
Jack
Mail
Tace
Umbo

5 letters:
Armet
Bevor
Cuish
Culet
Curat
Fauld
Jambe
Jupon
Nasal
Petta
Tasse
Visor
Vizor

6 letters:
Beaver
Byrnie
Camail
Corium
Couter
Crinet
Cuisse
Curiet

Gorget
Greave
Gusset
Helmet
Jamber
Poleyn
Secret
Taslet
Tasset
Thorax
Tonlet
Tuille
Voider

7 letters:
Ailette
Basinet
Besagew
Brasset
Buckler
Casspir
Corslet
Cuirass
Hauberk
Jambart
Jambeau
Lamboys
Panoply
Placcat
Placket
Poitrel

Roundel
Sabaton
Ventail

8 letters:
Barbette
Bascinet
Chaffron
Chamfron
Chanfron
Chausses
Corselet
Gauntlet
Jazerant
Pauldron
Pavloron
Plastron
Pouldron
Solleret
Spaudler
Vambrace

9 letters:
Chamfrain
Garderobe
Garniture
Habergeon
Jesserant
Lance rest
Nosepiece

Sword belt
Vantbrass

10 letters:
Brigandine
Cataphract
Coat-of-mail

11 letters:
Breastplate
Genouillère
Mentonnière

Art

ART STYLES AND MOVEMENTS

2 letters:
Op

3 letters:
Pop

4 letters:
Clip
Dada
Deco
Fine
Kano

5 letters:
Cobra
Dedal
Nabis
Tatum
Virtu

6 letters:
Bonsai
Brücke
Cubism
Daedal
Gothic
Kitsch
Rococo
Trouvé
Ukiyo-e

7 letters:
Art Deco
Baroque
Bauhaus

Dadaism
Daedale
De Stijl
Fauvism
Flemish
Kinetic
Minimal
Montage
New Wave
Norwich
Nouveau
Optical
Orphism
Plastic
Realism
Relievo
Sienese
Tachism
Trivium

8 letters:
Abstract
Futurism
Mandorla
Nazarene
Tachisme
Trecento

9 letters:
Mannerism
Modernism
Primitive
Still-life
Symbolism
Tenebrism
Toreutics
Vorticism

10 letters:
Arte Povera
Art Nouveau
Bloomsbury
Classicism
Commercial
Conceptual
Decorative
Jugendstil
Naturalism
Postmodern
Quadratura
Quadrivium
Romanesque
Surrealism
Synthetism

11 letters:
Chiaroscuro
Divisionism
Performance
Perigordian
Pointillism
Psychedelic
Romanticism
Suprematism
Synchronism
Trompe l'oeil

12 letters:
Clair-obscure
Clare-obscure
Neoclassical

13 letters:
Expressionism

Impressionism
Impressionist
Neoclassicism
Neoplasticism
Postmodernism
Pre-Raphaelite

14 letters:
Abstractionism
Barbizon School
Constructivism

Der Blaue Reiter

16 letters:
Neoimpressionism

17 letters:
Postimpressionism

21 letters:
Abstract expressionism

ART EQUIPMENT

3 letters:
Ink

5 letters:
Brush
Chalk
Easel
Glaze
Paint

6 letters:
Canvas
Crayon
Ground
Pastel

Pencil

7 letters:
Acrylic
Palette
Spatula
Varnish

8 letters:
Airbrush
Charcoal
Fixative
Oil paint
Paintbox
Spray gun

9 letters:
Lay figure

10 letters:
Linseed oil
Paintbrush
Sketchbook

11 letters:
Watercolour

12 letters:
Drawing paper
Palette knife

Arthurian legend

CHARACTERS IN ARTHURIAN LEGEND

4 letters:
Bors

5 letters:
Nimue

6 letters:
Arthur
Elaine
Gawain
Merlin
Modred

7 letters:
Caradoc
Galahad
Gawayne
Igraine
Launfal
Tristan
Viviane

8 letters:
Bedivere
Lancelot
Parsifal

Perceval
Tristram

11 letters:
Morgan Le Fay

14 letters:
Gareth of Orkney
Launcelot du Lac
Uther Pendragon

16 letters:
The Lady of the Lake

PLACES IN ARTHURIAN LEGEND

6 letters:	7 letters:	8 letters:	9 letters:	11 letters:
Avalon	Astolat	Tintagel	Lyonnesse	Glastonbury
	Camelot			

Artists

3 letters:
Arp, *Hans*
Arp, *Jean*
Cox, *David*
Dix, *Otto*
Dou, *Gerrit*
Fry, *Roger*
Gui, *Xia*
Nay, *Ernst Wilhelm*
Ono, *Yoko*
Ray, *Man*

4 letters:
Bell, *Vanessa*
Boyd, *Arthur*
Caro, *Anthony*
Cole, *Thomas*
Cuyp, *Aelbert*
Dadd, *Richard*
Dalí, *Salvador*
Done, *Ken*
Doré, *Gustave*
Dufy, *Raoul*
Etty, *William*
Gabo, *Naum*
Gill, *Eric*
Goya (y Lucientes), *Francisco José de*
Gris, *Juan*
Gros, *Antoine Jean*
Hals, *Frans*
Hunt, *William Holman*
John, *Augustus*
John, *Gwen*
Klee, *Paul*
Kuei, *Hsia*
Kuyp, *Aelbert*
Lely, *Peter*

Long, *Richard*
Marc, *Franz*
Miró, *Joan*
Nash, *Paul*
Opie, *John*
Phiz *(Hablot Knigh Browne)*
Rees, *Lloyd*
Reni, *Guido*
Rosa, *Salvator*
West, *Benjamin*
Zorn, *Anders*

5 letters:
Aiken, *John MacDonald*
Appel, *Karel*
Bacon, *Francis*
Bakst, *Leon Nikolayevich*
Balla, *Giacomo*
Beuys, *Joseph*
Blake, *Peter*
Blake, *William*
Bosch, *Hieronymus*
Brown, *Ford Madox*
Buren, *Daniel*
Burra, *Edward*
Corot, *Jean Baptiste Camille*
Crane, *Walter*
Crome, *John*
Danby, *Francis*
David, *Jacques Louis*
Degas, *Hilaire Germain Edgar*
Denis, *Maurice*
Dulac, *Pierre Charles*
Dürer, *Albrecht*
Ensor, *James*
Ernst, *Max*
Freud, *Lucian*

Gorky, *Arshile*
Grant, *Duncan*
Greco, *El*
Grosz, *George*
Hirst, *Damien*
Hoare, *William*
Homer, *Winslow*
Hooch, *Pieter de*
Johns, *Jasper*
Kitaj, *Ron B(rooks)*
Klimt, *Gustav*
Kline, *Franz*
Leech, *John*
Léger, *Fernand*
Lewis, *Wyndham*
Lippi, *Filippino*
Lotto, *Lorenzo*
Lowry, *L(awrence) S(tephen)*
Manet, *Edouard*
Monet, *Claude Oscar*
Moore, *Henry*
Morse, *Samuel Finley Breese*
Moses, *Grandma*
Munch, *Edvard*
Myron
Nolan, *Sidney*
Nolde, *Emil*
Olley, *Margaret*
Olsen, *John*
Orpen, *Sir William*
Oudry, *Jean Baptiste*
Pilon, *Germain*
Piper, *John*
Poons, *Larry*
Puget, *Pierre*
Redon, *Odilon*
Riley, *Bridget*
Rodin, *Auguste*
Runge, *Philipp Otto*
Seago, *Edward*
Shahn, *Ben*
Sloan, *John*
Smith, *David*
Steen, *Jan*
Steer, *Philip Wilson*

Stoss, *Veit*
Tatum, *Mary*
Watts, *George Frederick*
Zumbo, *Gaetano Giulio*

6 letters:
Albers, *Josef*
Andrei, *Rublev*
Andrei, *Rublyov*
Benton, *Thomas Hart*
Boudin, *Eugène*
Braque, *Georges*
Bratby, *John*
Buffet, *Bernard*
Butler, *Reg*
Calder, *Alexander*
Callot, *Jacques*
Campin, *Robert*
Canova, *Antonio*
Clouet, *François*
Clouet, *Jean*
Copley, *John*
Cotman, *John*
Coypel, *Antoine*
De Goya, *Francisco*
Derain, *André*
De Wint, *Peter*
Dobell, *William*
D'Orsay, *Count Alfred Guillaum Gabriel*
Eakins, *Thomas*
Fuseli, *Henry*
Gérard, *François*
Giotto *(di Bondone)*
Greuze, *Jean Baptiste*
Guardi, *Francesco*
Haydon, *Benjamin Robert*
Herman, *Sali*
Hopper, *Edward*
Houdon, *Jean Antoine*
Ingres, *Jean Auguste Dominique*
Knight, *Laura*
Lebrun, *Charles*
Le Nain, *Antoine*
Le Nain, *Louis*
Le Nain, *Mathieu*

Mabuse, *Jan*
Martin, *John*
Massys, *Quentin*
Millet, *Jean François*
Moreau, *Gustave*
Morris, *William*
Newman, *Barnett*
O'Keefe, *Georgia*
Oliver, *Isaac*
Orozco, *José Clemente*
Palmer, *Samuel*
Pisano, *Andrea*
Pisano, *Giovanni*
Pisano, *Nicola*
Potter, *Paulus*
Ramsay, *Allan*
Renoir, *Pierre Auguste*
Ribera, *Jusepe de*
Rivera, *Diego*
Romano, *Giulio*
Romney, *George*
Rothko, *Mark*
Rubens, *Peter Paul*
Scopas
Sendak, *Maurice*
Sesshu, *Toyo*
Seurat, *Georges*
Signac, *Paul*
Sisley, *Alfred*
Sluter, *Claus*
Stubbs, *George*
Tanguy, *Yves*
Tatlin, *Vladimir*
Tissot, *James Jacques Joseph*
Titian
Turner, *J(oseph) M(allord) W(illiam)*
Vasari, *Giorgio*
Villon, *Jacques*
Warhol, *Andy*
Wilson, *Richard*
Wright, *Joseph*
Zeuxis

7 letters:
Acconci, *Vito*

Alberti, *Leon Battista*
Allston, *Washington*
Apelles
Audubon, *John James*
Balthus *(Balthasar Klossowski de Rola)*
Bellini, *Giovanni*
Bernini, *Gian Lorenzo*
Bomberg, *David*
Bonheur, *Rosa*
Bonnard, *Pierre*
Borduas, *Paul*
Borglum, *Gutzon*
Boucher, *Francois*
Brassaï, *Gyula*
Bruegel, *Jan*
Bruegel, *Pieter*
Cassatt, *Mary*
Cellini, *Benvenuto*
Cézanne, *Paul*
Chagall, *Marc*
Chardin, *Jean-Baptiste Siméon*
Christo
Cimabue, *Giovanni*
Collier, *John*
Courbet, *Gustave*
Cranach, *Lucas*
Daumier, *Honoré*
Da Vinci, *Leonardo*
De Hooch, *Pieter*
De Hoogh, *Pieter*
Delvaux, *Paul*
Duchamp, *Marcel*
Epstein, *Jacob*
Flaxman, *John*
Fouquet, *Jean*
Gauguin, *Paul*
Gibbons, *Grinling*
Hobbema, *Meindert*
Hockney, *David*
Hofmann, *Hans*
Hogarth, *William*
Hokusai, *Katsushika*
Holbein, *Hans*
Hoppner, *John*
Kneller, *Godfrey*

Kossoff, *Leon*
Lindsay, *Norman Alfred William*
Lorrain, *Claude*
Maillol, *Aristide*
Martens, *Conrad*
Martini, *Simone*
Matisse, *Henri*
Meldrum, *Max*
Memlinc, *Hans*
Memling, *Hans*
Millais, *John Everett*
Morisot, *Berthe*
Morland, *George*
Murillo, *Bartolomé Esteban*
Nattier, *Jean Marc*
Orcagna, *Andrea di Cionne*
Parrish, *Maxfield*
Pasmore, *Victor*
Patinir, *Joachim*
Peruzzi, *Baldassare*
Pevsner, *Antoine*
Phidias
Picabia, *Francis*
Picasso, *Pablo*
Pigalle, *Jean Baptiste*
Pollock, *Jackson*
Poussin, *Nicolas*
Preston, *Margaret*
Proesch, *Gilbert*
Prud'hon, *Pierre Paul*
Pucelle, *Jean*
Rackham, *Arthur*
Raeburn, *Henry*
Raphael
Rouault, *Geroges*
Russolo, *Luigi*
Sargent, *John Singer*
Schiele, *Egon*
Severni, *Gino*
Sickert, *Walter Richard*
Soutine, *Chaim*
Spencer, *Stanley*
Teniers, *David*
Tiepolo, *Giambattista*
Uccello, *Paolo*

Utamaro, *Kitigawa*
Utrillo, *Maurice*
Van Dyck, *Anthony*
Van Eyck, *Jan*
Van Gogh, *Vincent*
Van Rijn, *Rembrandt Harmensz*
Vecchio, *Palma*
Vermeer, *Jan*
Watteau, *Jean Antoine*
Zeuxian
Zoffany, *Johann*

8 letters:
Angelico, *Fra*
Annigoni, *Pietro*
Auerbach, *Frank*
Beckmann, *Max*
Boccioni, *Umberto*
Bramante, *Donato*
Brancusi, *Constantin*
Breughel, *Jan*
Breughel, *Pieter*
Bronzino, *Agnolo*
Brueghel, *Jan*
Brueghel, *Pieter*
Carracci, *Agostino*
Carracci, *Annibale*
Carracci, *Ludovico*
Chadwick, *Lynn*
Daguerre, *Louis*
Daubigny, *Charles François*
De La Tour, *Georges*
Delaunay, *Robert*
De Ribera, *José*
Di Cosimo, *Piero*
Di Duccio, *Agostino*
Drysdale, *George Russell*
Dubuffet, *Jean*
Eastlake, *Sir Charles Lock*
Ghiberti, *Lorenzo*
Giordano, *Luca*
González, *Julio*
Hamilton, *Richard*
Jongkind, *Johan Barthold*
Jordaens, *Jacob*

Kirchner, *Ernst Ludwig*
Landseer, *Edwin*
Lawrence, *Thomas*
Leighton, *Frederic*
Leonardo
Lipchitz, *Jacques*
Lysippus
Magritte, *René*
Malevich, *Kasimir Severinovich*
Mantegna, *Andrea*
Masaccio *(Thomasso Giovanni di Simone Guidi)*
Mondrian, *Piet*
Munnings, *Alfred*
Nevinson, *Christopher Richard Wynne*
Paolozzi, *Eduardo*
Passmore, *George*
Patenier, *Joachim*
Perceval, *John*
Perugino, *Pietro*
Piranesi, *Giambattista*
Pissarro, *Camille*
Pontormo, *Jacopo Carucci*
Reynolds, *Joshua*
Rockwell, *Norman*
Rossetti, *Dante Gabriel*
Rousseau, *Henri Julien*
Rousseau, *Théodore*
Ter Borch, *Gerard*
Thorburn, *Archibald*
Topolski, *Feliks*
Van Goyen, *Jan*
Vasarely, *Victor*
Veronese, *Paolo*
Whistler, *James Abbott McNeill*
Whiteley, *Brett*
Zurbarán, *Francisco*

9 letters:
Altdorfer, *Albrecht*
Bartholdi, *Frédéric August*
Beardsley, *Aubrey Vincent*
Bonington, *Richard Parkes*
Canaletto *(Giovanni Antonio Canal)*
Carpaccio, *Vittore*

Cavallini, *Pietro*
Constable, *John*
Correggio, *Antonio Allegri da*
Da Cortona, *Pietro*
Da Messina, *Antonello*
De Chirico, *Giorgio*
De Kooning, *Willem*
Delacroix, *Eugène*
Delaroche, *Paul*
Donatello *(Donato di Betto Bardi)*
Feininger, *Lyonel*
Fragonard, *Jean Honoré*
Friedrich, *Caspar David*
Géricault, *Théodore*
Giorgione, *Giorgio Barbarelli*
Grünewald, *Isaak*
Hiroshige, *Ando*
Kandinsky, *Wassily*
Kauffmann, *Angelica*
Kokoschka, *Oscar*
Kuniyoshi, *Utagawa*
Lehmbruck, *Wilhelm*
Mestrovic, *Ivan*
Nicholson, *Ben*
Nollekens, *Joseph*
Oldenburg, *Claes*
Pisanello
Rembrandt *(Harmensz van Rijn)*
Rodchenko, *Alexander Mikhailovich*
Roubiliac, *Louis-François*
Roubillac, *Louis-François*
Siqueiros, *David Alfaro*
Thornhill, *James*
Velázquez, *Diego Rodríguez de Silva y*

10 letters:
Alma-Tadema, *Lawrence*
Archipenko, *Aleksandr Porfiryevich*
Arcimboldo, *Giuseppe*
Bonnington, *Richard Parkes*
Botticelli, *Sandro*
Buonarroti, *Michelangelo*
Burne-Jones, *Edward*
Da Corregio, *Antonio Allegri*
Da Fabriano, *Gentile*

De Vlaminck, *Maurice*
Giacometti, *Alberto*
Guillaumin, *Armand*
Mackintosh, *Charles Rennie*
Michelozzo, *Michelozzi*
Modigliani, *Amedeo*
Moholy-Nagy, *László*
Motherwell, *Robert*
Polyclitus
Polygnotus
Praxiteles
Rowlandson, *Thomas*
Schongauer, *Martin*
Schwitters, *Kurt*
Signorelli, *Luca*
Sutherland, *Graham*
Tintoretto, *Jacopo*
Van der Goes, *Hugo*
Van de Velde, *Adriaen*
Van de Velde, *Willem*

11 letters:
Bartolommeo, *Fra*
Callimachus
De Chavannes, *Pierre Puvis*
Del Barbiere, *Domenico*
Della Robbia, *Andrea*
Della Robbia, *Luca*
Domenichino *(Domenico Zampien)*
Fairweather, *Ian*
Gentileschi, *Artemisia*
Ghirlandaio, *Domenico*
Giambologna *(Jean de Boulogne)*
Terbrugghen, *Hendrik*
Thorvaldsen, *Bertel*
Van Ruisdael, *Jacob*
Van Ruysdael, *Salomen*

Vigée-Lebrun, *Élisabeth*

12 letters:
Da Caravaggio, *Michelangelo Merisi*
De Champaigne, *Philippe*
Della Quercia, *Jacopa*
Fantin-Latour, *Henri*
Gainsborough, *Thomas*
Lichtenstein, *Roy*
Michelangelo *(Michelagniolo di Lodovico Buonarriti)*
Parmigianino *(Girolano Francesco Maria Mazzola)*
Pinturicchio *(Bernardino di Betto)*
Rauschenberg, *Robert*
Van der Weyden, *Rogier*
Winterhalter, *Franz Xaver*

13 letters:
Del Pollaiuolo, *Antonio*
Del Pollaiuolo, *Piero*
Del Verrocchio, *Andrea*
Di Buoninsegna, *Duccio*
Messerschmidt, *Franz Xavier*

14 letters:
Da Castelfranco, *Giorgione*
Della Francesca, *Piero*
Gaudier-Brzeska, *Henri*

16 letters:
Gilbert and George

17 letters:
De Toulouse-Lautrec, *Henri Marie Raymond*

Asteroids

4 letters:	**5 letters:**	**6 letters:**
Eros	Ceres	Aurora
Iris	Doris	Chiron
Juno	Vesta	Cybele
		Davida

Europa
Hektor
Hermes
Hygiea
Icarus
Pallas
Psyche
Sylvia
Thisbe
Ursula

7 letters:
Eunomia
Fortuna

8 letters:
Bamberga
Chariklo
Hermione
Hesperia
Phaethon

9 letters:
Herculina
Patientia

10 letters:
Euphrosyne
Interamnia

Astrology terms

2 letters:
MC

3 letters:
Air

4 letters:
Cusp
Fire

5 letters:
Earth
Fixed
House
Stars
Trine
Water

6 letters:
Aspect
Square
Zodiac

7 letters:
Element
Mutable
Sun sign

8 letters:
Cardinal
Quintile
Star sign

9 letters:
Ascendant
Ascendent

Horoscope
Midheaven

10 letters:
Birthchart
Descendant
Descendent
Opposition

11 letters:
Conjunction
Satellitium

12 letters:
Ruling planet

Astronomy

ASTRONOMERS

4 letters:
Hale, *Alan*
Oort, *Jan*
Pond, *John*
Rees, *Martin*
Ryle, *Martin*

5 letters:
Bliss, *Nathaniel*
Brahe, *Tycho*

Dyson, *Frank*
Encke, *Johann Franz*
Hoyle, *Sir Fred(erick)*
Jeans, *Sir James Hopwood*
Meton
Moore, *Patrick*
Reber, *Grote*
Roche, *Edouard*

6 letters:
Bessel, *Friedrich Wilhelm*
Halley, *Edmund*
Hewish, *Antony*
Hubble, *Edwin*
Kepler, *Johannes*
Lovell, *Sir (Alfred Charles) Bernard*

7 letters:
Bradley, *James*
Cassini, *Giovanni*
Celsius, *Anders*
Eudoxus
Galileo, *Galilei*
Huggins, *Sir William*
Khayyam, *Omar*
Laplace, *Pierre Simon de*
Lockyer, *Sir Joseph Norman*
Ptolemy *(Claudius Ptolemaeus)*
Woolley, *Richard*

8 letters:
Almagest
Callipic
Christie, *William*
Herschel, *Caroline*

Herschel, *William*

9 letters:
Eddington, *Sir Arthur*
Flamsteed, *John*
Leverrier, *Urbain Jean Joseph*
Maskelyne, *Nevil*
Sosigenes

10 letters:
Copernicus, *Nicolas*
Hipparchus
Wolfendale, *Arnold*

11 letters:
Aristarchus
Biddell Airy, *George*
Graham Smith, *Francis*

12 letters:
Eratosthenes
Spencer Jones, *Harold*

13 letters:
Schwarzschild, *Karl*

ASTRONOMY TERMS

3 letters:
Jet
Ray

4 letters:
Apse
Coma
Cusp
Limb
Mass
Node
Nova
Pole
Ring
Star
Tide

5 letters:
Apsis
Basin
Burst
Comet
Crust
Dwarf
Epoch
Flare
Giant
Lunar
Maria
Nadir
Orbit
Quiet
Rupes
Saros

Solar
Space
Spray
Train

6 letters:
Albedo
Aurora
Bolide
Colure
Corona
Cosmic
Crater
Ejecta
Facula
Galaxy
Merger

Meteor
Nebula
Octant
Plages
Quasar
Rising
Spinar
Syzygy
Zenith

7 letters:
Apapsis
Apolune
Appulse
Aureola
Aureole
Azimuth
Cluster
Ellipse
Equator
Equinox
Farside
Inertia
Ingress
New moon
Nucleus
Perigee
Plerion
Primary
Quarter
Radiant
Sextile
Spicule
Stellar
Sunspot

8 letters:
Aerolite
Altitude
Analemma
Aphelion
Asteroid
Cislunar
Crescent

Dynamics
Emersion
Evection
Filament
Fireball
Loadstar
Lodestar
Mass loss
Meridian
Nearside
Northing
Nutation
Parallax
Red giant
Regolith
Rotation
Solstice
Southing
Spherule
Universe

9 letters:
Aerospace
Anthelion
Black drop
Black hole
Chondrite
Collapsar
Companion
Cosmogony
Cosmology
Eccentric
Ecosphere
Ephemeris
Exosphere
Flocculus
Immersion
Light year
Magnitude
Meteorite
Meteoroid
Moonquake
Obliquity
Percentre

Periapsis
Planetary
Planetoid
Polar axis
Protostar
Ring plain
Satellite
Secondary
Shell star
Spacetime
Star cloud
Supernova
Variation
White hole

10 letters:
Achondrite
Aerosphere
Almacantar
Almucantar
Astrobleme
Atmosphere
Barycentre
Binary star
Brown dwarf
Elongation
Extinction
Inequality
Insolation
Ionosphere
Luminosity
Mesosphere
Metal ratio
Oblateness
Opposition
Periastron
Perihelion
Precession
Prominence
Quadrature
Revolution
Supergiant
Terminator
Tidal force

Triple star
White dwarf

11 letters:
Apocynthion
Chemosphere
Circumlunar
Circumpolar
Circumsolar
Colour index
Conjunction
Culmination
Evolved star
Gravitation
Heliosphere
Inclination
Inner planet
Major planet
Metallicity
Meteor storm
Missing mass
Neutron star
Observatory
Occultation
Open cluster
Outer planet
Photosphere
Protogalaxy
Protoplanet
Radio source
Retardation
Singularity
Solar system
Stellar wind
Troposphere

12 letters:
Asteroid belt
Chromosphere
Interstellar
Lunar eclipse
Mass transfer
Meteor shower
Multiple star
Planetesimal

Plasmasphere
Proper motion
Sidereal time
Solar eclipse
Spectral type
Sunspot cycle
Supercluster
Telluric line
Thermosphere
Tidal capture
Total eclipse
Tropical year
Variable star

13 letters:
Blue straggler
Circumstellar
Constellation
Magnetosphere
Moving cluster
Red supergiant
Scintillation
Seyfert galaxy
Solar constant
Solar spectrum
Spectral class
Sublunar point
Subsolar point
Symbiotic star
Synodic period
Tidal friction
Universal time

14 letters:
Annular eclipse
Aurora borealis
Escape velocity
Galactic centre
Inferior planet
Interplanetary
Molecular cloud
Northern lights
Partial eclipse
Reciprocal mass
Southern lights

Superior planet
Total magnitude
Vertical circle
Zenith distance

15 letters:
Aurora australis
Cepheid variable
Galactic equator
Meridian passage
Meteoroid stream
Nucleosynthesis
Orbital elements
Orbital velocity
Planetary system
Ptolemaic system
Strömgren sphere
Substellar point
Visual magnitude

16 letters:
Coordinate system
Copernican system
Galactic rotation
Naked singularity
Penumbral eclipse
Stellar evolution
Stellar structure

17 letters:
Physical libration
Pulsating universe
Pulsating variable
Shepherd satellite
Terrestrial planet

18 letters:
Chandrasekhar limit
Heliocentric system
North celestial pole
Northern hemisphere
North polar distance
Planetary alignment
Quasi-stellar object
South celestial pole

Southern hemisphere
South polar distance
Velocity dispersion

19 letters:
Cataclysmic variable
Oscillating universe
Schwarzschild radius

See also:
➤ **Asteroids** ➤ **Atmosphere, layers of** ➤ **Comets** ➤ **Galaxies**
➤ **Meteor showers** ➤ **Planets** ➤ **Satellites**
➤ **Stars and constellations**

20 letters:
Effective temperature

23 letters:
Transient lunar phenomena

24 letters:
Precession of the equinoxes

Athletic events

5 letters:
Relay

6 letters:
Discus
Hammer

7 letters:
Hurdles
Javelin
Shot put

Walking

8 letters:
High jump
Long jump
Marathon

9 letters:
Decathlon
Pole vault
Triathlon

10 letters:
Heptathlon
Pentathlon
Triple jump

12 letters:
Half marathon
Orienteering
Steeplechase

19 letters:
Cross-country running

Atmosphere, layers of

10 letters:
Ionosphere
Mesosphere
Ozone layer

11 letters:
Ozonosphere
Troposphere

12 letters:
Stratosphere
Thermosphere

Aviation terms

3 letters:
SBA
Yaw

4 letters:
Bank

Bunt
Crab
Dive
Gate
Hunt
Loop

Mach
Rake
Roll
Spin
Taxi
Trim

5 letters:
Ditch
Glide
Pilot
Pitch
Stack

Stall

6 letters:
Cruise
Drogue
Redeye
Reheat
Runway

7 letters:
Air miss
Airside
Batsman
Ceiling
Copilot
Feather
Landing
Loading
Overfly
Takeoff
Taxiway
Yaw axis

8 letters:
Airspeed
Anhedral
Approach
Attitude
Clearway
Dihedral
Flameout
In-flight
Landside
Nose dive
Roll axis

Sideslip
Snap roll
Subsonic
Tailspin
Wide-body
Wingover

9 letters:
Autopilot
Chandelle
Crash-dive
Crash-land
Fly-by-wire
Immelmann
Navigator
Overshoot
Pitch axis
Power dive
Sonic boom

10 letters:
Aerobatics
Barrel roll
Bird strike
Flight path
Shockstall
Supersonic
Undershoot

11 letters:
Air corridor
Groundspeed
Vapour trail
Victory roll

12 letters:
Approach path
Autorotation
Belly landing
Boarding pass
Redeye flight
Sound barrier

13 letters:
Charter flight
Contact flight
Head-up display
Immelmann turn

14 letters:
Automatic pilot
Holding pattern
Pancake landing

15 letters:
Scheduled flight

17 letters:
Air traffic control

20 letters:
Standard beam approach

23 letters:
Flight management
  systems

Bb

Back words

2 letters:
Ah / Ha
Am / Ma
At / Ta
Eh / He
Em / Me
Er / Re
Ha / Ah
He / Eh
Ho / Oh
Ma / Am
Me / Em
Mp / Pm
No / On
Oh / Ho
On / No
Pm / Mp
Re / Er
Ta / At

3 letters:
And / Dna
Are / Era
Bad / Dab
Bag / Gab
Ban / Nab
Bat / Tab
Ben / Neb
Bid / Dib
Big / Gib
Bin / Nib
Bog / Gob
Boy / Yob
Bud / Dub
Bun / Nub

Bus / Sub
But / Tub
Cam / Mac
Cor / Roc
Dab / Bad
Dag / Gad
Dal / Lad
Dam / Mad
Dew / Wed
Dib / Bid
Dim / Mid
Dna / And
Dog / God
Doh / Hod
Don / Nod
Dot / Tod
Dub / Bud
Eel / Lee
Era / Are
Gab / Bag
Gad / Dag
Gal / Lag
Gas / Sag
Gel / Leg
Gib / Big
Git / Tig
Gob / Bog
God / Dog
Got / Tog
Gum / Mug
Gut / Tug
Hay / Yah
Hod / Doh
Jar / Raj
Lad / Dal

Lag / Gal
Lap / Pal
Lee / Eel
Leg / Gel
Mac / Cam
Mad / Dam
Map / Pam
May / Yam
Mid / Dim
Mug / Gum
Nab / Ban
Nap / Pan
Neb / Ben
Net / Ten
Nib / Bin
Nip / Pin
Nit / Tin
Nod / Don
Not / Ton
Now / Won
Nub / Bun
Owt / Two
Pal / Lap
Pam / Map
Pan / Nap
Par / Rap
Pat / Tap
Pay / Yap
Per / Rep
Pin / Nip
Pit / Tip
Pot / Top
Pus / Sup
Put / Tup
Raj / Jar

Rap / Par
Rat / Tar
Raw / War
Rep / Per
Roc / Cor
Rot / Tor
Sag / Gas
Saw / Was
Sub / Bus
Sup / Pus
Tab / Bat
Tap / Pat
Tar / Rat
Ten / Net
Tig / Git
Tin / Nit
Tip / Pit
Tod / Dot
Tog / Got
Ton / Not
Top / Pot
Tor / Rot
Tub / But
Tug / Gut
Tup / Put
Two / Owt
War / Raw
Was / Saw
Way / Yaw
Wed / Dew
Won / Now
Yah / Hay
Yam / May
Yap / Pay
Yaw / Way

Yob / Boy

4 letters:
Abut / Tuba
Agas / Saga
Ajar / Raja
Auks / Skua
Avid / Diva
Bard / Drab
Bats / Stab
Bird / Drib
Bonk / Knob
Brag / Garb
Buns / Snub
Burg / Grub
Buts / Stub
Cram / Marc
Dart / Trad
Deem / Meed
Deep / Peed
Deer / Reed
Deus / Sued
Dial / Laid
Diva / Avid
Doom / Mood
Door / Rood
Drab / Bard
Draw / Ward
Dray / Yard
Drib / Bird
Dual / Laud
Edam / Made
Edit / Tide
Emir / Rime
Emit / Time
Ergo / Ogre
Et al / Late
Evil / Live
Flog / Golf
Flow / Wolf
Gals / Slag
Garb / Brag
Girt / Trig
Gnat / Tang
Gnus / Sung

Golf / Flog
Grub / Burg
Gulp / Plug
Gums / Smug
Guns / Snug
Hoop / Pooh
Keel / Leek
Keep / Peek
Knob / Bonk
Laid / Dial
Lair / Rial
Late / Etal
Laud / Dual
Leek / Keel
Leer / Reel
Liar / Rail
Live / Evil
Loop / Pool
Loot / Tool
Macs / Scam
Made / Edam
Maps / Spam
Marc / Cram
Mart / Tram
Maws / Swam
Meed / Deem
Meet / Teem
Mood / Doom
Moor / Room
Naps / Span
Nets / Sten
Nips / Spin
Nuts / Stun
Ogre / Ergo
Pals / Slap
Pans / Snap
Part / Trap
Paws / Swap
Peed / Deep
Peek / Keep
Pees / Seep
Pets / Step
Pins / Snip
Plug / Gulp
Pooh / Hoop

Pool / Loop
Pots / Stop
Prat / Tarp
Rail / Liar
Raja / Ajar
Raps / Spar
Rats / Star
Reed / Deer
Reel / Leer
Rial / Lair
Rime / Emir
Rood / Door
Room / Moor
Saga / Agas
Saps / Spas
Scam / Macs
Seep / Pees
Skua / Auks
Slag / Gals
Slap / Pals
Smug / Gums
Snap / Pans
Snip / Pins
Snot / Tons
Snub / Buns
Snug / Guns
Spam / Maps
Span / Naps
Spar / Raps
Spas / Saps
Spat / Taps
Spin / Nips
Spit / Tips
Spot / Tops
Stab / Bats
Star / Rats
Sten / Nets
Step / Pets
Stew / Wets
Stop / Pots
Stub / Buts
Stun / Nuts
Sued / Deus
Sung / Gnus
Swam / Maws

Swap / Paws
Sway / Yaws
Swot / Tows
Tang / Gnat
Taps / Spat
Tarp / Prat
Teem / Meet
Tide / Edit
Time / Emit
Tips / Spit
Tons / Snot
Tool / Loot
Tops / Spot
Tort / Trot
Tows / Swot
Trad / Dart
Tram / Mart
Trap / Part
Trig / Girt
Trot / Tort
Tuba / Abut
Ward / Draw
Wets / Stew
Wolf / Flow
Yard / Dray
Yaws / Sway

5 letters:
Debut / Tubed
Decaf / Faced
Decal / Laced
Deeps / Speed
Denim / Mined
Devil / Lived
Draws / Sward
Faced / Decaf
Fires / Serif
Keels / Sleek
Knits / Stink
Laced / Decal
Lager / Regal
Leper / Repel
Lever / Revel
Lived / Devil
Loops / Spool

Loots / Stool
Mined / Denim
Nonet / Tenon
Pacer / Recap
Parts / Strap
Pools / Sloop
Ports / Strop
Rebut / Tuber
Recap / Pacer
Regal / Lager
Remit / Timer
Repel / Leper
Revel / Lever
Roñes / Señor
Señor / Roñes
Serif / Fires
Sleek / Keels
Sloop / Pools
Smart / Trams
Snaps / Spans
Snips / Spins
Spans / Snaps
Speed / Deeps
Spins / Snips
Spool / Loops
Spots / Stops
Sprat / Tarps
Stink / Knits
Stool / Loots
Stops / Spots
Stows / Swots
Strap / Parts
Straw / Warts
Strop / Ports
Sward / Draws
Swots / Stows
Tarps / Sprat
Tenon / Nonet
Timer / Remit
Trams / Smart
Tubed / Debut
Tuber / Rebut
Warts / Straw

6 letters:
Denier / Reined
Diaper / Repaid
Drawer / Reward
Looter / Retool
Pilfer / Reflip
Pupils / Slipup
Recaps / Spacer
Redraw / Warder
Reflip / Pilfer
Reflow / Wolfer
Reined / Denier
Reknit / Tinker
Rennet / Tenner
Repaid / Diaper
Retool / Looter
Reward / Drawer
Sleets / Steels
Slipup / Pupils
Sloops / Spools
Snoops / Spoons
Spacer / Recaps
Spools / Sloops
Spoons / Snoops
Sports / Strops
Steels / Sleets
Strops / Sports
Tenner / Rennet
Tinker / Reknit
Warder / Redraw
Wolfer / Reflow

7 letters:
Amaroid / Diorama
Deifier / Reified
Deliver / Reviled
Dessert / Tressed
Diorama / Amaroid
Gateman / Nametag
Nametag / Gateman
Reified / Deifier
Reknits / Stinker
Reviled / Deliver
Stinker / Reknits
Tressed / Dessert

8 letters:
Desserts / Stressed
Redrawer / Rewarder

Rewarder / Redrawer
Stressed / Desserts

Bacteria

4 letters:
MRSA

5 letters:
Cocci
Staph
Strep

6 letters:
Aerobe
Operon
Vibrio

7 letters:
Bacilli
Lysogen

8 letters:
Listeria
Pathogen
Spirilla

9 letters:
Peritrich
Serogroup

Spirulina

10 letters:
Salmonella

11 letters:
Pasteurella

13 letters:
Streptococcus

Bags

3 letters:
Bum
Cod
Ice
Net
Sea
Tea

4 letters:
Body
Caba
Cool
Dime
Grip
Poke
Port
Sack
Tote

5 letters:
Amaut
Amowt
Bulse
Cabas

Dilli
Dilly
Ditty
Doggy
Jelly
Jiffy®
Nunny
Pikau
Pouch
Purse
Scrip
Water

6 letters:
Bergen
Carpet
Clutch
Duffel
Kitbag
Oxford
Sachet
Saddle
Sponge
Tucker

Valise
Vanity
Wallet

7 letters:
Alforja
Carrier
Daypack
Dorothy
Handbag
Holdall
Satchel
Shopper
Sporran
Weekend
Workbag

8 letters:
Backpack
Carryall
Crumenal
Knapsack
Pochette
Reticule

Ridicule
Rucksack
Shoulder
Sleeping
Suitcase
Survival

9 letters:
Briefcase
Carpetbag
Gladstone
Haversack
Overnight
Saddlebag
Vanity box

10 letters:
Diplomatic
Portmantle
Portmantua
Sabretache
Vanity case

11 letters:
Portmanteau

Ballet

BALLETS

5 letters:
Manon
Rodeo

6 letters:
Bolero
Carmen
Façade
Ondine
Onegin
Parade

7 letters:
Giselle
Masques
Orpheus

8 letters:
Coppélia
Firebird
Les Noces
Serenade

Swan Lake

9 letters:
Les Biches
Mayerling
Spartacus

10 letters:
Cinderella
La Bayadère
Nutcracker
Petroushka

11 letters:
Billy the Kid

12 letters:
Les Sylphides
Rite of Spring
Scheherazade

14 letters:
Romeo and Juliet
Sleeping Beauty

16 letters:
Enigma Variations
La Fille mal gardée

17 letters:
Appalachian Spring

18 letters:
L'après-midi d'un
  faune

19 letters:
La Boutique Fantasque

20 letters:
Midsummer Night's
  Dream

BALLET STEPS AND TERMS

3 letters:
Pas

4 letters:
Jeté
Plié

5 letters:
Adage
Battu
Brisé
Coupé
Decor
Passé
Tombé

6 letters:
Adagio
Aplomb
Ballon
Chassé
Croisé
Dégagé
Ecarté
En l'air
Failli
Ouvert
Pointe
Relevé

7 letters:
Allegro
Allongé

Balancé
Ciseaux
Déboulé
Échappé
Emboîté
Soutenu
Turn-out

8 letters:
Absolute
Abstract
Assemblé
Attitude
Ballonné
Ballotté
Batterie
Cabriole

Demi-plié
En dedans
En dehors
En pointe
Figurant
Glissade
Pas coupé
Romantic
Sickling
Sur place
Temps lié
Toe-dance

9 letters:
Arabesque
Ballerina
Battement

Classical
Cou-de-pied
Détournée
Dévelopée
Elevation
Entrechat
Pas de chat
Pas de deux
Pirouette
Raccourci
Temps levé
Variation

10 letters:
Changement
Demi-pointe
En couronne
Foudroyant
Grand écart
Grande plié
Pas ciseaux
Pas de brisé
Pas échappé
Soubresaut
Tour en l'air

11 letters:
Ballet blanc
Contretemps
Pas ballotté
Pas de bourée
Pas de chassé
Ports de bras
Rond de jambe
Terre à terre

12 letters:
Ballet de cour
Croisé devant
Enchaînement
Gargouillade

13 letters:
Ballet d'action
En tire-bouchon
Pas de sissonne
Temps de cuisse
Temps de flèche

14 letters:
Benesh notation
Croisé derrière

Entrée de ballet
Premier danseur
Prima ballerina
Temps de poisson
Temps dévelopée

15 letters:
Cecchetti method

16 letters:
Pas de bourée couru
Première
  danseuse
Stepanov notation
Von Laban notation

17 letters:
Changement de pieds
Fouetté en tournant

21 letters:
Défilé de corps de ballet

22 letters:
Prima ballerina assoluta

Ball games

4 letters:
Golf
Polo
Pool

5 letters:
Fives

6 letters:
Boules
Hockey
Soccer
Squash
Tennis

7 letters:
Bowling
Croquet
Hurling
Netball
Pinball
Pyramid
Snooker

8 letters:
Baseball
Football
Goalball
Handball
Korfball
Lacrosse

Pushball
Rounders
Softball
Subbuteo®

9 letters:
Badminton
Bagatelle
Billiards
Crazy golf
Paintball
Punchball

10 letters:
Volleyball

11 letters:
Bumble-puppy

12 letters:
Bar billiards

15 letters:
Australian Rules
Pocket billiards

16 letters:
American football
Canadian football
Piggy in the middle

Baseball teams

11 letters:
Chicago Cubs
New York Mets

12 letters:
Boston Red Sox
Tampa Bay Rays
Texas Rangers

13 letters:
Anaheim Angels
Atlanta Braves
Detroit Tigers
Houston Astros

14 letters:
Cincinnati Reds

Florida Marlins
Minnesota Twins
New York Yankees
San Diego Padres

15 letters:
Chicago White Sox
Colorado Rockies
Seattle Mariners
Toronto Blue Jays

16 letters:
Baltimore Orioles
Cleveland Indians
Kansas City Royals
Los Angeles Angels
Milwaukee Brewers

Oakland Athletics
St Louis Cardinals

17 letters:
Los Angeles Dodgers
Pittsburgh Pirates

18 letters:
San Francisco Giants

19 letters:
Arizona Diamondbacks
Washington Nationals

20 letters:
Philadelphia Phillies

Basketball Teams

8 letters:
Utah Jazz

9 letters:
Miami Heat

11 letters:
Phoenix Suns

12 letters:
Atlanta Hawks
Chicago Bulls
Orlando Magic

13 letters:
Boston Celtics

Denver Nuggets
Indiana Pacers
New Jersey Nets
New York Knicks

14 letters:
Detroit Pistons
Houston Rockets
Milwaukee Bucks
Toronto Raptors

15 letters:
Dallas Mavericks
Sacramento Kings
San Antonio Spurs

16 letters:
Charlotte Bobcats
Los Angeles Lakers
Memphis Grizzlies

17 letters:
New Orleans Hornets
Philadelphia 76ers
Washington Wizards

18 letters:
Cleveland Cavaliers
Los Angeles Clippers
Seattle SuperSonics

19 letters:	20 letters:	21 letters:
Golden State Warriors	Portland Trail Blazers	Minnesota Timberwolves

Bats

5 letters:	8 letters:	11 letters:
Fruit	Serotine	Barbastelle
		Pipistrelle
6 letters:	9 letters:	
Kalong	Flying fox	12 letters:
	Horseshoe	False vampire
7 letters:		
Noctule	10 letters:	13 letters:
Vampire	Hammerhead	Insectivorous

Battles

Battle	Year
Aboukir Bay *or* Abukir Bay	1798
Actium	31 B.C.
Agincourt	1415
Alamo	1836
Armageddon	
Arnhem	1944
Atlantic	1939-45
Austerlitz	1805
Balaklava *or* Balaclava	1854
Bannockburn	1314
Barnet	1471
Bautzen	1813
Belleau Wood	1918
Blenheim	1704
Borodino	1812
Bosworth Field	1485
Boyne	1690
Britain	1940
Bulge	1944-45
Bull Run	1861;1862
Bunker Hill	1775
Cannae	216 B.C.
Chapultepec	1847
Crécy	1346
Culloden	1746
Dien Bien Phu	1954
Edgehill	1642

Battle	Year
El Alamein	1942
Falkirk	1298; 1746
Flodden	1513
Gettysburg	1863
Guadalcanal	1942-3
Hastings	1066
Hohenlinden	1800
Imphal	1944
Inkerman	1854
Issus	333 B.C.
Jemappes	1792
Jena	1806
Killiecrankie	1689
Kursk	1943
Ladysmith	1899-1900
Le Cateau	1914
Leipzig	1813
Lepanto	1571
Leyte Gulf	1944
Little Bighorn	1876
Lützen	1632
Majuba Hill	1881
Manassas	1861; 1862
Mantinea *or* Mantineia	418 B.C.; 362 B.C.
Marathon	490 B.C.
Marengo	1800
Marston Moor	1644
Missionary Ridge	1863
Naseby	1645
Navarino	425 B.C.
Omdurman	1898
Passchendaele	1917
Philippi	42 B.C.
Plains of Abraham	1759
Plassey	1757
Plataea	479 B.C.
Poltava	1709
Prestonpans	1745
Pydna	168 B.C.
Quatre Bras	1815
Ramillies	1706
Roncesvalles	778
Sadowa *or* Sadová	1866
Saint-Mihiel	1918

Battle	Year
Salamis	480 B.C.
Sedgemoor	1685
Sempach	1386
Shiloh	1862
Shipka Pass	1877-78
Somme	1916; 1918
Stalingrad	1941-42
Stamford Bridge	1066
Stirling Bridge	1297
Tannenberg	1410; 1914
Tewkesbury	1471
Thermopylae	480 B.C.
Tobruk	1941; 1942
Toulouse	1814
Trafalgar	1805
Trenton	1776
Verdun	1916
Vitoria	1813
Wagram	1809
Waterloo	1815
Ypres	1914; 1915; 1917; 1918
Zama	202 B.C.

Bays

2 letters:
MA

3 letters:
Ise

4 letters:
Pigs
Vigo
Wick

5 letters:
Algoa
Bonny
Byron
Casco
Dvina
False
Fleet

Fundy
Glace
Green
Hawke
Herne
Horse
James
Korea
Milne
Omura
Osaka
Shark
Sligo
Suvla
Table
Tampa
Tokyo
Urado

6 letters:
Abukir
Ariake
Baffin
Bantry
Bengal
Biscay
Botany
Broken
Callao
Colwyn
Daphne
Dublin
Galway
Golden
Hawke's
Hudson
Jervis
Lobito

Manila
Mobile
Newark
Tasman
Toyama
Tralee
Ungava
Vyborg
Walvis

7 letters:
Aboukir
Cape Cod
Delagoa
Delogoa
Dundalk
Florida
Jiazhou
Montego
Moreton
New York
Pegasus
Poverty
Setúbal
Swansea
Thunder
Walfish
Whitley

8 letters:
Biscayne
Buzzards

Cardigan
Delaware
Georgian
Hangzhou
Quiberon
San Pedro
Santiago

9 letters:
Bay of Acre
Bay of Pigs
Bombetoka
Discovery
Encounter
Famagusta
Frobisher
Guanabara
Inhambane
Kuskokwim
Magdalena
Morecambe
St Austell

10 letters:
Bay of Cádiz
Bay of Fundy
Bay of Vlorë
Caernarvon
Carmarthen
Chesapeake
Cienfuegos
Guantánamo

Lützow-Holm

11 letters:
Bay of Bengal
Bay of Biscay
Bay of Gdansk
Bay of Naples
Bay of Plenty
Port Phillip

12 letters:
Bay of Kaválla
Narragansett
San Francisco

13 letters:
Bay of Campeche
Bay of St Michel
Corpus Christi
Massachusetts
Passamaquoddy

14 letters:
Bay of Gibraltar

16 letters:
Bay of Trincomalee

18 letters:
Bay of Espírito Santo

Beans and other pulses

3 letters:	**5 letters:**	Adzuki	Snow pea
Red	Black	Butter	
	Bobby	French	**8 letters:**
4 letters:	Broad	Kidney	Borlotti
Dhal	Field	Lentil	Chick pea
Gram	Green	Runner	Garbanzo
Lima	Pinto	String	Split pea
Mung			
Navy	**6 letters:**	**7 letters:**	**9 letters:**
Soya	Adsuki	Haricot	Black-eyed

Cannelini
Flageolet
Mangetout
Petit pois
Pigeon pea

Puy lentil
Red kidney
Red lentil

11 letters:
Green lentil

12 letters:
Black-eyed pea

Marrowfat pea
Sugar snap pea

17 letters:
Continental lentil

Beds

3 letters:
Air
Box
Cot
Day
Mat

4 letters:
Bunk
Camp
Cott
Crib
Kang
Lilo®
Loft
Sofa
Twin

5 letters:
Berth
Couch
Divan
Field
Futon
Water

6 letters:
Cradle
Double
Litter
Murphy
Pallet
Put-u-up
Single
Sleigh

7 letters:
Amenity
Charpoy
Feather
Folding
Hammock
Trestle
Truckle
Trundle

8 letters:
Apple-pie
Bassinet
Captain's
Carrycot
Foldaway
Hospital
King-size
Mattress

Platform

9 letters:
Couchette
King-sized
Paillasse
Palliasse
Queen-size
Shake down
Stretcher

10 letters:
Four-poster
Queen-sized

11 letters:
Procrustean

Beetles

3 letters:
Bee
Dor
May
Oil

4 letters:
Bark
Cane
Dorr
Dung
Flea
Gold
Huhu
June

King
Leaf
Mall
Maul
Pill
Rose
Rove
Stag

5 letters:
Bacon
Black
Click
Clock
Jewel

Roach
Snout
Tiger
Water

6 letters:
Batler
Carpet
Chafer
Diving
Dor-fly
Elater
Gregor
Ground
Hammer

Larder
Mallet
May bug
Museum
Potato
Scarab
Sexton
Sledge
Spider
Weevil

7 letters:
Asiatic
Blister
Burying
Cabinet
Cadelle
Carrion
Elmbark
Elytron
Elytrum
Firefly
Goldbug
Goliath
Hop-flea
Hornbug
June bug
Ladybug
Leather
Skelter
Soldier
Vedalia

8 letters:
Ambrosia
Bum-clock
Cardinal
Colorado
Curculio
Darkling
Glow-worm
Hercules
Japanese
Ladybird
Longhorn
Māori bug
Scarabee
Skipjack
Snapping
Tortoise
Wireworm

9 letters:
Buprestis
Cantharis
Carpet bug
Christmas
Cockroach
Furniture
Goldsmith
Kekerengu
Longicorn
Pea weevil
Pinchbuck
Scavenger

Timberman
Tumble-bug
Whirligig
Woodborer

10 letters:
Bean weevil
Boll weevil
Bombardier
Churchyard
Cockchafer
Deathwatch
Dumbledore
Long-horned
Rhinoceros
Rose chafer
Spanish fly
Turnip-flea

11 letters:
Bloody-nosed
Typographer

12 letters:
Buzzard-clock
Sledge-hammer

16 letters:
Devil's
 coach-horse

Bets and Betting Systems

3 letters:
Win

4 letters:
Ante
Back
Flag
Tote

5 letters:
Heinz
Place

6 letters:
Banker
Chance
Double
Parlay
Patent

Single
Treble
Trixie
Yankee

7 letters:
A cheval
Each-way
Goliath
Lucky 7

Lucky 15
Lucky 31
Lucky 63
Rounder
Tricast

Quadrella
Scorecast
Super flag
Union Jack
Up-and-down

12 letters:
Correct score
Podium finish
Treble chance

16 letters:
Race dual forecast
Reversed forecast

8 letters:
Antepost
Canadian
Forecast
Perfecta
Quinella
Trifecta

10 letters:
Martingale
Parimutuel
Roundabout
Round Robin
Superfecta
Super Heinz

18 letters:
Combination tricast

19 letters:
Combination forecast

9 letters:
Asian line
Goal crazy

11 letters:
Accumulator
Super Yankee

Bible

BOOKS OF THE BIBLE: OLD TESTAMENT

3 letters:
Job

4 letters:
Amos
Ezra
Joel
Ruth

5 letters:
Hosea
Jonah
Kings
Micah

Nahum

6 letters:
Daniel
Esther
Exodus
Haggai
Isaiah
Joshua
Judges
Psalms
Samuel

7 letters:
Ezekiel

Genesis
Malachi
Numbers
Obadiah

8 letters:
Habakkuk
Jeremiah
Nehemiah
Proverbs

9 letters:
Leviticus
Zechariah
Zephaniah

10 letters:
Chronicles

11 letters:
Deuteronomy

12 letters:
Ecclesiastes
Lamentations

13 letters:
Song of Solomon

BOOKS OF THE BIBLE: NEW TESTAMENT

4 letters:
Acts
John
Jude
Luke
Mark

5 letters:
James
Peter
Titus

6 letters:
Romans

7 letters:
Hebrews
Matthew
Timothy

8 letters:
Philemon

9 letters:
Ephesians
Galatians

10 letters:
Colossians
Revelation

11 letters:	Philippians	13 letters:
Corinthians		Thessalonians

BOOKS OF THE BIBLE: APOCRYPHA

5 letters:	8 letters:	Song of the Three
Tobit	Manasseh	
		16 letters:
6 letters:	9 letters:	Daniel and Susanna
Baruch	Maccabees	
Esdras		20 letters:
Judith	14 letters:	Daniel, Bel and the
Wisdom	Ecclesiasticus	Snake

CHARACTERS IN THE BIBLE

3 letters:	Noah	Moses	Martha
Dan	Paul	Nahum	Midian
Eve	Ruth	Naomi	Miriam
Gad	Saul	Peter	Naboth
Ham	Seth	Sarah	Nathan
Job	Shem	Simon	Nimrod
Lot		Tobit	Philip
	5 letters:	Uriah	Rachel
4 letters:	Aaron		Reuben
Abel	Ammon	6 letters:	Salome
Adam	Asher	Andrew	Samson
Ahab	David	Balaam	Samuel
Amos	Dinah	Baruch	Simeon
Boaz	Dives	Belial	Thomas
Cain	Elias	Caspar	Zilpah
Cush	Enoch	Daniel	
Enos	Hagar	Dorcas	7 letters:
Esau	Herod	Elijah	Abigail
Ezra	Hiram	Elisha	Abraham
Jael	Hosea	Esther	Absalom
Jehu	Isaac	Gideon	Ananias
Joab	Jacob	Gilead	Deborah
Joel	James	Haggai	Delilah
John	Jesse	Hannah	Ephraim
Jude	Jonah	Isaiah	Ezekiel
Kush	Jonas	Jephte	Gabriel
Leah	Jubal	Jethro	Goliath
Levi	Judah	Joseph	Ishmael
Luke	Laban	Joshua	Japheth
Mark	Magus	Josiah	Jezebel
Mary	Micah	Judith	Lazarus

Malachi	Jeremiah	Nabonidus	Jesus Christ
Matthew	Jeroboam	Nathanael	Melchizedek
Meshach	Jonathan	Nicodemus	Prodigal Son
Obadiah	Lot's wife	Tubal-cain	
Rebecca	Manasseh	Zachariah	**12 letters:**
Solomon	Matthias	Zacharias	Melchisedech
Susanna	Melchior	Zechariah	Queen of Sheba
Thadeus	Mordecai	Zephaniah	
Zachary	Naphtali		**13 letters:**
Zebedee	Nehemiah	**10 letters:**	Good Samaritan
Zebulun	Potiphar	Achitophel	Judas Iscariot
	Shadrach	Ahithophel	Mary Magdalene
8 letters:	Thaddeus	Belshazzar	
Abednego	Zedekiah	Holofernes	**14 letters:**
Barabbas		Methuselah	John the Baptist
Benjamin	**9 letters:**	Virgin Mary	Nebuchadnezzar
Caiaphas	Ahasuerus		Nebuchadrezzar
Habakkuk	Balthazar	**11 letters:**	Tetragrammaton
Hezekiah	Bathsheba	Bartholomew	Whore of Babylon
Issachar	Beelzebub	Gog and Magog	
Jephthah	Boanerges	Jehoshaphat	

PLACE NAMES IN THE BIBLE

2 letters:	Ophir	Galilee	Bethlehem
On	Sodom	Gehenna	Capernaum
		Jericho	Jerusalem
4 letters:	**6 letters:**	Samaria	Land of Nod
Aram	Ararat	Shittim	
Cana	Bashan	Topheth	**10 letters:**
Eden	Canaan		Arimathaea
Gath	Goshen	**8 letters:**	Gethsemane
Gaza	Judaea	Aceldama	Wilderness
Moab	Shiloh	Bethesda	
	Shinar	Golgotha	**12 letters:**
	Tadmor	Gomorrah	Garden of Eden
5 letters:	Tophet	Gomorrha	Rabbath Ammon
Babel		Nazareth	
Horeb	**7 letters:**		**18 letters:**
Judah	Antioch	**9 letters:**	Land of milk and
Judea	Calvary	Arimathea	honey

TYPES OF BIBLE

2 letters:	OT	**3 letters:**	RSV
AV	RV	NEB	
NT		NIV	

4 letters:	Missal	Vulgate	King James
NRSV	Tanach		Taverners
Whig	Targum	8 letters:	
	Wyclif	Cromwell	10 letters:
5 letters:	Zurich	Good News	Pentateuch
Douai		Mazarine	Septuagint
Douay	7 letters:	Peshitta	
Itala	Bamberg	Peshitto	12 letters:
	Cranmer	Polyglot	Antilegomena
6 letters:	Hexapla	Wycliffe	
Family	Mazarin		14 letters:
Geneva	Midrash	9 letters:	Revised Version
Gideon	Peshito	Apocrypha	
Gospel	Psalter	Coverdale	16 letters:
Italic	Tyndale	Jerusalem	King James version

Bicycles

BICYCLE PARTS

4 letters:	6 letters:	8 letters:	Saddlebag
Bell	Saddle	Crossbar	
		Mudguard	10 letters:
5 letters:	7 letters:		Handlebars
Pedal	Pannier	9 letters:	Mileometer
Wheel	Rat-trap	Kickstand	Stabilizer

| 11 letters: | | 12 letters: | |
| Bicycle pump | | Bicycle chain | |

TYPES OF BICYCLE

3 letters:	8 letters:	Fairy cycle
BMX	Roadster	Velocipede
6 letters:	9 letters:	12 letters:
Tandem	Autocycle	Exercise bike
		Mountain bike
7 letters:	10 letters:	
Bicycle	All-terrain	13 letters:
Chopper	Boneshaker	Penny-farthing

Biochemists

3 letters:
Dam, *Henrik Carl Peter*

4 letters:
Cori, *Carl Ferdinand*

Cori, *Gerti*
Funk, *Casimir*
Funk, *Kazimierz*
Katz, *Bernard*

5 letters:
Bloch, *Konrad Emil*
Boyer, *Herbert*
Cohen, *Stanley*
Doisy, *Edward Adelbert*
Krebs, *Sir Hans Adolf*
Monod, *Jaques Lucien*
Moore, *Stanford*
Ochoa, *Severo*
Stein, *William H(oward)*
Synge, *Richard*

6 letters:
Beadle, *George Wells*
De Duve, *Christian*
Domagk, *Gerhard*
Florey, *Sir Howard Walter*
Holley, *Robert W(illiam)*
Martin, *Archer*
Mullis, *Kary Banks*
Oparin, *Alexandr*
Porter, *Rodney*
Sanger, *Frederick*
Sumner, *James B(atcheller)*

7 letters:
Buchner, *Eduard*
Edelman, *Gerald M(aurice)*
Fleming, *Sir Alexander*
Gilbert, *Walter*
Haworth, *Norman*
Hopkins, *Sir Frederick Gowland*
Kendrew, *John C(owdery)*
Khorana, *Har Gobind*
Macleod, *John James Richard*
Rodbell, *Martin*
Stanley, *Wendell Meredith*
Waksman, *Selman Abraham*
Warburg, *Otto Heinrich*

8 letters:
Anfinsen, *Christian Boehmer*
Chargaff, *Erwin*
Kornberg, *Arthur*
Meyerhof, *Otto Fritz*
Northrop, *John H(oward)*

9 letters:
Bergstrom, *Sune K(arl)*
Butenandt, *Adolf Friedrich Johann*
Ferdinand, *Max Perutz*
Nirenberg, *Marshall W(arren)*

10 letters:
Samuelsson, *Bengt*

Biology

BRANCHES OF BIOLOGY

6 letters:
Botany

7 letters:
Ecology
Zoology

8 letters:
Biometry
Cytology

Genetics
Taxonomy

9 letters:
Histology

10 letters:
Biophysics
Biostatics
Morphology

Organology
Somatology
Teratology

11 letters:
Aerobiology
Agrobiology
Biodynamics
Cryobiology

12 letters:
Astrobiology
Bacteriology
Biochemistry
Biogeography
Cytogenetics
Microbiology

Oceanography
Organography
Parasitology
Photobiology
Radiobiology
Sociobiology
Stoichiology

13 letters:
Actinobiology
Chronobiology
Palaeontology
Photodynamics

BIOLOGY TERMS

3 letters:
DNA
Egg
RNA

4 letters:
Bone
Cell
Gene
Ovum
Root
Seed
Skin
Soil

5 letters:
Blood
Class
Clone
Fruit
Genus
Gland
Gonad
Order
Organ
Sperm
Spore
Virus

6 letters:
Albino
Allele
Dorsal
Embryo
Enzyme
Family

Flower
Foetus
Fossil
Fungus
Gamete
Growth
Hybrid
Muscle
Phylum
Pollen
Zygote

7 letters:
Aerobic
Biomass
Diploid
Haploid
Hormone
Kingdom
Meiosis
Mitosis
Nucleus
Osmosis
Progeny
Protein
Puberty
Species
Ventral
Vitamin

8 letters:
Anterior
Bacteria
Division
Dominant
Heredity

Mutation
Parasite
Pathogen
Pectoral
Predator
Ribosome
Skeleton

9 letters:
Anaerobic
Cytoplasm
Diffusion
Digestion
Ecosystem
Epidermis
Evolution
Excretion
Food chain
Gestation
Life cycle
Ovulation
Pollution
Posterior
Pregnancy
Recessive
Symbiosis

10 letters:
Chromosome
Conception
Copulation
Krebs cycle
Metabolism
Protoplasm
Vertebrate
Viviparous

11 letters:
Allelomorph
Blood vessel
Circulation
Codominance
Cold-blooded
Environment
Germination
Inheritance
Pollination
Propagation
Respiration
Warm-blooded
X-chromosome
Y-chromosome

12 letters:
Assimilation
Fermentation
Invertebrate
Menstruation
Reproduction
Spermatozoon

13 letters:
Agglutination
Binary fission
Fertilization
Hermaphrodite
Metamorphosis
Nitrogen cycle
Translocation
Transpiration

14 letters:
Photosynthesis

Poikilothermic

16 letters:
Natural selection

17 letters:
Circulatory system
Ribose nucleic acid

18 letters:
Sexual reproduction

19 letters:
Asexual reproduction

20 letters:
Deoxyribonucleic acid

BIOLOGISTS

3 letters:
May, *Robert McCredie*
Orr, *John Boyd*

4 letters:
Berg, *Paul*
Koch, *Robert*

5 letters:
Cohen, *Stanley*
Crick, *Francis Harry Compton*
Krebs, *Hans Adolf*

6 letters:
Beadle, *George Well*
Bordet, *Jules*
Carrel, *Alexis*
Carson, *Rachel*

Claude, *Albert*
Darwin, *Charles (Robert)*
Haller, *Albrecht*
Harvey, *William*
Huxley, *Andrew Fielding*
Huxley, *Julian*
Huxley, *Thomas Henry*
Kinsey, *Alfred*
Mendel, *Gregor*
Morgan, *Thomas Hunt*
Watson, *James Dewey*

7 letters:
Dawkins, *Richard*
Fleming, *Alexander*
Haeckel, *Ernst Heinrich*
Kendrew, *John*
Pasteur, *Louis*
Shatten, *Gerald*

8 letters:
Delbrück, *Max*
Dulbecco, *Renato*
Franklin, *Rosalind*
Linnaeus
Von Linné, *Carl*

9 letters:
Baltimore, *David*
Von Haller, *Albrecht*

10 letters:
Denisovich, *Trofim*
Dobzhansky, *Theodosius*

14 letters:
Van Leeuwenhoek, *Anton*

See also:
➤ **Bacteria** ➤ **Enzymes** ➤ **Hormones** ➤ **Membranes**
➤ **Proteins** ➤ **Sugars**

Birds

2 letters:	Jay	Pie	Cirl	Eyas
Ka	Kae	Ree	Cobb	Fung
	Kea	Roc	Cock	Gled
3 letters:	Mag	Ruc	Coly	Guan
Ani	Maw	Tit	Coot	Guga
Auk	Mew	Tui	Crax	Gull
Boo	Nun		Crow	Hawk
Cob	Oil	**4 letters:**	Dove	Hern
Emu	Owl	Barb	Emeu	Huma
Fum	Pea	Chat	Erne	Ibis

Iynx	Whip	Micky	Solan	Conure
Jynx	Wren	Mimus	Soree	Corbie
Kagu	Xema	Mohua	Spink	Coucal
Kaka	Yale	Monal	Sprug	Cuckoo
Kite	Yite	Mulga	Squab	Culver
Kiwi		Murre	Stare	Curlew
Knot	**5 letters:**	Mynah	Stilt	Cushat
Koel	Agami	Nandu	Stint	Darter
Kora	Ardea	Nelly	Stork	Dikkop
Lark	Ariel	Noddy	Sugar	Dipper
Loon	Bennu	Ousel	Swift	Drongo
Lory	Booby	Ouzel	Sylph	Duiker
Lyre	Bosun	Ox-eye	Terek	Dunlin
Mina	Buteo	Peggy	Tewit	Duyker
Monk	Capon	Pekan	Topaz	Elanet
Myna	Chook	Pewit	Twite	Evejar
Otis	Colin	Picus	Umber	Falcon
Pavo	Colly	Piper	Umbre	Fulmar
Pawn	Cooee	Pipit	Urubu	Gambet
Pern	Crake	Pitta	Veery	Gander
Piet	Crane	Poaka	Vireo	Gannet
Pink	Diver	Poker	Wader	Garuda
Pown	Eagle	Potoo	Whaup	Gentle
Pyot	Egret	Prion	Widow	Gentoo
Rail	Finch	Quail	Wonga	Gillar
Rhea	Fleet	Quest	Yaffa	Go-away
Roch	Galah	Quist		Godwit
Rook	Galar	Raven	**6 letters:**	Gooney
Ruff	Glede	Reeve	Amazon	Goslet
Runt	Goose	Rifle	Aquila	Grakle
Ruru	Goura	Robin	Avocet	Grouse
Rype	Grebe	Rotch	Avoset	Hagden
Shag	Heron	Ryper	Bantam	Hagdon
Skua	Hobby	Saker	Barbet	Haglet
Smee	Homer	Scape	Bishop	Hermit
Sora	Isaac	Scart	Bittor	Hoopoe
Swan	Junco	Scaup	Bittur	Houdan
Taha	Kight	Scops	Bonxie	Jabiru
Tara	Liver	Scray	Boubou	Jaçana
Teal	Lowan	Scrub	Brolga	Jaegar
Tern	Macaw	Serin	Bulbul	Jaeger
Tody	Madge	Shama	Canary	Kakapo
Tuli	Manch	Sitta	Chough	Karoro
Weka	Mavis	Skart	Chukar	Kereru
Whio	Merle	Snipe	Condor	Kokako

Kotare
Kotuku
Lahore
Lanner
Leipoa
Linnet
Lintie
Locust
Loriot
Lourie
Lungie
Magpie
Martin
Menura
Merlin
Merops
Missel
Mistle
Monaul
Mopoke
Mossie
Motmot
Musket
Nandhu
Nandoo
Oriole
Osprey
Parrot
Parson
Pavone
Peahen
Peewee
Peewit
Pernis
Petrel
Phoebe
Pigeon
Pipipi
Plover
Pouter
Progne
Puffin
Pukeko
Pullet
Queest

Quelea
Quoist
Redcap
Redleg
Reeler
Roller
Scamel
Scarth
Scaury
Scraye
Sea-cob
Sea-mew
Seapie
Shrike
Simara
Simorg
Simurg
Siskin
Skarth
Smeath
Soland
Sorage
Strich
Sultan
Sylvia
Tailor
Takahe
Tarcel
Tassel
Tauhou
Tewhit
Thrush
Tom-tit
Toucan
Towhee
Trogon
Turaco
Turbit
Tyrant
Tystie
Verdin
Wading
Walker
Waxeye
Weaver

Whidah
Whydah
Willet
Woosel
Yaffle
Ynambu
Yucker
Zoozoo

7 letters:
Amokura
Anhinga
Antbird
Apostle
Apteryx
Axebird
Babbler
Bécasse
Bittern
Bittour
Blighty
Bluecap
Blue-eye
Blue jay
Bluetit
Boobook
Bullbat
Bunting
Buphaga
Bushtit
Bustard
Buzzard
Cacique
Cariama
Catbird
Chewink
Chicken
Coal tit
Coletit
Colibri
Corella
Cotinga
Courlan
Courser
Cowbird

Creeper
Crombec
Cropper
Cumulet
Diamond
Dinorus
Dottrel
Dovekie
Dunnock
Emu-wren
Fantail
Fern-owl
Fig-bird
Finfoot
Flicker
Frigate
Gobbler
Goburra
Gorcrow
Goshawk
Grackle
Grallae
Grey jay
Hacklet
Hadedah
Hagbolt
Hagdown
Halcyon
Hemipod
Hoatzin
Humming
Ice-bird
Jacamar
Jackdaw
Jacobin
Kahawai
Kamichi
Kestrel
Killdee
Kinglet
Lapwing
Leghorn
Limpkin
Manakin
Marabou

Martlet
Mesites
Minivet
Mudlark
Ortolan
Oscires
Ostrich
Pandion
Peacock
Peafowl
Pelican
Penguin
Phoenix
Pickmaw
Piculet
Pinnock
Pintado
Pintail
Pochard
Pockard
Poe-bird
Poussin
Poy-bird
Quetzal
Rainbow
Rasores
Redpoll
Redwing
Regulus
Rooster
Rosella
Rotchie
Ruddock
Sakeret
Sawbill
Scooper
Scourie
Sea-mell
Seriema
Simurgh
Sirgang
Sitella
Skimmer
Skylark
Snow-cap

Soldier
Spadger
Sparrow
Squacco
Staniel
Stinker
Sturnus
Sunbird
Swallow
Tanager
Tarrock
Tattler
Teacher
Teuchat
Tiercel
Tinamou
Titanis
Titlark
Titling
Tokahea
Totanus
Touraco
Tumbler
Tweeter
Vulture
Vulturn
Wagtail
Warbler
Waxbill
Waxwing
Whooper
Widgeon
Wimbrel
Witwall
Wood hen
Woosell
Wren-tit
Wrybill
Wryneck
Yang-win

8 letters:
Aasvogel
Accentor
Adjutant

Aigrette
Alcatras
Altrices
Amadavat
Aquiline
Arapunga
Avadavat
Barnacle
Bee-eater
Bellbird
Blackcap
Bluebird
Blue duck
Blue-wing
Boatbill
Boattail
Bobolink
Bobwhite
Buln-buln
Bush wren
Capuchin
Caracara
Cardinal
Cargoose
Cheewink
Chirn-owl
Cockatoo
Coquette
Curassow
Dabchick
Didapper
Dip-chick
Dobchick
Dotterel
Estridge
Fauvette
Fernbird
Firebird
Fish-hawk
Flamingo
Gambetta
Gang-gang
Garefowl
Garganey
Great tit

Greenlet
Grosbeak
Guacharo
Hackbolt
Hangbird
Hangnest
Hawfinch
Hazelhen
Hemipode
Hernshaw
Hill myna
Hoactzin
Hornbill
Kakariki
Killdeer
Kingbird
Kiskadee
Koromako
Landrail
Lanneret
Laverock
Longspur
Lorikeet
Lovebird
Lyrebird
Macaroni
Magotpie
Makomako
Māori hen
Marsh tit
Megapode
Mire-drum
Miromiro
Morepork
Murrelet
Nightjar
Nuthatch
Ovenbird
Oxpecker
Paradise
Parakeet
Peetweet
Percolin
Petchary
Pheasant

Philomel
Pihoihoi
Podargus
Poorwill
Puffbird
Quarrian
Quarrion
Rainbird
Rallidae
Redshank
Redstart
Reedbird
Reedling
Reed-wren
Ricebird
Rifleman
Ringdove
Ringtail
Riroriro
Rock dove
Sandpeep
Scolopar
Screamer
Shake-bag
Shoebill
Silktail
Skua-gull
Snowbird
Stanniel
Starling
Struthio
Surfbird
Swiftlet
Tantalus
Tapacolo
Tapaculo
Teru-tero
Thrasher
Thresher
Throstle
Tick-bird
Titmouse
Tom-noddy
Toucanet
Tragopan

Trembler
Troopial
Troupial
Umbrella
Umbrette
Waldropp
Water-hen
Weka rail
Wheatear
Whimbrel
Whinchat
Whitecap
White-eye
Woodchat
Woodcock
Wood ibis
Woodlark
Woodwale
Yoldring
Zopilote

9 letters:
Accipiter
Aepyornis
Albatross
Aylesbury
Baldicoot
Baltimore
Beccaccia
Beccafico
Bergander
Blackbird
Blackcock
Blackhead
Blackpoll
Bowerbird
Brambling
Broadbill
Brown duck
Brown kiwi
Bullfinch
Campanero
Cassowary
Chaffinch
Chatterer

Chickadee
Coachwhip
Cockateel
Cockatiel
Cormorant
Corncrake
Crocodile
Crossbill
Currawong
Cushie-doo
Dowitcher
Estreldid
Fieldfare
Fig-pecker
Firecrest
Fledgling
Francolin
Friarbird
Frogmouth
Gallinule
Gerfalcon
Gier-eagle
Goldcrest
Goldfinch
Goosander
Grassquit
Green leek
Grenadier
Guillemot
Happy Jack
Helldiver
Heronshaw
Icteridae
Impundulu
Jacksnipe
Kittiwake
Lintwhite
Little auk
Little owl
Mallemuck
Merganser
Mistletoe
Mollymawk
Mousebird
Nighthawk

Nutjobber
Olive-back
Ossifraga
Ossifrage
Pardalote
Parrakeet
Partridge
Peaseweep
Peregrine
Phalarope
Pictarnie
Pied goose
Policeman
Porphyrio
Ptarmigan
Razorbill
Redbreast
Red grouse
Red siskin
Riflebird
Ring ouzel
Rosy finch
Salangane
Sandpiper
Sapsucker
Scansores
Sea-turtle
Secretary
Seedeater
Sheldrake
Shoveller
Silvereye
Skunk-bird
Snakebird
Solitaire
Sooty tern
Spoonbill
Standgale
Stock dove
Stonechat
Storm-cock
Swart-back
Swordbill
Talegalla
Thickhead

Thick-knee
Thornbill
Trochilus
Trumpeter
Turnstone
Volucrine
Water rail
Willow tit
Wind-hover
Xanthoura

10 letters:
Aberdevine
Arctic tern
Bananaquit
Banded rail
Bearded tit
Bell magpie
Bishopbird
Black robin
Bluebreast
Blue grouse
Bluethroat
Brain-fever
Bubbly-jock
Budgerigar
Bush canary
Bush shrike
Butter-bump
Cape pigeon
Chiffchaff
Crested tit
Demoiselle
Dickcissel
Didunculus
Dollarbird
Ember-goose
Eyas-musket
Flycatcher
Fringillid
Goatsucker
Gobemouche
Grassfinch
Greenfinch
Greenshank

Guinea fowl
Hen harrier
Honeyeater
Honey guide
Hooded crow
Jungle fowl
Kingfisher
Kookaburra
Magpie lark
Marsh-robin
Meadowlark
Night heron
Noisy miner
Nutcracker
Pettichaps
Pettychaps
Piwakawaka
Pratincole
Quaker-bird
Racket-tail
Rafter-bird
Regent-bird
Rhampastos
Rhinoceros
Roadrunner
Rockhopper
Rock pigeon
Saddleback
Saddlebill
Sage grouse
Sanderling
Sandgrouse
Sand martin
Scandaroon
Shearwater
Sheathbill
Sicklebill
Silverbill
Silver gull
Snowy egret
Song thrush
Spatchcock
Stone-snipe
Sun bittern
Tailorbird

Tanagridae
Tree-runner
Tropicbird
Turtledove
Water crake
Water ouzel
Wattlebird
Weaverbird
Whisky-jack
Whisky-john
White heron
Wild turkey
Wonga-wonga
Woodpecker
Wood pigeon
Yaffingale
Yellowlegs
Yellowtail
Yellowyite
Zebra finch

11 letters:
Black cuckoo
Black grouse
Bokmakierie
Bristlebird
Butcherbird
Button quail
Cape sparrow
Carrion crow
Coppersmith
Corn bunting
Gnatcatcher
Grallatores
Green plover
Grey warbler
Happy family
Honeysucker
House martin
Hummingbird
Java sparrow
King penguin
Leatherhead
Lily-trotter
Little grebe

Magpie goose
Meadow pipit
Mockingbird
Moss-bluiter
Moss-cheeper
Nightingale
Pied wagtail
Plain turkey
Plantcutter
Pyrrhuloxia
Reed bunting
Reed warbler
Scissortail
Snow bunting
Song sparrow
Stone curlew
Storm petrel
Stymphalian
Tawny pippit
Thunderbird
Titipounamu
Tree creeper
Tree sparrow
Wall creeper
Water thrush
Whitethroat
Wonga pigeon
Woodcreeper
Woodswallow
Wood warbler
Yellow-ammer
Zebra parrot

12 letters:
Bronze-pigeon
Brown creeper
Bustard quail
Capercaillie
Capercailzie
Chimney swift
Cliff swallow
Collared dove
Cuckoo-shrike
Drongo-cuckoo
Drongo-shrike

Flower-pecker
Golden oriole
Hedge sparrow
Homing pigeon
Honey creeper
House sparrow
Marsh harrier
Missel thrush
Mistle thrush
Mosquito hawk
Mountain duck
Mourning dove
Murray magpie
Painted finch
Pallid cuckoo
Paradise duck
Peppershrike
Piping shrike
Plains turkey
Putangitangi
Ring-dotterel
Ringed plover
Ruffed grouse
Sage-thrasher
Sandwich tern
Sedge warbler
Serpent-eater
Spotted crake
Standard-wing
Stonechatter
Stormy petrel
Throstle-cock
Whippoorwill
Willow grouse
Willy wagtail
Yellowhammer
Yellowthroat
Yellow-yowley

13 letters:
Bushman's clock
Chaparral cock
Cock-of-the-rock
Crow blackbird
Gouldian finch

Indigo bunting
Long-tailed tit
Major Mitchell
Numidian crane
Owlet nightjar
Oyster-catcher
Pintado petrel
Pipiwharauroa
Plantain-eater
Settler's clock
Swamp pheasant
Topknot pigeon
Whistling duck
White cockatoo
Whooping crane
Willow warbler

14 letters:
Banded dotterel
Bird of paradise
Chimney swallow
Cockatoo-parrot
Emperor penguin
Manx shearwater
Noisy friarbird
Ortolan bunting
Pheasant coucal
Pie-billed grebe
Ringneck parrot
Robin redbreast
Satin bowerbird
Scarlet tanager
Superb blue wren
Superb lyrebird
Tawny frogmouth
Welcome swallow
Woodchat shrike

15 letters:
American ostrich
Australian crane
Baltimore oriole
Blackbacked gull
Blue-wattled crow
Boat-billed heron

Cape Barren goose
Chipping sparrow
Chuck-will's-widow
Demoiselle crane
Green woodpecker
Laughing jackass
Native companion
Purple gallinule
Rainbow lorikeet
Red-backed shrike
Regent bowerbird
Rough-legged hawk
Shining starling

16 letters:
Black-fronted tern
Californian quail
Cardinal grosbeak
Loggerhead shrike
Metallic starling
New Zealand pigeon
Piping crow-shrike
Regent honeyeater
Roseate spoonbill
Spotted sandpiper
White-fronted tern

17 letters:
Great crested grebe
Pectoral sandpiper
Port Lincoln parrot
Spotted flycatcher

18 letters:
Bronze-winged cuckoo
Great northern diver
Grey-crowned babbler
Red-backed sandpiper
Red-legged partridge
Ring-necked pheasant
Rough-legged buzzard

19 letters:
Leadbeater's cockatoo
Purple-breasted finch

White-crowned sparrow

Yellowtail kingfisher

20 letters:
Great brown kingfisher
Rose-breasted grosbeak

22 letters:
Sulphur-crested cockatoo

EXTINCT BIRDS

3 letters:	6 letters:	9 letters:	13 letters:
Moa	Piopio	Solitaire	Archaeopteryx

4 letters:	8 letters:	11 letters:	15 letters:
Dodo	Great auk	Archaeornis	Passenger pigeon
Huia	Notornis	Ichthyornis	

See also:
➤ **Ducks** ➤ **Fowl** ➤ **Hawks** ➤ **Prey, birds of** ➤ **Sea birds**

Birthstones

Month	Stone	Month	Stone
January	Garnet	July	Ruby
February	Amethyst	August	Peridot, Sardonyx
March	Aquamarine, Bloodstone	September	Sapphire
		October	Opal, Tourmaline
April	Diamond	November	Topaz
May	Emerald	December	Turquoise, Zircon
June	Pearl, Alexandrite, Moonstone		

Biscuits

3 letters:	5 letters:	Hobnob	Pig's ear
Nut	ANZAC	Jumbal	Pretzel
Sea	Marie	Oliver	Ratafia
Tea	Matzo	Parkin	Rich tea
	Pilot	Perkin	Tararua
4 letters:	Sable	Tim Tam	
Bake	Ship's		8 letters:
Farl	Tuile	7 letters:	Amaretto
Kiss	Wafer	Bannock	Ameretti
Nice	Water	Bourbon	Biscotti
Puff		Cracker	Captain's
Rusk	6 letters:	Fairing	Charcoal
Soda	Cookie	Oatcake	Cracknel
Tack	Empire	Osborne	Flapjack

Hardtack
Macaroon
Mattress
Poppadom
Poppadum
Teiglach
Zwieback

9 letters:
Abernethy
Dandyfunk
Digestive

Garibaldi
Ginger nut
Jaffa cake®
Lebkuchen
Petit four
Shortcake
Sweetmeal

10 letters:
Bath Oliver
Brandy snap
Butterbake
Crispbread

Dunderfunk
Florentine
Ginger snap
Love letter
Shortbread

12 letters:
Caramel wafer
Cream cracker
Custard Cream
Langue de chat

13 letters:
Graham cracker

14 letters:
Gingerbread man

15 letters:
Tollhouse cookie

18 letters:
Chocolate
 digestive

Black and white shades

3 letters:
Ash
Jet

4 letters:
Grey
Iron

5 letters:
Black

Cream
Ebony
Ivory
Pearl
Putty
Raven
Sable
Slate
Stone
White

6 letters:
Pewter
Silver

8 letters:
Charcoal
Eggshell
Gunmetal
Off-white
Platinum

9 letters:
Steel grey

10 letters:
Pitch-black

11 letters:
Oyster white

Blemishes

3 letters:
Zit

4 letters:
Boil
Mole
Scab
Scar
Spot
Wart

5 letters:
Stain

6 letters:
Callus
Naevus
Pimple

7 letters:
Freckle

Pustule
Verruca

8 letters:
Pockmark

9 letters:
Birthmark
Blackhead
Carbuncle

Whitehead

13 letters:
Discoloration

14 letters:
Strawberry mark

Blood cells

9 letters:
Haemocyte
Leucocyte

Macrocyte
Microcyte
Polymorph

10 letters:
Lymphocyte

11 letters:
Erythrocyte
Poikilocyte

12 letters:
Reticulocyte

24 letters:
Phagocytic white blood cell

Blue, shades of

3 letters:
Sky

4 letters:
Aqua
Bice
Cyan
Navy
Nile
Saxe
Teal

5 letters:
Azure
Clear
Perse
Royal
Saxon
Slate

Steel

6 letters:
Berlin
Cantab
Cobalt
Indigo
Oxford
Petrol
Pewter
Powder
Saxony
Welkin

7 letters:
Celeste
Duck-egg
Gentian
Nattier

Peacock
Watchet

8 letters:
Bleuâtre
Caesious
Cerulean
Eggshell
Electric
Lavender
Mazarine
Midnight
Prussian
Sapphire
Stafford
Wedgwood®

9 letters:
Cambridge
Germander
Robin's egg
Turquoise

10 letters:
Aquamarine
Copenhagen
Cornflower
Heliotrope
Periwinkle

11 letters:
Clair de lune
Lapis lazuli
Ultramarine

Board games

2 letters:
Go

3 letters:
I-go

4 letters:
Life
Ludo
Risk

5 letters:
Chess
Halma

6 letters:
Cluedo®

7 letters:
Reversi

8 letters:
Chequers
Draughts
Monopoly®
Scrabble®

9 letters:
Acey-deucy
Bagatelle
Parcheesi®
Solitaire

10 letters:
Backgammon
Game of Life

Kriegspiel
Speed chess

11 letters:
Fox and geese

13 letters:
Trivial Pursuit

14 letters:
Lightning chess
Nine men's morris
Shove-halfpenny

15 letters:
Chinese chequers

16 letters:
Snakes and ladders

Boats and ships

1 letter:
Q

2 letters:
MY
PT
VJ

3 letters:
Ark
Cat
Cog
Cot
Dow
Gig
Hoy
MTB
Red
Tub
Tug

4 letters:
Argo
Bark
Brig
Buss
Cock
Dhow
Dory
Duck
Grab
Junk
Koff
Maxi
Nina
Pink
Pont
Pram
Prau
Proa
Punt
Raft

Ro-ro
Saic
Scow
Snow
Tall
Tern
Trow
Yawl
Zulu

5 letters:
Aviso
Barge
Broke
Camel
Canal
Canoe
Coble
Coper
Crare
Dandy
Dingy
Drake
E-boat
Ferry
Funny
Jolly
Kayak
Ketch
Laker
Liner
Moses
Oiler
Pinky
Pinto
Prore
Púcán
Q-boat
Razee
Sabot
Scoot
Screw
Scull

Shell
Skiff
Sloop
Snow
Swamp
Tramp
U-boat
Umiak
Whiff
Xebec
Yacht
Zabra
Zebec

6 letters:
Argosy
Banker
Barque
Bateau
Bawley
Beagle
Bethel
Bireme
Boatel
Borley
Bounty
Caïque
Carack
Carvel
Castle
Coaler
Cobble
Cooper
Crayer
Cutter
Decker
Dingey
Dinghy
Dogger
Droger
Dromon
Drover
Dugout
Flotel

Frigot
Galiot
Galley
Gay-you
Hooker
Jigger
Launch
Lorcha
Lugger
Masula
Narrow
Nuggar
Oomiak
Packet
Pedalo
Pequod
Pinkie
Pirate
Pitpan
Pulwar
Puteli
Randan
Rowing
Sampan
Sandal
Schuit
Schuyt
Sealer
Settee
Slaver
Tanker
Tartan
Tender
Tonner
Torpid
Trader
Wangan
Wangun
Whaler
Wherry
Zebeck

7 letters:
Airboat
Belfast
Bidarka
Bumboat
Capital
Caravel
Carrack
Carract
Carrect
Catboat
Clipper
Coaster
Collier
Coracle
Counter
Crabber
Cruiser
Currach
Curragh
Dredger
Drifter
Drogher
Dromond
Factory
Felucca
Fishing
Floatel
Flyboat
Foyboat
Frigate
Gabbard
Gabbart
Galleas
Galleon
Galliot
Galloon
Geordie
Gondola
Gunboat
Jet-boat
Jetfoil
Liberty

Lighter
Lymphad
Man o' war
Masoola
Mistico
Monitor
Mudscow
Oomiack
Patamar
Pearler
Pelican
Pinnace
Piragua
Pirogue
Polacca
Polacre
Pontoon
Revenge
Rowboat
Sailing
Scooter
Shallop
Sharpie
Sounder
Steamer
Stew-can
Tartane
Titanic
Torpedo
Towboat
Trawler
Trireme
Tugboat
Vedette
Victory
Vidette
Wanigan
Warship

8 letters:
Acapulco
Bilander
Billyboy
Cabotage
Cockboat

Corocore
Corocoro
Corvette
Dahabieh
Faldboat
Faltboat
Fireboat
Flatboat
Foldboat
Galleass
Galliass
Gallivat
Hoveller
Ice yacht
Indiaman
Ironclad
Keelboat
Lifeboat
Longboat
Longship
Mackinaw
Man-of-war
Mary Rose
Masoolah
Merchant
Monohull
Outboard
Pinafore
Sailboat
Savannah
Schooner
Shanghai
Showboat
Skipjack
Surfboat
Trimaran

9 letters:
Auxiliary
Bucentaur
Catamaran
Cutty Sark
Dahabeeah
Dahabiyah
Dahabiyeh

Destroyer
Dromedary
First-rate
Freighter
Frigatoon
Houseboat
Hydrofoil
Klondiker
Klondyker
Lapstrake
Lapstreak
Leviathan
Lightship
Lusitania
Mayflower
Minelayer
Monoxylon
Motorboat
Multihull
Outrigger
Oysterman
Peter-boat
Powerboat
Shear-hulk
Sheer-hulk
Speedboat
Steamboat
Steamship
Submarine
Temeraire
Troopship
Vaporetto
Whale-back
Whaleboat

10 letters:
Bathyscape
Bathyscaph
Battleship
Bermuda rig
Brigantine
Cockleboat
Fourmaster
Golden Hind
Hydroplane

Icebreaker
Knockabout
Minehunter
Motor yacht
Paddleboat
Purse-seine
Quadrireme
Sandsucker
Santa Maria
Track-scout
Trekschuit
Triaconter
Windjammer

11 letters:
Barquantine
Barquentine
Bathyscaphe
Bellerophon
Berthon-boat
Bulk carrier
Cockleshell
Dreadnaught
Dreadnought
Merchantman
Minesweeper
Penteconter
Quinquereme
Sidewheeler
Skidbladnir
Submersible
Supertanker
Threedecker
Three-master
Weathership

12 letters:
Cabin cruiser
Deepwaterman
Fore-and-after
Great Eastern
Landing craft
Marie Celeste
Motor torpedo
Square-rigger

Stern-wheeler

13 letters:
Battlecruiser
Paddle steamer
Revenue cutter
Ship of the line

14 letters:
Ocean greyhound
Vaucluse junior

15 letters:
Aircraft carrier
Destroyer escort

16 letters:
Pocket battleship

20 letters:
Torpedo-boat destroyer

See also:
➤ **Ships, parts of**

Body, parts of

Part of the body	Technical name	Related adjective
Abdomen	-	Abdominal
Adenoids	Pharyngeal tonsil	Adenoid *or* adenoidal
Alimentary canal	-	-
Ankle	Talus	-
Anus	-	Anal
Appendix	Vermiform appendix	Appendicular
Arm	Brachium	Brachial
Armpit	Axilla	Axillary
Artery	-	Arterial
Back	-	Dorsal
Belly	Venter	Ventral
Bladder	Urinary bladder	Vesical
Blood	-	Haemal, haemic, *or* haematic
Bone	Os	Osseous, osteal, *or* osteoid
Brain	Encephalon	Cerebral
Breast	-	-
Buttocks	Nates	Natal *or* gluteal
Caecum	-	Caecal
Calf	-	-
Capillary	-	Capillary
Cervix	-	Cervical
Cheek	Gena	Genal
Chest	-	Pectoral
Chin	-	Genial *or* mental
Clitoris	-	Clitoral
Colon	-	Colonic
Duodenum	-	Duodenal
Ear	-	Aural
Elbow	-	-

Part of the body	Technical name	Related adjective
Epiglottis	-	Epiglottal
External ear	Auricle *or* pinna	-
Eye	-	Ocular *or* ophthalmic
Eyebrow	-	Superciliary
Eyelash	Cilium	Ciliary
Eyelid	-	Palpebral
Fallopian tube	Oviduct	Oviducal *or* oviductal
Finger	-	Digital
Fingernail	-	Ungual *or* ungular
Fist	-	-
Follicle	-	Follicular
Fontanelle *or* fontanel	-	-
Foot	Pes	Pedal
Forearm	-	Cubital
Forehead	-	Frontal
Foreskin	Prepuce	Preputial
Gall bladder	-	-
Gland	-	Adenoid
Glottis	-	Glottic
Groin	-	Inguinal
Gullet	Oesophagus	Oesophageal
Gum	Gingiva	Gingival
Hair	-	-
Half-moon	Lunula *or* lunule	-
Hamstring	-	Popliteal
Hand	Manus	Manual
Hard palate	-	-
Head	Caput	Capital
Heart	-	Cardiac
Heel	-	-
Hip	-	-
Ileum	-	Ileac *or* ileal
Inner ear *or* internal ear	Labyrinth	-
Instep	-	-
Intestine	-	Alvine
Jaw	-	Gnathic *or* gnathal
Jejunum	-	Jejunal
Jugular vein	-	-
Kidney	-	Renal *or* nephritic
Knee	Genu	Genicular
Knuckle	-	-
Labia majora	-	Labial
Labia minora	-	Labial
Large intestine	-	-

Part of the body	Technical name	Related adjective
Leg	Crus	Crural
Lip	-	Labial
Liver	-	Hepatic
Loin	Lumbus	Lumbar
Lung	-	Pulmonary
Lymph cell	Lymphocyte	-
Lymph node	-	-
Midriff	Diaphragm	-
Mons pubis	-	-
Mons veneris	-	-
Mouth	-	Stomatic
Nape	Nucha	Nuchal
Navel or omphalos	Umbilicus	Umbilical
Neck	Cervix	Cervical
Nerve	-	Neural
Nerve cell	Neuron or neurone	Neuronic
Nipple or teat	Mamilla or papilla	Mamillary
Nose	-	Nasal
Nostril	Naris	Narial or narine
Occiput	-	Occipital
Ovary	-	Ovarian
Pancreas	-	Pancreatic
Penis	-	Penile
Pharynx	-	Pharyngeal
Pubes	-	Pubic
Rectum	-	Rectal
Red blood cell	Erythrocyte	Erythrocytic
Ribcage	-	-
Scalp	-	-
Scrotum	-	Scrotal
Shin	-	-
Shoulder	-	-
Side	-	-
Skin	Cutis	Cutaneous
Small intestine	-	-
Soft palate	-	-
Sole	-	Plantar
Spleen	-	Lienal or splenetic
Stomach	-	Gastric
Tear duct	Lacrimal duct	-
Temple	-	Temporal
Tendon	-	-
Testicle	-	Testicular
Thigh	-	Femoral or crural

Part of the body	Technical name	Related adjective
Thorax	-	Thoracic
Throat	-	Guttural, gular, *or* jugular
Thumb	Pollex	Pollical
Toe	-	-
Toenail	-	Ungual *or* ungular
Tongue	Lingua	Lingual *or* glottic
Tonsil	-	Tonsillar *or* tonsillary
Torso	-	-
Transverse colon	-	-
Trunk	-	-
Umbilical cord	Umbilicus	-
Ureter	-	Ureteral *or* ureteric
Urethra	-	Urethral
Vagina	-	Vaginal
Vein	Vena	Venous
Vocal cords	Glottis	Glottal
Voice box	Larynx	Laryngeal
Vulva	-	Vulval, vulvar, *or* vulvate
Waist	-	-
White blood cell	Leucocyte	Leucocytic
Windpipe	Trachea	Tracheal *or* tracheate
Womb	Uterus	Uterine
Wrist	Carpus	-

See also:
➤ **Blood cells** ➤ **Bones** ➤ **Brain, parts of** ➤ **Ear, parts of**
➤ **Eye** ➤ **Glands** ➤ **Heart, parts of** ➤ **Humours of the body**
➤ **Membranes** ➤ **Muscles** ➤ **Nerves** ➤ **Organs** ➤ **Teeth**
➤ **Veins**

Bombs

3 letters:
IED

4 letters:
Atom
Nail

5 letters:
A-bomb
Dirty
Mills

6 letters:
Fusion
Petrol

7 letters:
Cluster
Grenade
Neutron
Nuclear
Plastic

8 letters:
Bouncing
Hydrogen

10 letters:
Incendiary

11 letters:
Blockbuster
Depth charge
Hand grenade
Stun grenade

15 letters:
Molotov cocktail

16 letters:
Bangalore torpedo

Bones

Bone	Nontechnical name
Astragalus	Anklebone
Calcaneus	Heel bone
Carpal	Wrist
Carpus	Wrist
Centrum	-
Clavicle	Collarbone
Coccyx	-
Costa	Rib
Cranium	Brainpan
Cuboid	-
Ethmoid	-
Femur	Thighbone
Fibula	-
Frontal	-
Hallux	-
Humerus	Funny
Hyoid	-
Ilium	-
Incus	Anvil
Innominate	Hipbone
Ischium	-
Malar	Cheek
Malleus	Hammer
Mandible	Lower jawbone
Mastoid	-
Maxilla	Upper jawbone
Metacarpal	-
Metatarsal	-
Metatarsus	-
Nasal	Nose
Occipital	-
Parietal	-
Patella	Kneecap
Pelvis	-
Phalanx	-
Pubis	-
Radius	-
Rib	-
Sacrum	-
Scapula	Shoulder blade
Skull	-
Sphenoid	-

Bone	Nontechnical name
Spinal column *or* spine	Backbone
Stapes	Stirrup
Sternum	Breastbone
Talus	Anklebone
Tarsal	-
Tarsus	-
Temporal	-
Tibia	Shinbone
Trapezium	-
Ulna	-
Vertebra	-
Vertebral column	Backbone
Zygomatic	Cheekbone

Books

TYPES OF BOOK

3 letters:
Log

4 letters:
A to Z
Hymn
Road
Song

5 letters:
Album
Atlas
Bible
Comic
Diary
E-book
Novel
Score

6 letters:
Annual
Gradus
Jotter
Ledger
Manual
Missal

Phrase
Prayer
Primer
Reader

7 letters:
Almanac
Anatomy
Bibelot
Cookery
Grammar
Journal
Lexicon
Logbook
Novella
Ordinal
Peerage
Psalter
Service
Speller
Statute
Who's who

8 letters:
Armorial

Baedeker
Bestiary
Breviary
Brochure
Casebook
Copybook
Exercise
Grimoire
Handbook
Notebook
Register
Textbook
Wordbook
Workbook
Yearbook

9 letters:
Anthology
Biography
Catalogue
Catechism
Companion
Directory
Formulary
Gazetteer
Guidebook

Monograph
Novelette
Reference
Scrapbook
Storybook
Thesaurus
Vade mecum

10 letters:
Compendium
Dictionary
Electronic
Lectionary
Miscellany
Photonovel
Prospectus
Sketchbook

11 letters:
Coffee-table
Commonplace
Concordance

12 letters:
Confessional
Dispensatory
Encyclopedia
Graphic novel

13 letters:
Autobiography
Encyclopaedia
Pharmacopoeia

18 letters:
Telephone directory

PARTS OF A BOOK

4 letters:
Back
Leaf
Page
Tail

5 letters:
Blurb
Cover
Folio
Index
Plate
Proem
Recto
Spine
Verso

6 letters:
Errata
Gutter
Margin
Rubric

7 letters:
Binding
Chapter
Flyleaf
Preface
Prelims
Wrapper

8 letters:
Addendum
Appendix
Colophon
Contents

Endpaper
Epigraph
Epilogue
Fore-edge
Foreword
Glossary
Prologue
Slipcase

9 letters:
Afterword
Half-title
Interleaf
Title page

10 letters:
Back matter
Corrigenda
Dedication

Dust jacket
Postscript

11 letters:
Front matter
Running head

12 letters:
Bibliography
Frontispiece
Illustration
Introduction
Prolegomenon

15 letters:
Acknowledgments
Table of contents

Botany

BRANCHES OF BOTANY

8 letters:
Algology
Bryology
Mycology

9 letters:
Carpology

10 letters:
Dendrology
Floristics

11 letters:
Agrostology
Astrobotany
Ethnobotany
Phytography
Pteridology

12 letters:
Archeobotany
Palaeobotany
Phytogenesis

13 letters:
Archaeobotany

14 letters:
Phytogeography
Phytopathology

17 letters:
Palaeoethnobotany

BOTANY TERMS

3 letters:
Key

Nut
Sap

4 letters:
Axil

Axis
Bulb

Corm
Leaf
Pith
Root
Seed
Stem

5 letters:
Auxin
Berry
Calyx
Fruit
Hilum
Ovary
Ovule
Sepal
Shoot
Spore
Stoma
Style
Testa
Tuber
Xylem

6 letters:
Anther
Carpel
Corona
Cortex
Flower
Lamina
Legume
Phloem
Pistil
Pollen
Raceme
Runner
Spadix
Stamen
Stigma
Stolon

7 letters:
Cambium
Corolla
Cuticle
Plumule
Radicle
Rhizome
Root cap
Rosette
Seed pod
Tropism

8 letters:
Filament
Lenticel
Meristem
Root hair
Seedcase

9 letters:
Cotyledon
Epidermis
Foliation
Guard cell
Gynaecium
Mesophyll
Micropyle
Operculum

10 letters:
Abscission
Androecium
Geotropism
Integument
Receptacle
Root nodule
Seed vessel
Sporangium

11 letters:
Androgynous
Archegonium
Chlorophyll
Chloroplast
Dicotyledon
Germination
Pollination
Seed capsule

12 letters:
Hydrotropism
Phototropism

13 letters:
Inflorescence
Monocotyledon
Translocation
Transpiration

14 letters:
Nastic movement
Photosynthesis
Vascular bundle

15 letters:
Self-pollination
Spongy mesophyll
Wind pollination

16 letters:
Cross-pollination

17 letters:
Insect pollination
Palisade mesophyll

22 letters:
Vegetative reproduction

BOTANISTS

3 letters:
Ray, *John*

5 letters:
Banks, *Joseph*

Brown, *Robert*

6 letters:
Carver, *George Washington*
Darwin, *Charles (Robert)*
Hooker, *Joseph Dalton*
Hooker, *William Jackson*
Mendel, *Gregor Johann*

7 letters:
Bellamy, *David (James)*

De Vries, *Hugo*
Eichler, *August Wilhelm*

8 letters:
Linnaeus
Von Linné, *Carl*

10 letters:
De Candolle, *Auguste Pyrame*
Tradescant, *John*

See also:
➤ **Algae** ➤ **Ferns** ➤ **Fungi** ➤ **Grasses** ➤ **Lilies** ➤ **Mosses**
➤ **Palms** ➤ **Plants** ➤ **Seaweeds** ➤ **Shrubs** ➤ **Trees**

Bottles

5 letters:
Flask
Gourd
Phial
Water

6 letters:
Carboy
Caster
Flacon

Flagon
Lagena
Nansen
Stubby
Woulfe

7 letters:
Ampulla
Feeding

8 letters:
Decanter
Demijohn
Half-jack
Hot-water
Screw top

9 letters:
Miniature

10 letters:
Pycnometer
Soda siphon

11 letters:
Marie-Jeanne
Vinaigrette

Boxes

4 letters:
Case
Coin
Deed
Nest
Poor
Wine

5 letters:
Bulla
Chest
Ditty
Glory

Glove
Grass
Music
Trunk

6 letters:
Ballot
Carton
Casket
Coffer
Coffin
Hatbox
Haybox

Pounce
Saggar
Vanity
Window

7 letters:
Bandbox
Caisson
Cracket
Honesty
Keister
Pillbox
Pouncet

Saltbox
Sandbox
Soapbox

8 letters:
Dispatch
Matchbox
Paintbox
Solander

9 letters:
Cartouche
Papeterie

Strongbox
Tinderbox

Boxing weights

Weight	Amateur	Professional
Paperweight	-	40.6 kg
Minimumweight	-	47.6 kg
Light flyweight	49 kg	49 kg
Flyweight	52 kg	50.8 kg
Bantamweight	56 kg	53.5 kg
Featherweight	57 kg	57.2 kg
Junior lightweight	-	59 kg
Lightweight	60 kg	61 kg
Light welterweight	63.5 kg	63.5 kg
Welterweight	67 kg	66.6 kg
Light middleweight	71 kg	70 kg
Middleweight	75 kg	72.5 kg
Light heavyweight	81 kg	79.4 kg
Cruiserweight	-	90.7 kg
Heavyweight	91 kg	+88.5 kg
Superheavyweight	+91 kg	-

Brain, parts of

6 letters:
Vermis

8 letters:
Amygdala
Cerebrum
Meninges
Midbrain
Thalamus

9 letters:
Brainstem

10 letters:
Afterbrain
Broca's area
Cerebellum
Grey matter
Pineal body

11 letters:
Frontal lobe
Hippocampus
Pons Varolli
White matter

12 letters:
Diencephalon
Hypothalamus
Infundibulum
Limbic system
Optic chiasma
Parietal lobe
Temporal lobe

13 letters:
Central sulcus
Choroid plexus
Mamillary body
Occipital lobe

Wernicke's area

14 letters:
Cerebral cortex
Corpus callosum
Myelencephalon
Pituitary gland
Substantia alba
Third ventricle

15 letters:
Fourth ventricle

16 letters:
Cerebral aqueduct
Medulla oblongata

18 letters:
Cerebrospinal fluid

Breads

3 letters:
Bap
Bun
Cob
Nan
Pan
Rye

4 letters:
Corn
Loaf
Naan
Puri
Roll
Roti
Soda

5 letters:
Bagel
Black
Brown
Matza
Matzo
Panko

Pitta
Plain
Plait
White

6 letters:
Beigel
Coburg
Damper
French
Gluten
Hallah
Indian
Matzah
Matzoh
Muffin

7 letters:
Bloomer
Brioche
Buttery
Challah
Chapati
Granary®

Long tin
Paratha
Popover
Stollen
Wheaten

8 letters:
Baguette
Barm cake
Chapatti
Ciabatta
Corn pone
Focaccia
Poppadom
Poppadum
Quartern
Split tin
Tortilla

9 letters:
Barmbrack
Batch loaf
Croissant
Farmhouse

Fruit loaf
Schnecken
Sourdough
Square tin
Wholemeal

10 letters:
Billy-bread
Bridge roll
Johnny cake
Unleavened
Whole-wheat

11 letters:
Cottage loaf
French stick

12 letters:
Griddlebread
Half-quartern
Pumpernickel

Bridges

BRIDGES

4 letters:
Skye
Tyne

5 letters:
Tower

6 letters:
Humber
London
Rialto
Severn

7 letters:
Rainbow

8 letters:
Brooklyn
Waterloo

9 letters:
Forth Road
Halfpenny

10 letters:
Golden Gate
Millennium
Oakland Bay

11 letters:
Westminster

12 letters:
Forth Railway

13 letters:
Bridge of Sighs
Sydney Harbour

17 letters:
Clifton Suspension

19 letters:
Gateshead Millennium

TYPES OF BRIDGE

4 letters:
Deck
Snow
Turn

5 letters:
Pivot
Swing
Truss

6 letters:
Bailey

7 letters:
Balance
Bascule
Clapper
Flyover
Pontoon
Viaduct

8 letters:
Aqueduct

9 letters:
Box-girder

10 letters:
Cantilever
Drawbridge
Footbridge

Suspension

11 letters:
Cable-stayed

12 letters:
Counterpoise

British forces

RANKS OF THE ARMY/ROYAL MARINES

5 letters:
Major

6 letters:
Marine

7 letters:
Captain
Colonel
General
Private

8 letters:
Corporal

Sergeant

9 letters:
Brigadier

10 letters:
Lieutenant

12 letters:
Field Marshal
Major General
Officer Cadet

13 letters:
Lance Corporal
Staff Sergeant

14 letters:
Colour Sergeant
Warrant Officer

17 letters:
Lieutenant Colonel
Lieutenant General

RANKS OF THE ROYAL NAVY

7 letters:
Admiral
Captain

9 letters:
Commander
Commodore

10 letters:
Able Rating
Lieutenant
Midshipman

11 letters:
Leading Rate
Rear Admiral
Vice Admiral

12 letters:
Petty Officer

13 letters:
Sub-Lieutenant

14 letters:
Warrant Officer

17 letters:
Admiral of the Fleet
Chief Petty Officer

19 letters:
Lieutenant Commander

RANKS OF THE ROYAL AIR FORCE

10 letters:
Air Marshal

12 letters:
Air Commodore
Group Captain

13 letters:
Flying Officer
Wing Commander

14 letters:
Air Vice-Marshal
Squadron Leader

15 letters:
Air Chief Marshal
Marshal of the RAF

16 letters:
Flight Lieutenant

Brown, shades of

3 letters:
Bay
Dun
Tan

4 letters:
Buff
Drab
Ecru
Fawn
Fusc
Rust
Sand
Sore
Teak

5 letters:
Abram
Amber
Beige
Camel
Cocoa
Cream
Hazel
Henna

Khaki
Liver
Mocha
Mousy
Sable
Sepia
Soare
Taupe
Tawny
Tenné
Umber

6 letters:
Almond
Auburn
Bisque
Bistre
Bronze
Burnet
Coffee
Copper
Fallow
Ginger
Nutmeg
Rufous

Russet
Sienna
Sorrel
Walnut

7 letters:
Biscuit
Brindle
Caramel
Caromel
Filemot
Fulvous
Fuscous
Neutral
Oatmeal
Oxblood
Vandyke

8 letters:
Brunette
Chestnut
Cinnabar
Cinnamon
Mahogany
Mushroom

Nutbrown
Philamot

9 letters:
Butternut
Chocolate
Pygmalion
Seal brown

10 letters:
Burnt umber
Café au lait
Centennial
Coromandel
Terracotta
Testaceous

11 letters:
Burnt sienna

13 letters:
Tortoiseshell

Buddhism

3 letters:
Zen

4 letters:
Jodo

5 letters:
Foism

Sima
Soto

Geluk
Kagyü
Sakya

6 letters:
Rinjai
Tendai

7 letters:
Lamaism
Nyingma

8 letters:
Hinayana

Mahayana
Nichiren

9 letters:
Theravada
Vajrayana

10 letters:
Soka Gakkai

16 letters:
Pure Land Buddhism

Bugs

4 letters:
Lace

5 letters:
Māori
Mealy
Stink
Water

6 letters:
Bedbug
Chinch
Cicada
Cicala

Damsel
Debris
Shield

7 letters:
Kissing
Spittle

9 letters:
Harlequin

10 letters:
Froghopper
Leaf-hopper

Pond-skater

11 letters:
Water skater

12 letters:
Water boatman
Water strider

13 letters:
Spittle insect
Water scorpion

Buildings and monuments

5 letters:
Kaaba

6 letters:
Big Ben
Louvre
Masada
Mosque

7 letters:
Beehive
Knossos
Kremlin
Lateran
Vatican

8 letters:
Alhambra
Barbican

Basilica
Cenotaph
Holyrood
Monument
Pentagon
Taj Mahal

9 letters:
Charminar
Hermitage

10 letters:
The Gherkin
White House

11 letters:
Eiffel Tower
Scone Palace
Summerhouse

12 letters:
Althorp House
Mansion House

13 letters:
Arc de Triomphe
Crystal Palace
Élysée Palace
Forbidden City
Holyroodhouse
Lambeth Palace
Longleat House
Nelson's Column
Tower of London

14 letters:
Admiralty House
Blenheim Palace
Sagrada Familia

15 letters:
Angel of the North
Edinburgh Castle

16 letters:
Buckingham Palace
Cleopatra's Needle
Guggenheim Museum
Kensington Palace
Sydney Opera House
Westminster Abbey

17 letters:
Saint James's Palace

18 letters:
Hampton Court Palace
Houses of Parliament
Leaning Tower of Pisa
Palace of Versailles

19 letters:
Empire State Building

Businesspeople

4 letters:
Benz, *Karl Friedrich*
Bond, *Alan*
Boot, *Sir Jesse*
Cook, *Thomas*
Ford, *Henry*
Jobs, *Steven Paul*
Mond, *Sir Robert Ludwig*
Shah, *Eddy*
Slim, *Carlos*
Tate, *Sir Henry*

5 letters:
Astor, *Lord John Jacob*
Dawes, *Charles Gates*
Dyson, *James*
Flynt, *Larry*
Forte, *Lord Charles*
Frick, *Henry Clay*
Gates, *Bill*
Getty, *Jean Paul*
Grade, *Michael*
Heinz, *Henry John*
Honda, *Soichiro*
Jones, *Digby*
Krupp, *Friedrich*
Laker, *Sir Freddie*
Lyons, *Sir Joseph*
Marks, *Lord Simon*
Rolls, *Charles Stewart*
Royce, *Sir Henry*

Sieff, *Lord Israel*
Sugar, *Baron Alan*
Trump, *Donald*
Zeiss, *Carl*

6 letters:
Ashley, *Laura*
Austin, *Lord Herbert*
Boeing, *William Edward*
Butlin, *Billy*
Conran, *Sir Terence*
Cunard, *Sir Samuel*
Dunlop, *John Boyd*
Farmer, *Sir Tom*
Glazer, *Malcolm*
Hammer, *Armand*
Hanson, *Lord James*
Hilton, *Conrad*
  Nicholson
Hoover, *William Henry*
Hughes, *Howard*
Hulton, *Sir Edward*
Lipton, *Sir Thomas*
Mittal, *Lakshmi*
Morris, *William Richard (Viscount*
  Nuffield)
Ogilvy, *David*
Packer, *Kerry*
Ratner, *Gerald Irving*
Turner, *Ted*
Warner, *Harold*

7 letters:
Agnelli, *Giovanni*
Arnault, *Bernard*
Barclay, *Sir David*
Barclay, *Sir Frederick*
Barclay, *Robert*
Branson, *Sir Richard*
Buffett, *Warren*
Bugatti, *Ettore*
Burrell, *Sir William*
Cadbury, *George*
Citroën, *André Gustave*
Douglas, *Donald*
Goodwin, *Sir Fred*
Kennedy, *Joseph Patrick*
Lebedev, *Alexander*
Maxwell, *Robert*
Murdoch, *Rupert*
Onassis, *Aristotle*
Roddick, *Dame Anita Lucia*
Tiffany, *Charles Lewis*

8 letters:
Birdseye, *Clarence*
Carnegie, *Andrew*

Christie, *James*
Guinness, *Sir Benjamin Lee*
Michelin, *André*
Olivetti, *Adriano*
Pulitzer, *Joseph*
Rowntree, *Joseph*
Sinclair, *Sir Clive*
Southeby, *John*
Zaharoff, *Sir Basil*

9 letters:
Firestone, *Harvey Samuel*
Sainsbury, *Lord Alan*
Selfridge, *Harry Gordon*
Woolworth, *Frank Winfield*

10 letters:
Abramovich, *Roman*
Rothschild, *Meyer Amschel*
Vanderbilt, *Cornelius*

11 letters:
Beaverbrook, *Lord Max*
Harvey-Jones, *Sir John Henry*
Rockefeller, *John Davison*

Butterflies and moths

2 letters:	Leaf	Friar	Yucca
Io	Luna	Ghost	Zebra
	Meal	Gipsy	
3 letters:	Monk	Grass	6 letters:
Bag	Puss	Gypsy	Antler
Bee	Wave	Heath	Apollo
Fox		House	Bogong
Nun	5 letters:	Owlet	Bugong
Owl	Argus	Regal	Burnet
Wax	Atlas	Snout	Calico
	Brown	Swift	Carpet
4 letters:	Comma	Thorn	Codlin
Arch	Dryad	Tiger	Copper
Bell	Eggar	Tinea	Dagger
Blue	Egger	Umber	Diadem
Goat	Fairy	White	Ermine
Hawk	Flour	Y-moth	Herald

Hermit
Kitten
Lackey
Lappet
Lichen
Magpie
Morpho
Muslin
Noctua
Pieris
Psyche
Sphinx
Thecla
Turnip
Veneer
Winter
Yellow

7 letters:
Abraxas
Admiral
Bagworm
Buff-tip
Cabbage
Clothes
Codling
Drinker
Emperor
Festoon
Flannel
Hook-tip
Kallima
Leopard
Lobster
Monarch
Noctuid
Old lady
Peacock
Pug-moth
Pyralid
Ringlet
Silver-Y
Skipper
Stamper
Sulphur

Thistle
Tortrix
Tussock
Unicorn
Vanessa
Zygaena

8 letters:
Birdwing
Black eye
Black tip
Bobowler
Bombycid
Cardinal
Cecropia
Cinnabar
Dart-moth
Forester
Geometer
Goldtail
Grayling
Hesperid
Milkweed
Oak-egger
Peppered
Saturnia
Silkworm
Sphingid
Tapestry
Tineidae
Vapourer
Wainscot

9 letters:
Arctiidae
Atlas blue
Bath white
Brimstone
Brown-tail
Carpenter
Clearwing
Cleopatra
Commodore
Geometrid
Golden tip

Hackberry
Honeycomb
Notodonta
Orange-tip
Pyralidae
Salt marsh
Saturniid
Scavenger
Swordtail
Underwing
Wall brown
Wood white

10 letters:
Adonis blue
Arctic blue
Arran brown
Black satyr
Black witch
Bush beauty
Common blue
Crimson tip
Death's-head
Fritillary
Gate-keeper
Grass jewel
Hairstreak
Large white
Leafroller
Plain tiger
Polyphemus
Privet hawk
Red admiral
Silverline
Silverspot
Small white
Yellowtail

11 letters:
Amanda's blue
Diamondback
Forest queen
Grass yellow
Hummingbird
Large copper

Meadow brown
Painted lady
Parnassians
Pyromorphid
Swallowtail

12 letters:
Cabbage white
Cactoblastis
Dotted border
Kentish glory
Lymantriidae
Marbled white
Red underwing
Sallow-kitten
Speckled wood

White admiral

13 letters:
Blinded sphinx
Chalk-hill blue
Clouded yellow
Giant silkworm
Mother-of-pearl
Mother Shipton
Mourning cloak
Pearl crescent
Processionary
Purple emperor
Tortoiseshell
Woodland brown

14 letters:
Death's-head hawk
Lemon traveller
Mountain beauty
Painted empress
Pandora's sphinx
Two-tailed pasha

15 letters:
Great sooty satyr
Yellow underwing

16 letters:
Camberwell beauty
Clifden nonpareil
Tiger swallowtail

Cc

Cakes and pastries

3 letters:
Bun
Nut
Oil
Pan
Set

4 letters:
Baba
Farl
Kueh
Pone
Puff
Puri
Rock
Roti
Rout
Rusk
Slab
Soul
Tart

5 letters:
Angel
Babka
Cream
Donut
Fairy
Farle
Fudge
Genoa
Lardy
Latke
Layer
Poori

Pound
Rosti
Scone
Sushi
Tansy
Tipsy
Torte
Wafer

6 letters:
Almond
Carrot
Cherry
Coburg
Cotton
Dainty
Dundee
Eccles
Eclair
Gateau
Girdle
Hockey
Johnny
Jumbal
Jumble
Kuchen
Marble
Muffin
Parkin
Simnel
Sponge
Tablet
Waffle
Wonder
Yumyum

7 letters:
Baklava
Banbury
Bannock
Brioche
Brownie
Carcake
Chapati
Chupati
Coconut
Cruller
Crumpet
Cupcake
Fritter
Galette
Jannock
Jumbles
Kruller
Linseed
Madeira
Oatmeal
Pancake
Paratha
Pavlova
Pikelet
Pomfret
Ratafia
Rum baba
Savarin
Stollen
Teacake
Vetkoek
Wedding

8 letters:
Agnus dei
Birthday
Black bun
Chapatti
Chillada
Chupatty
Doughnut
Dumpling
Flapjack
Macaroon
Meringue
Mince pie
Napoleon
Pandowdy
Sandwich
Seedcake
Teabread
Tortilla
Turnover

9 letters:
Angel food
Barmbrack
Buckwheat
Chocolate
Christmas
Chupattie
Clapbread
Cream puff
Croquette
Drop scone
Fruitcake
Kugelhopf
Lamington

Madeleine
Panettone
Petit four
Puftaloon
Queencake
Sally Lunn
Swiss roll

10 letters:
Battenberg
Battenburg
Coffee kiss
Devil's food
Frangipane
Frangipani
Koeksister

Ladyfinger
Pontefract
Puftaloona
Religieuse
Upside-down

11 letters:
Gingerbread
Hot cross bun
Linzer torte
Profiterole
Sachertorte

12 letters:
Bakewell tart
Danish pastry

French pastry
Maid of honour
Millefeuille
Singing hinny
Sponge finger

13 letters:
Genoese sponge

14 letters:
Selkirk bannock
Victoria sponge

17 letters:
Black forest gateau

Calendars

4 letters:
Maya

5 letters:
Bahá'í
Hindu
Lunar
Roman
Solar

6 letters:
Coptic
Fiscal
Hebrew
Jewish
Julian

7 letters:
Chinese

Iranian
Islamic
Persian
Tibetan

8 letters:
Japanese

9 letters:
Arbitrary
Gregorian
Lunisolar
Malayalam

19 letters:
French Revolution

Cameras

CAMERA PARTS

4 letters:
Body
Lens

6 letters:
Tripod

7 letters:
Hot shoe
Shutter

8 letters:
Aperture

Flash gun
Lens hood
Sprocket
Zoom lens

9 letters:
Amplifier
Macro lens
Self-timer
Telephoto
Wide angle

10 letters:
Autowinder
Viewfinder

12 letters:
Synchroflash

13 letters:
Accessory shoe
Extension ring
Iris diaphragm
Telephoto lens
Wide-angle lens

| 14 letters: | Intervalometer | 17 letters: |
| Automatic focus | Shutter release | Automatic exposure |

TYPES OF CAMERA

3 letters:	Webcam	8 letters:	10 letters:
Box		Polaroid	Programmed
	7 letters:		
4 letters:	Brownie	9 letters:	12 letters:
Cine	Compact	Automatic	Subminiature
	Digital	Camcorder	
6 letters:	Pinhole	Miniature	13 letters:
Candid	Process	Steadicam	Point and shoot
Reflex		Swing-back	

Canals

3 letters:	7 letters:	11 letters:
Suo	Corinth	Bridgewater
	Welland	Canal du Midi
4 letters:		Dortmund-Ems
Erie	8 letters:	Houston Ship
Göta	Berezina	
Kiel		12 letters:
Suez	9 letters:	Canal do Norte
	Champlain	
5 letters:		14 letters:
Grand	10 letters:	Manchester Ship
	Caledonian	
6 letters:	Grand Union	17 letters:
Moscow	Mittelland	Canal de São Gonçalo
Panama	Rhine-Herne	New York State Barge
Twente		

Capes

3 letters:	Naze	North	Reinga
Cod	Race	Parry	Sontag
Hoe	Roca	Sable	Ushant
May	Scaw	Sandy	
Ras	Skaw	Verde	7 letters:
	Vert	Wrath	Agulhas
4 letters:			Comorin
Fear	5 letters:	6 letters:	Delgado
Hogh	Byron	Helles	Leeuwin
Horn	Canso	Lizard	Matapan

Runaway	Hatteras	Guardafui	**10 letters:**
Western	Palatine	Lindesnes	Beachy Head
	Palliser	Southwest	Finisterre
8 letters:		St Vincent	
Farewell	**9 letters:**	Trafalgar	**11 letters:**
Flattery	Canaveral		Fairweather
Good Hope	Dungeness		

Capitals

Capital	Country, region, state, etc
Abidjan	Ivory Coast
Abu Dhabi	United Arab Emirates
Abuja	Nigeria
Accra	Ghana
Addis Ababa	Ethiopia
Adelaide	South Australia
Agana	Guam
Akita	Japan
Albany	New York (state capital)
Algiers	Algeria
Amman	Jordan
Amsterdam	Netherlands
Andorra la Vella	Andorra
Angkor	Cambodia
Ankara	Turkey
Annapolis	Maryland
Antananarivo	Madagascar
Antioch	Ancient Syria
Apia	Samoa
Ashkhabad	Turkmenistan
Asmara	Eritrea
Astana	Kazakhstan
Asunción	Paraguay
Athens	Greece
Atlanta	Georgia
Austin	Texas
Baghdad	Iraq
Baku	Azerbaijan
Bamako	Mali
Bandar Seri Begawan	Brunei
Bangalore	Karnataka, India
Bangkok	Thailand
Bangui	Central African Republic

Capital	**Country, region, state, etc**
Banjul	Gambia
Barnaul	Altai Krai, Russia
Barquisemoto	Lara, Venezuela
Barranquilla	Atlántico, Colombia
Basseterre	St Kitts and Nevis
Bastia	Haute-Corse, Corsica
Baton Rouge	Louisiana
Beijing *or* Peking	People's Republic of China
Beira	Sofala, Mozambique
Beirut *or* Beyrouth	Lebanon
Belfast	Northern Ireland
Belgrade	Yugoslavia (Serbia and Montenegro)
Belmopan	Belize
Berlin	Germany
Berne	Switzerland
Besançon	France
Bishkek	Kyrgyzstan
Bissau	Guinea-Bissau
Bloemfontein	Judicial capital of South Africa
Blois	Loir-et-Cher, France
Bogotá	Colombia
Bonn	Federal Republic of Germany (formerly)
Brasília	Brazil
Bratislava	Slovakia
Brazzaville	Congo (Republic of)
Bridgetown	Barbados
Brisbane	Queensland, Australia
Brno	Moravia, Czech Republic
Bruges	West Flanders, Belgium
Brussels	Belgium
Bucharest	Romania
Budapest	Hungary
Buenos Aires	Argentina
Bujumbura	Burundi
Caen	Basse-Normandie, France
Cagliari	Sardinia
Cairo	Egypt
Calcutta	West Bengal, India
Cali	Valley of the Cauca, Colombia
Canberra	Australia
Cape Town	Legislative capital of South Africa
Caracas	Venezuela
Carcassonne	Aude, France
Cardiff	Wales

Capital	Country, region, state, etc
Cartagena	Bolivar, Colombia
Castries	St Lucia
Cayenne	French Guiana
Changsha	Hunan, China
Charleston	West Virginia
Chengdu	Sichuan, China
Chennai	Tamil Nadu, India
Chiba	Chiba, Japan
Chonju	North Jeolla, S. Korea
Cienfuegos	Cuba
Cochabamba	Cercado, Bolivia
Colombo	Sri Lanka
Colón	Colón, Panama
Conakry or Konakry	Guinea
Concepcion	Biobío, Chile
Copenhagen	Denmark
Córdoba	Córdoba, Spain
Cosenza	Cosenza, Italy
Cotonou	Benin
Cremona	Cremona, Italy
Cúcuta	Norte de Santander, Colombia
Cuenca	Ecuador
Cuernavaca	Morelos, Mexico
Cuiabá	Mato Grosso, Brazil
Dakar	Senegal
Damascus	Syria
Darwin	Northern Territory, Australia
Debrecen	Hadjú-Bihar, Hungary
Delhi	India
Denpasar	Bali
Dhaka or Dacca	Bangladesh
Dili	East Timor
Djibouti or Jibouti	Djibouti or Jibouti
Dodoma	Tanzania
Doha	Qatar
Douglas	Isle of Man
Dublin	Republic of Ireland
Dushanbe	Tajikistan
Edinburgh	Scotland
Enugu	Enugu, Nigeria
Faro	The Algarve, Portugal
Fort-de-France	Martinique
Freetown	Sierra Leone

Capital	Country, region, state, etc
Funafuti	Tuvalu
Funchal	Madeira
Gaborone	Botswana
Georgetown	Guyana
Grozny	Chechnya
Guangzhou	Guangdong, China
Guatemala City	Guatemala
Haikou	Hainan, China
Hamilton	Bermuda
Hangzhou	Zhejiang, China
Hanoi	Vietnam
Harare	Zimbabwe
Havana	Cuba
Helsinki	Finland
Heraklion *or* Eraklion	Crete
Hobart	Tasmania
Honiara	Solomon Islands
Honolulu	Hawaii
Ibadan	Oyo State, Nigeria
Iloilo City	Iloilo, Philippines
Ipoh	Perak, Malaysia
Iquique	Tarapacó, Chile
Islamabad	Pakistan
Istanbul *or* Constantinople	Turkey (formerly)
Jaén	Jaén Spain
Jaffna	Jaffna, Sri Lanka
Jakarta *or* Djakarta	Indonesia
Jambi City	Jambi, Indonesia
Jerusalem	Israel
Jos	Plateau State, Nigeria
Juneau	Alaska
Kabul	Afghanistan
Kampala	Uganda
Karachi	Sind, Pakistan
Katmandu *or* Kathmandu	Nepal
Katsina	Katsina, Nigeria
Kayseri	Kayseri, Turkey
Kerman	Kerman, Iran
Khartoum *or* Khartum	Sudan
Kiel	Schleswig-Holstein, Germany
Kiev	Ukraine
Kigali	Rwanda
Kingston	Jamaica

Capital	Country, region, state, etc
Kingstown	St Vincent and the Grenadines
Kinshasa	Congo (Democratic Republic of)
Kirkwall	Orkney Islands
Kisangani	Tshopo, Congo
Kishinev	Moldova
Kisumu	Nyanza, Kenya
Kobe	Honshu, Japan
Koror	Palau
Kota Bharu	Kelantan, Malaysia
Kuala Lumpur	Malaysia
Kuwait	Kuwait
Lagos	Nigeria (formerly)
Lambaréné	Moyen-Ogooué, Gabon
La Paz	Administrative capital of Bolivia
La Spezia	La Spezia, Italy
Lassa *or* Lhasa	Tibet
Leningrad, St Petersburg, *or* Petrograd	Russia (formerly)
Libreville	Gabon
Lilongwe	Malawi
Lima	Peru
Linz	Upper Austria, Austria
Lisbon	Portugal
Little Rock	Arkansas, U.S.A.
Ljubljana	Slovenia
Lomé	Togo
London	United Kingdom
Luanda	Angola
Lusaka	Zambia
Luxembourg	Luxembourg
Madrid	Spain
Majuro	Marshall Islands
Malabo	Equatorial Guinea
Malé	Maldives
Managua	Nicaragua
Manama	Bahrain
Manila	Philippines
Maputo	Mozambique
Maseru	Lesotho
Mathura	Braj Bhoomi, India
Mbabane	Swaziland
Memphis	Egypt, Old Kingdom
Mexico City	Mexico
Minna	Niger State, Nigeria
Minsk	Belarus

Capital	Country, region, state, etc
Mogadishu	Somalia
Monaco-Ville	Monaco
Monrovia	Liberia
Montevideo	Uruguay
Moroni	Comoros
Moscow	Russia
Mumbai	India
Muscat	Oman
Mutare	Manicaland, Zimbabwe
Nairobi	Kenya
Nakuru	Rift Valley Province, Kenya
Namibe	Namibe, Angola
Nanning	Guangxi, China
Nashville	Tennessee
Nassau	Bahamas
Ndjamena	Chad
New Delhi	India
Niamey	Niger
Nicosia	Cyprus
Nineveh	Ancient Assyrian empire
Nouakchott	Mauritania
Nuku'alofa	Tonga
Nuuk	Greenland
Oaxaca	Oaxaca, Mexico
Olympia	Washington state
Orense	Orense, Spain
Orleans	Loiret, France
Oslo	Norway
Ottawa	Canada
Ouagadougou	Burkina-Faso
Palermo	Sicily
Palikir	Micronesia
Panama City	Panama
Pandemonium *or* Pandaemonium	Hell
Paramaribo	Suriname
Paris	France
Persepolis	Ancient Persia
Perugia	Umbria, Italy
Phnom Penh	Cambodia
Pishpek	Kirghizia
Ponta Delgada	Azores, Portugal
Port-au-Prince	Haiti
Port Louis	Mauritius
Port Moresby	Papua New Guinea

Capital	Country, region, state, etc
Port of Spain	Trinidad and Tobago
Porto Novo	Benin
Port Vila	Vanuatu
Prague	Czech Republic
Praia	Cape Verde
Pretoria	Administrative capital of South Africa
Pristina	Kosovo (Federal Republic of Yugoslavia)
Providence	Rhode Island
Pyongyang	North Korea
Quetta	Balochistan, Pakistan
Quito	Ecuador
Rabat	Morocco
Reykjavik	Iceland
Riga	Latvia
Rio	Rio de Janeiro, Brazil
Rio Branco	Acre, Brazil
Riyadh	Saudi Arabia
Rome	Italy
Roseau	Dominica
Safi	Doukkala-Abda, Morocco
Samarkand	Mongol Empire (14th century)
San'a	Yemen
San Cristobal	Táchira, Venezuela
San José	Costa Rica
San Juan	Puerto Rico
San Marino	San Marino
San Salvador	El Salvador
Santiago	Chile
Santo Domingo	Dominican Republic
São Tomé	São Tomé and Principe
Sarajevo	Bosnia and Herzegovina
Ségou	Ségou, Mali
Segovia	Segovia, Spain
Sekondi-Takoradi	Western Region, Ghana
Sendai	Tohoku, Japan
Seoul	South Korea
Seville	Andalusia, Spain
Shijiazhuang	Hebai, China
Sidi-bel Abbes	Sidi-bel Abbes, Algeria
Siena	Siena, Italy
Singapore	Singapore
Skopje	Macedonia
Sofia	Bulgaria
Sokoto	Sokoto, Nigeria

Capital	Country, region, state, etc
St George's	Grenada
St John's	Antigua and Barbuda
Stockholm	Sweden
Stuttgart	Baden-Württemberg, Germany
Sucré	Legislative and judicial capital of Bolivia
Susa	Ancient Persia (Achaemenid dynasty)
Suva	Fiji
Sydney	New South Wales, Australia
Szczecin	West Pomerania, Poland
Tabora	Tabora, Tanzania
Taipei	Taiwan
Tallinn	Estonia
Tarawa	Kiribati
Tashkent	Uzbekistan
Tbilisi	Georgia
Tegucigalpa	Honduras
Tehran *or* Teheran	Iran
Tel Aviv	Israel
Terni	Terni, Italy
Thebes	Ancient Egypt (18th dynasty)
Thimphu *or* Thimbu	Bhutan
Tirana	Albania
Tokyo	Japan
Topeka	Kansas
Trebizond	Trebizond, Turkey
Tripoli	Libya
Tunis	Tunisia
Ujung Pandang	South Sulawesi, Indonesia
Ufa	Bashkiria, Russia
Ulan Bator	Mongolia
Urumqi	Xinjiang Uyghur, China
Vaasa	Ostrobothnia, Finland
Vaduz	Liechtenstein
Valencia	Valencia, Spain
Valladolid	Castilla-Léon, Spain
Valletta	Malta
Valparaiso	Valparaiso, Chile
Van	Van, Turkey
Vatican City	Vatican City
Vicenza	Vicenza, Italy
Victoria	Seychelles
Vienna	Austria
Vientiane	Laos
Vilnius	Lithuania

Capital	Country, region, state, etc
Vitoria	Álava, Spain
Wad Medani	Al Jazirah, Sudan
Warsaw	Poland
Washington DC	United States of America
Wellington	New Zealand
Wiesbaden	Hesse, Germany
Windhoek	Namibia
Winnipeg	Manitoba, Canada
Wuhan	Hubei, China
Xanthus	Ancient Lycia
Xian	Shaanxi, China
Yakutsk	Sakha, Russia
Yamoussoukro	Côte d'Ivoire
Yangon (Rangoon)	Myanmar (Burma)
Yaoundé *or* Yaunde	Cameroon
Yaren	Nauru
Yerevan	Armenia
Zagreb	Croatia
Zaragoza	Aragon, Spain

Caps

3 letters:
Mob
Taj
Tam

4 letters:
Blue
Caul
Coif
Cope
Cowl
Flat
Kepi

5 letters:
Beret
Chaco
Chape
Cloth
Kippa
Mutch
Pagri

Quoif
Shako
Toque
Tuque
Turk's

6 letters:
Abacot
Amorce
Barret
Berret
Biggin
Blakey
Calpac
Chapka
Cornet
Czapka
Dunce's
Forage
Gandhi
Granny
Jockey

Juliet
Kalpak
Kipput
Kiss-me
Morion
Pileus
Pinner
Square
Toorie

7 letters:
Bathing
Bellhop
Bendigo
Biretta
Bycoket
Calotte
Calpack
Chapeau
Chechia
Fatigue
Grannie

Kippoth
Liberty
Monteer
Montero
Morrion
Newsboy

8 letters:
Balmoral
Baseball
Capeline
Chaperon
Garrison
Havelock
Monmouth
Phrygian
Puggaree
Schapska
Skullcap
Stocking
Thinking
Trencher

Yarmulka
Yarmulke
Zuchetto

9 letters:
Balaclava

Glengarry
Trenchard

10 letters:
Cockernony
Kilmarnock

11 letters:
Bonnet-rouge
Deerstalker
Kiss-me-quick
Mortar-board
Tam-o'-shanter

12 letters:
Cheese-cutter
Davy Crockett

Cards

CARD GAMES

3 letters:
Loo
Nap

4 letters:
Faro
Skat
Snap
Solo

5 letters:
Cinch
Monte
Ombre
Poker
Rummy
Stops
Whist

6 letters:
Boston
Bridge
Casino
Chemmy
Écarté
Euchre
Hearts
Piquet
Quinze

Switch

7 letters:
Bezique
Canasta
Cooncan
Old maid
Pinocle
Pontoon
Seven up

8 letters:
Baccarat
Canfield
Conquian
Cribbage
Gin rummy
Napoleon
Patience
Penuchle
Penuckle
Pinochle
Slapjack

9 letters:
Blackjack
Solo whist
Spoilfive
Stud poker

10 letters:
Strip poker

11 letters:
Chemin-de-fer
Five hundred
Rouge et noir

12 letters:
Rubber bridge

13 letters:
Auction bridge
Happy families

14 letters:
Contract bridge

15 letters:
Duplicate bridge

16 letters:
Trente et quarante

17 letters:
Beggar-my-neighbour

BRIDGE TERMS

4 letters:
East
Ruff
Slam

West

5 letters:
Dummy

North
South
Trick
Trump

6 letters:
Double
Rubber

7 letters:	8 letters:	9 letters:	10 letters:
Finesse	Contract	Grand slam	Little slam
No-trump	Redouble	Singleton	Vulnerable
		Small slam	Yarborough

POKER TERMS

3 letters:	5 letters:	Straddle	10 letters:
See	Flush	Straight	Royal flush
Shy	Raise		
		9 letters:	13 letters:
4 letters:	8 letters:	Full house	Straight flush
Ante	Showdown		
Pair	Stand pat		

OTHER CARD TERMS

3 letters:	King	Knave	8 letters:
Ace	Suit	Queen	Diamonds
Cut	Trey		Face card
	Wild	6 letters:	
4 letters:		Hearts	9 letters:
Deal	5 letters:	Misere	Court card
Deck	Clubs	Revoke	
Hand	Deuce	Spades	
Jack	Joker		

Carnivores

3 letters:	Dingo	Bobcat	Red fox
Cat	Genet	Chetah	Serval
Dog	Hyena	Corsac	Teledu
Fox	Otter	Cougar	Weasel
	Ounce	Coyote	
4 letters:	Panda	Ermine	7 letters:
Bear	Potto	Fennec	Caracal
Coon	Rasse	Ferret	Cheetah
Eyra	Ratel	Grison	Genette
Lion	Sable	Hyaena	Glutton
Lynx	Skunk	Jackal	Grey fox
Mink	Stoat	Jaguar	Grizzly
Puma	Tayra	Kit fox	Leopard
Wolf	Tiger	Margay	Linsang
	Zibet	Marten	Meerkat
5 letters:		Nanook	Panther
Civet	6 letters:	Ocelot	Polecat
Dhole	Badger	Racoon	Raccoon

Rooikat
Sun bear
Zorilla
Zorille

8 letters:
Aardwolf
Carcajou
Grey wolf
Kinkajou
Kolinsky
Mongoose
Sea otter
Swift fox
Tiger cat
Warrigal
Zibeline

9 letters:
Arctic fox
Binturong
Black bear
Brown bear
Cacomixle
Catamount
Hog badger
Honey bear
Ichneumon
Native dog
Palm civet
Polar bear
Silver fox
Sloth bear
Wolverine

10 letters:
Cacomistle
Desert lynx
Giant panda
Jaguarondi
Jaguarundi
Kodiak bear
Otter shrew
Pine marten
Prairie dog
Raccoon dog
Strandwolf
Timber wolf

11 letters:
Grizzly bear
Prairie wolf

Snow leopard
Stone marten
Sweet marten

12 letters:
Catamountain
Cat-o'-mountain
Cinnamon bear
Mountain lion
Spotted hyena

13 letters:
Hognosed skunk
Laughing hyena

See also:
➤ **Cats** ➤ **Dogs**

Carpets and rugs

5 letters:
Kilim

6 letters:
Durrie
Kirman
Numdah
Wilton

7 letters:
Ingrain

8 letters:
Aubusson
Chenille

9 letters:
Axminster

Broadloom
Flat-woven

10 letters:
Bukhara rug
Persian rug

12 letters:
Turkey carpet

13 letters:
Kidderminster
Persian carpet

14 letters:
Brussels carpet

Carriages and carts

3 letters:
Cab
Car
Fly
Gig
Rig

4 letters:
Bier
Cart

Chay
Coch
Drag
Ekka
Pung
Rath
Shay
Sled
Trap
Wain

5 letters:
Bandy
Brake
Buggy
Coach
Coupé
Ratha
Sulky
Tonga
Wagon

6 letters:
Berlin
Britka
Calash
Chaise
Charet
Dennet
Do-si-do
Drosky
Fiacre

			10 letters:
Gharry	Caroche	Curricle	Four-in-hand
Go-cart	Chariot	Equipage	Post chaise
Hansom	Chassis	Pochaise	Stagecoach
Herdic	Dogcart	Quadriga	Tim-whiskey
Jampan	Dos-a-dos	Rickshaw	
Landau	Droshky	Rockaway	11 letters:
Limber	Growler	Sociable	Hurly-hacket
Pochay	Norimon	Stanhope	Jaunting car
Random	Phaeton	Tarantas	
Remise	Tilbury	Victoria	12 letters:
Sledge	Vetture		Covered wagon
Spider	Vis-à-vis	9 letters:	
Surrey	Voiture	Britschka	13 letters:
Tandem	Whiskey	Buckboard	Désobligeante
Troika		Cabriolet	Spider phaeton
Whisky	8 letters:	Gladstone	
	Barouche	Horseless	14 letters:
7 letters:	Brougham	Jaunty car	Conestoga wagon
Berline	Cape cart	Landaulet	
Britska	Carriage	Tarantass	15 letters:
Britzka	Carriole	Wagonette	Prairie schooner
Calèche	Carryall	Whirligig	
Cariole	Clarence	Whisky gig	

Cars

TYPES OF CAR

2 letters:	4 letters:	5 letters:	Super
BL	Audi	Astra	Turbo
DR	Biza	Buick	
GT	Drag	Coupé	6 letters:
MG	Fiat	Honda	Aquada
RR	Ford	Lexus	Austin
VW	Golf	Mazda	Beetle
	Jeep®	Micro	Bubble
3 letters:	Kart	Panda	Bumper
4WD	Lada	Prowl	Caparo
BMW	Limo	Racer	Dodgem®
Cab	Merc	Rolls	Estate
Elf	Mini	Scion	Hearse
GTi	Opel	Sedan	Hot-rod
JZR	SEAT	Skoda	Hummer®
Kia	Tank	Smart®	Hybrid
MPV		Squad	Invicta
SUV		Stock	Jaguar

Jetcar
Lancia
Morris
Muscle
Nissan
Patrol
Ragtop
Roller
Saloon
Sports
Suzuki
Tourer
Toyota

7 letters:
Bugatti
Citroen
Compact

Company
Cortina
Daimler
Ferrari
Formula
Hardtop
Hillman
Hyundai
Lagonda
Peugeot
Porsche
Renault
Sunbeam
Veteran
Vintage

8 letters:
Cadillac

Dragster
Drophead
Fastback
Hot hatch
Mercedes
Roadster
Vauxhall

9 letters:
Cabriolet
Connaught
Hatchback
Landaulet
Land Rover
Limousine
Notchback
Supermini
Two-seater

10 letters:
Subcompact
Volkswagen

11 letters:
Aston Martin
Convertible
Mitsubishi
People mover
Stretch-limo

12 letters:
Station wagon
Three-wheeler

13 letters:
People carrier

CAR PARTS

3 letters:
ABS
Fan
Top

4 letters:
Axle
Body
Boot
Bulb
Coil
Cowl
Door
Fuse
Gear
Hood
Horn
Jack
Lock
Plug
Roof
Seat
Sump
Tank
Trim

Tyre
Wing

5 letters:
Brake
Choke
Crank
Light
Pedal
Valve
Wheel

6 letters:
Air bag
Big end
Bonnet
Bumper
Clutch
Engine
Fascia
Fender
Gasket
Grille
Heater
Hubcap

Piston
Points
Sat-Nav
Towbar
Window

7 letters:
Ammeter
Ashtray
Battery
Bearing
Chassis
Exhaust
Fan belt
Fog lamp
Fuse box
Gearbox
Hard top
Mud flap
Oil pump
Soft top
Springs
Starter
Sunroof
Wing nut

8 letters:
Brake pad
Camshaft
Cylinder
Demister
Dipstick
Flywheel
Headrest
Ignition
Manifold
Odometer
Radiator
Seat belt
Silencer
Sprocket
Tailgate
Tailpipe
Wheel nut

9 letters:
Crankcase
Dashboard
Fuel gauge
Gear lever
Gearshift

Generator
Handbrake
Hands-free
Headlight
Indicator
Little end
Milometer
Oil filter
Petrol cap
Radius arm
Rear light
Taillight
Wheel trim

10 letters:
Alternator
Brake light
Bucket seat
Crankshaft
Disc brakes
Door handle
Driveshaft
Mileometer
Petrol tank
Safety belt
Spare wheel

Suspension
Torsion bar
Wheel brace
Windscreen
Wing mirror

11 letters:
Accelerator
Anti-roll bar
Carburettor
Distributor
Hazard light
Luggage rack
Numberplate
Parcel shelf
Petrol gauge
Speedometer

12 letters:
Cylinder head
Parking light
Sunshine roof
Transmission

13 letters:
Connecting rod

Cruise control
Shock absorber
Steering wheel

14 letters:
Automatic
  choke
Childproof lock
Convertible top
Distributor cap
Radiator grille
Rear-view mirror
Reversing light
Steering column
Universal joint

15 letters:
Windscreen wiper

16 letters:
Glove compartment
Oil-pressure gauge

18 letters:
Catalytic converter

INTERNATIONAL CAR REGISTRATION LETTERS

Letter(s)	Country	Letter(s)	Country
A	Austria	BS	Bahamas
ADN	Yemen	BUR	Myanmar
AFG	Afghanistan	BW	Botswana
AL	Albania	BY	Belarus
AM	Armenia	C	Cuba
AND	Andorra	CDN	Canada
AUS	Australia	CH	Switzerland
B	Belgium	CI	Côte d'Ivoire
BD	Bangladesh	CL	Sri Lanka
BDS	Barbados	CO	Colombia
BG	Bulgaria	CR	Costa Rica
BH	Belize	CY	Cyprus
BOL	Bolivia	CZ	Czech Republic
BR	Brazil	D	Germany
BRN	Bahrain	DK	Denmark
BRU	Brunei	DOM	Dominican Republic

Letter(s)	Country	Letter(s)	Country
DY	Benin	KZ	Kazakhstan
DZ	Algeria	L	Luxembourg
E	Spain	LAO	Laos
EAK	Kenya	LAR	Libya
EAT	Tanzania	LB	Liberia
EAU	Uganda	LS	Lesotho
EAZ	Zanzibar	LT	Lithuania
EC	Ecuador	LV	Latvia
ES	El Salvador	M	Malta
EST	Estonia	MA	Morocco
ET	Egypt	MAL	Malaysia
ETH	Ethiopia	MC	Monaco
F	France	MEX	Mexico
FIN	Finland	MGL	Mongolia
FJI	Fiji	MK	Macedonia
FL	Liechtenstein	MNE	Montenegro
FR	Faeroe Islands	MOC	Mozambique
G	Gabon	MS	Mauritius
GB	United Kingdom	MW	Malawi
GBA	Alderney	N	Norway
GBG	Guernsey	NA	Netherlands Antilles
GBJ	Jersey	NAM	Nambia
GBM	Isle of Man	NEP	Nepal
GBZ	Gibraltar	NIC	Nicaragua
GCA	Guatemala	NL	Netherlands
GH	Ghana	NZ	New Zealand
GR	Greece	OMAN	Oman
GUY	Guyana	P	Portugal
H	Hungary	PA	Panama
HK	Hong Kong	PE	Peru
HKJ	Jordan	PK	Pakistan
HR	Croatia	PL	Poland
I	Italy	PNG	Papua New Guinea
IL	Israel	PY	Paraguay
IND	India	Q	Qatar
IR	Iran	RA	Argentina
IRL	Republic of Ireland	RB	Botswana
IRQ	Iraq	RC	Taiwan
IS	Iceland	RCA	Central African Republic
J	Japan	RCB	Congo Republic
JA	Jamaica	RCH	Chile
K	Cambodia	RG	Guinea
KS	Kyrgyzstan	RH	Haiti
KWT	Kuwait	RI	Indonesia

Letter(s)	Country	Letter(s)	Country
RIM	Mauritania	TG	Togo
RL	Lebanon	TJ	Tajikistan
RM	Madagascar	TN	Tunisia
RMM	Mali	TR	Turkey
RN	Niger	TT	Trindad and Tobago
RO	Romania	UA	Ukraine
ROK	South Korea	UAE	United Arab Emirates
ROU	Uruguay	USA	United States of America
RP	Philippines	UZ	Uzbekistan
RSM	San Marino	V	Vatican City
RU	Burundi	VN	Vietnam
RUS	Russian Federation	WAG	Gambia
RWA	Rwanda	WAL	Sierra Leone
S	Sweden	WAN	Nigeria
SA	Saudi Arabia	WD	Dominica
SD	Swaziland	WG	Grenada
SGP	Singapore	WL	St Lucia
SK	Slovakia	WS	Western Samoa
SLO	Slovenia	WV	St Vincent and the Grenadines
SME	Surinam		
SN	Senegal	YAR	Yemen
SO	Somalia	YU	Yugoslavia
SRB	Serbia	YV	Venezuela
SUD	Sudan	Z	Zambia
SWA	Namibia	ZA	South Africa
SY	Seychelles	ZRE	Zaire
SYR	Syria	ZW	Zimbabwe
T	Thailand		

Cartoon characters

3 letters:
Doc
Ren
Tom

4 letters:
Dino
Kyle
Stan

5 letters:
Bambi
Bluto

Dopey
Dumbo
Goofy
Happy
Itchy
Jerry
Kenny
Pluto
Snowy

6 letters:
Bam-Bam
Boo-Boo

Grumpy
Krusty
Popeye
Shaggy
Sleepy
Sneezy
Stimpy
Tigger
Tintin
Top Cat

7 letters:
Bashful

Cartman
Muttley
Pebbles
Swee' Pea

8 letters:
Andy Capp
Olive Oyl
Scratchy
Yogi Bear

9 letters:
Betty Boop
Daffy Duck
Elmer Fudd
Scooby-Doo
Sylvester
Tweety-Pie

10 letters:
Donald Duck
Joe Swanson

Meg Griffin
Roadrunner

11 letters:
Bart Simpson
Betty Rubble
Lisa Simpson
Lois Griffin
Mickey Mouse
Minnie Mouse
Ned Flanders
Sideshow Bob
Wile E Coyote
Yosemite Sam

12 letters:
Barney Rubble
Brian Griffin
Chris Griffin
Homer Simpson
Marge Simpson
Peter Griffin

13 letters:
Dick Dastardly
Glenn Quagmire
Maggie Simpson
Officer Dibble
Stewie Griffin
The Hooded Claw
Winnie the Pooh

14 letters:
Cleveland Brown
Foghorn Leghorn
Fred Flintstone
Speedy Gonzalez

15 letters:
Penelope Pitstop
Wilma Flintstone

19 letters:
Groundskeeper Willie

Cases

3 letters:
Bin
Box
Keg
Pod

4 letters:
Aril
Beer
Bere
Etui
Flan
Grip
Hull
Husk
Port

5 letters:
Ascus
Blimp

Burse
Calyx
Chase
Crate
Crust
Etwee
Frame
Ocrea
Theca
Trunk
Volva

6 letters:
Basket
Cachet
Chitin
Cocoon
Locket
Lorica
Manche

Ochrea
Penner
Quiver
Red box
Sheath
Telium
Valise
Walise
Wallet

7 letters:
Cabinet
Capsule
Compact
Elytron
Hanaper
Hold-all
Humidor
Keister
Nacelle

Sheathe
Six-pack
Sporran
Toolbox
Wardian

8 letters:
Bundwall
Canister
Cartouch
Cellaret
Dispatch
Flapjack
Indusium
Nutshell
Scabbard
Tantalus
Tea-chest
Vasculum

9 letters:
Cartouche
Cartridge
Chrysalis
Croustade

Housewife
Papeterie

10 letters:
Canterbury

Phylactery
Sabretache

12 letters:
Plummer-block

Castles

3 letters:
Man

4 letters:
Cheb
Drum
More
Rait
Trim

5 letters:
Aydon
Blois
Cabra
Cahir
Conwy
Corfe
Dinan
Hever
Leeds
Spain
Torún
Upnor
Vaduz

6 letters:
Brodie
Cawdor
Dublin
Durham
Farney
Forfar
Glamis
Kilkea
Ludlow
Raglan
Rothes

Stuart

7 letters:
Amboise
Arundel
Ashford
Barnard
Beeston
Belvoir
Blarney
Braemar
Canossa
Chillon
Colditz
Crathes
Culzean
Despair
Harlech
Lincoln
Otranto
Schloss
Skipton
St Mawes
Warwick
Windsor

8 letters:
Balmoral
Balvenie
Bamburgh
Bastille
Berkeley
Bunratty
Carbonek
Darnaway
Doubting
Egremont

Elephant
Elsinore
Kilkenny
Killaghy
Leamaneh
Malahide
Malperdy
Monmouth
Pembroke
Portlick
Rackrent
Reculver
Richmond
Stirling
Stokesay
Taymouth
Tintagel
Urquhart
Wartburg

9 letters:
Beaumaris
Dangerous
Dunnottar
Dunsinane
Edinburgh
Esterháza
Inverness
Kilravock
Lancaster
Leicester
Pendennis
Restormel
Sherborne
Trausnitz
Vincennes

10 letters:
Caernarfon
Caerphilly
Carmarthen
Heidelberg
Kenilworth
Launceston
Pontefract

11 letters:
Aberystwyth
Carisbrooke

Eilean Donan
Gormenghast
Scarborough

12 letters:
Berkhamstead
Caerlaverock
Château-Raoul
Dunstaffnage
Fotheringhay
Herstmonceux
Rock of Cashel

13 letters:
Ballindalloch
Carrickfergus

14 letters:
Ashby de la Zouch

16 letters:
Berwick-upon-Tweed

Cathedrals in the UK

3 letters:
Ely

4 letters:
Peel

5 letters:
Derby
Isles
Leeds
Ripon
Truro
Wells

6 letters:
Bangor
Brecon
Dundee
Durham
Exeter
Oxford

7 letters:
Arundel
Bristol
Cardiff
Chester
Clifton
Dornoch

Glasgow
Lincoln
Newport
Norwich
Salford
St Asaph
St John's
St Mary's
St Paul's
Swansea
Wrexham

8 letters:
Aberdeen
Bradford
Carlisle
Coventry
Hereford
Llandaff
Plymouth
St Albans
St Davids

9 letters:
Blackburn
Brentwood
Edinburgh
Guildford
Inverness

Lancaster
Leicester
Lichfield
Liverpool
Newcastle
Rochester
Salisbury
Sheffield
Southwark
St Andrews
Wakefield
Worcester

10 letters:
Birmingham
Canterbury
Chelmsford
Chichester
Gloucester
Manchester
Nottingham
Portsmouth
Shrewsbury
Winchester

11 letters:
Northampton
Westminster
York Minster

12 letters:	13 letters:	16 letters:
Christ Church	Middlesbrough	Southwell Minster
Peterborough	St Edmundsbury	

Cats

BREEDS OF CAT

3 letters:
Rex

4 letters:
Manx

5 letters:
Tabby

6 letters:
Angora
Havana

7 letters:
Burmese
Persian
Ragdoll
Siamese
Turkish

9 letters:
Himalayan
Maine Coon

10 letters:
Abyssinian

11 letters:
Colourpoint
Russian blue

13 letters:
Bengal leopard
Tortoiseshell

17 letters:
American shorthair

FAMOUS CATS

3 letters:
Tom

4 letters:
Bast
Jinx

5 letters:
Bucky
Felix
Fritz
Hodge
Salem

6 letters:
Arthur
Bastet
Ginger

Huckle
Muessa
Selima
Top Cat

7 letters:
Bagpuss
Lucifer
Slipper

8 letters:
Garfield
Lady Jane
Scratchy
Snowball

9 letters:
Mehitabel
Mistigris

Thomasina
Tobermory

10 letters:
Grizabella
Heathcliff

11 letters:
Bombalurina
Cat in the Hat
Cheshire Cat
Mungojerrie
Puss-in-Boots
Snagglepuss

13 letters:
Fat Freddy's Cat

Cattle and other artiodactyls

2 letters:		3 letters:	
Ox	Zo	Cow	Dzo
			Elk

Gnu
Goa
Kob
Pig
Yak
Zho

4 letters:
Axis
Boar
Bull
Deer
Gaur
Goat
Ibex
Kudu
Oont
Oryx
Pudu
Sika
Stag
Tahr
Thar
Zebu

5 letters:
Addax
Argal
Ariel
Bison
Bongo
Bubal
Camel
Eland
Gayal
Goral
Izard
Jacob
Llama
Moose
Nagor
Nyala

Okapi
Oribi
Saiga
Serow
Sheep
Takin

6 letters:
Alpaca
Aoudad
Argali
Bharal
Chital
Dik-dik
Duiker
Duyker
Impala
Koodoo
Nilgai
Reebok
Rhebok
Sambar
Sambur
Vicuña
Wapiti

7 letters:
Alpacca
Blaubok
Blesbok
Brocket
Bubalis
Buffalo
Bushpig
Carabao
Caracul
Caribou
Chamois
Gazelle
Gemsbok
Gerenuk
Giraffe

Grysbok
Guanaco
Jumbuck
Karakul
Kongoni
Kouprey
Markhor
Mouflon
Muntjac
Muntjak
Nilghau
Nylghau
Peccary
Red deer
Roe deer
Sassaby
Wart hog
Water ox

8 letters:
Antelope
Babirusa
Boer goat
Bontebok
Boschbok
Bushbuck
Markhoor
Moufflon
Mule deer
Musk deer
Reedbuck
Reindeer
Steenbok
Wild boar

9 letters:
Blacktail
Dromedary
Hartbeest
Marshbuck
Mouse deer
Pronghorn

Razorback
Springbok
Waterbuck

10 letters:
Camelopard
Chevrotain
Hartebeest
Jacob sheep
Wildebeest

11 letters:
Barking deer
Cape buffalo
Kashmir goat

12 letters:
Hippopotamus
Klipspringer
Mountain goat
Water buffalo

13 letters:
Bactrian camel
Sable antelope

14 letters:
Père David's deer

15 letters:
White-tailed deer

16 letters:
Chinese water deer

17 letters:
Harnessed
  antelope
Rocky Mountain
  goat

See also:
➤ **Cows** ➤ **Pigs** ➤ **Sheep**

Cattle, breeds of

4 letters:
Aver
Gyal
Neat
Nout
Nowt
Soum
Sowm
Stot

5 letters:
Devon
Heard
Kerry
Kraal
Kyloe
Luing
Owsen
Store
Wagyu

6 letters:
Ankole
Catalo

Dexter
Durham
Jersey
Rother
Sussex

7 letters:
Brahman
Cattalo
Kouprey
Lairage
Lincoln
Red Poll

8 letters:
Alderney
Ayrshire
Charbray
Friesian
Galloway
Gelbvieh
Guernsey
Hereford
Highland

Holstein
Limousin
Longhorn
Normandy

9 letters:
Charolais
Friesland
Illawarra
Red Polled
Shorthorn
Simmental
Teeswater

10 letters:
Africander
Brown Swiss
Piemontese
Simmenthal
Welsh black

11 letters:
Chillingham

12 letters:
Norwegian Red

13 letters:
Aberdeen Angus
Texas longhorn

14 letters:
Belted Galloway
Santa Gertrudis

16 letters:
Blonde d'Aquitaine
Holstein Friesian
Meuse-Rhine-
  Ijssel

18 letters:
Illawarra
  shorthorn

Chairs

3 letters:
Pew
Tub

4 letters:
Bath
Camp
Cane
Club
Deck
Easy
Form
Pouf
Wing

5 letters:
Bench
Sedan
Stool
Súgán
Swing

6 letters:
Barrel
Basket
Bosun's
Carver
Corner
Curule
Dining
Estate

Garden
Jampan
Morris
Pouffe
Rocker
Settee
Settle
Swivel
Throne

7 letters:
Beanbag
Berbice
Bergère
Dos-à-dos
Folding

Guérite
Hassock
Jampani
Lounger
Ottoman
Rocking
Windsor

8 letters:
Armchair
Bar stool
Bentwood
Birthing
Campaign
Captain's
Cathedra

Electric
Fauteuil
Jampanee
Recliner
Straight
Wainscot

9 letters:
Banquette

Butterfly
Director's
Highchair
Opsitbank
Reclining

10 letters:
Bucket seat
Fiddle-back

Ladder-back
Music stool
Piano stool
Wheelchair
Window seat

11 letters:
Gestatorial

12 letters:
Milking stool

13 letters:
Shooting stick
Windsor rocker

14 letters:
Platform rocker

Champagne bottles

Bottle	Capacity	Bottle	Capacity
Magnum	2 bottles	Salmanazar	6 magnums
Jeroboam	2 magnums	Balthazar	8 magnums
Rehoboam	3 magnums	Nebuchadnezzar	10 magnums
Methuselah	4 magnums		

Channels

3 letters:
Fox

5 letters:
Bashi
Malta
North

6 letters:
Beagle

Queen's

7 letters:
Bristol
English
Jamaica
Kennedy
Robeson
Yucatán

8 letters:
Anguilla
Spithead

9 letters:
Old Bahama
St George's

10 letters:
Mozambique

11 letters:
Solway Firth

12 letters:
Saint George's

14 letters:
Molucca Passage

Cheeses

3 letters:
Ewe
Fet
Oka
Pot

4 letters:
Blue
Brie
Curd
Edam
Feta

Goat
Hard
Skyr
Tofu
Yarg

5 letters:
Caboc
Cream
Derby
Esrom
Fynbo

Goats'
Gouda
Islay
Kenno
Quark
Samsø

6 letters:
Cantal
Chèvre
Damson
Dunlop

Ermite
Junket
Orkney
Romano
Tilsit

7 letters:
Boursin
Chaumes
Cheddar
Chessel
Cottage

Crowdie
Fontina
Gjetost
Gruyère
Havarti
Kebbock
Kebbuck
Limburg
Munster
Mycella
Ricotta
Sapsago
Stilton®

8 letters:
American
Bel Paese
Blue vein
Cheshire
Emmental
Halloumi
Huntsman
Muenster
Parmesan

Pecorino
Raclette
Taleggio
Tornegus
Vacherin
Vignotte

9 letters:
Amsterdam
Appenzell
Blue Vinny
Camembert
Emmenthal
Ilchester
Jarlsberg®
Killarney
Leicester
Limburger
Lymeswold®
Mousetrap
Port-Salut
Provolone
Reblochon
Roquefort

Sage Derby
Saint Agur

10 letters:
Blue Vinney
Bonchester
Caerphilly
Cambazolla
Canestrato
Danish blue
Dolcelatte
Emmentaler
Gloucester
Gorgonzola
Lanark Blue
Lancashire
Mascarpone
Mozzarella
Neufchâtel
Red Windsor
Stracchino

11 letters:
Blue Stilton

Coulommiers
Dunsyre Blue
Emmenthaler
Ribblesdale
Wensleydale

12 letters:
Bavarian blue
Bleu de Bresse
Caciocavallo
Fromage frais
Monterey jack
Red Leicester

13 letters:
Bleu d'Auvergne

14 letters:
Blue Shropshire

16 letters:
Double Gloucester

Chefs

3 letters:
Hom, *Kenneth*

4 letters:
Diat, *Louis*
Gray, *Rose*
Kerr, *Graham*
Puck, *Wolfgang*
Roux, *Albert*
Roux, *Michel*
Spry, *Constance*

5 letters:
Beard, *James*
Blanc, *Raymond*
David, *Elizabeth*
Floyd, *Keith*
Leith, *Prue*

Nairn, *Nick*
Sardi, *Vincent*
Smith, *Delia*
Soyer, *Alexis*
Stein, *Rick*
White, *Marco Pierre*

6 letters:
Mrs Beeton
Bocuse, *Paul*
Elliot, *Rose*
Farmer, *Fannie*
Lawson, *Nigella*
Oliver, *Jamie*
Patten, *Marguerite*
Ramsay, *Gordon*
Rhodes, *Gary*
Slater, *Nigel*

7 letters:
Cradock, *Fanny*
Grigson, *Jane*
Jaffrey, *Madhur*

8 letters:
Grossman, *Loyd*
Harriott, *Ainsley*
Mosimann, *Anton*
Paterson, *Jennifer*

9 letters:
Carluccio, *Antonio*
Claiborne, *Craig*
Delmonico, *Lorenzo*
Escoffier, *Auguste*
McCartney, *Linda*
Prudhomme, *Paul*

10 letters:
Blumenthal, *Heston*

13 letters:
Dickson-Wright, *Clarissa*

15 letters:
Worrall-Thompson, *Anthony*

21 letters:
Fearnley-Whittingstall, *Hugh*

Chemical elements

Chemical element	Symbol	Atomic number
Hydrogen	H	1
Helium	He	2
Lithium	Li	3
Beryllium	Be	4
Boron	B	5
Carbon	C	6
Nitrogen	N	7
Oxygen	O	8
Fluorine	F	9
Neon	Ne	10
Sodium	Na	11
Magnesium	Mg	12
Aluminium *or* aluminum	Al	13
Silicon	Si	14
Phosphorus	P	15
Sulphur *or* sulfur	S	16
Chlorine	Cl	17
Argon	Ar	18
Potassium	K	19
Calcium	Ca	20
Scandium	Sc	21
Titanium	Ti	22
Vanadium	V	23
Chromium	Cr	24
Manganese	Mn	25
Iron	Fe	26
Cobalt	Co	27
Nickel	Ni	28
Copper	Cu	29
Zinc	Zn	30
Gallium	Ga	31
Germanium	Ge	32
Arsenic	As	33
Selenium	Se	34
Bromine	Br	35
Krypton	Kr	36

Chemical element	Symbol	Atomic number
Rubidium	Rb	37
Strontium	Sr	38
Yttrium	Y	39
Zirconium	Zr	40
Niobium	Nb	41
Molybdenum	Mo	42
Technetium	Tc	43
Ruthenium	Ru	44
Rhodium	Rh	45
Palladium	Pd	46
Silver	Ag	47
Cadmium	Cd	48
Indium	In	49
Tin	Sn	50
Antimony	Sb	51
Tellurium	Te	52
Iodine	I	53
Xenon	Xe	54
Caesium *or* cesium	Cs	55
Barium	Ba	56
Lanthanum	La	57
Cerium	Ce	58
Praseodymium	Pr	59
Neodymium	Nd	60
Promethium	Pm	61
Samarium	Sm	62
Europium	Eu	63
Gadolinium	Gd	64
Terbium	Tb	65
Dysprosium	Dy	66
Holmium	Ho	67
Erbium	Er	68
Thulium	Tm	69
Ytterbium	Yb	70
Lutetium *or* lutecium	Lu	71
Hafnium	Hf	72
Tantalum	Ta	73
Tungsten *or* wolfram	W	74
Rhenium	Re	75
Osmium	Os	76
Iridium	Ir	77
Platinum	Pt	78
Gold	Au	79
Mercury	Hg	80

Chemical element	Symbol	Atomic number
Thallium	Tl	81
Lead	Pb	82
Bismuth	Bi	83
Polonium	Po	84
Astatine	At	85
Radon	Rn	86
Francium	Fr	87
Radium	Ra	88
Actinium	Ac	89
Thorium	Th	90
Protactinium	Pa	91
Uranium	U	92
Neptunium	Np	93
Plutonium	Pu	94
Americium	Am	95
Curium	Cm	96
Berkelium	Bk	97
Californium	Cf	98
Einsteinium	Es	99
Fermium	Fm	100
Mendelevium	Md	101
Nobelium	No	102
Lawrencium	Lr	103
Rutherfordium	Rf	104
Dubnium	Db	105
Seaborgium	Sg	106
Bohrium	Bh	107
Hassium	Hs	108
Meitnerium	Mt	109
Darmstadtium	Ds	110
Roentgenium	Rg	111

Chemistry

BRANCHES OF CHEMISTRY

7 letters:
Nuclear
Organic
Zymurgy

8 letters:
Chemurgy
Kinetics
Physical

9 letters:
Inorganic

10 letters:
Analytical

12 letters:
Biochemistry
Geochemistry

Zoochemistry

13 letters:
Cytochemistry
Stoichiometry

14 letters:
Astrochemistry
Histochemistry

Neurochemistry
Petrochemistry
Phonochemistry
Photochemistry
Phytochemistry
Radiochemistry

15 letters:
Immunochemistry

Stereochemistry
Thermochemistry

16 letters:
Electrochemistry

Magnetochemistry

CHEMISTRY TERMS

2 letters:
PH

3 letters:
Fat
Gas
Ion
Oil
Ore

4 letters:
Acid
Atom
Base
Bond
Foam
Fuel
Mole
Salt
Soap

5 letters:
Alloy
Anion
Anode
Chain
Ester
Ether
Inert
Metal
Solid
Sugar

6 letters:
Alkali
Alkane
Cation
Dilute
Fusion
Isomer
Liquid

Proton

7 letters:
Alcohol
Cathode
Crystal
Element
Fission
Formula
Halogen
Isotope
Mineral
Mixture
Monomer
Neutral
Neutron
Nucleus
Organic
Plastic
Polymer
Reagent
Soluble
Solvent
Valency

8 letters:
Analysis
Catalyst
Compound
Electron
Emulsion
Equation
Inert gas
Molarity
Molecule
Noble gas
Nonmetal
Reaction
Solution

9 letters:
Allotrope
Amino acid
Corrosion
Diffusion
Electrode
Fatty acid
Inorganic
Insoluble
Ionic bond
Metalloid
Oxidation
Reduction
Saturated
Synthesis

10 letters:
Atomic mass
Combustion
Hydrolysis
Ionization
Lanthanide
Litmus test
Suspension

11 letters:
Alkali metal
Evaporation
Hydrocarbon
Precipitate
Sublimation
Unsaturated

12 letters:
Atomic number
Boiling point
Carbohydrate
Concentrated
Condensation
Covalent bond
Distillation

Electrolysis
Fermentation
Melting point

13 letters:
Chain reaction
Periodic table
Radioactivity
Redox reaction

14 letters:
Brownian motion
Chromatography
Electrovalency
Saponification

15 letters:
Crystallization
Transition metal

16 letters:
Rare-earth
  element

17 letters:
Van der Waals
  forces

18 letters:
Alkaline earth
  metal

20 letters:
Substitution
  reaction

CHEMISTS

4 letters:
Auer, *Karl*
Caro, *Heinrich*
Curl, *Robert*
Davy, *Humphrey*
Hahn, *Otto*
Hall, *Charles Martin*
Hill, *Archibald Vivian*
Kipp, *Petrus Jacobus*
Mond, *Ludwig*
Swan, *Joseph Wilson*
Todd, *Alexander Robert*
Urey, *Harold Clayton*

5 letters:
Abney, *William*
Adams, *Roger*
Aston, *Francis William*
Baumé, *Antoine*
Black, *James (Whyte)*
Black, *Joseph*
Bosch, *Carl*
Boyle, *Robert*
Brown, *Herbert Charles*
Curie, *Marie*
Curie, *Pierre*
Dakin, *Henry*
Debye, *Peter Joseph Wilhelm*
Dewar, *James*
Dumas, *Jean-Baptiste André*
Eigen, *Manfred*
Ernst, *Richard Robert*
Haber, *Fritz*
Henry, *William*
Hooke, *Robert*
Kroto, *Harold*
Libby, *Willard Frank*
Nobel, *Alfred Bernhard*
Prout, *William*
Soddy, *Frederick*

6 letters:
Baeyer, *Johann*

Barton, *Derek*
Brandt, *Georg*
Bunsen, *Robert Wilhelm*
Calvin, *Melvin*
Carver, *George Washington*
Dalton, *John*
Draper, *John William*
Liebig, *Justus*
Morley, *Edward Williams*
Müller, *Paul Hermann*
Mullis, *Kary Banks*
Nernst, *Walther Hermann*
Perutz, *Max Ferdinand*
Porter, *George*
Proust, *Joseph Louis*
Ramsay, *William*
Schiff, *Hugo*
Solvay, *Ernest*
Tizard, *Henry*
Werner, *Alfred*
Wöhler, *Friedrich*
Woulfe, *Peter*

7 letters:
Abelson, *Philip*
Andrews, *Thomas*
Bergius, *Friedrich (Karl Rudolph)*
Buchner, *Eduard*
Castner, *Hamilton Young*
Crookes, *William*
Faraday, *Michael*
Fischer, *Emil Hermann*
Fischer, *Ernst Otto*
Fischer, *Hans*
Gadolin, *Johan*
Gomberg, *Moses*
Guthrie, *Samuel*
Helmont, *Jan*
Hodgkin, *Dorothy Crowfoot*
Leblanc, *Nicolas*
Macadam, *John*
Ostwald, *Wilhelm*
Pasteur, *Louis*

Pauling, *Linus Carl*
Piccard, *Jean Félix*
Scheele, *Karl Wilhelm*
Seaborg, *Glenn Theodore*
Von Babo, *Lambert*
Warburg, *Otto Heinrich*
Ziegler, *Carl*

8 letters:
Beckmann, *Ernst Otto*
Grignard, *Victor*
Langmuir, *Irving*
Lipscomb, *William*
Mulliken, *Robert Sanderson*
Newlands, *John Alexander*
Sabatier, *Paul*
Silliman, *Benjamin*
Smithson, *James*
Sorensen, *Soren Peter Lauritz*
Van't Hoff, *Jacobus Hendricus*
Weizmann, *Chaim*
Woodward, *R(obert) B(urns)*

9 letters:
Arrhenius, *Svante August*
Baekeland, *Leo*
Berzelius, *Jons*
Butenandt, *Adolf Frederick Johann*
Cavendish, *Henry*

Cornforth, *John Warcup*
Gay-Lussac, *Joseph Louis*
Lavoisier, *Antoine Laurent*
Pelletier, *Pierre Joseph*
Priestley, *Joseph*
Prigogine, *Ilya*
Strassman, *Fritz*
Von Baeyer, *Johann Friedrich Wilhelm Adolf*
Von Hevesy, *George*
Zsigmondy, *Richard Adolf*

10 letters:
Chardonnet, *(Louis Marie) Hilaire Bernigaud*
Erlenmeyer, *Emil*
Mendeleyev, *Dmitri Ivanovich*
Van Helmont, *Jean Baptiste*

11 letters:
Hinshelwood, *Cyril*

13 letters:
Von Stradonitz, *(Friedrich) August Kekulé*

25 letters:
Von Nagyrapolt
Szent-Gyorgyi, *Albert*

See also:
➤ **Acids** ➤ **Alcohols** ➤ **Alkalis** ➤ **Alloys**
➤ **Chemical elements** ➤ **Compounds** ➤ **Crystals**
➤ **Hydrocarbons** ➤ **Minerals** ➤ **Molecules** ➤ **Ores**
➤ **Salts** ➤ **Silicas and silicates** ➤ **Subatomic particles** ➤ **Sugars**

Chess

CHESS PIECES

Piece	Abbreviation	Piece	Abbreviation
Bishop	B	King's rook	KR
King	K	Knight	N
King's bishop	KB	Pawn	P
King's knight	KN	Queen	Q

Piece	Abbreviation
Queen's bishop	QB
Queen's knight	QN
Queen's rook	QR

CHESS PLAYERS

UNDISPUTED WORLD CHAMPIONS

Chess player	Term title held	Country
Wilhelm Steinitz	1886-94	Austria
Emanuel Lasker	1894-1921	Germany
José Raúl Capablanca	1921-27	Cuba
Alexander Alekhine	1927-35, 1937-46	Soviet Union
Max Euwe	1935-37	Netherlands
Mikhail Botvinnik	1948-57, 1958-60, 1961-63	Soviet Union
Vasily Smyslov	1957-58	Soviet Union
Mikhail Tal	1960-61	Latvia
Tigran Petrosian	1963-69	Soviet Union
Boris Spassky	1969-72	Soviet Union
Bobby Fischer	1972-75	United States
Anatoly Karpov	1975-85	Soviet Union
Garry Kasparov	1985-1993	Soviet Union/Russia
Vladimir Kramnik	2006-2007	Russia
Viswanathan Anand	2007-	India

FIDE WORLD CHAMPIONS

Chess player	Term title held	Country
Anatoly Karpov	1993-99	Russia
Alexander Khalifman	1999-2000	Russia
Viswanathan Anand	2000-2002	India
Ruslan Ponomariov	2002-2004	Ukraine
Rustam Kasimdzhanov	2004-2005	Uzbekistan
Veselin Topalov	2005-2006	Bulgaria

CLASSICAL WORLD CHAMPIONS

Chess player	Term title held	Country
Garry Kasparov	1993-2000	Russia
Vladimir Kramnik	2000-2006	Russia

Chinaware

4 letters:	Ware	Derby	Spode®
Goss		Hizen	Wally
Ming	**5 letters:**	Imari	
Waly	Delft	Seric	

6 letters:
Kaolin
Minton

Dresden
Limoges
Meissen

Etrurian
Wedgwood®

10 letters:
Rockingham
Rusticware
Willowware

7 letters:
Crackle
Doulton

8 letters:
Coalport
Eggshell

9 letters:
Cameoware
Porcelain

Christian denominations and sects

5 letters:
Amish

7 letters:
Mormons

9 letters:
Adventism
Calvinism
Methodism
Quakerism
Shakerism

10 letters:
Anabaptism

11 letters:
Anglicanism
Catholicism
Lutheranism

12 letters:
Coptic Church
Unitarianism

13 letters:
Baptist Church
Protestantism
Salvation Army

14 letters:
Evangelicalism
Maronite Church
Moravian Church
Orthodox Church
Pentecostalism

15 letters:
Byzantine Church
Episcopal Church
Latter-day Saints
Presbyterianism

16 letters:
Christian Science
Plymouth Brethren
Roman Catholicism
Society of Friends

17 letters:
Congregationalism
Jehovah's Witnesses
Unification Church

18 letters:
Christadelphianism
New Jerusalem Church

19 letters:
Dutch Reformed Church
Greek Orthodox Church
Seventh-Day Adventism

20 letters:
United Reformed Church

21 letters:
Eastern Orthodox Church
Russian Orthodox Church

Cinema and television

2 letters:
TV

3 letters:
Act
BBC
Cue
DVD

Fan
ITV
LCD
Set

4 letters:
Cast
Crew

Film
Hero
Mike
Part
Play
Plot
Role
Shot

Show
Star
Unit

5 letters:
Actor
Cable
Drama

Enact
Extra
Flick
Movie
Odeon
Oscar
Radio
Scene
Telly
Video

6 letters:
Blu-ray
Camera
Ceefax
Cinema
Comedy
Critic
Make up
Movies
Rushes
Screen
Script
Serial
Series
Sit com
Studio
Talkie
TV show

7 letters:
Actress
Cartoon
Compere
Feature
Film set
Flicker
Heroine
Musical
Network
Perform
Phone-in
Pop star
Portray
Present

Produce
Sponsor
Tragedy
Trailer
YouTube

8 letters:
Audience
Bioscope
Chat show
Cinerama
Comedian
Director
Festival
Film club
Film crew
Film star
Fruit pie
Newsreel
Pictures
Premiere
Producer
Quiz show
Tape deck
Telecast
Telefilm

9 letters:
Blue movie
Broadcast
Cameraman
Character
Direction
Entertain
Exhibitor
Film actor
Film extra
Film-strip
Flash-back
Goggle-box
Guest star
Interview
Movie-goer
Movie show
Movie star

Performer
Photoplay
Programme
Projector
Recording
Rehearsal
Soap opera
Spectacle
Title role
Voice-over

10 letters:
Commercial
Crowd scene
Home-movies
Horror film
Horse opera
Microphone
Movie actor
Needle time
Newscaster
Newsreader
On location
Performing
Production
Screenplay
Silent film
Television
The critics

11 letters:
Broadcaster
Credit title
Documentary
Echo chamber
Entertainer
Feature film
Performance
Picture show
Radio caster
Sound effect
Talking film
Technicolor

12 letters:
Academy Award
Cinéma vérité
Clapperboard
Film festival
Picture house
Scriptwriter
Show business
Silver screen
Stereoscopic

13 letters:
Chinese puzzle
Cinematograph
Cine projector
Clapperboards
Continuity man
Entertainment
Global village

Motion picture
Nouvelle Vague
Picture palace
Tape recording
Telerecording
Television set
Videocassette
Video recorder

14 letters:
Cinematography
Closed circuits
Continuity girl
Feature picture
Features editor
High definition
Moving pictures
Question master
Supporting cast

Supporting film
Supporting part
Supporting role
Television play
Third Programme

15 letters:
Animated cartoon
Cable television
Cinematographer
Cinematographic
Documentary film
French subtitles
Peak viewing time
Situation comedy
Slapstick comedy
Spot advertising

Cities

4 letters:
Baku
Bari
Bonn
Brno
Cork
Gifu
Giza
Graz
Homs
Hull
Ipoh
Kano
Kiel
Kiev
Kobe
Lima
Lodz
Nice
Omsk
Oran
Oslo
Riga
Rome

5 letters:
Accra
Adana
Amman
Basle
Basra
Belem
Berne
Bursa
Cairo
Chiba
Dacca
Davao
Delhi
Essen
Genoa
Gorky
Haifa
Halle
Hanoi
Izmir

Kabul
Kazan
Kyoto
Lagos
La Paz
Leeds
Lyons
Malmo
Mecca
Miami
Milan
Mosul
Omaha
Osaka
Padua
Paris
Patna
Perth
Poona
Quito
Rabat
Sakai
Seoul

Sofia
Surat
Tampa
Tokyo
Tomsk
Tunis
Turin

6 letters:
Aachen
Abadan
Aleppo
Ankara
Asmara
Athens
Austin
Baroda
Beirut
Berlin
Bilbao
Bochum
Bogota
Bombay

Boston
Bremen
Cracow
Dallas
Dayton
Denver
Dublin
Dundee
Durban
El Paso
Frunze
Fukoka
Fushun
Gdansk
Geneva
Harbin
Havana
Ibadan
Indore
Jaipur
Kanpur
Kansas
Khulna
Kumasi
Lahore
Lisbon
London
Luanda
Lübeck
Lusaka
Madras
Madrid
Magpur
Málaga
Malang
Manila
Mexico
Moscow
Multan
Munich
Mysore
Nantes
Naples
Newark
Odessa

Oporto
Ottawa
Oxford
Panama
Peking
Penang
Poznan
Prague
Puebla
Quebec
Santos
Shiraz
St Paul
Sydney
Tabriz
Taipei
Talinn
Toledo
Venice
Verona
Vienna
Warsaw
Zagreb
Zürich

7 letters:
Abidjan
Algiers
Antwerp
Atlanta
Baghdad
Bangkok
Barnaul
Belfast
Bologna
Brescia
Bristol
Buffalo
Caracas
Cardiff
Chengtu
Chicago
Cologne
Colombo
Córdoba

Corunna
Detroit
Donetsk
Dresden
Firenze
Foochow
Glasgow
Gwalior
Hamburg
Hanover
Houston
Irkutsk
Isfahan
Jakarta
Kalinin
Karachi
Kharkov
Kowloon
Kwangju
La Plata
Leipzig
Lucknow
Managua
Memphis
Messina
Mombasa
Nairobi
Nanking
New York
Oakland
Palermo
Phoenix
Rangoon
Rosario
San Jose
San Juan
Santa Fe
Sapporo
Saratov
Seattle
Seville
Soochow
Stettin
St Louis
Taranto

Tbilisi
Teheran
Tel Aviv
Toronto
Trieste
Tripoli
Utrecht

8 letters:
Aberdeen
Adelaide
Amritsar
Auckland
Augsburg
Belgrade
Bordeaux
Bradford
Brasilia
Brisbane
Brussels
Budapest
Bulawayo
Cagliari
Calcutta
Campinas
Canberra
Capetown
Columbus
Coventry
Curitiba
Damascus
Dortmund
Duisborg
Edmonton
Florence
Gorlovka
Hague, The
Haiphong
Hamilton
Hangchow
Helsinki
Honolulu
Istanbul
Katmandu
Katowice

Khartoum
Kingston
Kinshasa
Kumamoto
Kweiyang
Mandalay
Mannheim
Montreal
Murmansk
Nagasaki
Oklahoma
Peshawar
Plymouth
Portland
Port Said
Pretoria
Richmond
Salonika
Salt Lake
San Diego
Santiago
Sao Paulo
Sarajevo
Shanghai
Sholapur
Srinagar
Tashkent
Tientsin
Toulouse
Winnipeg
Yokohama

9 letters:
Ahmedabad
Allahabad
Amagasaki
Amsterdam
Archangel
Asahikawa
Astrakhan
Baltimore
Bangalore
Barcelona
Brunswick
Bucharest

Cambridge
Cartagena
Chengchow
Chihuahua
Cleveland
Des Moines
Edinburgh
Fort Worth
Frankfurt
Guatemala
Guayaquil
Hamamatsu
Hiroshima
Hyderabad
Jerusalem
Karlsruhe
Krasnodar
Krivoi Rog
Kuibyshev
Kwangchow
Las Palmas
Leicester
Leningrad
Liverpool
Magdeburg
Maracaibo
Marrakesh
Melbourne
Milwaukee
Nuremberg
Pyongyang
Reykjavik
Rotterdam
Salisbury
Samarkand
Saragossa
Sheffield
Singapore
Stockholm
Stuttgart
Vancouver
Volgograd
Wuppertal

10 letters:
Addis Ababa
Alexandria
Baton Rouge
Birmingham
Bratislava
Canterbury
Casablanca
Chittagong
Cincinnati
Coimbatore
Copenhagen
Düsseldorf
Gothenburg
Jamshedpur
Los Angeles
Louisville
Manchester
Marseilles
Montevideo
New Orleans
Nottingham
Pittsburgh
Portsmouth
Rawalpindi
Sacramento
San Antonio
Strasbourg
Sunderland
Sverdlovsk
Tananarive
Valparaiso
Washington
Wellington

11 letters:
Baranquilla
Buenos Aires
Chelyabinsk
Dar-es-Salaam
Guadalajara
Kuala Lumpur
Mar del Plata
Novosibirsk
Pondicherry

Rostov-on-Don
San Salvador
Southampton
Vladivostok

12 letters:
Barquisimeto
Bloemfontein
Braunschweig
Indianapolis

Jacksonville
Johannesburg
Magnitogorsk
Philadelphia
Port-au-Prince
Rio de Janeiro
San Francisco
Santo Domingo
Stoke-on-Trent

13 letters:
Gelsenkirchen
Karl-Marx-Stadt
Port Elizabeth
Shihkiachwang
Wolverhampton

14 letters:
Dnepropetrovsk

Clothing

ARTICLES OF CLOTHING

3 letters:
Aba
Alb
Tie

4 letters:
Abba
Body
Bubu
Coat
Gown
Haik
Hose
Izar
Kilt
Muff
Rami
Robe
Sari
Sash
Shoe
Slop
Sock
Toga
Vest
Wrap

5 letters:
Abaya
Ao dai
Apron

Burka
Burqa
Cardy
Chaps
Cimar
Cotta
Dress
Ephod
Fanon
Frock
Gilet
Glove
Ihram
Jupon
Kanga
Kanzu
Levis
Pareu
Pilch
Plaid
Ramée
Ramie
Ruana
Saree
Shawl
Shift
Shirt
Smock
Stola
Stole
Tanga

Thong
Tunic

6 letters:
Barrow
Basque
Bikini
Blouse
Bodice
Bolero
Boubou
Braces
Caftan
Cardie
Chador
Chimer
Cilice
Coatee
Cossie
Cravat
Dirndl
Dolman
Exomis
Garter
Gyvies
Halter
Jacket
Jerkin
Jersey
Jibbah
Jubbah

Jumper
Kaftan
Kameez
Kaross
Khanga
Kimono
Kittel
Mantle
Mitten
Peplos
Rochet
Sarong
Serape
Shorts
Skivvy
Tabard
Tallit
Tights
Trunks
T-shirt
Zephyr

7 letters:
Baldric
Blouson
Bourkha
Burnous
Bustier
Busuuti
Catsuit
Chapeau

Chuddah
Chuddar
Chudder
Costume
Dashiki
Djibbah
Doublet
Exomion
Hauberk
Leotard
Maillot
Manteau
Necktie
Nightie
Overall
Pajamas
Paletot
Pallium
Partlet
Pelisse
Pyjamas
Rompers
Shalwar
Singlet
Soutane
Sporran
Sunsuit
Surcoat

Sweater
Tank top
Tube top
Tunicle
Unitard
Wrapper
Yashmac
Yashmak

8 letters:
Bathrobe
Bodysuit
Cardigan
Chasuble
Chausses
Codpiece
Culottes
Dalmatic
Foot muff
Galluses
Gambeson
Himation
Jump suit
Negligée
Overcoat
Pashmina
Peignoir
Pelerine

Pullover
Scapular
Sundress
Surplice
Swimsuit
Tee shirt

9 letters:
Cover-slut
Dungarees
Housecoat
Loincloth
Mandilion
Mandylion
Nightgown
Overskirt
Pantihose
Pantyhose
Sanbenito
Shell suit
Waistcoat

10 letters:
Chaparajos
Chaparejos
Cote-hardie
Cummerbund
Jeistiecor

Kummerbund
Nightdress
Nightshirt
Oversleeve
Salopettes
Suspenders

11 letters:
Bathing suit
Bib and brace
Breechcloth
Dreadnought

12 letters:
Body stocking
Dressing gown
Undergarment

14 letters:
Bathing costume
Swimming trunks

15 letters:
Swimming
 costume

PARTS OF CLOTHING

3 letters:
Arm
Hem
Leg

4 letters:
Cuff
Hood
Seam
Tail

Yoke

5 letters:
Dicky
Jabot
Lapel
Train
Waist

6 letters:
Armlet
Bodice
Collar
Gusset
Lining
Pocket
Sleeve

7 letters:
Armhole
Flounce
Hemline

8 letters:
Neckline
Shoulder

9 letters:
Epaulette
Waistline

10 letters:
Buttonhole

11 letters:
Patch pocket
Shawl collar

TYPES OF CLOTHING

4 letters:
Hose

5 letters:
Mufti
Slops

6 letters:
Armour
Civies

Livery
Samfoo

7 letters:
Civvies
Hosiery
Uniform
Weepers

8 letters:
Black tie
Fatigues
Froufrou
Knitwear
Lingerie
Neckwear

Skivvies
Swimwear
White tie

9 letters:
Beachwear
Clericals
Coveralls
Long-coats
Millinery
Nightwear
Sackcloth
Separates

Underwear

10 letters:
Canonicals
Fancy dress
Sportswear

11 letters:
Baby clothes
Coordinates
Long clothes
Underthings
Widow's weeds

12 letters:
Evening dress
Morning dress
Nightclothes
Overgarments

13 letters:
Academic dress
Highland dress
Undergarments

16 letters:
Swaddling clothes

See also:
➤ **Caps**   ➤ **Coats and cloaks**   ➤ **Dresses**   ➤ **Hats**   ➤ **Hoods**
➤ **Jackets**   ➤ **Scarves**   ➤ **Shirts**   ➤ **Shoes and boots**
➤ **Skirts**   ➤ **Socks and tights**   ➤ **Suits**   ➤ **Sweaters**
➤ **Ties and cravats**   ➤ **Trousers and shorts**   ➤ **Underwear**

Clouds

3 letters:
Fog

4 letters:
Haze
Mist

5 letters:
Storm

6 letters:
Cirrus
Nimbus

7 letters:
Cumulus
Strat(o)us

8 letters:
Water-dog
Woolpack

9 letters:
Goat's hair
Mare's tail

11 letters:
Altocumulus
Altostratus
False cirrus
Thunderhead

12 letters:
Cirrocumulus
Cirrostratus
Cumulonimbus
Nimbostratus

13 letters:
Fractocumulus
Fractostratus
Stratocumulus

Clubs

3 letters:
RAC

4 letters:
Bath
Golf

5 letters:
Disco
Slate
Youth

6 letters:
Brook's
Cotton

Drones
Guards
Jockey
Kitcat
Monday
Reform
Rotary
Savage

Savile
White's

7 letters:
Adelphi
Almack's
Boodles
Carlton

Cavalry
Country
Garrick
Hampden
Jacobin
Kiwanis
Leander
Variety

8 letters:	10 letters:	Caterpillar	14 letters:
Atheneum	Crockford's	Discotheque	Constitutional
Hell-fire	Devonshire		United Services
Rotarian	Landsdowne	12 letters:	
	Oddfellows	Conservative	15 letters:
9 letters:	Travellers		National Liberal
Athenaeum		13 letters:	
Beefsteak	11 letters:	Junior Carlton	
	Army and Navy	Thatched House	

Clubs and bats

3 letters:	Polt	7 letters:	10 letters:
Bat		Bourdon	Knobkerrie
	5 letters:		Nightstick
4 letters:	Basto	8 letters:	Nulla-nulla
Cosh	Lathi	Bludgeon	Shillelagh
Kiri	Waddy	Shillala	
Mace		Trunnion	12 letters:
Maul	6 letters:		Quarterstaff
Mell	Alpeen	9 letters:	
Mere	Cudgel	Blackjack	13 letters:
Meri	Kierie	Knobstick	Life preserver
Patu	Priest	Truncheon	

Coats and cloaks

3 letters:	Mink	Jelab	Anorak
Aba	Polo	Jemmy	Capote
Box	Rail	Jupon	Chimer
Car	Sack	Lammy	Coatee
Fur	Seal	Loden	Covert
Mac	Tail	Manta	Dolman
Top	Tent	Palla	Domino
	Toga	Parka	Duffel
4 letters:	Warm	Pilch	Duster
Abba	Wool	Sable	Fleece
Capa		Sagum	Fun fur
Cape	5 letters:	Tails	Jacket
Cope	Abaya		Jerkin
Hair	Acton	6 letters:	Joseph
Hood	Amice	Abolla	Kaross
Jack	Dress	Achkan	Lammie
Jump	Frock	Afghan	Mantle
Mack	Grego	Anarak	Parkee

Peplum
Poncho
Raglan
Riding
Tippet
Trench
Tuxedo
Ulster
Vestry
Visite

7 letters:
Admiral
Burnous
Cassock
Chimere
Chlamys
Chuddah
Chuddar
Crombie®
Cutaway
Galabea
Galabia
Hacking
Jellaba
Manteel
Mantlet
Matinee
Morning
Mozetta
Paenula
Paletot
Pallium

Peacoat
Pelisse
Posteen
Rocklay
Rokelay
Sarafan
Slicker
Snorkel
Spencer
Surcoat
Surtout
Swagger
Topcoat
Zamarra
Zamarro

8 letters:
Barathea
Bathrobe
Benjamin
Burberry®
Burnoose
Burnouse
Capuchin
Cardinal
Chasuble
Djellaba
Galabieh
Gambeson
Hall-robe
Haqueton
Himation
Jellabah

Jodhpuri
Mackinaw
Mantelet
Mantilla
Overcoat
Peignoir
Poshteen
Raincoat
Revestry
Scapular
Sherwani
Taglioni
Tailcoat
Vestiary

9 letters:
Balmacaan
Caracalla
Chlamydes
Coat dress
Djellabah
Gabardine
Gaberdine
Gallabeah
Greatcoat
Hacqueton
Housecoat
Inverness
Macintosh
Newmarket
Opera hood
Pea jacket
Petersham

Redingote
Sheepskin
Sou'wester
Undercoat

10 letters:
Fearnaught
Fearnought
Gallabiyah
Gallabiyeh
Mackintosh
Opera cloak
Roquelaure
Ulsterette
Waterproof
Windjammer
Wrap-rascal

11 letters:
Dreadnaught
Dreadnought
Swallowtail

12 letters:
Chesterfield
Dressing gown
Mousquetaire
Paludamentum
Prince Albert

13 letters:
Swallow-tailed

Coins

1 letter:	**3 letters:**	Fin	Lev	Sen	**4 letters:**
D	Ban	Flu	Lew	Sol	Anna
	Bar	Hao	Mil	Som	Baht
2 letters:	Bob	Jun	Mna	Sou	Bani
As	Cob	Kip	Moy	Won	Birr
DM	Dam	Lat	Ore	Yen	Buck
Kr	Ecu	Lei	Pul	Zuz	Cedi
Rd	Fen	Lek	Pya		Cent
Xu	Fil	Leu	Red		Chon

Dibs	Spur	Laari	Sucre
Dime	Tael	Laree	Sycee
Doit	Taka	Leone	Tenge
Dong	Tala	Liard	Tetri
Dram	Toea	Litas	Thebe
Duro	Vatu	Livre	Tical
Euro	Yuan	Louis	Ticky
Fiat	Zack	Lumma	Tolar
Fils		Lyart	Toman
Inti	**5 letters:**	Maile	Tyiyn
Jack	Agora	Manat	Zaire
Jane	Angel	Maneh	Zimbi
Jiao	Asper	Marka	Zloty
Kina	Aurar	Mohur	
Kobo	Baiza	Mongo	**6 letters:**
Kuna	Bekah	Mopus	Aureus
Kyat	Belga	Naira	Balboa
Lari	Bodle	Nakfa	Bawbee
Lion	Broad	Ngwee	Bender
Lira	Brown	Noble	Bezant
Loti	Butat	Obang	Boddle
Lwei	Butut	Oscar	Byzant
Maik	Chiao	Paisa	Canary
Mark	Colon	Paolo	Centas
Merk	Conto	Pence	Copeck
Mina	Crore	Pengo	Couter
Obol	Crown	Penie	Dalasi
Para	Daric	Penni	Danace
Paul	Dibbs	Penny	Deaner
Peag	Dinar	Plack	Décime
Peni	Dobra	Pound	Denier
Peso	Ducat	Razoo	Derham
Pice	Eagle	Rider	Dirham
Pula	Eyrir	Royal	Dirhem
Puli	Franc	Rubel	Dodkin
Punt	Fugio	Ruble	Dollar
Rand	Gerah	Rupee	Double
Real	Groat	Sceat	Drachm
Reis	Grosz	Scudo	Ekuele
Rial	Haler	Scute	Escudo
Riel	Hauer	Semis	Filler
Rock	Krona	Sente	Florin
Ryal	Krone	Shand	Forint
Sene	Kroon	Soldo	Gilder
Slog	Kurus	Souon	Gourde

Guinea
Gulden
Halala
Haleru
Heller
Hryvna
Jitney
Kobang
Koruna
Kroner
Kroona
Kwacha
Kwanza
Lepton
Likuta
Loonie
Makuta
Mancus
Markka
Mawpus
Pa'anga
Pagoda
Pataca
Pennia
Peseta
Pesewa
Poisha
Qintar
Rappen
Rouble
Rupiah
Santim
Satang
Sceatt
Seniti
Sequin
Shekel
Sickle
Siglos
Stater
Stiver
Stotin
Talent
Tanner
Tester

Teston
Thaler
Tickey
Toonie
Tugrik
Turner
Vellon
Wakiki

7 letters:
Afghani
Austral
Bolivar
Cardecu
Carolus
Centavo
Chetrum
Cordoba
Crusado
Drachma
Ekpwele
Guarani
Guilder
Hryvnya
Jacobus
Joannes
Kreuzer
Lempira
Metical
Millime
Milreis
Moidore
Ostmark
Ouguiya
Patrick
Piastre
Piefort
Pistole
Pollard
Quarter
Quetzal
Ringgit
Ruddock
Rufiyaa
Sextans

Solidus
Spanker
Tambala
Testoon
Testril
Thrimsa
Thrymsa
Tughrik
Unicorn
Xerafin

8 letters:
Brockage
Cardecue
Cruzeiro
Denarius
Doubloon
Ducatoon
Emalengi
Farthing
Groschen
Johannes
Kreutzer
Louis d'or
Maravedi
Millieme
Napoleon
Ngultrum
Nuevo sol
Picayune
Pistolet
Planchet
Portague
Portigue
Quadrans
Rigmarie
Semuncia
Sesterce
Shilling
Skilling
Solidare
Stotinka
Xeraphin
Zecchino

9 letters:
Boliviano
Britannia
Centesimo
Dandiprat
Dandyprat
Didrachma
Dupondius
Lilangeni
Luckpenny
Pistareen
Rennminbi
Rix-dollar
Rose noble
Schilling
Sovereign
Spur-royal
Yellowboy
Zwanziger

10 letters:
Broadpiece
Chervonets
Krugerrand
Portcullis
Reichsmark

11 letters:
Deutschmark
Sword-dollar
Tetradrachm

12 letters:
Antoninianus

13 letters:
Rennminbi yuan

18 letters:
Maria Theresa
 dollar

Collective nouns

Noun	Collective noun
Actors	Company
Aldermen	Bench, guzzle
Bakers	Tabernacle
Bishops	Bench
Critics	Shrivel
Directors	Board
Eggs	Clutch
Flowers	Bouquet
Inventions	Budget
Judges	Bench
People	Audience, crowd, congregation, horde, mob
Poems	Garland
Policemen	Posse
Prisoners	Gang
Remedies	Rabble
Rumours	Nest
Sailors	Crew
Ships	Fleet
Stories	Anthology
Thieves	Gang
Workmen	Gang

Collectors and enthusiasts

Collector/enthusiast	Object
Ailurophile	Cats
Arctophile	Teddy bears
Audiophile	High-fidelity sound reproduction
Automobilist	Cars
Bibliophile	Books
Brolliologist	Umbrellas
Campanologist	Bell-ringing
Cartophilist	Cigarette cards
Cruciverbalist	Crosswords
Deltiologist	Picture postcards
Discophile	Gramophone records
Fusilatelist	Phonecards
Herbalist	Herbs
Lepidopterist	Moths and butterflies
Medallist	Medals
Numismatist	Coins
Oenophile	Wine

Collector/enthusiast	Object
Paranumismatist	Coin-like objects
Philatelist	Stamps
Phillumenist	Matchbox labels
Phraseologist	Phrases
Scripophile	Share certificates
Vexillologist	Flags
Zoophile	Animals

Colleges

3 letters:
New

4 letters:
City
Dana
Eton
Fife
Iona
Reed
Snow
Taft
York

5 letters:
Bates
Chase
Clare
Green
Jesus
Keble
King's
Oriel
Peace
Ripon
Salem
Smith
Union
Wells

6 letters:
Bethel
Boston
Darwin

Durham
Exeter
Geneva
Girton
Gordon
Hebrew
Ithaca
Merton
Queen's
Selwyn
Thomas
Vassar
Wadham

7 letters:
Amherst
Aquinas
Balliol
Barnard
Bedford
Bermuda
Bowdoin
Chatham
Christ's
Concord
Cornell
Cypress
Douglas
Downing
Emerson
Erskine
Kellogg
Linacre
Lincoln

New Hall
Newnham
St Anne's
St Cross
St Hugh's
St John's
St Paul's
Trinity
Wolfson

8 letters:
All Souls
Bryn Mawr
Carleton
Columbia
Emmanuel
Findhorn
Hamilton
Hastings
Hertford
Homerton
Illinois
Imperial
Lewisham
Longwood
Magdalen
Meredith
Monmouth
National
Nuffield
Pembroke
Robinson
St Hilda's
St Peter's

9 letters:
Brasenose
Churchill
Clare Hall
Claremont
Gateshead
Guildford
Hampshire
Haverford
Kalamazoo
Lafayette
Magdalene
Manhattan
Mansfield
Newcastle
St Antony's
St Edmund's
Templeton
Wellesley
Worcester

10 letters:
Chesapeake
Goldsmith's
Greyfriars
Heidelberg
Hughes Hall
Huntingdon
Middlebury
Paul Smith's
Peterhouse
Somerville
St Stephen's
University

Washington

11 letters:
Blackfriars
Campion Hall
Fitzwilliam
King Alfred's
Regent's Park
Springfield
Trinity Hall

12 letters:
Christ Church
Sidney Sussex
St Benet's Hall
St Catharine's
St Catherine's
St Edmund Hall
Wycliffe Hall

13 letters:
Corpus Christi
Lucy Cavendish

16 letters:
Gonville and Caius
Harris Manchester
Lady Margaret Hall

See also:
➤ **Degrees**   ➤ **Education terms**   ➤ **Ivy League universities**
➤ **Oxbridge colleges**   ➤ **Schools**

Colours

3 letters:
Jet
Red
Tan

4 letters:
Anil
Blue
Ecru
Fawn
Gold
Grey
Iris
Jade
Navy
Onyx
Opal
Pink
Plum
Puce
Rose
Ruby
Rust
Sage
Sand
Sloe

5 letters:
Amber
Beige
Black
Brown
Cocoa
Coral
Cream
Ebony
Green
Hazel
Henna
Ivory
Khaki
Lemon
Lilac
Mauve
Ocher
Ochre
Olive
Peach
Pearl
Sepia
Slate
Taupe
Topaz
Umber

White

6 letters:
Auburn
Blonde
Bottle
Bronze
Canary
Cerise
Cherry
Claret
Cobalt
Copper
Indigo
Maroon
Orange
Purple
Russet
Salmon
Silver
Violet
Walnut
Yellow

7 letters:
Apricot
Avocado

Biscuit
Caramel
Crimson
Emerald
Fuchsia
Gentian
Magenta
Mustard
Oxblood
Saffron
Scarlet
Vermeil

8 letters:
Burgundy
Charcoal
Chestnut
Cinnamon
Eau de nil
Lavender
Magnolia
Mahogany
Raw umber
Santalin
Sapphire
Viridian

9 letters:
Aubergine
Chocolate
Olive drab
Pistachio
Tangerine

Turquoise
Vermilion

10 letters:
Aquamarine

Burnt umber
Chartreuse
Cobalt blue
Terracotta

11 letters:
Burnt sienna
Lemon yellow
Ultramarine

Comedians

3 letters:
Dee, *Jack*
Fry, *Stephen*
Kay, *Peter*
Ray, *Ted*
Wax, *Ruby*

4 letters:
Ali G
Ball, *Lucille*
Barr, *Roseanne*
Cook, *Peter*
Dodd, *Ken*
Hill, *Benny*
Hill, *Harry*
Hope, *Bob*
Hudd, *Roy*
Idle, *Eric*
Marx, *Chico*
Marx, *Groucho*
Marx, *Harpo*
Marx, *Zeppo*
Pegg, *Simon*
Sims, *Joan*
Took, *Barry*
Wall, *Max*
Wise, *Ernie*
Wood, *Victoria*

5 letters:
Abbot, *Russ*
Allen, *Dave*
Allen, *Woody*
Askey, *Arthur*
Benny, *Jack*
Borge, *Victor*

Brand, *Jo*
Brand, *Russell*
Bruce, *Lenny*
Burns, *George*
Chase, *Chevy*
Cohen, *Sacha Baron*
Cosby, *Bill*
David, *Larry*
Drake, *Charlie*
Elton, *Ben*
Emery, *Dick*
Goons, *The*
Hardy, *Jeremy*
Hardy, *Oliver*
Henry, *Lenny*
Hicks, *Bill*
Horne, *Kenneth*
James, *Sidney*
Jones, *Griff Rhys*
Jones, *Spike*
Jones, *Terry*
Leary, *Denis*
Lewis, *Jerry*
Lloyd, *Harold*
Moore, *Dudley*
Myers, *Mike*
Oddie, *Bill*
Palin, *Michael*
Pryor, *Richard*
Robey, *Sir George*
Sayle, *Alexei*
Smith, *Linda*
Smith, *Mel*
Starr, *Freddie*
Sykes, *Eric*
Worth, *Harry*

6 letters:
Abbott, *Bud*
Bailey, *Bill*
Barker, *Ronnie*
Carrey, *Jim*
Cleese, *John*
Coogan, *Steve*
Cooper, *Tommy*
Dawson, *Les*
De Vito, *Danny*
Fields, *W(illiam) C(laude)*
French, *Dawn*
Garden, *Graeme*
Howerd, *Frankie*
Izzard, *Eddie*
Junkin, *John*
Keaton, *Buster*
Laurel, *Stan*
Laurie, *Hugh*
Lehrer, *Tom*
Martin, *Steve*
Mayall, *Rik*
Merton, *Paul*
Murphy, *Eddie*
Proops, *Greg*
Reeves, *Vic*
Ullman, *Tracey*
Wilson, *Owen*
Wisdom, *Norman*

7 letters:
Aykroyd, *Dan*
Baddiel, *David*
Belushi, *John*
Bentine, *Michael*
Bremner, *Rory*

Carrott, *Jasper*
Chaplin, *Charlie*
Chapman, *Graham*
Charles, *Craig*
Corbett, *Ronnie*
Crystal, *Billy*
Edwards, *Jimmy*
Enfield, *Harry*
Everett, *Kenny*
Feldman, *Marty*
Gervais, *Ricky*
Goodman, *John*
Grammer, *Kelsey*
Hancock, *Tony*
Handley, *Tommy*
Jacques, *Hattie*
Manning, *Bernard*
Matthau, *Walter*
Newhart, *Bob*
Rushton, *Willie*
Secombe, *Harry*
Sellers, *Peter*
Stiller, *Ben*

Tarbuck, *Jimmy*
Toksvig, *Sandi*
Ustinov, *Sir Peter*

8 letters:
Coltrane, *Robbie*
Connolly, *Billy*
Costello, *Lou*
Goldberg, *Whoopi*
Groening, *Matt*
McIntyre, *Michael*
Milligan, *Spike*
Mortimer, *Bob*
Sadowitz, *Jerry*
Saunders, *Jennifer*
Seinfeld, *Jerry*
Sessions, *John*
Williams, *Kenneth*
Williams, *Robin*

9 letters:
Edmondson, *Adrian*
Humphries, *Barry*

Monkhouse, *Bob*
Morecambe, *Eric*
Whitfield, *June*

10 letters:
Pete and Dud
Stephenson, *Pamela*
Whitehouse, *Paul*

11 letters:
Monty Python
Terry-Thomas

12 letters:
Brooke-Taylor, *Tim*

14 letters:
Rowan and Martin

15 letters:
The Marx Brothers
The Three Stooges

Comets

4 letters:
West
Wild

8 letters:
Borrelly
Hale-Bopp

Kohoutek
McNaught

9 letters:
Hyakutake
Ikeya-Seki
Oort cloud

11 letters:
Swift-Tuttle

12 letters:
Halley's Comet

13 letters:
Shoemaker-Levy

19 letters:
Schwassmann-
  Wachmann

Commonwealth members

5 letters:
Ghana
India
Kenya
Malta
Nauru
Samoa
Tonga

6 letters:
Belize
Brunei
Canada
Cyprus
Guyana
Malawi
Tuvalu
Uganda

Zambia

7 letters:
Grenada
Jamaica
Lesotho
Namibia
Nigeria
St Lucia

Vanuatu

8 letters:
Barbados
Botswana
Cameroon
Dominica
Kiribati
Malaysia

Maldives
Pakistan
Sri Lanka
Tanzania
Zimbabwe

9 letters:
Australia
Mauritius
Singapore
Swaziland
The Gambia

10 letters:
Bangladesh
Mozambique
New Zealand
Seychelles
The Bahamas

11 letters:
Sierra Leone
South Africa

13 letters:
United Kingdom

14 letters:
Papua New Guinea
Solomon Islands

15 letters:
St Kitts and Nevis

17 letters:
Antigua and Barbuda
Trinidad and Tobago

25 letters:
St Vincent and The
  Grenadines

Communications

2 letters:
IT
PA

3 letters:
BCD
Cue
Dah
Dit
Dot
DVD
FAQ
Fax
FTP
IAP
ICT
ISP
LAN
Net
Out
TMT
URL
WAN
WAP
Web
XML

4 letters:
Alfa
Byte
CCTA
Code
Dash
Data
E-CRM
E-FIT
HTML
Java
Link
Mail
Mast
Over
Page
SGML
Site
Spam
WiFi
Worm

5 letters:
Bleep
Carry
Comms
Crier
Datum

DOVAP
Email
Flame
GMDSS
Inbox
Media
Modem
Pager
Radar
Radio
Stamp
Telex
Virus

6 letters:
Aerial
Browse
Cipher
Codify
Convey
Decode
Direct
Encode
Letter
Mayday
Medium
Nettie
Newbie

Outbox
Return
Server
Sitrep
Syncom
Trojan
Usenet

7 letters:
Bleeper
Braille
Browser
Courier
Decrypt
DEW line
Digital
Dossier
En clair
Encrypt
Entropy
Evernet
E-wallet
Lurking
Message
Meta tag
Nethead
Netizen
Network

Tapping
Telecom
Webcast
Web page
Website

8 letters:
Anti-site
Blocking
Boob tube
Chatroom
Codeword
Computer
Coverage
Data bank
Database
Decipher
Diaphone
Dispatch
Disperse
E-address
Envelope
E-payment
Ethernet
Firewall
Internet
Intranet
Listen in
Minidish
New media
Postmark
Register
Registry
Semaphor
Talkback
Wireless

9 letters:
Aldis lamp
Bandwidth
Bluetooth
Broadband
Cybercafé
Digital TV
Direction

Directory
E-commerce
Facsimile
Frequency
Hypertext
Mass media
Morse code
Paperless
Royal Mail
Satellite
Snail mail
Telephone
Telephony
Time-stamp

10 letters:
Beam aerial
Come across
Correspond
Dead letter
Degenerate
Fax machine
JavaScript
Media event
Memorandum
Multimedia
Netiquette
Silicon Fen
Ticker tape
Ultrafiche
Undirected

11 letters:
Address book
Chain letter
Communicate
Cryptograph
Dactylology
Mailing list
Mobile phone
Safe surfing
Silicon Glen

12 letters:
Cause célèbre

Conversation
Cryptography
Email address
Multichannel
Registration
Silicon Alley
Silver surfer

13 letters:
Bandspreading
Communication
Communicative
Correspondent
Cryptanalysis
Dead letter box
Dispatch rider
Online banking
Rural delivery
Satellite dish
Silicon Valley

14 letters:
Conversational
Correspondence
Electronic mail
Registered post

16 letters:
Recorded delivery

17 letters:
Branch instruction
Desktop publishing
General Post Office

18 letters:
Bottom-up processing
Exclusive OR circuit
Wireless networking

20 letters:
Digital versatile disk

21 letters:
Information technology

23 letters:
Internet Service Provider

Compass and cardinal points

COMPASS POINTS

Name	Abbreviation
North	N
North by East	N by E
North North East	NNE
North East by North	NE by N
North East	NE
North East by East	NE by E
East North East	ENE
East by North	E by N
East	E
East by South	E by S
East South East	ESE
South East by East	SE by E
South East	SE
South East by South	SE by S
South South East	SSE
South by East	S by E
South	S
South by West	S by W
South South West	SSW
South West by South	SW by S
South West	SW
South West by West	SW by W
West South West	WSW
West by South	W by S
West	W
West by North	W by N
West North West	WNW
North West by West	NW by W
North West	NW
North West by North	NW by N
North North West	NNW
North by West	N by W

CARDINAL POINTS

Name	Related adjective	Name	Related adjective
North	Arctic *or* boreal	South	Meridional *or* austral
East	Oriental	West	Occidental *or* hesperidan

Composers

CLASSICAL COMPOSERS

3 letters:
Bax, *Arnold*

4 letters:
Adam, *Adolphe*
Arne, *Thomas*
Bach, *Carl Philipp Emanuel*
Bach, *Johann Christian*
Bach, *Johann Christoph Friedrich*
Bach, *Johann Sebastian*
Bach, *Wilhelm Friedemann*
Berg, *Alban*
Blow, *John*
Bull, *John*
Byrd, *William*
Cage, *John*
Dima, *Gheorghe*
Ives, *Charles*
Lalo, *Édouard*
Nono, *Luigi*
Orff, *Carl*
Pärt, *Arvo*
Peri, *Jacopo*
Raff, *Joachim*
Ward, *David*
Weir, *Judith*
Wolf, *Hugo*

5 letters:
Adams, *John*
Alwyn, *William*
Auber, *Daniel François Espirit*
Auric, *Georges*
Balfe, *Michael William*
Berio, *Luciano*
Biber, *Heinrich*
Bizet, *Georges*
Bliss, *Arthur*
Bloch, *Ernest*
Boito, *Arrigo*
Boyce, *William*
Brian, *Havergal*

Bruch, *Max*
Crumb, *George*
D'Indy, *Vincent*
Dukas, *Paul*
Dupré, *Marcel*
Dutch, *Jan Pieterszoon Sweelinck*
Elgar, *Edward*
Fauré, *Gabriel*
Field, *John*
Finzi, *Gerald*
Glass, *Philip*
Gluck, *Christoph Willibald*
Grieg, *Edvard*
Harty, *Sir (Herbert) Hamilton*
Haydn, *Franz Joseph*
Haydn, *Michael*
Henze, *Hans Werner*
Holst, *Gustav*
Ibert, *Jacques*
Jones, *Daniel*
Lawes, *Henry*
Lawes, *William*
Lehár, *Franz*
Liszt, *Franz*
Lloyd, *George*
Locke, *Matthew*
Loewe, *Karl*
Lully, *Jean Baptiste*
Nyman, *Michael*
Ogdon, *John*
Parry, *Hubert*
Prout, *Ebenezer*
Ravel, *Maurice*
Reger, *Max*
Reich, *Steve*
Rieti, *Vittorio*
Rossi, *Luigi*
Satie, *Erik*
Smyth, *Ethel*
Sousa, *John Philip*
Suppe, *Franz von*
Tosti, *Francesco Paolo*

Verdi, *Giuseppi*
Watts, *Isaac*

6 letters:
Alfven, *Hugo*
Arnold, *Malcolm*
Azione
Barber, *Samuel*
Bartók, *Béla*
Boulez, *Pierre*
Brahms, *Johannes*
Bridge, *Frank*
Burney, *Charles*
Busoni, *Ferruccioni*
Carter, *Eliot*
Carver, *Robert*
Casals, *Pablo*
Chopin, *Frédéric*
Clarke, *Jeremiah*
Coates, *Eric*
Czerny, *Karl*
Davies, *Peter Maxwell*
Delius, *Frederick*
Doráti, *Antal*
Duparc, *Henri*
Dvořák, *Antonín*
Enesco, *Georges*
Farmer, *John*
Flotow, *Friedrich Freiherr von*
Franck, *César*
German, *Sir Edward*
Glière, *Reinhold*
Glinka, *Mikhail Ivanovich*
Gounod, *Charles François*
Gurney, *Ivor*
Halévy, *Fromental*
Handel, *George Frederick*
Harris, *Roy*
Hummel, *Johann Nepomuk*
Joplin, *Scott*
Kodály, *Zoltán*
Lassus, *Orlandus*
Ligeti, *György*
Mahler, *Gustav*
Martin, *Frank*

Mingus, *Charles*
Morley, *Thomas*
Mozart, *Leopold*
Mozart, *Wolfgang Amadeus*
Ogolon
Rameau, *Jean Philippe*
Rubbra, *Edmund*
Schütz, *Heinrich*
Straus, *Oscar*
Tallis, *Thomas*
Thomas, *Ambroise*
Varèse, *Edgar or Edgard*
Wagner, *Richard*
Walton, *William*
Webern, *Anton*

7 letters:
Albéniz, *Isaac*
Allegri, *Gregorio*
Antheil, *George*
Bantock, *Granville*
Bellini, *Vincenzo*
Bennett, *Richard Rodney*
Berlioz, *Hector*
Berners, *Gerald*
Borodin, *Aleksandr Porfirevich*
Britten, *Benjamin*
Brubeck, *Dave (David Warren)*
Copland, *Aaron*
Corelli, *Arcangelo*
Debussy, *Claude*
De Falla, *Manuel*
Delibes, *Léo*
De Lisle, *Claude Joseph Rouget*
Des Prés, *Josquin*
Di Lasso, *Orlando*
Dowland, *John*
Duruflé, *Maurice*
Gibbons, *Orlando*
Górecki, *Henryk*
Ireland, *John*
Janáček, *Leoš*
Joachim, *Joseph*
Knussen, *Oliver*
Krommer, *Franz*

Kubelik, *Raphael*
Lambert, *Constant*
Lutyens, *Elisabeth*
Martinů, *Bohuslav*
Menotti, *Gian Carlo*
Milhaud, *Darius*
Nicolai, *Carl Otto Ehrenfried*
Nielsen, *Carl*
Poulenc, *Francis*
Puccini, *Giacomo*
Purcell, *Henry*
Purnell, *Alton*
Quilter, *Roger*
Rodrigo, *Joaquín*
Romberg, *Sigmund*
Rossini, *Gioacchino Antonio*
Roussel, *Albert*
Salieri, *Antonio*
Schuman, *William*
Simpson, *Robert*
Smetana, *Bedřich*
Stainer, *John*
Strauss, *Johann*
Strauss, *Richard*
Tartini, *Giuseppe*
Tavener, *John*
Thomson, *Virgil*
Tippett, *Michael*
Vivaldi, *Antonio*
Warlock, *Peter*
Weelkes, *Thomas*
Wellesz, *Egon*
Xenakis, *Yannis*

8 letters:
Alaleona, *Domenico*
Albinoni, *Tomaso*
Benjamin, *Arthur*
Berkeley, *Lennox*
Bonporti, *Francesco Antonio*
Bruckner, *Anton*
Chabrier, *Emmanuel*
Chausson, *Ernest*
Cimarosa, *Domenico*
Couperin, *François*

De Lassus, *Roland*
Gabrieli, *Andrea*
Gabrieli, *Giovanni*
Gershwin, *George*
Gesualdo, *Carlo*
Glazunov, *Aleksandr Konstantinovich*
Goossens, *Eugene*
Grainger, *Percy*
Granados, *Enrique*
Holliger, *Heinz*
Honegger, *Arthur*
Korngold, *Erich*
Kreutzer, *Conradin*
Maconchy, *Elizabeth*
Marcello, *Benedetto*
Marenzio, *Luca*
Martland, *Steve*
Mascagni, *Pietro*
Massenet, *Jules Émile Frédéric*
Messager, *André*
Messiaen, *Olivier*
Musgrave, *Thea*
Ockeghem, *Johannes*
Paganini, *Niccolò*
Panufnik, *Andrzej*
Respighi, *Ottorino*
Schnabel, *Artur*
Schubert, *Franz*
Schumann, *Clara*
Schumann, *Robert*
Scriabin, *Aleksandr Nikolayvich*
Sessions, *Roger*
Sibelius, *Jean*
Stanford, *Charles*
Taverner, *John*
Telemann, *Georg Philipp*
Von Weber, *Carl Maria*
Williams, *Ralph Vaughan*

9 letters:
Balakirev, *Mily Alexeyevich*
Beethoven, *Ludwig van*
Bernstein, *Leonard*
Bocherini, *Luigi*
Boulanger, *Nadia*

Broughton, *Bruce*
Buxtehude, *Dietrich*
Carpenter, *John Alden*
Chaminade, *Cecile*
Cherubini, *Luigi*
De Machaut, *Guillaume*
Donizetti, *Gaetano*
Dunstable, *John*
Dutilleux, *Henri*
Ginastera, *Alberto*
Hildegard *of Bingen*
Hindemith, *Paul*
Klemperer, *Otto*
MacMillan, *James*
Meyerbeer, *Giacomo*
Offenbach, *Jacques*
Pachelbel, *Johann*
Pergolesi, *Giovanni Battista*
Prokofiev, *Sergei Sergeyevich*
Scarlatti, *Alessandro*
Scarlatti, *Domenico*
Schnittke, *Alfred*
Takemitsu, *Toru*
Tortelier, *Paul*
Von Flotow, *Friedrich*
Whitehead, *Gillian*
Zemlinsky, *Alexander*

10 letters:
Birtwistle, *Harrison*
Canteloube, *Joseph*
De Victoria, *Tomás Luis*
Monteverdi, *Claudio*
Mussorgsky, *Modest Petrovich*
Paderewski, *Ignace Jan*
Palestrina, *Giovanni Pierluigi da*
Penderecki, *Krzystof*
Ponchielli, *Amilcare*
Praetorius, *Michael*
Rawsthorne, *Alan*

Rubinstein, *Anton Grigorevich*
Saint-Saëns, *Camille*
Schoenberg, *Arnold*
Sculthorpe, *Peter*
Stravinsky, *Igor Fyodorovich*
Villa-Lobos, *Heitor*
Williamson, *Malcolm*

11 letters:
Butterworth, *George*
Charpentier, *Gustave*
Charpentier, *Marc-Antoine*
Frescobaldi, *Girolamo*
Fürtwangler, *Wilhelm*
Humperdinck, *Englebert*
Leoncavallo, *Ruggiero*
Lutosławski, *Witold*
Mendelssohn, *Fanny*
Mendelssohn, *Felix*
Rachmaninov, *Sergei Vassilievich*
Stockhausen, *Karlheinz*
Szymanowski, *Karol*
Tchaikovsky, *Pyotr Ilyich*
Theodorakis, *Mikis*
Von Dohnányi, *Ernst*
Wolf-Ferrari, *Ermanno*

12 letters:
Dallapiccola, *Luigi*
Khachaturian, *Aram Ilyich*
Rostropovich, *Mstislav Leopoldovich*
Shostakovich, *Dmitri Dmitriyevich*

14 letters:
Jaques-Dalcroze, *Émile*
Rimsky-Korsakov, *Nikolai Andreyevich*

15 letters:
Coleridge-Taylor, *Samuel*

POPULAR COMPOSERS, SONGWRITERS, AND LYRICISTS

4 letters:
Baez, *Joan*
Bart, *Lionel*

Brel, *Jacques*
Cahn, *Sammy*
Duke, *Vernon*

Hart, *Lorenz*
John, *Elton*
Kern, *Jerome (David)*

King, *Carole*
Mann, *Barry*
Monk, *Thelonious (Sphere)*
Rice, *Tim*
Webb, *Jimmy*
Weil, *Cynthia*

5 letters:
Arlen, *Harold*
Barry, *John*
Bowie, *David*
Brown, *Nacio Herb*
Cohan, *George*
Cohen, *Leonard*
Dixon, *Willie*
Dylan, *Bob*
Handy, *W(illiam) C(hristopher)*
Jarre, *Maurice*
Jobim, *Antonio Carlos*
Loewe, *Frederick*
Pomus, *Doc*
Shore, *Howard*
Simon, *Paul*
Styne, *Jule*
Waits, *Tom*
Weill, *Kurt*

6 letters:
Berlin, *Irving*
Coward, *Noel*
Dozier, *Lamont*
Foster, *Stephen*
Goffin, *Gerry*
Herman, *Jerry*
Jagger, *Mick*

Lehrer, *Tom*
Lennon, *John*
Lerner, *Alan Jay*
Lieber, *Jerry*
McColl, *Ewan*
McColl, *Kirsty*
McHugh, *Jimmy*
Nelson, *Willie*
Parker, *Charlie*
Porter, *Cole*
Strong, *Barrett*
Warren, *Harry*
Wilson, *Brian*

7 letters:
Babbitt, *Milton*
Gilbert, *W(illiam) S(chwenck)*
Guthrie, *Woody*
Holland, *Brian*
Holland, *Eddie*
Johnson, *Robert*
Lilburn, *Douglas*
Loesser, *Frank*
Mancini, *Henry*
Manilow, *Barry*
Novello, *Ivor*
Rodgers, *Richard*
Romberg, *Sigmund*
Stoller, *Mike*
Youmans, *Vincent*

8 letters:
Anderson, *Laurie*
Coltrane, *John*
Gershwin, *George*

Hamlisch, *Marvin*
Mitchell, *Joni*
Morrison, *Van*
Richards, *Keith*
Robinson, *William 'Smokey'*
Sondheim, *Stephen*
Sullivan, *Arthur*
Williams, *Hank*
Williams, *John*

9 letters:
Bacharach, *Burt*
Bernstein, *Leonard*
Ellington, *Duke*
Goldsmith, *Jerry*
Ledbetter, *Huddie 'Leadbelly'*
McCartney, *Paul*
Strayhorn, *Billy*
Toussaint, *Allen*
Van Heusen, *Johnny*
Whitfield, *Norman*

10 letters:
Carmichael, *Hoagy*
Goldenthal, *Elliot*
Livingston, *Jay*

11 letters:
Hammerstein, *Oscar*
Lloyd-Webber, *Andrew*

13 letters:
Kristofferson, *Kris*

Compounds

3 letters:	EDTA	Urea	Amino
Azo	Enol		Azide
	Haem	**5 letters:**	Azine
4 letters:	Heme	Allyl	Azole
Alum	Tepa	Amide	Diazo
Dopa	TEPP	Amine	Diene

Dimer
Diode
Erbia
Ester
Furan
Halon
Imide
Imine
Lipid
Olein
Oxide
Oxime
Potin
Pyran
Sarin
Tabun
Thiol
Trona
Vinyl

6 letters:
Acetal
Alkane
Alkene
Arsine
Baryta
Borane
Calque
Cetane
Chrome
Cresol
Diazin
Epimer
Fluate
Glycol
Halide
Haloid
Hexene
Isatin
Isomer
Ketone
Lithia
Malate
Niello
Phenol

Pinene
Potash
Purine
Pyrene
Retene
Silane
Speiss
Tartar
Tetryl
Thymol
Triene
Trimer
Uranyl

7 letters:
Acetone
Acridin
Aglycon
Ammonia
Benzene
Betaine
Bromide
Caliche
Calomel
Camphor
Caprate
Carbide
Chelate
Choline
Cinerin
Creatin
Cumarin
Cyanide
Diamine
Diazine
Diazole
Dioxide
Dvandva
Epoxide
Erinite
Ethanol
Eugenol
Fenuron
Flavone
Hormone

Hydrate
Hydride
Indican
Indoxyl
Inosine
Lactate
Menthol
Metamer
Monomer
Nitrite
Oxazine
Peptone
Polymer
Protein
Quassia
Quinoid
Quinone
Realgar
Skatole
Steroid
Sulfide
Syncarp
Taurine
Terpene
Toluene
Tritide
Uridine
Wolfram

8 letters:
Acridine
Aglycone
Aldehyde
Alizarin
Arginine
Butyrate
Catenane
Chloride
Chromene
Coenzyme
Coumarin
Creatine
Cyanogen
Datolite
Dieldrin

Dopamine
Farnesol
Fluoride
Glycogen
Haloform
Hydroxyl
Iodoform
Isologue
Ketoxime
Lecithin
Massicot
Melamine
Monoxide
Pentosan
Peroxide
Piperine
Psilocin
Ptomaine
Pyrazole
Pyruvate
Racemate
Retinoid
Rock-alum
Rotenone
Selenate
Silicide
Siloxane
Sodamide
Stilbene
Sulphide
Sulphone
Tautomer
Tetroxid
Thiazide
Thiazine
Thiazole
Thiotepa
Thiourea
Thyroxin
Titanate
Triazine
Triazole
Trilling
Tyramine
Urethane

Xanthate
Xanthine
Ytterbia
Zirconia

9 letters:
Aflatoxin
Alicyclic
Aliphatic
Anhydride
Auranofin
Biguanide
Capsaicin
Carbazole
Carnitine
Caseinate
Cellulose
Cementite
Cortisone
Deuteride
Dipeptide
Disulfram
Endorshin
Ferrocene
Flavanone
Glycoside
Guanosine
Haematein
Histamine
Hydrazide
Hydroxide

Imidazole
Impsonite
Ionophore
Isoniazid
Monoamine
Pentoxide
Perborate
Phenoxide
Pheromone
Phosphide
Phthalate
Piperonal
Polyamine
Porphyrin
Prussiate
Qinghaosu
Quercetus
Quinidine
Quinoline
Serotonin
Tetroxide
Thyroxine
Valproate
Verapamil
Veratrine

10 letters:
Amphoteric
Argyrodite
Dimethoate
Disulphide

Endosulfan
Enkephalin
Isocyanate
Lumisterol
Mercaptide
Nucleoside
Phenacaine
Picrotoxin
Piperazine
Piperidine
Propionate
Putrescine
Pyrethrine
Pyrogallol
Tatpurusha
Tetracaine
Thimerosal
Tocopherol

11 letters:
Acetanilide
Amphetamine
Coprosterol
Dimercaprol
Diphosphate
Electrolyte
Fluorescein
Glutathione
Hydrocarbon
Neostigmine
Sesquioxide

Trichlorfon
Trichloride

12 letters:
Carbohydrate
Formaldehyde
Haematoxylin
Hydrastinine
Hydroquinone
Permanganate
Polyurethane
Quinalizarin
Triglyceride
Trimethadine

13 letters:
Catecholamine
Cycloheximide
Isoproterenol
Metronidazole
Nortriptyline
Plastoquinone
Trinucleotide

14 letters:
Oxyhaemoglobin
Polycarboxylic
Polyunsaturate
Tribomoethanol
Trihalomethane

Computer games

3 letters:
Jak
RPG

4 letters:
Doom
Halo
Myst

6 letters:
Action

Driver
Far Cry
MMPORG
Shogun

7 letters:
RockMan
Shooter
SimCity
The Sims
Top Spin

8 letters:
Half-Life
Max Payne
Ragnarok
Star Wars
Strategy
Total War
Warcraft
Xenosaga

9 letters:
Ace Combat
Adventure
Bejeweled
Guild Wars
Homeworld
Spy Hunter
StarCraft
Wii Sports

10 letters:
Angry Birds
Call of Duty
Dragon Fire
Fight Night
Fire Emblem
Primal Rage
Redemption
Simulation
Terminator

11 letters:
Ghost Master
Gran Turismo
Ninja Gaiden
Role playing

12 letters:
Age of Wonders

Apocalyptica
City of Heroes
Final Fantasy
Resident Evil
Return to Arms
Viewtiful Joe

13 letters:
Medal of Honour
Rise of Nations

14 letters:
Ace Yeti Trapper
Ancient Empires
Backyard Skater
Beyond Divinity
Grand Theft Auto
Massive Assault
Metal Gear Solid

Prince of Persia

15 letters:
Freedom Fighters
Pro Rugby Manager
Red Dead Revolver
Samurai Warriors
World of Warcraft

16 letters:
Sonic the Hedgehog
Unreal Tournament

17 letters:
Red Dead Redemption

18 letters:
Railsport Challenge
Super Mario Brothers

Computers

COMPUTER PARTS

3 letters:
ALU
CPU
MTU
VDU

4 letters:
Case
Chip
DIMM
Disk
DRAM
Port
SIMM

5 letters:
Modem
Mouse
SDRAM

6 letters:
DDR-RAM

Dongle
Memory
Screen
Webcam

7 letters:
Console
Counter
Encoder
Monitor
Printer
Scanner
Speaker
USB port

8 letters:
Disk unit
Emulator
Joystick
Keyboard
LCD panel

9 letters:
Cartridge
Digitizer
Disk drive
DVD reader
DVD writer
Hard drive
Interface
Processor
Sound card
Trackball

10 letters:
CD-rewriter
CD-Rom drive
Control key
Daisywheel
Floppy disk
Transistor

11 letters:
Line printer

Motherboard
Multiplexor
Optical disk

12 letters:
Coaxial cable
Graphics card
Laser printer

13 letters:
Digital camera

14 letters:
Flatbed scanner
Microprocessor
Optical scanner

16 letters:
Magnetic tape unit

17 letters:
Integrated circuit

Visual display unit

18 letters:
Digital audio player

19 letters:
Arithmetic logic unit
Printed circuit board

21 letters:
Central processing unit

22 letters:
Optical character reader

24 letters:
Analogue-digital converter

COMPUTER TERMS

2 letters:
AI
I/O
IT
PC

3 letters:
Bit
BPI
Bug
Bus
CAD
CAE
CAI
CAL
CAM
CAT
CBT
CIM
COL
COM
DAC
DMA
DOS®
Dpi
DTP
FAT
FTP
Gif
ICL
IDE
Job
LAN
Mac

OCR
OEM
PDA
Pdf
RAM
ROM

Run
SAM
Sim
USB
WAN
WAP
XML

4 letters:
ADSL
Area
Bomb
Boot
Byte
Cast
CISC
Code
Data
Dump
Echo
Edit
Exit
File
Flag
Gate
Giga-
GIGO
Host

HTML
Icon
IKBS
iPad
ISDN
Jpeg
Kilo-
Load
Loop
Mega-
Menu
Midi
Mpeg
Node
Open
PROM
RISC
SCSI
SGML
Sort
UNIX®
Wi-Fi
WIMP
Word
Worm

5 letters:
Array
ASCII
Brain
CD-Rom
Clock
Crash
Cyber

Cycle
Datel®
Digit
Earom
E-mail
Eniac
EPROM
ERNIE
Field
Flops
Fuzzy
Input
JANET
Key in
Log in
Macro
Micro
Patch
Pixel
Queue
Rerun
Reset
Sense
Stack
Store
Tally
Tower
Virus
Voxel
Warez

6 letters:
Access
Analog

Applet
Backup
Buffer
Bundle
Busbar
CADCAM
CADMAT
Caster
Cookie
Cursor
Device
Driver
Duplex
Earcon
EBCDIC
Editor
EEPROM
Figure
Hacker
Holmes
Hot key
Infect
Joypad
Kludge
Laptop
Legacy
Linker
Log out
Module
Online
OR gate
Output
Packet
Parser

Phreak
Prompt
Read in
Reboot
Record
Scroll
Server
Sprite
String
SWITCH
Syntax
System
Tablet
TAURUS
Toggle
Uptime
Window
Wizard
Zmodem

7 letters:
ActiveX
Address
AND gate
Browser
Capture
Chipset
Clip art
Command
Corrupt
Counter
Databus
Default
Desktop
Digital
Freenet
Gateway
Hotlist
Install
Keyword
Lapheld
Manager
Measure
Network
NOR gate

NOT gate
Notwork
Numlock
Offline
Package
Palette
Palmtop
Pointer
Power up
Process
Program
Read out
Routine
Run time
Time out
Turnkey
Utility
Vaccine
WYSIWYG

8 letters:
Analogue
Assemble
Autosave
Backbone
Beta-test
Black box
Calculus
Checksum
Chiphead
Compiler
Constant
Data bank
Database
Digitize
Document
Download
Downsize
Down time
Emulator
Estimate
Extranet
Fail-safe
Filename
Firewall

FireWire
Firmware
Freeware
Function
Gigabyte
Graphics
Hard card
Hard copy
Hardware
Hardwire
Idle time
Internet
Intranet
Kilobyte
Language
Listserv
Liveware
Location
Megabyte
Morphing
NAND gate
Nyetwork
Optimize
Overflow
Password
Platform
Popunder
Portable
Printout
Protocol
Pushdown
Realtime
Reckoner
Skinning
Software
TALISMAN
Terabyte
Terminal
Topology
Tristate
Variable
Wavefile
Wild card
Wireless

9 letters:
Algorithm
Alpha-test
Assembler
Authoring
Bandwidth
Bluetooth
Bootstrap
Broadband
Bus master
Calculate
Character
Co-routine
Cybercafé
Cyberpunk
Dataglove
Debugging
Directory
Dithering
Dot matrix
Ecommerce
Floptical
Flowchart
Groupware
Handshake
Hard-wired
Hypertext
Interface
Interrupt
Logic bomb
Mainframe
Multi-user
Parameter
Power down
Procedure
Processor
Retrieval
Rogue site
Shareware
Smart card
Statement
Trackball
Underflow
User group

10 letters:
3D graphics
Access time
Address bus
Choke route
Cobweb site
Compatible
Core memory
Cyberspace
Encryption
Fileserver
Hypermedia
Initialize
Integrator
Linked list
Main memory
Menu-driven
Patch board
Programmer
README file
Robustness
Scratchpad
Server farm
Stand-alone
Subroutine
Throughput
Transcribe
Translator
Transputer
Voice input
Webcasting

11 letters:
Base address
Binary digit
Bits per inch
Cache memory
Clickstream
Computerate
Computerize
Concordance
Cut and paste
Cybernetics
Data capture

Dots per inch
File manager
Function key
Greybarland
Help screens
Input device
Input/output
Instruction
Interactive
Interpreter
Machine code
Mail bombing
Memory stick
Multiaccess
NAND circuit
Parity check
Plug and play
Screensaver
Shared logic
Spreadsheet
Superserver
Systems disk
Telecottage
Time sharing
Trackerball
Work station

12 letters:
Anti-aliasing
Architecture
Backing store
Digital fount
Disassembler
Dumb terminal
Error message
Expert system
Global search
Housekeeping
Logic circuit
Minicomputer
Mobile device
Remote access
Reserved word
Script kiddie
Search engine

Shell program
Telesoftware
World Wide Web

13 letters:
Audio response
Bulletin board
Configuration
Data structure
Decision table
Escape routine
Expansion slot
Memory mapping
Microcomputer
Multi-threaded
Neurocomputer
Object program
Point and click
Query language
Queuing theory
Source program
Storage device
Supercomputer
Turnkey system
Virtual memory
Voice response
Word processor

14 letters:
Binary notation
Communications
Condition codes
Cross assembler
Data processing
Data protection
Digital imaging
Digital mapping
Document reader
Electronic mail
Hybrid computer
Magnetic bubble
Microprocessor
Neural computer
Number-cruncher
Plug compatible

Read only memory
Source document
Teleprocessing
Text processing
User-defined key
Virtual address
Virtual reality
Virtual storage
Volatile memory
Web development

15 letters:
Absolute address
Archival storage
Automatic repeat
Batch processing
Command language
Computer science
Control commands
Digital computer
Fifth-generation
Machine learning
Machine readable
Operating system
Packet-switching
Palmtop computer
Storage capacity
Store and forward
Systems analysis

16 letters:
Analogue computer
Assembly language
Computer graphics
Digital watermark
Distributed logic
Electronic office
Hand-held computer
Image enhancement
Interactive video
Local area network
Logic programming
Low-level language
Multiprogramming
Notebook computer

Personal computer
Program generator
Program statement
Sequential access
Serial processing
Voice recognition

17 letters:
Branch instruction
Desktop publishing
Development system
Front-end processor
High-level language
Speech recognition
Top-down processing
Visual programming

18 letters:
Application program
Bottom-up processing
Database management
Direct memory access
Exclusive OR circuit
Incremental plotter
Machine translation
Parallel processing
Random access memory
Real-time processing
Serial access memory

19 letters:
Computer-aided design
Computer typesetting
Direct-access storage
Disk operating system®
Hexadecimal notation
Incremental recorder
Intelligent terminal
Polymorphic function
Programming language
Random-access storage
Software engineering

20 letters:
Computer aided trading

Computer conferencing
Concurrent processing
Dataflow architecture
Electronic publishing
File transfer protocol
Restricted users group

21 letters:
Computer-aided learning
Computer-aided teaching
Computer-based training
Decision support system
Information technology

22 letters:
Artificial intelligence
Graphical user interface

23 letters:
Computer-aided management

24 letters:
Computer-aided engineering
Computer-aided instruction
Computer-aided manufacture
Computer-assisted learning
Computer input on microfilm

25 letters:
Distributed array processor
Windows icons menus pointers

26 letters:
Programmable read only memory

28 letters:
Random Instruction Set Computer

29 letters:
Complex instruction set computer
Computer integrated manufacture
Original equipment manufacturer
Reduced instruction set computer
Small Computer Systems Interface

31 letters:
Intelligent knowledge-based system

32 letters:
Floating-point operations per second

33 letters:
Computer-aided design and
  manufacture

34 letters:
Electronic flight information systems

41 letters:
Extended binary-coded decimal-
  interchange code

COMPUTER SCIENTISTS

4 letters:
Cray, *Seymour*
Jobs, *Steve*

5 letters:
Aiken, *Howard*
Gates, *Bill*

6 letters:
Eckert, *John Presper*
Turing, *Alan Mathison*

7 letters:

Babbage, *Charles*
Mauchly, *John W.*

8 letters:
Lovelace, *Ada (Countess of)*
Sinclair, *Clive*

9 letters:
Hollerith, *Herman*

10 letters:
Berners-Lee, *Tim*
Von Neumann, *John*

See also:
➤ **Computer games** ➤ **Internet domain names** ➤ **Programming languages**

Confectionery

3 letters:
Gem
Gum

4 letters:
Jube
Kiss
Mint
Rock

5 letters:
Candy
Dolly

Fudge
Halva
Lolly
Taffy

6 letters:
Bonbon
Button
Cachou
Comfit
Confit
Dainty
Dragée

Halvah
Humbug
Jujube
Nougat
Sorbet
Sundae
Tablet
Toffee

7 letters:
Brittle
Caramel
Fondant

Gumdrop
Halavah
Lozenge
Panocha
Praline
Sherbet
Truffle

8 letters:
Acid drop
All-sorts
Bull's eye
Licorice

Lollipop
Marzipan
Noisette
Pastille
Peardrop
Scroggin
Stickjaw

9 letters:
Blackball
Chocolate
Fruit drop
Jelly baby
Jelly bean
Lemon drop
Liquorice

Marchpane

10 letters:
Brandyball
Candyfloss
Chewing gum
Coconut ice
Gob-stopper
Nanaimo bar
Peppermint
Pick and mix
Soft-centre

11 letters:
Barley sugar
Boiled sweet

Marshmallow
Toffee apple

12 letters:
Burnt-almonds
Butterscotch

13 letters:
Fruit pastille

14 letters:
Turkish delight

20 letters:
Hundreds and thousands

Containers for liquids

3 letters:
Can
Jar
Jug
Keg
Tin

4 letters:
Butt
Cask
Tube

5 letters:
Flask
Gourd
Tinny

6 letters:
Barrel

Bottle
Carafe
Carton
Coldie
Firkin
Flagon
Magnum
Stubby

7 letters:
Amphora
Ampulla
Pitcher
Polypin

8 letters:
Decanter
Gallipot
Hogshead

Jeroboam
Rehoboam
Screw-top
Tantalus

9 letters:
Balthazar
Miniature

10 letters:
Half-bottle
Methuselah
Percolator
Salmanazar

14 letters:
Nebuchadnezzar

Continents

4 letters:
Asia

6 letters:
Africa
Europe

9 letters:
Australia

10 letters:	12 letters:	South America
Antarctica	North America	

Cookery

GENERAL COOKERY TERMS

3 letters:	Icing	Sippet	Marinade
Fry	Knead	Smoked	Marinate
Ice	Ladle		Meunière
	Offal	**7 letters:**	Mirepoix
4 letters:	Paste	À la king	Scramble
Bake	Poach	À la mode	Tandoori
Bard	Purée	Caterer	Teriyaki
Boil	Roast	Cobbler	Unsmoked
Chef	Sauce	Cuisine	
Cook	Sauté	Curried	**9 letters:**
Dice	Steam	Custard	Antipasto
Ghee	Stock	Garnish	Au naturel
Jerk	Sweat	Giblets	Blackened
Lard	Tikka	Goulash	Carbonado
Luau	Yeast	Lardoon	Casserole
Mash		Liaison	Char-grill
Mask	**6 letters:**	Marengo	Cook-chill
Meze	Au lait	Marmite	Entremets
Rise	Barbie	Newburg	Fricassee
Roux	Batter	Parboil	Lyonnaise
Soup	Blanch	Rissole	Macedoine
Stew	Braise	Roulade	Oven-ready
Whip	Coddle	Supreme	Salipicon
	Commis	Timbale	Tenderize
5 letters:	Corned	Topping	Undressed
Au jus	Creole		Wholemeal
Barde	Entrée		
Baste	Fajita	**8 letters:**	**10 letters:**
Broth	Fillet	Au gratin	Caramelise
Cured	Flambé	Barbecue	Jardinière
Dough	Fondue	Browning	Médaillons
Farci	Goujon	Chasseur	Medallions
Flour	Lardon	Colander	Parmentier
Fumet	Leaven	Consommé	Provençale
Glacé	Mornay	Cookbook	Rijstaffel
Glaze	Panada	Dressing	Royal icing
Grate	Potage	En croute	Stroganoff
Gravy	Ragout	Gelatine	Unleavened
Grill	Season	Julienne	Wholewheat

11 letters:
Chafing dish
Cookery book
En brochette
Graham flour
Hors d'oeuvre

12 letters:
Boil-in-the-bag
Confectioner
Sweet-and-sour

13 letters:
Silver service

14 letters:
Cuisine minceur
Wholemeal flour

15 letters:
Nouvelle cuisine

CUISINES AND COOKING STYLES

4 letters:
Ital
Thai

5 letters:
Balti
Greek
Halal
Tapas
Vegan

6 letters:
French
Fusion
Indian
Kosher
Tex-Mex

7 letters:
Chinese
Italian
Mexican
Seafood
Sichuan
Turkish

8 letters:
Fast food
Japanese
Szechuan

9 letters:
Cantonese
Caribbean
Malaysian

Provençal

10 letters:
Cordon bleu
Indonesian
Vegetarian

11 letters:
Californian
Home cooking

12 letters:
Haute cuisine

13 letters:
Gutbürgerlich
International

Mediterranean

14 letters:
Cuisine minceur

15 letters:
Nouvelle cuisine

19 letters:
Molecular
  gastronomy

Counties

ENGLISH COUNTIES

4 letters:
Kent

5 letters:
Devon
Essex

6 letters:
Dorset
Durham
Surrey

7 letters:
Bristol
Cumbria

Norfolk
Rutland
Suffolk

8 letters:
Cheshire
Cornwall
Somerset

9 letters:
Berkshire
Hampshire
Wiltshire

10 letters:
Derbyshire
East Sussex
Lancashire
Merseyside
Shropshire
West Sussex

11 letters:
Isle of Wight
Oxfordshire
Tyne and Wear

12 letters:
Bedfordshire

Lincolnshire
Warwickshire
West Midlands

13 letters:
Greater London
Herefordshire
Hertfordshire
Staffordshire
West Yorkshire

14 letters:
Cambridgeshire
Leicestershire
Northumberland
North Yorkshire
South Yorkshire
Worcestershire

15 letters:
Buckinghamshire
Gloucestershire

Nottinghamshire

16 letters:
Northamptonshire

17 letters:
Greater Manchester

21 letters:
East Riding of Yorkshire

FORMER ENGLISH COUNTIES

4 letters:
Kent

5 letters:
Devon
Essex

6 letters:
Dorset
Durham
Surrey

7 letters:
Norfolk
Rutland

8 letters:
Cheshire
Cornwall
Somerset

9 letters:
Berkshire
Hampshire
Wiltshire

10 letters:
Cumberland
Derbyshire
East Sussex
Lancashire
Shropshire
West Sussex

11 letters:
East Suffolk
Oxfordshire
Westmorland
West Suffolk

12 letters:
Bedfordshire
Lincolnshire
Warwickshire

13 letters:
East Yorkshire
Greater London
Herefordshire
Hertfordshire
Staffordshire

West Yorkshire

14 letters:
Leicestershire
Northumberland
North Yorkshire
Worcestershire

15 letters:
Buckinghamshire
Gloucestershire
Nottinghamshire

16 letters:
Northamptonshire

25 letters:
Huntingdon and
  Peterborough

26 letters:
Cambridgeshire and Isle
  of Ely

SCOTTISH COUNTIES

4 letters:
Fife

5 letters:
Angus

Moray

6 letters:
Orkney

7 letters:
Falkirk

8 letters:
Highland

Shetland
Stirling

10 letters:
Dundee City

Eilean Siar — Western Isles
Inverclyde
Midlothian

13 letters:
Aberdeenshire
Argyll and Bute
North Ayrshire
South Ayrshire

11 letters:
East Lothian
Glasgow City
West Lothian

15 letters:
City of Edinburgh
Perth and Kinross
Scottish Borders

12 letters:
Aberdeen City
East Ayrshire
Renfrewshire

16 letters:
Clackmannanshire
East Renfrewshire
North Lanarkshire
South Lanarkshire

18 letters:
East Dunbartonshire
West Dunbartonshire

19 letters:
Dumfries and Galloway

FORMER SCOTTISH COUNTIES

4 letters:
Bute
Fife

5 letters:
Angus
Banff
Moray
Nairn

6 letters:
Argyll
Dundee
Orkney

7 letters:
Glasgow
Kinross

8 letters:
Aberdeen
Ayrshire
Roxburgh

Shetland

9 letters:
Caithness
Edinburgh

10 letters:
Banffshire
Kincardine
Midlothian
Nairnshire
Perthshire
Sutherland

11 letters:
East Lothian
Lanarkshire
West Lothian

12 letters:
Berwickshire
Kinross-shire
Peeblesshire

Renfrewshire
Selkirkshire
Wigtownshire

13 letters:
Aberdeenshire
Dumfriesshire
Roxburghshire
Stirlingshire

14 letters:
Dunbartonshire
Inverness-shire

15 letters:
Kincardineshire
Ross and Cromarty

16 letters:
Clackmannanshire

18 letters:
Kirkcudbrightshire

WELSH COUNTIES (POST-1998)

5 letters:
Conwy
Powys

7 letters:
Cardiff
Gwynedd
Newport
Swansea

Torfaen
Wrexham

8 letters:
Anglesey

Bridgend

10 letters:
Caerphilly
Ceredigion

Flintshire

12 letters:
Blaenau Gwent
Denbighshire

13 letters:
Merthyr Tydfil
Monmouthshire
Pembrokeshire

15 letters:
Carmarthenshire

Neath Port Talbot
Vale of Glamorgan

16 letters:
Rhondda, Cynon, Taff

FORMER WELSH COUNTIES

5 letters:
Clwyd
Dyfed
Gwent
Powys

7 letters:
Gwynedd

12 letters:
Mid Glamorgan

13 letters:
West Glamorgan

14 letters:
South Glamorgan

NORTHERN IRISH COUNTIES

4 letters:
Down

6 letters:
Antrim
Armagh
Tyrone

9 letters:
Fermanagh

11 letters:
Londonderry

REPUBLIC OF IRELAND COUNTIES

4 letters:
Cork
Mayo

5 letters:
Cavan
Clare
Kerry
Laois

Louth
Meath
Sligo

6 letters:
Carlow
Dublin
Galway
Offaly

7 letters:
Donegal
Kildare
Leitrim
Wexford
Wicklow

8 letters:
Kilkenny

Limerick
Longford
Monaghan

9 letters:
Roscommon
Tipperary
Waterford
Westmeath

Countries

4 letters:
Chad
Cuba
Fiji
Iran
Iraq
Laos
Mali
Oman
Peru
Togo

5 letters:
Belau
Benin
Chile
Congo
Egypt
Gabon
Ghana
Haiti
India
Italy

Japan
Kenya
Libya
Malta
Nauru
Nepal
Niger
Qatar
Samoa
Spain
Sudan

Syria
Tonga
Wales
Yemen

6 letters:
Angola
Belize
Bhutan
Brazil
Brunei

Canada
Cyprus
France
Gambia
Greece
Guinea
Guyana
Israel
Jordan
Kuwait
Latvia
Malawi
Mexico
Monaco
Norway
Panama
Poland
Russia
Rwanda
Serbia
Sweden
Taiwan
Turkey
Tuvalu
Uganda
Zambia

7 letters:
Albania
Algeria
Andorra
Armenia
Austria
Bahamas
Bahrain
Belarus
Belgium
Bolivia
Burundi
Comoros
Croatia
Denmark
Ecuador
England
Eritrea

Estonia
Finland
Georgia
Germany
Grenada
Hungary
Iceland
Jamaica
Lebanon
Lesotho
Liberia
Moldova
Morocco
Myanmar
Namibia
Nigeria
Romania
Senegal
Somalia
St Lucia
Surinam
Tunisia
Ukraine
Uruguay
Vanuatu
Vietnam

8 letters:
Barbados
Botswana
Bulgaria
Cambodia
Cameroon
Colombia
Djibouti
Dominica
Ethiopia
Honduras
Kiribati
Malaysia
Mongolia
Pakistan
Paraguay
Portugal
Scotland

Slovakia
Slovenia
Sri Lanka
Tanzania
Thailand
Zimbabwe

9 letters:
Argentina
Australia
Cape Verde
Costa Rica
East Timor
Greenland
Guatemala
Indonesia
Kirghizia
Lithuania
Macedonia
Mauritius
Nicaragua
San Marino
Singapore
Swaziland
Venezuela

10 letters:
Azerbaijan
Bangladesh
El Salvador
Kazakhstan
Kyrgyzstan
Luxembourg
Madagascar
Mauritania
Micronesia
Montenegro
Mozambique
New Zealand
North Korea
Puerto Rico
Seychelles
South Korea
Tajikistan
Uzbekistan

Yugoslavia

11 letters:
Afghanistan
Burkina Faso
Côte d'Ivoire
Netherlands
Philippines
Saudi Arabia
Sierra Leone
South Africa
Switzerland
Vatican City

12 letters:
Guinea-Bissau
Turkmenistan

13 letters:
American Samoa
Czech Republic
Liechtenstein
United Kingdom

14 letters:
Papua New Guinea
Solomon Islands

15 letters:
Marshall Islands

Northern Ireland
St Kitts and Nevis

16 letters:
Equatorial Guinea

17 letters:
Antigua and Barbuda
Dominican Republic
Republic of Ireland
Trinidad and Tobago

18 letters:
Republic of Maldives
São Tomé and Principe
United Arab Emirates

20 letters:
Bosnia and Herzegovina

21 letters:
United States of America

22 letters:
Central African Republic
People's Republic of China

25 letters:
St Vincent and the Grenadines

See also:
➤ **Commonwealth members** ➤ **Dependencies** ➤ **European Union** ➤ **Republics**

Cows

2 letters:	**4 letters:**	Muley	Mulley
Zo	Zebu	Stirk	Rother
3 letters:	**5 letters:**	**6 letters:**	**7 letters:**
Dun	Colly	Crummy	Kouprey
Zho	Kyloe	Dexter	Redpoll
	Milch	Heifer	
	Mooly	Jersey	

8 letters:
Alderney
Galloway
Guernsey
Hereford

9 letters:
Charolais
Red Sindhi
Simmental
Teeswater

11 letters:
Rother-beast

See also:
➤ **Cattle, breeds of**

Crafts

5 letters:
Batik

6 letters:
Sewing

7 letters:
Crochet
Macramé
Pottery
Weaving

8 letters:
Basketry
Ceramics
Knitting
Knotwork
Quilling
Quilting
Spinning
Tapestry

9 letters:
Decoupage
Patchwork

10 letters:
Crewelwork
Embroidery
Raffia work
Sugarcraft
Wickerwork

11 letters:
Calligraphy
Cloisonnage
Dressmaking
Needlepoint

12 letters:
Basket-making

15 letters:
Flower arranging

Cricket

CRICKETERS

3 letters:
Dev, *Kapil*
Fry, *C(harles) B(urgess)*
May, *Peter*

4 letters:
Ames, *Leslie*
Bird, *Richard 'Dicky'*
Boon, *David*
Cook, *Alastair*
Hick, *Graham*
Khan, *Imran*
Lara, *Brian*
Lock, *Tony*
Snow, *John*
Vaas, *Chaminda*

5 letters:
Broad, *Stuart*
Croft, *Colin*
Dhoni, *Mahendra Singh*
Evans, *Godfrey*
Gooch, *Graham*
Gough, *Darren*
Gower, *David*
Grace, *W(illiam) G(ilbert)*
Greig, *Tony*
Hobbs, *Sir Jack*
Knott, *Alan*
Laker, *Jim*
Lloyd, *Clive Hubert*
Marsh, *Rodney*
Patil, *Sandeep Madhusuda*
Prior, *Matthew*
Singh, *Harbhajan*

Singh, *Yuvraj*
Smith, *M(ichael) J(ohn) K(night)*
Tyson, *Frank*
Walsh, *Courtney*
Warne, *Shane*
Waugh, *Mark*
Waugh, *Steve*

6 letters:
Akhtar, *Shoaib*
Bailey, *Trevor*
Barnes, *Sydney*
Benaud, *Richie*
Bishan, *Bedi*
Border, *Allan*
Botham, *Ian*
Cronje, *Hansie*
Dexter, *Ted*
Donald, *Allan*
Dravid, *Rahul*
Flower, *Andrew*
Garner, *Joel*
Hadlee, *Sir Richard*
Hayden, *Matthew*
Haynes, *Desmond*
Hutton, *Sir Len*
Kallis, *Jacques*
Kambli, *Vinod*
Kumble, *Anil*
Laxman, *V(angipurappu) V(enkata) S(ai)*
Lillee, *Dennis*
Loader, *Peter*
Mankad, *Mulvantrai Himatlal 'Vinoo'*
McCabe, *Stanley*
Olonga, *Henry*
Rhodes, *Jonty*
Sehwag, *Virender*
Sobers, *Sir Garfield*
Styris, *Scott*
Thorpe, *Graham*
Turner, *Glenn*
Wardle, *Johnny*
Weekes, *Sir Everton*
Younis, *Waqar*

7 letters:
Ambrose, *Curtly*
Boycott, *Geoffrey*
Bradman, *Sir Donald*
Compton, *Denis*
Cowdrey, *Sir Colin*
Dilshan, *Tillakaratne*
Fleming, *Stephen*
Gambhir, *Gautum*
Ganguly, *Sourav*
Gatting, *Mike*
Hammond, *Walter*
Hussein, *Nasser*
Jardine, *Douglas*
Larwood, *Harold*
Malinga, *Lasith*
McGrath, *Glenn*
Miandad, *Javed*
O'Reilly, *Bill*
Pollock, *Shaun*
Srinath, *Javagal*
Statham, *Brian*
Stewart, *Alec*
Strauss, *Andrew*
Thomson, *Jeffrey*
Trueman, *Fred*
Tufnell, *Phil*
Umrigar, *Pahelam Ratanji*
Wadekar, *Ajit Laxman*
Walcott, *Sir Clyde*
Worrell, *Sir Frank*

8 letters:
Amarnath, *Lala*
Amarnath, *Mohinder*
Amarnath, *Surinder*
Anderson, *James (Jimmy)*
Atherton, *Mike*
Brearley, *Michael*
Chappell, *Greg*
Chappell, *Ian*
Gavaskar, *Sunil*
Graveney, *Tom*
Houghton, *Dave*
Lindwall, *Ray*

Marshall, *Malcolm*
Mohammad, *Hanif*
Richards, *Viv*

9 letters:
D'Oliveira, *Basil Lewis*
Gilchrist, *Adam*
Gillespie, *Jason*
Greenidge, *Gordon*
Manjrekar, *Sanjay Vijay*
Ranatunga, *Arjuna*
Sutcliffe, *Herbert*
Tendulkar, *Sachin*
Underwood, *Derek*

10 letters:
Azharuddin, *Mohammed*
Barrington, *Ken*

Greatbatch, *Mark*
Jayasuriya, *Sanath*
Sangakkara, *Kumar*
Vengsarkar, *Dilip Balwant*

11 letters:
Heyhoe-Flint, *Rachel*
Jayawardene, *Mahela*
Trescothick, *Marcus*

12 letters:
Inzamam-ul-Haq
Muralitharan, *Muttiah*
Ranjitsinhji, *K(umar) S(hri)*

13 letters:
Chandrasekhar, *Bhagwat Subramaniam*

CRICKET TERMS

2 letters:
In

3 letters:
Bat
Bye
Cut
Out
Pad
Run
Six

4 letters:
Bail
Ball
Bowl
Duck
Edge
Four
Hook
Over
Pull
Seam
Slip
Spin

Wide

5 letters:
Ashes
Catch
Drive
Extra
Glide
Gully
Mid on
Pitch
Stump
Sweep
Swing
Umpie

6 letters:
Appeal
Bowled
Bowler
Bumper
Caught
Covers
Crease
Doosra

Glance
Googly
Leg bye
Long on
Maiden
Mid off
No ball
On side
Opener
Run out
Single
Slider
Snicko
Teesra
Umpire
Wicket
Yorker

7 letters:
Arm ball
Batsman
Bouncer
Century
Declare
Fielder

Fine leg
Flipper
Fly slip
Hawk-eye®
Hot spot
Innings
Leg side
Leg slip
Long hop
Long leg
Long off
Off side
Stumped

8 letters:
Bodyline
Boundary
Chinaman
Follow on
Full toss
Leg break
Off break
Short leg
Third man

9 letters:
Fieldsman
Hit wicket
Mid wicket
Slog sweep
Square leg
Test match

10 letters:
Cover point
Extra cover
Fast bowler
Golden duck

Maiden over
Silly mid on
Topspinner
Twelfth man

11 letters:
Backspinner
Silly mid off
Snickometer

12 letters:
Twenty-Twenty
Wicketkeeper

13 letters:
Nightwatchman

14 letters:
Duckworth-Lewis
Opening batsman

15 letters:
Leg before wicket

Crime terms

2 letters:
Do
Go

3 letters:
GBH
Job
Rap
Sin

4 letters:
Abet
Gaol
Heat
Jail
Life
Rape
View

5 letters:
Admit
Alibi
Arson
Atone
Bribe
Caper
Cough
Crime
Do for

Fraud
Guilt
Panel
Remit
Steal
Sting
Theft
Thief
TWOC

6 letters:
Acquit
Bigamy
Charge
Commit
Degree
Detect
Exposé
Felony
Finger
Guilty
Hijack
Incest
Indict
Infect
Murder
Piracy
Punish
Record

Turn in
Verbal
Wanted

7 letters:
Assault
Battery
Bribery
Burglar
Confess
Convict
Cover-up
Find out
Forgery
Impeach
Larceny
Mugging
Offence
Penance
Pentito
Perjury
Robbery
Soldier
Treason
Villain

8 letters:
Acqittal
Barratry

Burglary
Conspire
Criminal
Homicide
Infamous
Innocent
Litigate
Murderer
Offender
Penology
Poaching
Prisoner
Sabotage
Stalking
Thriller
Tu quoque
War crime

9 letters:
Accessory
Admission
Blackmail
Blasphemy
Criminate
Desertion
Detective
Embracery
Extortion
Guiltless

Hate crime
Implicate
Innocence
Inside job
Not proven
Penal code
Pilfering
Principal
Red-handed
Terrorism
Vandalism
Whodunnit
Wrongdoer

10 letters:
Accomplice
Accusation
Bail bandit
Commission
Commitment
Conspiracy
Conviction
Corruption
Cybercrime
Delinquent
Entrapment
Indictable
Indictment
Kidnapping
Litigation

Misconduct
Perpetrate
Petty theft
Punishment
Recidivism

11 letters:
Conspirator
Criminology
Delinquency
Hooliganism
Incriminate
Infanticide
Investigate
Law-and-order
Lawlessness
Premeditate

12 letters:
Death penalty
Denunciation
Embezzlement
Extraditable
Life sentence
Manslaughter
Misadventure
Misdemeanour

13 letters:
Drug smuggling

Housebreaking
Identity theft
Premeditation
Public nuisance
Reinvestigate
Transgression

15 letters:
Computer hacking
Crime passionnel
Indecent assault
Victimless crime

16 letters:
Bill of indictment
Culpable homicide
Private detective
White-collar crime

17 letters:
Capital punishment

19 letters:
Justifiable homicide

20 letters:
Identification parade

21 letters:
Corporate manslaughter

Crime writers

3 letters:
Poe, *Edgar Allan*

4 letters:
Kerr, *Philip*
Vine, *Barbara*

5 letters:
Block, *Lawrence*
Child, *Lee*
Doyle, *Arthur Conan*
James, *P(hyllis) D(orothy)*

Nesbø, *Jo*

6 letters:
Dexter, *Colin*
Greene, *Graham*
Peters, *Ellis*
Rankin, *Ian*
Sayers, *Dorothy L(eigh)*

7 letters:
Andrews, *Sarah*
Bateman, *Colin*

Crispin, *Edmund*
Francis, *Dick*
Grisham, *John*
Hammett, *Dashiell*
Hiaasen, *Carl*
Larsson, *Stieg*
Mankell, *Henning*
Rendell, *Ruth*
Simenon, *Georges (Joseph Christian)*
Wallace, *Edgar (Richard Horatio)*

8 letters:
Chandler, *Raymond*
Christie, *Dame Agatha (Mary Clarissa)*
Connelly, *Michael*
Connolly, *John*

Cornwell, *Patricia*
Friedman, *Kinky*
McDermid, *Val*
Mitchell, *Gladys*

9 letters:
Allingham, *Margery*
Brookmyre, *Christopher*
Highsmith, *Patricia*
Patterson, *James*

10 letters:
Wiesenthal, *Simon*

11 letters:
McCall Smith, *Alexander*

Critics

4 letters:
Agee, *James*
Frye, *Northrop*
Ross, *Jonathan*
Said, *Edward*
Self, *Will*
Shaw, *George Bernard*

5 letters:
Bloom, *Harold*
Booth, *Wayne*
Burke, *Kenneth*
Carey, *John*
De Man, *Paul*
Greer, *Bonnie*
Greer, *Germaine*
Hegel, *Georg W(ilhelm) F(riedrich)*
Lodge, *David (John)*
Plato
Ronay, *Egon*
Tynan, *Kenneth*
Weber, *Max*
Woolf, *(Adeline) Virginia*

6 letters:
Barker, *Harley Granville*

Berlin, *Isaiah*
Bhabha, *Homi K.*
Brooks, *Cleanth*
Clarke, *Oz*
Horace
Lawson, *Mark*
Leavis, *F(rank) R(aymond)*
Milnes, *Rodney*
Morley, *Paul*
Norman, *Barry*
Norman, *Emma*
Orwell, *George*
Parker, *Dorothy*
Paulin, *Tom*
Ruskin, *John*
Sartre, *Jean-Paul*
Sewell, *Brian*
Sontag, *Susan*

7 letters:
Bakhtin, *Mikhail*
Barthes, *Roland*
Carlyle, *Thomas*
Chomsky, *Noam*
Derrida, *Jacques*
Forster, *E(dward) M(organ)*

Goolden, *Jilly*
Kermode, *Frank*
Nabokov, *Vladimir (Vladimirovich)*

8 letters:
Benjamin, *Walter*
Bradbury, *Malcolm*
Eagleton, *Terry*
Foucault, *Michel*
Longinus
Plotinus
Sedgwick, *Eve Kosofsky*

9 letters:
Aristotle

Showalter, *Elaine*
Winterson, *Jeanette*

10 letters:
De Beauvoir, *Simone*
Greenblatt, *Stephen*
Lewis-Smith, *Victor*

11 letters:
Bogdanovich, *Peter*

12 letters:
Wittgenstein, *Ludwig*

Crosses

3 letters:
Red
Tau

4 letters:
Ankh
Crux
Iona
Iron
Rood
Tree

5 letters:
Fiery
Greek
Latin
Papal
Pommé
Rouen

6 letters:
Ansate
Barbée
Botone
Celtic
Chiasm
Fitché

Fleury
Fylfot
Geneva
George
Graded (Calvary)
Moline
Pattée
Potent
Raguly
Trefly

7 letters:
Botonne
Calvary
Chiasma
Eleanor
Maltese
Patonce
Potence
Rarulée
Saltier
Saltire

8 letters:
Cercelée
Crosslet
Crucifix

Globical
Holy rood
Lorraine
Military
Millvine
Pectoral
Quadrate
Southern
St Peter's
Svastika
Swastika
Victoria

9 letters:
Encolpion
Jerusalem
St Andrew's
St George's

10 letters:
Canterbury
Clover-leaf
Crux ansata
St Anthony's

11 letters:
Constantine

Patriarchal

12 letters:
Pattée formée

13 letters:
Cross crosslet

14 letters:
Archiepiscopal

15 letters:
Russian Orthodox

Crustaceans

4 letters:
Crab
Craw

5 letters:
Koura
Krill
Prawn

6 letters:
Cyprid
Cypris
Isopod
Marron
Scampi
Scampo
Shrimp
Slater

7 letters:
Camaron
Copepod
Cyclops
Decapod

Foot-jaw
Gribble
Limulus
Lobster
Macrura
Squilla

8 letters:
Amphipod
Barnacle
Cirriped
Cirripid
Crawfish
Crayfish
Cumacean
Decapoda
King crab
Land crab
Nauplius
Nephrops
Pagurian
Sand flea
Scorpion

9 letters:
Beach flea
Cirripede
Euphausia
Fishlouse
King prawn
Langouste
Ostracoda
Phyllopod
Schizopod
Sea spider
Water flea
Woodlouse

10 letters:
Brachyuran
Cladoceran
Hermit crab
Oyster crab
Robber crab
Sand hopper
Sand shrimp
Spider crab
Stomatopod

11 letters:
Langoustine
Rock lobster

12 letters:
Branchiopoda
Entomostraca
Spiny lobster

13 letters:
Goose barnacle
Horseshoe crab
Malacostracan
Norway lobster
Opossum shrimp
Rhizocephalan
Soft-shell crab

14 letters:
Dublin Bay prawn

16 letters:
Freshwater shrimp

Crystals

4 letters:
Lead
Rock
Spar

5 letters:
Beryl
Druse
Glass

Macle
Nicol
Prism
Purin

6 letters:
Liquid
Purine
Quartz

Silica

7 letters:
Baccara
Cumarin
Epitaxy

8 letters:
Baccarat

Coumarin
Dendrite
Jarosite
Melamine
Pinacoid
Pinakoid
Sorbitol
Trichite
Trilling

9 letters:
Hemitrope
Love-arrow
Rubicelle
Snowflake

Triclinic
Xenocryst

10 letters:
Phenocryst

Rhinestone
Watch-glass

12 letters:
Enantiomorph

15 letters:
Allotriomorphic

Cupboards and cabinets

4 letters:
Safe

5 letters:
Ambry
Chest
Press
Shelf
Stand

6 letters:
Buffet
Bureau
Closet
Dooket
Drawer

Larder
Locker
Lowboy
Pantry

7 letters:
Armoire
Cabinet
Commode
Console
Dresser
Étagère
Highboy
Tallboy
Vitrine
Whatnot

8 letters:
Bookcase
Cellaret
Credenza
Wardrobe

9 letters:
Garderobe
Sideboard

10 letters:
Canterbury
Chiffonier
Encoignure

11 letters:
Chiffonnier

12 letters:
Chest-on-chest
Clothes-press
Welsh dresser

13 letters:
Court cupboard
Credence table
Filing cabinet
Medicine chest

14 letters:
Chest of drawers
Coolgardie safe

Cups and other drinking vessels

3 letters:
Cup
Mug
Nut
Pot
Tig
Tot
Tyg

4 letters:
Dish
Horn

5 letters:
Calix
Cruse
Cylix
Glass

Hanap
Kylix
Tazza

6 letters:
Beaker
Copita
Cotyle
Fingan
Finjan
Goblet
Loving
Noggin
Porrón
Quaich
Rhyton
Tassie

7 letters:
Canteen
Chalice
Cyathus
Scyphus
Stirrup
Tankard
Tea-dish
Tumbler

8 letters:
Pannikin
Schooner
Tantalus
Tastevin

9 letters:
Cantharus

Demitasse
Moustache

10 letters:
Monstrance

11 letters:
Water bottle

14 letters:
Champagne flute

Cups and trophies

2 letters:
FA

4 letters:
UEFA

5 letters:
Davis
Fairs
Ryder
World

8 letters:
America's
Calcutta
European

Currencies

Country	Currency
Afghanistan	Afghani
Albania	Lek
Algeria	Algerian dinar
Andorra	Euro
Angola	Kwanza
Antigua and Barbuda	East Caribbean dollar
Argentina	Peso
Armenia	Dram
Australia	Australian dollar
Austria	Euro
Azerbaijan	Manat
Bahamas	Bahamian dollar
Bahrain	Dinar
Bangladesh	Taka
Barbados	Barbados dollar
Belarus	Rouble
Belgium	Euro
Belize	Belize dollar
Benin	CFA franc
Bhutan	Ngultrum
Bolivia	Boliviano
Bosnia-Herzegovina	Convertible marka
Botswana	Pula
Brazil	Real
Brunei	Brunei dollar
Bulgaria	Lev
Burkina-Faso	CFA franc
Burundi	Burundi franc
Cambodia	Riel
Cameroon	CFA franc
Canada	Canadian dollar
Cape Verde	Escudo
Central African Republic	CFA franc

Country	Currency
Chad	CFA franc
Chile	Peso
China	Yuan
Colombia	Peso
Comoros	Comorian franc
Congo (Democratic Republic of)	Congolese franc
Congo (Republic of)	CFA franc
Costa Rica	Cólon
Côte d'Ivoire	CFA franc
Croatia	Kuna
Cuba	Peso
Cyprus	Euro
Czech Republic	Koruna
Denmark	Krone
Djibouti	Djibouti franc
Dominica	East Caribbean dollar
Dominican Republic	Peso
East Timor	US dollar
Ecuador	US dollar
Egypt	Pound
El Salvador	Cólon
Equatorial Guinea	CFA franc
Eritrea	Nakfa
Estonia	Euro
Ethiopia	Birr
Fiji	Fiji dollar
Finland	Euro
France	Euro
French Guiana	French franc
Gabon	CFA franc
Gambia	Dalasi
Germany	Euro
Ghana	Cedi
Greece	Euro
Greenland	Danish krone
Grenada	East Caribbean dollar
Guatemala	Quetzal
Guinea	Guinea franc
Guinea-Bissau	CFA franc
Guyana	Guyana dollar
Haiti	Gourde
Honduras	Lempira
Hungary	Forint
Iceland	Krona

Country	Currency
India	Rupee
Indonesia	Rupiah
Iran	Rial
Iraq	Dinar
Ireland (Republic of)	Euro
Israel	Shekel
Italy	Euro
Jamaica	Jamaican dollar
Japan	Yen
Jordan	Dinar
Kazakhstan	Tenge
Kenya	Shilling
Kirghizia	Som
Kiribati	Australian dollar
Kosovo	Dinar; euro
Kuwait	Dinar
Kyrgyzstan	Som
Laos	Kip
Latvia	Lat
Lebanon	Pound
Lesotho	Loti
Liberia	Liberian dollar
Libya	Dinar
Liechtenstein	Swiss franc
Lithuania	Litas
Luxembourg	Euro
Macedonia	Denar
Madagascar	Malagasy franc
Malawi	Kwacha
Malaysia	Ringgit
Maldives (Republic of)	Rufiyaa
Mali	CFA franc
Malta	Euro
Marshall Islands	US dollar
Mauritania	Ouguiya
Mauritius	Rupee
Mexico	Peso
Micronesia	US dollar
Moldova	Leu
Monaco	Euro
Mongolia	Tugrik
Montenegro	Euro
Montserrat	East Caribbean dollar
Morocco	Dirham

Country	Currency
Mozambique	Metical
Myanmar	Kyat
Namibia	Namibian dollar
Nauru	Australian dollar
Nepal	Rupee
Netherlands	Euro
New Zealand	New Zealand dollar
Nicaragua	Córdoba
Niger	CFA franc
Nigeria	Naira
North Korea	Won
Norway	Krone
Oman	Rial
Pakistan	Rupee
Palau	US dollar
Panama	Balboa
Papua New Guinea	Kina
Paraguay	Guarani
Peru	New sol
Philippines	Philippine peso
Poland	Zloty
Portugal	Euro
Qatar	Riyal
Romania	Leu
Russia	Rouble
Rwanda	Rwanda franc
St Kitts and Nevis	East Caribbean dollar
St Lucia	East Caribbean dollar
St Vincent and the Grenadines	East Caribbean dollar
Samoa	Tala
San Marino	Euro
São Tomé and Principe	Dobra
Saudi Arabia	Riyal
Senegal	CFA franc
Seychelles	Rupee
Sierra Leone	Leone
Singapore	Singapore dollar
Slovakia	Euro
Slovenia	Euro
Solomon Islands	Solomon Islands dollar
Somalia	Shilling
South Africa	Rand
South Korea	Won
Spain	Euro

Country	Currency
Sri Lanka	Rupee
Sudan	Dinar
Surinam	Guilder
Swaziland	Lilangeni
Sweden	Krona
Switzerland	Swiss franc
Syria	Pound
Taiwan	Taiwan dollar
Tajikistan	Somoni
Tanzania	Shilling
Thailand	Baht
Togo	CFA franc
Tonga	Pa'anga
Trinidad and Tobago	Trinidad and Tobago dollar
Tunisia	Dinar
Turkey	Turkish lira
Turkmenistan	Manat
Tuvalu	Australian dollar
Uganda	Shilling
Ukraine	Hryvna
United Arab Emirates	Dirham
United Kingdom	Pound sterling
United States of America	US dollar
Uruguay	Peso
Uzbekistan	Sum
Vanuatu	Vatu
Vatican City	Euro
Venezuela	Bolívar
Vietnam	Dong
Yemen	Riyal
Yugoslavia (Serbia)	Dinar
Zambia	Kwacha
Zimbabwe	Zimbabwe dollar

Curries

4 letters:
Dhal
Phal

5 letters:
Balti
Bhuna
Kofta

Korma
Tikka

6 letters:
Achari
Bhoona
Chasni
Karahi

Madras
Masala
Pathia
Sambar

7 letters:
Biryani
Dhansak

Dopiaza
Jaipuri
Nentara
Pasanda
Red Thai

8 letters:
Jalfrezi

Massaman
Phanaeng
Tandoori
Vindaloo

9 letters:
Green Thai
Rogan josh

9 letters:
Yellow Thai

11 letters:
Tikka masala

Cutting tools

3 letters:
Axe
Bit
Saw

4 letters:
Adze

5 letters:
Dicer
Flymo®
Lance
Mower

6 letters:
Carver
Chisel
Grater
Jigsaw
Padsaw
Ripsaw
Scythe
Shaver
Shears
Sickle

7 letters:
Chopper

Cleaver
Coulter
Handsaw
Scissor

8 letters:
Engraver

9 letters:
Secateurs

11 letters:
Ploughshare

Dd

Dams

4 letters:
Guri
Hume
Pati

5 letters:
Aswan
Nurek
Rogun

6 letters:
Hoover
Inguri
Itaipu

Kariba
Vaiont

7 letters:
Benmore

8 letters:
Chapetón

9 letters:
Aswan High

10 letters:
Glen Canyon

11 letters:
Grand Coulee
Three Gorges

13 letters:
Grande Dixence
Vishvesvaraya

16 letters:
Syncrude Tailings

Dance

DANCES

3 letters:
Fan
Gig
Hay
Hey
Ice
Jig
Lap
Pas
Poi
Sun
Tap
Toe
War

4 letters:
Alma

Ball
Barn
Bump
Clog
Dump
Fado
Folk
Foot
Fris
Frug
Giga
Go-go
Haka
Hora
Hula
Jive
Jota

Juba
Juke
Kolo
Lion
Mosh
Nach
Pogo
Polo
Rave
Reel
Shag
Slam
Soca
Spin
Stag
Step
Taxi

Trip

5 letters:
Belly
Bogle
Brawl
Break
Caper
Carol
Ceili
Ceroc®
Conga
Disco
Dolin
Fling
Furry
Galop

Ghost
Gigue
Gopak
Horah
Limbo
Loure
Mambo
Mooch
Natch
Paspy
Pavan
Paven
Pavin
Polka
Raver
Round
Rumba
Salsa
Samba
Shake
Skank
Snake
Stomp
Strut
Sword
Tango
Twist
Valse
Vogue
Volta
Waltz
Whirl

6 letters:
Almain
Apache
Ballet
Bolero
Boogie
Boston
Branle
Canary
Cancan
Cha-cha
Do-si-do

Fading
Floral
Friska
German
Gigolo
Hustle
Jump-up
Kathak
Lavolt
Maenad
Maxixe
Minuet
Morris
Nautch
Oberek
Pavane
Petipa
Redowa
Shimmy
Spring
Square
Trophe
Valeta
Veleta
Watusi
Zapata

7 letters:
Baladin
Ballant
Beguine
Bourrée
Bransle
Brantle
Calypso
Cantico
Capuera
Carioca
Ceilidh
Coranto
Cossack
Country
Courant
Csardas
Czardas

Farruca
Forlana
Foxtrot
Furlana
Gavotte
Halling
Hetaera
Hetaira
Hoedown
Lambada
Lancers
Ländler
Lavolta
Macaber
Macabre
Maypole
Mazurka
Moresco
Morisco
Morrice
Moshing
Musette
Old-time
One-step
Pericon
Planxty
Polacca
Popping
Pyrrhic
Ridotto
Romaika
Roundel
Roundle
Sardana
Sashaya
Saunter
Shuffle
St Vitus
Tanagra
Tordion
Trenise
Trip hop
Two-step
Watutsi
Ziganka

8 letters:
Baladine
Ballroom
Bayadère
Boogaloo
Bunny hug
Cachucha
Cakewalk
Canticoy
Capoeira
Chaconne
Corybant
Coryphee
Cotillon
Courante
Egg-dance
Excuse-me
Fandango
Flamenco
Flip-flop
Galliard
Habanera
Hardcore
Hay-de-guy
Haymaker
Heythrop
Hoolican
Hornpipe
Hula-hula
Irish jig
Joncanoe
Junkanoo
Kantikoy
Kazachok
Kazatzka
Krumping
Lindy hop
Macarena
Marinera
Matachin
Medicine
Merengue
Murciana
Orchesis
Pierette

Rigadoon
Rigaudon
Robotics
Ronggeng
Saraband
Snowball
Soft-shoe
Toyi-toyi
Trippant
Trucking
Vogueing

9 letters:
Allemande
Ballabile
Bergamask
Bergomask
Bossa nova
Breakdown
Butterfly
Caballero
Cha-cha-cha
Cotillion
Ecossaise
Eightsome
Farandole
Formation
Gallopade
Hoolachan
Jitterbug
Kathakali
Malagueña
Pas de deux
Paso doble
Passepied
Paul Jones
Polonaise
Poussette
Quadrille

Quickstep
Ring-shout
Roundelay
Siciliano
Sink-a-pace
Sugarfoot
Tambourin
Tripudium
Variation
Zapateado

10 letters:
Antimasque
Breakdance
Carmagnole
Charleston
Cinque-pace
Corroboree
Gay Gordons
Hay-de-guise
Hay-de-guyes
Hey-de-guise
Hokey cokey
Nautch-girl
Passamezzo
Petronella
Saltarello
Seguidilla
Sicilienne
Sinke-a-pace
Strathspey
Tarantella
Trenchmore
Tripudiate
Turkey trot
Tyrolienne

11 letters:
Antistrophe

Black bottom
Body popping
Buck and wing
Contradance
Contredanse
Cracovienne
Lambeth walk
Palais glide
Passacaglia
Pastourelle
Schottische
Shimmy-shake
Terpsichore
Varsovienne

12 letters:
Bharat Natyam
Labanotation
Passemeasure
Passy-measure
Robot dancing
Saltatorious
Virginia reel

13 letters:
Eightsome reel
Highland fling

14 letters:
Jack-in-the-green
Strip the willow

18 letters:
Sir Roger de Coverley

20 letters:
Dashing White Sergeant

GENERAL DANCE STEPS AND TERMS

3 letters:		**4 letters:**	
Box	Set	Lock	Time
Pas		Spin	

5 letters:
Basic
Glide
Score
Steps

6 letters:
Chaine
Chassé
Dosado
Dosido
Gancho

In step
Phrase
Rhythm

7 letters:
Feather
Pas seul
Routine
Shuffle

8 letters:
Enchufla

Heel turn
Keep step
Moonwalk
Sequence
Slip step
Telemark

9 letters:
Out of step
Promenade

10 letters:
Grand chain
Pigeonwing

11 letters:
Comprimario
Pas de basque
Progressive

12 letters:
Choreography

See also:
➤ **Ballet**   ➤ **Ballet steps and terms**

Degrees

Degree	Abbreviation
Bachelor of Agriculture	BAgr
Bachelor of Arts	BA
Bachelor of Commerce	BCom
Bachelor of Dental Surgery	BDS
Bachelor of Divinity	BD
Bachelor of Education	BEd
Bachelor of Engineering	BEng
Bachelor of Law	BL
Bachelor of Laws	LLB
Bachelor of Letters	BLitt
Bachelor of Medicine	BM *or* MB
Bachelor of Music	BMus, MusB, *or* MusBac
Bachelor of Pharmacy	BPharm
Bachelor of Philosophy	BPhil
Bachelor of Science	BSc
Bachelor of Surgery	BS
Diploma in Education	DipEd
Doctor of Dental Surgery *or* Science	DDS *or* DDSc
Doctor of Divinity	DD
Doctor of Laws	LLD
Doctor of Letters *or* Literature	DLitt *or* LittD
Doctor of Medicine	MD
Doctor of Music	DMus, MusD, *or* MusDoc
Doctor of Philosophy	PhD
Higher National Certificate	HNC

Higher National Diploma	HND
Master of Arts	MA
Master of Education	MEd
Master of Laws	LLM
Master of Letters	MLitt
Master of Music	MMus
Master of Philosophy	MPhil
Master of Science	MSc
Master of Surgery	MCh
Master of Technology	MTech
Ordinary National Certificate	ONC
Ordinary National Diploma	OND

Dependencies

4 letters:
Guam
Niue

5 letters:
Aruba
Macau (S.A.R.)
Undof

6 letters:
Jersey

7 letters:
Bermuda
Mayotte
Réunion
Tokelau

8 letters:
Anguilla
Guernsey
Hong Kong (S.A.R.)
Jan Mayen
Svalbard

9 letters:
Aksai Chin
East Timor
Gibraltar
Greenland

Isle of Man
Wake Atoll

10 letters:
Antarctica
Guadeloupe
Martinique
Montserrat
Puerto Rico

11 letters:
Baker Island
Cook Islands
Kingman Reef
Saint Helena

12 letters:
Bouvet Island
Cocos Islands
Europa Island
Faroe Islands
French Guiana
Jarvis Island
New Caledonia
Palmyra Atoll

13 letters:
American Samoa
Bassas da India
Cayman Islands

Howland Island
Islas Malvinas
Johnston Atoll
Midway Islands
Navassa Island
Norfolk Island
Virgin Islands

14 letters:
Keeling Islands
Paracel Islands
Spratly Islands
Tromelin Island

15 letters:
Christmas Island
Coral Sea Islands
Falkland Islands
French Polynesia
Glorioso Islands
Pitcairn Islands
Wallis and Futuna

16 letters:
Clipperton Island
Juan de Nova Island

19 letters:
Netherlands Antilles

20 letters:
British Virgin Islands

21 letters:
Turks and Caicos
  Islands

22 letters:
Northern Mariana
  Islands
Saint Pierre and Miquelon

24 letters:
Ashmore and Cartier Islands

27 letters:
British Indian Ocean Territory

29 letters:
Heard Island and McDonald Islands

31 letters:
French Southern and Antarctic Lands

38 letters:
South Georgia and the South Sandwich
  Islands

Deserts

4 letters:
Gobi
Thar

6 letters:
Gibson
Libyan
Mohave
Mojave
Nubian
Sahara
Sertao

7 letters:
Arabian
Atacama
Kara Kum

8 letters:
Kalahari
Kyzyl Kum

9 letters:
Dasht-e-Lut
Dasht-i-Lut

10 letters:
Great Sandy
Rub'al Khali

11 letters:
Death Valley

13 letters:
Great Victoria

15 letters:
Taklimakan Shama

Desserts and sweet dishes

3 letters:
Ice
Pav
Pud

4 letters:
Duff
Eve's
Fool
Milk
Plum
Rice
Sago

Suet
Tart
Whip

5 letters:
Black
Bombe
Coupe
Crème
Crêpe
Hasty
Jello
Jelly

Kulfi
Pease
Slump
Sweet
Tansy
Torte

6 letters:
Afters
Blintz
Gâteau
Junket
Kissel

Mousse
Panada
Pashka
Queen's
Sorbet
Sowens
Sponge
Stodge
Summer
Sundae
Trifle
Yogurt

7 letters:
Cabinet
Caramel
Cassata
Cobbler
College
Compote
Crumble
Custard
Dessert
Fondant
Fritter
Furmety
Furmity
Panocha
Parfait
Pavlova
Popover
Pudding
Sabayon
Soufflé
Spumone
Spumoni
Steamed
Strudel
Tapioca
Tartlet

8 letters:
Bavarois
Cocktail
Dumpling
Flummery
Fromenty
Fruit cup
Frumenty

Furmenty
Ice cream
Pandowdy
Plum duff
Roly-poly
Semolina
Sillabub
Stickjaw
Syllabub
Tiramisu
Vacherin
Water ice

9 letters:
Charlotte
Christmas
Cranachan
Shortcake
White hass
Yorkshire

10 letters:
Blancmange
Brown Betty
Cheesecake
Fruit salad
Nesselrode
Peach Melba
Shoofly pie
Tarte tatin
White hause
White hawse
Zabaglione

11 letters:
Athole Brose

Atholl Brose
Baked Alaska
Banana split
Crème brûlée
Easter-ledge
Spotted dick
Tutti-frutti

12 letters:
Butterscotch
Crème caramel
Crêpe suzette
Île Flottante

13 letters:
Bavarian cream
Marrons glacés

14 letters:
Bread and butter
Charlotte russe

15 letters:
Clootie dumpling

16 letters:
Death by chocolate

17 letters:
Black Forest gateau
Mississippi mud pie

18 letters:
Knickerbocker glory
Neapolitan ice cream

Detectives

4 letters:
Monk

7 letters:
Maigret

Spender
Taggart

8 letters:
Ironside

Sam Spade

9 letters:
Dick Tracy
Donald Lam

Jack Regan
Joe Friday
Lew Archer
Nancy Drew
Nero Wolfe
Vic Mackey

10 letters:
Jane Marple
Mike Hammer
Paul Temple
Perry Mason

11 letters:
Charlie Chan
Ellery Queen
Father Brown
Jim Bergerac
Jim Rockford
Lord Peter Wimsey
Travis McGee

12 letters:
George Carter
Jimmy McNulty
Sergeant Cuff
Simon Templar
V I Warshawski

13 letters:
Albert Campion
C Auguste Dupin
Hercule Poirot
Jonathan Creek
Kinky Friedman
Kurt Wallander
Philip Marlowe

14 letters:
Brother Cadfael
Charlie Resnick
Inspector Morse
Inspector Rebus

Sherlock Holmes

15 letters:
Eddie Shoestring
Inspector Bucket
Lieutenant Kojak

16 letters:
Inspector Wexford

17 letters:
Inspector Clouseau
Inspector Lestrade
Lieutenant Columbo
Marcus Didius Falco

19 letters:
Commissario Brunetti

Devils and demons

4 letters:
Beng

5 letters:
Hades
Iblis
Satan

6 letters:
Belial
Mammon

Plutus

7 letters:
Abaddon
Bheliar
Clootie
Gehenna
Lucifer
Mastema
Old Nick
Sammael

Shaitan

8 letters:
Apollyon
Baphomet
Diabolos
Diabolus

9 letters:
Beelzebub
Cacodemon

Old Cloots

10 letters:
Demogorgon
Lord of Lies
Malebolgia

14 letters:
Mephistopheles

Dialects

2 letters:
Wu

3 letters:
Eye
Min

Twi

4 letters:
Amoy
Burr
Erse

Manx
Norn
Pedi
Taal
Tyke

5 letters:
Attic
Doric
Eldin
Eolic
Ionic

Joual
Koine
Ladin
Scots

6 letters:
Aeolic
Basuto
Damara
Gascon
Khalka
Mackem
Norman
Parsee
Patois
Picard
Scouse
Syriac
Tuscan

7 letters:
Arcadic
Brummie
Chicano
Cockney
Estuary

Geechee
Geordie
Jockney
Konkani
Lallands
Prakrit
Riffian
Romansh
Yealdon

8 letters:
Friulian
Hegelian
Pitmatic
Romansch
Yenglish
Yinglish

9 letters:
Alemannic
Castillian
Landsmaal
Langue d'oc
Low German
Potteries
Ruthenian

10 letters:
Franconian
Langue d'oil
Langue d'oui

11 letters:
Appalachian
Langobardic
Maltenglish

12 letters:
Gallo-Romance
Old Icelandic

13 letters:
Rhaeto-Romance

14 letters:
Hiberno-English
Old North French

19 letters:
Black Country English

21 letters:
Received Pronunciation

Diarists

3 letters:
Nin, *Anaïs*

4 letters:
Gide, *André (Paul Guillaume)*

5 letters:
Frank, *Anne*
Pepys, *Samuel*

6 letters:
Burney, *Fanny*
Evelyn, *John*

7 letters:
Kilvert, *Francis*

8 letters:
Fielding, *Helen (Bridget Jones)*
Townsend, *Sue (Adrian Mole)*

9 letters:
Delafield, *E M*
Grossmith, *George and Weedon (Charles Pooter)*

10 letters:
Wordsworth, *Dorothy*

11 letters:
Rivers-Moore, *Marion*

12 letters:
Bashkirtseff, *Marie*

Dinosaurs

8 letters:
Allosaur
Mosasaur
Stegodon
Theropod

9 letters:
Apatosaur
Archosaur
Hadrosaur
Iguanodon
Oviraptor
Pterosaur
Stegodont
Stegosaur
Trachodon

10 letters:
Allosaurus
Ankylosaur
Brontosaur
Ceratosaur
Dimetrodon
Diplodocus

Dromiosaur
Elasmosaur
Iguanodont
Megalosaur
Mosasaurus
Plesiosaur
Pteranodon
Titanosaur

11 letters:
Apatosaurus
Atlantosaur
Brachiosaur
Dolichosaur
Hadrosaurus
Ichthyosaur
Pterodactyl
Stegosaurus
Titanothere
Triceratops
Tyrannosaur

12 letters:
Ankylosaurus

Brontosaurus
Ceratosaurus
Dromiosaurus
Elasmosaurus
Megalosaurus
Plesiosaurus
Titanosaurus
Velociraptor

13 letters:
Atlantosaurus
Brachiosaurus
Compsognathus
Dolichosaurus
Ichthyosaurus
Protoceratops
Tyrannosaurus

16 letters:
Pachycephalosaur

Directors

3 letters:
Lee, *Ang*
Lee, *Spike*
Ray, *Satyajit*
Woo, *John*

4 letters:
Coen, *Ethan*
Coen, *Joel*
Ford, *John*
Hall, *Peter*
Hill, *George Roy*
Lang, *Fritz*
Lean, *David*
Penn, *Arthur*
Reed, *Carol*

Roeg, *Nicholas*
Tati, *Jacques*
Weir, *Peter*
Wise, *Robert*

5 letters:
Allen, *Woody*
Brook, *Peter*
Capra, *Frank*
Carné, *Marcel*
Clair, *René*
Dante, *Joe*
Demme, *Jonathan*
Fosse, *Bob*
Gance, *Abel*
Hawks, *Howard*

Ivory, *James*
Kaige, *Chen*
Kazan, *Elia*
Leigh, *Mike*
Leone, *Sergio*
Loach, *Ken*
Lucas, *George*
Lumet, *Sidney*
Lynch, *David*
Malle, *Louis*
Mamet, *David*
Noyce, *Philip*
Pabst, *G(eorge) W(ilhelm)*
Parer, *Damien*
Reitz, *Edgar*
Roach, *Hal*

Scott, *Ridley*
Stone, *Oliver*
Vadim, *Roger*
Vidor, *King*
Wajda, *Andrei*
Yimou, *Zhang*

6 letters:
Altman, *Robert*
Badham, *John*
Beatty, *Warren*
Besson, *Luc*
Brooks, *Mel*
Buñuel, *Luis*
Burton, *Tim*
Corman, *Roger*
Cuarón, *Alfonso*
Curtiz, *Michael*
De Sica, *Vittoria*
De Vito, *Danny*
Donner, *Richard*
Dreyer, *Carl*
Forbes, *Bryan*
Forman, *Milös*
Frears, *Stephen*
Godard, *Jean-Luc*
Guitry, *Sacha*
Haneke, *Michael*
Herzog, *Werner*
Huston, *John*
Jarman, *Derek*
Jordan, *Neil*
Kasdan, *Lawrence*
Keaton, *Buster*
Landis, *John*
Lester, *Richard*
Méliès, *Georges*
Mendes, *Sam*
Miller, *George*
Miller, *Jonathon Wolfe*
Ophüls, *Max*
Pagnol, *Marcel*
Parker, *Alan*
Powell, *Michael*
Reiner, *Carl*

Reiner, *Rob*
Renoir, *Jean*
Rohmer, *Eric*
Romero, *George*
Siegel, *Don*
Welles, *Orson*
Wilder, *Billy*
Winner, *Michael*

7 letters:
Aldrich, *Robert*
Asquith, *Anthony*
Bergman, *Ingmar*
Berkoff, *Steven*
Boorman, *John*
Bresson, *Robert*
Cameron, *James*
Campion, *Jane*
Chabrol, *Claude*
Cocteau, *Jean*
Coppola, *Francis Ford*
De Mille, *Cecil B(lount)*
De Palma, *Brian*
Edwards, *Blake*
Fellini, *Federico*
Fleming, *Victor*
Forsyth, *Bill*
Gilliam, *Terry*
Guthrie, *Tyrone*
Jackson, *Peter*
Kaufman, *Philip*
Kubrick, *Stanley*
McBride, *Jim*
Nichols, *Mike*
Olivier, *Laurence*
Pollack, *Sydney*
Puttnam, *David*
Redford, *Robert*
Resnais, *Alain*
Ritchie, *Guy*
Rivette, *Jacques*
Robbins, *Tim*
Russell, *Ken*
Sennett, *Mack*
Sturges, *Preston*

Van Sant, *Gus*
Wenders, *Wim*

8 letters:
Anderson, *Lindsay*
Anderson, *Wes*
Columbus, *Chris*
Eastwood, *Clint*
Friedkin, *William*
Grierson, *John*
Griffith, *D(avid) W(ark)*
Kurosawa, *Akira*
Levinson, *Barry*
Merchant, *Ismail*
Minnelli, *Vincente*
Pasolini, *Pier Paolo*
Polanski, *Roman*
Pudovkin, *Vsevolod*
Scorsese, *Martin*
Truffaut, *François*
Visconti, *Luchino*
Von Trier, *Lars*
Zemeckis, *Robert*

9 letters:
Almódovar, *Pedro*
Antonioni, *Michelangelo*
Armstrong, *Gillian*
Carpenter, *John*
Dovzhenko, *Aleksandr Petrovitch*
Greenaway, *Peter*
Hitchcock, *Alfred*
Minghella, *Anthony*
Mizoguchi, *Kenji*

Peckinpah, *Sam*
Preminger, *Otto*
Spielberg, *Steven*
Stevenson, *Robert*
Tarantino, *Quentin*
Tarkovsky, *Andrei*
Tavernier, *Bertrand*
Zinnemann, *Fred*

10 letters:
Bertolucci, *Bernardo*
Cronenberg, *David*
Eisenstein, *Sergei Mikhailovich*
Fassbinder, *Rainer Werner*
Kieslowski, *Krzysztof*
Littlewood, *Joan*
Mankiewicz, *Joseph*
Rossellini, *Roberto*
Soderbergh, *Steven*
Zeffirelli, *Franco*

11 letters:
Bogdanovich, *Peter*
Mackendrick, *Alexander*
Pressburger, *Emeric*
Riefenstahl, *Leni*
Schlesinger, *John*
Von Stroheim, *Erich*

12 letters:
Attenborough, *Richard*
Stanislavski, *Konstantin*
Von Sternberg, *Josef*

Disciples

4 letters:
John
Jude

5 letters:
James (*the Great*)
James (*the Less*)
Judas

Peter
Simon

6 letters:
Andrew
Philip
Thomas

7 letters:
Matthew

11 letters:
Bartholomew

Diseases

2 letters:
CD
ME
MS
TB
VD

3 letters:
ALD
BSE
CFS
Flu
Gid
Haw
MND
Pip
Pox
Rot
TSE
Wog

4 letters:
Acne
Ague
AIDS
Boba
Bots
Bunt
Clap
Cold
Conk
Gout
Kuru
Loco
Lues
Lyme
Roup
SARS
Scab
Yaws

5 letters:
Bang's
Brand
Braxy
Ebola
Edema
Ergot
Favus
Gapes
Lupus
Lurgi
Lurgy
Mesel
Mumps
Ngana
Palsy
Pinta
Polio
Pott's
Sprue
Surra
Tinea
Weil's

6 letters:
Anbury
Angina
Asthma
Blight
Blotch
Cancer
Canker
Caries
Chagas'
Chorea
Cowpox
Crohn's
Cruels
Dartre
Dengue
Dropsy
Eczema
Farcin
Goitre
Grapes

Graves'
Heaves
Herpes
Income
Iritis
Johne's
Lampas
Mad cow
Meazel
Mildew
Morbus
Nagana
Oedema
Otitis
Paget's
Q fever
Quinsy
Rabies
Sapego
Scurvy
Spavin
Still's
Sweeny
Thrush
Typhus
Ulitis
Urosis
Warble
Zoster

7 letters:
Anthrax
Apraxia
Ascites
Bird flu
Bright's
British
Bulimia
Caisson
Cholera
Coeliac
Colitis
Crewels

Dourine
Earache
Founder
Glue ear
Hansen's
Hard pad
Hydatid
Icterus
Lampers
Leprosy
Lockjaw
Lumbago
Maidism
Malaria
Marburg
Measles
Megrims
Mooneye
Moor-ill
Murrain
Myiasis
Pébrine
Pinkeye
Porrigo
Prurigo
Purples
Purpura
Pyaemia
Quittor
Ratbite
Rickets
Roaring
Rosette
Rubella
Scabies
Scrapie
Sequela
Serpigo
Sitfast
Sycosis
Tetanus
Tetters
Typhoid

Uraemia
Uveitis
Variola
Wilson's

8 letters:
Addison's
Alastrim
Anorexia
Aortitis
Basedow's
Beriberi
Blackleg
Bornholm
Bull nose
Bursitis
Carditis
Clubroot
Coxalgia
Cushing's
Cynanche
Cystitis
Diabetes
Dutch elm
Economo's
Epilepsy
Ergotism
Fishskin
Fowl pest
Glanders
Glaucoma
Grand mal
Gummosis
Hidrosis
Hodgkin's
Hookworm
Impetigo
Jaundice
Kala-azar
Loose-cut
Lumpy jaw
Lymphoma
Mastitis
Menière's
Minamata

Myopathy
Myxedema
Osteitis
Pellagra
Petit mal
Phthisis
Phytosis
Pleurisy
Progeria
Pullorum
Rachitis
Raynaud's
Red water
Rhinitis
Ringbone
Ringworm
Rose-rash
Sciatica
Scrofula
Seedy toe
Shingles
Smallpox
Staggers
Suppeago
Swayback
Swine flu
Swinepox
Syphilis
Tay-Sachs
Toe crack
Trachoma
Trembles
Venereal
Vincent's
Vulvitis
Windgall
Zoonosis

9 letters:
Acariasis
Arthritis
Bilharzia
Brown lung
Calenture
Chancroid

Chin cough
Chloracne
Chlorosis
Christmas
Cirrhosis
Dhobi itch
Diarrhoea
Diathesis
Distemper
Dysentery
Emphysema
Enteritis
Exanthema
Gastritis
Glossitis
Gonorrhea
Hepatitis
Idiopathy
Influenza
Ixodiasis
Kawasaki's
Laminitis
Lathyrism
Leucaemia
Leukaemia
Loose smut
Malanders
Milk fever
Myxoedema
Nephritis
Nephrosis
Newcastle
Pellagrin
Pemphigus
Phlebitis
Pneumonia
Porphyria
Psoriasis
Pyorrhoea
Retinitis
Sand crack
Sapraemia
Scratches
Siderosis
Silicosis

Sinusitis
Splenitis
Strangles
Sunstroke
Synovitis
Tarantism
Tick fever
Trichosis
Tularemia
Urticaria
Vaginitis
Vagotonia
Varicosis
Varioloid
Whistling

10 letters:
Absinthism
Acromegaly
Alcoholism
Alzheimer's
Amoebiasis
Asbestosis
Ascariasis
Autoimmune
Babesiosis
Bagassosis
Bell's palsy
Black Death
Broken wind
Bronchitis
Byssinosis
Cellulitis
Chickenpox
Common cold
Dandy-fever
Dermatitis
Diphtheria
Ebola virus
Erysipelas
Fibrositis
Filariasis
Framboesia
Gingivitis
Gonorrhoea

Heartwater
Hemophilia
Hepatitis A
Hepatitis B
Hog cholera
Ichthyosis
Impaludism
Laryngitis
Lassa fever
Leuchaemia
Limber-neck
Lou Gehrig's
Louping ill
Mallanders
Mallenders
Meningitis
Moniliasis
Muscardine
Myasthenia
Narcolepsy
Neuropathy
Ornithosis
Parkinson's
Pityriasis
Rinderpest
Salmonella
Scarlatina
Scleriasis
Seborrhoea
Shell shock
Springhalt
Stomatitis
Stringhalt
Swamp fever
Swine fever
Texas fever
Tularaemia
Urethritis
Valvulitis

11 letters:
Anthracosis
Brittle-bone
Brucellosis
Cardiopathy

Coccidiosis
Consumption
Dead fingers
Farmer's lung
Green monkey
Haemophilia
Hebephrenia
Huntington's
Hypothermia
Jungle fever
Kwashiorkor
Listeriosis
Myxomatosis
Parasitosis
Pharyngitis
Psittacosis
Rickettsial
Salpingitis
Sarcoidosis
Scleroderma
Scrub typhus
Septicaemia
Spina bifida
Spondylitis
Thoroughpin
Tonsillitis
Trench fever
Trench mouth
Trichinosis
Utriculitis
Yellow fever

12 letters:
Aeroneurosis
Alkaptonuria
Anaplasmosis
Appendicitis
Athlete's foot
Avitaminosis
Bilharziasis
Bilharziosis
Black measles
Bush sickness
Constipation
Cor pulmonale

Encephalitis
Endocarditis
Enterobiasis
Fascioliasis
Finger and toe
Foot-and-mouth
Furunculosis
Gallsickness
Herpes zoster
Hoof-and-mouth
Legionnaire's
Milk sickness
Molybdenosis
Motor neurone
Osteomalacia
Osteoporosis
Pericarditis
Quarter crack
Ratbite fever
Sarcomatosis
Scarlet fever
Schizothymia
Sclerodermia
Shaking palsy
Sheep measles
Splenomegaly
Spotted fever
Thalassaemia
Tuberculosis
Typhoid fever
Uncinariasis

13 letters:
Actinomycosis
Blind staggers
Bronchiolitis
Bubonic plague
Elephantiasis
Enterocolitis
Genital herpes
German measles
Greensickness
Herpes simplex
Labyrinthitis
Leichmaniasis

Leishmaniasis
Leishmaniosis
Leptospirosis
Lupus vulgaris
Moon blindness
Non-A hepatitis
Non-B hepatitis
Osteomyelitis
Panleucopenia
Poliomyelitis
Polycythaemia
Reye's syndrome
Salmonellosis
Schizophrenia
Serum sickness
Syringomyelia
Toxoplasmosis
Tsutsugamushi
Undulant fever
Whooping cough

14 letters:
Bulimia nervosa
Cardiomyopathy
Coal miner's lung
Conjunctivitis
Cystic fibrosis
Diverticulitis
Encephalopathy
Glandular fever
Histoplasmosis
Hypothyroidism
Kaposi's sarcoma
Leucodystrophy
Onchocerciasis
Osteoarthritis
Pneumoconiosis
Relapsing fever
Rheumatic fever
Senile dementia
Spirochaetosis
Sporotrichosis
St Anthony's Fire
Swine vesicular
Trichomoniasis

Trichophytosis
Variola porcina
Vincent's angina
Vulvovaginitis

15 letters:
Agranulocytosis
Ancylostomiasis
Ankylostomiasis
Anorexia nervosa
Atherosclerosis
Blackwater fever
Burkitt lymphoma
Double pneumonia
Equine distemper
Gastroenteritis
Pleuropneumonia
Schistosomiasis
Strongyloidosis
Sydenham's chorea
Trypanosomiasis

16 letters:
Actinodermatitis
Anchylostomiasis
Arteriosclerosis
Bronchopneumonia
Burkitt's lymphoma
Creutzfeldt-Jakob
Erythroblastosis
Hodgkin's lymphoma
Ménière's syndrome
Myasthenia gravis
Paratyphoid fever
Saint Vitus's dance
Sleeping sickness
Strongyloidiasis
Sweating sickness
Tourette syndrome

17 letters:
Encephalomyelitis
Haemoglobinopathy
Huntington's chorea
Multiple sclerosis

Muscular dystrophy
Osteitis deformans
Presenile dementia
Radiation sickness
Sickle-cell anaemia

18 letters:
Cerebellar syndrome
Coccidioidomycosis
Exophthalmic goitre
Glomerulonephritis
Lupus erythematosus
Pelvic inflammatory
Toxic shock syndrome

19 letters:
Infectious hepatitis
Korsakoff's psychosis
Non-Hodgkin's lymphoma
Rheumatoid arthritis

20 letters:
Adrenoleukodystrophy
Carpal tunnel syndrome

Necrotising fasciitis

21 letters:
Decompression sickness

22 letters:
Chronic fatigue syndrome

23 letters:
Bacillary white diarrhoea
Equine infectious anaemia
Infectious mononucleosis

24 letters:
Myalgic encephalomyelitis

25 letters:
Rocky Mountain spotted fever
Seasonal affective disorder

30 letters:
Bovine spongiform encephalopathy

Dishes

3 letters:	Soup	Cutie	Pilaf
Fry	Stew	Daube	Pilao
Pan	Taco	Dolma	Pilau
Pie	Tofu	Fry-up	Pilaw
Poi	Udon	Gomer	Pilow
		Grits	Pizza
4 letters:	**5 letters:**	Gruel	Poori
Dent	Balti	Kasha	Quorn®
Flan	Belle	Kebab	Raita
Fool	Bhaji	Kibbe	Ramen
Hash	Bitok	Knish	Roast
Lanx	Brawn	Kofta	Rojak
Mess	Brose	Korma	Sabji
Olla	Broth	Laksa	Salad
Paté	Champ	Maror	Salmi
Puri	Chips	Paten	Sango
Soba	Crêpe	Patin	Satay
Soss	Curry	Patty	Split

Sushi
Tamal
Thali
Tikka
Toast

6 letters:
Apollo
Bharta
Blintz
Bredie
Bridie
Burgoo
Canapé
Coddle
Cook-up
Croute
Cuscus
Entrée
Faggot
Fondue
Haggis
Hotpot
Houmus
Hummus
Humous
Kimchi
Kishke
Laggen
Laggin
Luggie
Mousse
Muesli
Nachos
Omelet
Paella
Pakora
Panada
Patera
Patine
Pilaff
Pirogi
Pot pie
Quiche
Ragout

Salmis
Samosa
Sanger
Sarmie
Scampi
Scouse
Sowans
Sowens
Subgum
Tagine
Tamale
Tsamba
Won ton

7 letters:
Biriani
Bobotie
Bouchée
Burrito
Calzone
Ceviche
Chafing
Charger
Cocotte
Comport
Compote
Crowdie
Crubeen
Crumble
Custard
Cuvette
Dariole
Dhansak
Dopiaza
Egg roll
Epergne
Fajitas
Falafel
Fel-a-fel
Flasket
Foo yong
Foo Yung
Friture
Goulash
Grav lax

Haroset
Lasagne
Mousaka
Navarin
Padella
Pad Thai
Piccata
Polenta
Pottage
Poutine
Ramekin
Rarebit
Ravioli
Risotto
Rissole
Roulade
Sashimi
Scallop
Seviche
Skirlie
Sosatie
Soufflé
Stir-fry
Stottie
Stovies
Tartlet
Tempura
Terrine
Timbale
Tostada
Zamponi

8 letters:
Brandade
Calabash
Caponata
Chop suey
Chow mein
Consommé
Coolamon
Coq au vin
Coquille
Couscous
Crostini
Dolmades

Entremes
Escargot
Feijoada
Fish cake
Gado-gado
Halloumi
Haroseth
Kedgeree
Keftedes
Kickshaw
Kouskous
Kreplach
Kromesky
Mahi-mahi
Matelote
Mazarine
Meat loaf
Mirepoix
Moussaka
Omelette
Pandowdy
Pannikin
Pastrami
Pirozhki
Porridge
Pot-au-feu
Pot roast
Quenelle
Raclette
Ramequin
Salpicon
Sandwich
Scrapple
Shashlik
Sillabub
Souvlaki
Steak pie
Sukiyaki
Syllabub
Teriyaki
Tomalley
Tortilla
Tsatsiki
Tzatziki
Yakimono

Yakitori

9 letters:
Carbonara
Casserole
Cassoulet
Compotier
Croquette
Curry puff
Egg-fo-yang
Enchilada
Entremets
Forcemeat
Fricassee
Galantine
Game chips
Gravad lax
Guacamole
Hamburger
Howtowdie
Irish stew
Jambalaya
Lobscouse
Madrilène
Manicotti
Matelotte
Mutton pie
Osso bucco
Pastitsio
Pepper pot
Reistafel
Rijstafel
Rillettes
Schnitzel
Scotch egg
Scotch pie
Shashlick
Souvlakia
Succotash
Surf 'n' turf
Tyropitta
Vol-au-vent

10 letters:
Avgolemono

Baked beans
Blanquette
Bombay duck
Bruschetta
Cacciatore
Cottage pie
Coulibiaca
Couscousou
Doner kebab
Egg-foo-yung
Fish finger
Fish supper
Hotchpotch
Jugged hare
Koulibiaca
Laver bread
Minestrone
Mixed grill
Nasi goreng
Parmigiana
Pease brose
Provencale
Quesadilla
Red pudding
Rijsttafel
Salmagundi
Salmagundy
Sauerkraut
Scaloppine
Scaloppini
Shish kebab
Smørrebrød
Spankopita
Spitchcock
Spring roll
Stroganoff
Vegeburger

11 letters:
Buck-rarebit
Caesar salad
Chicken Kiev
Chimichanga
Clam chowder
Cock-a-leekie

Corn chowder
Cullen skink
Frankfurter
French toast
Fritto misto
Gefilte fish
Hominy grits
Olla podrida
Palm-oil chop
Ratatouille
Saltimbocca
Sauerbraten
Sausage roll
Scotch broth
Smorgasbord
Spanakopita
Spanish rice
Spanokopita
Suet pudding
Vichyssoise
Welsh rabbit

12 letters:
Cheeseburger
Club sandwich
Cockie-leekie
Cornish pasty
Eggs Benedict
Fish and chips
Forfar bridie
Gefüllte fish
Mulligatawny
Open sandwich
Parmigianino
Pease pudding
Prawn cracker
Shepherd's pie
Steak tartare
Taramasalata
Veggieburger
Waldorf salad
Welsh rarebit
White pudding

13 letters:
Prairie oyster
Rumbledethump
Salade niçoise
Scrambled eggs
Toad-in-the-hole

14 letters:
Beef stroganoff
Chilli con carne
Lobster Newburg
Macaroni cheese
Mock turtle soup
Quiche lorraine
Rumbledethumps

15 letters:
Beef bourguignon
Bubble and squeak

Ploughman's lunch

16 letters:
Blanquette de veau
Boeuf bourguignon
Lancashire hotpot
Lobster thermidor
Moules marinieres
Yorkshire pudding

17 letters:
Angels-on-horseback
Cauliflower cheese
Devils-on-horseback
Steak-and-kidney pie

21 letters:
Steak-and-kidney pudding

Divination

METHODS OF DIVINATION

4 letters:
Dice

5 letters:
Runes
Tarot

6 letters:
I Ching

7 letters:
Dowsing
Scrying

9 letters:
Astrology
Palmistry
Sortilege
Tea leaves

10 letters:
Numerology

12 letters:
Clairvoyance

13 letters:
Crystal gazing

MEANS OF DIVINATION

Name	Object used
Ailuromancy	Cats
Alphitomancy	Wheat *or* barley cakes
Arachnomancy	Spiders
Astragalomancy	Dice
Bibliomancy	Passages from books
Cartomancy	Cards
Catoptromancy	Mirror
Ceromancy	Melted wax
Chiromancy	Hands
Cleidomancy	Suspended key
Crithomancy	Freshly baked bread

Name	Object used
Cromniomancy	Onions
Crystallomancy	Crystal ball
Dactylomancy	Suspended ring
Geomancy	Earth, sand, *or* dust
Hippomancy	Horses
Hydromancy	Water
Lampadomancy	Oil lamps
Lithomancy	Precious stones
Lychnomancy	Flames of wax candles
Molybdomancy	Molten lead
Necromancy	The dead
Oneiromancy	Dreams
Ornithomancy	Birds
Pegomancy	Sacred pool
Pyromancy	Fire *or* flames
Radiesthesia	Pendulum
Rhabdomancy	Rod *or* wand
Sciomancy	Ghosts
Tasseography	Tea leaves
Theomancy	God
Tyromancy	Cheese

Dogs

3 letters:
Cur
Lab
Pom
Pug

4 letters:
Barb
Bush
Chow
Dane
Kuri
Peke
Puli
Stag
Tosa

5 letters:
Akita
Alans

Apsos
Boxer
Brach
Cairn
Coach
Corgi
Husky
Spitz
Spoor

6 letters:
Afghan
Bandog
Barbet
Beagle
Blanch
Borzoi
Briard
Chenet
Cocker

Collie
Eskimo
Goorie
Kelpie
Messan
Pariah
Poodle
Pye-dog
Saluki
Scotch
Setter
Shough
Sleuth
Talbot
Teckel
Vizsla
Westie
Yorkie

7 letters:
Basenji
Boerbul
Bouvier
Brachet
Bulldog
Courser
Griffon
Harrier
Lurcher
Maltese
Maremma
Mastiff
Mongrel
Pointer
Prairie
Raccoon
Samoyed
Sapling
Scottie

Shar-Pei
Sheltie
Shih-tzu
Showghe
Spaniel
Terrier
Volpino
Whippet

8 letters:
Aardwolf
Aberdeen
Airedale
Alsatian
Blenheim
Bratchet
Carriage
Chow-chow
Doberman
Elkhound
Foxhound
Huntaway
Keeshond
Komondor
Labrador
Landseer
Malamute
Malemute
Papillon
Pekinese
Pembroke
Pinscher
Samoyede
Scottish
Sealyham
Springer
Warragal
Warrigal

9 letters:
Blue merle
Buckhound
Chihuahua
Coonhound
Dachshund

Dalmatian
Deerhound
Gazehound
Great Dane
Greyhound
Kerry blue
Lhasa apso
Pekingese
Red setter
Retriever
Schnauzer
Staghound
St Bernard
Wolfhound

10 letters:
Bedlington
Bloodhound
Blue cattle
Blue heeler
Bruxellois
Fox terrier
Otterhound
Pomeranian
Rottweiler
Schipperke
Tripehound
Weimaraner
Welsh corgi

11 letters:
Afghan hound
Basset hound
Bichon Frise
Bull mastiff
Bull terrier
Irish setter
Jack Russell
Rough collie
Skye terrier
Sydney silky

12 letters:
Belvoir hound
Border collie

Cairn terrier
Field spaniel
Gordon setter
Irish terrier
Japanese tosa
Newfoundland
Saint Bernard
Water spaniel
Welsh terrier
West Highland

13 letters:
Affenpinscher
Alpine spaniel
Bearded collie
Border terrier
Boston terrier
Cocker spaniel
Dandie Dinmont
English setter
French bulldog
Scotch terrier
Sussex spaniel

14 letters:
Clumber spaniel
Egyptian basset
German shepherd
Irish wolfhound
Norfolk terrier
Norwich terrier
Pit bull terrier

15 letters:
Aberdeen terrier
Airedale terrier
Alaskan malamute
Blenheim spaniel
Blue Gascon hound
Cuban bloodhound
Golden retriever
Highland terrier
Japanese spaniel
Lakeland terrier
Mexican hairless

Sealyham terrier
Springer spaniel

16 letters:
Australian cattle
Doberman pinscher
Italian greyhound
Kerry blue terrier
Persian greyhound
Pyrenean mountain
Russian wolfhound
Shetland sheepdog
Yorkshire terrier

17 letters:
Australian terrier
Bedlington terrier
Dobermann-pinscher
Irish water spaniel
Labrador retriever
Manchester terrier
Norwegian elkhound

Wire-haired terrier

18 letters:
Black-and-tan terrier
Jack Russell terrier
King Charles spaniel
Old English sheepdog
Rhodesian ridgeback

20 letters:
Dandie Dinmont terrier
Queensland blue heeler

22 letters:
American pit bull terrier
Australian silky terrier
Norfolk springer spaniel

24 letters:
Staffordshire bull terrier
West Highland white terrier

Drama

2 letters:
No

3 letters:
Noh

5 letters:
Farce

6 letters:
Comedy
Kabuki
Sitcom
Sketch

7 letters:
Tragedy

8 letters:
Jacobean

9 letters:
Kathakali
Melodrama
Soap opera

10 letters:
Shadow play

11 letters:
Kitchen sink
Mystery play
Passion play
Tragicomedy

12 letters:
Costume drama
Costume piece
Grand Guignol
Morality play

13 letters:
Street theatre

14 letters:
Revenge tragedy

15 letters:
Comedy of manners
Situation comedy

16 letters:
Commedia dell'arte
Theatre of cruelty

17 letters:
Restoration Comedy

18 letters:
Theatre of the absurd

Dramatists

2 letters:
Fo, *Dario*

3 letters:
Fry, *Christopher Harris*
Gay, *John*
Kyd, *Thomas*

4 letters:
Amos, *Robert*
Bond, *Edward*
Ford, *John*
Gray, *Oriel*
Hare, *David*
Inge, *William Motter*
Lyly, *John*
Shaw, *George Bernard*

5 letters:
Albee, *Edward (Franklin)*
Behan, *Brendan*
Burke, *Gregory*
Bryne, *John*
Eliot, *T(homas) S(tearns)*
Elton, *Ben*
Esson, *Louis*
Friel, *Brian*
Genet, *Jean*
Gogol, *Nikolai Vasilievich*
Grieg, *David*
Havel, *Václav*
Hayes, *Alfred*
Ibsen, *Henrik*
Lorca, *Federico García*
Mamet, *David*
Odets, *Clifford*
Orton, *Joe*
Otway, *Thomas*
Synge, *(Edmund) J(ohn) M(illington)*
Udall, *Nicholas*
Wilde, *Oscar (Fingal O'Flahertie Wills)*
Yeats, *W(illiam) B(utler)*

6 letters:
Adamov, *Arthur*
Barrie, *J(ames) M(atthew)*
Beynon, *Richard*
Brecht, *Bertolt (Eugen Friedrich)*
Bridie, *James (Osborne Henry Mavor)*
Brieux, *Eugene*
Coward, *Noël (Pierce)*
Dekker, *Thomas*
De Vega, *Lope*
Dryden, *John*
Ennuis, *Quintus*
Goethe, *Johann Wolfgang von*
Greene, *Robert*
Hebbel, *(Christian) Friedrich*
Hewett, *Dorothy*
Howard, *Sidney*
Jonson, *Ben(jamin)*
Kaiser, *George*
Lawler, *Ray*
Miller, *Arthur*
Oakley, *Barry*
O'Casey, *Sean*
O'Neill, *Eugene (Gladstone)*
Pinero, *Arthur Wing*
Pinter, *Harold*
Porter, *Hal*
Racine, *Jean (Baptiste)*
Ramsay, *Allan*
Sartre, *Jean-Paul*
Seneca, *Lucius Annaeus*
Wilder, *Thornton*

7 letters:
Anouilh, *Jean*
Arrabal, *Fernando*
Beckett, *Samuel (Barclay)*
Chapman, *George*
Chekhov, *Anton Pavlovich*
Gilbert, *W(illiam) S(chwenk)*
Goldoni, *Carlo*
Heywood, *Thomas*
Hibberd, *Jack*

Ionesco, *Eugène*
Kushner, *Tony*
Lyndsay, *David*
Marlowe, *Christopher*
Marston, *John*
McGrath, *John*
Molière
Osborne, *John*
Patrick, *John*
Plautus, *Titus Maccius*
Pushkin, *Aleksander Sergeyevich*
Romeril, *John*
Rostand, *Edmond*
Russell, *Willy*
Seymour, *Alan*
Shaffer, *Peter*
Shepard, *Sam*
Soyinka, *Wole*
Terence
Webster, *John*

8 letters:
Beaumont, *Francis*
Congreve, *William*
Farquhar, *George*
Fletcher, *John*
Lochhead, *Liz*
Menander
Priestly, *J(ohn) B(oynton)*
Rattigan, *Terence (Mervyn)*
Schiller, *Johann Christoph Friedrich von*
Shadwell, *Thomas*
Sheridan, *Richard Brinsley*
Sherwood, *Robert*
Stoppard, *Tom*
Vanbrugh, *Sir John*
Wedekind, *Frank*
Williams, *Tennessee*

Wycherly, *William*

9 letters:
Aeschylus
Ayckbourn, *Alan*
Bleasdale, *Alan*
Centlivre
Corneille, *Pierre*
De la Barca, *Pedro Calderón*
Euripides
Giraudoux, *(Hippolyte) Jean*
Goldsmith, *Oliver*
Hauptmann, *Gerhart Johann Robert*
Massinger, *Philip*
Middleton, *Thomas*
Sackville, *Thomas*
Sophocles

10 letters:
Drinkwater, *John*
Galsworthy, *John*
Pirandello, *Luigi*
Strindberg, *August*
Williamson, *David Keith*

11 letters:
Maeterlinck, *Count Maurice*
Shakespeare, *William*

12 letters:
Aristophanes
Beaumarchais, *Pierre Augustin Caron de*

14 letters:
De Beaumarchais, *Pierre Augustin Caron*

Dresses

4 letters:
Coat
Midi
Sack

Sari

5 letters:
Burka

Pinny
Saree
Shift
Tunic

6 letters:
Caftan
Chiton
Dirndl
Jumper
Kaftan
Kimono
Mantua
Muu-muu
Nighty
Sheath

7 letters:
Busuuti
Chemise
Gymslip
Nightie
Sweater

Tea gown
Wedding

8 letters:
Ballgown
Cocktail
Negligée
Peignoir
Pinafore
Sundress

9 letters:
Cheongsam
Maxidress
Minidress
Nightgown
Nightrobe
Overdress

10 letters:
Microdress
Nightdress
Nightshirt
Shirtdress
Shirtwaist

11 letters:
Riding habit

12 letters:
Shirtwaister

13 letters:
Button-through
Mother Hubbard

Drinks

2 letters:
It

3 letters:
Ale
Ava
Cha
Cup
Dão
Dop
Gin
Ice
IPA
Keg
Kir
Mum
Nog
Pop
Rum
Rye
Tea
Vin

4 letters:
Arak
Asti
Beef
Bock
Brut
Bull
Bush
Cava
Coke®
Cola
Corn
Dram
Flip
Gavi
Grog
Herb
Hock
Java
Kava
Kola
Korn
Kvas
Malt

Marc
Maté
Mead
Mild
Milk
Mint
Nipa
Nogg
Ouzo
Palm
Pils
Port
Purl
Raki
Rosé
Rosy
Sack
Saké
Saki
Sekt
Soda
Soma
Sour
Sura

Tent
Tutu
Yill

5 letters:
Anise
Anjou
Assam
Bingo
Black
Blend
Bohea
Bombo
Brown
Bumbo
China
Cider
Cocoa
Congo
Crème
Crush
Cyder
Decaf
Fitou

Float
Fruit
Glogg
Grain
Grass
Green
Guest
Haoma
Heavy
Hogan
Hooch
Hyson
Irish
Juice
Julep
Kefir
Kirsh
Kvass
Lager
Latte
Ledum
Lemon
Light
Lirac
Mâcon
Mauby
Meath
Medoc
Meths
Mirin
Mobby
Mocha
Mosel
Mulse
Nappy
Negus
Noyau
Pekoe
Pepsi®
Perry
Pinot
Plain
Polly
Pombe
Punch

Quass
Rakee
Rhine
Rioja
Roero
Rueda
Rully
Rummy
Salop
Senna
Shake
Shrub
Sixty
Sling
Soave
Stout
Straw
Syrah
Tavel
Tizer®
Toddy
Tokay
Tonic
Twist
Vimto®
Vodka
Water
Wheat
White
Xeres
Yerba

6 letters:
Arrack
Atomic
Bandol
Barley
Barolo
Barsac
Beaune
Bishop
Bovril®
Brandy
Burton
Busera

Cahors
Canary
Carema
Cassis
Caudle
Cauker
Ceylon
Chaser
Claret
Coffee
Cognac
Congou
Cooler
Cooper
Crusta
Doctor
Eggnog
Eighty
Enzian
Export
Frappé
Gaelic
Gibson
Gimlet
Ginger
Glayva®
Grappa
Graves
Gueuze
Herbal
Indian
Kaffir
Kahlua
Kenyan
Kephir
Kirsch
Kölsch
Koumis
Kumiss
Kümmel
Lambic
Lisbon
Málaga
Malibu®
Meathe

Merlot
Mescal
Midori
Mocker
Mojito
Muscat
Nectar
Nobbie
Oolong
Orgasm
Orgeat
Oulong
Pastis
Pernod®
Poitín
Porter
Posset
Poteen
Pulque
Quincy
Redeye
Ribena®
Rickey
Samshu
Saumur
Scotch
Shandy
Sherry
Shiraz
Squash
Stingo
Strega
Taffia
Tisane
Tokaji
Waragi
Whisky
Yaqona
Zombie
Zythum

7 letters:
Absinth
Akvavit
Alcopop

Alicant	Jasmine	Shebeen	Cold duck
Amarone	Koumiss	Sherbet	Condrieu
Amoroso	Koumyss	Sherris	Daiquiri
Aniseed	Lapsang	Shnapps	Dog's nose
Aquavit	Limeade	Shooter	Drambuie®
Arabica	Liqueur	Sidecar	Dubonnet®
Auslese	Madeira	Slammer	Earl Grey
Bacardi®	Malmsey	Sloe gin	Eau de vie
Banyuls	Margaux	Special	Espresso
Bastard	Marsala	Stengah	Espumoso
Bellini	Martini®	Stinger	Essencia
Bitters	Mineral	Swizzle	Faugères
Blended	Moselle	Tequila	Frascati
Bourbon	Negroni	Tio Pepe®	Fruit tea
Bucelas	Oenomel	Turkish	Galliano®
Cachaca	Oloroso	Twankay	Geropiga
Campari®	Orvieto	Vouvray	Gigondas
Catawba	Pale ale		Gin sling
Chablis	Palinka	**8 letters:**	Gluhwein
Chanoyu	Parrina	Absinthe	Highball
Chianti	Perrier®	Advocaat	Hollands
Chinese	Persico	Aleberry	Home brew
Cinzano®	Pilsner	Amaretto	Hydromel
Cobbler	Pink gin	Ambrosia	Iron brew
Collins	Pomerol	Anisette	Jerepigo
Cordial	Pommard	Apéritif	Jurançon
Cowslip	Quetsch	Armagnac	Kabinett
Curaçao	Ratafee	Bairrada	Labrador
Curaçoa	Ratafia	Bergerac	Lemonade
Daquiri	Real ale	Bordeaux	Lemon tea
Dark rum	Red-root	Brouilly	Light ale
Draught	Retsina	Brown ale	Lucozade®
Eggflip	Rhenish	Bucellas	Mahogany
Eiswein	Robusta	Bullshot	Malvasia
Essence	Rooibos	Burgundy	Malvesie
Fendant	Russian	Cabernet	Montilla
Fleurie	Sambuca	Café noir	Muscadel
Fustian	Samshoo	Calvados	Muscadet
Gaillac	Sangria	Camomile	Muscatel
Guarana	Sazerac	Champers	Palm wine
Gunfire	Schnaps	Charneco	Paraguay
Herb tea	Scrumpy	Ciderkin	Pauillac
Hokonui	Seltzer	Club soda	Persicot
Instant	Seventy	Coca-Cola®	Pilsener
Italian	Shebean	Cocktail	Pink lady

Pinotage
Pradikat
Prunelle
Red biddy
Resinata
Resinate
Rice beer
Rice wine
Riesling
Root beer
Saketini
Sambucca
Sancerre
Sangaree
Sauterne
Schnapps
Sillabub
Skokiaan
Smoothie
Snowball
Souchong
Sour mash
Spätlese
Spremuta
Spritzer
Spumante
Switchel
Syllabub
Tia Maria®
Trappist
Verdelho
Vermouth
White rum
Witblitz

9 letters:
Alexander
Americano
Applejack
Aqua vitae
Ayahuasco
Bacharach
Badminton
Bardolino
Bourgogne

Bourgueil
Brazilian
Buck's fizz
Chamomile
Champagne
Chocolate
Christmas
Claret cup
Cointreau®
Colombian
Corbières
Côte Rôtie
Cream soda
Cuba libre
Falernian
Firewater
Framboise
Fumé Blanc
Gattinara
Gingerade
Ginger ale
Gladstone
Grenadine
Gunpowder
Hard cider
Hermitage
Hippocras
Hoccamore
Lambrusco
Lambswool
Languedoc
Macchiato
Malvoisie
Manhattan
Margarita
Meersault
Metheglin
Meursault
Milk punch
Milk shake
Milk stout
Minervois
Mint julep
Mirabelle
Muscadine

Nor'wester
Orangeade
Pinot noir
Rauchbier
Rusty Nail
Sauternes
Sauvignon
Slivovitz
Snakebite
Soda water
St Emilion
Sundowner
Tarragona
Triple sec
Van der Hum
Weissbier
Whisky mac
White lady
Zinfandel

10 letters:
Apple juice
Barbaresco
Barley wine
Beaujolais
Bloody Mary
Bull's Blood
Buttermilk
Café au lait
Cappuccino
Chambertin
Chardonnay
Chartreuse®
Constantia
Costa Rican
Darjeeling
Dry martini
Elderberry
Frangelico
Fruit juice
Genevrette
Ginger beer
Ginger wine
Hochheimer
Hogan-mogen

Lolly water
Malt liquor
Manzanilla
Maraschino
Mochaccino
Montrachet
Moscow Mule
Mulled wine
Peter-see-me
Piesporter
Piña colada
Poppy water
Pousse-café
Rosé d'Anjou
Russian tea
Saint-Véran
Shandygaff
Single malt
Spruce beer
Sweet stout
Tanglefoot
Tom Collins
Valdepeñas
Vatted malt
Verdicchio
Vichy water
Vinho Verde
Weizenbier

11 letters:
Aguardiente
Amontillado
Apple brandy
Barley water
Benedictine
Bitter lemon
Black and tan
Black velvet
Boiler-maker
Continental
Crusted port
Egri Bikaver
Frappuccino
French roast
Half-and-half

Irish coffee
Kirshwasser
Lemon squash
Lime cordial
Monbazillac
Niersteiner
Orange juice
Orange pekoe
Pinot Grigio
Post-and-rail
Pouilly-Fumé
Rosso Cònero
Rüdesheimer
Saint-Julien
Screwdriver
Scuppernong
Skinny latte
Soapolallie
Steinberger
Tom-and-Jerry
Tomato juice
Whiskey sour
Yerba de Maté

12 letters:
Asti Spumante
Barbera d'Albi
Barbera d'Asti
Bière de Garde
Black Russian
Blue mountain
Cherry brandy
Christmas ale
Colheita Port
Côtes du Rhône
Crème de cacao
Gaelic coffee
Grand Marnier®
Hot chocolate
Humpty-dumpty
Ice-cream soda
India Pale Ale
Irish whiskey
Johannisberg
Kirschwasser

Liqueur Tokay
Marcobrunner
Mineral water
Moscato d'Asti
Old-fashioned
Perrier water®
Saint-Émilion
Saint-Estèphe
Sarsaparilla
Seltzer water
Valpolicella
Vin ordinaire
Vosne-Romanée

13 letters:
Amendoa Amarga
Blanc de blancs
Crème de menthe
Decaffeinated
Eau des creoles
Entre-Deux-Mers
Liebfraumilch
Liqueur Muscat
Long Island Tea
Mâcon-Villages
Peach schnapps
Pessac-Léognan
Planter's punch
Pouilly-Fousse
Pouilly-Fuissé
Prairie oyster
Sixty shilling

14 letters:
Crémant d'Alsace
Crémant de Loire
Eighty shilling
Elderberry wine
French vermouth
Gewürztraminer
Herbal infusion
Johannisberger
John Barleycorn
Quarts de Chaume

Singapore sling
Tokay-Pinot Gris
Veuve Jacquolot

Cabernet Sauvignon
Nuits-Saint-Georges
Peppermint cordial

15 letters:
Alcohol-free beer
Applejack brandy
Brandy Alexander
Cask-conditioned
Crozes-Hermitage
Grange Hermitage
Grapefruit juice
Italian vermouth
Lachryma Christi
Lapsang Souchong
Salice Salentino
Seventy shilling
Southern Comfort®

18 letters:
Blanquette de Limoux
Cask-conditioned ale
Coteaux du Tricastin
Teroldego Rotaliano

19 letters:
Dandelion and burdock

20 letters:
Bottle-conditioned ale
Brunello di Montalcino
Côte de Beaune-Villages
Trockenbeerenauslese

16 letters:
Gevrey-Chambertin
Harvey Wallbanger
Non-alcoholic beer

21 letters:
Montepulciano d'Abruzzo

23 letters:
Muscat de Beaumes-de-Venise
Slow Screw Against the Wall

17 letters:
Bailey's Irish Cream®
Beaujolais nouveau
Bereich Bernkastel
Bottle-conditioned

25 letters:
Vino Nobile di Montepulciano

Drugs and drug terms

1 letter:	Cop	LSD	**4 letters:**
E	DET	Man	Acid
H	DMT	MLD	Adam
Q	EPO	Mud	Alum
	Eve	PCP®	Ara-A®
2 letters:	Fix	Pop	Bang
Do	Hit	Pot	Blow
LD	Hop	Qat	Bong
OD	Ice	STP	Bust
	INH	Tab	Bute
3 letters:	Jag	Tea	Buzz
Ana	Kat		Coca
Bud	Kif		Coke

Dopa
Dope
Dose
Drop
Gear
Gone
Goof
Hard
Hash
Head
Hemp
High
Hype
Junk
Khat
Kick
Line
Mass
MDMA
Mkat
Nail
Narc
Oral
Scag
Sida
Snow
Soap
Soft
Soma
Tina
Toke
Toot
Trip
Unit
User
Wine
Wrap

5 letters:
Aloes
Aloin
Benny
Bhang
Candy
Crack

Crank
Dagga
Dexie
Ganja
Grass
Green
Habit
Hocus
Hop up
Intal®
Joint
L-dopa
Lit up
Local
Mummy
NSAID
Opium
Pills
Poppy
Quina
Roach
Route
Rutin
Salep
Salop
Salts
Score
Skunk
Smack
Smoke
Snort
Speed
Splay
Stash
Stuff
Sugar
Sulfa
Taxol
Tonic
Upper
Vomit
Wafer

6 letters:
Amulet

Amytal®
Ativan®
Bombed
Bromal
Bummer
Burned
Charas
Cocain
Cook up
Curare
Curari
Dealer
Dosage
Downer
Dragée
Dry out
Elixir
Emetic
Get off
Heroin
Hooked
Inulin
Ipecac
Jack up
Joypop
Junkie
Kaolin
Liquor
Loaded
Make it
Mescla
Monkey
Mummia
Nod out
Normal
Number
Opiate
Peyote
Pituri
Popper
Prozac®
Pusher
Reefer
Remedy
Roofie

Saloop
Skin up
Spaced
Spirit
Spliff
Squill
Step on
Stoned
Sulpha
Turn on
Valium®
Viagra®
Wasted
Weight
Zonked

7 letters:
Alcohol
Anodyne
Araroba
Argyrol®
Aspirin
Atabrin
Atebrin®
Atropin
Blocker
Botanic
Calomel
Cardiac
Cascara
Charlie
Chillum
Churrus
Cocaine
Codeine
Crank up
Damiana
Dapsone
Ecbolic
Ecstasy
Errhine
Ethical
Eucaine
Exhaust
Extract

Guarana
Hashish
Hemagog
Hemlock
Henbane
Hepatic
Hophead
Hyped up
Hypnone
Insulin
Jellies
Kaoline
Librium®
Linctus
Metopon
Miltown®
Mixture
Mogadon®
Morphia
Nervine
Pareira
Patulin
Pep pill
Pessary
Placebo
Pothead
Quinine
Reactor
Rhatany
Salicin
Seconal®
Shoot up
Skin-pop
Smashed
Steroid
Styptic
Suramin
Swacked
Synergy
Tetanic
Topical
Trional
Turpeth
Vehicle
Veronal®

Vinegar
Wrecked

8 letters:
Acidhead
Adjuvant
Antabuse®
Antidote
Aromatic
Atabrine®
Ataraxic
Atenolol
Atropine
Autacoid
Bacterin
Banthine
Barbital
Benadryl®
Bioassay
Blockade
Caffeine
Cannabis
Cinchona
Cohobate
Comedown
Cortisol
Curarine
Designer
Diazepam
Diuretic
Emulsion
Endermic
Ephedrin
Excitant
External
Fentanyl
Freebase
Goofball
Hyoscine
Hypnotic
Inhalant
Ketamine
Krameria
Laetrile
Laudanum

Laxative
Lenitive
Mainline
Meow-Meow
Mersalyl
Mescalin
Methadon
Miticide
Moonrock
Morphine
Naloxone
Naproxin
Narcotic
Nembutal®
Neomycin
Nepenthe
Nicotine
Nystatin
Opium den
Orlistat
Overdose
Oxytocic
Pectoral
Positive
Psilocin
Pulmonic
Reaction
Relaxant
Retrovir®
Rifampin
Roborant
Salicine
Santonin
Scammony
Scopolia
Sedative
Serevent®
Snowball
Spansule
Specific
Switch on
Terebene
Tetronal
Thiazide
Tincture

Tolerant
Valerian
Vesicant
Viricide
Wormseed
Zerumbet
Zolpidem

9 letters:
Acyclovir
Addiction
Addictive
Analeptic
Analgesic
Angel dust
Anovulant
Antrycide
Arsenical
Ataractic
Attenuant
Augmentin
Azedarach
Barbitone
Berberine
Biguanide
Botanical
Bring down
Busulphan
Calmative
Captopril
Carbachol
Cathartic
Cisplatin
Clonidine
Clozapine
Corticoid
Cortisone
Crackhead
Cyclizine
Cytotoxin
Decoction
Demulcent
Digitalis
Dramamine®
Electuary

Ephedrine
Excipient
Expellant
Expellent
Febrifuge
Foscarnet
Frusemide
Galenical
Glycoside
Goa powder
Hemagogue
Ibuprofen
Inotropic
Iprindole
Isoniazid
Jaborandi
Lorazepam
Magistral
Marihuana
Marijuana
Menstruum
Mepacrine
Merbromin
Mercurial
Mescaline
Methadone
Mydriasis
Novocaine®
Nux vomica
Officinal
Oleoresin
Paludrine®
Paregoric
Pethidine
Phenytoin
Practolol
Purgative
Quercetin
Quercitin
Quinidine
Quinquina
Reserpine
Resolvent
Revulsive
Safflower

Scopoline
Senna leaf
Senna pods
Sensitise
Sensitize
Signature
Smackhead
Soporific
Spaced out
Speedball
Stimulant
Strung out
Sudorific
Synergism
Synergist
Tamoxifen
Temazepam
Teniacide
Teniafuge
Totaquine
Tretinoin
Tricyclic
Trinitrum
Verapamil
Vermifuge
Vulnerary
Wych hazel
Yohimbine

10 letters:
Abirritant
Absorption
Acedapsone
Acetanilid
Agrypnotic
Alterative
Amantadine
Ampicillin
Anesthetic
Antagonist
Antibiotic
Antiemetic
Antimonial
Antipyrine
Anxiolytic

Astringent
Atracurium
Bacitracin
Belladonna
Benzedrine®
Benzocaine
Biological
Bufotenine
Chalybeate
Cholagogue
Cimetedine
Cimetidine
Cinchonine
Clofibrate
Clomiphene
Cold turkey
Colestipol
Confection
Connection
Convulsant
Dependency
Depressant
Disulfiram
Ergotamine
Ethambutol
Euphoriant
Formestane
Get through
Haemagogue
Helminthic
Hemostatic
Hypodermic
Imipramine
Indapamide
Iproneazid
Irinotecan
Isoniazide
Ivermectin
Ketoprofin
Lethal dose
Long-acting
Medication
Mefloquine
Meperidine
Mephedrone

Methridine
Methyldopa
Mickey Finn
Nalbuphine
Natorphine
Nifedipine
Nitrazepam
Olanzapine
Painkiller
Palliative
Papaverine
Parenteral
Penicillin
Pentaquine
Phenacaine
Phenacetin
Phenformin
Potash alum
Potentiate
Prednisone
Preventive
Primaquine
Probenecid
Psilocybin
Quinacrine
Rifampicin
Salbutamol
Selegiline
Side effect
Space cadet
Speedfreak
Spermicide
Stramonium
Sucralfate
Taeniacide
Taeniafuge
Terramycin®
Thiouracil
Unofficial
Vagotropic
Vesicatory
Witch hazel
Withdrawal
Ziduvudine

11 letters:
Acetanilide
Acriflavine
Adiaphorous
Allopurinol
Aminobutene
Amphetamine
Amyl nitrite
Anaesthetic
Antifebrile
Antimycotic
Antipyretic
Antitussive
Aphrodisiac
Apomorphine
Barbiturate
Beta-blocker
Bitter aloes
Bupivacaine
Cantharides
Carbimazole
Carminative
Chloroquine
Chrysarobin
Cinnarizine
Clenbuterol
Clindamycin
Contrayerva
Deserpidine
Diamorphine
Diaphoretic
Distalgesic
Embrocation
Emmenagogue
Expectorant
Fluconazole
Gemfibrozil
Haemostatic
Haloperidol
Hydralazine
Hyoscyamine
Indometacin
Ipecacuanha
Ipratropium
Isoxsuprine

Laughing gas
Magic bullet
Masticatory
Meprobamate
Methicillin
Neuroleptic
Nikethamide
Paracetamol
Paraldehyde
Pentamidine
Pentazocine
Pravastatin
Propranolol
Proprietary
Psychedelic
Psychodelic
Purple heart
Restorative
Sanguinaria
Scopolamine
Sensitivity
Short-acting
Succedaneum
Suppository
Suppurative
Thalidomide
Theobromine
Tolbutamide
Tous-les-mois
Trituration
Tropomyosin
Tumefacient
Varenicline
Vasodilator
Vinblastine
Vincristine

12 letters:
ACE inhibitor
Aldesleukine
Alexipharmic
Alpha-blocker
Anistreplase
Anthelmintic
Antimalarial

Antiperiodic
Arsphenamine
Azathioprine
Chlorambucil
Clotrimazole
Control group
Cyclopropane
Cyclosporin-A
Decongestant
False saffron
Fluid extract
Fluorouracil
Fluphenazine
Glue-sniffing
Gonadotropin
Guanethidine
Hallucinogen
Idiosyncrasy
Incompatible
Indomethacin
Intoxicating
Mecamylamine
Methaqualone
Methotrexate
Mifepristone
Nitrous oxide
Perphenazine
Physotigmine
Prednisolone
Prescription
Promethazine
Prophylactic
Psychoactive
Radio mimetic
Recreational
Solvent abuse
Sorbefacient
Spermatocide
Streptomycin
Stupefacient
Tetracycline
Tranquilizer
Trimethoprim
Venepuncture
Venipuncture

13 letters:
Abortifacient
Amitriptyline
Anaphrodisiac
Anthelminthic
Antihistamine
Antispasmodic
Carbamazepine
Contraceptive
Co-trimoxazole
Depressomotor
Knockout drops
Magic mushroom
Materia medica
Mind-expanding
Nortriplyline
Penicillamine
Phencyclidine
Phenothiazine
Pyrimethamine
Sulphadiazine
Suxamethonium
Sympatholytic
Tachyphylaxis
Thiabendazole
Tranquilliser
Tranquillizer
Triamcinolone
Vasoinhibitor
Vinca alkaloid

14 letters:
Anticonvulsant
Antidepressant
Antimetabolite
Antiphlogistic
Bendrofluozide
Benzodiazepine
Bronchodilator
Butyrhophenone
Cascara sagrada
Chlorothiazide
Chlorpromazine
Chlorpropamide
Chlorthalidone

Contraindicate
Dimenhydrinate
Flucloxacillin
Hydrocortisone
Hypersensitive
Mean lethal dose
Mercaptopurine
Norethisterone
Over-the-counter
Pentobarbitone
Phenacyclidine
Phenobarbitone
Phenylbutazone
Rochelle powder
Seidlitz powder
Sulfamethazine
Sulphadimidine
Sulphanilamide
Sulphathiozole
Sulphisoxazole

15 letters:
Acetophenetidin
Alkylating agent
Anticholinergic
Bioavailability
Chloramphenicol
Dinitrogen oxide
Local anesthetic
Methamphetamine
Phenolphthalein
Psychotomimetic
Seidlitz powders
Shooting gallery
Sodium Pentothal®
Sympathomimetic
Vasoconstrictor

16 letters:
Anti-inflammatory
Blow someone's mind
Chemoprophylaxis
Chlordiazepoxide
Hypodermic needle
Local anaesthetic

Median lethal dose
Symphathomimetic
Thiopental sodium

17 letters:
Calcium antagonist
Chlortetracycline
Dextroamphetamine
Diethyltryptamine
General anesthetic
Hypodermic syringe
Immunosuppressive
Minimum lethal dose
Pentylenetetrazol
Thiopentone sodium

18 letters:
Dimethyltryptamine
General anaesthetic
Intermediate-acting
Sildenafil citrate

Withdrawal symptoms

19 letters:
Acetylsalicylic acid
Sodium pentabarbital

20 letters:
Pentobarbitone sodium

21 letters:
Procaine hydrochloride

23 letters:
Meperidene hydrochloride

24 letters:
Lysergic acid diethylamide

28 letters:
Nonsteroidal anti-inflammatory

Ducks

4 letters:
Blue
Musk
Smee
Smew
Sord
Surf
Teal
Wood

5 letters:
Eider
Ruddy
Scaup

6 letters:
Garrot
Hareld
Herald
Runner
Scoter

Smeath
Smeeth
Tufted
Wigeon

7 letters:
Flapper
Gadwall
Mallard
Muscovy
Pintail
Pochard
Spatula
Widgeon

8 letters:
Bald-pate
Garganey
Mandarin
Oldsquaw
Paradise

Ring-bill
Shelduck
Shoveler

9 letters:
Aylesbury
Bergander
Golden-eye
Goosander
Greenhead
Harlequin
Sheldrake
Shoveller
Sprigtail
Whistling
Whitewing

10 letters:
Bufflehead
Canvasback
Long-tailed

Surfscoter

11 letters:
Ferruginous

12 letters:
Velvet scoter

Dwarfs

3 letters:
Doc

5 letters:
Dopey
Happy

6 letters:
Grumpy
Sleepy
Sneezy

7 letters:
Bashful

Dyes

3 letters:
Azo
Vat

4 letters:
Anil
Chay
Choy
Ikat
Kohl
Wald
Weld
Woad
Wold

5 letters:
Aweto
Batik
Chaya
Chica
Congo
Eosin
Grain
Henna
Shaya
Sumac
Woald

6 letters:
Archil
Battik
Cobalt
Corkir

Crotal
Direct
Flavin
Fustet
Fustic
Fustoc
Gambir
Indigo
Kamala
Kermes
Korkir
Madder
Orcein
Orchil
Raddle
Sumach
Tannin
Tie-dye

7 letters:
Alkanet
Camwood
Crocein
Crottle
Cudbear
Engrain
Flavine
Fuchsin
Gambier
Indican
Indoxyl
Indulin
Magenta

Mauvein
Para-red
Puccoon
Sunfast
Valonia

8 letters:
Catechin
Cinnabar
Fuchsine
Indamine
Induline
Mauveine
Nigrosin
Orchella
Purpurin
Pyronine
Safranin
Stilbene
Stone-rag
Stone-raw
Turnsole
Xanthium
Xylidine

9 letters:
Cochineal
Envermeil
Indirubin
Myrobalan
Nigrosine
Phthalein
Primuline

Quinoline
Rhodamine
Rosanilin
Safranine

10 letters:
Anthracene
Azobenzine
Carthamine
Quercitron

Resorcinol
Rosaniline
Tartrazine
Tropaeolin
Trypan blue

11 letters:
Incarnadine
Ultramarine

13 letters:
Anthraquinone
Canthaxanthin

14 letters:
Dinitrobenzene

15 letters:
Phenolphthalein

See also:
➤ **Pigments**

Ee

Ear, parts of

5 letters:
Ancus
Incus
Pinna

6 letters:
Meatus
Stapes
Tragus

7 letters:
Cochlea
Eardrum
Ear lobe
Malleus

Saccule
Utricle

8 letters:
Tympanum

10 letters:
Oval window

11 letters:
Round window

12 letters:
Organ of Corti

13 letters:
Auditory canal
Auditory nerve

14 letters:
Eustachian tube

16 letters:
Tympanic membrane

18 letters:
Semicircular canals

21 letters:
External auditory canal

Earth's crust

4 letters:
Sial
Sima

7 letters:
Oceanic

8 letters:
Basement

11 letters:
Continental
Lithosphere
Lower mantle
Upper mantle

13 letters:
Asthenosphere

14 letters:
Transition zone

24 letters:
Mohorovicíc
  discontinuity

Eating habits

Food	Name of habit
Fellow humans	Anthropophagic *or* anthropophagous
Bees	Apivorous
Other members of the same species	Cannibalistic
Meat	Carnivorous

Food	Name of habit
Fruit	Carpophagous, frugivorous, *or* fruitarian
Dead and rotting flesh	Carrion
Dung	Coprophagous
Earth	Geophagous
Plants	Herbivorous
Wood	Hylophagous
Insects	Insectivorous
Mud	Limivorous
Large pieces of food	Macrophagous
Only one food	Monophagous
Fungi	Mycetophagous
Ants	Myrmecophagous
Nectar	Nectarivorous
Nuts	Nucivorous
Meat and plants	Omnivorous
Raw food	Omophagic *or* omophagous
Fish	Piscivorous
Gods	Theophagous
No animal products	Vegan
No flesh	Vegetarian
Animals	Zoophagous

Ecclesiastical terms

1 letter:
R
S
V
X
Y

2 letters:
BV
CE
DG
DV
HC
MS
PB
PP
RR
Sr
SS
St

VG
VW
Xn
XP
Xt

3 letters:
Abp
Alb
BVM
Cup
Dip
Fra
God
IDN
IHS
Lay
LDS
Mgr
Nun

Par
Pie
Pit
Pix
Pye
Pyx
Rev
See
Sta
STD
Ste
Sun
Use
Ven
Vow
WCC
Zen

4 letters:
Abbé

Alms
Ambo
Amen
Apse
Bans
Bapt
Beat
Bell
Cell
Chap
C of E
Cope
Cowl
Crib
Cure
Dame
Dean
Dove
Ebor
Eccl

Fall
Fold
Font
Hadg
Hajj
Halo
Holy
Host
Hymn
Idol
Kirk
Laic
Lent
Mass
Monk
None
Pall
Revd
Rite
Rood
Rule
Sain
Seal
Sext
Sign
Sion
Slip
Suff
Text
Veil
V Rev
Wake
Whit
Xmas
Xnty
YMCA
Yule
YWCA
Zion

5 letters:
Abbey
Abbot
Agape
Allah

Altar
Ambry
Amice
Amish
Angel
Banns
Bedel
Bible
Bless
Canon
Carol
Catho
Cense
Chant
Choir
Clerk
Close
Cloth
Credo
Creed
Cross
Cruet
Crypt
Curse
Deify
Deism
Deist
Deity
Demon
Denom
Devil
Dirge
Dogma
Dowry
Druid
Elder
Elect
Epiph
Exeat
Faith
Flock
Friar
Frock
Glebe
Glory

Godly
Grace
Hindu
Hours
House
Islam
Jesus
Jewry
Karma
Koran
Laity
Laver
Maker
Manna
Manse
Matin
Miter
Mitre
Mt Rev
Myrrh
Nones
Offer
Order
Padre
Pagan
Papal
Paten
Patin
Pietà
Piety
Plate
Prior
Psalm
Pyxis
Rabbi
Saint
Satan
Stall
Stole
Stoop
Stoup
Suffr
Synod
Teind
Tithe

Title
Trump
Vigil
Wafer

6 letters:
Abbacy
Abbess
Advent
Almuce
Anoint
Anthem
Archbp
Assume
Aumbry
Austin
Beadle
Bishop
Cantor
Censer
Chapel
Cherub
Chrism
Christ
Church
Clergy
Cleric
Coming
Common
Crèche
Curacy
Curate
Curtal
Deacon
Devout
Divine
Dossal
Dragon
Easter
Eparch
Exarch
Exodus
Father
Ferial
Friary

Fundie
Gloria
Gnosis
God man
Godson
Gospel
Gradin
Hallow
Harrow
Heaven
Hebrew
Heresy
Homily
Housel
Hymnal
Impose
Intone
Israel
Jesuit
Jewish
Judaic
Lavabo
Lector
Legend
Lenten
Lesson
Litany
Living
Marian
Martyr
Matins
Maundy
Mormon
Mosaic
Moslem
Mosque
Mother
Muslim
Novice
Nuncio
Oblate
Octave
Office
Old man
Ordain

Orders
Papacy
Papism
Papist
Parish
Parson
Pastor
Patron
Paynim
Person
Postil
Prayer
Preach
Priest
Priory
Proper
Pulpit
Purify
Purple
Quaker
Redeem
Revert
Ritual
Rosary
Rt Revd
Rubric
Sacral
Sacred
Schism
Season
Secret
Sermon
Server
Sexton
Shiite
Shinto
Shrine
Shroud
Simony
Sinful
Sinner
Sister
Solemn
Stigma
Sufism

Sunday
Suttee
Talmud
Tantra
Taoism
Te Deum
Temple
Theism
Tippet
Tongue
Venite
Verger
Vesper
Vestal
Vestry
Virgin
Votary
Warden

7 letters:
Aaronic
Acolyte
Agrapha
Ampulla
Anagoge
Apostle
Article
Ascetic
Asperse
Atheism
Atheist
Bahaism
Bambino
Baptism
Baptist
Baptize
Benison
Blessed
Brother
Canonry
Cantuar
Cassock
Cenacle
Chalice
Chancel

Chantry
Chapter
Chrisom
Classis
Cluniac
Collate
Collect
College
Commune
Confess
Confirm
Conform
Convent
Council
Counsel
Crosier
Crozier
Deanery
Decanal
Defrock
Deified
Devotee
Diocese
Dissent
Dominie
Element
Epistle
Eremite
Errancy
Evangel
Evil One
Expiate
Frontal
Genesis
Gentile
Glorify
Gnostic
Godhead
Godhood
Halidom
Hassock
Heathen
Holy day
Holy Joe
Hosanna

Idolize
Immerse
Incense
Infulae
Inspire
Introit
Jainism
Jehovah
Judaism
Kenosis
Kerygma
Kirkman
Labarum
Lady Day
Laicize
Liturgy
Low Mass
Lustral
Madonna
Maniple
Martyry
Mattins
Maurist
Messiah
Minster
Miracle
Mission
Monkery
Monkish
Mortify
Mourner
Movable
Mystery
Notitia
Nunhood
Nunnery
Old Nick
Oratory
Ordinal
Our Lady
Parlour
Paschal
Pauline
Peccant
Penance

Pietism
Pilgrim
Pontiff
Prebend
Prelacy
Prelate
Present
Primacy
Primate
Profane
Prophet
Proverb
Provide
Puritan
Ramadan
Recluse
Rectory
Regular
Reredos
Respond
Retable
Revival
Sabbath
Sacring
Sanctum
Sanctus
Saviour
Secular
Sedilia
Service
Species
Sponsor
Spousal
Station
Stylite
Tantric
Titulus
Tribune
Trinity
Unction
Unfrock
Vatican
Vespers
Whitsun
Worship

Xmas Day
Yule log
Zionism

8 letters:
Abbatial
Ablution
Advowson
Affusion
Agnus Dei
Alleluia
Altar boy
Anathema
Anglican
Antiphon
Beadsman
Bedesman
Benefice
Brownist
Buddhism
Buddhist
Canonist
Canonize
Canon law
Canticle
Cardinal
Cathedra
Catholic
Celibacy
Cellarer
Cenobite
Chancery
Chapelry
Chaplain
Charisma
Chasuble
Cherubim
Choirboy
Christen
Ciborium
Clerical
Cloister
Coenacle
Colloquy
Creation

Crucifix
Deaconry
Dedicate
Devotion
Diaconal
Dies Irae
Diocesan
Diriment
Disciple
Disfrock
Docetism
Doxology
Druidess
Druidism
Ecce Homo
Ecclesia
Emmanuel
Empyrean
Epiphany
Epistler
Evensong
Expiable
Faithful
Footpace
Fraction
Frontlet
Galilean
Gallican
Godchild
God's acre
Godsquad
Guardian
Hail Mary
Hallowed
Heavenly
Hierarch
Hieratic
High Mass
Holiness
Holy City
Holy Land
Holy rood
Holy Week
Hymn book
Immanent

Immanuel	Sanctify	Calvinism	Establish
Jacobite	Sanctity	Calvinist	Eucharist
Jubilate	Sarum use	Candlemas	Exarchate
Lavatory	Scapular	Canonical	Expectant
Libellee	Sentence	Cantorial	Expiation
Lord's Day	Separate	Capitular	Expiatory
Lustrate	Silenced	Catechism	Formalism
Lutheran	Simoniac	Catechize	Formulary
Man of God	Sinecure	Cathedral	Godfather
Maronite	Son of God	Celebrant	Godmother
Marriage	Suffrage	Celestial	Godparent
Menology	Superior	Christian	Gospeller
Ministry	Tantrism	Christmas	Graveyard
Miserere	Tertiary	Churchman	Hagiarchy
Mohammed	Thurible	City of God	Halloween
Monachal	Thurifer	Claustral	Hallowmas
Monastic	Tithable	Clergyman	Hermitage
Monition	Traditor	Clericals	Hierarchy
Monkhood	Transept	Cloistral	High altar
Nativity	Unchurch	Coadjutor	Holocaust
Oblation	Unhallow	Coenobite	Holy Ghost
Offering	Veronica	Collation	Holy Grail
Ordinand	Versicle	Collative	Holy water
Ordinary	Vesperal	Collegium	Homiletic
Orthodox	Vestment	Comforter	Immersion
Paradise	Viaticum	Commendam	Impeccant
Parament	Vicarage	Communion	Incensory
Parclose	Vicarial	Conciliar	Incumbent
Pastoral		Confessor	Institute
Pelagian	**9 letters:**	Confirmed	Interdict
Penitent	Adoration	Dalai Lama	Jerusalem
Pericope	Alleluiah	Damnation	Last rites
Piacular	Allelujah	Deaconess	Lay sister
Postlude	Ambrosian	Dei gratia	Libellant
Priestly	Antiphony	Diaconate	Liturgics
Prophesy	Apostolic	Dimissory	Liturgist
Province	Archangel	Directory	Love feast
Psalmody	Aspersion	Discalced	Low Sunday
Redeemer	Augustine	Dissenter	Martinmas
Registry	Avoidance	Dog collar	Martyrdom
Response	Baptistry	Dominical	Mercy seat
Reverend	Beelzebub	Easter Day	Methodism
Rigorism	Bishopric	Ecumenism	Methodist
Rogation	Blasphemy	Epiclesis	Millenary
Sacristy	Born-again	Episcopal	Miscreant

Missioner
Monastery
Mortal sin
Novitiate
Obedience
Offertory
Officiant
Officiate
Our Father
Out sister
Paraclete
Parochial
Parsonage
Pastorate
Patriarch
Patrimony
Patristic
Patrology
Patroness
Pentecost
Perdition
Pluralism
Plurality
Pluralize
Polyptych
Precentor
Preceptor
Predicant
Prelatism
Presbyter
Proselyte
Provision
Quakerism
Recession
Reconcile
Reconvert
Reformism
Religieux
Religious
Reliquary
Remission
Ritualism
Ritualize
Rubrician
Rural dean

Sacrament
Sacrarium
Sacrifice
Sacrilege
Sacristan
Saint's day
Salvation
Sanctuary
Scientist
Seneschal
Shintoism
Solemnize
Spiritual
Succentor
Succursal
Suffragan
Surrogate
Sutteeism
Synagogue
Testament
Tradition
Translate
Venerable
Venial sin
Vestryman
Vicariate
Yom Kippur

10 letters:
Act of faith
Allhallows
Altar cloth
Amen corner
Antinomian
Antiphonal
Apostolate
Archbishop
Archdeacon
Archpriest
Asceticism
Ascription
Assumption
Athanasian
Bar mitzvah
Benedicite

Benedictus
Canonicals
Canonicate
Canonicity
Canto fermo
Catechumen
Ceremonial
Chancellor
Childermas
Churchgoer
Circumcise
Cloistered
Conference
Confessant
Confession
Confirmand
Conformist
Conformity
Connection
Consecrate
Consistory
Conventual
Dedication
Deo gratias
Deo volente
Devotional
Discipline
Ecumenical
Enthusiasm
Enthusiast
Episcopacy
Episcopate
Evangelism
Evangelist
Evangelize
Fellowship
Fenestella
Free Church
Gnosticize
Good Friday
Gospel oath
Hagiolatry
Halleluiah
Hallelujah
Hierocracy

High Church
High Priest
Holy Family
Holy orders
Holy Spirit
Homiletics
Horologium
House group
House of God
Idolatrize
Impanation
Impeccable
Insufflate
Intinction
Invitatory
Invocation
Irreligion
Lammastide
Last Supper
Lay brother
Lectionary
Limitarian
Liturgical
Lord's table
Magnificat
Metropolis
Millennium
Miscreance
Misericord
Missionary
Mother's Day
Ordination
Palm Sunday
Pancake Day
Pilgrimage
Pontifical
Prayer book
Preachment
Prebendary
Presbytery
Priesthood
Profession
Protestant
Providence
Provincial

Puritanism
Religieuse
Requiescat
Reredorter
Responsory
Retrochoir
Reunionist
Revelation
Revivalism
Revivalist
Sacerdotal
Sacrosanct
Sanctified
Sanctitude
Scriptures
Secularize
Sexagesima
Shrovetide
Sisterhood
Solifidian
Subreption
Subsellium
Superaltar
Tabernacle
Twelfth Day
Unhallowed
Unhouseled
Versicular
Vigil light
Visitation
Whit Monday
Whit Sunday

11 letters:
All Souls' Day
Antependium
Antiphonary
Archdiocese
Aspersorium
Augustinian
Benediction
Beneficiary
Blasphemous
Book of hours
Brotherhood

Calefactory
Cardinalate
Catholicism
Celtic cross
Christening
Christingle
Churchwoman
Clericalism
Cockleshell
Coessential
Commandment
Communicant
Communicate
Contemplate
Conventicle
Convocation
Crucifixion
Evangelical
Externalism
Gloria Patri
Glossolalia
Goddaughter
Hare Krishna
House church
Immanentism
Impropriate
Incarnation
Incorporeal
Independent
Institution
Irreligious
Jesus Christ
Judgment Day
Lord of Hosts
Lord's Prayer
Lord's Supper
Martyrology
Millenarian
Monasticism
Monseigneur
Mother of God
Oecumenical
Parish clerk
Parishioner
Paschal Lamb

Passiontide
Passion Week
Patron saint
Pelagianism
Pentecostal
Preparation
Priestcraft
Prodigal Son
Proselytize
Protomartyr
Purificator
Rastafarian
Recessional
Ritualistic
Sabbatarian
Sacramental
Sanctus bell
Scriptorium
Stabat Mater
Sursum corda
Temporality
Thaumaturge
Twelfthtide
Whitsuntide
Year of grace
Zen Buddhism

12 letters:
Advent Sunday
All Saints' Day
Anathematize
Annunciation
Apostolic See
Archdeaconry
Ascension Day
Ash Wednesday
Body of Christ
Chapel of ease
Chapterhouse
Christmas Day
Christmas Eve
Churchwarden
Circuit rider
Concelebrate
Confessional

Confirmation
Confucianism
Congregation
Deconsecrate
Disestablish
Dispensation
Ecclesiastic
Ecclesiology
Eleanor Cross
Episcopalian
Episcopalism
Good Shepherd
Heteroousian
Holy Saturday
Holy Thursday
Immersionism
Independency
Intercession
Judgement Day
Kyrie eleison
Last Judgment
Messeigneurs
Metropolitan
Ministration
Most Reverend
New Testament
Non-Christian
Obedientiary
Old Testament
Palingenesis
Patriarchate
Presbyterian
Presentation
Presentative
Procathedral
Processional
Providential
Quadragesima
Real presence
Residentiary
Rogation Days
Satisfaction
Satisfactory
Septuagesima
Spirituality

Spiritualize
Spy Wednesday
Subapostolic
Subscription
Sunday school
Superhumeral
Thanksgiving
Traducianism
Twelfth Night
Very Reverend
Vicar general
Well dressing
Winding sheet

13 letters:
Allhallowtide
Apostles' Creed
Archbishopric
Archidiaconal
Ascensiontide
Autocephalous
Baptism of fire
Burnt offering
Canonical hour
Contemplation
Contemplative
Corpus Christi
Credence table
Day of Judgment
Divine service
Ecclesiolatry
Excommunicate
Gift of tongues
Glorification
Holy Communion
Incardination
Last Judgement
Mater dolorosa
Metrical psalm
Mortification
Nonpractising
Passion Sunday
Premillennial
Protestantism
Quadragesimal

Quinquagesima
Right Reverend
Roman Catholic
Sacerdotalism
Salvation Army
Sanctuary lamp
Shrove Tuesday
Spoiled priest
Trinity Sunday
Unconsecrated

14 letters:
Archidiaconate
Archiepiscopal
Article of faith
Day of Judgement
Ecclesiastical
Exclaustration
Extracanonical
Fundamentalism
Gregorian chant
Indifferentism
Intercommunion
Maundy Thursday
Millenarianism
Orthodox Church
Parish register
Peculiar people
Pontifical Mass
Rastafarianism
Recording Angel
Reverend Mother
Sacramentalism
Sacramentarian
Territorialism

15 letters:
Act of contrition
Archiepiscopate
Athanasian Creed
Church of England
Dominical letter
Ecclesiasticism
Excommunication
Father confessor

General Assembly
Jehovah's Witness
Mothering Sunday
Presbyterianism
Ten Commandments

16 letters:
Apostolic Fathers
Blessed Sacrament
Church of Scotland
Patriarchal cross
Premillennialism
Prince of Darkness
Saint Swithin's Day
Sustentation fund

17 letters:
Communion of saints
Established Church
Saint Andrew's Cross
Speaking in tongues

18 letters:
College of Cardinals
Establishmentarian
Stations of the Cross

19 letters:
Gloria in Excelsis Deo

22 letters:
World Council of Churches

27 letters:
Ecclesiastical Commissioners
Purification of the Virgin Mary

Economics

BRANCHES OF ECONOMICS

7 letteers:
Welfare

10 letters:
Agronomics
Industrial

11 letters:
Cliometrics

12 letters:
Bioeconomics
Econometrics

14 letters:
Macroeconomics
Microeconomics
Neuroeconomics

15 letters:
Economic history

16 letters:
Political economy

ECONOMICS TERMS

2 letters:
HP

3 letters:
Bid
GDP
GNP
Pay
PEP
Tax
UBR
VAT

4 letters:
Bank
Boom
Cash
Debt
Duty
Hire
Loan
MCAs
Mint
PAYE
PSBR
Rent
Shop
Wage

5 letters:
Asset

Lease
Money
Price
Sales
Share
Slump
Stock
Trade
Trust
Yield

6 letters:
Barter
Budget
Cartel
Credit
Demand
Export
Import
Income
Labour
Lender
Market
Merger
Patent
Picket
Profit
Retail
Salary
Saving
Supply

Tariff
Wealth

7 letters:
Autarky
Bad bank
Boycott
Capital
Dumping
Duopoly
Embargo
Finance
Freight
Funding
Hedging
Holding
Invoice
Lockout
Payroll
Pension
Premium
Revenue
Subsidy
Surplus
Synergy
Trustee
Utility

8 letters:
Base rate
Capacity

Consumer
Currency
Discount
Dividend
Earnings
Employee
Employer
Exchange
Freeport
Hoarding
Hot money
Interest
Junk bond
Monopoly
Mortgage
Offshore
Overtime
Producer
Recovery
Sub-prime
Supplier
Takeover
Taxation
Tax haven
Training

9 letters:
Commodity
Deflation
Franchise
Free rider

Free trade
Income tax
Insurance
Liability
Liquidity
Means test
Mediation
Middleman
Net profit
Oligopoly
Overheads
Piecework
Portfolio
Rationing
Recession
Recycling
Reflation
Trademark
Unit trust

10 letters:
Automation
Bankruptcy
Bear market
Bull market
Capitalism
Closed shop
Commission
Depression
Divestment
Employment
Fiscal drag
Fiscal year
Fixed costs
Forfaiting
Game theory
Green money
Insolvency
Investment
Monetarism
Pawnbroker
Production
Redundancy
Share issue
Tax evasion

Trade union
Wholesaler

11 letters:
Arbitration
Capital good
Central bank
Competition
Consumption
Cooperative
Corporation
Devaluation
Durable good
Expenditure
Fixed assets
Foreclosure
Gross profit
Index-linked
Indirect tax
Intangibles
Legal tender
Liquid asset
Liquidation
Money supply
Overheating
Overmanning
Pension fund
Poverty trap
Premium bond
Public works
Pump priming
Revaluation
Savings bank
Self service
Shareholder
Share market
Shop steward
Social costs
Speculation
Stagflation
Stockbroker
Stock market
Stop-go cycle
Transaction
Underwriter

12 letters:
Balance sheet
Black economy
Bridging loan
Buyer's market
Clearing bank
Common market
Consumer good
Cost of living
Credit crunch
Customs union
Depreciation
Deregulation
Discount rate
Disinflation
Dutch disease
Earned income
Entrepreneur
Exchange rate
Fiscal policy
Five-Year Plan
Gold standard
Hard currency
Hire purchase
Human capital
Interest rate
Joint venture
Labour market
Laisser faire
Laissez faire
Mercantilism
Merchant bank
Mixed economy
Moonlighting
National debt
Pay-as-you-earn
Productivity
Profit margin
Rent controls
Risk analysis
Soft currency
Stock control
Tax avoidance
Terms of trade
Too big to fail

Trade barrier
Unemployment
Welfare state

13 letters:
Budget deficit
Business cycle
Credit squeeze
Discount house
Financial year
Free trade area
Free trade zone
Futures market
Income support
Invisible hand
Listed company
Market failure
Multinational
Primary sector
Privatization
Profitability
Profit sharing
Protectionism
Public finance
Public utility
Ratchet effect
Seller's market
Sequestration
Service sector
Stock exchange
Unit of account
Value-added tax
Variable costs
Wage restraint

14 letters:
Balanced budget
Balance of trade
Barriers to exit
Command economy
Commercial bank
Corporation tax
Credit controls
Current account
Deposit account

Disequilibrium
Economic growth
Economic policy
Fringe benefits
Full employment
Gains from trade
Government bond
Hyperinflation
Infrastructure
Inheritance tax
Mass production
Monetary policy
National income
Nondurable good
Planned economy
Public interest
Quality control
Regional policy
Self-employment
Simple interest
Specialization
Tangible assets
Unearned income
Venture capital
Working capital

15 letters:
Barriers to entry
Building society
Diversification
Fixed investment
Friendly society
Marginal revenue
Marginal utility
Nationalization
National product
Per capita income
Private property
Purchasing power
Rationalization
Self-sufficiency
Share price index

16 letters:
Demand management

Disposable income
Division of labour
Economies of scale
Industrial estate
Industrial policy
Industrial sector
Instalment credit
Intangible assets
Invisible balance
Management buy-out
Medium of exchange
Retail price index
Standard of living

17 letters:
Balance of payments
Chamber of Commerce
Cost effectiveness
Cost-push inflation
Credit default swap
Economic sanctions
Free-market economy
Gilt-edged security
Industrial dispute
International debt
Joint-stock company
Private enterprise
Public expenditure
Subsidiary company

18 letters:
Diminishing returns
Environmental audit
Import restrictions
Inflationary spiral
Perfect competition
Personal equity plan
Quantitative easing
Socio-economic group
Trade-weighted index

19 letters:
Cost-benefit analysis
Deindustrialization
Demand-pull inflation

Industrial relations
Labour theory of value
Macroeconomic policy
Microeconomic policy
Progressive taxation
Shadow banking system
Stabilization policy
Supply-side economics
Unemployment benefit
Uniform business rate
Vertical integration
Worker participation

20 letters:
Collective bargaining
Comparative advantage
Greenfield investment
Gross domestic product
Gross national product
Imperfect competition
Information agreement
Profit-and-loss account
Rational expectations
Residual unemployment
Seasonal unemployment

21 letters:
Foreign exchange market
Forward exchange market
Horizontal integration
International reserves
Polluter pays principle
Voluntary unemployment

22 letters:
Conspicuous consumption
Institutional investors
Prices and incomes policy
Recommended retail price
Research and development
Structural unemployment

23 letters:
Fixed exchange-rate system
Foreign exchange controls

25 letters:
Intellectual property right
Natural rate of unemployment
Public-sector debt repayment
Restrictive labour practice

26 letters:
Floating exchange-rate system

27 letters:
Medium-term financial strategy
Monetary compensatory amounts

28 letters:
Collateralized debt obligation
International competitiveness

30 letters:
National insurance contributions

32 letters:
Public-sector borrowing requirement

ECONOMICS SCHOOLS AND THEORIES

7 letters:
Chicago
Marxism

8 letters:
Austrian

9 letters:
Classical

10 letters:
Monetarism

11 letters:
Physiocrats
Reaganomics
Rogernomics
Thatcherism

12 letters:
Keynesianism
Mercantilism
Neoclassical

15 letters:
NeoKeynesianism

ECONOMISTS

4 letters:
Hume, *David*
Marx, *Karl*
Mill, *James*
Mill, *John Stuart*
Ward, *Dame Barbara (Mary)*
Webb, *Sidney*
West, *Arthur Lewis*

5 letters:
Passy, *Frédéric*
Singh, *Manmohan*
Smith, *Adam*
Weber, *Max*

6 letters:
Angell, *Norman*
Bright, *John*
Cobden, *Richard*
Coombs, *Nuggett*
Delors, *Jacques*
Frisch, *Ragnar*
George, *Henry*
Jevons, *William Stanley*
Keynes, *John Maynard*
Laffer, *Arthur*
Monnet, *Jean*
Myrdal, *Gunnar*
Pareto, *Vilfredo*
Turgot, *Anne Robert Jacques*
Veblen, *Thorstein*

7 letters:
Bagehot, *Walter*

Cournot, *Augustin*
D' Oresme, *Nicole*
Douglas, *C(lifford) H(ugh)*
Krugman, *Paul*
Kuznets, *Simon*
Leacock, *Stephen Butler*
Malthus, *Thomas Robert*
Quesnay, *François*
Ricardo, *David*
Toynbee, *Arnold*
Wootton, *Barbara (Frances)*

8 letters:
Beccaria, *Cesare Bonesana*
Friedman, *Milton*
Mansholt, *Sicco Leendert*
Marshall, *Alfred*
Phillips, *A(lban) W(illiam) H(ousego)*
Rathenau, *Walther*
Stiglitz, *Joseph*
Von Hayek, *Friedrich August*
Von Mises, *Ludwig*

9 letters:
Beveridge, *William Henry*
Galbraith, *J(ohn) K(enneth)*
Tinbergen, *Jan*

10 letters:
De Sismondi, *Jean Charles Léonard Simonde*
Papandreou, *Andreas (George)*
Schumacher, *Ernst Friedrich*
Schumpeter, *Joseph*

Education terms

2 letters:			4 letters:	
UE	Dux	ONC	Co-ed	Fail
	GCE	PTA	CPVE	GCSE
	GPS	SCE	Crib	Gown
3 letters:	Jig	Set	Dean	Hall
COP	LMS	Wag	Exam	Hood
Don	NCT			Mich

Pass
Pipe
SATS
Term
Test
Year

5 letters:
Class
Dunce
Entry
Essay
Expel
Flunk
Gaudy
Grade
Grant
Hooky
House
Lines
Lycée
Mitch
Mocks
Pandy
Resit
Shell
Sizar
Stage
Tutee
Tutor
Union

6 letters:
A level
Alumna
Bedder
Binary
Bursar
Campus
Credit
Degree
Docent
Fellow
Ferule
Greats

Higher
Honors
Hookey
Incept
Infant
Junior
Master
Matric
Ofsted
O grade
O level
Pedant
Porter
Reader
Recess
Rector
Regent
Remove
Report
Second
Senate
Senior
Stream
Thesis
Truant
Warden

7 letters:
Adviser
Advisor
Alumnus
Banding
Battels
Boarder
Bursary
Crammer
Deanery
Dominie
Donnish
Dropout
Educate
Faculty
Federal
Fresher
Honours

Janitor
Lecture
Marking
Midterm
Prefect
Prelims
Primers
Proctor
Provost
Seminar
Session
Subject
Teach-in
Tuition

8 letters:
A bursary
Academic
Accredit
Aegrotat
B bursary
Comedown
Commoner
Delegacy
Dunce cap
Emeritus
Exercise
External
Freshman
Graduand
Graduate
Headship
Homework
Internal
Key stage
Lecturer
Lettered
Manciple
Mistress
Parietal
Redbrick
Remedial
Semester
Send down
Sorority

Transfer
Tutorial
Wrangler

9 letters:
Assistant
Associate
Bubs grade
Bursarial
Catalogue
Catchment
Classmate
Classroom
Collegial
Collegian
Detention
Education
Extension
Gymnasium
Moderator
Muck-up day
Principal
Professor
Reception
Registrar
Rusticate
Schoolman
Sixth form
Sophomore
Speech day
Sports day
Statement
Trimester

10 letters:
Assignment
Bursarship
Chancellor
Collegiate
Coursework
Curricular
Curriculum
Department
Easter term
Eleven-plus

Exhibition
Extramural
Fellowship
Free school
Graded post
Graduation
Grant-in-aid
Headmaster
High school
Hilary term
Imposition
Instructor
Intramural
Invigilate
Prepositor
Prospectus
Readership
Recreation
Sabbatical
Scholastic
Schoolmarm
Supervisor
Transcript
Unstreamed

11 letters:
Coeducation
Convocation
Educational
Examination
Housefather
Housemaster
Housemother
In residence
Invigilator
Lower school
Matriculate
Progressive
Trinity term
Upper school

12 letters:
Accumulation
Chapterhouse
Commencement

Congregation
Core subjects
Dissertation
Exhibitioner
Headmistress
Open learning
Postgraduate
Privatdocent
Schoolleaver
Schoolmaster
Self-educated
Subprincipal

13 letters:
Advanced level
Baccalaureate
Boarding house
Cuisenaire rod®
Full professor
Lowerclassman
Matriculation
Mature student
Ordinary grade
Ordinary level
Professoriate
Schoolteacher
Standard Grade
Summa cum laude
Undergraduate

14 letters:
Common Entrance
Family grouping
Headmastership
Liaison officer
Michaelmas term
Sandwich course
Schoolmistress
Student teacher
Tutorial system
Vice chancellor

15 letters:
Advisory teacher
Cross-curricular

Extracurricular
Grant-maintained
Hall of residence
Interscholastic
Refresher course
Regius professor
Tertiary bursary

16 letters:
Campus university
Foundation school
Further education
Headmistress-ship
Junior common room
Middle common room
Senior common room
Sixth-form college
Vertical grouping

17 letters:
Level of attainment
Literae humaniores
Local examinations
School Certificate
Visiting professor

18 letters:
Great Public Schools
National Curriculum
Punishment exercise
University entrance

19 letters:
Conductive education
Record of achievement
Summative assessment

20 letters:
Continuous assessment

21 letters:
City technology college

23 letters:
Nuffield teaching project

Standard assessment tasks

University entrance examination

24 letters:
Certificate of Proficiency
Local management of schools
Parent teacher association

27 letters:
Ordinary National Certificate

29 letters:
General Certificate of Education

30 letters:
Scottish Certificate of Education

35 letters:
Certificate of Pre-vocational Education

38 letters:
General Certificate of Secondary
  Education

Electronics terms

3 letters:
Bar
Bus
CCD
Eye
Key
LCD
LED
Pad

4 letters:
Bell
Bulb
Card
Chip
Coil
Cord
Dial
Disc
Duct
Flex
Fuse
Gate
Gobo
Jack
Lead
Lobe
Loop
Mike
Neon

Plug
Port
Slug
Tube
Wire

5 letters:
Array
Balun
Cable
Choke
Clock
Coder
Diode
Donor
Drain
Latch
Maser
Mixer
Motor
Plate
Shunt
Spool
Tuner
Valve
Wafer
Wiper

6 letters:
Aerial

Bridge
Buffer
Busbar
Button
Buzzer
Bypass
Carbon
Driver
Feeder
Heater
Mosaic
Needle
Outlet
Phasor
Pick-up
Radome
Scaler
Screen
Sensor
Sheath
Sleeve
Slicer
Socket
Stator
Stylus
Switch
Triode
Woofer

7 letters:
Acetate
Adaptor
Antenna
Battery
Bimorph
Booster
Breaker
Bushing
Capstan
Charger
Chassis
Chopper
Clipper
Console
Counter
Coupler
Crystal
Display
Divider
Element
Emitter
Exciter
Excitor
Fuse box
Gyrator
Harness
Igniter
Krytron
Limiter

Mag tape
Monitor
Negator
Pentode
Reactor
Scanner
Speaker
Tetrode
Tone arm
Trimmer
Tweeter

8 letters:
Acceptor
Black box
Detector
Diffuser
Digitron
Envelope
Expander
Filament
Heat sink
Ignitron
Inverter
Live wire
Magic eye
Neon lamp
Orthicon
Radiator
Receiver
Recorder
Repeater
Resistor
Rheostat
Sleeving
Slip ring
Solenoid
Varactor
Varistor
Vibrator

9 letters:
Amplifier
Autometer
Autotimer

Bolometer
Call alarm
Capacitor
Cartridge
Choke coil
Component
Condenser
Conductor
Contactor
Delay line
Drift tube
Dummy load
Dynamotor
Equalizer
Flame lamp
Fluxmeter
Hygristor
Image tube
Kinescope
Labyrinth
Leyden jar
Light bulb
Magnetron
Metal tape
Microchip
Nixie tube
Optophone
Phono plug
Phototube
Pilot lamp
Plugboard
Plumbicon
Power pack
Rectifier
Reflector
Resnatron
Resonator
Sequencer
Spark coil
Tesla coil
Thyratron
Thyristor
Turntable
Voltmeter
Wattmeter

10 letters:
Acorn valve
Alternator
Banana plug
Breadboard
Camera tube
Chrome tape
Commutator
Comparator
Compressor
Controller
Coulometer
Esaki diode
Goniometer
Harmonizer
Hydrophone
LCD display
LED display
Microphone
Mimic panel
Moving coil
Multimeter
NOT circuit
Oscillator
Patch board
Photodiode
P-n junction
Push button
Radio valve
Reproducer
Rhumbatron
Screen grid
Servomotor
Shadow mask
Sodium lamp
Solar panel
Stabilizer
Suppressor
Switchgear
Thermistor
Time switch
Transducer
Transistor
Trip switch
Vacuum tube

Variometer
Voltameter
Wander plug
Welding rod
Zener diode

11 letters:
Anticathode
Autochanger
Cat's whisker
Cold cathode
Electric eye
Faraday cage
Interrupter
Junction box
Knife switch
Loading coil
Loudspeaker
Microswitch
Motherboard
NAND circuit
Open circuit
Picture tube
Ring circuit
Silicon chip
Space heater
Storage tube
Strobe tuner
Switchboard
Tickler coil
Transformer
Tunnel diode
Voltammeter

12 letters:
Bow collector
Circuit board
Coaxial cable
Electrometer
Electron tube
Friction tape
Magnetic tape
Microcircuit
Oscillograph
Oscilloscope

Preamplifier
Squirrel cage
Standard cell
Toggle switch

13 letters:
Crystal pick-up
Discharge tube
Discriminator
Electric motor
Image orthicon
Induction coil
Low-pass filter
Mercury switch
Multivibrator
Potentiometer
Quartz crystal
Record-changer
Rhombic aerial
Ripple control
Semiconductor
Tumbler switch

14 letters:
Band-pass filter
Circuit breaker
Heating element
High-pass filter
Image converter
Induction motor
Long-wire aerial
Magnetic pick-up
Magnetic stripe
Mesh connection
Motor generator
Noise generator
Peltier element
Power amplifier
Printed circuit
Schmitt trigger
Servomechanism
Star connection
Television tube
Trickle charger
Turbogenerator

Universal motor
Voltage divider

15 letters:
Alloyed junction
Autotransformer
Bleeder resistor
Bridge rectifier
Cavity resonator
Class-A amplifier
Class-B amplifier
Class-C amplifier
Crystal detector
Drift transistor
Electric circuit
Local oscillator
Majority carrier
Minority carrier
Phototransistor
Shuttle armature
Signal generator
Thermionic valve

16 letters:
Carbon microphone
Gas-discharge tube
Image intensifier
Potential divider
Ribbon microphone
Silicon rectifier
Smoothing circuit
Sodium-vapour lamp
Spark transmitter
Spectrum analyser
Synchronous motor
Transmission line

17 letters:
Crystal microphone
Electrostatic lens
Equivalent circuit
Full-wave rectifier
Ground-plane aerial
Integrated circuit
Lightning arrester

Photoelectric cell

18 letters:
Dynatron oscillator
Electronic ignition
I-type semiconductor
Junction transistor
Light-emitting diode
Lightning conductor
Travelling-wave tube

19 letters:
Epitaxial transistor
Parametric amplifier
Parametric equalizer
Pulse height analyser
Seven-segment display

20 letters:
Liquid-crystal display
Multichannel analyser

Operational amplifier
Relaxation oscillator
Synchronous converter

21 letters:
Electric-discharge lamp
Field-effect transistor
Residual current device

22 letters:
Electrostatic generator
Intrinsic semiconductor

24 letters:
Analogue-digital converter

26 letters:
Silicon-controlled rectifier

32 letters:
Steam-generating heavy-water reactor

Embroidery stitches

3 letters:
Fly

4 letters:
Back
Barb
Coil
Fern
Post
Rice
Stem

5 letters:
Briar
Catch
Chain
Coral
Cross
Daisy
Greek
Satin

Split

6 letters:
Basque
Beaded
Berlin
Cast on
Cretan
Crewel
Damask
Eyelet
Ladder
Scroll

7 letters:
Berwick
Blanket
Bullion
Chevron
Chinese
Convent

Feather
Kloster
Outline
Plaited
Running
Russian
Sampler
Sham Hem

8 letters:
Pekinese
Scottish
Wheatear

9 letters:
Arrowhead
Crow's-foot
Lazy Daisy
Open Chain
Quilt Knot

10 letters:
Buttonhole
Casalguidi
French Knot
German Knot
Portuguese
Roman Chain
Whipped Fly

11 letters:
Caterpillar
Double Cross
Herringbone
Montenegrin
Renaissance
Ribbed Wheel
Spider-wheel
Threaded Fly

Whipped Back
Whipped Stem
Zigzag Chain

12 letters:
Ghiordes Knot
Russian Cross
Twisted Chain
Whipped Chain

13 letters:
Buttonhole Bar
Closed Feather
Porto Rico rose

14 letters:
Crossed corners
Feathered Chain

Whipped Running

15 letters:
Buttonhole Wheel
Threaded Running

16 letters:
Closed Buttonhole

17 letters:
Crossed Buttonhole
Threaded Arrowhead
Woven Spider's Wheel

18 letters:
Twisted Lattice Band

Emperors

TITLES OF EMPERORS

3 letters:
Imp
Rex

4 letters:
Inca
King
Tsar

5 letters:
Kesar
Mpret
Negus
Rosco
Ruler
Shang
Tenno

6 letters:
Kaiser
Keasar
Mikado
Purple
Sultan

9 letters:
Sovereign
Yoshihito

12 letters:
Boris Godunov

15 letters:
Ivan the Terrible

FAMOUS EMPERORS

3 letters:
Leo

4 letters:
John
Ming
Nero
Otho
Otto
Pu-yi
Wu Di

5 letters:
Akbar
Asoka
Babur
Gaius
Henry
Jimmu
Kesar
Meiji
Negus
Nerva
Pedro

Rosco
Shang
Tenno
Titus

6 letters:
Bao Dai
Caesar
George
Joseph
Kaiser
Keaser

Manuel
Trajan
Valens
Yong Lo

7 letters:
Akihito
Charles
Francis
Gratian
Hadrian
Leopold

Lothair
Menelik
Severus
William

8 letters:
Agramant
Augustan
Augustus
Aurelian
Caligula
Claudius
Commodus
Hirohito
Matthias
Napoleon
Octavian
Qian Long
Theodore
Tiberius
Valerian
Xuan Zong

9 letters:
Agramante

Atahualpa
Aurangzeb
Bonaparte
Caracalla
Diomitian
Ferdinand
Frederick
Heraclius
Justinian
Montezuma
Shah Jahan
Vespasian
Vitellius

10 letters:
Barbarossa
Dessalines
Diocletian
Franz Josef
Kublai Khan
Maximilian
Meiji Tenno
Theodosius
Theophilus

Wenceslaus

11 letters:
Charlemagne
Constantine
Genghis Khan
Valentinian

13 letters:
Akbar the Great
Antoninus Pius
Haile Selassie
Peter the Great

16 letters:
Germanicus Caesar

17 letters:
Napoleon Bonaparte
Ras Tafari Makonnen

19 letters:
Frederick Barbarossa

Engineering

TYPES OF ENGINEERING

5 letters:
Civil
Naval

6 letters:
Mining

7 letters:
Genetic
Nuclear
Process
Traffic

8 letters:
Chemical
Military

Sanitary

9 letters:
Aerospace

10 letters:
Automotive
Electrical
Ergonomics
Hydraulics
Mechanical
Production
Structural

11 letters:
Electronics

Geotechnics

12 letters:
Aerodynamics
Aeronautical
Agricultural
Astronautics
Cosmonautics
Mechatronics

13 letters:
Computer-aided
Environmental
Fluid dynamics

14 letters:
Bioengineering

ENGINEERS

4 letters:
Ader, *Clement*
Arup, *Ove*
Otto, *Nikolaus*
Watt, *James*

5 letters:
Baird, *John Logie*
Tesla, *Nikola*

6 letters:
Brunel, *Isambard*
Eiffel, *Gustave*
Fokker, *Anthony*
McAdam, *John*
Savery, *Thomas*

Wallis, *Barnes*
Wankel, *Felix*

7 letters:
Brinell, *Johan*
Heinkel, *Tesla*
Junkers, *Hugo*
Marconi, *Guglielmo*
Parsons, *Charles*
Rogallo, *Francis*
Siemens, *Ernst*
Telford, *Thomas*
Whittle, *Frank*

8 letters:
Bessemer, *Henry*
Brindley, *James*

Kennelly, *Arthur*
Samarski, *V.E*
Sikorsky, *Igor*
Sinclair, *Clive*
Stirling, *Robert*
Von Braun, *Wernher*

9 letters:
Armstrong, *William*
Cockerell, *Christopher*
Whitworth, *Joseph*

10 letters:
Stephenson, *George*
Trevithick, *Richard*

Entertainment

TYPES OF ENTERTAINMENT

3 letters:
Gig

4 letters:
Agon
Ball
Fair
Fête
Film
Gala
Play
Rave
Show

5 letters:
Dance
Farce
Feast
Gaudy
Levee
Magic
Opera

Party
Revue
Rodeo

6 letters:
Ballet
Barnum
Circus
Comedy
Kermis
Masque
Review
Sitcom
Soiree

7 letters:
Airshow
Banquet
Busking
Cabaret
Ceilidh
Charade

Concert
Ice show
Karaoke
Kirmess
Musical
Reading
Recital
Ridotto
Tragedy
Tumbler
Tummler
Variety
Waltzer

8 letters:
All-dayer
Après-ski
Aquashow
Carnival
Cotillon
Juggling
Operetta

Road show
Showgirl
Sideshow
Singsong
Zarzuela

9 letters:
Conjuring
Cotillion
Fireworks
Floor show
Light show
Melodrama
Mind candy
Music hall
Pantomime
Pop singer
Raree show
Reception
Slapstick
Slide show
Video game

10 letters:
Acrobatics
Aerobatics
All-nighter
Antimasque
Escapology
Exhibition
Masked ball
Puppet show
Recitation
Shadow play
Striptease
Vaudeville
Whist drive

11 letters:
Bear-baiting
Fashion show
Funambulism
Galanty show
Garden party
Slot machine
Wall of death

12 letters:
Bullfighting
Cockfighting
Minstrel show
Pyrotechnics
Son et lumière

13 letters:
Burlesque show
Fete champetre
Street theatre
Ventriloquism

14 letters:
Warehouse party

16 letters:
Tightrope-walking

18 letters:
Command performance

TYPES OF ENTERTAINER

4 letters:
Diva
Fool

5 letters:
Actor
Clown
Mimic

6 letters:
Artist
Busker
Dancer
Guiser
Jester
Mummer
Singer

7 letters:
Acrobat
Actress
Artiste
Auguste
Juggler
Trouper
Tumbler

8 letters:
Comedian
Conjurer
Funnyman
Gracioso
Jongleur
Magician
Minstrel
Musician
Show girl

Stripper

9 letters:
Fire eater
Harlequin
Lion tamer
Performer
Puppeteer
Raconteur
Strongman
Tragedian

10 letters:
Chorus girl
Comedienne
Go-go dancer
Prima donna
Ringmaster
Unicyclist

11 letters:
Equilibrist
Funambulist
Illusionist
Merry-andrew
Stripteaser
Tragedienne

12 letters:
Circus artist
Escapologist
Exotic dancer

Impersonator
Organ-grinder
Snake charmer
Vaudevillian

13 letters:
Bareback rider
Contortionist
Impressionist
Trapeze artist
Ventriloquist

14 letters:
Prima ballerina
Sword swallower

15 letters:
Strolling player
Tightrope walker

17 letters:
Quick-change artist

PLACES OF ENTERTAINMENT

3 letters:
Zoo

4 letters:
Hall
Lido

5 letters:
Arena
Disco

6 letters:
Big top
Cinema
Circus
Museum

7 letters:
Funfair
Gallery

Marquee
Niterie
Stadium
Theatre

8 letters:
Ballroom
Carnival
Coliseum
Waxworks

9 letters:
Bandstand
Bingo hall
Colosseum
Dance hall
Music hall
Nightclub
Nightspot

10 letters:
Auditorium
Fairground
Opera house
Social club
Vaudeville

11 letters:
Concert hall

12 letters:
Amphitheatre

13 letters:
Leisure centre

15 letters:
Amusement arcade

Enzymes

3 letters:
ACE

5 letters:
Dnase
Lyase
Lysin
Renin

6 letters:
Cytase
DNAase
Kinase
Ligase
Lipase
Mutase
Papain

Pepsin
Rennin
Urease
Zymase

7 letters:
Amylase
Apyrase

Caseane
Cyclase
Enolase
Erepsin
Guanase
Hydrase
Inulase
Lactase

Maltase
Oxidase
Pectase
Pepsine
Plasmin
Ptyalin
Trypsin

8 letters:
Aldolase
Arginase
Bromelin
Catalase
Diastase
Elastase
Esterase
Lysozyme
Nuclease
Permease
Protease
Steapsin
Synthase
Thrombin

9 letters:
Amylopsin
Autolysin
Bromelain
Cathepsin
Cellulase

Deaminase
Hydrolase
Invertase
Isomerase
Oxygenase
Reductase
Sulfatase
Trehalase
Urokinase

10 letters:
Allosteric
Hexokinase
Kallikrein
Luciferase
Pancreatin
Peroxidase
Peroxisome
Polymerase
Proteinase
Saccharase
Subtilisin
Sulphatase
Tyrosinase

11 letters:
Carboxylase
Chymopapain
Collagenase
Dipeptidase

Glucosidase
Histaminase
Phosphatase
Restriction
Transferase

12 letters:
Asparaginase
Carbohydrase
Chymotrypsin
Enterokinase
Fibrinolysin
Flavoprotein
Ribonuclease
Transaminase

13 letters:
Decarboxylase
Galactosidase
Oxdoreductase
Streptokinase
Topoisomerase
Transcriptase

14 letters:
Cholinesterase
Creatine kinase
Pectinesterase
Streptodornase
Thromboplastin

Equestrianism

EQUESTRIAN EVENTS AND SPORTS

4 letters:
Hunt
Oaks
Polo

5 letters:
Ascot
Derby
Joust
Plate

7 letters:
Classic
Jump-off
Meeting

8 letters:
Dressage
Eventing
Gymkhana
Races, the

9 letters:
Badminton
Cavalcade
Puissance

10 letters:
Picnic race
Saint Leger
Sweepstake

11 letters:
Buckjumping
Horse racing
Race meeting
Showjumping
Sweepstakes

12 letters:
Claiming race

Point-to-point
Steeplechase

13 letters:
Grand National
Harness racing
Kentucky Derby
Nursery stakes

16 letters:
Three-day eventing

18 letters:
One Thousand Guineas
Two Thousand Guineas

CLASSIC ENGLISH HORSE RACES

Race	Course	Distance
One Thousand Guineas (fillies)	Newmarket	One mile
Two Thousand Guineas (colts)	Newmarket	One mile
Derby (colts)	Epsom	One and a half miles
The Oaks (fillies)	Epsom	One and a half miles
St. Leger (colts and fillies)	Doncaster	One and three quarter miles

HORSE RACING TERMS

3 letters:
Nap

4 letters:
Away
Card
Colt
Draw
Flat
Gate
Head
Neck
Pole
Post
Turf
Wire

5 letters:
Break
Chase
Fence
Filly
Going
Handy
Pacer
Place

Plate
Sweat
Track

6 letters:
Boring
Chaser
Come in
Course
Faller
Finish
Flight
Hurdle
Impost
Jockey
Length
Maiden
Novice
Plater
Scurry
Stakes
Stayer

7 letters:
Also-ran
Classic

Each way
Furlong
Meeting
Paddock
Roughie
Scratch
Starter
Steward
Stretch
Sweat up
Trainer
Weigh in

8 letters:
Dead heat
Distance
Handicap
Hurdling
Milepost
Race card
Straight
Ticktack
Unplaced
Walkover
Yearling

9 letters:
Allowance
Break away
Dope sheet
Objection
Pacemaker
Short head

10 letters:
Apprentice
Flat jockey
Flat racing
Green horse
Jockey Club
Jump jockey
Pacesetter
Silver ring

11 letters:
Accumulator

Daily double
Handicapper
Harness race
Home stretch
Photo finish
Selling race
Winning post

12 letters:
Auction plate
Claiming race
Home straight
National Hunt
Point-to-point
Starting gate
Starting post
Steeplechase
Straightaway
Trotting race

13 letters:
Blanket finish
Starting price
Unseated rider

14 letters:
Across-the-board
Starting stalls

15 letters:
Ante post betting
Stewards' inquiry

16 letters:
Clerk of the course
Clerk of the scales

19 letters:
Under starter's orders

TYPES OF JUMP

4 letters:
Gate
Wall

6 letters:
Planks

8 letters:
Hog's back

9 letters:
Water jump

10 letters:
Double oxer
Triple bars

11 letters:
Narrow stile

12 letters:
Post and rails

13 letters:
Brush and rails
Parallel poles

European Union

Year	Country
1952	Belgium
1952	France
1952	Germany
1952	Italy
1952	Luxembourg
1952	The Netherlands
1973	Denmark
1973	Republic of Ireland
1973	United Kingdom
1981	Greece

Year	Country
1986	Portugal
1986	Spain
1995	Austria
1995	Finland
1995	Sweden
2004	Cyprus
2004	Czech Republic
2004	Estonia
2004	Hungary
2004	Latvia
2004	Lithuania
2004	Malta
2004	Poland
2004	Slovakia
2004	Slovenia
2007	Bulgaria
2007	Romania

Explorers

3 letters:

Fox	1812–93	New Zealand

4 letters:

Byrd, *Richard E*	1888–1957	US
Cook, *Captain James*	1728–79	British
Dias, *Bartolomeu*	c. 1450–1500	Portuguese
Diaz, *Bartolomeu*	c. 1450–1500	Portuguese
Eyre, *Edward John*	1815–1901	British
Gama, *Vasco da*	c. 1469–1524	Portuguese
Grey, *George*	1812–98	British
Hume, *Hamilton*	1797–1873	Australian
Park, *Mungo*	1771–c.1806	Scottish
Polo, *Marco*	c. 1254–1324	Venetian
Ross, *Sir James Clark*	1800–62	British
Soto, *Hernando de*	c. 1496–1542	Spanish

5 letters:

Baker, *Sir Samuel White*	1821–93	British
Barth, *Heinrich*	1821–65	German
Boone, *Daniel*	1735–1820	US
Bruce, *James*	1730–94	British
Burke, *Robert O'Hara*	1820–61	Irish

Cabot, *John (Giovanni Caboto)*	c. 1450–c.1500	Italian
David, *Edgeworth*	1858–1954	Australian
Fuchs, *Sir Vivian*	1908–99	British
Laird, *Macgregor*	1808–61	Scottish
Oates, *Lawrence Edwards Grace*	1880–1912	British
Parry, *William*	1790–1855	British
Peary, *Robert Edwin*	1856–1920	US
Ponce, *Juan*	1460–1521	Spanish
Scott, *Robert Falcon*	1868–1912	British
Speke, *John Hanning*	1827–64	British
Sturt, *Charles*	1795–1869	British
Wills, *William*	1834–1861	Australian

6 letters:

Baffin, *William*	1584–1622	English
Balboa, *Vasco Núñez de*	c.1475–1517	Spanish
Bering, *Vitus*	1681–1741	Danish
Brazza, *Pierre Paul François Camille Savorgnan de*	1852–1905	French
Brooke, *Sir James*	1803–68	British
Burton, *Sir Richard*	1821–90	British
Cabral, *Pedro*	1460–1526	Portuguese
Cortés, *Hernán(do)*	1485–1547	Spanish
Lawson, *William*	1774–1850	Australian
Nansen, *Fridtjof*	1861–1930	Norwegian
Stuart, *John McDouall*	1815–66	Scottish
Tasman, *Abel*	1603–c.1659	Dutch

7 letters:

Barents, *Willem*	c. 1550–97	Dutch
Cartier, *Jacques*	1491–1557	French
Córdoba, *Francisco Hernández de*	d. 1517 or 1526	Spanish
Covilhã, *Pêro da*	c. 1460–after 1526	Portuguese
Dampier, *William*	1652–1715: English	
Fiennes, *Sir Ranulph*	1944–	British
Frémont, *John C*	1813–90	US
Hillary, *Sir Edmund*	1919–2008	New Zealand
La Salle, *Robert Cavalier, Sieur de*	1643–87	French
McClure, *Sir Robert John le Mesurier*	1807–73	Irish
Raleigh, *Sir Walter*	1554–1618	British
Stanley, *Sir Henry Morton*	1841–1904	British
Wilkins, *Sir George Hubert*	1888–1958	British
Wrangel, *Ferdinand Petrovich, Baron von*	1794–1870	Russian

8 letters:

Amundsen, *Roald*	1872–1928	Norwegian
Barentsz, *Willem*	c. 1550–97	Dutch
Columbus, *Christopher*	1451–1506	Italian
Cousteau, *Jacques Yves*	1910–97	French
Flinders, *Matthew*	1774–1814	English
Franklin, *Sir John*	1786–1847	British
Hargrave, *Lawrence*	1850–1915	Australian
Humboldt, *Alexander von*	1769–1859	German
Magellan, *Ferdinand*	1480–1521	Portuguese
Marchand, *Jean Baptiste*	1863–1934	French
Mitchell, *Thomas*	1792–1855	Australian
Vespucci, *Amerigo*	1454–1512	Italian

9 letters:

Champlain, *Samuel de*	1567–1635	French
Frobisher, *Sir Martin*	c. 1535–94	English
Iberville, *Pierre le Moyne, Sieur d'*	1661–1706	French-Canadian
Leichardt, *Ludwig*	1813–48	German
Mackenzie, *Alexander*	1764–1820	Scottish
Marquette, *Jacques*	1637–75	French
Rasmussen, *Knud Johan Victor*	1879–1933	Danish
Vancouver, *George*	1757–98	English
Wentworth, *William*	1793–1872	Australian

10 letters:

Erik the Red	late 10th Century	Norwegian
Shackleton, *Sir Ernest Henry*	1874–1922	British

11 letters:

Livingstone, *David*	1813–73	Scottish
Ponce de Leon, *Juan*	1460–1521	Spanish
Vasco da Gama	c. 1469–1524	Portuguese

12 letters:

Leif Ericson	975–1020	Icelandic

14 letters:

Bellingshausen, *Fabian Gottlieb,* *Baron von*	1778–1852	Russian

Explosives

2 letters:	**3 letters:**	PLX
HE	Cap	RDX

TNT

4 letters:
ANFO
Mine
TATP

5 letters:
Agene
Jelly
Petar

6 letters:
Amatol
Dualin
Petard
Semtex®
Tetryl
Tonite
Trotyl

7 letters:
Ammonal

Cordite
Dunnite
Grenade
Warhead

8 letters:
Cheddite
Fireball
Firedamp
Firework
Landmine
Melinite
Roburite
Saucisse
Thermite
Xyloidin

9 letters:
Gelignite
Guncotton
Gunpowder
Xyloidine

10 letters:
Aquafortis
Euchlorine

11 letters:
Firecracker

12 letters:
Thunderflash

14 letters:
Nitroglycerine

15 letters:
Trinitrobenzene

16 letters:
Bangalore torpedo

Eye

PARTS OF THE EYE

3 letters:
Rod

4 letters:
Cone
Iris
Lens

5 letters:
Fovea
Pupil

6 letters:
Cornea
Retina
Sclera

7 letters:
Choroid
Eyeball

8 letters:
Chorioid

9 letters:
Blind spot

10 letters:
Optic nerve

11 letters:
Ciliary body
Conjunctiva

12 letters:
Ocular muscle
Vitreous body

13 letters:
Aqueous humour

14 letters:
Retinal vessels
Vitreous humour

18 letters:
Suspensory ligament

AFFLICTIONS OF THE EYE

6 letters:
Albugo
Iritis
Miosis
Myosis
Nebula
Xeroma

7 letters:
Lazy eye
Leucoma
Scotoma
Thylose
Tylosis
Wall-eye

8 letters:
Cataract
Coloboma
Diplopia
Glaucoma

Hemiopia
Pearl eye
Synechia
Thylosis
Trachoma

9 letters:
Amblyopia
Ametropia
Ceratitis
Entropion
Keratitis
Lippitude
Micropsia
Nystagmus
Retinitis
Scotomata

10 letters:
Asthenopia
Nyctalopia

Presbyopia
Stigmatism
Strabismus
Teichopsia
Tritanopia

11 letters:
Aniseikonia
Astigmatism
Hemeralopia
Hemianopsia

12 letters:
Exophthalmus
Heterotropia

13 letters:
Anisomatropia
Hypermetropia
Xerophthalmia

Ff

Fabrics

3 letters:
Abb
Fur
Net
Rep
Say
Web

Rund
Shag
Silk
Slop
Sulu
Tick
Wool

4 letters:
Aida
Baft
Ciré
Cord
Doek
Drab
Duck
Felt
Fent
Gair
Haik
Harn
Huck
Hyke
Ikat
Jean
Kelt
Knit
Lace
Lamé
Lawn
Leno
Line
Mull
Nude
Puke

5 letters:
Atlas
Baize
Batik
Beige
Binca
Budge
Chino
Crape
Crash
Crepe
Denim
Dobby
Drill
Duroy
Fanon
Foulé
Frisé
Gauze
Gunny
Haick
Honan
Jaspe
Kanga
Kente
Khadi
Khaki

Kikoi
Linen
Lisle
Llama
Loden
Lurex®
Lycra®
Moiré
Mongo
Mungo
Ninon
Orlon®
Panne
Perse
Piqué
Plaid
Plush
Poult
Rayon
Satin
Scrim
Serge
Slops
Stuff
Stupe
Surah
Surat
Surge
Tabby
Tamin
Tammy
Terry
Tibet
Toile
Towel

Tulle
Tweed
Tweel
Twill
Union
Voile
Wigan

6 letters:
Aertex®
Alpaca
Angora
Armure
Barège
Battik
Beaver
Bouclé
Broche
Burlap
Burnet
Burrel
Byssus
Caddis
Calico
Camlet
Camlot
Canvas
Chintz
Cilice
Cloqué
Coburg
Cotton
Coutil
Crepon
Cubica

Cyprus
Dacron®
Damask
Devoré
Dimity
Domett
Dossal
Dossel
Dowlas
Dralon®
Duffel
Duffle
Dupion
Durrie
Etamin
Faille
Fannel
Fleece
Frieze
Gloria
Greige
Gurrah
Haique
Harden
Herden
Hodden
Humhum
Hurden
Jersey
Kersey
Khanga
Kincob
Lampas
Madras
Medley
Melton
Merino
Mohair
Mongoe
Moreen
Muslin
Nankin
Oxford
Pongee
Poplin

Rateen
Ratine
Runner
Russel
Russet
Samite
Satara
Sateen
Saxony
Sendal
Shalli
Sherpa
Shoddy
Sindon
Soneri
Stroud
Tamine
Tartan
Thibet
Tricot
Tussah
Tusser
Velour
Velure
Velvet
Vicuna
Wadmal
Wincey
Winsey

7 letters:
Abattre
Acrilan®
Alepine
Baracan
Batiste
Brocade
Bunting
Cabbage
Cambric
Camelot
Challie
Challis
Cheviot
Chiffon

Crombie
Cypress
Delaine
Dhurrie
Doeskin
Dornick
Drabbet
Drapery
Droguet
Drugget
Duvetyn
Etamine
Façonné
Fannell
Fishnet
Flannel
Foulard
Fustian
Galatea
Genappe
Gingham
Gore-Tex®
Grogram
Hessian
Holland
Hopsack
Jaconet
Jamdani
Khaddar
Kitenge
Leather
Lockram
Marabou
Mockado
Nankeen
Oilskin
Organza
Orleans
Ottoman
Paisley
Percale
Rabanna
Raploch
Raschel
Ratteen

Rattine
Sacking
Sagathy
Satinet
Schappe
Silesia
Sinamay
Spandex
Stammel
Suiting
Tabaret
Tabinet
Taffeta
Ticking
Tiffany
Tussore
Veiling
Velours
Viyella®
Wadmaal
Webbing
Woolsey
Worsted
Zanella

8 letters:
Algerine
American
Armozeen
Armozine
Arresine
Bagheera
Barathea
Barracan
Bayadere
Bird's-eye
Bobbinet
Brocatel
Buckskin
Cameline
Cashmere
Casimere
Celanese
Chambray
Chamelot

Chenille
Ciclaton
Corduroy
Corporal
Coteline
Coutille
Cretonne
Diamanté
Drabette
Duchesse
Dungaree
Duvetine
Duvetyne
Eolienne
Gambroon
Gossamer
Homespun
Jacquard
Jeanette
Lambskin
Lava-lava
Lustring
Mackinaw
Mantling
Marcella
Marocain
Mazarine
Moleskin
Moquette
Nainsook
Organdie
Osnaburg
Paduasoy
Pashmina
Prunella
Prunelle
Prunello
Rodevore
Sarcenet
Sarsenet
Shabrack
Shalloon
Shantung
Sheeting
Shirting

Sicilian
Spun silk
Swanskin
Tabbinet
Tarlatan
Terylene®
Toilinet
Whipcord
Wild silk
Zibeline

9 letters:
Balzarine
Bengaline
Bombasine
Bombazine
Calamanco
Cassimere
Cerecloth
Charmeuse®
Ciclatoun
Corporale
Cottonade
Crepoline
Crimplene®
Crinoline
Evenweave
Farandine
Filoselle
Folk weave
Gaberdine
Georgette
Grenadine
Grosgrain
Haircloth
Horsehair
Huckaback
Indiennes
Levantine
Mandylion
Marseille
Matelassé
Messaline
Nun's cloth
Organzine

Paramatta
Penistone
Percaline
Persienne
Petersham
Piña cloth
Polyester
Ravenduck
Sailcloth
Satinette
Sharkskin
Silkaline
Stockinet
Swan's-down
Tarpaulin
Towelling
Tricotine
Velveteen
Wire gauze
Worcester
Zibelline

10 letters:
Balbriggan
Broadcloth
Brocatelle
Candlewick
Farrandine
Fearnaught
Fearnought
Ferrandine
Florentine
India print
Kerseymere
Lutestring
Marseilles
Monk's cloth
Mousseline
Needlecord
Parramatta
Peau de soie
Polycotton
Ravensduck
Seersucker
Shabracque

Sicilienne
Tattersall
Toilinette
Tuftaffeta
Winceyette

11 letters:
Abercrombie
Cheesecloth
Cloth of gold
Covert cloth
Dotted Swiss
Drap-de-berry
Dreadnought
Hammercloth
Harris Tweed®
Interfacing
Kendal green
Marquisette
Poult-de-soie
Sempiternum
Stockinette
Stretch knit
Swiss muslin

12 letters:
Brilliantine
Cavalry twill
Crepe de chine
Donegal tweed
Leather-cloth
Slipper satin

13 letters:
Cotton flannel
Gros de Londres
Jacquard weave
Linsey-woolsey

14 letters:
Paisley pattern

See also:
➤ **Materials**   ➤ **Silks**

Fates

6 letters:	7 letters:	8 letters:
Clotho	Atropos	Lachesis

Fencing terms

4 letters:	Prime	Parade	9 letters:
Mask	Reach	Quarte	Backsword
Volt	Sabre	Quinte	Repechage
	Sixte	Tierce	
5 letters:	Terce	Touché	11 letters:
Carte	Touch		Singlestick
Feint		7 letters:	
Guard	6 letters:	Seconde	
Parry	Bracer	Septime	
Piste	Octave		

Ferns

3 letters:	6 letters:	8 letters:	Cryptogam
Oak	Azolla	Adiantum	Dicksonia
	Meadow	Aspidium	Filicales
4 letters:	Nardoo	Barometz	Rock brake
Hard	Pteris	Bungwall	
Lady	Shield	Ceterach	10 letters:
Male	Silver	Cinnamon	Maidenhair
Tara		Fishbone	Pepperwort
Tree	7 letters:	Marsilea	Spleenwort
	Bladder	Marsilia	Venus's-hair
5 letters:	Bracken	Moonwort	
Beech	Buckler	Mosquito	11 letters:
Cycad	Cyathea	Mulewort	Hart's-tongue
Filmy	Elkhorn	Pillwort	Nephrolepis
Grape	Filices	Rachilla	
Marsh	Isoetes	Schizaea	12 letters:
Ponga	Osmunda	Staghorn	Adder's-tongue
Punga	Parsley		Ophioglossum
Royal	Polypod	9 letters:	
Sword	Walking	Asparagus	13 letters:
	Wall rue	Asplenium	Scolopendrium
	Woodsia	Bird's nest	

Festivals

3 letters:
Eid
Mod
Tet

4 letters:
Feis
Gaff
Holi
Mela
Noel
Obon
Puja
Utas
Yule

5 letters:
Doseh
Druid
Hosay
Litha
Mabon
Miraj
Pasch
Pesah
Pooja
Purim
Seder
Vesak
Wesak

6 letters:
Adonia
Ashura
Bairam
Dewali
Divali
Diwali
Easter
Eostra
Fringe
Hosein
Imbolc

Lammas
Ostara
Pardon
Pesach
Pongal
Poojah
Shrove
Sukkot
Yomtov

7 letters:
Al Hijra
Baisaki
Beltane
Gregory
Harvest
Holy-ale
Kermess
Kermiss
Kirmess
Lady-day
Lemural
Lemuria
Matsuri
Palilia
Potlach
Samhain
Vinalia

8 letters:
Al Hijrah
Baisakhi
Bayreuth
Biennale
Cerealia
Chanukah
Dassehra
Dionysia
Encaenia
Epiphany
Hanukkah
Hock-tide
Id-al-fitr

Lag b'Omer
Panegyry
Passover
Shabuath
Shavuath
Tanabata
Yuletide

9 letters:
Aldeburgh
Candlemas
Chanukkah
Church-ale
Crouchmas
Eid Al-Adha
Eid Al-Fitr
Hallowmas
Navaratra
Navaratri
Pentecost
Thargelia
Up-Helly-Aa
Yom Arafat

10 letters:
Ambarvalia
Childermas
Eisteddfod
Lughnasadh
Lupercalia
Merry-night
Michaelmas
Quirinalia
Saturnalia
Semi-double
Shrovetide
Terminalia
Visitation

11 letters:
Anthesteria

12 letters:
All Saints' Day
Circumcision
Day of the Dead
Lailat-ul-Qadr
Lesser Bairam
Panathenaean

Rosh Hashanah
Simchat Torah
Thesmophoria

13 letters:
Corpus Christi

Greater Bairam
Laylat-al-Miraj

14 letters:
Shemini Atzeret

Fibres

3 letters:
Tow

4 letters:
Bass
Bast
Coir
Flax
Hemp
Herl
Jute
Noil
Pita
Pons
Pulu
Rami
Rhea

5 letters:
Abaca

Buaze
Bwazi
Istle
Ixtle
Kapok
Kenaf
Noils
Nylon
Orlon®
Ramee
Viver
Watap

6 letters:
Aramid
Arghan
Cotton
Cuscus
Dralon®
Kevlar®

Kittul
Maguey
Strick

7 letters:
Acrilan®
Acrylic
Cantala
Filasse
Funicle
Gore-Tex®
Monofil
Pontine
Tampico
Whisker

8 letters:
Elastane
Henequen
Henequin

Monomode
Peduncle
Piassaba
Piassava
Pine-wool
Sunn-hemp
Toquilla

9 letters:
Courtelle®
Desmosome

10 letters:
Spherulite

11 letters:
Monkey-grass

14 letters:
Corpus callosum

Figures of speech

5 letters:
Irony

6 letters:
Aporia
Climax
Simile
Tmesis
Zeugma

7 letters:
Analogy
Kenning
Litotes
Meiosis
Sarcasm

8 letters:
Allusion
Anaphora
Chiasmus

Emphasis
Metaphor
Metonymy
Oxymoron
Pleonasm

9 letters:
Apophasis
Assonance
Cataphora
Hendiadys

Hypallage
Hyperbole
Inversion
Prolepsis
Syllepsis

10 letters:
Anastrophe
Antithesis
Apostrophe
Epanaphora
Gemination
Hyperbaton
Paralipsis
Repetition
Spoonerism
Synecdoche

11 letters:
Anacoluthia
Anadiplosis
Antiphrasis
Antonomasia
Aposiopesis
Catachresis
Exclamation
Malapropism
Paraleipsis
Parenthesis
Periphrasis
Prosopopeia

12 letters:
Alliteration
Epanorthosis

Onomatopoeia
Polysyndeton
Prosopopoeia

14 letters:
Circumlocution

15 letters:
Personification

16 letters:
Hysteron proteron

18 letters:
Rhetorical question

Film and television

1 letter:
A
U

2 letters:
AA
HD
PG

3 letters:
BFI
CGI
Cut
Dub
DVD
LCD
Pan
SFX
VHS
Zap

4 letters:
BBFC
Boom
Edit

Emmy
Grip
HDTV
IMAX
Sync
TiVo

5 letters:
Anime
BAFTA
Cameo
Frame
Oscar
Short
Weepy

6 letters:
Action
Biopic
Blu-ray
B movie
Co-star
Editor
Gaffer
Razzie

Repeat
Romcom
Sequel
X-rated

7 letters:
Animate
Backlot
Betacam
Cable TV
Credits
Fleapit
Footage
Key grip
Prequel
Ratings
Trailer
Western
Zapping

8 letters:
Actioner
Art house
Bratpack
Britpack

Game show
Long shot
Stuntman
Subtitle
Talk show
Typecast

9 letters:
Animation
Big screen
Bollywood
Celluloid
Cinematic
Digital TV
Docu-drama
Flashback
Footprint
Hollywood
LCD screen
Reality TV
Road movie
Satellite
Set-top box
Stop-frame

10 letters:
Access card
Adult movie
Blue screen
Body double
Chick flick
Flat screen
Home cinema
Neorealism
Screen test
Slow motion
Snuff movie
Soundtrack
Stop-motion
Storyboard
Video nasty
Widescreen

11 letters:
Channel-surf
Chapter stop

Cinemascope
Cliffhanger
Freeze-frame
Independent
Reality show
Satellite TV
Small screen
Synthespian

12 letters:
Animatronics
Cinematheque
Plasma screen
Screenwriter
Slasher movie
Sneak preview

13 letters:
Interactive TV
Motion capture
Remote control

Satellite dish

14 letters:
Channel-surfing
High definition
Postproduction
Shooting script
Special effects

16 letters:
Spaghetti western

17 letters:
Digital television

19 letters:
Satellite television

21 letters:
Interactive television

Fireworks

3 letters:
SIB

4 letters:
Cake
Mine
Pioy

5 letters:
Gerbe
Peeoy
Pioye
Squib

Wheel

6 letters:
Banger
Fizgig
Maroon
Petard
Rocket

7 letters:
Cracker
Serpent

8 letters:
Fountain
Pinwheel
Sparkler

9 letters:
Girandole
Skyrocket
Whizzbang

10 letters:
Cherry bomb

11 letters:
Bengal light
Roman candle
Tourbillion

14 letters:
Catherine wheel

First names

BOYS

3 letters:				
Abe	Ben	Ger	Jan	Len
Alf	Bob	Gus	Jim	Leo
Ali	Dan	Guy	Joe	Luc
	Don	Ian	Kim	Mat

Max	Evan	Raul	Bruce
Nat	Ewan	Rémy	Bruno
Ned	Fred	Rene	Caleb
Nye	Gene	Rhys	Carlo
Ray	Gert	Rick	Cecil
Reg	Gwyn	Rolf	Celio
Rex	Hans	Rory	Chris
Rob	Hugh	Ross	Cliff
Roy	Hugo	Rudi	Clive
Sam	Iain	Ryan	Colin
Sid	Ivan	Sa'id	Cyril
Tam	Ivor	Saul	Cyrus
Ted	Jack	Sean	Danny
Tim	Jake	Stan	Darby
Tom	Jean	Theo	D'Arcy
Val	Jeff	Toby	David
Vic	Jock	Tony	Davie
Viv	John	Walt	Denis
Wal	José	Will	Derek
Wim	Josh	Yves	Diego
	Juan		Dodie
4 letters:	Karl		Dylan
Abel	Kurt	**5 letters:**	Eamon
Abie	Leon	Aaron	Eddie
Adam	Liam	Abdul	Edgar
Alan	Luca	Adolf	Elias
Aldo	Luke	Ahmed	Eliot
Alex	Marc	Aidan	Ellis
Amos	Mark	Alain	Elmer
Andy	Matt	Alfie	Émile
Avis	Mick	Algie	Enoch
Bart	Mike	Allan	Ernie
Bert	Muir	Allen	Ernst
Bill	Neal	Alvin	Errol
Carl	Neil	André	Felix
Chad	Nick	Angus	Frank
Clem	Noel	Anton	Franz
Dave	Olaf	Artur	Fritz
Dick	Otto	Barry	Garry
Dirk	Owen	Basil	Garth
Drew	Paco	Benny	Gavin
Duke	Paul	Bernd	Geoff
Earl	Pepe	Billy	Georg
Egon	Pete	Bobby	Giles
Eric	Phil	Boris	Guido
		Brian	

Harry
Hasan
Heinz
Henri
Henry
Hiram
Inigo
Jacky
Jacob
Jaime
Jakob
Jamal
James
Jamie
Jason
Jerry
Jesse
Jesús
Jimmy
Jorge
Jules
Keith
Kevin
Klaus
Lance
Lenny
Lewis
Lloyd
Louis
Luigi
Manny
Marco
Mario
Marty
Miles
Moses
Myles
Niall
Nicky
Nigel
Orson
Oscar
Pablo
Paddy
Paolo

Pedro
Perce
Percy
Perry
Peter
Piero
Ralph
Robin
Rodge
Roger
Romeo
Rufus
Serge
Simon
Steve
Tariq
Terry
Tomás
Vijay
Vince
Wayne

6 letters:
Adrian
Adrien
Albert
Aldous
Alexis
Alfred
Andrés
Andrew
Antony
Archie
Arnaud
Arnold
Arthur
Arturo
Aubrey
Austin
Aylwin
Barney
Benoît
Billie
Calvin
Carlos

Caspar
Cedric
Claude
Connor
Conrad
Damian
Daniel
Darsey
Deepak
Dermot
Didier
Dieter
Donald
Dougal
Dudley
Dugald
Duncan
Dustin
Dwight
Edmund
Edward
Egbert
Enrico
Ernest
Esmond
Eugene
Fergus
Gareth
Gaston
George
Gerald
Gideon
Gilles
Gordon
Graham
Gregor
Hamish
Harold
Harvey
Hector
Helmut
Hilary
Horace
Howard
Hubert

Hugues
Hunter
Ingram
Irving
Isaiah
Israel
Jackie
Jasper
Javier
Jeremy
Jerome
Johann
Joseph
Joshua
Josiah
Julian
Julien
Julius
Jürgen
Justin
Kenelm
Larrie
Laurie
Leslie
Lester
Lionel
Lucius
Ludwig
Luther
Magnus
Mahmud
Manuel
Marcel
Marcus
Marius
Martin
Melvin
Melvyn
Merlin
Mervyn
Michel
Mickey
Miguel
Murray
Nathan

	7 letters:	Giorgio	Solomon
Norman	Abraham	Godfrey	Spencer
Norris	Alberto	Gregory	Stanley
Oliver	Alfonso	Herbert	Stefano
Osbert	Alfredo	Horatio	Stephan
Oswald	Alister	Ibrahim	Stephen
Petrus	Ambrose	Jacques	Stewart
Philip	Andreas	Jeffrey	Terence
Pierre	Anthony	Joachim	Thibaut
Rainer	Antoine	Joaquin	Thierry
Rashid	Antonio	Kenneth	Timothy
Reuben	Baldwin	Lachlan	Umberto
Robert	Barnaby	Laurent	Valerie
Rodney	Bernard	Leonard	Vaughan
Roland	Bertram	Leopold	Vincent
Ronald	Brendan	Lindsey	Wallace
Rupert	Cameron	Lorenzo	Wilfred
Samuel	Carlton	Luciano	Wilhelm
Sanjiv	Charles	Malcolm	William
Selwyn	Charlie	Matthew	Windsor
Sergio	Clement	Maurice	Winston
Sidney	Clemmie	Maxwell	Wyndham
Stefan	Desmond	Michael	Youssef
Steven	Diarmid	Montagu	
Stuart	Dominic	Murdoch	8 letters:
Sydney	Douglas	Mustafa	Abdullah
Thomas	Ebeneza	Neville	Alasdair
Trevor	Edmondo	Nicolas	Alastair
Ulrich	Edoardo	Norbert	Aloysius
Victor	Édouard	Obadiah	Augustus
Vikram	Emanuel	Olivier	Benedict
Vivian	Erasmus	Pascual	Benjamin
Wallis	Estéban	Patrice	Bernabas
Walter	Étienne	Patrick	Bernardo
Warner	Ezekiel	Placido	Bertrand
Warren	Fabrice	Quentin	Charlton
Werner	Filippo	Raphael	Clarence
Wesley	Francis	Raymond	Claudius
Wilbur	Gabriel	Richard	Clifford
Willie	Geordie	Rodrigo	Consuelo
Willis	Georges	Rolando	Cuthbert
Xavier	Geraint	Rudolph	Dietrich
Yasser	Gerhard	Rudyard	Emmanuel
Yehudi	Giacomo	Russell	Fabrizio
	Gilbert	Sigmund	Farquhar

Fernando
François
Geoffrey
Giovanni
Giuliano
Giuseppe
Heinrich
Hercules
Humphrey
Johannes
Jonathan
Jonathon
Lancelot
Laurence
Lawrence
Leonardo
Llewelyn
Marcello
Matthias
Matthieu

Montague
Morrison
Mortimer
Muhammed
Nicholas
Octavius
Odysseus
Percival
Philippe
Randolph
Reginald
Roderick
Salvador
Santiago
Sherlock
Silvanus
Sinclair
Somerset
Stéphane
Theodore

Timothée
Wolfgang

9 letters:
Alejandro
Alexander
Alexandre
Alphonsus
Archibald
Augustine
Christian
Cornelius
Dominique
Ethelbert
Ferdinand
Francesco
Frederick
Friedrich
Gottfried

Grégroire
Guillaume
Marmaduke
Nathaniel
Peregrine
Sebastian
Sébastien
Siegfried
Sylvester

10 letters:
Alessandro
Christophe
Maximilian
Montgomery

11 letters:
Bartholomew
Christopher

GIRLS

3 letters:
Ada
Amy
Ana
Ann
Bab
Bea
Bel
Dot
Ena
Eva
Eve
Fay
Flo
Gay
Ger
Ina
Isa
Jan
Joy
Kay
Kim
Kit

Liv
Liz
Lyn
May
Meg
Nan
Net
Pam
Pat
Peg
Pen
Pip
Pru
Rae
Sal
Sis
Sue
Tam
Una
Ute
Val
Zoe

4 letters:
Alba
Ally
Alma
Anke
Anna
Anne
Babs
Bess
Beth
Cara
Ceri
Ciss
Cleo
Dawn
Dora
Edna
Ella
Elma
Elsa
Emma
Enid
Gabi

Gail
Gill
Gina
Gita
Gwen
Hope
Inge
Iona
Iris
Jane
Jean
Jess
Jill
Joan
Judy
June
Kate
Leah
Lena
Lily
Lisa
Lois
Lola

Lucy
Lynn
Mary
Maud
Myra
Nell
Nina
Nita
Olga
Oona
Rene
Rita
Romy
Rosa
Rose
Ruby
Ruth
Sara
Tess
Tina
Vera
Zara

5 letters:

Abbie	Effie	Leila	Peggy	Bertha
Adele	Elise	Leona	Penny	Bianca
Aggie	Eliza	Libby	Polly	Billie
Agnes	Ellen	Liese	Renée	Blaise
Ailie	Ellis	Linda	Rhoda	Brenda
Ailsa	Elsie	Lindy	Rhona	Bryony
Alice	Emily	Lorna	Sadie	Carmen
Aline	Ethel	Lotte	Sally	Carole
Amber	Faith	Lucia	Sandy	Carrie
Anita	Fanny	Luisa	Sarah	Cécile
Annie	Fiona	Lydia	Sofia	Céline
April	Fleur	Lynne	Sonia	Cherry
Avril	Flora	Mabel	Sonja	Cheryl
Beata	Freda	Madge	Susan	Claire
Becca	Gerda	Maeve	Susie	Concha
Bella	Ginny	Magda	Sybil	Daphne
Berry	Grace	Mamie	Tania	Davina
Beryl	Greta	Marge	Tanya	Debbie
Betsy	Hazel	Margo	Tatum	Denise
Betty	Heidi	Maria	Thora	Dianne
Biddy	Helen	Marie	Tilly	Doreen
Carla	Helga	Marta	Tracy	Dulcie
Carol	Hetty	Marty	Vicky	Easter
Cathy	Hilda	Maude	Viola	Edwina
Celia	Honor	Mavis	Wanda	Eileen
Chloe	Irene	Merle	Wendy	Eilidh
Chris	Isaac	Milly		Elaine
Clara	Jacky	Mitzi	**6 letters:**	Elinor
Clare	Janet	Moira	Agatha	Elisha
Coral	Janey	Molly	Aileen	Elodie
Corin	Jayne	Morag	Alexis	Elvira
Daisy	Jemma	Moray	Alicia	Emilia
D'Arcy	Jenny	Morna	Alison	Esther
Debby	Jesse	Myrna	Althea	Eunice
Delia	Josie	Nancy	Amanda	Evadne
Diana	Joyce	Nanny	Amelia	Evelyn
Diane	Julia	Naomi	Amélie	Fatima
Dilys	Julie	Nelly	Andrea	Gertie
Dinah	Karen	Netty	Angela	Gladys
Dolly	Katja	Nicky	Arabel	Gloria
Donna	Kiera	Nicol	Arline	Gretel
Doris	Kitty	Norma	Astrid	Gwenda
Edith	Kylie	Patty	Athene	Hannah
Edwin	Laura	Paula	Audrey	Hattie
	Laure	Pearl	Aurora	Hélène

Hester
Hilary
Imogen
Indira
Ingrid
Isabel
Isobel
Isolde
Jackie
Jamila
Janice
Jeanne
Jemima
Jessie
Joanna
Joanne
Judith
Juliet
Kirsty
Krista
Leonie
Lesley
Lilian
Lolita
Lottie
Louisa
Louise
Madhur
Maggie
Maisie
Marcia
Margie
Marian
Marina
Marion
Martha
Maxine
Minnie
Miriam
Monica
Morgan
Morrie
Morris
Morven
Muriel

Myrtle
Nadine
Nessie
Nettie
Nicola
Nicole
Noelle
Odette
Oonagh
Oriana
Paloma
Pamela
Petula
Phoebe
Rachel
Raquel
Regina
Renata
Robina
Rowena
Roxana
Sabina
Sabine
Salome
Sandra
Selina
Serena
Sharon
Sheena
Sheila
Silvia
Simone
Sophia
Sophie
Stella
Sylvia
Tamsin
Thelma
Tricia
Trixie
Trudie
Ulrike
Ursula
Verity
Violet

Vivian
Winnie
Yvette
Yvonne

7 letters:
Abigail
Adriana
Alfreda
Annabel
Annette
Antonia
Ariadne
Aurelia
Barbara
Beatrix
Belinda
Bernice
Bettina
Blanche
Bridget
Bronwen
Camilla
Camille
Candida
Carolyn
Cecilia
Celeste
Chantal
Charity
Charlie
Chrissy
Christy
Clarice
Claudia
Colette
Corinna
Corinne
Cynthia
Deborah
Deirdre
Dolores
Dorothy
Eleanor
Elspeth

Estella
Eugenia
Fenella
Florrie
Flossie
Frances
Gertrud
Gillian
Giselle
Gwyneth
Harriet
Heather
Isadora
Jasmine
Jessica
Jocelyn
Josette
Juliana
Justine
Katrina
Kirstie
Kristin
Lavinia
Leonora
Letitia
Lillian
Lindsey
Linette
Lucille
Lucinda
Manuela
Margery
Marilyn
Martina
Martine
Matilda
Maureen
Melanie
Melissa
Mildred
Mirabel
Miranda
Modesty
Myfanwy
Natalie

Natasha
Ophelia
Ottilie
Pauline
Perdita
Petrina
Phyllis
Queenie
Rebecca
Roberta
Rosalie
Sabrina
Shelagh
Shelley
Shirley
Siobahn
Susanna
Suzanne
Theresa
Valerie
Vanessa
Yolande

8 letters:
Adrienne
Angeline
Arabella
Beatrice
Beverley
Brigitta
Brigitte
Carlotta
Carolina
Caroline
Cathleen
Catriona
Charmian
Claribel
Clarissa
Claudine
Clemence
Collette
Conchita
Consuela
Cordelia

Cressida	Meredith	Annabella	Sempronia
Danielle	Michaela	Cassandra	Seraphina
Dominica	Michelle	Catherina	Stephanie
Dorothea	Patience	Catherine	Veronique
Drusilla	Patricia	Charlotte	
Euphemia	Penelope	Christina	**10 letters:**
Felicity	Perpetua	Christine	Alessandra
Florence	Primrose	Constance	Antoinette
Francine	Prudence	Elizabeth	Christabel
Georgina	Prunella	Esmerelda	Christelle
Gertrude	Rosalind	Francesca	Christiana
Hermione	Rosamund	Françoise	Christiane
Isabelle	Rosemary	Gabrielle	Clementine
Iseabail	Samantha	Genevieve	Concepción
Jeanette	Scarlett	Geraldine	Emmanuelle
Jeannine	Theodora	Gwendolyn	Jacqueline
Jennifer	Veronica	Henrietta	Lieselotte
Juliette	Victoria	Jacquetta	Margherita
Kathleen	Violette	Josephine	Marguerite
Lorraine	Virginia	Katharine	Petronella
Madeline	Virginie	Madeleine	Wilhelmina
Magdalen	Winifred	Magdalene	
Marcella		Millicent	**11 letters:**
Margaret	**9 letters:**	Mirabelle	Bernadettte
Marianne	Alejandra	Nicolette	Constantine
Marigold	Alexandra	Phillippa	
Marjorie	Anastasia	Priscilla	
Mercedes	Anastasie	Rosabella	

Fish

2 letters:	Dib	Rig	Chad	Gump
Ai	Dog	Sar	Char	Hake
Id	Eel	Tai	Chub	Harl
	Gar	Top	Chum	Hoki
3 letters:	Ged		Coho	Huso
Aua	Hag	**4 letters:**	Cray	Huss
Ayu	Ice	Bass	Cusk	Jack
Bar	Ide	Blay	Dace	Kelt
Bib	Koi	Bley	Dare	Keta
But	Lax	Brim	Dart	Lant
Cat	Lob	Brit	Dory	Leaf
Cod	Par	Butt	Fugu	Ling
Cow	Pod	Carp	Gade	Luce
Dab	Ray	Cero	Goby	Lump

Maid
Maze
Moki
Mort
Opah
Orfe
Parr
Peal
Peel
Pike
Pogy
Pope
Pout
Raun
Rawn
Rigg
Rudd
Ruff
Scad
Scar
Scat
Scup
Seer
Seir
Shad
Sild
Slip
Snig
Sole
Star
Tope
Trot
Tuna
Tusk
Woof

5 letters:
Ablet
Ahuru
Allis
Angel
Apode
Barra
Basse
Betta

Bleak
Bream
Brill
Bully
Capon
Charr
Cisco
Clown
Cobia
Cohoe
Coley
Cuddy
Danio
Dorad
Doras
Doree
Dorse
Elops
Elver
Fluke
Gadus
Gibel
Grunt
Guppy
Jewie
Jurel
Koaea
Laker
Lance
Loach
Lythe
Maise
Maize
Manta
Masus
Mease
Molly
Moray
Murre
Murry
Nerka
Padle
Perai
Perca
Perch

Pilot
Piper
Pirai
Platy
Pogge
Porae
Porgy
Powan
Prawn
Roach
Roker
Ruffe
Saith
Sargo
Saury
Scrod
Sewen
Sewin
Shark
Sheat
Skate
Slope
Smelt
Snoek
Snook
Solen
Speck
Sprat
Sprod
Tench
Tetra
Toado
Togue
Torsk
Trout
Tunny
Umber
Wahoo
Whiff
Wirra
Witch
Yabby
Zebra

6 letters:
Alevin
Allice
Anabas
Angler
Araara
Archer
Ballan
Barbel
Belone
Beluga
Bigeye
Blenny
Bonito
Bounce
Bowfin
Braise
Braize
Bumalo
Burbot
Callop
Caplin
Caranx
Caribe
Cheven
Clupea
Cockle
Comber
Conger
Conner
Cottus
Cudden
Cuddie
Cuddin
Cunner
Cuttle
Darter
Dentex
Diodon
Dipnoi
Discus
Doctor
Dorado
Dun-cow
Finnac

Finnan
Flying
Fogash
Fumado
Gadoid
Garvie
Gilgie
Goramy
Grilse
Groper
Gulper
Gunnel
Gurami
Gurnet
Haddie
Hapuka
Hapuku
Hassar
Inanga
Jerker
Jilgie
Kelpie
Kipper
Kokopu
Labrus
Lancet
Launce
Lizard
Louvar
Lunker
Mad Tom
Mahsir
Maomao
Marari
Marlin
Meagre
Medaka
Medusa
Megrim
Milter
Minnow
Morgay
Mudcat
Mullet
Murena

Nerite
Nigger
Oyster
Paddle
Paidle
Pakoko
Parore
Parrot
Patiki
Pholas
Pillie
Piraña
Piraya
Plaice
Podley
Pollan
Porgie
Puffer
Rawaru
Red cod
Redfin
Remora
Robalo
Roughy
Runner
Saithe
Salmon
Samlet
Samson
Sander
Sardel
Sargus
Sauger
Saurel
Scampi
Sea-bat
Sea-owl
Seeder
Serran
Shanny
Sheath
Shiner
Skelly
Sparid
Sucker

Tailor
Tarpon
Tautog
Toitoi
Tomcod
Trygon
Turbot
Twaite
Ulicon
Ulikon
Vendis
Weever
Wirrah
Wrasse
Yabbie
Zander
Zingel

7 letters:
Alewife
Anchovy
Anemone
Asterid
Azurine
Batfish
Beardie
Bellows
Bergylt
Bloater
Bluecap
Blue cod
Boxfish
Brassie
Buffalo
Bummalo
Cabezon
Capelin
Catfish
Cavalla
Cavally
Ceviche
Cichlid
Codfish
Copepod
Cowfish

Crappie
Croaker
Crucian
Crusian
Cutlass
Dogfish
Eelfare
Eelpout
Escolar
Findram
Finnack
Finnock
Flattie
Garfish
Garpike
Garvock
Geelbek
Gemfish
Goldeye
Gourami
Grouper
Growler
Grunion
Gudgeon
Gurnard
Gwiniad
Gwyniad
Haddock
Hagdown
Hagfish
Halibut
Herling
Herring
Hirling
Hogfish
Homelyn
Houting
Ichthys
Inconnu
Javelin
Jewfish
Kahawai
Keeling
Koi carp
Kokanee

Lampern
Lamprey
Lampuki
Lantern
Lingcod
Lobster
Lyomeri
Mahseer
Medacca
Merling
Mojarra
Mooneye
Morwong
Mudfish
Muraena
Oarfish
Old-wife
Oolakan
Opaleye
Osseter
Oulakan
Oulicon
Panchax
Pandora
Pegasus
Pigfish
Pinfish
Piranha
Pollack
Pollock
Pomfret
Pompano
Ragfish
Rasbora
Ratfish
Rat-tail
Redfish
Rock cod
Rorqual
Sand dab
Sand eel
Sardine
Sawfish
Scalare
Scallop

Sculpin
Sea bass
Sea-cock
Sea-dace
Sea-moth
Sea-pike
Sea-star
Sea-wife
Sillock
Skegger
Skipper
Sleeper
Snapper
Sockeye
Sparoid
Speldin
Sterlet
Sunfish
Surgeon
Teleost
Tiddler
Tilapia
Titling
Torgoch
Torpedo
Ulichon
Vendace
Walleye
Warehou
Whipray
Whiting
Wide-gab

8 letters:
Albacore
Anableps
Arapaima
Asteroid
Atherine
Ballahoo
Bay trout
Billfish
Black cod
Blind eel
Bloodfin

Blowfish	Graining	Rockfish	Wolffish
Blueback	Grayling	Rockling	Wollamai
Bluefish	Hackbolt	Roncador	Wollomai
Bluegill	Hairtail	Rosefish	
Blue moki	Halfbeak	Saibling	**9 letters:**
Blue nose	Hard-head	Sailfish	Alfonsino
Boarfish	Holostei	Saltfish	Amberjack
Bonefish	Hornbeak	Sardelle	Anabantid
Brisling	Hornpout	Scabbard	Anchoveta
Bullhead	Jackfish	Sciaenid	Angelfish
Bullhorn	John Dory	Scorpion	Argentine
Cabezone	Kabeljou	Scuppaug	Barracuda
Cabrilla	Kelpfish	Sea bream	Black bass
Cardinal	Killfish	Sea-devil	Blackfish
Cavefish	Kingfish	Sea horse	Blindfish
Characid	Kingklip	Sea-lemon	Bony bream
Characin	Kukukuma	Sea perch	Bull trout
Chimaera	Lionfish	Sea raven	Butterfly
Climbing	Luderick	Sea robin	Cascadura
Coalfish	Lumpfish	Sea snail	Ceratodus
Corkwing	Lungfish	Sea trout	Chaetodon
Cucumber	Mackerel	Sergeant	Chavender
Cyprinid	Mahi-mahi	Serranus	Clingfish
Dealfish	Mangrove	Skipjack	Clupeidae
Devil ray	Manta ray	Smear-dab	Coregonus
Dragonet	Mata Hari	Snake-eel	Coryphene
Drumfish	Menhaden	Sparling	Devilfish
Eagle-ray	Milkfish	Stenlock	Gaspereau
Escallop	Monkfish	Stingray	Glassfish
Eulachon	Moonfish	Stonecat	Globefish
Fallfish	Mulloway	Sturgeon	Goldfinny
Fighting	Nannygai	Tarakihi	Goldsinny
Filefish	Nennigai	Tarwhine	Golomynka
Flatfish	Nine-eyes	Teraglin	Goosefish
Flathead	Oulachon	Terakihi	Greenbone
Flounder	Paradise	Tilefish	Greenling
Four-eyed	Patutuki	Toadfish	Grenadier
Four-eyes	Pickerel	Trevalla	Haberdine
Frogfish	Pilchard	Trevally	Hornyhead
Ganoidei	Pipefish	Tropical	Hottentot
Gillaroo	Pirarucu	Tubenose	Houndfish
Gilthead	Redbelly	Tullibee	Ichthyoid
Goatfish	Red bream	Weakfish	Jacksmelt
Gobiidae	Rock bass	Whitling	Jewelfish
Goldfish	Rock-cook	Wobegong	Kabeljouw

Killifish
Labyrinth
Lamper eel
Latimeria
Lemon sole
Menominee
Mudhopper
Neon tetra
Pikeperch
Placoderm
Porbeagle
Porcupine
Quillback
Red mullet
Red salmon
Roussette
Sand lance
Scaldfish
Schnapper
Scorpaena
Selachian
Shubunkin
Siluridae
Slickhead
Snailfish
Snakehead
Snipefish
Solenette
Spadefish
Spearfish
Speldring
Stargazer
Steelhead
Steenbras
Stingaree
Stockfish
Stone bass
Stonefish
Surfperch
Surmullet
Swellfish
Swordfish
Swordtail
Thornback
Threadfin

Tittlebat
Tommy ruff
Topminnow
Trachinus
Troutfish
Trunkfish
Whitebait
White-bass
Whitefish
Wobbegong
Wobbygong
Wreckfish
Yellowfin

10 letters:
Archerfish
Barracoota
Barracouta
Barramunda
Barramundi
Bitterling
Black bream
Black perch
Bombay duck
Bottlehead
Brook trout
Brown trout
Butterfish
Candlefish
Cockabully
Coelacanth
Coral trout
Cornetfish
Cyclostome
Damselfish
Demoiselle
Dollarfish
Etheostoma
Fingerling
Flutemouth
Giant perch
Groundling
Guitarfish
Horned pout

King salmon
Lumpsucker
Māori chief
Maskalonge
Maskanonge
Maskinonge
Midshipman
Mirror carp
Mossbunker
Mudskipper
Needlefish
Nurse-hound
Ouananiche
Paddlefish
Pakirikiri
Parrotfish
Pearl perch
Rabbitfish
Red emperor
Red snapper
Ribbonfish
Rock salmon
Rudderfish
Scopelidae
Sea lamprey
Sea-poacher
Sea-surgeon
Serrasalmo
Sheepshead
Shovelnose
Silverfish
Silverside
Springfish
Squeteague
Teleostome
Titarakura
Tommy rough
Tripletail
Yellow jack
Yellowtail

11 letters:
Bluefin tuna
Chondrostei
Dolly Varden

Electric eel
Golden perch
Istiophorus
Lake herring
Lepidosiren
Maskallonge
Moorish idol
Murray perch
Muskellunge
Ostracoderm
Oxyrhynchus
Plagiostome
Pumpkinseed
Salmon trout
Scolopendra
Sea scorpion
Seventy-four
Silver belly
Silversides
Sleeper goby
Smooth hound
Soldierfish
Stickleback
Stone roller
Surgeonfish
Triggerfish
Trumpetfish
Whiting pout
Yellow-belly

12 letters:
Baggie minnow
Ballan-wrasse

Elasmobranch
Father lasher
Heterosomata
Histiophorus
Mangrove Jack
Miller's thumb
Mouthbreeder
Native salmon
Orange roughy
Ox-eye herring
Plectognathi
Rainbow trout
River lamprey
Silver salmon
Skipjack tuna
Squirrelfish
Walleyed pike
Yarra herring

13 letters:
Armed bullhead
Black kingfish
Black rockfish
Brown bullhead
Chinook salmon
Climbing perch
Flying gurnard
Horse mackerel
Leatherjacket
Northern porgy
Quinnat salmon
Sailor's choice
Sergeant Baker

Sergeant major
Speckled trout

14 letters:
Largemouth bass
Orange chromide
School mackerel
Smallmouth bass

15 letters:
Crossopterygian
Freshwater bream
Siamese fighting
Spanish mackerel
Spotted mackerel

16 letters:
Australian salmon

17 letters:
Queensland halibut

18 letters:
Queensland kingfish
Queensland lungfish

19 letters:
Queensland trumpeter

22 letters:
Short-spined sea
  scorpion

See also:
➤ **Seafood** ➤ **Sharks**

Flags

7 letters:
Saltire

8 letters:
Lone Star

Old Glory
Swastika

9 letters:
Betsy Ross

Blue Peter
Maple Leaf
Red Dragon
Red Duster
Rising Sun

Tricolore
Tricolour
Union Jack

10 letters:
Blue Ensign
Bonnie Blue
Jolly Roger
Lonely Star
Single Star

11 letters:
Golden Arrow
White Duster

12 letters:
Federal Cross
Herring Salad
Stars and Bars

13 letters:
Southern Cross

14 letters:
Flag of the South

15 letters:
Cross of St George
Hammer and Sickle
Stainless Banner
Stars and Stripes

18 letters:
Skull and crossbones

Flies

3 letters:
Bee
Bot
Fly
Fox

4 letters:
Bulb
Bush
Cleg
Deer
Dung
Frit
Gnat
Horn
Moth
Pium
Zimb

5 letters:
Alder
Aphid
Aphis
Baker
Black
Brize
Crane
Drake
Drone
Flesh
Fruit

Hover
Musca
Nymph
Onion
Sedge
Snake
Snipe
Zebub

6 letters:
Blowie
Botfly
Breese
Breeze
Caddis
Carrot
Dayfly
Dragon
Gadfly
Mayfly
Medfly
Motuca
Mutuca
Needle
Pomace
Robber
Stable
Thrips
Tipula
Tsetse
Tzetze

Warble
Willow

7 letters:
Antlion
Beetfly
Blowfly
Brommer
Bushfly
Chalcid
Cluster
Diptera
Gallfly
Grannom
Harvest
Hessian
Lantern
Mangold
Sandfly
Spanish
Tabanid
Tachina
Vinegar
Watchet

8 letters:
Assassin
Bedstead
Blackfly
Dutchman

Glossina
Greenfly
Horsefly
Housefly
Lacewing
Mosquito
Ox-warble
Scorpion
Simulium
Stonefly
Whitefly

9 letters:
Bean aphid
Bee killer
Blue-arsed
Damselfly
Dobsonfly
Dragonfly
Greenhead
Homoptera

Ichneumon
Jock Scott
Sciaridae
Screwworm
Syrphidae

10 letters:
Bluebottle
Cecidomyia
Drosophila
Plant louse
Silverhorn

11 letters:
Apple blight
Buffalo gnat
Greenbottle
Plecopteran

12 letters:
Cheesehopper

Green blowfly
Jenny-spinner
Trichopteran

13 letters:
Cheese skipper
Daddy-longlegs

14 letters:
American blight

15 letters:
Welshman's button

18 letters:
Mediterranean fruit

19 letters:
Devil's darning-needle

Flowers

4 letters:
Aloe
Arum
Cyme
Disa
Flag
Gold
Gool
Gule
Irid
Iris
Lily
Pink
Rose

5 letters:
Agave
Aster
Brook
Bugle
Camas

Daisy
Enemy
Hosta
Lotus
Lupin
Oxlip
Padma
Pansy
Peony
Phlox
Poppy
Stock
Tansy
Toran
Tulip
Umbel
Yulan

6 letters:
Acacia
Adonis

Arabis
Azalea
Betony
Cactus
Camash
Camass
Corymb
Crants
Crocus
Dahlia
Gollan
Henbit
Madder
Maguey
Mallow
Nuphar
Onagra
Orchid
Paeony
Pompom
Pompon

Protea
Safety
Scilla
Sesame
Silene
Smilax
Spadix
Tassel
Torana
Vernal
Violet
Yarrow
Zinnia

7 letters:
Aconite
Alyssum
Anemone
Arbutus
Astilbe
Begonia

Bugloss
Burdock
Campion
Cowslip
Dog rose
Freesia
Fuchsia
Fumaria
Gentian
Gilt-cup
Glacier
Godetia
Golland
Gowland
Hemlock
Ipomoea
Jasmine
Jonquil
Kikumon
Lobelia
Melilot
Petunia
Picotee
Primula
Quamash
Ragweed
Rampion
Saffron
Sulphur
Verbena

8 letters:
Abutilon
Acanthus
Amaranth
Argemone
Asphodel
Aubretia
Aubrieta
Bignonia
Bindi-eye
Bluebell
Camellia
Camomile
Carolina

Clematis
Cyclamen
Daffodil
Floscule
Foxglove
Gardenia
Geranium
Gillyvor
Glory-pea
Harebell
Hepatica
Hibiscus
Hyacinth
Kok-sagyz
Larkspur
Lavender
Magnolia
Mandrake
Marigold
Marjoram
Myosotis
Oleander
Oxtongue
Primrose
Samphire
Scabious
Snowdrop
Stapelia
Sweet pea
Trollius
Tuberose
Turnsole
Valerian
Wisteria
Woodbine

9 letters:
Amaryllis
Aubrietia
Bald-money
Belamoure
Buttercup
Calendula
Carnation
Celandine

Chamomile
Clianthus
Columbine
Dandelion
Desert pea
Digitalis
Edelweiss
Eglantine
Gessamine
Gladiolus
Groundsel
Hellebore
Hollyhock
Hydrangea
Jessamine
Melampode
Monkshood
Narcissus
Pimpernel
Pre-vernal
Rudbeckia
Santonica
Saxifrage
Speedwell
Strobilus
Sunflower
Tiger lily
Water lily

10 letters:
Aspidistra
Bellamoure
Busy Lizzie
Cornflower
Coronation
Delphinium
Gypsophila
Heart's-ease
Heliotrope
Immortelle
Marguerite
Nasturtium
Oxeye daisy
Pentstemon
Poinsettia

Snapdragon
Stavesacre
Sweetbrier
Tibouchine
Touch-me-not
Wallflower
Willowherb

11 letters:
Bog asphodel
Bur-marigold
Cotoneaster
Forget-me-not
Gilliflower
Gillyflower
Guelder-rose
London pride
Loose-strife
Meadowsweet

Ragged robin
Wintergreen
Wood anemone

12 letters:
Hortus siccus
Morning-glory
None-so-pretty
Old man's beard
Sweet william
Tradescantia

13 letters:
African violet
Babe-in-a-cradle
Bougainvillea
Chrysanthemum
Grape hyacinth
Passionflower

14 letters:
Black-eyed Susan
Cardinal flower
Cooktown orchid
Love-in-idleness

15 letters:
Christmas cactus
Lily of the valley
Michaelmas daisy
Sturt's desert pea

16 letters:
Deadly nightshade
Love-lies-bleeding
Scarlet pimpernel

See also:
➤ **Lilies**

Football

TERMS USED IN (ASSOCIATION) FOOTBALL

2 letters:
FA
OG

3 letters:
Bar
Cap
Net
Nil
SFA
SFL
SPL

4 letters:
Back
FIFA
Foul
Goal

Half
Mark
Pass
Post
Save
Shot
Trap
UEFA
Wall
Wing

5 letters:
Cross
Derby
Dummy

6 letters:
Corner

Cut out
Goalie
Lay off
Nutmeg
One-two
Onside
Square
Tackle
Winger

7 letters:
Booking
Bye kick
Caution
Clasico
Dribble
Forward
Goal net

Kick off
Offside
Own goal
Penalty
Playoff
Red card
Referee
Striker
Sweeper
Throw in

8 letters:
Crossbar
Defender
Free kick
Fullback
Full time
Goal area

Goal kick
Goalpost
Halfback
Half time
Handball
Left back
Linesman
Long ball
Midfield
Pass-back
Reserves
Route One
Spot kick
Transfer
Wall pass

9 letters:
Added time
Aggregate
Breakaway
Clearance
Extra time
Finishing
Inswinger
Non-league
Promotion
Right back

Score draw
Target man
Touchline

10 letters:
Ballplayer
Ballwinner
Catenaccio
Centre half
Corner kick
Goalkeeper
Injury time
Inside left
Midfielder
Penalty box
Relegation
Sending-off
Six-yard box
Substitute
Yellow card

11 letters:
Half way line
Inside right
Offside trap
Ordering-off
Outside left

Penalty area
Penalty kick
Penalty spot
Six-yard line

12 letters:
Centre circle
Outside right
Stoppage time

13 letters:
Centre forward
International
Sliding tackle
Total football

14 letters:
Aggregate score
Direct free kick

15 letters:
Penalty shoot-out

16 letters:
Assistant referee
Indirect free kick
Professional foul

TERMS USED IN AUSTRALIAN RULES FOOTBALL

3 letters:
AFL

4 letters:
Goal
Mark
Rove
Ruck

5 letters:
Flank
Footy
Point
Rover

6 letters:
Behind
Rub out
Stanza

7 letters:
Quarter
Throw in

8 letters:
Boundary
Eighteen, the
Follower
Free kick
Guernsey

Half-back
Handball
Shepherd
Stab kick

9 letters:
Ruckrover
Scrimmage

10 letters:
Back pocket
Behind line
Behind post
Goal umpire
Shirt front

11 letters:	12 letters:	14 letters:
Aussie Rules	Twentieth man	Aerial ping-pong
Field umpire		
Half-forward	13 letters:	24 letters:
Interchange	Forward pocket	Australian Football
	Nineteenth man	League

TERMS USED IN AMERICAN FOOTBALL

3 letters:	7 letters:	Touchdown
Run	Defense	
	End zone	10 letters:
4 letters:	Lineman	Cornerback
Down	Offense	Incomplete
Line	Pigskin	Line backer
Pass	Shotgun	Point after
Play		
Punt	8 letters:	11 letters:
Rush	Complete	Quarterback
Sack	Football	Running back
Snap	Fullback	Special team
	Gridiron	
5 letters:	Halfback	12 letters:
Blitz	Overtime	Defensive end
Block	Tight end	Interception
Guard	Turnover	Wide receiver
	9 letters:	13 letters:
6 letters:	Backfield	Defensive back
Center	Field goal	
Kicker	Scrimmage	15 letters:
Punter	Secondary	Line of scrimmage
Safety	Super Bowl	
Tackle	Touchback	

FOOTBALL CLUBS

EUROPEAN FOOTBALL CLUBS

4 letters:	Braga	Monaco	CFR Cluj
Ajax	Lazio		Hamburg
Genk	Parma	7 letters:	
Lyon	Porto	AC Milan	8 letters:
Roma		Auxerre	Besiktas
	6 letters:	Benfica	Juventus
5 letters:	Brugge	Beveren	Valencia
Basel	Lierse	Brondby	

9 letters:
AEK Athens
Barcelona
Bursaspor
Celta Vigo
Feyenoord
MSK Zilina
Schalke 04
Stuttgart
Villareal

10 letters:
Anderlecht
Copenhagen
Dynamo Kiev
Heerenveen
Inter Milan
Olympiacos
Real Madrid
Rubin Kazan

11 letters:
Ferencvaros
Galatasaray
Rapid Vienna
RCD Mallorca

12 letters:
Bayern Munich
Dinamo Zagreb
PSV Eindhoven
Real Sociedad
Sparta Prague
Werder Bremen

13 letters:
Austria Vienna
Hapoel Tel-Aviv
Panathinaikos
Spartak Moscow

14 letters:
Paris St Germain
Twente Enschede

15 letters:
Lokomotiv Moscow
Red Star Belgrade
Shakhtar Donetsk
Steaua Bucharest

16 letters:
Borussia Dortmund
Partizan Belgrade

17 letters:
Deportivo La Coruna

18 letters:
Olympique Marseille

UK FOOTBALL CLUBS

Club	Nickname	Ground
Aberdeen	Dons	Pittodrie
Arsenal	Gunners	Emirates
Aston Villa	Villa	Villa Park
Birmingham City	Blues	St Andrews
Blackburn Rovers	Rovers	Ewood Park
Blackpool	Seasiders	Bloomfield Road
Bolton	Trotters	Reebok Stadium
Bradford	Bantams	Valley Parade
Bristol City	Robins	Ashton Gate
Burnley	Clarets	Turf Moor
Cardiff	Bluebirds	Cardiff City Stadium
Celtic	Celts, Hoops, Tic	Celtic Park, Parkhead
Charlton	Addicks	The Valley
Chelsea	Pensioners, Blues	Stamford Bridge
Coventry City	Sky Blues	Ricoh Arena
Crewe	Railwaymen	Alexandra Stadium, Gresty Road
Crystal Palace	Eagles	Selhurst Park
Derby County	Rams	Pride Park
Dundee	Dark Blues	Dens Park
Dundee United	Tangerines	Tannadice
Dunfermline Athletic	Pars	East End Park

Club	Nickname	Ground
Everton	Toffee Men	Goodison Park
Fulham	Cottagers	Craven Cottage
Gillingham	Gills	Priestfield Stadium
Hamilton Academical	Accies	New Douglas Park
Hearts	Jambos, Jam Tarts	Gorgie Road
Hibernian	Hibs, Hibees	Easter Road
Inverness Caledonian Thistle	Caley, The Jags	Tulloch Caledonian Stadium
Ipswich	Blues, Tractor Boys	Portman Road
Kilmarnock	Killie	Rugby Park
Leeds United	United	Elland Road
Leicester City	Foxes	Walkers Stadium
Leyton Orient	Orient	Brisbane Road
Liverpool	Reds	Anfield
Livingston	Thistle, Wee Jags	Almondvale Stadium
Manchester City	City	City of Manchester Stadium
Manchester United	Reds, Red Devils	Old Trafford
Middlesbrough	Boro	Riverside Stadium
Millwall	Lions	The Den
Motherwell	Steelmen, Well	Fir Park
Newcastle United	Magpies, Toon	St James Park
Norwich	Canaries	Carrow Road
Nottingham Forest	Forest	City Ground
Partick Thistle	Jags	Firhill
Peterborough	Posh	London Road
Portsmouth	Pompey	Fratton Park
Preston	Lilywhites	Deepdale
Queen of the South	The Doonhamers	Palmerston Park
Queen's Park Rangers	QPR	Loftus Road
Rangers	Gers, The Blues, (Teddy) Bears	Ibrox
Reading	Royals, Biscuitmen	Madejski Stadium
Ross County	Staggies	Victoria Park Stadium
Rotherham	Merry Millers	Don Valley
St Johnstone	The Saints	McDiarmid Park
St Mirren	The Buddies	St Mirren Park
Sheffield United	Blades	Bramall Lane
Sheffield Wednesday	Owls	Hillsborough
Southampton	Saints	The Dell
Stenhousemuir	The Warriors	Ochilview Park
Stoke	Potteries	Britannia Stadium
Sunderland	Rokerites	Stadium of Light
Tottenham Hotspur	Spurs	White Hart Lane
Tranmere Rovers	Super Whites, Rovers	Prenton Park

Club	Nickname	Ground
Walsall	Saddlers	Bescot Stadium
Watford	Hornets	Vicarage Road
West Bromwich Albion	Throstles, Raggies	The Hawthorns
West Ham United	Hammers	Upton Park
Wigan Athletic	Latics	JJB Stadium
AFC Wimbledon	Dons, Wombles	Kingsmeadow
Wolverhampton Wanderers	Wolves	Molineux

FOOTBALLERS

3 letters:
Law, *Dennis*

4 letters:
Ball, *Alan*
Best, *George*
Caca
Cech, *Petr*
Dean, *Dixie*
Didi
Duff, *Damien*
Eto'o, *Samuel*
Figo, *Luis*
Gray, *Eddie*
Hunt, *Roger*
Kaka
Owen, *Michael*
Pele
Repp, *Johnny*
Rush, *Ian*
Toni, *Luca*
Xavi
Zoff, *Dino*

5 letters:
Adams, *Tony*
Banks, *Gordon*
Giggs, *Ryan*
Giles, *John*
Greig, *John*
Henry, *Thierry*
Hurst, *Geoff*
Keane, *Robbie*
Messi, *Lionel*

Moore, *Bobby*
Pires, *Robert*
Puyol, *Carles*
Rossi, *Paulo*
Terry, *John*
Tévez, *Carlos*
Totti, *Francisco*
Villa, *David*

6 letters:
Baggio, *Roberto*
Barnes, *John*
Baxter, *Jim*
Bowles, *Stan*
Cooper, *Davie*
Crespo, *Hernan*
Cruyff, *Johann*
Drogba, *Didier*
Finney, *Tom*
Forlán, *Diego*
Ginola, *David*
Graham, *George*
Gullit, *Ruud*
Hansen, *Alan*
Heskey, *Emil*
Hoddle, *Glen*
Horton, *Jim*
Keegan, *Kevin*
Lawton, *Tommy*
Mackay, *Dave*
Maicon
McNeil, *Billy*
McStay, *Paul*
Milito, *Diego*

Muller, *Gerd*
Puskas, *Ferenc*
Robson, *Brian*
Rooney, *Wayne*
Seaman, *David*
Stiles, *Nobby*
St John, *Ian*
Torres, *Fernando*
Viduka, *Mark*
Vieira, *Patrick*
Wright, *Billy*
Wright, *Ian*
Yashin, *Lev*
Zidane, *Zinedine*

7 letters:
Alberto, *Carlos*
Beckham, *David*
Bremner, *Billy*
Cantona, *Eric*
Charles, *John*
Di Canio, *Paulo*
Eusebio
Francis, *Trevor*
Gemmell, *Archie*
Gemmell, *Tommy*
Gerrard, *Steven*
Gilzean, *Alan*
Greaves, *Jimmy*
Iniesta, *Andrés*
Lampard, *Frank*
Larsson, *Henrik*
Lineker, *Gary*
Lorimer, *Peter*

Mannion, *Wilf*
McCoist, *Ally*
Platini, *Michel*
Rivaldo
Ronaldo
Ronaldo, *Cristiano*
Scholes, *Paul*
Shearer, *Alan*
Shilton, *Peter*
Souness, *Graeme*
Toshack, *John*
Waddell, *Willie*

8 letters:
Bergkamp, *Dennis*
Charlton, *Bobby*
Charlton, *Jack*
Dalglish, *Kenny*
Fontaine, *Just*

Heighway, *Steve*
Jennings, *Pat*
Johnston, *Willie*
Maradona, *Diego*
Matthaus, *Lothar*
Sneijder, *Wesley*
Socrates

9 letters:
Archibald, *Steve*
Cannavaro, *Fabio*
Collymore, *Stan*
DiStefano, *Alfredo*
Gascoigne, *Paul*
Henderson, *Willie*
Jairzinho
Johnstone, *Jimmy*
Klinsmann, *Jurgen*
Lofthouse, *Nat*

Van Basten, *Marco*
Van der sar, *Edwin*

10 letters:
Battistuta, *Gabriel*
Djourkaeff, *Youri*
McClintock, *Frank*
Ronaldinho
Schillacci, *Toto*

11 letters:
Beckenbauer, *Franz*

12 letters:
Blanchflower, *Danny*

13 letters:
Van Nistelrooy, *Ruud*

Foreign words and phrases

3 letters:
Ami
Jeu
Mot

4 letters:
À bas
Abbé
Doge
Gene
In re
Lied
Vivo

5 letters:
Ab ovo
Addio
À deux
Ad hoc
Adios
Ad lib
Ad rem
Adsum

À gogo
Aidos
Apage
Arras
Assai
Buffo
Ca ira
Canto
Corno
Desto
Dolce
Domus
École
Étude
Grave
Largo
Lento
Lycée
Mores
Obiit
Per se
Plaza
Pleno

Reich
Salle
Segno
Segue
Sordo
Tacet
Torte
Tutti
Usine

6 letters:
Abattu
Abrege
Agrege
Allons
Aperçu
À terre
Aubade
Au fait
Au fond
Avanti
Avenir
Bel air

Bêtise
Bon mot
Bon ton
Cortes
Crible
Da capo
Dégagé
Déja vu
De jure
Der Tag
Emptor
En fête
Fi donc
Flèche
Giusto
Grazia
Ibidem
In vivo
Legato
Lieder
Maison
Mañana
Nobile

Ottava
Palais
Posada
Presto
Rubato
Sempre
Subito
Tenuto
Torero
Troppo
Vivace

7 letters:
Acharne
Ad astra
Ad finem
Ad litem
À droite
Ad vivum
Affaire
Affiche
Agaçant
À gauche
Agitato
À jamais
À la mode
Alcaide
Alcalde
Al conto
Altesse
Animato
A priori
À quatre
Attacca
Au mieux
Auslese
Bas bleu
Battuta
Berceau
Bonjour
Bonsoir
Bourrée
Bravura
Calando
Cantina

Canzona
Canzone
Caramba
Chambre
Chanson
Château
Chez moi
Clavier
Codetta
Comedia
Con brio
Con moto
Couloir
Cui bono
D'accord
Danseur
Ébauche
En prise
En route
Ex aequo
Fagotto
Farceur
Fermata
Friture
Furioso
Gestalt
Giocoso
Gouache
Haut ton
Ich dien
In utero
In vacuo
In vitro
Ländler
Laus Deo
Märchen
Morceau
Morendo
Palazzo
Pas seul
Peccavi
Pension
Pesante
Piacere
Plafond

Pomposo
Pro rata
Qui vive
Ragazza
Rathaus
Rigsdag
Riksdag
Rondeau
Rondino
Rosalio
Roulade
Schloss
Sine die
Sordino
Sub rosa
Tant pis
Vibrato

8 letters:
Abat jour
Abat-voix
Ad summum
Agaçerie
Agrément
À la carte
Alta moda
Apéritif
A piacere
Après ski
À quoi bon
Au gratin
Au revoir
Autobahn
Aux armes
À volonté
Banlieue
Bel canto
Bien-être
Bona fide
Bout-rime
Chez nous
Col legno
Con amore
Con fuoco
Coryphée

Cum laude
Dal segno
Danseuse
Déjeuner
Démarche
Deus vult
Dies irae
Distrait
Doloroso
Duettino
Enceinte
Entresol
Estancia
Et cetera
Excerpta
Ex gratia
Faubourg
Fine Gael
Gendarme
Grand mal
Hacienda
Hic jacet
Idée fixe
Leggiero
Maestoso
Maggiore
Mala fide
Mal de mer
Mandamus
Mea culpa
Moderato
Mon repos
Mot juste
Ostinato
Par avion
Parlando
Parlante
Pro forma
Raisonné
Rara avis
Ripiendo
Ritenuto
Sayonara
Scordato
Semplice

Serenata
Sobranje
Spianato
Staccato
Sub poena
Trouvère
Una corda
Vorspiel

9 letters:
À bon droit
Aborigine
A cappella
Ad hominem
Ad libitum
Ad nauseam
Ad valorem
A fortiori
Alla breve
Alma mater
Âme perdue
Anschluss
Antipasto
À outrance
Arc-en-ciel
Aria buffa
Assez bien
Au courant
Au naturel
Au secours
Ausgleich
Autopista
Autoroute
Bal masque
Beaux arts
Beaux yeux
Bel esprit
Belle amie
Ben venuto
Bête noire
Bon marché
Bon vivant
Bon viveur
Bon voyage
Bundesrat

Bundestag
Buona sera
Cantabile
Carpe diem
Cauchemar
Cave canem
Centumvir
Coup d'état
Das heisst
Dei gratia
De rigueur
Dolce vita
En famille
En passant
Et tu, Brute
Flute-a-bec
Folketing
Gemütlich
Glissando
Grandioso
Grand prix
Haut monde
Inter alia
Ipse dixit
Ipso facto
Landsting
Leitmotiv
Mardi Gras
Meden agan
Mezza voce
Nisi prius
Obbligato
Objet d'art
Pari passu
Pas de deux
Passepied
Per capita
Per contra
Petit four
Piacevole
Piangendo
Politburo
Pro patria
Pro re nata
Ricercare

Rus in urbe
Scherzoso
Sforzando
Siciliana
Sine prole
Smerzando
Solfeggio
Sostenuto
Sotto voce
Spiritoso
Sub judice
Sub specie
Succès fou
Tant mieux
Taoiseach
Tête-à-tête
Tout à fait
Tout court
Vers libre
Volkslied
Vox humana

10 letters:
À bon marché
Absente reo
Ad absurdum
Ad vizandum
Affettuoso
Aficionado
Alla Franca
Allargando
All tedesca
Anno Domini
Art nouveau
Au pis aller
Autostrada
Avant garde
Bar mitzvah
Bêche-de-mer
Ben trovato
Billet doux
Bon appetit
Buon giorno
Café au lait
Camino real

Canto fermo
Canzonetta
Certiorari
Cinquepace
Confiserie
Con sordini
Con spirito
Cordon bleu
Danke schön
Deo gratias
Deo volente
Dernier cri
Eisteddfod
Feuilleton
Fianna Fáil
Forte piano
Gesundheit
In excelsis
In extremis
Jardinière
Jus commune
Jus gentium
Lebensraum
Magnum opus
Mezzo forte
Mezzo piano
Nom-de-plume
Opera buffa
Ottava rima
Perdendosi
Pied-à-terre
Plat du jour
Ponticello
Prima facie
Prix unique
Pro hac vice
Quid pro quo
Recitativo
Ritardando
Ritornelle
Ritornello
Scherzando
Scordatura
Seguidilla
Semper idem

Sens unique
Sine qua non
Stringendo
Sui generis
Table d'hôte
Terra firma
Thé dansant
Tiergarten
Tout de même
Tremolando
Ultra vires
Urbi et orbi
Villanella

11 letters:
Accelerando
Ad infinitum
Aetatis suae
Aide-mémoire
Allez-vous en
Alto-relievo
Amor patriae
Amour-propre
À nos moutons
A posteriori
Arcades ambo
Arrivederci
Au contraire
Avec plaisir
À votre santé
Belle époque
Bien entendu
Bonne bouche
Boutonnière
Capriccioso
Carte du jour
Cavo-relievo
Che sera sera
Comme il faut
Concertante
Contra punto
Contredanse
Coram populo
Crème brûlée
Dail Eireann

Decrescendo
Degringoler
De haut en bas
De profundis
Ex hypothesi
Ex post facto
Femme fatale
Fieri facias
Fin de siècle
Fritto misto
Hasta mañana
In medias res
In principio
Lèse majesté
Lignum vitae
Litterateur
Mise en scène
Motu proprio
Musica ficta
Ne plus ultra
Nihil obstat
Nom de guerre
Nous verrons
Obiter dicta
Objet trouvé
Opera bouffe
Papier-mâché
Pas de quatre
Pax vobiscum
Politbureau
Raison d'être
Rellentando
Savoir-faire
Schottische
Smörgasbord
Summum bonum
Tempo giusto
Tempus fugit
Tertium quid
Tout le monde
Und so weiter
Vivacissimo

12 letters:
Acciaccatura

Amicus curiae
Ancien régime
Ante meridiem
Appassionata
Appoggiatura
À quatre mains
Arrière-garde
Ave atque vale
Ballon d'essai
Basso-relievo
Buenas noches
Carte blanche
Cause célèbre
Caveat emptor
Compos mentis
Concertstück
Conseil d'état
Contra mundum
Crème caramel
Degringolade
Donnerwetter
Doppelganger
Eppur si muove
Experto crede
Fait accompli
Ferae naturae
Feu d'artifice
Force majeure
Gesellschaft
Glockenspiel
Habeas corpus
Hasta la vista
Haute couture
Homme du monde
Honoris causa
Hors concours
Hors de combat
Hors d'oeuvres
Hotel de ville
Laissez-faire
Lapsus calami
Lite pendente
Mezzo-relievo
Modus vivendi
Obiter dictum

Opéra comique
Piobaireachd
Pollice verso
Pons asinorum
Porte-cochère
Porte-monnaie
Quelque chose
Rien ne va plus
Salle à manger
Sauve qui peut
S'il vous plait
Terminus a quo
Zigeunerlied

13 letters:
Ab urbe condita
Aggiornamento
À la bonne heure
À propos de rien
Ariston metron
Arrière pensée
Avant-gardiste
Avis au lecteur
Basso profondo
Champs Élysées
Cogito ergo sum
Corps de ballet
Corpus delicti
Couleur de rose
Crème de menthe
Croix de guerre
Cum grano salis
Deux ex machina
Éminence grise
Exempli gratia
Ex proprio motu
Faites vos jeux
Fête champêtre
Force de frappe
In vino veritas
Laissez-passer
Lapsus linguae
Magna cum laude
Mirabile dictu
Modus operandi

Multum in parvo
Nolens vivendi
Noli-me-tangere
Nolle prosequi
Nouvelle Vague
Nulli secundus
Palais de danse
Poisson d'avril
Quartier latin
Schadenfreude
Succès d'estime
Summa cum laude
Très au sérieux

14 letters:
A minori ad majus
Annus mirabilis
Auf Wiedersehen
Bureau de change
Ceteris paribus
Crème de la crème
Deuxième Bureau
Dis aliter visum
Divide et impera
Dolce far niente
Double entendre
Ejusdem generis
Enfant terrible
Et in Arcadia ego
Facile princeps
Hapax legomenon
Homme d'affaires
In loco parentis
Ipsissima verba
Maxima cum laude
Ne obliviscaris
Obiit sine prole
Petit bourgeois
Terminus ad quem
Terra incognita
Tertius gaudens
Valet de chambre

15 letters:
Ad misericordiam

Amende honorable
À propos de bottes
Argumentum ad rem
Cherchez la femme

Cordon sanitaire
Crime passionnel
Gaudeamus igitur
Mutatis mutandis

Persona non grata
Rem acu tetigisti

Fossils

5 letters:
Amber

6 letters:
Eozoon
Olenus

7 letters:
Exuviae
Ichnite
Zoolite

8 letters:
Ammonite
Baculite
Blastoid
Calamite
Conchite
Conodont
Eohippus
Mosasaur
Pliosaur
Ram's horn
Scaphite
Solenite
Volulite
Volutite
Wood-opal

9 letters:
Belemnite
Buccinite
Ceratodus
Chondrite
Cordaites
Encrinite
Goniatite
Ichnolite
Miliolite
Muscalite
Nummulite
Ostracite
Patellite
Phytolite
Serpulite
Stigmaria
Strombite
Tellinite
Trilobite
Turbinate
Turrilite

10 letters:
Blastoidea
Eurypterus
Graptolite
Lingulella
Mosasauros

Orthoceras
Osteolepis
Plesiosaur
Pliohippus
Pterygotus
Sigillaria
Snakestone

11 letters:
Gongiatites
Ichthyolite
Ostracoderm

12 letters:
Pythonomorph
Sinanthropus
Stromatolite
Uintatherium

13 letters:
Titanotherium
Zinganthropus

14 letters:
Conchyliaceous

15 letters:
Ichthyodurolite

Fowl

3 letters:
Cob
Hen
Ree

4 letters:
Cock
Coot
Duck
Gnow
Kora

Nene
Smew
Swan
Teal

5 letters:
Capon
Chock
Chook
Eider
Ember

Goose
Layer
Quail
Reeve
Rumpy
Scaup
Solan

6 letters:
Ancona
Bantam
Boiler
Brahma
Cochin
Eirack
Guinea
Houdan
Jungle
Pullet
Rumkin
Sitter
Sultan
Sussex
Tappit
Turkey
Wigeon

7 letters:
Campine
Chicken
Dorking

Gadwall
Greylag
Hamburg
Leghorn
Mallard
Minorca
Moorhen
Partlet
Pintado
Pintail
Pochard
Poulard
Redhead
Rooster
Sawbill
Sea duck
Sumatra
Whooper
Widgeon

8 letters:
Baldpate
Blue duck
Cockerel
Hamburgh
Langshan
Marsh hen
Megapode
Musk duck
Mute swan
Pheasant

Screamer
Shelduck
Shoveler
Wood duck

9 letters:
Black swan
Blue goose
Eider duck
Faverolle
Goldeneye
Goosander
Merganser
Orpington
Partridge
Pertelote
Ruddy duck
Scaup duck
Snow goose
Welsummer
Wyandotte

10 letters:
Andalusian
Australorp
Bufflehead
Burrow-duck
Canvasback
Chittagong
Mallee fowl
Spatchcock

Spitchcock

11 letters:
Bewick's swan
Brissle-cock
Brush turkey
Canada goose
Magpie goose
Muscovy duck
Scrub turkey
Whooper swan

12 letters:
Greylag goose
Mandarin duck
New Hampshire
Paradise duck
Plymouth Rock
Velvet scoter

13 letters:
Barnacle goose
Buff Orpington
Harlequin duck
Trumpeter swan
Whistling swan

14 letters:
American wigeon
Rhode Island Red

Fruits

3 letters:
Fig
Haw
Hep
Hip
Hop
Jak

4 letters:
Akee
Bael

Bito
Date
Gage
Gean
Jack
Kaki
Kiwi
Lime
Pear
Pepo
Plum

Pome
Sloe
Sorb
Star
Tuna
UGLI®

5 letters:
Anana
Anona
Apple

Assai
Berry
Bread
Choko
Gourd
Grape
Guava
Jaffa
Lemon
Lichi
Lotus

Mango
Melon
Nancy
Naras
Nashi
Nelis
Olive
Papaw
Peach
Prune
Rowan
Whort

6 letters:
Almond
Ananas
Babaco
Banana
Banian
Banyan
Carica
Casaba
Cherry
Chocho
Citron
Citrus
Damson
Durian
Durion
Emblic
Feijoa
Kiwano®
Lichee
Litchi
Longan
Loquat
Lychee
Mammee
Medlar
Narras
Nelies
Orange
Papaya
Pawpaw
Pepino

Pepper
Pomelo
Pruine
Quince
Raisin
Russet
Samara
Sapota
Sharon
Squash
Sweety
Tomato
Wampee

7 letters:
Apricot
Avocado
Boquila
Bramble
Bullace
Cedrate
Chayote
Crab-nut
Cumquat
Geebung
Genipap
Kumquat
Leechee
Litchee
Manjack
Morello
Naartje
Passion
Pimento
Pinguin
Poperin
Pumpkin
Pupunha
Ruddock
Satsuma
Soursop
Sultana
Sweetie
Tangelo
Winesap

8 letters:
Abricock
Apricock
Bergamot
Bilberry
Blimbing
Boxberry
Calabash
Dewberry
Fraughan
Goosegog
Hagberry
Hastings
Hedgehog
Kalumpit
Mandarin
May apple
Minneola
Mulberry
Physalis
Plantain
Rambutan
Sebesten
Shaddock
Sunberry
Sweetsop
Tamarind
Tayberry
Victoria

9 letters:
Algarroba
Apple-john
Asian pear
Aubergine
Bakeapple
Beach plum
Blaeberry
Blueberry
Cantaloup
Carambola
Chempaduk
Cherimoya
Cranberry
Greengage

Haanepoot
Hackberry
Jackfruit
Japan plum
Love apple
Mirabelle
Muskmelon
Myrobalan
Naseberry
Nectarine
Neesberry
Ogen melon
Ortanique
Persimmon
Pineapple
Plumdamas
Poppering
Raspberry
Rockmelon
Sapodilla
Saskatoon
Shadberry
Snowberry
Sour gourd
Star-apple
Tamarillo
Tangerine
Tomatillo
Victorine
Whimberry

10 letters:
Blackberry
Breadfruit
Calamondin
Canteloupe
Cherimoyer
Chokeberry
Clementine
Cloudberry
Elderberry
Galia melon
Gooseberry
Granadilla
Grapefruit

Grenadilla
Jargonelle
Loganberry
Mangosteen
Pick-cheese
Redcurrant
Scaldberry
Sour cherry
Strawberry
Tree tomato
Watermelon
Youngberry

11 letters:
Anchovy pear
Avocado pear
Black cherry
Blood orange
Boysenberry
Chokecherry
Heart cherry
Hesperidium
Huckleberry
Jaffa orange
Marionberry
Navel orange

Pampelmoose
Pampelmouse
Pomegranate
Pompelmoose
Pompelmouse
Prickly pear
Salmonberry
Sweet cherry
Winter melon

12 letters:
Bartlett pear
Bergamot pear
Blackcurrant
Cassaba melon
Concord grape
Custard apple
Sea buckthorn
Serviceberry
Thimbleberry
Victoria plum
White currant
Whortleberry
Williams pear

13 letters:
Alligator pear
Honeydew melon
Morello cherry
Sapodilla plum
Seville orange

14 letters:
Cape gooseberry
Conference pear
Queensland blue
Worcesterberry

15 letters:
Beurre Hardy pear
Bigarreau cherry
Bon Chretien pear
Cantaloupe melon
Charentais melon

16 letters:
Blackheart cherry
Strawberry tomato

17 letters:
Chinese gooseberry

Fungi

3 letters:
Cup

4 letters:
Bunt
Rust
Smut

5 letters:
Black
Ergot
Favus
Honey
Jelly
Morel
Mould

Mucor
Spunk
Yeast

6 letters:
Agaric
Amadou
Dry rot
Elf-cup
Empusa
Ink-cap
Mildew
Miller
Peziza
Torula
Wax cap

Wet rot

7 letters:
Amanita
Blewits
Boletus
Bracket
Candida
Jew's ear
Milk cap
Monilia
Phallus
Pythium
Russula
Tarspot
Truffle

8 letters:
Ambrosia
Bootlace
Clubroot
Death cap
Death-cup
Fuss-ball
Fuzz-ball
Merulius
Mushroom
Noble rot
Puccinia
Puckfist
Puffball
Rhizopus
Rhytisma

Sariodes
Sickener
Tremella
Tuckahoe
Ustilago

9 letters:
Beefsteak
Blackknot
Cramp ball
Earthstar
Eumycetes
Funnel cap
Horsehair
Mucorales
Shaggy cap
Stinkhorn
Toadstool

10 letters:
Gibberella
Liberty cap

Oak-leather
Orange-peel
Rust fungus
Shoestring
Sooty mould
Yellow rust

11 letters:
Anthracnose
Aspergillus
Chantarelle
Chanterelle
Cladosporum
Craterellus
Ithyphallus
Jelly fungus
Penicillium
Phycomycete
Saprolegnia
Sulphur tuft
Velvet shank

12 letters:
Cryptococcus
Discomycetes
Horn of plenty
Hypersarcoma
Trichophyton
Wood hedgehog

13 letters:
Bracket fungus
Magic mushroom
Saccharomyces
Witches' butter

14 letters:
Wood woollyfoot

15 letters:
Bird's-nest fungus
Dermatophytosis
Destroying angel

Furies

6 letters:
Alecto

7 letters:
Megaera

9 letters:
Tisiphone

Furniture

TYPES OF FURNITURE

6 letters:
Canopy
Litter
Screen
Tester

7 letters:
Bedpost
Epergne
Lectern
Trolley

8 letters:
Bedstead

Hatstand
Vanitory

9 letters:
Coatstand
Footstool
Girandola
Girandole
Hallstand
Headboard
Washstand

10 letters:
Dumbwaiter

Vanity unit

11 letters:
Cheval glass

13 letters:
Longcase clock
Umbrella stand

16 letters:
Grandfather clock
Grandmother clock

FURNITURE STYLES

5 letters:
Saxon
Tudor

6 letters:
Empire
Gothic
Norman
Shaker

7 letters:
Art Deco
Bauhaus
Puritan
Regency

8 letters:
Georgian
Jacobean
Medieval

9 letters:
Cape Dutch
Edwardian
Queen Anne
Victorian

10 letters:
Louis Seize

11 letters:
Elizabethan

Louis Quinze
Louis Treize
New Georgian
Restoration

12 letters:
Greek Revival
Second Empire

13 letters:
Louis Quatorze

14 letters:
William and Mary

FURNITURE DESIGNERS

4 letters:
Adam, *Robert*
Heal, *Ambrose*
Kent, *William*

5 letters:
Aalto, *Alvar*
Bevan, *Charles*
Jones, *Inigo*
Jones, *William*
Klint, *Kaara*
Marot, *Daniel*
Phyfe, *Duncan*
Pugin, *Augustus*
Smith, *George*

6 letters:
Breuer, *Marcel Lajos*

Burges, *William*
Morris, *William*
Voysey, *Charles*

8 letters:
Sheraton, *Thomas*

9 letters:
Pergolesi, *Michael Angelo*

10 letters:
Mackintosh, *Charles Rennie*

11 letters:
Chippendale, *Thomas*
Hepplewhite, *George*

Gg

Galaxies

4 letters:
Arp's

5 letters:
Bode's
Draco
Dwarf
Giant
Helix
Radio
Virgo

6 letters:
Baade's
Carafe
Carina
Cygnus
Fornax
Maffei
Quasar
Spiral
Zwicky

7 letters:
Barbon's
Cluster
Garland

Pancake
Regular
Seyfert
Spindle

8 letters:
Aquarius
Barnard's
Bear's Paw
Black Eye
Circinus
Holmberg
Lacertid
Milky Way
Papillon
Pinwheel
Reinmuth
Sculptor
Seashell
Sombrero

9 letters:
Andromeda
Blue fuzzy
Capricorn
Cartwheel
Centaurus

Great Wall
Irregular

10 letters:
Elliptical
Horologium
Local Group

12 letters:
Supercluster

13 letters:
Burbidge Chain

15 letters:
Exclamation Mark

17 letters:
Ambartsumian's Knot

19 letters:
Mini Magellanic cloud

20 letters:
Large Magellanic Cloud
Small Magellanic Cloud

Games

2 letters:	3 letters:	Maw	Put	War
Eo	Cat	Nap	Swy	
Go	Hob	Nim	Tag	**4 letters:**
RU	Loo	Pit	Tig	Base

Brag
Bull
Crap
Dibs
Fa-fi
Faro
Goff
Golf
Grab
I-spy
Keno
Kino
Loto
Ludo
Main
Mora
Polo
Pool
Putt
Ruff
Scat
Skat
Snap
Solo
Taws
Vint

5 letters:
Bingo
Bocce
Bowls
Catch
Chess
Cinch
Craps
Darts
Fives
Goose
Halma
House
Jacks
Keeno
Lotto
Lurch
Merel

Meril
Monte
Morra
Noddy
Novum
Omber
Ombre
Poker
Quino
Rebus
Roque
Rummy
Shogi
Spoof
Tarok
Tarot
Trugo
Two-up
Whisk
Whist

6 letters:
Animal
Basset
Beetle
Boston
Boules
Casino
Chemmy
Clumps
Crambo
Ecarté
Euchre
Fantan
Footer
Gammon
Gobang
Gomoku
Hockey
Hoopla
Hurley
Kitcat
Merell
Pelota
Piquet

Quinze
Quoits
Raffle
Shinny
Shinty
Soccer
Socker
Squash
Tipcat
Uckers
Vigoro

7 letters:
Anagram
Ba'spiel
Bezique
Braemar
Camogie
Canasta
Cassino
Charade
Codille
Conkers
Coon-can
Croquet
Curling
Diabolo
Hangman
Hurling
In-and-In
Jai Alai
Jukskei
Kabaddi
Lottery
Mahjong
Mancala
Marbles
Matador
Muggins
Netball
Old Maid
Pachisi
Pallone
Peekabo
Pharaoh

Pinball
Plafond
Primero
Rackets
Reversi
Ring taw
Seven-up
Snooker
Squails
Statues
Tangram
Vingt-un
War game

8 letters:
Acrostic
All-fours
Baccarat
Bumpball
Canfield
Charades
Chouette
Cottabus
Cribbage
Dominoes
Fivepins
Football
Forfeits
Handball
Klondike
Klondyke
Korfball
Leapfrog
Mah-jongg
Monopoly®
Ninepins
Nintendo®
Octopush
Pachinko
Pall-mall
Pastance
Patience
Peekaboo
Pegboard
Penneech

Penneeck
Penuchle
Petanque
Ping-pong
Pinochle
Pintable
Pope Joan
Reversis
Rolypoly
Roulette
Rounders
Sack race
Scrabble®
Skipping
Skittles
Slapjack
Softball
Sphairee
Subbuteo®
Teetotum
Tray-trip
Tredille
Trictrac
Verquere
Verquire
Wall game

9 letters:
Badminton
Bagatelle
Billiards
Black-cock
Black-jack
Broomball
Crossword
Duplicate
Fillipeen
Hopscotch
Jingo-ring
Lanterloo
Level-coil
Logogriph
Matrimony
Mistigris
Mumchance

Newmarket
Or mineral
Paintball
Parcheesi®
Pelmanism
Punchball
Quadrille
Quidditch®
Simon says
Solitaire
Spoilfive
Stoolball
Tip-and-run
Tredrille
Twenty-one
Vegetable
Vingt-et-un

10 letters:
Angel-beast
Basketball
Bouillotte
Candlepins
Cat's cradle
Deck tennis
Dumb Crambo
Five-stones

Handy-dandy
Horseshoes
Jackstones
Jackstraws
Knurr-spell
Lansquenet
Paddleball
Phillipina
Phillipine
Philopoena
Spillikins
Tablanette
Tchoukball
Thimblerig
Tricktrack
Troll-madam
Trou-madame
Volley-ball

11 letters:
Barley-brake
Battleships
Bumble-puppy
Catch-the-ten
Hide-and-seek
Racquetball
Rouge et noir

Sancho-pedro
Shovelboard
Speculation
Tick-tack-toe
Tiddlywinks
Troll-my-dame

12 letters:
Bar billiards
Caber tossing
Commonwealth
Consequences
Housey-housey
Jigsaw puzzle
Knur and spell
One-and-thirty
Pitch-and-toss
Shuffleboard
Span-farthing
Troll-my-dames

13 letters:
Blind man's buff
French cricket
Musical chairs
Postman's knock
Prisoner's base

Scavenger hunt

14 letters:
British bulldog
Crown and anchor
Ducks and drakes
Follow-my-leader
Shove-halfpenny
Snip-snap-snorum
Three-card monte

15 letters:
Chinese whispers
Crossword puzzle
King of the castle
Russian roulette
The Minister's Cat
Twenty questions

16 letters:
Trente-et-
  quarante

17 letters:
Noughts and
  crosses

See also:
➤ **Board games**   ➤ **Chess pieces**   ➤ **Computer games**

Gases

1 letter:	RN	**4 letters:**	**5 letters:**	Water
H	VX	Coal	Argon	Xenon
O		Damp	Calor®	
	3 letters:	Flue	Ether	**6 letters:**
2 letters:	Air	Mace®	Marsh	Arsine
BZ	CNG	Neon	Nerve	Biogas
CN	LNG	Tail	Ozone	Bottle
CS	LPG	Tear	Radon	Butane
He	Nox	Town	Sarin	Butene
Kr	SNG		Soman	Ethane
Ne			Tabun	Ethene

Ethine
Helium
Ketene
Oilgas
Olefin
Oxygen
Plasma
Sewage
Silane
Thoron
V-agent

7 letters:
Ammonia
Argonon
Blister
Bottled
Coal-oil
Crypton
Fluorin
Krypton
Methane
Mofette
Mustard
Natural
Olefine
Propane
Propene
Stibine

8 letters:
Chlorine
Cyanogen
Diborane
Etherion
Ethylene

Firedamp
Fluorine
Hydrogen
Laughing
Lewisite
Nitrogen
Phosgene
Producer

9 letters:
Acetylene
Afterdamp
Butadiene
Chokedamp
Phosphine
Propylene
Protostar
Solfatara
Synthesis
Whitedamp

10 letters:
Diphosgene
Greenhouse

11 letters:
Methylamine
Nitric oxide

12 letters:
Carbonic-acid
Diazomethane
Electrolytic
Formaldehyde
Nitrous oxide
Oxyacetylene

13 letters:
Carbon dioxide
Methyl bromide
Vinyl chloride

14 letters:
Carbon monoxide
Hydrogen iodide
Methyl chloride
Sulphur dioxide

15 letters:
Hydrogen bromide
Nitrogen dioxide
Nitrogen mustard

16 letters:
Hydrogen chloride
Hydrogen fluoride
Hydrogen sulphide
Synthetic natural

17 letters:
Compressed natural
Tetrafluoroethene

18 letters:
Liquefied petroleum

19 letters:
Tetrafluoroethylene

23 letters:
Dichlorodifluoromethane

Gemstones

2 letters:	**4 letters:**	**5 letters:**		
ID	Jade	Agate	Prase	Jargon
	Onyx	Balas	Topaz	Jasper
3 letters:	Opal	Beryl		Jaspis
Jet	Ruby	Idaho	**6 letters:**	Morion
	Sard	Pearl	Garnet	Plasma
			Iolite	Pyrope

Quartz
Sphene
Spinel
Zircon

7 letters:
Cat's-eye
Citrine
Diamond
Emerald
Girasol
Girosol
Helidor
Jacinth
Jadeite
Jargoon
Kunzite
Peridot
Sardine
Smaragd

8 letters:
Adularia
Amethyst
Corundum
Diopside
Fire opal
Girasole
Hawk's-eye

Heliodor
Hyacinth
Melanite
Menilite
Peridote
Sapphire
Sardonyx
Sunstone
Titanite

9 letters:
Almandine
Amazonite
Andradite
Aventurin
Black opal
Cairngorm
Carnelian
Cornelian
Cymophane
Demantoid
Hessonite
Hiddenite
Liver opal
Moonstone
Morganite
Moss agate
Rhodolite
Rubellite

Spodumene
Starstone
Tiger's eye
Turquoise
Uvarovite

10 letters:
Andalusite
Aquamarine
Avanturine
Aventurine
Bloodstone
Chalcedony
Chrysolite
Heliotrope
Indicolite
Indigolite
Odontolite
Rhinestone
Rose quartz
Staurolite
Topazolite
Tourmaline

11 letters:
Alexandrite
Chrysoberyl
Chrysoprase
Lapis lazuli

Smoky quartz
Spessartite
Verd antique
Vesuvianite

12 letters:
Colorado ruby
Dumortierite
Grossularite
Spanish topaz

13 letters:
Bone turquoise
Colorado topaz
Water sapphire
White sapphire

15 letters:
Oriental emerald

17 letters:
Oriental
  almandine

20 letters:
Madagascar
  aquamarine
New Zealand
  greenstone

Generals

3 letters:
Ike *(Dwight David Eisenhower)*
Lee, *Robert E(dward)*

4 letters:
Foch, *Ferdinand*
Haig, *Douglas*

5 letters:
Booth, *William*
Condé, *Louis de Bourbon, Prince de*
De Wet, *Christian*
Grant, *Ulysses Simpson*

Monty *(Bernard Montgomery)*
Smuts, *Jan*
Wolfe, *James*

6 letters:
Brooke, *Alan*
Custer, *George Armstrong*
Franco, *Francisco*
Gordon, *Charles George*
Joshua
Leslie, *David*
Napier, *Lord Robert*
Patton, *George*

Paulus, *Friedrich*
Pompey
Powell, *Colin*
Raglan, *Fitzroy James Henry Somerset*
Rommel, *Erwin*
Scipio, *Publius Cornelius*
Zhukov, *Georgy*

7 letters:
Agrippa, *Marcus Vipsanius*
Allenby, *Viscount Edmund*
Blücher, *Gebhard Leberecht von*
Bradley, *Omar*
Crassus, *Marcus Licinius*
Gamelin, *Maurice Gustave*
Hadrian
Sherman, *William Tecumseh*
Turenne

8 letters:
Agricola, *Gnaeus Julius*
De Gaulle, *Charles (André Joseph Marie)*
Hannibal
Marshall, *George Catlett*
Montcalm, *Louis Joseph de*
Napoleon *(Bonaparte)*
Pershing, *Johh Joseph*
Pinochet, *Augusto*

Shrapnel, *Henry*
Stilwell, *Joseph Warren*
Stratton, *Charles Sherwood*
Tom Thumb *(Charles Sherwood Stratton)*

9 letters:
Agamemnon
Antigonus
Antipater
Boulanger, *George Ernest Jean Marie*
Kitchener, *Earl Herbert*
Lafayette, *Marie Joseph, Marquis de*
Macarthur, *Douglas*
Rundstedt, *Gerd von*

10 letters:
Alcibiades
Cornwallis, *Charles, Marquis*
Eisenhower, *Dwight D(avid) (Ike)*
Hindenburg, *Paul von*
Holofernes
Ludendorff, *Erich*
Montgomery, *Bernard*
Stroessner, *Alfredo*

11 letters:
Schwarzkopf, *Norman*

Geography

BRANCHES OF GEOGRAPHY

5 letters:
Human

7 letters:
Geology
Orology

8 letters:
Pedology
Physical

9 letters:
Chorology
Hydrology
Orography
Political

10 letters:
Demography
Glaciology
Oceanology
Seismology

Topography

11 letters:
Cartography
Chorography
Climatology
Geopolitics
Meteorology
Vulcanology

12 letters:
Biogeography
Oceanography

13 letters:
Geomorphology

GEOGRAPHY TERMS AND FEATURES

3 letters:
Bay
Col
Cwm
Map
Tor

4 letters:
Core
Crag
Dyke
Fell
Glen
Loch
Reef
Rill
Spit
Spur
Tarn
Veld
Wadi

5 letters:
Arête
Atlas
Atoll
Basin
Beach
Cliff
Crust
Delta
Fault
Fjord
Glade
Levée
Ocean
Ridge
Scree
Stack
Veldt

6 letters:
Canyon

Cirque
Coombe
Corrie
Crater
Desert
Ice cap
Isobar
Jungle
Lagoon
Mantle
Sierra
Spring
Steppe
Suburb
Tundra

7 letters:
Climate
Contour
Culvert
Equator
Erosion
Estuary
Glacier
Isobath
Isohyet
Isthmus
Meander
Moraine
New town
Rivulet
Sand bar
Savanna
Subsoil
Topsoil
Tropics
Tsunami
Volcano
Wetland

8 letters:
Crevasse
Eastings

Headland
Isotherm
Latitude
Oriental
Salt flat
Salt lake
Sandbank
Sand dune
Savannah
Snow line

9 letters:
Antipodes
Continent
Coral reef
Dormitory
Epicentre
Green belt
Longitude
Northings
North Pole
Pollution
Relief map
South Pole
Temperate
Waterfall
Watershed
Whirlpool

10 letters:
Atmosphere
Earthquake
Escarpment
Flood plain
Glaciation
Irrigation
Occidental
Ozone layer
Permafrost
Rainforest
Rain shadow
Rift valley
River basin

Third World
Water cycle
Water table
Weathering

11 letters:
Conurbation
Environment
Watercourse

12 letters:
Conservation
Urbanization

13 letters:
Afforestation
Deforestation
Global warming
Grid reference
Hanging valley
Precipitation

14 letters:
Infrastructure
Longshore drift
Ordnance Survey
Plate tectonics

15 letters:
Desertification

16 letters:
Continental drift
Continental shelf
Greenhouse effect

18 letters:
Mercator projection
Northern hemisphere
Southern hemisphere

21 letters:
International Date Line

GEOGRAPHERS

6 letters:
Kremer, *Gerhard*
Strabo

7 letters:
Hakluyt, *Richard*
Ptolemy

8 letters:
Mercator, *Gerardus*

9 letters:
Mackinder, *Sir Halford John*

Pausanias

10 letters:
Somerville, *Mary*

See also:
➤ **Canals** ➤ **Capes** ➤ **Capitals** ➤ **Channels** ➤ **Cities**
➤ **Continents** ➤ **Countries** ➤ **Deserts** ➤ **Earth's crust**
➤ **Hills** ➤ **Islands and island groups** ➤ **Lakes, lochs and loughs**
➤ **Peninsulas** ➤ **Ports** ➤ **Rivers** ➤ **Seas and oceans**
➤ **Sounds** ➤ **Straits** ➤ **Towns** ➤ **Volcanoes** ➤ **Waterfalls**

Geology

GEOLOGICAL ERAS

8 letters:
Cenozoic

10 letters:
Palaeozoic

11 letters:
Precambrian

Mesozoic

GEOLOGICAL PERIODS

7 letters:
Permian

8 letters:
Cambrian
Devonian
Jurassic

Silurian
Tertiary
Triassic

10 letters:	Ordovician	13 letters:
Cretaceous	Quaternary	Carboniferous

EPOCHS OF THE CENOZOIC ERA

6 letters:	8 letters:	9 letters:	11 letters:
Eocene	Holocene	Oligocene	Pleistocene
	Pliocene		
7 letters:		10 letters:	
Miocene		Palaeocene	

See also:
➤ **Earth's crust** ➤ **Minerals** ➤ **Rocks** ➤ **Stones**

Giants and giantesses

2 letters:	Mimir	Gabbara	Colbronde
Og	Talos	Geirred	Enceladus
	Talus	Goliath	Ephialtes
3 letters:	Thrym	Harapha	Gargantua
Gog		Skrymir	Lestrigon
	6 letters:		Leviathan
4 letters:	Coltys	8 letters:	Rounceval
Anak	Cottus	Ascapart	Tregeagle
Bran	Gefion	Bellerus	Tryphoeus
Otus	Krasir	Briareus	
Ymir	Pallas	Colbrand	10 letters:
	Tityus	Cormoran	Pantagruel
5 letters:	Triton	Cyclopes	Patagonian
Argus	Typhon	Ferragus	Polyphemus
Balan	Urizen	Hrungnir	
Balor		Slaygood	11 letters:
Cacus	7 letters:		Alifanfaron
Hymir	Antaeus	9 letters:	Blunderbore
Idris	Cyclops	Alcyoneus	Galligantus
Magog	Despair	Archiloro	

Glands

3 letters:	5 letters:	Scent	Tarsel	7 letters:
Oil	Green	Sweat	Testis	Adenoid
	Liver		Thymus	Adrenal
4 letters:	Lymph	6 letters:	Tonsil	Cowper's
Silk	Mucus	Ink-sac		Eccrine
	Ovary	Pineal		Mammary

Musk-sac
Nectary
Parotid
Parotis
Thyroid

8 letters:
Apocrine
Conarium
Exocrine
Lacrimal
Pancreas
Pope's eye

Prostate
Salivary
Testicle

9 letters:
Digestive
Endocrine
Epiphysis
Holocrine
Lachrymal
Meibomian
Pituitary
Sebaceous

Uropygial

10 letters:
Bartholin's
Hypophysis
Osmeterium
Suprarenal

11 letters:
Colleterial
Paranephros
Parathyroid
Prothoracic

12 letters:
Hypothalamus

13 letters:
Bulbourethral

18 letters:
Islets of
 Langerhans

19 letters:
Islands of
 Langerhans

Glass, types of

3 letters:
Cut

4 letters:
Eden
Jena
Lead
Milk
Opal
Spun
Vita
Wire

5 letters:
Crown
Flint
Float
Paste
Plate

Pyrex®
Silex
Smalt

6 letters:
Bottle
Cullet
Quartz
Smalto
Strass

7 letters:
Baccara
Crookes
Crystal
Favrile
Lalique
Murrine
Opaline

Perlite
Schmelz
Stained
Tektite
Tiffany
Triplex®
Vitrail

8 letters:
Baccarat
Murrhine
Obsidian
Pearlite
Venetian
Volcanic

9 letters:
Fulgurite
Lanthanum

Tachilite
Tachylite
Tachylyte
Waterford

10 letters:
Avanturine
Aventurine
Calcedonio
Latticinio
Millefiori
Mousseline
Pitchstone

12 letters:
Vitro-di-trina

Gods and Goddesses

AZTEC

3 letters:	**5 letters:**	**6 letters:**	**7 letters:**	**8 letters:**
Atl	Innan	Atlaua	Amimitl	Camaxtli
	Itzli	Paynal	Ehecatl	Centeotl
4 letters:	Teteo	Tlaloc	Omacatl	Chantico
Tena		Xolotl	Xilonen	Mayahuel
				Mixcoatl

Patecatl
Techlotl
Tonatiuh
Tzapotla
Xippilli

9 letters:
Coatlicue
Cochimetl
Ixtlilton
Techalotl
Tzintetol
Tzontemoc
Xipe Totec
Xiuhcoatl

10 letters:
Acolmiztli
Chiconahui
Cihuacoatl
Nanauatzin
Omecihuatl
Xochipilli

11 letters:
Huehueteotl
Itzpapalotl
Ometecuhtli
Tepeyollotl
Tlazolteotl
Uixtociuatl
Xiuhteuctli

12 letters:
Chicomecoatl
Coyolxauhqui
Malinalxochi
Quetzalcoatl
Tecciztecatl
Tezcatlipoca
Tlaltecuhtli
Xochiquetzal
Yacatecuhtli

13 letters:
Acolnahuacatl
Huixtocihuatl
Ilamatecuhtli

Macuilxochitl

14 letters:
Chicomexochtli
Itzlacoliuhque
Mictlantecutli
Tonacatecuhtli

15 letters:
Centzonuitznaua
Chalchiuhtlicue
Chalchiutotolin
Chalmecacihuilt
Huitzilopochtli

16 letters:
Mictlantecihuatl

17 letters:
Chalchiuhtlatonal

21 letters:
Tlahuixcalpantecuhtli

CELTIC

3 letters:
Anu
Dôn
Lir

4 letters:
Áine
Badb
Bíle
Bodb
Dana
Danu
Donn
Ériu
Esus
Fand
Llyr
Lugh
Medb

Ogma

5 letters:
Artio
Balor
Banba
Bóand
Dagda
Epona
Mabon
Macha
Midir
Núadu

6 letters:
Bécuma
Brigid
Nemain
Sirona

7 letters:
Belenus
Nechtan
Sequana
Taranis

8 letters:
Ceridwen
Manannán
Morrígan
Nemetona
Rhiannon
Rosmerta
Sucellus
Teutates

9 letters:
Arianrhod
Blodeuedd

Cernunnos
Manawydan

11 letters:
Nantosuelta
Óengus Mac Óc

14 letters:
Lleu Llaw Gyffes
Vagdavercustis

EGYPTIAN

2 letters:	**4 letters:**	**5 letters:**	Anubis
Ra	Isis	Horus	Hathor
Re	Maat	Thoth	Osiris
	Ptah		

3 letters:		**6 letters:**	**7 letters:**
Set		Amen-Ra	Serapis

GREEK

God or goddess	Area or place ruled
Aeolus	Winds
Aphrodite	Love and beauty
Apollo	Light, youth, and music
Ares	War
Artemis	Hunting and the moon
Asclepius	Healing
Athene *or* Pallas Athene	Wisdom
Bacchus	Wine
Boreas	North wind
Cronos	Fertility of the earth
Demeter	Agriculture
Dionysus	Wine
Eos	Dawn
Eros	Love
Fates	Destiny
Gaea *or* Gaia	The earth
Graces	Charm and beauty
Hades	Underworld
Hebe	Youth and spring
Hecate	Underworld
Helios	Sun
Hephaestus	Fire and metalworking
Hera	Queen of the gods
Hermes	Messenger of the gods
Horae *or* the Hours	Seasons
Hymen	Marriage
Hyperion	Sun
Hypnos	Sleep
Iris	Rainbow
Momus	Blame and mockery
Morpheus	Sleep and dreams
Nemesis	Vengeance
Nike	Victory
Pan	Woods and shepherds

Poseidon	Sea and earthquakes
Rhea	Fertility
Selene	Moon
Uranus	Sky
Zephyrus	West wind
Zeus	King of the gods

HINDU

4 letters:
Agni
Devi
Kali
Kama
Maya
Rama

Siva

5 letters:
Durga
Indra
Shiva
Ushas

6 letters:
Brahma
Ganesa
Varuna
Vishnu

7 letters:
Hanuman
Krishna
Lakshmi

INCAN

3 letters:
Apo

4 letters:
Inti

5 letters:
Huaca
Supay

6 letters:
Chasca
Ekkeko

Illapa

7 letters:
Paricia
Punchau
Vichama

8 letters:
Catequil
Cocomama
Coniraya
Copacati
Zaramama

9 letters:
Apu Illapu
Cavillaca
Mama Allpa
Mama Cocha
Mama Oello
Mama Pacha
Pariacaca
Urcaguary
Viracocha

10 letters:
Apu Punchau

Mama Quilla
Manco Capac
Pachacamac

11 letters:
Apocatequil

13 letters:
Chasca Coyllur
Ka-Ata-Killa Kon

MAYAN

2 letters:
Ix

3 letters:
Kan
K'in

4 letters:
Acan
Acat
Alom
Chac
Naum

Zotz

5 letters:
Ah Kin
Ah Mun
Ajbit
Balam
Bitol
Cauac
Cizin
Ixtab
Mulac
Tohil

Votan
Yaluk

6 letters:
Ah Peku
Ah Puch
Chamer
Coyopa
Cum Hau
Ghanan
Ixchel
Kianto
Tzakol

7 letters:
Ac Yanto
Ahau-Kin
Ah Ciliz
Ahmakiq
Ah Tabai
Ahulane
Cakulha
Ekchuah
Hunab Ku
Hun Came
Hurakan
Itzamna

Xaman Ek
Yum Caax

8 letters:
Ah Cancum
Ah Cun Can
Ah Cuxtal
Ah Hulneb
Cabaguil
Camaxtli
Camazotz
Caprakan
Colel Cab
Gucumatz
Ixzaluoh
Kukulcan

9 letters:
Ah Chuy Kak
Akhushtal
Chibirias
Hacha'kyum
Kan-xib-yui
Tlacolotl

10 letters:
Ah Chun Caan
Ah Muzencab
Ah Uuc Ticab
Hun Hunahpu
Kinich Ahau

11 letters:
Alaghom Naom

Cit Bolon Tum
Itzananohk'u
Ix Chebel Yax
Kan-u-Uayeyab
Nohochacyum

12 letters:
Backlum Chaam
Buluc Chabtan
Chac Uayab Xoc

13 letters:
Ah Bolom Tzacab
Colop U Uichkin

14 letters:
Ah Uincir Dz'acab

NORSE

3 letters:
Hel
Tyr

4 letters:
Frey
Hela
Idun
Loki
Odin

Thor
Tyrr

5 letters:
Aegir
Aesir
Bragi
Freya
Freyr
Frigg

Njord
Norns
Othin
Vanir

6 letters:
Balder
Freyja
Frigga
Ithunn

Njorth

7 letters:
Heimdal

8 letters:
Heimdall

9 letters:
Heimdallr

ROMAN

God or goddess	Area or place ruled
Aesculapius	Medicine
Apollo	Light, youth, and music
Aurora	Dawn
Bacchus	Wine
Bellona	War
Bona Dea	Fertility
Ceres	Agriculture
Cupid	Love
Cybele	Nature
Diana	Hunting and the moon
Faunus	Forests
Flora	Flowers
Janus	Doors and beginnings

God or goddess	Area or place ruled
Juno	Queen of the gods
Jupiter *or* Jove	King of the gods
Lares	Household
Luna	Moon
Mars	War
Mercury	Messenger of the gods
Minerva	Wisdom
Neptune	Sea
Penates	Storeroom
Phoebus	Sun
Pluto	Underworld
Quirinus	War
Saturn	Agriculture and vegetation
Sol	Sun
Somnus	Sleep
Trivia	Crossroads
Venus	Love
Victoria	Victory
Vulcan	Fire and metalworking

Golfers

3 letters:
Els, *Ernie*

4 letters:
Lyle, *Sandy*
Webb, *Karrie*

5 letters:
Braid, *James*
Faldo, *Nick*
Furyk, *Jim*
Hagen, *Walter*
Hogan, *Ben*
Jones, *Bobby*
Lopez, *Nancy*
Snead, *Sam*
Woods, *Tiger*

6 letters:
Carner, *JoAnne*
Cotton, *Henry*
Garcia, *Sergio*

Gibson, *Althea*
Langer, *Bernhard*
Lawrie, *Paul*
Morris, *Tom*
Nelson, *Byron*
Norman, *Greg*
Palmer, *Arnold*
Player, *Gary*
Taylor, *J H*
Vardon, *Harry*
Watson, *Tom*

7 letters:
Bradley, *Pat*
Jacklin, *Tony*
Sarazen, *Gene*
Stewart, *Payne*
Thomson, *Peter*
Trevino, *Lee*
Woosnam, *Ian*

8 letters:
Crenshaw, *Ben*
McDowell, *Graeme*
Nicklaus, *Jack*
Olazabal, *José-Maria*
Torrance, *Sam*
Westwood, *Lee*
Zaharias, *Babe*

9 letters:
Mickelson, *Phil*
Sörenstam, *Annika*
Whitworth, *Kathy*

10 letters:
Harrington, *Padraig*

11 letters:
Ballesteros, *Severiano*
Montgomerie, *Colin*

Golf terms

3 letters:
Ace
Bag
Cup
Cut
Lag
Lie
Par
Pin
Run
Tee
Top

4 letters:
Ball
Chip
Club
Draw
Duff
Fade
Fore
Grip
Half
Heel
Hole
Hook
Iron
Loft
Pull
Putt
Thin
Trap
Wood
Yips

5 letters:
Apron
Blade
Bogey
Carry
Divot
Drive
Eagle

Fluff
Gimme
Green
Hosel
Links
Rough
Round
Score
Shaft
Shank
Slice
Spoon
Swing
Tiger
Wedge

6 letters:
Bandit
Birdie
Borrow
Bunker
Caddie
Course
Dormie
Driver
Foozle
Hazard
Honour
Marker
Putter
Rabbit
Sclaff
Single
Stance
Stroke
Stymie
Waggle

7 letters:
Air shot
Fairway
Midiron
Scratch

Trolley

8 letters:
Approach
Back nine
Four-ball
Foursome
Green fee
Half shot
Handicap
Long iron
Medal tee
Plus twos
Recovery
Sand trap
Slow play
Take-away

9 letters:
Albatross
Backswing
Caddie car
Clubhouse
Downswing
Front nine
Greensome
Hole in one
Ladies' tee
Match play
Medal play
Pitch shot
Plus fours
Sand wedge
Score card
Short iron
Sweetspot
Threesome

10 letters:
Better-ball
Local rules
Rescue club
Stroke play

11 letters:
Casual water
Green keeper
Pitch and run
Play through

12 letters:
Driving range
Fresh air shot

Putting green

13 letters:
Pitching wedge
Practice swing
Rub of the green

14 letters:
Nine-hole course

Nineteenth hole

15 letters:
Royal and Ancient

16 letters:
Stableford system

Gorgons

6 letters:
Medusa

Stheno

7 letters:
Euryale

Governments

Name	Meaning
Absolutism	By an absolute ruler
Anarchy	Absence of government
Aristocracy	By nobility
Autarchy *or* autocracy	By an unrestricted individual
Bureaucracy	By officials
Communalism	By self-governing communities
Constitutionalism	According to a constitution
Corporatism	By corporate groups
Democracy	By the people
Despotism	By a despot or absolute ruler
Diarchy *or* dyarchy	By two rulers
Dictatorship	By dictator
Ergatocracy	By the workers
Gerontocracy	By old people
Gynaecocracy *or* gynarchy	By women
Hagiocracy *or* hagiarchy	By holy men
Heptarchy	By seven rulers
Hexarchy	By six rulers
Hierocracy *or* hierarchy	By priests
Imperialism	By an emperor or empire
Isocracy	By equals
Meritocracy	By rulers chosen according to ability
Mobocracy	By the mob
Monarchy	By monarch
Monocracy	By one ruler
Nomocracy	By rule of law
Ochlocracy	By mob

Name	Meaning
Octarchy	By eight rulers
Oligarchy	By the few
Pantisocracy	By all equally
Pentarchy	By five rulers
Plutocracy	By the rich
Pornocracy	By whores
Ptochocracy	By the poor
Quangocracy	By quangos
Slavocracy	By slaveholders
Squirearchy *or* squirarchy	By squires
Stratocracy	By the army
Technocracy	By experts
Tetrarchy	By four rulers
Theocracy *or* thearchy	By a deity
Triarchy	By three rulers
Tyranny	By a tyrant

Graces

6 letters:
Aglaia

Thalia

10 letters:
Euphrosyne

Grammatical cases

6 letters:
Dative

7 letters:
Elative
Oblique

8 letters:
Ablative

Agentive
Ergative
Genitive
Illative
Locative
Vocative

9 letters:
Objective

10 letters:
Accusative
Nominative
Possessive
Subjective

12 letters:
Instrumental

Grand Prix circuits

3 letters:
Spa

5 letters:
Monza

6 letters:
Monaco

Sepang
Suzuka

7 letters:
Bahrain
Kyalami

8 letters:
Shanghai

9 letters:
Catalunya
Zandvoort

10 letters:
Albert Park
Interlagos

11 letters:
Brands Hatch
Hungaroring
Nurburgring
Silverstone

12 letters:
Indianapolis

13 letters:
Francorchamps

14 letters:
Hockenheimring
Jose Carlos Pace

Österreichring

16 letters:
Enzo e Dino Ferrari
Gilles Villeneuve
Nevers-Magny Cours

Grapes

3 letters:
Fox

5 letters:
Gamay
Pinot
Steen
Syrah
Tokay
Viura

6 letters:
Malbec
Merlot
Muscat
Shiraz
Spanna

7 letters:
Aligoté
Barbera
Catawba
Concord
Furmint
Hamburg
Malmsey
Sercial

8 letters:
Cabernet
Cinsault
Delaware
Dolcetto

Garnacha
Grenache
Hamburgh
Hanepoot
Honeypot
Malvasia
Malvesie
Marsanne
Moscatel
Muscadel
Muscatel
Nebbiolo
Pinotage
Riesling
Ruländer
Sémillon
Silvaner
Sylvaner
Verdelho
Viognier

9 letters:
Colombard
Haanepoot
Lambrusco
Malvoisie
Mourvèdre
Muscadine
Pinot gris
Pinot noir
Sauvignon
Scheurebe
Trebbiano

Ugni blanc
Véronique
Zinfandel

10 letters:
Chardonnay
Hárslevelü
Kékfrankos
Muscadelle
Negroamoro
Pinot blanc
Sangiovese
Sweet-water
Verdicchio

11 letters:
Chenin blanc
Pinot grigio
Scuppernong
Seyval blanc
Tempranillo

12 letters:
Laski rizling
Olasz rizling

13 letters:
Cabernet franc
Montepulciano
Müller-thurgau
Rhine riesling
Spätburgunder

14 letters:
Gewürztraminer
Sauvignon blanc
Tokay-Pinot Gris

Welschriesling

15 letters:
Grüner veltliner

17 letters:
Cabernet sauvignon

Grasses

3 letters:
Eel
Lop
Oat
Poa
Rye
Saw
Seg
Tef

4 letters:
Alfa
Bent
Cane
Cord
Crab
Culm
Dari
Diss
Doob
Dura
Hair
Kans
Knot
Lyme
Milo
Rami
Reed
Rice
Rips
Rusa
Salt
Snow
Stag
Star
Tape
Teff
Tell

Wire
Worm

5 letters:
Alang
Avena
Bahia
Blady
Canna
Chess
Cogon
Couch
Cutty
Dhura
Doura
Durra
Emmer
Flote
Goose
Grama
Halfa
Heath
Jawar
Jowar
Kunai
Lemon
Maize
Manna
Melic
Oryza
Pamir
Panic
Peach
Plume
Quack
Quick
Ramee
Ramie

Roosa
Sedge
Sisal
Spear
Spelt
Starr
Stipa
Storm
Sword
Wheat
Witch

6 letters:
Bamboo
Barley
Bennet
Bladey
Bromus
Buffel
Canary
Carpet
Clover
Cotton
Cuscus
Darnel
Dhurra
Eddish
Fescue
Fiorin
Jawari
Jowari
Kikuyu
Lalang
Lolium
Lucern
Marram
Marrum
Melick

Millet
Pampas
Phleum
Puszta
Quitch
Redtop
Ribbon
Scurvy
Scutch
Sesame
Toetoe
Toitoi
Twitch
Zoysia

7 letters:
Alfalfa
Bermuda
Bristle
Buffalo
Cannach
Clivers
Esparto
Feather
Foxtail
Heather
Johnson
Locusta
Lucerne
Matweed
Quaking
Sacaton
Sea-reed
Sorghum
Squitch
Timothy
Vetiver
Wallaby

Whangee
Whitlow
Wild oat
Wild rye
Zizania
Zostera

8 letters:
Barnyard
Cat's tail
Cleavers
Dactylis
Dogstail
Eelwrack
Elephant
Flinders
Kangaroo
Khuskhus
Materass
Paspalum
Rye-grass
Scorpion
Spinifex
Teosinte

9 letters:
Bluegrass
Cocksfoot
Corkscrew
Danthonia
Deergrass
Gama-grass
Harestail
Job's tears
Porcupine
Snowgrass
Sour-gourd

Sugar cane
Triticale

10 letters:
Brome-grass
Citronella
Cochlearia

Cortaderia
Miscanthus
Pennisetum
Persicaria

12 letters:
Kentucky blue
Squirrel-tail
Yorkshire fog

Greeks

4 letters:
Ajax
Nike

5 letters:
Homer
Momus
Timon
Zorba

6 letters:
Epirus
Euclid
Nestor
Nostos
Strabo

7 letters:
Orestes
Paestum
Pelopid
Perseus

Theseus

8 letters:
Achilles
Diomedes
Leonidas
Xenophon

9 letters:
Agamemnon
Aristides
Isocrates

Patroclus
Spartacus
Thersites

10 letters:
Archimedes
Pythagoras

11 letters:
Epaminondas

Green, shades of

3 letters:
Pea
Sea

4 letters:
Aqua
Cyan
Jade
Lime
Nile

Pine
Teal

5 letters:
Apple
Olive

6 letters:
Almond
Citron

7 letters:
Avocado
Celadon
Emerald
Lincoln

8 letters:
Eau de nil

9 letters:
Pistachio
Turquoise

10 letters:
Aquamarine
Chartreuse

Guns

2 letters:
BB
HA

3 letters:
BAR
Dag
Gat
Ray
Tea

Uzi®
Zip

4 letters:
Bolt
Bren
Burp
Colt
Owen
Pump

Rail
Riot
Spud
Sten
Stun
Tier

5 letters:
Flame
Fusil

Lewis
Luger®
Maxim
Radar
Rifle
Saker
Siege
Spear
Spray
Taser®

Tommy

6 letters:
Ack-ack
Archie
Barker
Bofors
Breech
Falcon
Fowler

Garand
Gingal
Jezail
Jingal
Magnum®
Mauser
Minnie
Minute
Mortar
Musket
Pistol
Pom-pom
Quaker
Roscoe
Squirt
Staple
Swivel
Tupelo

7 letters:
Bazooka
Bulldog
Bundook
Caliver
Carbine
Coehorn
Gatling
Gingall
Hackbut
Long Tom
Machine

Noonday
Pedrero
Pelican
Perrier
Shotgun

8 letters:
Amusette
Armalite®
Arquebus
Biscayan
Browning
Culverin
Deringer
Electron
Elephant
Falconet
Firelock
Howitzer
Oerlikon
Paderero
Paterero
Pederero
Petronel
Pistolet
Repeater
Revolver
Starting
Sterling
Thompson

9 letters:
Archibald
Automatic
Big Bertha
Brown Bess
Carronade
Chassepot
Chokebore
Derringer
Escopette
Flintlock
Forty-five
Harquebus
Matchlock
Morris Meg
Musketoon
Paintball
Sarbacane
Snaphance
Sterculia

10 letters:
Scatter-gun
Self-cocker
Six-shooter
Smoothbore
Snaphaunce

11 letters:
Blunderbuss

Garand rifle
Kalashnikov
Stern-cannon
Stern-chaser
Thirty eight

12 letters:
Anti-aircraft
Breech-loader
Enfield rifle
Fowlingpiece
Martini-Henry®
Mitrailleuse
Muzzle-loader
Trench mortar

13 letters:
Sub-machine-gun

15 letters:
Winchester rifle

16 letters:
Springfield rifle

21 letters:
Thompson
sub-machine
gun®

Gymnastic events

4 letters:
Beam

5 letters:
Rings

7 letters:
High bar

10 letters:
Horse vault

11 letters:
Pommel horse

12 letters:
Parallel bars

13 letters:
Horizontal bar

14 letters:
Asymmetric bars

Floor exercises
Side horse vault

18 letters:
Rhythmic gymnastics

Hh

Hairstyles

2 letters:
DA

3 letters:
Bob
Bun

4 letters:
Afro
Crop
Perm
Pouf

5 letters:
Plait

6 letters:
Marcel
Mullet

7 letters:
Beehive
Bunches
Buzz cut
Chignon
Corn row
Crew cut
Flat top

Mohican
Pageboy
Pigtail
Shingle

8 letters:
Bouffant
Eton crop
Ponytail
Razor-cut
Skinhead

9 letters:
Duck's arse
Pompadour

10 letters:
Dreadlocks
Feather-cut
French roll
Marcel wave

11 letters:
French pleat

13 letters:
Permanent wave

Harpies

5 letters:
Aello

7 letters:
Celaeno

Ocypete

Hats

3 letters:
Cap
Fez
Lum
Mob
Nab
Red
Taj
Tam
Tin
Tit
Top

4 letters:
Coif
Hard
Hood
Kepi
Poke
Silk
Sola
Tile
Topi
Ugly
Veil

5 letters:
Akuba
Ascot
Beany
Beret
Boxer
Busby
Crown
Curch
Derby
Envoy
Gibus

Mitre
Mutch
Opera
Pagri
Paper
Pilos
Salet
Shako
Snood
Solah
Straw
Tammy

Terai
Tiara
Topee
Toque
Tuque
Visor
Vizor

6 letters:
Akubra®
Anadem
Barret
Basher
Beanie
Beaver
Boater
Bonnet
Bowler
Breton
Calash
Calpac
Castor
Cloche
Cocked
Coolie
Cornet
Cowboy
Diadem
Fedora
Gaucho
Heaume
Helmet
Hennin
Kalpak
Lum-hat
Mobcap
Morion
Panama
Pilion
Pinner
Safari
Sailor
Salade
Sallet
Shacko

Shovel
Slouch
Sunhat
Titfer
Toorie
Topper
Tourie
Trilby
Turban
Wimple

7 letters:
Bandana
Bandeau
Basinet
Biretta
Bluecap
Caleche
Calotte
Calpack
Capouch
Capuche
Chaplet
Circlet
Commode
Coronet
Cossack
Crusher
Curchef
Earmuff
Flat cap
Frontal
Hattock
Homburg
Kufiyah
Laurels
Leghorn
Matador
Montero
Petasus
Picture
Pillbox
Pilleus
Plateau
Pork-pie

Profile
Puritan
Skimmer
Songkok
Stetson
Sundown
Tarbush
Tricorn

8 letters:
Babushka
Balmoral
Bandanna
Bascinet
Bearskin
Berretta
Blackcap
Capotain
Cloth cap
Coonskin
Dunce cap
Fool's cap
Frontlet
Havelock
Headband
Kaffiyeh
Keffiyeh
Mountie's
Mushroom
Nightcap
Planter's
Puggaree
Ramilies
Runcible
Skullcap
Snap-brim
Sola-topi
Sombrero
Tarboosh
Tarboush
Trencher
Tricorne
Tyrolean
Watch cap
Yarmulke

9 letters:
Astrakhan
Balaclava
Billycock
Bollinger
Broadbrim
Cartwheel
Cockle-hat
Dunstable
Forage cap
Gandhi cap
Glengarry
Headdress
Juliet cap
Nor'wester
Peaked cap
Ramillies
Shower cap
Sou'wester
Stovepipe
Sugarloaf
Sunbonnet
Tarbouche
Tarpaulin
Ten-gallon
Wide-awake

10 letters:
Balibuntal
Bluebonnet
Chimneypot
Fascinator
Liberty cap
Pith helmet
Poke bonnet
Sola-helmet

11 letters:
Baseball cap
Crash helmet
Deerstalker
Dolly Varden
Kamelaukion
Mortarboard
Phrygian cap

Stocking cap
Tam-o'-shanter
Trencher cap

12 letters:
Cheese cutter
Fore-and-after
Steeple-crown

15 letters:
Balaclava helmet

Hawks

4 letters:
Eyas
Kite
Nyas
Soar
Sore

5 letters:
Eagle
Hobby
Marsh
Soare

6 letters:
Auceps
Elanet

Falcon
Keelie
Lanner
Merlin
Musket
Osprey
Sorage
Tarsal
Tarsel
Tassel
Tercel

7 letters:
Buzzard
Cooper's
Goshawk

Haggard
Harrier
Kestrel
Sparrow
Staniel
Tarsell
Tiercel

8 letters:
Caracara
Lanneret
Ringtail
Tercelet

9 letters:
Gerfalcon

Gier-eagle
Ossifraga
Ossifrage
Peregrine
Sore-eagle
Wind-hover

10 letters:
Hen harrier

11 letters:
Accipitrine
Lammergeier

12 letters:
Marsh harrier

Heart, parts of

5 letters:
Aorta

6 letters:
Atrium
Septum

7 letters:
Auricle

8 letters:
Vena cava

9 letters:
Ventricle

13 letters:
Bicuspid valve
Pulmonary vein

14 letters:
Semilunar valve
Tricuspid valve

15 letters:
Pulmonary artery

Heraldry terms

2 letters:
Or

3 letters:
Bar
Fur
Vol

4 letters:
Bars

Base
Bend
Coue
Fess
File
Fret
Golp
Lion
Lyon
Orle

Pale
Pall
Paly
Pean
Pile
Semé
Urdé
Vair
Vert
Yale

5 letters:
Azure
Baton
Chief
Crest
Cross
Crown
Eagle
Fesse
Field

Flory
Fusil
Giron
Golpe
Gules
Gyron
Label
Party
Rebus
Sable

Scarp
Semée
Torse
Trick
Urdée

6 letters:
Argent
Armory
Bezant

Blazon	Armiger	**8 letters:**	Coat armour
Byzant	Bandeau	Bendwise	Coat of arms
Canton	Bearing	Blazonry	Cockatrice
Charge	Bezzant	Caboched	Cognisance
Checky	Bordure	Cicerone	Cognizance
Coupee	Cadency	Couchant	Difference
Coward	Chaplet	Crescent	Escutcheon
Dexter	Chevron	Crosslet	Fleur-de-lis
Empale	Compone	Emblazon	Fleur-de-lys
Erased	Compony	Guardant	King-of-arms
Ermine	Coronet	Hauriant	Lambrequin
Falcon	Dormant	Heraldic	Portcullis
Fecial	Endorse	Mantling	Pursuivant
Fetial	Gardant	Naissant	Quartering
Fillet	Garland	Octofoil	
Fleury	Gironny	Opinicus	**11 letters:**
Herald	Griffon	Ordinary	Achievement
Impale	Gyronny	Segreant	Canting arms
Lionel	Issuant	Sinister	Clarencieux
Lodged	Leopard	Tressure	Spread eagle
Mascle	Lozenge	Trippant	Subordinary
Moline	Lozengy	Umbrated	
Mullet	Martlet		**12 letters:**
Naiant	Nascent	**9 letters:**	Bend sinister
Norroy	Nombril	Abatement	Inescutcheon
Pallet	Passant	Dimidiate	
Parted	Purpure	Displayed	**13 letters:**
Potent	Quarter	Embattled	College of arms
Proper	Rampant	Hatchment	Matriculation
Sejant	Red Hand	Quartered	Officer of arms
Shield	Roundel	Quarterly	Voided lozenge
Verdoy	Roundle	Regardant	
Voided	Salient	Scutcheon	**14 letters:**
Volant	Saltire	Supporter	Armes parlantes
Vorant	Sea lion		Counter-passant
Wreath	Sejeant	**10 letters:**	Lyon King of Arms
Wyvern	Statant	Bloody Hand	Sun in splendour
	Trangle	Bluemantle	
7 letters:	Trundle	Cinquefoil	
Annulet	Urinant	Clarenceux	

Herbs, spices, and seasonings

3 letters:	Oca	Rue	**4 letters:**	Forb
Bay	Pia		Dill	Mace

Mint
Miso
Moly
Sage
Salt
Wort

5 letters:
Anise
Avens
Basil
Chive
Clove
Cress
Cumin
Eruca
Inula
Maror
Medic
Orval
Senna
Shoyu
Tacca
Tansy
Thyme
Typha
Yerba

6 letters:
Bennet
Borage
Capers
Chilli
Cummin
Exacum
Fennel
Ferula
Garlic
Ginger
Hyssop
Lovage
Madder
Nam pla
Nutmeg
Origan

Purpie
Savory
Sesame
Sorrel
Tamari
Wasabi
Willow
Yarrow

7 letters:
Aconite
Aniseed
Arugula
Bayleaf
Canella
Chervil
Coconut
Comfrey
Dittany
Felicia
Gentian
Gunnera
Madwort
Mustard
Oregano
Origane
Paprika
Parsley
Saffron
Salsify
Vervain

8 letters:
Allspice
Angelica
Bergamot
Cardamom
Centaury
Cilantro
Cinnamon
Costmary
Feverfew
Fireweed
Fluellin
Galangal

Knapweed
Mandrake
Marjoram
Origanum
Plantain
Purslane
Rosemary
Soapwort
Soy sauce
Staragen
Szechuan
Szechwan
Tarragon
Turmeric
Valerian
Wormwood

9 letters:
Asafetida
Calendula
Chamomile
Coriander
Echinacea
Eyebright
Fenugreek
Fish sauce
Galingale
Germander
Haworthia
Kalanchoe
Lamb's ears
Laserwort
Poppy seed
Pussytoes
Red pepper
Rhizocarp
Rocambole
Rodgersia
Soya sauce
Spearmint
Star anise
Tormentil

10 letters:
Asafoetida

Cassia bark
Lemon grass
Peppercorn
Pipsissewa
Rest-harrow
Sesame seed

11 letters:
Black pepper
Caraway seed
Coconut milk
Curry powder
Fines herbes
Garam masala
Laserpicium
Sweet cicely
White pepper

12 letters:
Aristolochia
Ornithogalum
Southernwood

13 letters:
Cayenne pepper
Good-King-Henry
Sunflower seed

14 letters:
Kaffir lime leaf

15 letters:
Alligator pepper
Five spice powder

18 letters:
Sichuan
 peppercorns

Hercules, labours of

Number	Labour
First	The slaying of the Nemean lion
Second	The slaying of the Lernaean hydra
Third	The capture of the hind of Ceryneia
Fourth	The capture of the wild boar of Erymanthus
Fifth	The cleansing of the Augean stables
Sixth	The shooting of the Stymphalian birds
Seventh	The capture of the Cretan bull
Eighth	The capture of the horses of Diomedes
Ninth	The taking of the girdle of Hippolyte
Tenth	The capture of the cattle of Geryon
Eleventh	The recovery of the golden apples of Hesperides
Twelfth	The taking of Cerberus

Heroes

3 letters:
Cid

4 letters:
Aitu
Ajax
Eric
Finn
Kami
Lion
Tell

5 letters:
Faust
Jason

6 letters:
Amadis
Cyrano
Fingal
Hector
Kaleva
Nestor
Oliver
Onegin
Roland
Rustem

Rustum
Sigurd

7 letters:
Alcides
Beowulf
Couplet
Lothair
Marmion
Paladin
Perseus
Rinaldo
Saladin
Tancred
Theseus
Tristam
Tristan
Ulysses
Volsung

8 letters:
Achilles
Crockett
Heracles
Hercules
Hiawatha
Leonidas

Meleager
Owlglass
Parsifal
Pericles
Roderego
Roderick
Superman
Tristram

9 letters:
Agamemnon
Cuchulain
Garibaldi
Lochinvar
Owleglass
Owspiegle
Siegfried

10 letters:
Cuchullain
Howleglass
Owlspiegle

11 letters:
Bellerophon
Finn MacCool
Tam o'Shanter

Triptolemus
White knight

12 letters:
Lemminkäinen

13 letters:
Vercingetorix

Hills

3 letters:
How
Kip
Kop
Law
Man
Nab
Pap
Puy
Tel
Tor

4 letters:
Bent
Chin
Cone
Fell
Kipp
Knot
Loma
Mesa
Peak
Pike
Pnyx
Sion
Tara
Tell

Zion

5 letters:
Bluff
Butte
Cleve
Gebel
Horst
Jebel
Kopje
Morro
Pingo
Wolds

6 letters:
Arafar
Broken
Bunker
Calvan
Coteau
Djebel
Mendip
Wrekin

7 letters:
Beverly

Caelian
Capitol
Drumlin
Hammock
Ludgate
Mamelon
Merrick
Nanatak
Silbury
Viminal

8 letters:
Aventine
Cemetery
Cheviots
Chiltern
Golgotha
Highgate
Lavender
Palatine
Pennines
Quirinal

9 letters:
Areopagus
Esquiline

Grampians
Helvellyn
Janiculum
Monadnock
Monticule
Quantocks

10 letters:
Capitoline
Lammermuir
North Downs
Saddleback
Tweedsmuir

11 letters:
Crag-and-tail
Otway Ranges

12 letters:
Golan Heights

16 letters:
Mount Lofty
 Ranges

Hindu denominations and sects

6 letters:
Saktas

8 letters:
Saivaism

11 letters:
Hare Krishna

Vaishnavism

Historians

4 letters:
Bede, *the Venerable*
Livy
Oman, *Sir Charles William Chadwick*

5 letters:
Acton, *John Emerich Edward Dalberg*
Clark, *Kenneth*
Green, *John Richard*
Pliny *(the Elder)*

Renan, *(Joseph) Ernest*
Wells, *H(erbert) G(eorge)*

6 letters:
Arrian
Beevor, *Anthony*
Bryant, *Sir Arthur (Wynne Morgan)*
Buckle, *Henry Thomas*
Camden, *William*
Froude, *James Anthony*
Gibbon, *Edward*
Gildas
Holmes, *Richard*
Schama, *Simon*
Taylor, *A(lan) J(ohn) P(ercivale)*
Thiers, *(Louis) Adolphe*

7 letters:
Asellio, *Sempronius*
Barnett, *Corelli*
Carlyle, *Thomas*
Sallust
Starkey, *David*
Tacitus
Toynbee, *Arnold Joseph*

8 letters:
Macaulay, *Thomas Babbington*
Plutarch
Ponsonby, *Lord Arthur*
Spengler, *Oswald*
Strachey, *(Giles) Lytton*
Thompson, *E P*
Xenophon

9 letters:
Herodotus
Suetonius
Trevelyan, *G(eorge) M(acaulay)*

10 letters:
Thucydides

11 letters:
Trevor-Roper, *Hugh*

13 letters:
Knickerbocker, *Diedrick*

18 letters:
Geoffrey of Monmouth

History

HISTORICAL CHARACTERS

3 letters:
Lee, *Robert E(dward)*

4 letters:
Cody, *William Frederick*
Cook, *Captain James*
Dong, *Mao Ze*
Khan, *Genghis*
King, *Martin Luther*
Polo, *Marco*

5 letters:
Drake, *Francis*
El Cid
James, *Jesse*
Jesus

Lenin, *Vladimir Ilyich*
Oates, *Lawrence Edward Grace*
Scott, *Robert Falcon*

6 letters:
Borgia, *Lucrezia*
Brutus
Buddha
Caesar, *Julius*
Cortés, *Hernando*
Custer, *George Armstrong*
Fawkes, *Guy*
Gandhi, *Mahatma*
Hickok, *James Butler*
Hickok, *Wild Bill*
Hitler, *Adolf*

Luther, *Martin*
Nelson, *Horatio*
Pompey
Stalin, *Joseph*
Stuart, *Charles Edward*
Wright, *Orville and Wilbur*
Zapata, *Emiliano*

7 letters:
À Becket, *Thomas*
Gagarin, *Yuri*
Guevara, *Che*
Lincoln, *Abraham*
Raleigh, *Walter*
Saladin
Trotsky, *Leon*
Tse-tung, *Mao*
Wallace, *William*

8 letters:
Augustus
Boadicea
Boudicca
Columbus, *Christopher*
Crockett, *Davy*
Cromwell, *Oliver*
Geronimo
Hannibal
Hiawatha
Mohammed
Muhammad
Pericles
Rasputin, *Grigori Efimovich*
Selassie, *Haile*
Socrates

9 letters:
Bonaparte, *Napoleon*
Churchill, *Winston*
Cleopatra
Garibaldi, *Giuseppe*
Joan of Arc
Montezuma
Mussolini, *Benito*

10 letters:
Antoinette, *Marie*
Crazy Horse
Mark Antony
Washington, *George*

11 letters:
Billy the Kid
Buffalo Bill
Charlemagne
Nightingale, *Florence*
Sitting Bull

12 letters:
Attila the Hun
Captain Oates
Clive of India
De Torquemada, *Tomás*

14 letters:
Alfred the Great
Robert the Bruce
The Black Prince

15 letters:
Hereward the Wake
Ivan the Terrible

16 letters:
Duke of Wellington
Gordon of Khartoum
Lawrence of Arabia

17 letters:
Alexander the Great
Catherine the Great
Mary, Queen of Scots

19 letters:
Bonnie Prince Charlie
Richard the Lionheart
Warwick the Kingmaker
William the Conqueror

HISTORICAL EVENTS

4 letters:
D-day

5 letters:
Alamo

7 letters:
Boer War
Cold War

8 letters:
Civil War
Crusades
Waterloo

9 letters:
Agincourt
Armistice
Great Trek
Hiroshima
Holocaust
Korean War
Long March
Trafalgar
Watergate

10 letters:
Black Death
Crimean War
Depression
Magna Carta
Suez Crisis
Vietnam War

11 letters:
Diet of Worms
Gordon Riots
Great Schism

Pearl Harbor
Reformation
Renaissance
Restoration

12 letters:
Bloody Sunday
Crystal Night
Easter Rising
Indian Mutiny
Potato Famine
Risorgimento

13 letters:
General Strike
Gunpowder Plot
Kristallnacht
Reign of Terror
Spanish Armada

14 letters:
Boston Tea Party
Boxer Rebellion
Napoleonic Wars
Norman Conquest
Peasants' Revolt
South Sea Bubble
Thirty Years' War
Wars of the Roses

15 letters:
Hundred Years War
Munich Agreement
Spanish Civil War
Wall Street Crash

16 letters:
American Civil War

Battle of Hastings
French Revolution
Peterloo Massacre

17 letters:
Gettysburg Address
Great Fire of London
Hungarian Uprising
Jacobite Rebellion
Russian Revolution

18 letters:
Cultural Revolution
Glorious Revolution
Spanish Inquisition
Treaty of Versailles

20 letters:
Industrial Revolution
Night of the Long Knives

22 letters:
The War between the
  States

23 letters:
Charge of the Light
  Brigade
Tiananmen Square
  Massacre

25 letters:
Declaration of
  Independence

26 letters:
Saint Valentine's Day
  Massacre

Homes

2 letters:	**3 letters:**	Huf	Inn	**4 letters:**
Ho	Cot	Hut	Mas	Bush

Casa
Chez
Cote
Crib
Dail
Digs
Drum
Flat
Gite
Hall
Home
Iglu
Izba
Keys
Mews
Pent
Rath
Safe
Semi
Slum
Tent
Tied
Town
York

5 letters:
Adobe
Booth
Cabin
Croft
Dacha
Dower
Frame
Hogan
Hotel
House
Hovel
Igloo
Konak
Lodge
Lords
Manor
Manse
Motel
Opera

Ranch
Shack
Tepee
Tower
Tudor
Tupek
Tupik
Usher
Villa
Wendy
Whare

6 letters:
Bhavan
Bhawan
Biggin
Bunker
Castle
Chalet
Custom
Des res
Duplex
Flotel
Garret
Grange
Hostel
Insula
Maison
Mobile
Mud hut
Orange
Palace
Prefab
Priory
Shanty
Stuart
Tavern
Wigwam

7 letters:
Althing
Barrack
Bastide
Caboose
Caravan

Chamber
Chapter
Charnel
Château
Commons
Convent
Cottage
Council
Crannog
Customs
Deanery
Embassy
Fashion
Flatlet
Habitat
Halfway
Hanover
Harbour
Knesset
Mansion
Meeting
Osborne
Rectory
Schloss
Starter
Stately
Terrace
Theatre
Trailer
Trinity
Windsor

8 letters:
Boarding
Bungalow
Burghley
Camboose
Clearing
Dwelling
Hacienda
Lagthing
Log cabin
Longleat
Montagne
Rest-home

Somerset
Tenement
Vicarage

9 letters:
Admiralty
Apartment
Bedsitter
Bundestag
But and ben
Clapboard
Consulate
Doss house
Earthship
Farmhouse
Flophouse
Houseboat
Lancaster
Long house
Mattamore
Odelsting
Parsonage
Penthouse
Roadhouse
Show house
Single-end
Straw-bale
Town house
Tree house

10 letters:
Back-to-back
Black house
Brownstone
Chatsworth
Commercial
Guest house
Heartbreak
Maisonette
Odelsthing
Parliament
Pied-à-terre
Studio flat

11 letters:
Cottage flat
Plantagenet
Shooting box

12 letters:
Broadcasting

Chattel house
Lake dwelling
Motor caravan
Weatherboard

13 letters:
Boarding house

14 letters:
Cape Cod cottage

15 letters:
Board-and-shingle
Duplex apartment

17 letters:
Bachelor
   apartment

Homophones

2 letters:
Be / Bee
By / Buy
Hi / High
Ho / Hoe
In / Inn
Lo / Low
Mo / Mow
No / Know
Oh / Owe
Pa / Pah
Pi / Pie
So / Sew
To / Two
We / Wee

3 letters:
Ail / Ale
Air / Heir
Ale / Ail
All / Awl
Arc / Ark
Ark / Arc
Awe / Ore
Awl / All
Aye / Eye
Baa / Bah
Bad / Bade
Bah / Baa
Bay / Bey
Bee / Be
Bey / Bay
Bow / Bough
Boy / Buoy
Bur / Burr

But / Butt
Buy / By
Can / Cannes
Coo / Coup
Cox / Cocks
Dam / Damn
Daw / Door
Dew / Due
Die / Dye
Doe / Dough
Due / Dew
Dug / Doug
Dun / Done
Dye / Die
Ewe / Yew
Eye / Aye
Few / Phew
Fin / Finn
Fir / Fur
For / Four
Fur / Fir
Gym / Jim
Haw / Whore
Hay / Hey
Hew / Hue
Hey / Hay
Him / Hymn
Hoe / Ho
Hue / Hew
Inn / In
Ion / Iron
Jam / Jamb
Jim / Gym
Key / Quay
Lax / Lacks

Lay / Ley
Lea / Leigh
Led / Lead
Lee / Lea
Ley / Lay
Lie / Lye
Loo / Lieu
Low / Lo
Lye / Lie
Mat / Matt
Mow / Mo
Nap / Knap
Nay / Neigh
Née / Nay
Net / Nett
New / Knew
Nix / Nicks
Nob / Knob
Not / Knot
Nun / None
Oar / Ore
Ode / Owed
One / Won
Ore / Oar
Our / Hour
Owe / Oh
Pah / Pa
Par / Parr
Pax / Packs
Pea / Pee
Pee / Pea
Per / Purr
Pie / Pi
Rap / Wrap
Red / Read

Rex / Wrecks
Roe / Row
Row / Roe
Rye / Wry
Sac / Sack
Set / Sett
Sew / So
Sic / Sick
Son / Sun
Spa / Spar
Sty / Stye
Sue / Sioux
Sum / Some
Sun / Son
Tax / Tacks
Tic / Tick
Toe / Tow
Ton / Tun
Too / To
Tor / Tore
Tow / Toe
Tun / Ton
Two / To
Urn / Earn
Use / Ewes
War / Wore
Wax / Whacks
Way / Whey
We'd / Weed
Wee / We
Wen / When
Wet / Whet
Wig / Whig
Win / Whin
Wit / Whit
Woe / Whoa
Won / One
Wry / Rye
Yew / Ewe

4 letters:
Airy / Eyrie
Alms / Arms
Ante / Anti
Anti / Ante

Aran / Arran
Arms / Alms
Away / Aweigh
Bade / Bad
Bail / Bale
Bait / Bate
Bald / Balled
Bale / Bail
Ball / Bawl
Balm / Barm
Bang / Bhang
Bare / Bear
Bark / Barque
Barm / Balm
Base / Bass
Bass / Base
Bate / Bait
Bawd / Board
Bawl / Ball
Bays / Baize
Bean / Been
Bear / Bare
Beat / Beet
Beau / Bow
Been / Bean
Beer / Bier
Beet / Beat
Bell / Belle
Berg / Burg
Bier / Beer
Bite / Bight
Blew / Blue
Blue / Blew
Boar / Bore
Bode / Bowed
Bold / Bowled
Bole / Bowl
Boos / Booze
Bore / Boar
Born / Borne
Bosh / Boche
Bowl / Bole
Brae / Bray
Bray / Brae
Bred / Bread

Buoy / Boy
Burg / Berg
Burr / Bur
Bury / Berry
Butt / But
Call / Caul
Cash / Cache
Cast / Caste
Caul / Call
Cede / Seed
Cell / Sell
Cent / Scent
Choc / Chock
Cite / Sight
Coal / Kohl
Coat / Cote
Coax / Cokes
Coin / Coign
Cops / Copse
Copt / Copped
Copy / Kopje
Cord / Chord
Core / Corps
Cork / Caulk
Cote / Coat
Coup / Coo
Cows / Cowes
Crew / Crewe
Curb / Kerb
Damn / Dam
Dane / Deign
Days / Daze
Daze / Days
Dear / Deer
Deer / Dear
Dire / Dyer
Done / Dun
Door / Daw
Dost / Dust
Doug / Dug
Dual / Duel
Duct / Ducked
Duel / Dual
Dust / Dost
Dyer / Dire

Earn / Urn
Eddy / Eddie
Eves / Eaves
Ewes / Use
Fain / Feign
Fair / Fare
Fare / Fair
Fate / Fête
Faun / Fawn
Fawn / Faun
Feat / Feet
Feet / Feat
Fête / Fate
Find / Fined
Finn / Fin
Firs / Furze
Flaw / Floor
Flea / Flee
Flee / Flea
Flew / Flue
Flex / Flecks
Floe / Flow
Flow / Floe
Flue / Flew
Fold / Foaled
Foul / Fowl
Four / For
Fowl / Foul
Gael / Gale
Gaff / Gaffe
Gage / Gauge
Gait / Gate
Gale / Gael
Gall / Gaul
Gate / Gait
Gaul / Gall
Gays / Gaze
Gaze / Gays
Gibe / Jibe
Gild / Guild
Gill / Jill
Gilt / Guilt
Guys / Guise
Hail / Hale
Hair / Hare

Hale / Hail
Hall / Haul
Hare / Hair
Hart / Heart
Haul / Hall
Heal / Heel
Hear / Here
Heel / Heal
Heir / Air
Herd / Heard
Here / Hear
Hide / Hied
Hied / Hide
High / Hi
Hire / Higher
Hoar / Whore
Hoes / Hose
Hold / Holed
Hole / Whole
Hose / Hoes
Hour / Our
Hymn / Him
Idle / Idol
Idol / Idle
Iron / Ion
Isle / Aisle
Jamb / Jam
Jibe / Gibe
Jill / Gill
Kail / Kale
Kale / Kail
Kerb / Curb
Knap / Nap
Knew / New
Knob / Nob
Knot / Not
Know / No
Kohl / Coal
Lade / Laid
Laid / Lade
Lain / Lane
Lama / Llama
Lane / Lain
Laps / Lapse
Laud / Lord

Lava / Larva
Lawn / Lorn
Lays / Laze
Laze / Leys
Lead / Led
Leaf / Lief
Leak / Leek
Leek / Leak
Lent / Leant
Levy / Levee
Leys / Laze
Liar / Lyre
Lief / Leaf
Lieu / Loo
Limb / Limn
Limn / Limb
Load / Lode
Loan / Lone
Lode / Lowed
Lone / Loan
Loos / Lose
Loot / Lute
Lord / Laud
Lorn / Lawn
Lose / Loos
Lute / Loot
Lynx / Links
Lyre / Liar
Made / Maid
Maid / Made
Mail / Male
Main / Mane
Male / Mail
Mane / Main
Mare / Mayor
Mark / Marque
Mask / Masque
Matt / Mat
Maze / Maize
Mead / Meed
Mean / Mien
Meat / Meet
Meed / Mead
Meet / Mete
Mete / Meet

Mews / Muse
Mien / Mean
Mind / Mined
Minx / Minks
Mist / Missed
Mite / Might
Moan / Mown
Moat / Mote
Mode / Mowed
Moor / More
More / Moor
Morn / Mourn
Mote / Moat
Mown / Moan
Muse / Mews
Must / Mussed
Nave / Knave
Need / Knead
Neil / Kneel
Nell / Knell
Nett / Net
None / Nun
Nose / Knows
Oral / Aural
Ours / Hours
Owed / Ode
Pact / Packed
Pail / Pale
Pain / Pane
Pair / Pear
Pale / Pail
Pall / Paul
Pane / Pain
Pare / Pair
Parr / Par
Past / Passed
Paul / Pall
Pawl / Pall
Pawn / Porn
Paws / Pause
Peak / Peek
Peal / Peel
Pear / Pair
Peat / Pete
Peek / Peak

Peel / Peal
Peer / Pier
Pete / Peat
Phew / Few
Pier / Peer
Plum / Plumb
Pole / Poll
Poll / Pole
Poof / Pouffe
Pore / Pour
Porn / Pawn
Pour / Pore
Pray / Prey
Prey / Pray
Pros / Prose
Purl / Pearl
Purr / Per
Quay / Key
Rack / Wrack
Rain / Rein
Rapt / Wrapped
Raze / Raise
Read / Red
Reed / Read
Rein / Rain
Rest / Wrest
Ring / Wring
Rite / Right
Road / Rode
Roam / Rome
Rode / Road
Role / Roll
Roll / Role
Rome / Roam
Rood / Rude
Room / Rheum
Root / Route
Rose / Rows
Rota / Rotor
Rote / Wrote
Rows / Rouse
Rude / Rood
Rues / Ruse
Ruff / Rough
Rung / Wrung

Ruse / Rues
Sack / Sac
Sail / Sale
Sale / Sail
Sane / Seine
Seam / Seem
Sear / Seer
Seed / Cede
Seek / Sikh
Seem / Seam
Seen / Scene
Seer / Sear
Sell / Cell
Serf / Surf
Sett / Set
Shoe / Shoo
Shoo / Shoe
Sick / Sic
Side / Sighed
Sign / Sine
Sikh / Seek
Sine / Sign
Size / Sighs
Slay / Sleigh
Sloe / Slow
Slow / Sloe
Soar / Sore
Sold / Soled
Sole / Soul
Some / Sum
Sore / Soar
Sort / Sought
Soul / Sole
Spar / Spa
Spec / Speck
Step / Steppe
Stye / Sty
Styx / Sticks
Surf / Serf
Swat / Swot
Swot / Swat
Tact / Tacked
Tail / Tale
Tale / Tail
Talk / Torque

Tare / Tear
Taut / Taught
Team / Teem
Tear / Tier
Teem / Team
Tern / Turn
Tick / Tic
Tide / Tied
Tied / Tide
Tier / Tear
Time / Thyme
Tire / Tyre
Toad / Towed
Told / Tolled
Tore / Tor
Tuba / Tuber
Tuna / Tuner
Turn / Tern
Tyre / Tire
Vain / Vein
Vale / Veil
Vane / Vain
Veil / Vale
Vein / Vain
Vial / Viol
Viol / Vial
Wade / Weighed
Wail / Whale
Wain / Wane
Wait / Weight
Wale / Whale
Wane / Wain
Ward / Warred
Ware / Where
Warn / Worn
Watt / What
Wave / Waive
Weak / Week
Wear / Ware
Weed / We'd
Week / Weak
Weld / Welled
Were / Whirr
What / Watt
When / Wen

Whet / Wet
Whey / Way
Whig / Wig
Whin / Win
Whit / Wit
Whoa / Woe
Who's / Whose
Wile / While
Wine / Whine
Won't / Wont
Wood / Would
Wore / War
Worn / Warn
Wrap / Rap
Yaws / Yours
Yoke / Yolk
Yolk / Yoke
Yore / You're
Your / Yore
Yule / You'll

5 letters:
Aisle / Isle
Aloud / Allowed
Altar / Alter
Alter / Altar
Arran / Aran
Auger / Augur
Aught / Ought
Augur / Auger
Aural / Oral
Baize / Bays
Balmy / Barmy
Barmy / Balmy
Baron / Barren
Based / Baste
Baste / Based
Beach / Beech
Beech / Beach
Belle / Bell
Berry / Bury
Berth / Birth
Betel / Beetle
Bhang / Bang
Bight / Bite

Birth / Berth
Board / Bored
Boche / Bosh
Booze / Boos
Bored / Board
Borne / Born
Bough / Bow
Bowed / Bode
Brake / Break
Bread / Bred
Break / Brake
Brews / Bruise
Brood / Brewed
Brows / Browse
Bruit / Brute
Brute / Bruit
Build / Billed
Cache / Cash
Calve / Carve
Canon / Cannon
Carat / Carrot
Carve / Calve
Caste / Cast
Caulk / Cork
Cause / Cores
Chard / Charred
Cheap / Cheep
Check / Czech
Cheep / Cheap
Chews / Choose
Chock / Choc
Choir / Quire
Chord / Cord
Chute / Shoot
Claws / Clause
Climb / Clime
Clime / Climb
Cocks / Cox
Coign / Coin
Cokes / Coax
Copse / Cops
Cores / Cause
Corps / Core
Court / Caught
Cowes / Cows

Cozen / Cousin
Creak / Creek
Creek / Creak
Crewe / Crew
Crews / Cruise
Crude / Crewed
Czech / Check
Deign / Dane
Derek / Derrick
Dough / Doe
Douse / Dowse
Dowse / Douse
Draft / Draught
Draws / Drawers
Droop / Drupe
Drupe / Droop
Eaves / Eves
Eddie / Eddy
Eerie / Eyrie
Eyrie / Eerie
Faint / Feint
Feign / Fain
Feint / Faint
Fined / Find
Flair / Flare
Flare / Flair
Floor / Flaw
Flour / Flower
Franc / Frank
Frank / Franc
Frays / Phrase
Friar / Frier
Frier / Friar
Furze / Firs
Gaffe / Gaff
Gauge / Gage
Gauze / Gores
Gores / Gauze
Grate / Great
Great / Grate
Groan / Grown
Groin / Groyne
Grown / Groan
Guest / Guessed
Guide / Guyed

Guild / Gild
Guilt / Gilt
Guise / Guys
Guyed / Guide
Heard / Herd
Heart / Hart
Hertz / Hurts
Hoard / Horde
Holed / Hold
Horde / Hoard
Horse / Hoarse
Hours / Ours
Hurts / Hertz
Islet / Eyelet
Knave / Nave
Knead / Need
Kneel / Neil
Knell / Nell
Knows / Nose
Kooky / Cookie
Kopje / Copy
Lacks / Lax
Lager / Laager
Lapse / Laps
Larva / Lava
Leach / Leech
Leads / Leeds
Leant / Lent
Least / Leased
Leech / Leach
Leeds / Leads
Leigh / Lea
Levee / Levy
Lewes / Lewis
Lewis / Lewes
Liken / Lichen
Links / Lynx
Llama / Lama
Lowed / Lode
Maize / Maze
Manor / Manner
Mayor / Mare
Medal / Meddle
Metal / Mettle
Meter / Metre

Metre / Meter
Might / Mite
Mined / Mind
Miner / Minor
Minks / Minx
Minor / Mynah
Moose / Mousse
Mourn / Morn
Mowed / Mode
Mucus / Mucous
Mynah / Minor
Naval / Navel
Navel / Naval
Neigh / Nay
Nicks / Nix
Night / Knight
Ought / Aught
Paced / Paste
Packs / Pax
Paste / Paced
Pause / Paws
Pawed / Pored
Peace / Piece
Pearl / Purl
Pedal / Peddle
Phlox / Flocks
Piece / Peace
Place / Plaice
Plain / Plane
Plane / Plain
Pleas / Please
Plumb / Plum
Pored / Pawed
Prays / Praise
Prise / Prize
Prize / Prise
Prose / Pros
Putty / Puttee
Quire / Choir
Raise / Raze
Reams / Rheims
Reign / Rain
Retch / Wretch
Revue / Review
Rheum / Room

Right / Write
Roads / Rhodes
Rotor / Rota
Rough / Ruff
Rouse / Rows
Route / Root
Sauce / Source
Saver / Savour
Scene / Seen
Scent / Cent
Scull / Skull
Seine / Sane
Semen / Seaman
Sewer / Sower
Shake / Sheik
Shear / Sheer
Sheer / Shear
Sheik / Shake
Shire / Shyer
Shoot / Chute
Shyer / Shire
Sighs / Size
Sight / Cite
Sioux / Sue
Skull / Scull
Soled / Sold
Sonny / Sunny
Sower / Sewer
Spade / Spayed
Speck / Spec
Staid / Stayed
Stair / Stare
Stake / Steak
Stalk / Stork
Stare / Stair
Steak / Stake
Steal / Steel
Steel / Steal
Sties / Styes
Stile / Style
Stoop / Stoup
Stork / Stalk
Story / Storey
Stoup / Stoop
Styes / Sties

Style / Stile
Suite / Sweet
Sunny / Sonny
Sweet / Suite
Sword / Soared
Tacks / Tax
Taper / Tapir
Tapir / Taper
Tenor / Tenner
Their / They're
There / Their
Threw / Through
Throe / Throw
Throw / Throe
Thyme / Time
Titan / Tighten
Towed / Toad
Troop / Troupe
Trust / Trussed
Tuber / Tuba
Tuner / Tuna
Venus / Venous
Waist / Waste
Waive / Wave
Waste / Waist
Waver / Waiver
Weald / Wield
Weigh / Way
Whale / Wale
Where / Ware
Which / Witch
While / Wile
Whine / Wine
Whirl / Whorl
Whirr / Were
White / Wight
Whole / Hole
Whore / Hoar
Whorl / Whirl
Whose / Who's
Wield / Weald
Wight / White
Witch / Which
World / Whirled
Would / Wood

Wrack / Rack
Wrest / Rest
Wring / Ring
Write / Right
Wrote / Rote
Wrung / Rung
You'll / Yule
You're / Yore
Yours / Yaws

6 letters:

Ascent / Assent
Assent / Ascent
Aweigh / Away
Balled / Bald
Baring / Bearing
Barque / Bark
Barren / Baron
Beetle / Betel
Billed / Build
Bolder / Boulder
Border / Boarder
Bowled / Bold
Breach / Breech
Breech / Breach
Brewed / Brood
Bridal / Bridle
Bridle / Bridal
Briton / Britain
Broach / Brooch
Brooch / Broach
Browse / Brows
Bruise / Brews
Callus / Callous
Cannes / Can
Cannon / Canon
Canvas / Canvass
Carrot / Carat
Caster / Castor
Castor / Caster
Caught / Court
Cellar / Seller
Censer / Censor
Censor / Censer
Cereal / Serial

Chased / Chaste

Chaste / Chased

Chilli / Chilly

Chilly / Chilli

Choler / Collar

Choose / Chews

Citrus / Citrous

Claude / Clawed

Clause / Claws

Clawed / Claude

Coarse / Course

Collar / Choler

Conker / Conquer

Cookie / Kooky

Copped / Copt

Corral / Chorale

Course / Coarse

Cousin / Cozen

Coward / Cowered

Crewed / Crude

Cruise / Crews

Cygnet / Signet

Cymbal / Symbol

Cyprus / Cypress

Denary / Deanery

Desert / Dessert

Dollar / Dolour

Dolour / Dollar

Ducked / Duct

Elicit / Illicit

Ensure / Insure

Ernest / Earnest

Eyelet / Islet

Father / Farther

Fillip / Philip

Fisher / Fissure

Flecks / Flex

Flocks / Phlox

Floury / Flowery

Flower / Flour

Foaled / Fold

Freeze / Frieze

Frieze / Freeze

Gallop / Gallup

Gallup / Gallop

Gamble / Gambol

Gambol / Gamble

Geezer / Geyser

Geyser / Geezer

Gilder / Guilder

Grater / Greater

Groyne / Groin

Hangar / Hanger

Hanger / Hangar

Hansom / Handsome

Heroin / Heroine

Higher / Hire

Hoarse / Horse

Hookah / Hooker

Hooker / Hookah

Insure / Ensure

Invade / Inveighed

Kernel / Colonel

Knight / Night

Laager / Lager

Leader / Lieder

Leased / Least

Lessen / Lesson

Lesson / Lessen

Lichen / Liken

Lieder / Leader

Lumbar / Lumber

Lumber / Lumbar

Manner / Manor

Marque / Mark

Marten / Martin

Martin / Marten

Masque / Mask

Meddle / Medal

Medlar / Meddler

Mettle / Metal

Missed / Mist

Mousse / Moose

Mucous / Mucus

Muscle / Mussel

Mussed / Must

Mussel / Muscle

Oriole / Aureole

Packed / Pact

Pallet / Palette

Passed / Past

Patten / Pattern

Peddle / Pedal

Pedlar / Peddler

Petrel / Petrol

Petrol / Petrel

Philip / Fillip

Phrase / Frays

Pistil / Pistol

Pistol / Pistil

Plaice / Place

Please / Pleas

Pouffe / Poof

Praise / Prays

Profit / Prophet

Puttee / Putty

Quarts / Quartz

Quartz / Quarts

Racket / Racquet

Ranker / Rancour

Revere / Revers

Revers / Revere

Review / Revue

Rheims / Reams

Rhodes / Roads

Rigger / Rigour

Rigour / Rigger

Ringer / Wringer

Roomer / Rumour

Rumour / Roomer

Savour / Saver

Schema / Schemer

Seaman / Semen

Seller / Cellar

Serial / Cereal

Sighed / Side

Signet / Cygnet

Sleigh / Slay

Slight / Sleight

Soared / Sword

Sought / Sort

Source / Sauce

Spayed / Spade

Stayed / Staid

Steppe / Step

Sticks / Styx
Storey / Story
Strait / Straight
Sucker / Succour
Sundae / Sunday
Sunday / Sundae
Symbol / Cymbal
Tacked / Tact
Taught / Taut
Tenner / Tenor
They're / Their
Throne / Thrown
Thrown / Throne
Tolled / Told
Torque / Talk
Troupe / Troop
Venous / Venus
Waists / Wastes
Waiver / Waver
Warred / Ward
Wastes / Waists
Weight / Wait
Welled / Weld
Wether / Whether
Whacks / Wax
Wither / Whither
Wrecks / Rex
Wretch / Retch
Wright / Right

7 letters:
Allowed / Aloud
Aureole / Oriole
Bearing / Baring
Boarder / Border
Boulder / Bolder
Britain / Briton
Callous / Callus
Canvass / Canvas
Ceiling / Sealing
Cession / Session
Charred / Chard
Chorale / Corral
Citrous / Citrus
Clanger / Clangour

Coarser / Courser
Colonel / Kernel
Conquer / Conker
Council / Counsel
Counsel / Council
Courser / Coarser
Cowered / Coward
Cubical / Cubicle
Cubicle / Cubical
Currant / Current
Current / Currant
Cypress / Cyprus
Deanery / Denary
Derrick / Derek
Descent / Dissent
Dessert / Desert
Dissent / Descent
Draught / Draft
Drawers / Draws
Earnest / Ernest
Elusive / Illusive
Farther / Father
Fissure / Fisher
Flowery / Floury
Gorilla / Guerrilla
Greater / Grater
Greaves / Grieves
Grieves / Greaves
Guessed / Guest
Guilder / Gilder
Heroine / Heroin
Humerus / Humorous
Illicit / Elicit
Literal / Littoral
Manikin / Mannequin
Marshal / Martial
Martial / Marshal
Meddler / Medlar
Morning / Mourning
Mustard / Mustered
Nightly / Knightly
Palette / Pallet
Pattern / Patten
Peddler / Pedlar
Pervade / Purveyed

Prophet / Profit
Racquet / Racket
Radical / Radicle
Radicle / Radical
Rancour / Ranker
Reining / Reigning
Schemer / Schema
Sealing / Ceiling
Session / Cession
Slaying / Sleighing
Sleight / Slight
Storied / Storeyed
Succour / Sucker
Summary / Summery
Summery / Summary
Through / Threw
Tighten / Titan
Trooper / Trouper
Trouper / Trooper
Trussed / Trust
Weather / Wether
Weighed / Wade
Whether / Wether
Whirled / World
Whither / Wither
Wrapped / Rapt
Wringer / Ringer

8 letters:
Brighten / Brighton
Brighton / Brighten
Clangour / Clanger
Discreet / Discrete
Discrete / Discreet
Formally / Formerly
Formerly / Formally
Handsome / Hansom
Humorous / Humerus
Illusive / Elusive
Knightly / Nightly
Lineally / Linearly
Linearly / Lineally
Littoral / Literal
Mourning / Morning
Mustered / Mustard

Overseas / Oversees
Oversees / Overseas
Populace / Populous
Populous / Populace
Purveyed / Pervade
Reigning / Reining
Sterling / Stirling
Stirling / Sterling
Storeyed / Storied
Straight / Strait
Windlass / Windless
Windless / Windlass

9 letters:
Guerrilla / Gorilla
Inveighed / Invade
Lightning / Lightening
Mannequin / Manikin
Principal / Principle

Principle / Principal
Sleighing / Slaying
Veracious / Voracious
Voracious / Veracious

10 letters:
Complement / Compliment
Compliment / Complement
Councillor / Counsellor
Counsellor / Councillor
Indiscreet / Indiscrete
Indiscrete / Indiscreet
Lightening / Lightning
Stationary / Stationery
Stationery / Stationary

13 letters:
Complementary / Complimentary
Complimentary / Complementary

Hoods

4 letters:	Pixie	**7 letters:**	Capuccio
Coif	Snood	Bashlik	Chaperon
Cope		Calèche	Trot-cozy
Cowl	**6 letters:**	Capuche	
	Almuce	Jacobin	**9 letters:**
5 letters:	Apache		Balaclava
Amaut	Biggin	**8 letters:**	Chaperone
Amice	Calash	Calyptra	Trot-cosey
Amowt	Mantle	Capeline	

Hormones

3 letters:	**7 letters:**	Bursicon	**9 letters:**
Sex	Gastrin	Ecdysone	Adrenalin®
	Inhibin	Estrogen	Corticoid
5 letters:	Insulin	Florigen	Cortisone
Auxin	Relaxin	Glucagon	Cytokinin
Kinin	Steroid	Juvenile	Endocrine
	Thyroid	Oestriol	Melatonin
6 letters:		Oestrone	Oestrogen
Growth	**8 letters:**	Oxytocin	Prolactin
	Androgen	Secretin	Secretion
	Autacoid	Thymosin	Serotonin

Thyroxine

10 letters:
Adrenaline
Calcitonin
Intermedin
Lactogenic
Lipotropin
Oestradiol

11 letters:
Aldosterone
Angiotensin
Epinephrine
Gibberellin
Luteinizing
Parathyroid
Progestogen
Somatomedin
Thyrotropin
Vasopressin

12 letters:
Androsterone
Antidiuretic
Biosynthesis
Corpus luteum
Gonadotropin

Luteotrophin
Noradrenalin
Pancreozymin
Progesterone
Secretagogue
Somatostatin
Somatotropin
Stilboestrol
Testosterone
Thyrotrophin

13 letters:
Gonadotrophic
Gonadotrophin
Noradrenaline
Prostaglandin
Somatotrophin

14 letters:
Corticosteroid
Corticosterone
Enterogastrone
Erythropoietin
Hydrocortisone

15 letters:
Cholecystokinin
Gibberellic acid

16 letters:
Triiodothyronine

18 letters:
Thyroid-stimulating

19 letters:
Deoxycorticosterone
Follicle-stimulating

20 letters:
Adrenocorticotrophic

22 letters:
Chorionic gonadotrophin

26 letters:
Trichlorophenoxyacetic
  acid

27 letters:
Interstitial-cell-
  stimulating
Luteinizing
  hormone-releasing

Horses

TYPES/BREEDS OF HORSE

2 letters:		Hack	Taki	Bevis
Kt	Rip	Jade	Turk	Bidet
	Tit	Mare	Weed	Borer
3 letters:		Plug	Wild	Caple
Ass	**4 letters:**	Pole	Yale	Capul
Bay	Arab	Pony	Yaud	Crock
Cob	Aver	Post		Favel
Don	Barb	Prad	**5 letters:**	Filly
Dun	Colt	Roan	Airer	Genet
Nag	Dale	Shan	Arion	Huçul
Pad	Deli	Snow	Arkle	Iomud
Pot	Fell	Stud	Batak	Konik
	Foal			

Lokai
Morel
Neddy
Night
Pacer
Pinto
Poler
Punch
Rogue
Screw
Seian
Shire
Spiti
Steed
Tacky
Takhi
Waler
Wheel
White
Zebra

6 letters:
Ambler
Basuto
Bayard
Breton
Bronco
Brumby
Calico
Canuck
Cayuse
Chaser
Cooser
Crollo
Curtal
Cusser
Danish
Exmoor
Favell
Garran
Garron
Gennet
Gidran
Hogget
Hunter

Jennet
Kanuck
Keffel
Lampos
Morgan
Mudder
Nonius
Novice
Pad-nag
Plater
Poster
Quagga
Randem
Remuda
Roarer
Rouncy
Runner
Sabino
Saddle
Shagya
Sorrel
Stayer
String
Summer
Tandem
Tarpan
Tracer
Vanner
Viatka

7 letters:
Beetewk
Bobtail
Burmese
Cavalry
Charger
Clipper
Courser
Cow pony
Criollo
Cuisser
Dappled
Eclipse
Eventer
Finnish

Flemish
Gelding
Hackney
Hobbler
Jutland
Kabarda
Klepper
Liberty
Manipur
Marengo
Marocco
Marwari
Morocco
Mustang
Palfrey
Piebald
Quarter
Rhenish
Saddler
Sheltie
Shirazi
Smudish
Spanker
Starter
Strelet
Suffolk
Sumpter
Swallow
Swinger
Trigger
Trooper
Walking
Wheeler
Yamoote
Zeeland
Zmudzin

8 letters:
Aquiline
Ardennes
Balearic
Bangtail
Bathorse
Boerperd
Camargue

Clay-bank
Cocktail
Dartmoor
Destrier
Eohippus
Fell pony
Friesian
Galloway
Gulf Arab
Highland
Holstein
Hyperion
Karabair
Karabakh
Karadagh
Kochlani
Limousin
Lusitano
Palomino
Polo pony
Schimmel
Shetland
Skewbald
Sleipnir
Springer
Stalking
Stallion
Stibbler
Turkoman
Warhorse
Warragal
Warragle
Warragul
Warregal
Warrigal
Welsh Cob
Whistler
Yarraman
Yearling

9 letters:
Akhal-Teke
Anglo-Arab
Appaloosa
Black Bess

Brabançon
Caballine
Carthorse
Clavileno
Coldblood
Connemara
Dales pony
Drayhorse
Esthonian
Fjord pony
Gringolet
Groningen
Houyhnhnm
Icelandic
Kladruber
Knabstrup
Miohippus
Mongolian
Oldenburg
Packhorse
Percheron
Pinzgauer
Racehorse
Rosinante
Rozinante
Schleswig
Tarbenian
Timor pony
Trakehner
Warmblood
Welsh pony
Workhorse

10 letters:
Andalusian

Bloodstock
Bucephalus
Buckjumper
Buttermilk
Clydesdale
Copenhagen
Gelderland
Hafflinger
Hanoverian
Kathiawari
Lipizzaner
Lippizaner
Pliohippus
Polish Arab
Przewalski
Show jumper
Stockhorse
Svadilfari
Zemaitukas

11 letters:
Anglo-Norman
High-stepper
Iceland pony
Mecklenburg
Merychippus
Persian Arab
Przewalski's
Running mate

12 letters:
Cleveland Bay
Dartmoor pony
Dutch Draught
Gudbrandsdal

Hambletonian
Highland pony
North Swedish
Orlov Trotter
Shetland pony
Standard Bred
Suffolk Punch
Thoroughbred

13 letters:
Hyracotherium
Kurdistan pony
New Forest pony
Russian saddle
Spanish Jennet
Stalking-horse

14 letters:
American Saddle
Polish Half-bred
Yorkshire Coach

15 letters:
American Quarter
Orlov Rostopchin
Swedish Ardennes

16 letters:
Tennessee Walking

17 letters:
Welsh Mountain pony

18 letters:
Polish Thoroughbred

LEGENDARY/FICTIONAL/HISTORICAL HORSES

5 letters:
Boxer

6 letters:
Bayard
Flicka
Silver

7 letters:
Pegasus
Trigger

8 letters:
Champion
Hercules
Mister Ed

Sleipnir
Traveler

9 letters:
Black Bess
El Fideldo
Incitatus
Rosinante

10 letters:
Bucephalus

11 letters:
Black Beauty

HORSE COLOURS

3 letters:	5 letters:	Sorrel	Palomino
Bay	Black		Skewbald
Dun	Cream	**7 letters:**	
	Mealy	Piebald	**10 letters:**
	Pinto		Dapplegrey
4 letters:		**8 letters:**	Fleabitten
Grey	**6 letters:**	Blue roan	
Roan	Albino	Chestnut	**14 letters:**
	Dapple	Claybank	Strawberry roan

HORSE MARKINGS

4 letters:	5 letters:	7 letters:	9 letters:
Snip	Blaze	Coronet	White face
Sock			
Star	**6 letters:**	**8 letters:**	
	Stripe	Stocking	

HORSE GAITS

4 letters:	5 letters:	7 letters:	11 letters:
Lope	Amble	Jog trot	Sitting trot
Pace			
Rack	**6 letters:**	**10 letters:**	**12 letters:**
Trot	Canter	Rising trot	Extended trot
Walk	Gallop	Single-foot	
	Prance		

HORSE PARTS

3 letters:	Tail	Muzzle	8 letters:
Bar	Tusk	Saddle	Buttress
Haw	Wall	Sheath	Chestnut
Toe			Coupling
	5 letters:	**7 letters:**	Diagonal
4 letters:	Croup	Brisket	Forehand
Back	Ergot	Counter	Forelock
Dock	Flank	Forearm	Near-fore
Frog	Loins	Foreleg	Near-hind
Heel	Shank	Gambrel	
Hock		Off-fore	**9 letters:**
Hoof	**6 letters:**	Off-hind	Hamstring
Mane	Barrel	Pastern	White line
Neck	Croupe	Quarter	
Poll	Gaskin	Shannon	**10 letters:**
Sole	Haunch	Withers	Cannon bone

Chin groove
Coffin bone
Splint bone

11 letters:
Coronet band
Second thigh

Stifle joint

12 letters:
Fetlock joint
Forequarters

PEOPLE ASSOCIATED WITH HORSES

3 letters:
Lad

5 letters:
Coper
Groom
Rider

6 letters:
Buster
Cowboy
Hussar
Jockey
Knight

Ostler

7 letters:
Cavalry
Currier
Equerry
Equites
Farrier
Knacker
Picador
Rustler
Saddler
Trainer

8 letters:
Cavalier
Coachman
Horseman
Wrangler

9 letters:
Caballero
Chevalier
Postilion
Postrider
Stable lad

10 letters:
Equestrian
Horsewoman
Jockey Club
Roughrider

12 letters:
Broncobuster
Equestrienne

14 letters:
Horse whisperer

TACK AND EQUIPMENT AND THEIR PARTS

3 letters:
Bar
Bit

4 letters:
Bard
Boot
Curb
Flap
Rein
Spur
Tack
Wisp

5 letters:
Barde
Cinch
Girth
Plate
Skirt
Trace

6 letters:
Bridle

Cantle
Day rug
Gag-bit
Halter
Numnah
Pelham
Pommel
Roller
Saddle
Twitch

7 letters:
Bridoon
Crupper
Curb bit
Gambado
Harness
Kneecap
Nosebag
Snaffle
Stirrup
Trammel

8 letters:
Blinkers
Browband
Cavesson
Chamfron
Hockboot
Hoof pick
Lip strap
Mane comb
Night rug
Noseband
Saddlery
Sliphead
Tail comb

9 letters:
Body brush
Breeching
Check rein
Curb chain
Curb reins
Curry comb
Front arch
Headpiece

Horseshoe
Nosepiece
Overcheck
Pad saddle
Saddlebag
Surcingle
Tailguard
Trappings

10 letters:
Cheek-piece
Crownpiece
Dandy brush
Girth strap
Kimblewick
Martingale
Sidesaddle
Snaffle bit
Stirrup bar
Throatlash
Water brush

11 letters:
Bearing rein

Breastplate
Saddlecloth
Stirrup iron
Summer sheet
Swingletree
Tail bandage
Throatlatch
Whiffletree
Whippletree

12 letters:
Anti-sweat rug
Double bridle

Plain snaffle
Stable rubber
Sweat scraper
Underblanket

13 letters:
Fulmer snaffle
New Zealand rug

14 letters:
Hackamore plate
Stirrup leather
Twisted snaffle

15 letters:
Weymouth curb bit

16 letters:
Split-eared bridle

20 letters:
Double-jointed snaffle

21 letters:
Jointed egg-butt snaffle

HORSES, RHINOS, AND OTHER PERISSODACTYLS

3 letters:
Ass

4 letters:
Mule

5 letters:
Horse

Kiang
Kulan
Tapir
Zebra

6 letters:
Donkey
Onager

7 letters:
Keitloa

8 letters:
Chigetai
Elephant

9 letters:
Dziggetai

10 letters:
Rhinoceros

13 letters:
White elephant

See also:
➤ **Races**

Household items

3 letters:
Bib
Box
Cup
Fan
Gas
Hob
Jar
Key
Log
Mop
Mug
Pan
Peg
Pot

Rug
Tap
Tin

4 letters:
Beam
Bell
Bowl
Bulb
Case
Coal
Dish
Door
Ewer
Flue

Fork
Fuel
Gong
Hi-fi
Hose
Iron
Jamb
Lamp
Lift
Lock
Oven
Pail
Pipe
Plug
Safe

Sash
Seat
Sink
Soap
Soda
Sofa
Spit
Tank
Tidy
Tile
Tray
Vase
Zarf

5 letters:
Apron
Ashet
Basin
Bench
Besom
Bidet
Blind
Board
Broil
Brush
Caddy
Chore
Cigar
Clock

Cloth
Cover
Crock
Cruet
Cruse
Diota
Doily
Duvet
Flask
Frame
Glass
Grate
Hinge
Juice
Knife
Ladle
Latch
Linen
Mixer
Mural
Paint
Panel
Poker
Quilt
Radio
Sheet
Shelf
Sieve
Spoon
Stove
Straw
Timer
Tongs
Torch
Towel
Trunk
Whisk

6 letters:
Aerial
Ash-bin
Ash-can
Awning
Basket
Beaker

Biggin
Bleach
Bluing
Boiler
Bucket
Bunker
Burner
Candle
Caster
Coffer
Colmar
Cooker
Cradle
Damper
Dishes
Dolium
Drawer
Duster
Egg-cup
Fender
Fiasco
Fingan
Flacon
Flagon
Fridge
Frieze
Gas-jet
Gas tap
Geyser
Grater
Hamper
Handle
Hearth
Heater
Ice-box
Jumble
Kaross
Kettle
Ladder
Lagena
Lintel
Locker
Log bin
Louvre
Mangle

Menage
Mincer
Mobile
Napkin
Patina
Pelmet
Pillow
Plaque
Polish
Pouffe
Pulley
Rhyton
Salver
Saucer
Scales
Sconce
Shovel
Shower
Skewer
Sponge
Starch
String
Switch
Teapot
Teaset
Tea-urn
Toy box
Trivet
Tureen
Vessel
Washer
Window
Wiring

7 letters:
Adaptor
Amphora
Ashtray
Bath tub
Bedding
Blanket
Bolster
Bouquet
Cake tin
Canteen

Ceiling
Chalice
Chamois
Chimney
Chopper
Cistern
Cleaver
Coaster
Coconut
Crystal
Cushion
Cutlery
Deed box
Dish mop
Doorway
Dustbin
Dust-pan
Faience
Fitting
Fixture
Furbish
Furnace
Fuse box
Gas-ring
Griddle
Hammock
Heating
Hickory
High tea
Hip bath
Holdall
Keyhole
Lacquer
Lagging
Lantern
Lattice
Matches
Oil lamp
Overall
Padella
Parquet
Pass-key
Pie-dish
Pitcher
Platter

Play pen
Pottery
Ramekin
Roaster
Samovar
Sanctum
Service
Serving
Shelves
Skillet
Spatula
Spy-hole
Stamnos
Steamer
Stewpot
Sundial
Sweeper
Tankard
Tea-cosy
Tea tray
Thermos
Thimble
Ticking
Toaster
Toby jug
Tool kit
Transom
Trellis
Trolley
Tumbler
Utensil
Valance
Varnish
Washday
Washtub
Worktop
Wringer

8 letters:
Atomiser
Ballcock
Barbecue
Bassinet
Bath cube
Bath soap

Bed cover
Bed linen
Bell pull
Billy can
Bird bath
Bookends
Cache-pot
Canister
Casement
Cauldron
Cigar box
Colander
Coverlet
Cream jug
Crockery
Cupboard
Cuspidor
Cut glass
Decanter
Doorbell
Doorknob
Doorpost
Doorstep
Doorstop
Driptray
Eggslice
Eggspoon
Eggtimer
Eggwhisk
Emulsion
Fanlight
Filament
Fireside
Firewood
Fixtures
Flat iron
Flour bin
Fly paper
Food-mill
Fuse-wire
Gallipot
Gas-meter
Handbell
Handrail
Hangings

Hip flask
Hollands
Homespun
Hot-plate
Immerser
Jelly bag
Jewel box
Kickshaw
Kindling
Linoleum
Matchbox
Mattress
Meatsafe
Monogram
Moth ball
Moulding
New broom
Ornament
Ovenware
Painting
Pannakin
Paraffin
Patty pan
Pendulum
Pipe rack
Polisher
Portrait
Pot plant
Radiator
Rosebowl
Saucepan
Scissors
Scrubber
Shoehorn
Shredder
Shutters
Side-door
Sink unit
Sitz bath
Skylight
Slop bowl
Slop pail
Snuff box
Soap dish
Soapsuds

Soft soap
Solarium
Spice jar
Spittoon
Squeezer
Strainer
Sunblind
Surround
Tablemat
Tapestry
Tea chest
Tea cloth
Teaspoon
Trapdoor
Underlay
Wainscot
Water jug
Water tap
Wig-block
Wireless
Yale lock

9 letters:
Ansaphone
Auto-timer
Baking tin
Barometer
Bath salts
Bath towel
Bay window
Bedspread
Beer glass
Blank door
Cakestand
Cantharus
Casserole
Chandlier
Chinaware
Cigarette
Clepsydra
Coffee cup
Container
Corkscrew
Crossbeam
Cullender

Demitasse
Desk light
Detergent
Directory
Dishcloth
Dish towel
Distemper
Dog basket
Doorplate
Drainpipe
Dust-sheet
Dutch oven
Dutch wife
Egg beater
Egg slicer
Eiderdown
Facecloth
Face towel
Fire alarm
Fireguard
Fire irons
Firelight
Fireplace
Fish knife
Fish slice
Flower pot
Foodmixer
Front door
Fruit bowl
Fruit dish
Frying pan
Gas burner
Gas cooker
Girandole
Glass door
Gold plate
Gravy boat
Hand towel
Hourglass
Housewife
Housework
Japanning
Jewel case
Joss-stick
Lamplight

Lampshade
Lampstand
Letterbox
Light bulb
Log basket
Loving cup
Master key
Mousetrap
Objet d'art
Panelling
Partition
Patchwork
Phone book
Pie-funnel
Place-card
Porcelain
Porringer
Punchbowl
Radiogram
Safety pin
Salad bowl
Sauceboat
Serviette
Shakedown
Shoeblack
Shower cap
Side light
Silver-wax
Slop basin
Soup plate
Soup spoon
Spin-drier
Sponge-bag
Staircase
Statuette
Steam iron
Steel wool
Storm door
Stovepipe
Sugar bowl
Swing door
Table lamp
Tableware
Tea kettle
Tea-waggon

Telephone
Threshold
Timepiece
Tinder-box
Tin opener
Toast-rack
Toilet bag
Underfelt
Wall clock
Wall light
Wallpaper
Washbasin
Washboard
Water butt
Water cock
Water pipe
Water tank
Wax polish
Whitewash
Window box
Wine glass

10 letters:
Abstergent
Alarm clock
Anthracite
Apple-cover
Baking bowl
Baking tray
Bedclothes
Bedsprings
Bellarmine
Boot polish
Bread board
Breadknife
Butter dish
Candelabra
Cassolette
Chafing pan
Chopsticks
Clothes peg
Coal-bucket
Coal-bunker
Coat-hanger
Coffee mill

Curtain rod
Deep-freeze
Dinner gong
Dishwasher
Doorhandle
Drawing pin
Dutch clock
Featherbed
Finger bowl
Fire-basket
Fire-escape
Firescreen
Fish kettle
Floor-cloth
Forcing bag
Fruit-knife
Glass-cloth
Gramophone
Grand piano
Hollow ware
Knickknack
Lamp socket
Letter-rack
Loose cover
Matchstick
Milk bottle
Mixing bowl
Musical box
Mustard pot
Napkin ring
Night-light
Nutcracker
Oven gloves
Paint-brush
Paper knife
Pepper mill
Percolator
Persian rug
Persiennes
Photograph
Pillowcase
Pillow slip
Pilot light
Pin cushion
Plate glass

Plate piece
Pot scourer
Pot scraper
Power point
Rain barrel
Ration book
Rolling pin
Rose-window
Salt cellar
Sealing wax
Silverware
Soap flakes
Soap powder
Spirit lamp
Step ladder
Storage jar
Strip-light
Tablecloth
Table-knife
Table-linen
Tablespoon
Tea service
Television
Thermostat
Time-switch
Tobacco jar
Toilet roll
Toilet soap
Toothbrush
Toothpaste
Transistor
Trinket box
Vanity lamp
Ventilator
Waffle-iron
Wall-socket
Warming pan
Washbasket
Wassai bowl
Watchglass
Water clock
Whisk broom
Window-pane
Window-sash
Window-seat

Window-sill
Wine basket
Wine bottle
Wine cooler
Wooden ware
Work basket
Worry beads

11 letters:
Airtight jar
Baking sheet
Broom handle
Butter-knife
Candelabrum
Candlestick
Centrepiece
Chafing dish
Cheese board
China figure
Chinoiserie
Clothes line
Clothes pole
Coal scuttle
Cookery book
Cooling tray
Counterpane
Cuckoo clock
Curtain hook
Curtain rail
Curtain ring
Dessert fork
Door-knocker
Earthenware
Eating irons
Elbowgrease
Family album
Firelighter
First-aid box
Floor polish
French chalk
Garden party
Garden swing
Hearth brush
Kitchen sink
Kitchen unit

Laundry room
Light switch
Linen basket
Loving spoon
Mantelpiece
Meat chopper
Meat cleaver
Metal polish
Non-stick pan
Oil painting
Oriental rug
Paperweight
Picture rail
Plant-holder
Pocket flask
Primus stove
Pudding bowl
Pumice stone
Record album
Roasting tin
Rotary whisk
Sauce bottle
Scouring pad
Serving dish
Shopping bag
Shower-cloth
Silver plate
Silver spoon
Skeleton key
Sliding door
Spring clean
Storm window
Table napkin
Tape measure
Tea-strainer
Thermometer
Vacuum flask
Vinaigrette
Washing line
Washing soap
Washing soda
Water closet
Water heater
Window blind
Window frame

Window-light
Wintergreen
Wooden spoon
Work-surface
Wrought iron

12 letters:
Adhesive tape
Antimacassar
Apron-strings
Ball of string
Bedside light
Bottle-opener
Bottom drawer
Bread curtain
Candleholder
Candle-sconce
Carpet beater
Carriage lamp
Carving-knife
Cheese-grater
Chiming clock
Chimney piece
Chimney-stack
Cigarette box
Clothes-brush
Clothes-drier
Clothes-horse
Companion set
Convex mirror
Cooking range
Dessert spoon
Disinfectant
Double boiler
Electric fire
Electric iron
Electric lamp
Extractor fan
Firelighters
Fireside seat
Flower holder
French polish
Hot water tank
Ironing board
Kettle-holder

Labour-saving
Light fitting
Looking-glass
Lunch counter
Magazine rack
Mulligatawny
Paraffin lamp
Passe-partout
Perambulator
Picnic basket
Picnic hamper
Picture frame
Place-setting
Pudding basin
Radiant plate
Record-player
Reel of cotton
Reel of thread
Refrigerator
Serving hatch
Serving spoon
Stain remover
Standard lamp
Swizzle stick
Table lighter
Table service
Talcum powder
Tape-recorder
Thermos flask
Toasting fork
Turkish towel
User-friendly
Visiting card
Washing board
Washing cloth

13 letters:
Backscratcher
Blanket stitch
Blotting paper
Candle snuffer
Carpet sweeper
Carriage clock
Chopping-block
Chopping-board

Clothes basket
Cocktail stick
Darning-needle
Dinner service
Draught screen
Electric mixer
Electric razor
Emulsion paint
Feather duster
Fire-resistant
Food processor
Household gods
Hurricane lamp
Lawn sprinkler
Microwave oven
Mowing-machine
Petrol lighter
Pinking-shears
Preserving-pan
Saratoga trunk
Sewing-machine
Smoothing iron
Soldering iron

Storage heater
Vacuum-cleaner
Venetian blind
Washing powder
Water softener

14 letters:
Cartridge-paper
Casement-window
Central heating
Chinese lantern
Cocktail shaker
Coconut-matting
Corrugated iron
Cut-throat razor
Electric cooker
Electric kettle
Electric shaver
Hot-water bottle
Hot-water system
Household goods
Household linen
Insulating tape

Kitchen utensil
Knitting-needle
Knives and forks
Luncheon basket
Pair of scissors
Patchwork quilt
Pressure-cooker
Scrubbing-brush
Spring cleaning
Spring mattress
Washing-machine

15 letters:
Cigarette holder
Combination lock
Corrugated paper
Electric blanket
Electric toaster
Immersion heater
Knitting-machine
Pencil sharpener
Photograph album
Weighing machine

Humours of the body

5 letters:	**6 letters:**	**9 letters:**	**10 letters:**
Blood	Phlegm	Black bile	Yellow bile

Huts

4 letters:
Shed
Skeo
Skio
Tilt

5 letters:
Banda
Booth
Bothy
Cabin
Hogan
Humpy

Igloo
Shack
Sheal
Shiel
Wilja

6 letters:
Bothie
Bustee
Chalet
Gunyah
Mia-mia
Nissen

Pondok
Rancho
Shanty
Succah
Sukkah
Tolsel
Tolsey
Tolzey
Wigwam
Wikiup
Wiltja
Wurley

Hydrocarbons

3 letters:
Wax

5 letters:
Alkyl
Arene
Diene
Gutta
Halon
Hexyl
Phene
Xylol

6 letters:
Aldrin
Alkane
Alkene
Alkyne
Butane
Butene
Cetane
Cubane
Decane
Dioxin
Ethane
Hexane
Hexene
Indene
Nonane

Octane
Pinene
Pyrene
Retene
Xylene

7 letters:
Amylene
Benzene
Heptane
Ligroin
Naphtha
Olefine
Pentane
Pentene
Polyene
Propane
Styrene
Terpene
Toluene

8 letters:
Camphane
Camphene
Carotene
Diphenyl
Hexylene
Isoprene
Limonene

Paraffin
Squalene
Stilbene
Triptane

9 letters:
Acetylene
Butadiene
Isobutane
Isooctane
Pentylene

10 letters:
Asphaltite
Mesitylene

11 letters:
Cycloalkane
Cyclohexane
Hatchettite
Naphthalene

12 letters:
Cyclopropane
Phenanthrene

15 letters:
Cyclopentadiene

Inflammations

3 letters:
Sty

4 letters:
Acne
Noma
Stye

5 letters:
Croup
Felon

6 letters:
Ancome
Angina
Bunion
Eczema
Garget
Iritis
Otitis
Quinsy
Thrush
Ulitis

7 letters:
Colitis
Ecthyma
Founder
Ignatis
Onychia
Pinkeye
Prurigo
Sunburn
Sycosis
Tylosis

Whitlow

8 letters:
Adenitis
Aortisis
Bursitis
Carditis
Cystisis
Fibrosis
Hyalitis
Mastitis
Metritis
Mycetoma
Myelitis
Myositis
Neuritis
Orchitis
Osteitis
Ovaritis
Phlegmon
Pleurisy
Pyelitis
Rachitis
Rhinitis
Uvulitis
Windburn

9 letters:
Arteritis
Arthritis
Balanitis
Cheilitis
Enteritis
Gastritis
Glossitis

Keratitis
Laminitis
Nephritis
Parotitis
Phlebitis
Phrenitis
Pneumonia
Proctitis
Pyorrhoea
Retinitis
Scleritis
Sinusitis
Splenitis
Strumitis
Synovitis
Typhlitis
Vaginitis

10 letters:
Asbestosis
Bronchitis
Cellulitis
Cervicitis
Dermatitis
Erysipelas
Fibrositis
Gingivitis
Hepatitis A
Hepatitis B
Intertrigo
Laryngitis
Meningitis
Oophoritis
Ophthalmia
Paronychia

Phlegmasia
Stomatitis
Tendinitis
Thrombosis
Tracheitis
Urethritis
Valvulitis
Vasculitis

11 letters:
Blepharitis
Farmer's lung
Mastoiditis
Myocarditis
Peritonitis
Pharyngitis
Prostatitis
Salpingitis
Shin splints
Spondylitis
Thoroughpin
Thyroiditis
Tonsillitis

12 letters:
Appendicitis
Encephalitis
Endocarditis
Folliculitis
Mesenteritis
Osteoporosis
Pancreatitis
Pericarditis
Polyneuritis
Swimmer's itch

13 letters:	14 letters:	16 letters:
Enterocolitis	Conjunctivitis	Bronchopneumonia
Labyrinthitis	Diverticulitis	
Osteomyelitis	Osteoarthritis	17 letters:
Perihepatitis	Vincent's angina	Encephalomyelitis
Perinephritis		Meningocephalitis
Periodontisis	15 letters:	
Perityphlitis	Gastroenteritis	
Tenosynovitis		

Inhabitants

Place	Inhabitant
Aberdeen	Aberdonian
Afghanistan	Afghan
Alabama	Alabaman *or* Alabamian
Alaska	Alaskan
Albania	Albanian
Alberta	Albertan
Algeria	Algerian
Alsace	Alsatian
American continent	American
American Samoa	American Samoan
Amsterdam	Amsterdammer
Anatolia	Anatolian
Andorra	Andorran
Angola	Angolan
Anjou	Angevin
Antigua	Antiguan
Argentina	Argentine *or* Argentinian
Arizona	Arizonan
Arkansas	Arkansan *or (informal)* Arkie
Armenia	Armenian
Asia	Asian
Assam	Assamese
Assyria	Assyrian
Australia	Australian *or (informal)* Aussie
Austria	Austrian
Azerbaijan	Azerbaijani *or* Azeri
Babylon	Babylonian
Bahamas	Bahamian
Bahrain	Bahraini
Bali	Balinese
Bangladesh	Bangladeshi
Barbados	Barbadian, Bajan *(informal)*, *or* Bim *(informal)*

Place	Inhabitant
Barbuda	Barbudan *or* Barbudian
Bavaria	Bavarian
Belarus *or* Byelorussia	Belarussian *or* Byelorussian
Belau	Belauan
Belgium	Belgian
Benin	Beninese *or* Beninois
Berlin	Berliner
Bhutan	Bhutanese
Birmingham	Brummie
Bohemia	Bohemian
Bolivia	Bolivian
Bordeaux	Bordelais
The Borders	Borderer
Bosnia	Bosnian
Boston	Bostonian *or (U.S. slang)* Bean-eater
Botswana	Botswanan
Brazil	Brazilian
Bristol	Bristolian
British Columbia	British Columbian
Brittany	Breton
Bulgaria	Bulgarian
Burgundy	Burgundian
Burkina-Faso	Burkinabe
Burma	Burmese
Burundi	Burundian
Byzantium	Byzantine
California	Californian
Cambodia	Cambodian
Cambridge	Cantabrigian
Cameroon	Cameroonian
Canada	Canadian *or (informal)* Canuck
Canada, Maritime Provinces	Downeaster
Cape Verde	Cape Verdean
Castile	Castilian
Catalonia	Catalan
The Caucasus	Caucasian
Cayman Islands	Cayman Islander
Chad	Chadian *or* Chadean
Chicago	Chicagoan
Chile	Chilean
China	Chinese
Circassia	Circassian
Colombia	Colombian
Colorado	Coloradan

Place	Inhabitant
Comoros Islands	Comorian
Congo Republic	Congolese
Connecticut	Nutmegger
Cork	Corkonian
Cornwall	Cornishman, Cornishwoman
Corsica	Corsican
Costa Rica	Costa Rican
Côte d'Ivoire	Ivorian *or* Ivorean
Croatia	Croat *or* Croatian
Cuba	Cuban
Cumbria	Cumbrian
Cyprus	Cypriot
Czechoslovakia	Czechoslovak *or* Czechoslovakian
Czech Republic	Czech
Delaware	Delawarean
Delphi	Pythian
Denmark	Dane
Devon	Devonian
Djibouti	Djiboutian *or* Djiboutien
Dominica	Dominican
Dominican Republic	Dominican
Dublin	Dubliner
Dundee	Dundonian
East Timor	East Timorese
Ecuador	Ecuadorean *or* Ecuadoran
Edinburgh	Edinburgher
Egypt	Egyptian
El Salvador	Salvadoran, Salvadorean, *or* Salvadorian
England	Englishman, Englishwoman
Ephesus	Ephesian
Equatorial Guinea	Equatorian
Eritrea	Eritrean
Estonia	Estonian
Ethiopia	Ethiopian
Europe	European
Euzkadi	Basque
Faeroe Islands	Faeroese
Falkland Islands	Falkland Islanders *or* Falklander
Fife	Fifer
Fiji	Fijian
Finland	Finn
Flanders	Fleming
Florence	Florentine
Florida	Floridian

Place	Inhabitant
France	Frenchman, Frenchwoman
French Guiana	Guianese
Friesland	Frisian
Friuli	Friulian
Gabon	Gabonese
Galicia	Galician
Galilee	Galilean
Galloway	Gallovidian
Galway	Galwegian
Gambia	Gambian
Gascony	Gascon
Genoa	Genoese
Georgia (country)	Georgian
Georgia (U.S. state)	Georgian
Germany	German
Ghana	Ghanaian *or* Ghanian
Glasgow	Glaswegian
Greece	Greek
Greenland	Greenlander
Grenada	Grenadian
Guam	Guamanian
Guatemala	Guatemalan
Guinea	Guinean
Guyana	Guyanese *or* Guyanan
Haiti	Haitian
Havana	Habanero
Hawaii	Hawaiian
Hesse	Hessian
Honduras	Honduran
Hungary	Hungarian *or* Magyar
Hyderabad state	Mulki
Ibiza	Ibizan
Iceland	Icelander
Idaho	Idahoan
Illinois	Illinoian *or* Illinoisian
India	Indian
Indiana	Indianan, Indianian, *or (informal)* Hoosier
Indonesia	Indonesian
Iowa	Iowan
Iran	Iranian
Iraq	Iraqi
Ireland	Irishman, Irishwoman
Isle of Man	Manxman, Manxwoman
Israel	Israeli

Place	Inhabitant
Italy	Italian
Jamaica	Jamaican
Japan	Japanese
Java	Javanese
Jordan	Jordanian
Kansas	Kansan
Karelia	Karelian
Kazakhstan	Kazakh
Kent (East)	Man, Woman of Kent
Kent (West)	Kentish Man, Woman
Kentucky	Kentuckian
Kenya	Kenyan
Kirghizia	Kirghiz
Korea	Korean
Kuwait	Kuwaiti
Lancashire	Lancastrian
Lancaster	Lancastrian
Laos	Laotian
Latvia	Latvian *or* Lett
Lebanon	Lebanese
Liberia	Liberian
Libya	Libyan
Liechtenstein	Liechtensteiner
Lincolnshire	Yellow belly *(dialect)*
Lithuania	Lithuanian
Liverpool	Liverpudlian *or (informal)* Scouse *or* Scouser
Lombardy	Lombard
London	Londoner *or* Cockney
Los Angeles	Angeleno
Louisiana	Louisianan *or* Louisianian
Luxembourg	Luxembourger
Lyon	Lyonnais
Macao	Macaonese
Macedonia	Macedonian
Madagascar	Madagascan *or* Malagasy
Madrid	Madrileño, Madrileña
Maine	Mainer *or* Downeaster
Majorca	Majorcan
Malawi	Malawian
Malaya	Malayan
Malaysia	Malaysian
Maldive Islands	Maldivian
Malta	Maltese
Manchester	Mancunian

Place	Inhabitant
Manitoba	Manitoban
Marquesas Islands	Marquesan
Mars	Martian
Marseilles	Marsellais
Marshall Islands	Marshall Islander
Martinique	Martiniquean
Maryland	Marylander
Massachusetts	Bay Stater
Mauritania	Mauritanian
Mauritius	Mauritian
Melanesia	Melanesian
Melbourne	Melburnian
Mexico	Mexican
Michigan	Michigander, Michiganite, *or* Michiganian
Micronesia	Micronesian
Milan	Milanese
Minnesota	Minnesotan
Mississippi	Mississippian
Missouri	Missourian
Moldavia	Moldavian
Monaco	Monegasque
Mongolia	Mongolian
Montana	Montanan
Montenegro	Montenegrin
Montserrat	Montserratian
Moravia	Moravian
Morocco	Moroccan
Moscow	Muscovite
Mozambique	Mozambican
Namibia	Namibian
Naples	Neapolitan
Nauru	Nauruan
Nebraska	Nebraskan
The Netherlands	Dutchman, Dutchwoman
New Brunswick	New Brunswicker
Newcastle upon Tyne	Geordie
New England	New Englander *or (informal)* Yankee *or* Downeaster
Newfoundland	Newfoundlander *or (informal)* Newfie
Newfoundland fishing village	Outporter
New Hampshire	New Hampshirite
New Jersey	New Jerseyan *or* New Jerseyite
New Mexico	New Mexican
New South Wales	New South Welshman, New South Welshwoman

Place	Inhabitant
New York	New Yorker *or* Knickerbocker
New Zealand	New Zealander, *or (informal)* Kiwi, *or* Enzedder
Nicaragua	Nicaraguan
Niger	Nigerien
Nigeria	Nigerian
Normandy	Norman
North Carolina	North Carolinian *or* Tarheel
North Dakota	North Dakotan
Northern Ireland	Northern Irishman, Northern Irishwoman
Northern Territory	Territorian
Northern Territory, northern part of	Top Ender
North Korea	North Korean
Northumbria	Northumbrian
Norway	Norwegian
Nova Scotia	Nova Scotian *or (informal)* Bluenose
Ohio	Ohioan
Okinawa	Okinawan
Oklahoma	Oklahoman *or (slang)* Okie
Oman	Omani
Ontario	Ontarian *or* Ontarioan
Oregon	Oregonian
Orkney	Orcadian
Oxford	Oxonian
Pakistan	Pakistani
Palestine	Palestinian
Panama	Panamanian
Papua New Guinea	Papua
Paraguay	Paraguayan
Paris	Parisian *or* Parisienne
Pennsylvania	Pennsylvanian
Persia	Persian
Perth	Perthite
Peru	Peruvian
The Philippines	Filipino
Poland	Pole
Pomerania	Pomeranian
Portugal	Portuguese
Prince Edward Island	Prince Edward Islander
Provence	Provençal
Prussia	Prussian
Puerto Rico	Puerto Rican
Qatar	Qatari
Quebec	Quebecer, Quebecker, *or* Quebecois

Place	Inhabitant
Queensland	Queenslander
Rhode Island	Rhode Islander
Rhodes	Rhodian
Rhodesia	Rhodesian
Rio de Janeiro	Cariocan
Romania	Romanian
Rome	Roman
Russian Federation	Russian
Ruthenia	Ruthenian
Rwanda	Rwandan
Samaria	Samaritan
San Marino	San Marinese *or* Sammarinese
Sardinia	Sardinian
Saskatchewan	Saskatchewanian
Saudi Arabia	Saudi *or* Saudi Arabian
Savoy	Savoyard
Saxony	Saxon
Scandinavia	Scandinavian
Scotland	Scot, Scotsman, Scotswoman, *or* Caledonian
Scottish Highlands	Highlander *or (old-fashioned)* Hielanman
Senegal	Senegalese
Serbia	Serb *or* Serbian
Seychelles	Seychellois
Shetland	Shetlander
Sierra Leone	Sierra Leonean
Sind	Sindhi
Singapore	Singaporean
Slovakia	Slovak
Slovenia	Slovene *or* Slovenian
Solomon Islands	Solomon Islander
South Africa	South African
South Australia	South Australian *or (informal)* Croweater
South Carolina	South Carolinian
South Dakota	South Dakota
South Korea	South Korean
Spain	Spaniard
Sri Lanka	Sri Lankan
Sudan	Sudanese
Suriname	Surinamese
Swaziland	Swazi
Sweden	Swede
Switzerland	Swiss
Sydney	Sydneysider
Sydney, Western suburbs of	Westie

Place	Inhabitant
Syria	Syrian
Taiwan	Taiwanese
Tajikistan	Tajik
Tanzania	Tanzanian
Tasmania	Tasmanian, *or (informal)* Tassie, *or* Apple Islander
Tennessee	Tennessean
Texas	Texan
Thailand	Thai
Thessalonika	Thessalonian
Tibet	Tibetan
Tobago	Tobagan *or* Tobagonian
Togo	Togolese
Tonga	Tongan
Trinidad	Trinidadian
Troy	Trojan
Tunisia	Tunisian
Turkey	Turk
Turkmenistan	Turkmen
Tuscany	Tuscan
Tuvalu	Tuvaluan
Tyneside	Geordie
Tyre	Tyrian
Uganda	Ugandan
Ukraine	Ukrainian
Ulster	Ulsterman, Ulsterwoman
Umbria	Umbrian
United Kingdom	Briton, Brit *(informal)*, *or* Britisher
United States of America	American, *or (informal)* Yank, *or* Yankee
Uruguay	Uruguayan
Utah	Utahan *or* Utahn
Uzbekistan	Uzbek
Venezuela	Venezuelan
Venice	Venetian
Vermont	Vermonter
Victoria	Victorian
Vienna	Viennese
Vietnam	Vietnamese
Virginia	Virginian
Wales	Welshman, Welshwoman
Washington	Washingtonian
Wearside	Mackem
Wessex	West Saxon
Western Australia	Western Australian, Westralian, *or (informal)* Sandgroper

Place	Inhabitant
Western Sahara	Sahwari
West Virginia	West Virginian
Winnipeg	Winnipegger
Wisconsin	Wisconsinite
Wyoming	Wyomingite
Yemen	Yemeni
Yorkshire	Yorkshireman, Yorkshirewoman
The Yukon	Yukoner
Zaire	Zairean
Zambia	Zambian
Zanzibar	Zanzibari
Zimbabwe	Zimbabwean

Insects

TYPES OF INSECT

3 letters:
Ant
Bee
Bot
Fly
Lac
Nit
Wax

4 letters:
Crab
Flea
Gnat
Grig
Kutu
Lice
Mite
Moth
Pium
Tick
Wasp
Weta
Zimb

5 letters:
Aphis
Cimex
Emmet

Louse
Midge
Ox-bot
Scale
Stick
Zebub

6 letters:
Acarid
Breeze
Capsid
Chigoe
Cicada
Cicala
Cootie
Day-fly
Earwig
Gadfly
Hopper
Hornet
Locust
Looper
Mantid
Mantis
Mayfly
Psocid
Psylla
Punkie

Redbug
Sawfly
Scarab
Slater
Spider
Tettix
Thrips
Walker
Weevil

7 letters:
Antlion
Buzzard
Chalcid
Chigger
Cornfly
Cricket
Daphnid
Ergates
Firefly
Gallfly
Grayfly
Hive-bee
Humbuzz
Katydid
Ladybug
Odonata
Oestrus

Oniscus
Phasmid
Pill-bug
Pyralis
Sandfly
Spectre
Stylops
Termite

8 letters:
Alderfly
Bollworm
Bookworm
Caseworm
Circutio
Coccidae
Crane-fly
Dipteras
Firebrat
Gall-wasp
Glossina
Greenfly
Horntail
Horsefly
Inchworm
Itchmite
Lacewing
Ladybird

Lygus bug
Mealybug
Metabola
Milliped
Mosquito
Myriapod
Puss-moth
Reduviid
Ruby-tail
Scarabee
Sheep ked
Silkworm
Snowflea
Stinkbug
Stonefly
Waterbug
Wheel bug
Whitefly
Wireworm
Woodworm

9 letters:
Ametabola
Body louse
Booklouse
Caddis-fly
Centipede
Clipshear

Cochineal
Cockroach
Compodeid
Crab louse
Croton bug
Damselfly
Dobsonfly
Dragonfly
Ephemerid
Hemiptera
Homoptera
Mecoptera
Millepede
Millipede
Rearhorse
Sheep tick
Tabanidae
Tiger-moth
Woodlouse

10 letters:
Apterygota
Bark mantis
Bluebottle

Caddis worm
Cankerworm
Casebearer
Chironomid
Clipshears
Cockchafer
Coleoptera
Collembola
Fan-cricket
Fen-cricket
Froghopper
Harvestman
Leaf-cutter
Leafhopper
Mallophaga
Orthoptera
Phylloxera
Plant-louse
Pond-skater
Psocoptera
Rhipiptera
Silverfish
Springtail
Thysanuran

Treehopper
Web spinner

11 letters:
Apple maggot
Bristletail
Cabbageworm
Dermopteran
Grasshopper
Greenbottle
Hymenoptera
Mole cricket
Neuropteran
Tiger-beetle
Trichoptera

12 letters:
Bishop's mitre
Dictyopteran
Heteropteran
Rhipidoptera
Strepsiptera
Sucking louse
Thousand-legs

Thysanoptera
Walking stick

13 letters:
Cotton stainer
Daddy-long-legs
Jenny-longlegs
Leatherjacket
Measuring worm
Praying mantis
Staphylinidae

15 letters:
German cockroach
Tent caterpillar

16 letters:
Periodical cicada

19 letters:
Seventeen-year
  locust

PARTS OF INSECTS

3 letters:
Jaw

4 letters:
Coxa

5 letters:
Femur
Ileum
Notum
Scape
Snout
Thigh
Tibia

6 letters:
Air sac
Arista
Cercus

Cirrus
Corium
Glossa
Labium
Labrum
Ligula
Proleg
Scutum
Stigma
Tarsus
Tegmen
Thorax

7 letters:
Antenna
Clasper
Clypeus
Elytron
Gonopod

Hamulus
Maxilla
Ocellus
Pedicel
Trachea

8 letters:
Forewing
Mandible
Pronotum
Spiracle

9 letters:
Flagellum
Proboscis
Prothorax
Pulvillus
Scutellum
Spinneret

Underwing

10 letters:
Acetabulum
Epicuticle
Exocuticle
Haustellum
Hemelytron
Mesothorax
Metathorax
Ovipositor
Prosternum
Trochanter

11 letters:
Compound eye
Endocuticle
Ventriculus

14 letters:
Proventriculus

16 letters:
Malpighian tubule

See also:
➤ **Ants, bees, and wasps** ➤ **Beetles** ➤ **Bugs** ➤ **Butterflies and moths** ➤ **Flies**

Instruments

3 letters:
Fan

4 letters:
Celt
Clam
Fork
Mike
Prog
Rasp
Rote
Tram

5 letters:
Brake
Fleam
Float
Gadge
Groma
Meter
Miser
Probe
Sonde
Wecht

6 letters:
Bougie
Broach
Etalon
Scythe
Strobe
Trocar

7 letters:
Alidade
Cadrans

Caltrop
Curette
Forceps
Pelican
Pointel
Probang
Scriber
Sextant
Spatula
Strigil
Swazzle
Swingle
Swozzle
Syringe
Trammel

8 letters:
Ablative
Barnacle
Diagraph
Dividers
Ecraseur
Odometer
Otoscope
Oximeter
Quadrant
Scissors
Strickle
Trephine
Waywiser

9 letters:
Alphonsin
Astrolabe
Atmometer
Auxometer

Barometer
Baryscope
Bolometer
Coelostat
Crows-bill
Cymograph
Dermatome
Dip-circle
Dropsonde
Eriometer
Haemostat
Heliostat
Hodometer
Konimeter
Machmeter
Manometer
Marigraph
Megascope
Metronome
Nocturnal
Potometer
Raspatory
Retractor
Rheometer
Tasimeter
Telemeter
Telescope
Tellurian
Tellurion
Tenaculum
Tonometer
Tripmeter
Voltmeter
Wavemeter

10 letters:
Almacantar
Almucantar
Altazimuth
Anemometer
Ceilometer
Clinometer
Colposcope
Cryophorus
Cystoscope
Fibrescope
Hydrometer
Hydroscope
Hygrometer
Hypsometer
Micrometer
Microphone
Pilliwinks
Protractor
Radiosonde
Spirograph
Spirometer
Tachigraph
Tachometer
Tensometer
Theodolite
Tribometer

11 letters:
Auxanometer
Chronograph
Chronometer
Chronoscope
Helicograph
Jacob's staff
Laparoscope

Pinnywinkle
Polarimeter
Rocketsonde
Seismograph
Solarimeter
Stauroscope
Stethoscope
Stroboscope
Synthesizer
Tacheometer
Tensiometer
Thermometer
Voltammeter

12 letters:
Aethrioscope
Bronchoscope
Cephalometer
Keraunograph
Myringoscope
Penetrometer
Pinniewinkle
Respirometer
Scarificator
Sensitometer
Spectroscope
Synchroscope

Turbidimeter
Zenith-sector

13 letters:
Tachistoscope

14 letters:
Interferometer
Ophthalmoscope

16 letters:
Sphygmomanometer

Insults and terms of abuse

2 letters:
'ho

3 letters:
Cow
Git
Mug
Nit
Oaf

4 letters:
Berk
Bozo
Clod
Clot
Coot
Dope
Dork
Drip
Fool
Geek
Jerk
Loon
Mong
Nerd
Nurd
Ogre
Prat
Scab

Slag
Tart
Twit
Wimp
Wuss

5 letters:
Bitch
Chump
Clown
Devil
Divvy
Dumbo
Dummy
Dunce
Dweeb
Eejit
Galah
Goose
Idiot
Moron
Ninny
Plank
Rogue
Twerp
Twirp
Wally
Whore

6 letters:
Anorak
Cretin
Dimwit
Donkey
Doofus
Drongo
Heifer
Mincer
Minger
Muppet
Nitwit
Numpty
Rascal
Thicko
Wretch

7 letters:
Airhead
Article
Bushpig
Cabbage
Charlie
Chicken
Chuckie
Dumb-ass
Fathead
Halfwit
Pillock

Plonker
Scutter
Slapper
Spanner
Wazzock

8 letters:
Bonehead
Dipstick
Doughnut
Imbecile
Numskull
Pea-brain
Scrubber

9 letters:
Bird-brain
Blockhead
Lamebrain
Numbskull
Scoundrel
Simpleton
Thickhead

10 letters:
Nincompoop

12 letters:
Cheeky monkey

Internet domain names

GENERAL DOMAIN NAMES

Abbreviation	Top-level domain
.aero	Air-transport industry
.arpa	Internet infrastructure
.asia	Asia-Pacific region
.biz	Business
.co	Commercial company (used with country)
.com	Commercial company
.coop	Cooperative
.edu	Educational establishment
.eu	European Union
.gov	Government organization
.info	General use
.int	International organization
.jobs	Companies
.mil	US military
.mobi	Mobile devices
.museum	Museum
.name	Individual user
.net	Company *or* organization
.org	Organization, usually nonprofit
.pro	Professionals (accountants, lawyers, etc.)
.tel	Internet communication services
.travel	Travel and tourism
.xxx	Adult entertainment

COUNTRY DOMAIN NAMES

Abbreviation	Country
.ac	Ascension Island
.ad	Andorra
.ae	United Arab Emirates
.af	Afghanistan
.ag	Antigua and Barbuda
.ai	Anguilla
.al	Albania
.am	Armenia
.an	Netherlands Antilles
.ao	Angola
.aq	Antarctica
.ar	Argentina
.as	American Samoa
.at	Austria
.au	Australia

Abbreviation	Country
.aw	Aruba
.az	Azerbaijan
.ba	Bosnia and Herzegovina
.bb	Barbados
.bd	Bangladesh
.be	Belgium
.bf	Burkina Faso
.bg	Bulgaria
.bh	Bahrain
.bi	Burundi
.bj	Benin
.bm	Bermuda
.bn	Brunei Darussalam
.bo	Bolivia
.br	Brazil
.bs	Bahamas
.bt	Bhutan
.bv	Bouvet Island
.bw	Botswana
.by	Belarus
.bz	Belize
.ca	Canada
.cc	Cocos (Keeling) Islands
.cd	Congo, Democratic Republic of the
.cf	Central African Republic
.cg	Congo, Republic of
.ch	Switzerland
.ci	Côte d'Ivoire
.ck	Cook Islands
.cl	Chile
.cm	Cameroon
.cn	China
.co	Colombia
.cr	Costa Rica
.cu	Cuba
.cv	Cape Verde
.cx	Christmas Island
.cy	Cyprus
.cz	Czech Republic
.de	Germany
.dj	Djibouti
.dk	Denmark
.dm	Dominica
.do	Dominican Republic

Abbreviation	Country
.dz	Algeria
.ec	Ecuador
.ee	Estonia
.eg	Egypt
.eh	Western Sahara
.er	Eritrea
.es	Spain
.et	Ethiopia
.fi	Finland
.fj	Fiji
.fk	Falkland Islands (Malvinas)
.fm	Micronesia, Federated States of
.fo	Faroe Islands
.fr	France
.ga	Gabon
.gd	Grenada
.ge	Georgia
.gf	French Guiana
.gg	Guernsey
.gh	Ghana
.gi	Gibraltar
.gl	Greenland
.gm	Gambia
.gn	Guinea
.gp	Equatorial Guinea
.gr	Greece
.gs	South Georgia and the South Sandwich Islands
.gt	Guatemala
.gu	Guam
.gw	Guinea-Bissau
.gy	Guyana
.hk	Hong Kong
.hm	Heard and McDonald Islands
.hn	Honduras
.hr	Croatia/Hrvatska
.ht	Haiti
.hu	Hungary
.id	Indonesia
.ie	Ireland
.il	Israel
.im	Isle of Man
.in	India
.io	British Indian Ocean Territory
.iq	Iraq

Abbreviation	Country
.ir	Iran (Islamic Republic of)
.is	Iceland
.it	Italy
.je	Jersey
.jm	Jamaica
.jo	Jordan
.jp	Japan
.ke	Kenya
.kg	Kyrgyzstan
.kh	Cambodia
.ki	Kiribati
.km	Comoros
.kn	Saint Kitts and Nevis
.kp	Korea, Democratic People's Republic of
.kr	Korea, Republic of
.kw	Kuwait
.ky	Cayman Islands
.kz	Kazakhstan
.la	Lao People's Democratic Republic
.lb	Lebanon
.lc	Saint Lucia
.li	Liechtenstein
.lk	Sri Lanka
.lr	Liberia
.ls	Lesotho
.lt	Lithuania
.lu	Luxembourg
.lv	Latvia
.ly	Libyan Arab Jamahiriya
.ma	Morocco
.mc	Monaco
.md	Moldova, Republic of
.mg	Madagascar
.mh	Marshall Islands
.mk	Macedonia, Former Yugoslav Republic of
.ml	Mali
.mm	Myanmar
.mn	Mongolia
.mo	Macau
.mp	Northern Mariana Islands
.mq	Martinique
.mr	Mauritania
.ms	Montserrat
.mt	Malta

Abbreviation	Country
.mu	Mauritius
.mv	Maldives
.mw	Malawi
.mx	Mexico
.my	Malaysia
.mz	Mozambique
.na	Namibia
.nc	New Caledonia
.ne	Niger
.nf	Norfolk Island
.ng	Nigeria
.ni	Nicaragua
.nl	Netherlands
.no	Norway
.np	Nepal
.nr	Nauru
.nu	Niue
.nz	New Zealand
.om	Oman
.pa	Panama
.pe	Peru
.pf	French Polynesia
.pg	Papua New Guinea
.ph	Philippines
.pk	Pakistan
.pl	Poland
.pm	St. Pierre and Miquelon
.pn	Pitcairn Island
.pr	Puerto Rico
.ps	Palestinian Territories
.pt	Portugal
.pw	Palau
.py	Paraguay
.qa	Qatar
.re	Reunion Island
.ro	Romania
.rs	Serbia
.ru	Russian Federation
.rw	Rwanda
.sa	Saudi Arabia
.sb	Solomon Islands
.sc	Seychelles
.sd	Sudan
.se	Sweden

Abbreviation	Country
.sg	St. Helena
.si	Slovenia
.sj	Svalbard and Jan Mayen Islands
.sk	Slovak Republic
.sl	Sierra Leone
.sm	San Marino
.sn	Senegal
.so	Somalia
.sr	Suriname
.st	São Tomé and Principe
.sv	El Salvador
.sy	Syrian Arab Republic
.sz	Swaziland
.tc	Turks and Caicos Islands
.td	Chad
.tf	French Southern Territories
.tg	Togo
.th	Thailand
.tj	Tajikistan
.tk	Tokelau
.tm	Turkmenistan
.tn	Tunisia
.to	Tongo
.tp	East Timor
.tr	Turkey
.tt	Trinidad and Tobago
.tv	Tuvalu
.tw	Taiwan
.tz	Tanzania
.ua	Ukraine
.ug	Uganda
.uk	United Kingdom
.um	US Minor Outlying Islands
.us	United States
.uy	Uruguay
.uz	Uzbekistan
.va	Holy See (Vatican City State)
.vc	Saint Vincent and the Grenadines
.ve	Venezuela
.vg	Virgin Islands (British)
.vi	Virgin Islands (USA)
.vn	Vietnam
.vu	Vanuatu
.wf	Wallis and Futuna Islands

Abbreviation	Country
.ws	Samoa
.ye	Yemen
.yt	Mayotte
.yu	Yugoslavia
.za	South Africa
.zm	Zambia
.zw	Zimbabwe

Invertebrates

3 letters:
Lug

4 letters:
Clam
Cone
Kina
Pipi
Worm

5 letters:
Ameba
Bardi
Bardy
Coral
Cunje
Gaper
Leech
Polyp
Squid
Ugari

6 letters:
Amoeba
Bardie
Chiton
Cockle
Cuttle
Mussel
Oyster
Quahog
Sea mat
Sea pen
Sponge

Tellin
Teredo

7 letters:
Bivalve
Blubber
Catworm
Crinoid
Daphnia
Decapod
Eelworm
Lobworm
Lugworm
Mollusc
Octopus
Piddock
Ragworm
Rotifer
Scallop
Sea lily
Sea wasp
Sunstar
Trepang
Tubifex

8 letters:
Ammonite
Annelida
Argonaut
Bryozoan
Clamworm
Cunjevoi
Echinoid
Gapeworm

Lancelet
Lungworm
Milleped
Nautilus
Parazoan
Pauropod
Pumpworm
Red coral
Sandworm
Sea mouse
Shipworm
Starfish
Tapeworm
Tube worm
Whipworm
White cat
Zoophyte

9 letters:
Amphioxus
Anthozoan
Arrowworm
Arthropod
Belemnite
Brandling
Centipede
Clabby-doo
Clappy-doo
Comb jelly
Cone shell
Devilfish
Earthworm
Gastropod
Hard-shell

Hydrozoan
Jellyfish
Lamp shell
Millepede
Millipede
Peritrich
Poriferan
Razor clam
Round clam
Roundworm
Sea slater
Sea squirt
Sea urchin
Soft-shell
Trilobite
Tusk shell
Water bear
Wheatworm
White worm
Woodborer

10 letters:
Animalcule
Balmain bug
Bêche-de-mer
Bluebottle
Brachiopod
Ctenophore
Cuttlefish
Echinoderm
Euripterid
Eurypterid
Gasteropod
Graptolite

Guinea worm
Horseleech
Liver fluke
Otter shell
Paddle worm
Protostome
Razor-shell
Scyphozoan
Sea anemone
Seed oyster
Stony coral
Tardigrade
Tooth shell
Venus shell
Vinegar eel
Water louse

11 letters:
Animalculum
Bladder worm
Bluff oyster

Feather star
Globigerina
Sea cucumber
Stomach worm
Vinegar worm
Water slater

12 letters:
Box jellyfish
Chicken louse
Gastropodart
Onychophoran
Trochelminth
Venus's-girdle

13 letters:
Crown-of-thorns
Hard-shell clam
Paper nautilus
Precious coral
Soft-shell clam

Water measurer

14 letters:
Pearly nautilus

15 letters:
Coat-of-mail shell

16 letters:
Water stick insect

17 letters:
Blue-ringed octopus
Chambered nautilus

18 letters:
Portuguese man-of-war
Venus's flower basket

21 letters:
Crown-of-thorns starfish

See also:
➤ **Insects** ➤ **Shellfish** ➤ **Snails, slugs, and other gastropods**
➤ **Spiders and other arachnids** ➤ **Worms**

Islands and island groups

2 letters:	**4 letters:**	Fair	Malé	Uist
TT	Amoy	Fiji	Maui	Ulva
	Aran	Guam	Mazu	Unst
3 letters:	Arru	Heat	Mona	Wake
Aru	Attu	Herm	Motu	Yell
Cos	Bali	Holy	Muck	
Diu	Biak	Hova	Mull	**5 letters:**
Fyn	Bute	Idse	Niue	Aland
Hoy	Calf	Iona	Oahu	Apple
Kos	Cebú	Java	Rhum	Arran
Man	Coll	Jolo	Rona	Aruba
May	Cook	Jura	Ross	Banka
Rat	Cuba	Keos	Saba	Banks
Rum	Dogs	King	Sark	Barra
Sea	Eigg	Line	Seil	Batan
Yap	Elba	Long	Skye	Belau
	Erin	Mahé	Truk	Belle

Bioko	Nauru	Banaba	Leucas	St. John
Bohol	Naxos	Bangka	Leukas	Stroma
Bonin	Nevis	Barrow	Levkás	Summer
Caldy	North	Bikini	Lipari	Tahiti
Canna	Oland	Borneo	Lizard	Taiwan
Capri	Ormuz	Bounty	Lombok	Thanet
Ceram	Panay	Butung	Madura	Thásos
Cheju	Páros	Caicos	Majuro	Tobago
Chios	Pemba	Canary	Marajó	Tresco
Clare	Qeshm	Canvey	Mercer	Tubuai
Cocos	Qishm	Cayman	Mersea	Tuvalu
Coney	Reil's	Ceylon	Midway	Unimak
Coral	Rhode	Chiloé	Negros	Ushant
Corfu	Samar	Cyprus	Ogygia	Veneti
Crete	Samoa	Devil's	Orkney	Virgin
Delos	Samos	Diomed	Paphos	Walney
Disko	Saria	Djerba	Patmos	
Ellis	Seram	Easter	Penang	**7 letters:**
Faial	South	Ellice	Pharos	Aeolian
Farne	Spice	Euboea	Philae	Aldabra
Faroe	Sumba	Flores	Pladdy	Amboina
Fayal	Sunda	Fraser	Ponape	Andaman
Foula	Thera	Hainan	Quemoy	Antigua
Funen	Thule	Harris	Raasay	Austral
Gigha	Timor	Hawaii	Ramsey	Bahamas
Haiti	Tiree	Hobart	Rhodes	Baranof
Handa	Tombo	Honshu	Rialto	Barbuda
Ibiza	Tonga	Hormuz	Rjukyu	Bardsey
Islay	Turks	Icaria	Robben	Basilan
Isola	Upolu	Imbros	Ryukyu	Battery
Jerba	Whale	Indies	Safety	Bedloe's
Kauai	White	Insula	Saipan	Bermuda
Kiska	Wight	Ionian	Saltee	Bonaire
Kuril	Youth	Ischia	Savaii	British
Lanai	Zante	Ithaca	Scilly	Cartier
Lewis		Jersey	Scyros	Celebes
Leyte	**6 letters:**	Kiushu	Sicily	Channel
Longa	Achill	Kodiak	Skerry	Chatham
Luing	Aegean	Kosrae	Skomer	Cipango
Lundy	Aegina	Kurile	Skyros	Corsica
Luzon	Amager	Kyushu	Snares	Crannog
Maewo	Andros	Labuan	Soemba	Curaçao
Malta	Avalon	Laputa	Soenda	Cythera
Matsu	Azores	Lemnos	Staffa	Diomede
Melos	Baffin	Lesbos	Staten	Emerald

Eriskay
Faeroes
Falster
Flannan
Frisian
Fur Seal
Gambier
Gilbert
Gotland
Grenada
Hawaiki
Hayling
Heimaey
Howland
Iceland
Ireland
Iwo Jima
Jamaica
Kerrera
Laaland
La Palma
Leeward
Liberty
Lismore
Lofoten
Lolland
Madeira
Majorca
Masbate
Mayotte
Mindoro
Minorca
Molokai
Moreton
Mykonos
Nicobar
Norfolk
Oceania
Okinawa
Orcades
Orkneys
Palawan
Palmyra
Phoenix
Rathlin

Réunion
Roanoke
Rockall
Salamis
San Juan
Sao Tomé
Scalpay
Sheppey
Shikoku
Skikoku
Society
Socotra
Solomon
St. Croix
Stewart
St. Kilda
St. Kitts
St. Lucia
Sumatra
Sumbawa
Surtsey
Tenedos
Tokelau
Tortola
Tortuga
Tuamotu
Tutuila
Vanuatu
Visayan
Volcano
Waihake
Western
Wrangel
Zealand
Zetland

8 letters:
Alcatraz
Alderney
Aleutian
Anglesey
Anguilla
Antilles
Atlantis
Auckland

Balearic
Barbados
Bathurst
Billiton
Blefuscu
Bora Bora
Bornholm
Canaries
Caroline
Catalina
Choiseul
Colonsay
Cyclades
Dominica
Falkland
Farquhar
Flinders
Foulness
Friendly
Gothland
Gottland
Guernsey
Hamilton
Hebrides
Hokkaido
Hong Kong
Jan Mayen
Kangaroo
Kermadec
Krakatau
Krakatoa
Ladrones
Lavongai
Lilliput
Lord Howe
Luggnagg
Mackinac
Mainland
Maldives
Mallorca
Marianas
Marquesa
Marshall
Melville
Mindanao

Miquelon
Moluccas
Mustique
Pelagian
Pitcairn
Portland
Pribilof
Principe
Sakhalin
Sardinia
Schouten
Shetland
Sjælland
Skokholm
Soembawa
Somerset
Sporades
Sri Lanka
St. Helena
St. Martin
Sulawesi
Sverdrup
Tasmania
Tenerife
Terceira
Thousand
Thursday
Trinidad
Tsushima
Unalaska
Venetian
Victoria
Viti Levu
Windward
Zanzibar

9 letters:
Admiralty
Alexander
Andreanof
Anticosti
Antipodes
Ascension
Barataria
Benbecula

Calf of Man
Chichagof
Christmas
Elephanta
Ellesmere
Falklands
Fortunate
Galápagos
Governors
Greenland
Hainan Tao
Halmahera
Innisfree
Jamestown
Kerguelen
Lampedusa
Lanzarote
Macquarie
Manhattan
Margarita
Marquesas
Mascarene
Mauritius
Melanesia
Nantucket
New Guinea
North Uist
Polynesia
Rangitoto
Rarotonga
Runnymede
Sao Miguel
Shetlands
Singapore
Sjaelland
South Uist
Stromboli
St. Tudwal's
St. Vincent
Teneriffe
Trobriand
Vancouver
Vanua Levu
Walcheren

10 letters:
Basse-Terre
Bermoothes
Campobello
Cape Breton
Cephalonia
Corregidor
Dodecanese
Formentera
Grand Manan
Grand Terre
Grenadines
Heligoland
Hispaniola
Isle Royale
Kiritimati
Langerhans
Madagascar
Manitoulin
Marinduque
Martinique
Micronesia
Montserrat
New Britain
New Georgia
New Ireland
Pescadores
Samothrace
Seychelles
Three Kings
West Indies
Whitsunday

11 letters:
Dry Tortugas
Florida Keys
Glubdubdrib
Grand Bahama
Grand Canary
Grande-Terre
Guadalcanal
Lakshadweep
Lindisfarne
Mount Desert
New Siberian

Pantelleria
Philippines
Poor Knights
San Salvador
Southampton
South Orkney
Spitsbergen

12 letters:
Bougainville
Cassiterides
Glubbdubdrib
Greater Sunda
Marie Galante
New Caledonia
Newfoundland
Nusa Tenggara
Prince Edward
San Cristóbal
Santa Barbara
South Georgia
Torres Strait

13 letters:
Espíritu Santo
Forneaux Group
Fuerteventura
Juan Fernández
New Providence
Prince of Wales
Santa Catalina
South Shetland
St. Christopher

14 letters:
D'Entrecasteaux
Franz Josef Land
Lesser Antilles
Lewis and Harris
Queen Charlotte
Queen Elizabeth
Tristan da Cunha
Turks and Caicos
Vestmannaeyjar

15 letters:
Greater Antilles
Lewis with Harris
Wallis and Futuna

16 letters:
French West Indies
Heard and McDonald

17 letters:
Andaman and Nicobar

Fernando de Noronha

19 letters:
Netherlands Antilles

Ivy League universities

4 letters:
Yale

5 letters:
Brown

7 letters:
Cornell

Harvard

8 letters:
Columbia

9 letters:
Princeton

16 letters:
Dartmouth College

24 letters:
University of
 Pennsylvania

Jj

Jackets

3 letters:
Bed
Cag
Mao
Pea
Tux

4 letters:
Baju
Boxy
Bush
Coat
Eton
Flak
Life
Mess
Sack

5 letters:
Acton
Bania
Biker
Cymar
Denim
Duvet
Gilet
Grego
Jupon
Nehru
Parka
Pilot
Polka
Shell
Shrug

Simar
Tunic
Wamus
Water

6 letters:
Amauti
Anorak
Báinín
Banian
Banyan
Basque
Battle
Blazer
Bolero
Bomber
Cagoul
Combat
Dinner
Dolman
Donkey
Jerkin
Kagool
Lumber
Monkey
Reefer
Sacque
Safari
Sports
Strait
Tabard
Tuxedo
Wammus
Wampus

Zouave

7 letters:
Amautik
Barbour®
Blouson
Cagoule
Doublet
Fustian
Hacking
Leather
Mae West
Matinée
Norfolk
Reefing
Simarre
Smoking
Spencer
Vareuse

8 letters:
Camisole
Cardigan
Gambeson
Gendarme
Haqueton
Mackinaw
Mandarin
Tailcoat
Toreador

9 letters:
Habergeon
Hacqueton

Newmarket
Pourpoint
Shortgown
Waistcoat

10 letters:
Body warmer
Bumfreezer

Carmagnole
Fearnought
Hug-me-tight
Windjammer

11 letters:
Afghanistan

Windbreaker®
Windcheater

12 letters:
Lumberjacket
Mackinaw coat

Jazz

JAZZ FORMS

3 letters:
Bop

4 letters:
Free
Scat
Trad

5 letters:
Swing

6 letters:
Modern

7 letters:
Hard bop
Ragtime

8 letters:
Highlife

9 letters:
Afro-Cuban
Dixieland
Gutbucket
West Coast

10 letters:
Mainstream
New Orleans

11 letters:
Barrelhouse
Thirdstream
Traditional

12 letters:
Boogie-woogie
Western swing

JAZZ MUSICIANS

3 letters:
Bix

4 letters:
Getz, *Stanley 'Stan'*
Pine, *Courtney*
Shaw, *Artie*

5 letters:
Basie, *William*
Davis, *Miles (Dewey)*
Haden, *Charles (Edward)*
Tatum, *Art (Arthur Tatum)*

6 letters:
Bechet, *Leon Bismarcke*
Bechet, *Sidney*
Blakey, *Art(hur)*

Garner, *Erroll*
Gordon, *Dexter*
Mingus, *Charles 'Charlie'*
Oliver, *Joseph*
Waller, *Fats (Thomas Waller)*

7 letters:
Brubeck, *Dave*
Coleman, *Ornette*
Hampton, *Lionel*
Hawkins, *Coleman*
Jarrett, *Keith*
Vaughan, *Sarah (Lois)*

8 letters:
Coltrane, *John (William)*
Marsalis, *Wynton*
Peterson, *Oscar (Emmanuel)*

9 letters:
Carpenter, *John Alden*
Christian, *Charlie*
Dankworth, *John (Philip William)*
Grappelli, *Stéphane*
Lyttelton, *Humphrey*

10 letters:
Count Basie
Fitzgerald, *Ella*
King Oliver

JAZZ TERMS

3 letters:
Gig

4 letters:
Band
Cool
Jazz
Jive
Riff
Skin

5 letters:
Combo
Jazzy
Major
Minor
Sound
Stomp
Swing

Vocal

6 letters:
Hepcat
Jazz up
Number
Vibist

7 letters:
Bassist
Big band
Hipster
Jug band
Sideman
Stomper

8 letters:
Slap bass
Vocalist

9 letters:
Augmented
Jitterbug
Mouldy fig
Ring-shout
Saxophone

10 letters:
Added sixth
Diminished
Jam session
Ninth chord
Vibraphone

13 letters:
Eleventh chord

15 letters:
Thirteenth chord

Jewish denominations and sects

7 letters:
Zionism

8 letters:
Hasidism

9 letters:
Chasidism

Hassidism

10 letters:
Chassidism

13 letters:
Reform Judaism

14 letters:
Liberal Judaism

15 letters:
Orthodox Judaism

19 letters:
Conservative Judaism

Judges

3 letters:
Ito, *Lance A(llan)*

4 letters:
Coke, *Sir Edward*
More, *Sir Thomas*

5 letters:
Draco
Judge, *Baron Igor*
Solon

Woolf, *Lord Henry*

6 letters:
Gideon
Holmes, *Oliver Wendell*
Hutton, *Lord (James) Brian (Edward)*
Irvine, *Lord Alexander*
Mackay, *Lord James*
Warren, *Earl*

7 letters:
Birkett, *Sir Norman*
Deborah
De Burgh, *Hubert*
Denning, *Lord Alfred*
Jephtha
Pickles, *James*
Roy Bean
Solomon

8 letters:
Falconer, *Lord Charles*
Hailsham, *Viscount Quintin McGarel Hogg*
Jeffreys, *Lord George*
Lawrence, *Sir Geoffrey*
Marshall, *Thurgood*

9 letters:
Judge Judy

10 letters:
Elwyn-Jones, *Lord Frederick*

13 letters:
Judge 'Joe' Dredd
Pontius Pilate

Kk

Kings

2 letters:
ER
Og

3 letters:
Asa
Ine
Lir
Log
Lud
Roi
Zog

4 letters:
Agag
Agis
Ahab
Brut
Ceyx
Cnut
Cole
Edwy
Fahd
Jehu
Lear
Nudd
Numa
Offa
Olaf
Rema
Saul

5 letters:
Asoka
Balak

Brute
Creon
Cyrus
David
Edgar
Edwin
Gyges
Henry
Herod
Hiram
Idris
Ixion
James
Lludd
Louis
Midas
Minos
Mpret
Ninus
Oscar
Penda
Priam
Rufus
Uther

6 letters:
Aegeus
Alfred
Alonso
Amasis
Arthur
Attila
Baliol
Brutus
Canute

Caspar
Casper
Cheops
Clovis
Darius
Duncan
Edmund
Egbert
Faisal
Farouk
Fergus
George
Harald
Harold
Hassan
Hyksos
Letsie
Lucomo
Ludwig
Memnon
Mswati
Nestor
Oberon
Ogyges
Oswald
Paphos
Philip
Ramses
Rhesus
Robert
Rudolf
Xerxes

7 letters:
Acestes

Baldwin
Balliol
Beowulf
Busiris
Caradoc
Casimir
Cecrops
Croesus
Elidure
Evander
Kenneth
Macbeth
Malcolm
Oedipus
Ptolemy
Pyrrhus
Rameses
Richard
Servius
Solomon
Stephen
Tarquin
Umberto
William

8 letters:
Abdullah
Cambyses
Cophetua
Endymion
Ethelred
Hezekiah
Jereboam
Jonathan
Leonidas

Melchior
Menander
Menelaus
Milesius
Odysseus
Rehoboam
Tantalus
Thyestes
Tigranes
Waldener
Zedekiah

9 letters:
Agamemnon
Ahasuerus
Alexander
Atahualpa
Athelstan
Balthazar
Bretwalda
Brian Boru
Conchobar
Cunobelin

Cymbeline
Ethelbert
Ferdinand
Florestan
Frederick
Gargantua
Pygmalion
Ras Tafari
Tarquinus
Theodoric
Vortigern
Wenceslas

10 letters:
Belshazzar
Cadwaladar
Caractacus
Maximilian
Ozymandias
Wenceslaus

11 letters:
Charlemagne

George Tupou
Hardicanute
Jehoshaphat
John Balliol
Mithridates
Sennacherib

12 letters:
Ashurbanipal
Wayland Smith

13 letters:
Chulalongkorn
Servius Tullus

14 letters:
Nebuchadnezzar
Robert the Bruce
Tigrath-pileser
Uther Pendragon

18 letters:
Gruffydd ap Llywelyn

Kitchen equipment

3 letters:
Aga®
Pot
Wok

4 letters:
Fork
Olla
Oven

5 letters:
Grill
Knife
Ladle
Mould
Ricer
Sieve
Spoon
Whisk

6 letters:
Barbie
Cooker
Girdle
Grater
Juicer
Kettle
Masher
Peeler
Scales
Tagine
Teapot

7 letters:
Blender
Cake tin
Chip pan
Flan tin
Griddle

Loaf tin
Poacher
Ramekin
Skillet
Spatula
Spurtle
Steamer
Tandoor
Timbale
Toaster

8 letters:
Barbecue
Colander
Egg whisk
Icing bag
Jelly bag
Pot-au-feu
Saucepan

Strainer
Teaspoon

9 letters:
Bain-marie
Cafetiere
Casserole
Coffeepot
Corkscrew
Egg beater
Fish slice
Frying pan
Gravy boat
Mandoline
Mezzaluna
Microwave
Sauce boat
Tin-opener

10 letters:
Baking tray
Bread knife
Chopsticks
Liquidizer
Mixing bowl
Nutcracker
Pepper mill
Percolator
Rolling pin
Rotisserie
Tablespoon
Tenderizer

11 letters:
Cooling rack

Wooden spoon

12 letters:
Bottle opener
Carving knife
Deep fat fryer
Dessertspoon
Double boiler
Measuring jug
Pastry cutter
Toasting fork

13 letters:
Chopping board
Coffee grinder
Food processor

Ice-cream maker
Lemon squeezer
Microwave oven

14 letters:
Double saucepan
Juice extractor

15 letters:
Fan-assisted oven
Mortar and pestle

17 letters:
Batterie de cuisine

Knights

3 letters:
Kay

4 letters:
Bors

5 letters:
Guyon
Pinel

6 letters:
Bliant
Cambel
Gareth
Gawain
Lionel

Melius
Modred
Ritter

7 letters:
Accolon
Artegal
Caradoc
Galahad
Launfal
Orlando
Paladin
Tristan

8 letters:
Alphagus

Banneret
Bedivere
Calidore
Lancelot
Maecenas
Palmerin
Parsifal
Perceval
Percival
Tristram
Vavasour

9 letters:
Aguecheek
Britomart

Caballero
Launcelot
Lochinvar
Lohengrin
Pharamond
Valvassor

10 letters:
Don Quixote
Tannhauser

11 letters:
Perceforest

Knitting stitches

3 letters:
Box
Rib

4 letters:
Moss
Purl

Seed
Slip

5 letters:
Cable

6 letters:
Garter

7 letters:
Layette

8 letters:
Pavilion
Stocking

9 letters:
Garter rib

10 letters:
Double moss
Double seed
Mistake rib

Knots

3 letters:
Bow
Tie

4 letters:
Bend
Flat
Loop
Love
Mesh
Reef
Slip
Wale
Wall

5 letters:
Hitch
Mouse
Picot
Quipu
Thumb
Water

6 letters:
Clinch
French
Granny
Lover's
Prusik
Shroud
Square

Moss panels

11 letters:
Diagonal rib

7 letters:
Barrell
Bowknot
Bowline
Cat's paw
Crochet
Diamond
Gordian
Rosette
Running
Sailor's
Windsor

8 letters:
Hangman's
Overhand
Slipknot
Surgeon's
Truelove

9 letters:
Bowstring
Half-hitch
Sheet bend
Swab hitch
Turk's-head

10 letters:
Becket bend
Clove hitch
Fisherman's

Roman stripe

13 letters:
Fisherman's rib

Girth hitch
Hawser bend
Monkey fist
Sheepshank
Stevedore's
Truelover's

11 letters:
Carrick bend
Englishman's
Magnus hitch
Timber hitch

12 letters:
Harness hitch
Rolling hitch
Weaver's hitch

13 letters:
Figure of eight
Matthew Walker
Slippery hitch

14 letters:
Blackwall hitch
Englishman's tie
Fisherman's bend
Running bowline

LI

Lakes, lochs and loughs

2 letters:
No

3 letters:
Ard
Awe
Ewe
Tay
Van
Zug

4 letters:
Bala
Biel
Bled
Chad
Como
Earn
Erie
Erne
Eyre
Fyne
Kivu
Mead
Ness
Nyos
Taal
Tana
Thun
Tien

5 letters:
Allen
Atlin
Cowan

Frome
Garda
Gatún
Huron
Ilmen
Léman
Leven
Lochy
Lower
Malar
Meech
Morar
Mungo
Mweru
Myall
Nam Co
Neagh
Nyasa
Onega
Patos
Playa
Poopó
Pskov
Sevan
Sween
Tahoe
Taupo
Tsana
Urmia
Volta

6 letters:
Albert
Annecy
Argyle

Averno
Baikal
Barlee
Bitter
Broads
Cayuga
Corrib
Edward
Geneva
George
Kariba
Ladoga
Laggan
Linnhe
Lomond
Lugano
Malawi
Miveru
Mobutu
Nakuru
Nam Tso
Nasser
Natron
Oneida
Peipus
P'o-yang
Rudolf
Saimaa
Te Anau
Tekapo
Tummel
Vanern
Wanaka
Zürich

7 letters:
Amadeus
Aral Sea
Avernus
Axolotl
Balaton
Balqash
Belfast
Dead Sea
Iliamna
Kara Kul
Katrine
Koko Nor
Kuku Nor
Lucerne
Managua
Nipigon
Ontario
Rannoch
Rotorua
Toronto
Torrens
Turkana

8 letters:
Balkhash
Bodensee
Carnegie
Dongting
Gairdner
Grasmere
Issyk-Kul
Kootenay
Lake Aral
Maggiore

Manitoba
Menindee
Menteith
Michigan
Naumachy
Okanagan
Onondaga
Regillus
Reindeer
Rosebery
Superior
Titicaca
Tonle Sap
Torridon
Veronica
Victoria
Wakatipu
Wanawaka
Winnipeg

9 letters:
Athabasca
Athabaska
Bangweulu
Champlain
Constance
Ennerdale
Everglade
Great Bear
Great Salt
Innisfree

Killarney
Macquarie
Manapouri
Maracaibo
Naumachia
Neuchâtel
Nicaragua
Nipissing
Qinghai Hu
Saint John
Serbonian
Thirlmere
Trasimeno
Ullswater
Wairarapa
Wast Water
Winnebago
Ysselmeer

10 letters:
Buttermere
Caspian Sea
Clearwater
Great Lakes
Great Slave
Hawes Water
Ijsselmeer
Malabo Pool
Miraflores
Mistassini
Okeechobee

Okefenokee
Saint Clair
Serpentine
Tanganyika
Washington
Windermere

11 letters:
Great Bitter
Lesser Slave
Stanley Pool

12 letters:
Derwentwater
Little Bitter
Memphremagog
Sea of Galilee
Waikaremoana

13 letters:
Bassenthwaite
Coniston Water
Crummock Water
Pontchartrain

14 letters:
Disappointment
Ennerdale Water
Lake of the Woods

Languages

AFRICAN LANGUAGES

2 letters:	Twi	Igbo	**5 letters:**
Ga		Krio	Bemba
Gã	**4 letters:**	Lozi	Chewa
	Akan	Luba	Duala
3 letters:	Beni	Nama	Dyula
Edo	Bini	Nuba	Fanti
Ewe	Efik	Nupe	Fulah
Ibo	Fang	Pedi	Galla
Luo	Fula	Susu	Ganda
Tiv	Hutu	Zulu	Hausa

Kongo
Masai
Moore
Mossi
Nyoro
Pondo
Sango
Shona
Sotho
Swazi
Temne
Tigré
Tonga
Venda
Wolof
Xhosa

6 letters:
Berber
Coptic
Damara
Fulani
Grikwa
Griqua
Herero
Ibibio
Kabyle
Kikuyu
Nyanja
Ovambo
Rwanda
Somali
Tsonga
Tswana
Tuareg

Yoruba

7 letters:
Adamawa
Amharic
Ashanti
Bambara
Barotse
Bashkir
Kirundi
Luganda
Malinke
Maninke
Namaqua
Ndebele
Sesotho
Songhai
Swahili

8 letters:
Chichewa
Fanagalo
Fanakalo
Kingwana
Malagasy
Matabele
Tigrinya
Tshiluba

9 letters:
Afrikaans
Hottentot

13 letters:
Northern Sotho

ASIAN LANGUAGES

3 letters:
Lao
Mon

4 letters:
Ainu
Cham
Moro
Naga
Nuri
Shan
Thai
Urdu

5 letters:
Dinka
Farsi
Gondi
Hindi
Karen
Kazak
Khmer
Malay
Oriya
Tamil

Tatar
Uigur
Uzbek
Yakut

6 letters:
Abkhaz
Adygei
Adyghe
Afghan
Arabic
Bihari
Brahui
Buriat
Buryat
Divehi
Evenki
Hebrew
Kafiri
Kalmyk
Kazakh
Korean
Lahnda
Lepcha
Manchu

Mishmi
Mongol
Nepali
Ostyak
Pashto
Pushto
Pushtu
Sindhi
Telegu
Telugu
Tungus
Uighur

7 letters:
Abkhazi
Aramaic
Balochi
Baluchi
Bengali
Burmese
Chinese
Chukchi
Chuvash
Dzongka
Iranian

Kalmuck
Kannada
Khalkha
Kirghiz
Kurdish
Marathi
Ossetic
Punjabi
Sogdian
Tadzhik
Tagalog
Tibetan
Turkman
Turkmen

8 letters:
Armenian
Assamese
Balinese
Canarese
Chukchee
Filipino
Gujarati
Gujerati
Gurkhali

Japanese
Javanese
Kanarese
Kashmiri
Mahratti
Mandarin
Ossetian
Tadzhiki
Turkoman

9 letters:
Abkhazian

Cantonese
Kabardian
Malayalam
Mongolian
Sinhalese

10 letters:
Circassian
Hindostani
Hindustani
Kara-Kalpak
Kazan Tatar

Malayalaam
Vietnamese

11 letters:
Azerbaijani
Hindoostani

15 letters:
Bahasa Indonesia

AUSTRALASIAN LANGUAGES

4 letters:
Krio
Motu

5 letters:
Dinka
Māori

6 letters:
Aranda
Fijian
Papuan
Samoan

Tongan

7 letters:
Moriori
Nauruan
Pintubi

8 letters:
Gurindji
Hawaiian
Hiri Motu
Tuvaluan
Warlpiri

9 letters:
Kamilaroi

10 letters:
Beach-la-Mar
Police Motu

13 letters:
Neo-Melanesian

20 letters:
Solomon Islands Pidgin

EUROPEAN LANGUAGES

4 letters:
Erse
Komi
Lapp
Manx

5 letters:
Czech
Dutch
Greek
Ladin
Vogul
Welsh

6 letters:
Basque
Bokmål
Breton
Cymric
Danish
French
Gaelic
German
Kymric
Ladino
Lallan
Magyar
Polish
Romany

Shelta
Slovak
Udmurt
Votyak
Zyrian

7 letters:
Catalan
Cornish
English
Finnish
Flemish
Frisian
Gagauzi
Italian

Lallans
Latvian
Lettish
Maltese
Mingrel
Mordvin
Nynorsk
Romanes
Romansh
Russian
Samoyed
Slovene
Sorbian
Spanish
Swedish

Turkish
Yiddish

8 letters:
Albanian
Bohemian
Cheremis
Croatian
Estonian
Faeroese
Friulian
Galician
Georgian
Karelian
Landsmål

Lusatian
Romanian
Romansch

9 letters:
Alemannic
Bulgarian
Castilian
Cheremiss
Hungarian
Icelandic
Norwegian
Provençal
Sardinian
Ukrainian

10 letters:
Lithuanian
Macedonian
Mingrelian
Portuguese
Serbo-Croat

12 letters:
Byelorussian

13 letters:
Serbo-Croatian

NORTH AMERICAN LANGUAGES

3 letters:
Fox
Ute

4 letters:
Crow
Erie
Hopi
Zuñi

5 letters:
Aleut
Creek
Haida
Huron
Osage
Piute
Sioux
Taino

6 letters:
Abnaki
Apache
Cayuga
Eskimo
Micmac
Mixtec
Mohave

Mohawk
Mojave
Navaho
Navajo
Nootka
Ojibwa
Oneida
Paiute
Pawnee
Pequot
Seneca

7 letters:
Arapaho
Caddoan
Catawba
Chinook
Choctaw
Mahican
Mohican
Shawnee
Tahltan
Tlingit

8 letters:
Aleutian
Algonkin
Cherokee

Cheyenne
Comanche
Delaware
Iroquois
Kwakiutl
Menomini
Nez Percé
Okanagan
Okanogan
Okinagan
Onondaga
Sahaptan
Sahaptin
Seminole
Shoshone
Shoshoni

9 letters:
Algonquin
Blackfoot
Chickasaw
Inuktitut
Sahaptian
Tuscarora
Winnebago

11 letters:
Assiniboine

Massachuset
Narraganset

12 letters:
Narragansett

13 letters:
Massachusetts

SOUTH AMERICAN LANGUAGES

4 letters:
Tupi

6 letters:
Aymara
Galibi
Kechua

7 letters:
Guarani
Nahuatl
Quechua
Quichua
Zapotec

8 letters:
Chibchan

10 letters:
Araucanian

ANCIENT LANGUAGES

4 letters:
Avar
Ge'ez
Inca
Maya
Norn
Pali

5 letters:
Aztec
Ionic
Koine
Latin
Mayan
Oscan
Punic
Vedic

6 letters:
Gothic
Hebrew
Libyan
Lycian
Lydian
Sabean
Syriac

7 letters:
Avestan
Avestic
Chaldee
Edomite

Elamite
Hittite
Pahlavi
Pehlevi
Pictish
Sabaean
Umbrian
Venetic
Wendish

8 letters:
Akkadian
Assyrian
Egyptian
Ethiopic
Etruscan
Faliscan
Frankish
Illyrian
Messapïc
Old Norse
Phrygian
Sanskrit
Scythian
Sumerian
Thracian
Ugaritic
Volscian

9 letters:
Canaanite
Langue d'oc

Messapian
Sabellian
Tocharian
Tokharian

10 letters:
Anglo-Saxon
Babylonian
Gallo-Roman
Himyaritic
Langue d'oïl
Phoenician

11 letters:
Celtiberian
Langobardic
Old Prussian
Osso-Umbrian

12 letters:
Ancient Greek
Gallo-Romance

13 letters:
Old High German

14 letters:
Thraco-Phrygian

17 letters:
Old Church Slavonic

ARTIFICIAL LANGUAGES

3 letters:
Ido

7 letters:
Volapuk

Volapük

9 letters:
Esperanto

11 letters:
Interlingua

LANGUAGE GROUPS

3 letters:
Gur
Kwa
San

4 letters:
Nakh
Veps

5 letters:
Bantu
Carib
Gumbo
Indic
Kwadi
Makah
Mande
Mayan
Munda
Ngoni
Nguni
Norse
Punca
Punka
Sintu
Ugric
Yuman

6 letters:
Altaic
Baltic
Celtic
Chadic
Cymric
Dardic
Eskimo

Finnic
Galibi
Inupik
Italic
Jivaro
Macusi
Na-Déné
Pahari
Panoan
Salish
Sherpa
Siouan
Sranan
Turkic
Uralic
Yakama

7 letters:
Caddoan
Euskara
Faroese
Guajiro
Hamitic
Hokkien
Ingrian
Inupiaq
Iranian
Khoisan
Kikapoo
Macushi
Mashona
Nilotic
Occitan
Oceanic
P-Celtic
Persian

Romance
Saharan
Sahrawi
Semitic
Shawnee
Sinitic
Sudanic
Voltaic
Wergaia

8 letters:
Albanian
Arawakan
Armenian
Brittoic
Creolian
Cushitic
Germanic
Hellenic
Kickapoo
Mampruli
Mikasuki
Moldovan
Mongolic
Mon-Khmer
Penutian
Rhaetian
Salishan
Slavonic
Tucanoan
Tungusic
Wakashan

9 letters:
Algonkian
Anatolian

Brythonic
Caucasian
Chari-Nile
Dravidian
Indo-Aryan
Iroquoian
Kartrehan
Muskogean
Semi-Bantu

10 letters:
Algonquian
Athabascan
Athabaskan
Athapascan
Athapaskan
Australian
Benue-Congo
Canaanitic
Halkomelem
Hindustani
Melanesian
Montagnais
Muskhogean
Niger-Congo
Polynesian
Potawatomi
Puna-pipogo
Sanskritic
Shoshonean
Uto-Aztecan
Wemba-wemba

11 letters:
Afro-Asiatic
East Iranian

Hokan-Siouan
Indo-Iranian
Indo-Pacific
Kordofanian
Micronesian
Nilo-Saharan
Oto-Manquean
Pama-Nyungan
Sino-Tibetan
Tupi-Guarani
West Iranian
Yuwaalaraay

12 letters:
Austronesian
East Germanic
Indo-European
Tibeto-Burman
West Atlantic
West Germanic
West Slavonic

13 letters:
Austro-Asiatic
Hamito-Semitic

North Germanic
Semito-Hamitic

15 letters:
Sahaptin-Chinook

16 letters:
Malayo-Polynesian

20 letters:
Trans-New Guinea
 phylum

Law

LAW TERMS

2 letters:
On

3 letters:
Ban
Bar
CAV
Doe
Dot
Jus
Run
Sue
Try
Use

4 letters:
Abet
Able
Aver
Avow
Bail
Bond
Case
Cite
Deed
Eyre
Fact
Feme
File

Find
Flaw
Free
Gist
Hear
Heir
Jury
Land
Lien
Mise
Mute
Nisi
Nude
Oath
Open
Oyer
Plea
Real
Rest
Riot
Rout
Rule
Sign
Sine
Soke
Sole
Suit
Term
Tort

Udal
Upon
User
View
Waif
Ward
Will
Writ

5 letters:
Abate
Adopt
Adult
Agist
Alibi
Array
Avoid
Award
Baron
Bench
Brief
Bring
Cause
Cheat
Chose
Close
Costs
Count
Court

Covin
Culpa
Demur
Devil
Donee
Donor
Dower
Droit
Enter
Estop
Evict
Folio
Grant
Grith
Heres
In fee
In rem
Issue
Joint
Judge
Jural
Jurat
Juror
Lapse
Libel
Limit
Manus
Mesne
Moral

Naked
Novel
Offer
Overt
Panel
Parol
Party
Petit
Petty
Plead
Posse
Privy
Proof
Prove
Pupil
Remit
Reply
Retry
Salvo
Sound
Squat
Stale
Swear
Tales
Tenor
Thing
Title
Trial
Venue
Waive
Waste
Wrong

6 letters:
Abator
Accrue
Accuse
Acquit
Action
Affirm
Affray
Allege
Amerce
Answer
Appeal

Assets
Assign
Attach
Attorn
Bailee
Bailor
Bigamy
Capias
Caveat
Cessor
Charge
Come on
Common
Custom
Cy pres
Decree
Defeat
De jure
Delict
Demand
Depose
Devise
Digest
Disbar
Docket
Domain
Duress
Enjoin
Equity
Escrow
Estray
Extend
Extent
Factor
Fiscal
Forest
Guilty
Haeres
Holder
In banc
Infant
Infirm
Injury
Intent
Junior

Jurist
Laches
Lawyer
Legist
Maihem
Malice
Matter
Mayhem
Merger
Merits
Motion
Nonage
Owelty
Pardon
Plaint
Prayer
Prefer
Queen's
Recoup
Rejoin
Relief
Remand
Remise
Report
Rescue
Retain
Return
Review
Ruling
Saving
Script
Socage
Suitor
Surety
Tender
Termer
Termor
Trover
Vacant
Vacate
Vendee
Vendor
Verify
Versus
Viewer

Waiver

7 letters:
Accused
Ad litem
Affiant
Alienee
Alienor
Alimony
Amnesty
Ancient
Approve
Arraign
Assault
Attaint
Bailiff
Bencher
Bequest
Capital
Caption
Case law
Caution
Circuit
Codicil
Commute
Condemn
Condone
Connive
Convene
Convert
Coroner
Counsel
Cruelty
Culprit
Custody
Damages
Damnify
Default
Defence
Deodand
Deraign
Detinue
Devolve
Dies non
Dismiss

Dissent	Nonsuit	Absolute	Executor
Dowable	Obscene	Act of God	Felo de se
Earnest	Onerous	Advocate	Feme sole
Empanel	Opening	Alienate	Fiducial
Engross	Portion	Alluvion	Forensic
Escheat	Precept	Appellee	Forjudge
Estreat	Presume	Assessor	Fungible
Examine	Privity	Assignee	Gravamen
Execute	Probate	Assignor	Guardian
Exhibit	Proceed	Attorney	Hand down
Ex parte	Process	Avulsion	Handling
Fiction	Purview	Bailable	Heirship
Filiate	Recital	Bailment	Heritage
Finding	Recover	Bailsman	Hung jury
Foreign	Relator	Bankrupt	Hypothec
Foreman	Release	Barratry	In camera
Forfeit	Replevy	Barretry	In escrow
Garnish	Residue	Bequeath	Innuendo
Grantee	Reverse	Bondsman	Insanity
Grantor	Scandal	Caveator	In specie
Hearing	Session	Chambers	Instruct
Hearsay	Settlor	Chancery	In venter
Heiress	Several	Citation	Ipso jure
Heritor	Slander	Complete	Issuable
Impanel	Sound in	Compound	Jeopardy
Implead	Stand by	Contempt	Jointure
Ingoing	Succeed	Contract	Judgment
In posse	Summary	Copyhold	Judicial
Inquest	Summons	Covenant	Juratory
Joinder	Suo jure	Darraign	Juristic
Juryman	Suo loco	Dead hand	Law Lords
Jus soli	Swear in	Decedent	Litigant
Justice	Tenancy	Deed poll	Mandamus
Justify	Testate	Demurrer	Material
Larceny	Testify	Deponent	Mistrial
Lawsuit	Triable	Detainer	Mittimus
Law term	Verdict	Disannul	Monopoly
Lex loci	Vesture	Disclaim	Mortmain
Manager	Vitiate	Distrain	Moveable
Mandate	Voucher	Distress	Novation
Mens rea	Warrant	Dividend	Nuisance
Misuser	Witness	Dotation	Oblivion
Movable		Estoppel	Occupant
Nol. pros.	**8 letters:**	Estovers	Ordinary
Non pros.	Abeyance	Evidence	Parcener

Peculium
Personal
Petition
Pleading
Post-obit
Premises
Presents
Promisee
Promisor
Propound
Pursuant
Question
Rebutter
Recorder
Recovery
Relation
Replevin
Reporter
Reprieve
Schedule
Scienter
Sentence
Sergeant
Serjeant
Solatium
Solution
Spinster
Stranger
Stultify
Subpoena
Sui juris
Swear out
Tenantry
Tipstaff
Tortious
Transfer
Traverse
Trespass
Tribunal
Variance
Voidable
Voir dire
Warranty

9 letters:
Abandonee
Accessary
Accessory
Accretion
Adjective
Adminicle
Affidavit
Affiliate
Alienable
Annulment
Appellant
Appellate
Appendant
Arbitrary
Assumpsit
Attainder
Authentic
Authority
Avoidance
Bailiwick
Barrister
Blasphemy
Bona fides
Briefless
Cartulary
Cassation
Challenge
Champerty
Collusion
Committal
Commonage
Common law
Competent
Complaint
Condition
Contumacy
Coparceny
Counselor
Coverture
Criminate
Custodian
Customary
Debatable
Declarant

Defalcate
Defendant
Demandant
Desertion
Determine
Devisable
Diligence
Disaffirm
Discharge
Discommon
Discovert
Discovery
Disforest
Distraint
Effectual
Equitable
Evocation
Exception
Execution
Executory
Executrix
Exemplify
Extradite
Fiduciary
Filiation
Foreclose
Forejudge
Garnishee
Gavelkind
Grand jury
Guarantee
Heritable
Immovable
Imperfect
Indemnity
Indenture
Instanter
Intention
Interdict
Intervene
Intestate
Jointress
Judge-made
Judgement
Judicable

Judiciary
Juridical
Jurywoman
Law French
Leasehold
Litigable
Mortgagee
Muniments
Nisi prius
Nolle pros.
Non liquet
Not guilty
Obreption
Occupancy
Onomastic
Pecuniary
Petit jury
Petty jury
Plaintiff
Pleadings
Precedent
Prescribe
Principal
Privilege
Proponent
Prosecute
Public law
Pupillage
Quitclaim
Recaption
Re-examine
Reference
Refresher
Rejoinder
Remission
Res gestae
Residuary
Sequester
Servitude
Severable
Severance
Signatory
Sine prole
Solemnity
Solicitor

Specialty
Stand down
Statement
Stipulate
Subrogate
Summation
Summing-up
Surcharge
Surrender
Testament
Testimony
Under oath
Venireman
Vexatious
Vindicate
Voluntary
Volunteer

10 letters:
Absente reo
Acceptance
Accusation
Actionable
Admissible
Advocation
Alienation
Ambulatory
Appearance
Assignment
Attachment
Automatism
Beneficial
Bill of sale
Case stated
Certiorari
Cessionary
Chargeable
Chartulary
Civil death
Coexecutor
Cognisable
Cognisance
Cognizable
Cognizance
Commitment

Commutable
Competence
Competency
Conclusion
Confiscate
Connivance
Consensual
Consortium
Constitute
Contraband
Contractor
Conversion
Conveyance
Convincing
Coparcener
Copyholder
Counsellor
Crown court
Cur. adv. vult
Dead letter
Decree nisi
Defamation
Defeasible
Deposition
Disinherit
Disorderly
Distrainee
Distringas
Emblements
Expectancy
Extinguish
Feme covert
Gratuitous
Ground rent
Hereditary
Homologate
Impartible
Impediment
In articles
Incapacity
In chancery
Inducement
Injunction
In personam
Institutes

Instrument
Intendment
Interplead
Inter vivos
Invalidate
Judicative
Judicatory
Judicature
Jus gentium
Left-handed
Lex scripta
Limitation
Lis pendens
Litigation
Magistrate
Memorandum
Misjoinder
Moratorium
Morganatic
Negligence
Next friend
Nonjoinder
Obligation
Perception
Peremptory
Personalty
Petitioner
Possessory
Predispose
Pre-emption
Preference
Prima facie
Private law
Privileged
Prize court
Proceeding
Propositus
Prosecutor
Recognisee
Recognisor
Recognizee
Recognizor
Repetition
Resolutive
Respondent

Returnable
Secularise
Secularize
Separation
Settlement
Smart money
Spoliation
Stated case
Statute law
Stillicide
Submission
Subreption
Surplusage
Suspension
Third party
Tort-feasor
Trial court
Ultra vires
Unilateral
Vindictive
Wager of law

11 letters:
Affiliation
Affirmation
Arbitration
Beneficiary
Commutation
Complainant
Composition
Constituent
Contentious
Continuance
Coparcenary
Corpus juris
Counterpart
Countersign
County court
Declaration
Declaratory
Dereliction
Descendable
Descendible
Disafforest
Discontinue

Distributee
Disturbance
Encumbrance
Enfranchise
Engrossment
Examination
Expropriate
Fieri facias
Forbearance
Fornication
Garnishment
Hypothecate
Incompetent
Incorporeal
Incriminate
Inheritance
Inquisition
Judges' rules
Jury process
Jus naturale
Justiciable
Law merchant
Leaseholder
Lex talionis
Locus standi
Maintenance
Malfeasance
Mare clausum
Mare liberum
Ministerial
Misfeasance
Mispleading
Necessaries
Nonfeasance
Nudum pactum
Port of entry
Presentment
Presumption
Preterition
Procuration
Procuratory
Prohibition
Prosecution
Protonotary
Provocation

Quo warranto
Replication
Reservation
Res judicata
Restitution
Scire facias
Self-defence
Sequestrate
Special case
Subrogation
Substantive
Surrebuttal
Surrebutter
Unalienable
Unavoidable
Ward of court
Year and a day

12 letters:
Accusatorial
Amicus curiae
Bona vacantia
Chance-medley
Chief justice
Codification
Compurgation
Constructive
Contributory
Conventional
Co-respondent
Coroner's jury
Counterclaim
Cross-examine
Denunciation
Determinable
Distribution
Earnest money
Encumbrancer
Extraditable
Force majeure
Grand larceny
Habeas corpus
Incapacitate
Indefeasible
Instructions

Interpleader
Jail delivery
Jurisconsult
Jurisprudent
Jus sanguinis
Justice court
Manslaughter
Misadventure
Notary public
Obiter dictum
Onus probandi
Pendente lite
Petit larceny
Petty larceny
Prescription
Prothonotary
Real property
Receivership
Recognisance
Recognizance
Surrejoinder
Testamentary
Traffic court
Unappealable
Uncovenanted
Unwritten law
Venire facias
Verification

13 letters:
A mensa et thoro
Articled clerk
Attorney-at-law
Body corporate
Breach of trust
Burden of proof
Certification
Change of venue
Civil marriage
Consideration
Consolidation
Corpus delicti
Countercharge
Determination
Documentation

Eminent domain
Extrajudicial
First offender
Inferior court
Inquisitorial
Interlocutory
Irrepleviable
Jurisprudence
Juvenile court
King's evidence
Legal medicine
Lex non scripta
Nolle prosequi
Paraphernalia
Paterfamilias
Paternity suit
Petty sessions
Premeditation
Primogeniture
Probable cause
Process-server
Question of law
Recrimination
Res adjudicata
Right of common
Self-executing
Sequestration
Sergeant at law
Serjeant at law
Treasure-trove

14 letters:
Arrest judgment
Barrister-at-law
Chamber counsel
Counselor-at-law
Decree absolute
Direct evidence
Examine-in-chief
Family Division
Fideicommissum
Irreplevisable
Justices in eyre
Mental disorder
Napoleonic Code

Nolo contendere
Non prosequitur
Plea bargaining
Posse comitatus
Property centre
Public defender
Public nuisance
Question of fact
Representation
State's evidence
Summary offence
Time immemorial
Ultimogeniture
Unincorporated
Utter barrister

15 letters:
Attorney general
Bill of attainder
Breach of promise
Carnal knowledge
Coroner's inquest
Disorderly house
Due process of law
Fideicommissary
Imprescriptable
Interrogatories
Non compos mentis
Official Referee
Oyer and terminer
Private nuisance
Quarter sessions
Res ipsa loquitur
Special pleading
Writ of execution

16 letters:
Affiliation order
Anton Piller order
Bill of indictment
Blasphemous libel
Breach of the peace
Conscience clause
Deferred sentence
Demisit sine prole

Dies non juridicus
Exemplary damages
Flagrante delicto
Forensic medicine
Goods and chattels
Magistrates' court
Mental impairment
Personal property
Public prosecutor
Restraining order
Statement of claim
Territorial court
Transitory action
Unlawful assembly
Without prejudice

17 letters:
Arrest of judgement
Compliance officer
Curia advisari vult
Disorderly conduct
False imprisonment
Insurable interest
Judgment by default
Justice of the peace
Persistent cruelty

18 letters:
Clerk to the justices
Corpus Juris Civilis
Cumulative evidence
In flagrante delicto
Judicial separation
Particulars of Claim
Pecuniary advantage
Place of safety order

19 letters:
Administration order
Challenge to the array
Challenge to the polls
Prosecuting attorney
Restrictive covenant
Specific performance
Summary jurisdiction

20 letters:
Court of first instance
Criminal conversation
Medical jurisprudence
Obtaining by deception
Psychopathic disorder
Statutory declaration
Voluntary arrangement

21 letters:
Indeterminate sentence
Unreasonable behaviour

22 letters:
Affiliation proceedings
Contributory negligence
Divorce from bed and board

23 letters:
Letters of administration

24 letters:
Diminished responsibility

26 letters:
Certificate of incorporation

LAW SITTINGS

6 letters:	Hilary	**7 letters:**	**10 letters:**
Easter		Trinity	Michaelmas

CRIMINAL LAW TERMS

5 letters:	Felon	Thief	**6 letters:**
Arson	Force	Utter	Felony
Entry	Theft		Suborn

7 letters:
Battery
Embrace
Forgery
Impeach
Perjure
Perjury
Riot Act
Robbery

8 letters:
Bailment
Burglary
Embracer
Infamous
True bill

9 letters:
Acquittal
Deception
Embraceor
Embracery
Felonious
Personate

10 letters:
Hard labour
Indictable
Indictment

12 letters:
Misdemeanant
Misdemeanour

13 letters:
Housebreaking

14 letters:
False pretences
Penal servitude

16 letters:
Actual bodily harm

18 letters:
Grievous bodily harm
Malice aforethought

PROPERTY LAW TERMS

3 letters:
Fee

4 letters:
Oust
Tail

5 letters:
Entry

6 letters:
Assure
Convey
Demise
Divest
Entail
Estate
Ouster
Result
Revert
Seisin
Seizin
Tenure
Vested

7 letters:
Abutter

Adverse
Appoint
Chattel
Deforce
Demesne
Descent
Devisee
Devisor
Enfeoff
Fee tail
Fixture
Heirdom

8 letters:
Abuttals
Amortise
Amortize
Disseise
Dominion
Dominium
Easement
Freehold
Heirloom
Hotchpot
Messuage
Remitter
Riparian

Survivor
Warranty

9 letters:
Abatement
Accession
Ademption
Appointee
Appointor
Disentail
Ejectment
Fee simple
Heir-at-law
Intrusion
Mortgager
Mortgagor
Partition
Party wall
Reconvert
Remainder
Reversion
Severalty

10 letters:
Betterment
Freeholder
Particular

Perpetuity
Transferee
Transferor

11 letters:
Advancement
Appointment
Chattel real
Reversioner
Transferrer

12 letters:
Appurtenance
Dilapidation
Heir apparent
Heriditament
Remainderman

13 letters:
Administrator

14 letters:
Administration
Vested interest

15 letters:
Abstract of title
Chattel personal
Unity of interest

16 letters:
Dominant tenement

Servient tenement

18 letters:
Equity of redemption
Power of appointment

SCOTS LAW TERMS

3 letters:
Feu

5 letters:
Agent
Poind
Pupil
Tutor

6 letters:
Assize
Decern
Delict
Depone
Desert
Fiscal
Notour
Repone
Sasine
Wadset

7 letters:
Aliment
Curator
Decreet
Feu duty
Mandate

8 letters:
Advocate
Continue
Defender
Hypothec
Law agent
Location
Lockfast
Poinding
Thirlage

9 letters:
Approbate
Avizandum
Interdict
Not proven
Tradition

10 letters:
Alimentary
Arrestment
Crown agent
Declarator
Repetition

11 letters:
Assignation

Fire raising
Sequestrate
Warrant sale

12 letters:
Interlocutor
Precognition

13 letters:
District court

14 letters:
Advocate Depute
Condescendence
Notour bankrupt
Sheriff officer

16 letters:
Culpable homicide
Multiplepoinding
Procurator fiscal

21 letters:
Approbate and reprobate

22 letters:
Justice of the peace court

Leather

3 letters:
Kid
Kip

4 letters:
Buff
Calf
Cuir
Hide

Napa
Roan
Yuft

5 letters:
Mocha
Nappa
Suede

6 letters:
Corium
Deacon
Levant
Nubuck®
Oxhide
Patent
Rexine®
Russia
Shammy

7 letters:
Box-calf

Chamois
Cowhide
Dogskin
Hog-skin
Kip-skin
Morocco
Pigskin
Rawhide
Saffian

8 letters:
Buckskin
Cabretta

Capeskin
Cheverel
Cordovan
Cordwain
Deerskin
Marocain
Maroquin
Rough-out
Shagreen

9 letters:
Chevrette
Crocodile

Horsehide
Sharkskin
Sheepskin

10 letters:
Checklaton
Shecklaton

11 letters:
Cuir-bouilli
Whitleather

Lilies

3 letters:
Day

4 letters:
Aloe
Arum
Corn
Lent
Lote
Sego

5 letters:
Calla
Camas
Lotus
Padma
Regal
Tiger
Water
Yucca

6 letters:
Camash
Camass
Canada
Crinum
Easter
Jacob's
Nerine
Nuphar
Smilax
Zephyr

7 letters:
African
Candock
Madonna
Nelumbo
Quamash

8 letters:
Asphodel
Galtonia
Martagon
Nenuphar
Phormium
Plantain
Trillium
Turk's cap
Victoria

9 letters:
Amaryllis
Colchicum
Colocasia
Herb-paris
Kniphofia

10 letters:
Agapanthus

Aspidistra
Belladonna
Fleur de lys
Haemanthus

11 letters:
Convallaria

12 letters:
Annunciation
Hemerocallis
Skunk cabbage
Solomon's seal

14 letters:
Chincherinchee

15 letters:
Star of Bethlehem

Literature

LITERATURE TERMS

2 letters:
SF

4 letters:
Coda

Epic
Myth
Plot
Saga

5 letters:
Beats
Cento
Drama
Essay

Fable
Gloss
Maxim
Motif
Novel

Roman
Story
Theme
Trope
Verse

6 letters:
Bathos
Comedy
Gothic
Legend
Parody
Pathos
Satire
Simile
Sketch
Theory
Thesis

7 letters:
Bombast
Byronic
Chiller
Conceit
Epistle
Epitaph
Erasure
Faction
Fantasy
Homeric
Imagery
Janeite
Joycean
Kenning
Lampoon
Novella
Polemic
Realism
Subplot
Subtext
Tragedy

8 letters:
Allegory
Allusion

Anti-hero
Aphorism
Archaism
Augustan
Causerie
Dialogue
Epilogue
Exegesis
Fabulist
Foreword
Futurism
Horatian
Jacobean
Kailyard
Kiddy lit
Metaphor
Narrator
Oxymoron
Pastiche
Pastoral
Samizdat
Swiftian
Vignette

9 letters:
Amphigory
Antinovel
Anti-roman
Brechtian
Bricolage
Cyberpunk
Decadence
Derridian
Dialectic
Discourse
Gongorism
Hellenism
Invective
Melodrama
Modernism
Narrative
Novelette
Pot-boiler

10 letters:
Amphigouri
Bakhtinian
Belletrist
Ciceronian
Classicism
Denouement
Dickensian
Johnsonian
Journalese
Juvenalian
Kafkaesque
Laurentian
Lawrentian
Mock-heroic
Mythopoeia
Naturalism
Nom de plume
Palindrome
Paraphrase
Picaresque
Plagiarism
Post-theory
Roman à clef
Short story
Spoonerism
Surrealism

11 letters:
Black comedy
Campus novel
Courtly love
Fantastique
Festschrift
Fin de siècle
Foucauldian
Hagiography
Historicism
Littérateur
Metafiction
Narratology
Pornography
Queer theory
Romanticism
Tragicomedy

12 letters:
Alliteration
Bibliography
Bodice-ripper
Hermeneutics
Magic realism
Metalanguage
New criticism
Nouveau roman
Onomatopoeia
Splatterpunk

13 letters:
Angry Young Men
Belles-lettres
Bildungsroman
Carnivalesque
Celtic Revival
Colloquialism
Expressionism
Marxist theory
Postmodernism

Structuralism
Sturm und Drang

14 letters:
Beat Generation
Bowdlerization
Cut-up technique
Deconstruction
Double entendre
Feminist theory
Figure of speech
Locus classicus
Lost Generation
Magical realism
New historicism
Science fiction

15 letters:
Bloomsbury group
Comedy of manners
Epistolary novel
Historical novel

Intertextuality
Post-colonialism

16 letters:
Commedia dell'arte
Death of the author
Hudibrastic verse
Sentimental novel
Socialist realism

17 letters:
Interior monologue
Literary criticism
Post-structuralism
Restoration comedy

19 letters:
Cultural materialism

21 letters:
Signifier and signified
Stream of consciousness

LITERARY CHARACTERS

Character	Book	Author
Captain Ahab	Moby Dick	Herman Melville
Aladdin	The Arabian Nights' Entertainments	Traditional
Alice	Alice's Adventures in Wonderland, Through the Looking-Glass	Lewis Carroll
Bridget Allworthy	Tom Jones	Henry Fielding
Squire Allworthy	Tom Jones	Henry Fielding
Blanch Amory	Pendennis	William Makepeace Thackeray
Harry Angstrom	Rabbit, Run et al.	John Updike
Artful Dodger	Oliver Twist	Charles Dickens
Jack Aubrey	Master and Commander et al.	Patrick O'Brian
Aunt Polly	Tom Sawyer	Mark Twain
Joe Bagstock	Dombey and Son	Charles Dickens
David Balfour	Kidnapped, Catriona	Robert Louis Stevenson
Mrs. Bardell	The Pickwick Papers	Charles Dickens
Barkis	David Copperfield	Charles Dickens
Jake Barnes	The Sun Also Rises	Ernest Hemingway

Character	Book	Author
Adam Bede	Adam Bede	George Eliot
Seth Bede	Adam Bede	George Eliot
Laura Bell	Pendennis	William Makepeace Thackeray
Elizabeth Bennet	Pride and Prejudice	Jane Austen
Jane Bennet	Pride and Prejudice	Jane Austen
Kitty Bennet	Pride and Prejudice	Jane Austen
Lydia Bennet	Pride and Prejudice	Jane Austen
Mary Bennet	Pride and Prejudice	Jane Austen
Mr. Bennet	Pride and Prejudice	Jane Austen
Mrs. Bennet	Pride and Prejudice	Jane Austen
Edmund Bertram	Mansfield Park	Jane Austen
Julia Bertram	Mansfield Park	Jane Austen
Lady Bertram	Mansfield Park	Jane Austen
Maria Bertram	Mansfield Park	Jane Austen
Sir Thomas Bertram	Mansfield Park	Jane Austen
Tom Bertram	Mansfield Park	Jane Austen
Biddy	Great Expectations	Charles Dickens
Charles Bingley	Pride and Prejudice	Jane Austen
Stephen Blackpool	Hard Times	Charles Dickens
Anthony Blanche	Brideshead Revisited	Evelyn Waugh
Leopold Bloom	Ulysses	James Joyce
Molly Bloom	Ulysses	James Joyce
Mr. Boffin	Our Mutual Friend	Charles Dickens
Mrs. Boffin	Our Mutual Friend	Charles Dickens
Farmer Boldwood	Far from the Madding Crowd	Thomas Hardy
Josiah Bounderby	Hard Times	Charles Dickens
Madeline Bray	Nicholas Nickleby	Charles Dickens
Alan Breck	Kidnapped, Catriona	Robert Louis Stevenson
Sue Bridehead	Jude the Obscure	Thomas Hardy
Miss Briggs	Vanity Fair	William Makepeace Thackeray
Dorothea Brooke	Middlemarch	George Eliot
Mr. Brooke	Middlemarch	George Eliot
Mr. Brownlow	Oliver Twist	Charles Dickens
Daisy Buchanan	The Great Gatsby	F. Scott Fitzgerald
Rosa Bud	Edwin Drood	Charles Dickens
Billy Budd	Billy Budd, Foretopman	Herman Melville
Mr. Bulstrode	Middlemarch	George Eliot
Bumble	Oliver Twist	Charles Dickens
Mrs. Cadwallader	Middlemarch	George Eliot
Carker	Dombey and Son	Charles Dickens

Character	Book	Author
Richard Carstone	Bleak House	Charles Dickens
Sydney Carton	A Tale of Two Cities	Charles Dickens
Mr. Casaubon	Middlemarch	George Eliot
Casby	Little Dorrit	Charles Dickens
Flora Casby	Little Dorrit	Charles Dickens
Dunstan Cass	Silas Marner	George Eliot
Godfrey Cass	Silas Marner	George Eliot
Lady Castlewood	Henry Esmond	William Makepeace Thackeray
Lord Castlewood	Henry Esmond	William Makepeace Thackeray
Holden Caulfield	The Catcher in the Rye	J. D. Salinger
Chadband	Bleak House	Charles Dickens
Constance Chatterley	Lady Chatterley's Lover	D. H. Lawrence
The Cheeryble Brothers	Nicholas Nickleby	Charles Dickens
Edward Chester	Barnaby Rudge	Charles Dickens
Sir James Chettam	Middlemarch	George Eliot
Chuffey	Martin Chuzzlewit	Charles Dickens
Frank Churchill	Emma	Jane Austen
Jonas Chuzzlewit	Martin Chuzzlewit	Charles Dickens
Martin Chuzzlewit	Martin Chuzzlewit	Charles Dickens
Ada Clare	Bleak House	Charles Dickens
Angel Clare	Tess of the D'Urbervilles	Thomas Hardy
Arthur Clennam	Little Dorrit	Charles Dickens
Humphry Clinker	Humphry Clinker	Tobias Smollett
William Collins	Pride and Prejudice	Jane Austen
Benjy Compson	The Sound and the Fury	William Faulkner
David Copperfield	David Copperfield	Charles Dickens
Emily Costigan	Pendennis	William Makepeace Thackeray
Bob Cratchit	A Christmas Carol	Charles Dickens
Henry Crawford	Mansfield Park	Jane Austen
Mary Crawford	Mansfield Park	Jane Austen
Bute Crawley	Vanity Fair	William Makepeace Thackeray
Miss Crawley	Vanity Fair	William Makepeace Thackeray
Mrs. Bute Crawley	Vanity Fair	William Makepeace Thackeray
Pitt Crawley	Vanity Fair	William Makepeace Thackeray
Rawdon Crawley	Vanity Fair	William Makepeace Thackeray

Character	Book	Author
Sir Pitt Crawley	Vanity Fair	William Makepeace Thackeray
Septimus Crisparkle	Edwin Drood	Charles Dickens
Vincent Crummles	Nicholas Nickleby	Charles Dickens
Jerry Cruncher	A Tale of Two Cities	Charles Dickens
Robinson Crusoe	Robinson Crusoe	Daniel Defoe
Captain Cuttle	Dombey and Son	Charles Dickens
Sebastian Dangerfield	The Ginger Man	J. P. Donleavy
Fitzwilliam Darcy	Pride and Prejudice	Jane Austen
Charles Darnay	A Tale of Two Cities	Charles Dickens
Elinor Dashwood	Sense and Sensibility	Jane Austen
John Dashwood	Sense and Sensibility	Jane Austen
Margaret Dashwood	Sense and Sensibility	Jane Austen
Marianne Dashwood	Sense and Sensibility	Jane Austen
Mrs. Henry Dashwood	Sense and Sensibility	Jane Austen
Dick Datchery	Edwin Drood	Charles Dickens
Fancy Day	Under The Greenwood Tree	Thomas Hardy
Lady Catherine de Bourgh	Pride and Prejudice	Jane Austen
Stephen Dedalus	A Portrait of the Artist as a Young Man, Ulysses	James Joyce
Sir Leicester Dedlock	Bleak House	Charles Dickens
Lady Dedlock	Bleak House	Charles Dickens
Madame Defarge	A Tale of Two Cities	Charles Dickens
Dick Dewy	Under The Greenwood Tree	Thomas Hardy
Mr. Dick	David Copperfield	Charles Dickens
Jim Dixon	Lucky Jim	Kingsley Amis
William Dobbin	Vanity Fair	William Makepeace Thackeray
Mr. Dombey	Dombey and Son	Charles Dickens
Florence Dombey	Dombey and Son	Charles Dickens
Don Quixote	Don Quixote de la Mancha	Miguel de Cervantes
Arabella Donn	Jude the Obscure	Thomas Hardy
Lorna Doone	Lorna Doone	R. D. Blackmore
Amy Dorrit *or* Little Dorrit	Little Dorrit	Charles Dickens
Fanny Dorrit	Little Dorrit	Charles Dickens
Tip Dorrit	Little Dorrit	Charles Dickens
William Dorrit	Little Dorrit	Charles Dickens
Edwin Drood	Edwin Drood	Charles Dickens
Bentley Drummle	Great Expectations	Charles Dickens
Catriona Drummond	Catriona	Robert Louis Stevenson

Character	Book	Author
Alec D'Urberville	Tess of the D'Urbervilles	Thomas Hardy
Tess Durbeyfield	Tess of the D'Urbervilles	Thomas Hardy
Catherine Earnshaw	Wuthering Heights	Emily Brontë
Hareton Earnshaw	Wuthering Heights	Emily Brontë
Hindley Earnshaw	Wuthering Heights	Emily Brontë
Anne Elliot	Persuasion	Jane Austen
Elizabeth Elliot	Persuasion	Jane Austen
Sir Walter Elliot	Persuasion	Jane Austen
Em'ly	David Copperfield	Charles Dickens
Eppie	Silas Marner	George Eliot
Esmeralda	Notre Dame de Paris	Victor Hugo
Beatrix Esmond	Henry Esmond	William Makepeace Thackeray
Henry Esmond	Henry Esmond	William Makepeace Thackeray
Estella	Great Expectations	Charles Dickens
Bathsheba Everdene	Far from the Madding Crowd	Thomas Hardy
Jane Eyre	Jane Eyre	Charlotte Brontë
Fagin	Oliver Twist	Charles Dickens
Andrew Fairservice	Rob Roy	Sir Walter Scott
Donald Farfrae	The Mayor of Casterbridge	Thomas Hardy
Jude Fawley	Jude the Obscure	Thomas Hardy
Edward Ferrars	Sense and Sensibility	Jane Austen
Huck or Huckleberry Finn	Tom Sawyer, Huckleberry Finn	Mark Twain
Miss Flite	Bleak House	Charles Dickens
Julia Flyte	Brideshead Revisited	Evelyn Waugh
Sebastian Flyte	Brideshead Revisited	Evelyn Waugh
Phileas Fogg	Around the World in Eighty Days	Jules Verne
Man Friday	Robinson Crusoe	Daniel Defoe
Sarah Gamp	Martin Chuzzlewit	Charles Dickens
Joe Gargery	Great Expectations	Charles Dickens
Jay Gatsby	The Great Gatsby	F. Scott Fitzgerald
Walter Gay	Dombey and Son	Charles Dickens
Solomon Gills	Dombey and Son	Charles Dickens
Louisa Gradgrind	Hard Times	Charles Dickens
Thomas Gradgrind	Hard Times	Charles Dickens
Tom Gradgrind	Hard Times	Charles Dickens
Mary Graham	Martin Chuzzlewit	Charles Dickens
Edith Granger	Dombey and Son	Charles Dickens
Dorian Gray	The Picture of Dorian Gray	Oscar Wilde
Mr. Grewgious	Edwin Drood	Charles Dickens
Mrs. Grundy	Speed the Plough	T. Morton

Character	Book	Author
Ben Gunn	Treasure Island	Robert Louis Stevenson
Chris Guthrie	Sunset Song et al.	Lewis Grassic Gibbon
Ham	David Copperfield	Charles Dickens
Richard Hannay	The Thirty-nine Steps et al.	John Buchan
Emma Haredale	Barnaby Rudge	Charles Dickens
John Harmon	Our Mutual Friend	Charles Dickens
James Harthouse	Hard Times	Charles Dickens
Miss Havisham	Great Expectations	Charles Dickens
Sir Mulberry Hawk	Nicholas Nickleby	Charles Dickens
Jim Hawkins	Treasure Island	Robert Louis Stevenson
Bradley Headstone	Our Mutual Friend	Charles Dickens
Heathcliff	Wuthering Heights	Emily Brontë
Uriah Heep	David Copperfield	Charles Dickens
Michael Henchard	The Mayor of Casterbridge	Thomas Hardy
Lizzy Hexam	Our Mutual Friend	Charles Dickens
Betty Higden	Our Mutual Friend	Charles Dickens
Sherlock Holmes	The Adventures of Sherlock Holmes et al.	Sir Arthur Conan Doyle
Humbert Humbert	Lolita	Vladimir Nabokov
Mr. Hyde	The Strange Case of Dr. Jekyll and Mr. Hyde	Robert Louis Stevenson
Injun Joe	Tom Sawyer	Mark Twain
Ishmael	Moby Dick	Herman Melville
Jaggers	Great Expectations	Charles Dickens
John Jarndyce	Bleak House	Charles Dickens
Bailie Nicol Jarvie	Rob Roy	Sir Walter Scott
John Jasper	Edwin Drood	Charles Dickens
Jeeves	My Man Jeeves et al.	P. G. Wodehouse
Dr. Jekyll	The Strange Case of Dr. Jekyll and Mr. Hyde	Robert Louis Stevenson
Mrs. Jellyby	Bleak House	Charles Dickens
Mrs. Jennings	Sense and Sensibility	Jane Austen
Jim	Huckleberry Finn	Mark Twain
Lord Jim	Lord Jim	Joseph Conrad
Jingle	The Pickwick Papers	Charles Dickens
Jo	Bleak House	Charles Dickens
Cissy Jupe	Hard Times	Charles Dickens
Joseph K.	The Trial	Franz Kafka
George Knightley	Emma	Jane Austen
Krook	Bleak House	Charles Dickens
Kurtz	Heart of Darkness	Joseph Conrad
Will Ladislaw	Middlemarch	George Eliot
Helena Landless	Edwin Drood	Charles Dickens

Character	Book	Author
Neville Landless	Edwin Drood	Charles Dickens
Edgar Linton	Wuthering Heights	Emily Brontë
Isabella Linton	Wuthering Heights	Emily Brontë
Dr. Livesey	Treasure Island	Robert Louis Stevenson
Tertius Lydgate	Middlemarch	George Eliot
Rob Roy Macgregor	Rob Roy	Sir Walter Scott
Randle P. McMurphy	One Flew Over the Cuckoo's Nest	Ken Kesey
Abel Magwitch	Great Expectations	Charles Dickens
Dr. Manette	A Tale of Two Cities	Charles Dickens
Lucie Manette	A Tale of Two Cities	Charles Dickens
Madame Mantalini	Nicholas Nickleby	Charles Dickens
The Marchioness	The Old Curiosity Shop	Charles Dickens
Jacob Marley	A Christmas Carol	Charles Dickens
Philip Marlowe	The Big Sleep et al.	Raymond Chandler
Silas Marner	Silas Marner	George Eliot
Stephen Maturin	Master and Commander et al.	Patrick O'Brian
Oliver Mellors	Lady Chatterley's Lover	D. H. Lawrence
Merdle	Little Dorrit	Charles Dickens
Mrs. Merdle	Little Dorrit	Charles Dickens
Wilkins Micawber	David Copperfield	Charles Dickens
Walter Mitty	The Secret Life of Walter Mitty	James Thurber
Lord Mohun	Henry Esmond	William Makepeace Thackeray
Monks	Oliver Twist	Charles Dickens
Dean Moriarty	On the Road	Jack Kerouac
Professor Moriarty	The Adventures of Sherlock Holmes et al.	Sir Arthur Conan Doyle
Dinah Morris	Adam Bede	George Eliot
Murdstone	David Copperfield	Charles Dickens
Mrs. Grundy	Hard Times	Charles Dickens
Baron Münchhausen	Münchhausen, Baron, Narrative of His Marvellous Travels	R. E. Raspe
Nancy	Oliver Twist	Charles Dickens
Little Nell	The Old Curiosity Shop	Charles Dickens
Captain Nemo	Twenty Thousand Leagues under the Sea	Jules Verne
Kate Nickleby	Nicholas Nickleby	Charles Dickens
Nicholas Nickleby	Nicholas Nickleby	Charles Dickens
Ralph Nickleby	Nicholas Nickleby	Charles Dickens
Newman Noggs	Nicholas Nickleby	Charles Dickens

Character	Book	Author
Susan Nipper	Dombey and Son	Charles Dickens
Kit Nubbles	The Old Curiosity Shop	Charles Dickens
Gabriel Oak	Far from the Madding Crowd	Thomas Hardy
Glorvina O'Dowd	Vanity Fair	William Makepeace Thackeray
Major O'Dowd	Vanity Fair	William Makepeace Thackeray
Mrs. O'Dowd	Vanity Fair	William Makepeace Thackeray
Francis Osbaldistone	Rob Roy	Sir Walter Scott
Rashleigh Osbaldistone	Rob Roy	Sir Walter Scott
George Osborne	Vanity Fair	William Makepeace Thackeray
Pancks	Little Dorrit	Charles Dickens
Sancho Panza	Don Quixote de la Mancha	Miguel de Cervantes
Sal Paradise	On the Road	Jack Kerouac
Passepartout	Around the World in Eighty Days	Jules Verne
Pecksniff	Martin Chuzzlewit	Charles Dickens
Charity Pecksniff	Martin Chuzzlewit	Charles Dickens
Mercy Pecksniff	Martin Chuzzlewit	Charles Dickens
Peggoty	David Copperfield	Charles Dickens
Arthur Pendennis	Pendennis	William Makepeace Thackeray
Helen Pendennis	Pendennis	William Makepeace Thackeray
Pew	Treasure Island	Robert Louis Stevenson
Samuel Pickwick	The Pickwick Papers	Charles Dickens
Ruth Pinch	Martin Chuzzlewit	Charles Dickens
Tom Pinch	Martin Chuzzlewit	Charles Dickens
Pip *or* Philip Pirrip	Great Expectations	Charles Dickens
Herbert Pocket	Great Expectations	Charles Dickens
Charles Pooter	The Diary of a Nobody	G. and W. Grossmith
Martin Poyser	Adam Bede	George Eliot
Mrs. Poyser	Adam Bede	George Eliot
Fanny Price	Mansfield Park	Jane Austen
J. Alfred Prufrock	Prufrock and Other Observations	T. S. Eliot
Pumblechook	Great Expectations	Charles Dickens
Quasimodo	Notre Dame de Paris	Victor Hugo
Queequeg	Moby Dick	Herman Melville
Daniel Quilp	The Old Curiosity Shop	Charles Dickens

Character	Book	Author
Roderick Random	Roderick Random	Tobias Smollett
Riah	Our Mutual Friend	Charles Dickens
Rogue Riderhood	Our Mutual Friend	Charles Dickens
Fanny Robin	Far from the Madding Crowd	Thomas Hardy
Mr. Rochester	Jane Eyre	Charlotte Brontë
Barnaby Rudge	Barnaby Rudge	Charles Dickens
Lady Russell	Persuasion	Jane Austen
Charles Ryder	Brideshead Revisited	Evelyn Waugh
Tom Sawyer	The Adventures of Tom Sawyer	Mark Twain
Scrooge	A Christmas Carol	Charles Dickens
Amelia Sedley	Vanity Fair	William Makepeace Thackeray
Jos Sedley	Vanity Fair	William Makepeace Thackeray
Tristram Shandy	The Life and Opinions of Tristram Shandy	Laurence Sterne
Becky or Rebecca Sharp	Vanity Fair	William Makepeace Thackeray
Bill Sikes	Oliver Twist	Charles Dickens
Long John Silver	Treasure Island	Robert Louis Stevenson
Harold Skimpole	Bleak House	Charles Dickens
Sleary	Hard Times	Charles Dickens
Smike	Nicholas Nickleby	Charles Dickens
Harriet Smith	Emma	Jane Austen
Winston Smith	1984	George Orwell
Augustus Snodgrass	The Pickwick Papers	Charles Dickens
Hetty Sorrel	Adam Bede	George Eliot
Lady Southdown	Vanity Fair	William Makepeace Thackeray
Mrs. Sparsit	Hard Times	Charles Dickens
Dora Spenlow	David Copperfield	Charles Dickens
Wackford Squeers	Nicholas Nickleby	Charles Dickens
Starbuck	Moby Dick	Herman Melville
Lucy Steele	Sense and Sensibility	Jane Austen
James Steerforth	David Copperfield	Charles Dickens
Lord Steyne	Vanity Fair	William Makepeace Thackeray
Esther Summerson	Bleak House	Charles Dickens
Dick Swiveller	The Old Curiosity Shop	Charles Dickens
Mark Tapley	Martin Chuzzlewit	Charles Dickens
Tartuffe	Tartuffe	Molière
Mr. Tartar	Edwin Drood	Charles Dickens

Character	Book	Author
Tarzan	Tarzan of the Apes	Edgar Rice Burroughs
Becky Thatcher	Tom Sawyer	Mark Twain
Montague Tigg	Martin Chuzzlewit	Charles Dickens
Tiny Tim	A Christmas Carol	Charles Dickens
Mrs. Todgers	Martin Chuzzlewit	Charles Dickens
Toots	Dombey and Son	Charles Dickens
Traddles	David Copperfield	Charles Dickens
Squire Trelawney	Treasure Island	Robert Louis Stevenson
Fred Trent	The Old Curiosity Shop	Charles Dickens
Job Trotter	The Pickwick Papers	Charles Dickens
Betsey Trotwood	David Copperfield	Charles Dickens
Sergeant Troy	Far from the Madding Crowd	Thomas Hardy
Tulkinghorn	Bleak House	Charles Dickens
Tracy Tupman	The Pickwick Papers	Charles Dickens
Thomas Tusher	Henry Esmond	William Makepeace Thackeray
Oliver Twist	Oliver Twist	Charles Dickens
Gabriel Varden	Barnaby Rudge	Charles Dickens
Dolly Varden	Barnaby Rudge	Charles Dickens
Mr. Veneering	Our Mutual Friend	Charles Dickens
Mrs. Veneering	Our Mutual Friend	Charles Dickens
Diggory Venn	Return of the Native	Thomas Hardy
Diana Vernon	Rob Roy	Sir Walter Scott
Rosamond Vincy	Middlemarch	George Eliot
Johann Voss	Voss	Patrick White
Eustacia Vye	Return of the Native	Thomas Hardy
George Warrington	Pendennis	William Makepeace Thackeray
Dr. Watson	The Adventures of Sherlock Holmes et al.	Sir Arthur Conan Doyle
Silas Wegg	Our Mutual Friend	Charles Dickens
Sam Weller	The Pickwick Papers	Charles Dickens
Wemmick	Great Expectations	Charles Dickens
Frank Wentworth	Persuasion	Jane Austen
Agnes Wickfield	David Copperfield	Charles Dickens
George Wickham	Pride and Prejudice	Jane Austen
Damon Wildeve	Return of the Native	Thomas Hardy
Bella Wilfer	Our Mutual Friend	Charles Dickens
John Willoughby	Sense and Sensibility	Jane Austen
Nathaniel Winkle	The Pickwick Papers	Charles Dickens
Dolly Winthrop	Silas Marner	George Eliot
Allan Woodcourt	Bleak House	Charles Dickens
Emma Woodhouse	Emma	Jane Austen

Character	Book	Author
Mr. Woodhouse	Emma	Jane Austen
Bertie Wooster	My Man Jeeves et al.	P. G. Wodehouse
Eugene Wrayburn	Our Mutual Friend	Charles Dickens
Jenny Wren	Our Mutual Friend	Charles Dickens
Clym Yeobright	Return of the Native	Thomas Hardy
Thomasin Yeobright	Return of the Native	Thomas Hardy
Yossarian	Catch-22	Joseph Heller
Yuri Zhivago	Doctor Zhivago	Boris Pasternak
Zorba *or* Alexis Zorbas	Zorba the Greek	Nikos Kazantzakis

See also:
➤ **Diarists** ➤ **Dramatists** ➤ **Musketeers** ➤ **Novelists**
➤ **Poetry** ➤ **Shakespeare** ➤ **Works of literature and music**
➤ **Writers**

Lizards

3 letters:
Eft
Jew

4 letters:
Abas
Gila
Newt
Sand
Tegu
Wall
Worm

5 letters:
Agama
Anole
Draco
Gecko
Guana
Skink

Snake
Teiid
Tokay
Varan

6 letters:
Anguis
Goanna
Horned
Iguana
Komodo
Leguan
Moloch
Worral
Worrel

7 letters:
Bearded
Frilled
Geckone

Lacerta
Leguaan
Monitor
Perenty
Stellio
Tuatara
Tuatera
Zandoli

8 letters:
Basilisk
Dinosaur
Hatteria
Menopome
Mosasaur
Perentie
Stellion
Sungazer
Teguexin
Whiptail

9 letters:
Blindworm
Chameleon
Galliwasp
Mastigure

10 letters:
Chuckwalla
Glass snake
Hellbender
Kabaragoya
Mosasaurus

11 letters:
Amphisboena
Blue-tongued
Brontosurus

12 letters:
Komodo dragon

Locomotives

7 letters:
Mallard

9 letters:
Blue Peter
Britannia

City Class
Hall Class
King Class

10 letters:
Black Class
The General

11 letters:
Golden Arrow
West Country

12 letters:
General Stamp
Merchant Navy

Schools Class

14 letters:
Flying Scotsman

15 letters:
Coronation Class

Midland Compound

16 letters:
Duke of Gloucester

19 letters:
Thomas the Tank Engine

London, boroughs of

5 letters:
Brent

6 letters:
Barnet
Bexley
Camden
Ealing
Harrow
Merton
Newham
Sutton

7 letters:
Bromley
Croydon
Enfield
Hackney
Lambeth

8 letters:
Haringey
Havering
Hounslow
Kingston
Lewisham
Richmond

9 letters:
Greenwich
Islington
Redbridge
Southwark

10 letters:
Hillingdon
Wandsworth

11 letters:
Westminster

12 letters:
Tower Hamlets

13 letters:
Waltham Forest

18 letters:
Barking and Dagenham

20 letters:
Hammersmith and
  Fulham
Kensington and Chelsea

Lovers

Antony and Cleopatra
Bonnie (Parker) and Clyde (Barrow)
Richard Burton and Elizabeth Taylor
Julius Caesar and Cleopatra
Casanova
Cathy and Heathcliffe
Dante and Beatrice
Darby and Joan
Dido and Aeneas
Don Juan
Edward VIII and Wallis Simpson
Eloise and Abelard
Harlequin and Columbine

Hero and Leander
Jane Eyre and Edward Rochester
Lancelot and Guinevere
Lochinvar and Ellen
Napoleon and Josephine
Scarlett O'Hara and Rhett Butler
Orpheus and Eurydice
Paris and Helen of Troy
Pelleas and Melisande
Petrarch and Laura
Porgy and Bess
Pyramus and Thisbe
Robin Hood and Maid Marian
Romeo and Juliet
Rosalind and Orlando
Samson and Delilah
Tosca and Cavaradossi
Tristan and Isolde
Troilus and Cressida
Zeus and Hera

Mm

Mammals, extinct

6 letters:
Apeman
Quagga
Tarpan

7 letters:
Aurochs
Mammoth

8 letters:
Creodont
Eohippus
Irish elk
Mastodon

9 letters:
Dinoceras
Dinothere
Megathere

10 letters:
Glyptodont
Uintathere

11 letters:
Nototherium
Titanothere

12 letters:
Chalicothere

13 letters:
Dryopithecine

14 letters:
Baluchitherium
Labyrinthodont

15 letters:
Sabre-toothed cat

17 letters:
Australopithecine
Sabre-toothed tiger

See also:
➤ **Anteaters and other edentates** ➤ **Antelopes** ➤ **Bats**
➤ **Carnivores** ➤ **Cats** ➤ **Cattle, breeds of** ➤ **Cows**
➤ **Dogs** ➤ **Horses** ➤ **Marsupials** ➤ **Monkeys, apes, and other**
primates ➤ **Pigs** ➤ **Rabbits and hares** ➤ **Rodents**
➤ **Seals** ➤ **Sea mammals** ➤ **Sheep** ➤ **Shrews and other**
insectivores ➤ **Whales and dolphins**

Mania

Mania	Object
Ablutomania	Washing
Agoramania	Open spaces
Ailuromania	Cats
Andromania	Men
Anglomania	England
Anthomania	Flowers
Apimania	Bees

Mania	Object
Arithmomania	Counting
Automania	Solitude
Autophonomania	Suicide
Balletomania	Ballet
Ballistomania	Bullets
Bibliomania	Books
Chionomania	Snow
Choreomania	Dancing
Chrematomania	Money
Cremnomania	Cliffs
Cynomania	Dogs
Dipsomania	Alcohol
Doramania	Fur
Dromomania	Travelling
Egomania	Your self
Eleuthromania	Freedom
Entheomania	Religion
Entomomania	Insects
Ergasiomania	Work
Eroticomania	Erotica
Erotomania	Sex
Florimania	Plants
Gamomania	Marriage
Graphomania	Writing
Gymnomania	Nakedness
Gynomania	Women
Hamartiomania	Sin
Hedonomania	Pleasure
Heliomania	Sun
Hippomania	Horses
Homicidomania	Murder
Hydromania	Water
Hylomania	Woods
Hypnomania	Sleep
Ichthyomania	Fish
Iconomania	Icons
Kinesomania	Movement
Kleptomania	Stealing
Logomania	Talking
Macromania	Becoming larger
Megalomania	Your own importance
Melomania	Music
Mentulomania	Penises
Micromania	Becoming smaller

Mania	Object
Monomania	One thing
Musicomania	Music
Musomania	Mice
Mythomania	Lies
Necromania	Death
Noctimania	Night
Nudomania	Nudity
Nymphomania	Sex
Ochlomania	Crowds
Oikomania	Home
Oinomania	Wine
Ophidiomania	Reptiles
Orchidomania	Testicles
Ornithomania	Birds
Phagomania	Eating
Pharmacomania	Medicines
Phonomania	Noise
Photomania	Light
Plutomania	Great wealth
Potomania	Drinking
Pyromania	Fire
Scribomania	Writing
Siderodromomania	Railway travel
Sitomania	Food
Sophomania	Your own wisdom
Thalassomania	The sea
Thanatomania	Death
Theatromania	Theatre
Timbromania	Stamps
Trichomania	Hair
Verbomania	Words
Xenomania	Foreigners
Zoomania	Animals

Marsupials

3 letters:
Roo

4 letters:
Dama
Euro
Marl
Tait

Tuan
Uroo

5 letters:
Bilby
Damar
Koala

Mardo
Marlu
Pongo
Quoll
Tungo
Yapok

6 letters:
Badger
Bobuck
Boodie
Cuscus
Glider
Jerboa
Kowari
Merrin
Mongan
Numbat
Possum
Quenda
Quokka
Tammar
Toolah
Tungoo
Warabi
Wogoit
Wombat
Woylie
Yapock

7 letters:
Bettong
Biggada
Dalgite
Dalgyte
Dasyure
Dibbler
Dunnart
Kultarr
Mulgara
Munning
Ningaui
Opossum
Potoroo
Wallaby
Wild cat
Wurrung
Yallara

8 letters:
Boongary
Burramys

Dasyurid
Duckbill
Forester
Kangaroo
Karrabul
Macropod
Platypus
Ringtail
Squeaker
Tiger cat
Toolache
Wallaroo
Wintarro
Wuhl-wuhl

9 letters:
Bandicoot
Boodie rat
Didelphia
Koala bear
Larapinta
Native cat
Pademelon
Petaurist
Phalanger
Thylacine
Wambenger

10 letters:
Antechinus
Diprotodon
Honey mouse
Native bear
Noolbenger
Notoryctes
Paddymelon
Phascogale
Red wallaby
Rock possum
Satanellus

11 letters:
Diprotodont
Fairy possum
Flying mouse

Hare-wallaby
Honey possum
Nototherium
Pygmy glider
Pygmy possum
Rat kangaroo
Red kangaroo
Rock wallaby
Sugar glider
Tcharibeena

12 letters:
Agile wallaby
Black wallaby
Fluffy glider
Grey forester
Marsupial cat
Parma wallaby
Pitchi-pitchi
River wallaby
Sandy wallaby
Scrub wallaby
Swamp wallaby
Tree kangaroo

13 letters:
Brush kangaroo
Feather glider
Marsupial mole
Rufous wallaby
Sooty kangaroo
Striped possum
Tasmanian wolf
Ursine dasyure

14 letters:
Banded anteater
Brown bandicoot
Flying squirrel
Forest kangaroo
Gunn's bandicoot
Jerboa kangaroo
Jungle kangaroo
Mallee kangaroo
Marsupial mouse

Mountain possum
Plains kangaroo
Ringtail possum
Squirrel glider
Tasmanian devil
Tasmanian tiger

15 letters:
Barred bandicoot
Bennett's wallaby
Brush-tail possum
Desert bandicoot
Flying phalanger
Golden bandicoot
Naked-nose wombat
Rabbit bandicoot
Whiptail wallaby

16 letters:
Antelope kangaroo
Hairy-nosed wombat
Musky rat-kangaroo
Red-necked wallaby
Ringtailed possum
Spotted native cat

17 letters:
Antilopine wallaby
Brindled bandicoot
Brush-tailed possum
Cannings' little dog
Desert-rat kangaroo
Great grey kangaroo
Grey's brush wallaby
Leadbeater's possum
Northern native cat
Pretty-face wallaby
Rufous rat-kangaroo

18 letters:
Black-faced kangaroo
Black-tailed wallaby
Brush-tailed bettong
Brush-tailed wallaby
Duck-billed platypus

Jerboa pouched mouse
Long-eared bandicoot
Long-nosed bandicoot
Pig-footed bandicoot

19 letters:
Darling Downs dunnart
Eastern brush wallaby
Eastern grey kangaroo
Green ringtail possum
Lesueur's rat-kangaroo
Mountain pygmy possum
Short-eared bandicoot
Short-nosed bandicoot
Western grey kangaroo
Yellow-bellied glider

20 letters:
Bennett's tree kangaroo
Burrowing rat-kangaroo
Rabbit-eared bandicoot

21 letters:
Lumholtz's tree kangaroo
Ring-tailed rock wallaby
Short-nosed rat kangaroo

22 letters:
Bridled nail-tail wallaby
Lemuroid ringtail possum
Northern brown bandicoot
Southern brown bandicoot
Yellow-footed antechinus

23 letters:
Crescent nail-tail wallaby
Mountain brushtail possum
Northern nail-tail wallaby
Yellow-footed rock wallaby

24 letters:
Tasmanian barred bandicoot

25 letters:
Crest-tailed marsupial mouse

26 letters:
Herbert River ringtail possum

Martial arts

MARTIAL ARTS

4 letters:
Judo
Kata
Sumo

5 letters:
Iai-do
Kendo
Kyudo
Wushu

6 letters:
Aikido
Chin Na
Karate
Kung fu
Tukido®

7 letters:
Hapkido
Ju jitsu
Ju-jutsu
Jukendo

8 letters:
Capoeira
Iai-jutsu
Jiu jitsu

Karate-do
Kravmaga
Muay Thai
Ninjitsu
Ninjutsu
Wing Chun

9 letters:
Shuai jiao
Tae kwon-do
Yari-jutsu

10 letters:
Jeet Kune Do
Kick boxing
Naginata-do
Thai boxing

11 letters:
Tai chi chuan

12 letters:
Tai chi qi gong
Tomiki aikido

13 letters:
Goju Kai karate
Goju Ryu karate

Hung Gar kung fu
Sumo wrestling
Wado Ryu karate

14 letters:
Ishin Ryu karate
Sankukai karate
Shito Ryu karate
Shotokai karate
Shotokan karate
Shukokai karate
Wing Tsun kung fu

16 letters:
Crane style kung fu
Ta Sheng Men kung fu
Tiger style kung fu

17 letters:
Monkey style kung fu

18 letters:
Kyokushinkai karate

24 letters:
Praying Mantis style
  kung fu

MARTIAL ARTS TERMS

Term	Meaning
Banzuke	list of sumo wrestlers according to rank
Basho	Sumo turnament
Bo	Staff
Bogu	Kendo armour
Bokuto	Kendo wooden sword
Budo *or* bushido	Warrior's way
Dan	Black belt grade

Term	Meaning
Do	Kendo breastplate
-do	The way
Dohyo	Sumo ring
Dojo	Practice room or mat
Gi	Suit
Hachimaki *or* tenugui	Kendo headcloth
Hakama	Divided skirt
Ippon	One competition point
Jiu-kumite	Freestyle karate competition
-jutsu	Fighting art
-ka	Student
Kama	Hand sickle
Kata	Sequence of techniques
Katana	Kendo sword
Katsu	Resuscitation techniques
Keikogi	Kendo jacket
Kesho-mawashi	Embroidered sumo apron
Ki, chi, *or* qi	Inner power
Kiai	Yell accompanying movement
Kihon	Repetition of techniques
Kote	Kendo gauntlets
Kyu	Student grade
Makiwara	Practice block
Mawashi	Sumo fighting belt
Men	Kendo mask
Nage-waza *or* tachi-waza	Ju jitsu competition
Naginata	Curved-blade spear
Ne-waza	Ju jitsu competition
Ninin-dori	Aikido competition
Ninja	Japanese trained assassin
Nunchaku	Hinged flails
Obi	Coloured belt
Ozeki	Sumo champion
Qi gong	Breath control
Randori kyoghi	Aikido competition
Rikishi	Sumo wrestler
Rokushakubo	Six-foot staff
Ryu	Martial arts school
Sai	Short trident
Samurai	Japanese warrior caste
Sensei	Teacher
Shinai	Kendo bamboo sword
Sifu	Teacher
Suneate	Naginata shin guards

Term	Meaning
Tanto randori	Aikido competition
Tare	Kendo apron
Te	Hand fighting
Ton-fa *or* tui-fa	Hardwood weapon
Tsuna	Sumo grand champion's belt
Waza-ari	Half competition point
Yari	Spear
Yokozuna	Sumo grand champion
Zanshin	Total awareness

Materials

3 letters:
Rep
Say

4 letters:
Lamé
Lawn
Tape
Wool

5 letters:
Crash
Denim
Linen
Lisle
Serge
Toile
Twill

6 letters:
Canvas
Cermet
Coburg
Dimity
Poplin
Russel

Soneri
Tusser

7 letters:
Batiste
Cambric
Ceramic
Chiffon
Flannel
Galatea
Genappe
Hessian
Oilskin
Sagathy
Satinet

8 letters:
Cretonne
Gossamer
Homespun
Illusion
Jeanette
Marocain
Moquette
Prunella
Toilinet

9 letters:
Calamanco
Cellulose
Charmeuse®
Fibrefill
Gaberdine
Macintosh
Pina-cloth
Polyester
Sackcloth
Stockinet
Swansdown
Tarpaulin
Towelling
Worcester

10 letters:
Fibreglass
Toilinette
Winceyette

11 letters:
Stockinette

Mathematics

BRANCHES OF MATHEMATICS

4 letters:
Pure

6 letters:
Conics

7 letters:
Algebra

Applied

8 letters:
Analysis
Calculus
Geometry
Topology

9 letters:
Set theory

10 letters:
Arithmetic
Game theory
Nomography

Statistics

11 letters:
Group theory

12 letters:
Number theory
Trigonometry

13 letters:
Chaos geometry

14 letters:
Boolean algebra

16 letters:
Integral calculus

17 letters:
Euclidean geometry
Numerical analysis
Probability theory

18 letters:
Analytical geometry
Coordinate geometry

20 letters:
Differential calculus
Non-Euclidean geometry

MATHEMATICAL TERMS

2 letters:
Pi

3 letters:
Arc
Log
Odd
Set
Sum

4 letters:
Area
Axis
Base
Cone
Cube
Cusp
Even
Mean
Mode
Node
Plus
Root
Sine
Surd
Zero

5 letters:
Angle
Chord
Curve
Digit
Graph
Helix
Index
Locus
Minus
Power
Prism
Proof
Ratio
Solid
Torus
Union
Value
X-axis
Y-axis
Z-axis

6 letters:
Binary
Circle
Cosine
Cuboid
Denary

Equals
Factor
Matrix
Median
Number
Oblong
Origin
Radian
Radius
Scalar
Secant
Sector
Sphere
Square
Subset
Vector
Volume

7 letters:
Average
Decagon
Decimal
Ellipse
Formula
Hexagon
Integer
Nonagon
Octagon

Open set
Polygon
Product
Rhombus
Scalene
Tangent

8 letters:
Addition
Algorism
Binomial
Constant
Cosecant
Cube root
Cylinder
Diagonal
Diameter
Division
Equation
Fraction
Function
Heptagon
Infinity
Integral
Operator
Parabola
Parallel
Pentagon
Quadrant
Quotient
Triangle
Variable

9 letters:
Algorithm
Closed set
Cotangent
Factorial
Frequency
Hyperbola
Isosceles
Logarithm
Numerator
Operation
Rectangle

Remainder
Slide rule
Trapezium

10 letters:
Acute angle
Concentric
Co-ordinate
Hemisphere
Hypotenuse
Octahedron
Percentage
Polyhedron
Polynomial
Real number
Reciprocal
Right angle
Semicircle
Square root

11 letters:
Coefficient
Denominator
Equilateral
Exponential
Icosahedron
Obtuse angle
Prime number
Probability
Reflex angle
Subtraction
Tetrahedron
Venn diagram

12 letters:
Common factor
Dodecahedron
Intersection
Universal set

13 letters:
Circumference
Complex number
Mandelbrot set

Natural number
Ordinal number
Parallelogram
Perfect number
Quadrilateral

14 letters:
Cardinal number
Multiplication
Proper fraction
Rational number
Vulgar fraction

15 letters:
Imaginary number

16 letters:
Improper fraction
Irrational number
Natural logarithm
Recurring decimal
Strange attractor

17 letters:
Common denominator
Pythagoras' theorem
Quadratic equation

18 letters:
Significant figures

19 letters:
Right-angled triangle

20 letters:
Cartesian coordinates
Lowest common multiple

21 letters:
Simultaneous equations

23 letters:
Lowest common
  denominator

MATHEMATICIANS

3 letters:
Dee, *John*
Lie, *Marius Sophus*

4 letters:
Hero
Kahn, *Herman*
Weyl, *Hermann*
Zeno *(of Elea)*

5 letters:
Aiken, *Howard Hathaway*
Bondi, *Hermann*
Boole, *George*
Comte, *Isidore Auguste*
Euler, *Leonhard*
Frege, *Gottlob*
Gauss, *Karl Friedrich*
Gibbs, *Josiah Willard*
Gödel, *Kurt*
Pitts, *Walter*

6 letters:
Agnesi, *Maria Gaetana*
Ampère, *André Marie*
Balmer, *Johann Jakob*
Bessel, *Friedrich Wilhelm*
Briggs, *Henry*
Cantor, *Georg*
Cauchy, *Augustin Louis*
Cayley, *Arthur*
Cocker, *Edward*
Darwin, *George Howard*
Euclid
Fermat, *Pierre De*
Gunter, *Edmund*
Halley, *Edmund*
Jacobi, *Karl Gustav Jacob*
Jevons, *William*
Kaluza, *Theodor*
Napier, *John*
Newton, *Isaac*
Pappus *of Alexandria*
Pascal, *Blaise*

Peirce, *Charles Sanders*
Penney, *William George*
Taylor, *Brook*
Thales
Turing, *Alan Mathison*
Wiener, *Norbert*

7 letters:
Babbage, *Charles*
D'Oresme, *Nicole*
Eudoxus *of Cnidus*
Fourier, *Jean Baptiste Joseph*
Galileo
Hawking, *Stephen William*
Hilbert, *David*
Khayyám, *Omar*
Laplace, *Pierre Simon*
Leibniz
Neumann, *John Von*
Pearson, *Karl*
Penrose, *Roger*
Poisson, *Siméon Denis*
Ptolemy
Pytheas
Riemann, *Georg Friedrich Bernhard*
Russell, *Bertrand*
Shannon, *Claude*

8 letters:
Archytas
Clausius, *Rudolf Julius*
Dedekind, *Julius Wilhelm Richard*
De Fermat, *Pierre*
Einstein, *Albert*
Goldbach, *Christian*
Hamilton, *William Rowan*
Lagrange, *Joseph Louis*
Legendre, *Adrien Marie*
Lovelace, *Ada*
Mercator, *Gerardus*
Playfair, *John*
Poincaré, *Jules Henri*

9 letters:
Bernoulli, *Daniel*
Bernoulli, *Jacques*
Bernoulli, *Jean*
Descartes, *René*
Dirichlet, *Peter Gustav Lejeune*
Dunstable, *John*
Fibonacci, *Leonardo*
Minkowski, *Hermann*
Whitehead, *Alfred North*

10 letters:
Apollonius *of Perga*
Archimedes
Diophantos
Kolmogorov, *Andrei Nikolaevich*
Pythagoras

Torricelli, *Evangelista*
Von Neumann, *John*

11 letters:
Anaximander
Lobachevsky, *Nikolai Ivanovich*
Von Leibnitz, *Gottfried Wilhelm*

12 letters:
De Maupertuis, *Pierre Louis Moreau*
Eratosthenes

13 letters:
Regiomontanus, *Johann Müller*

14 letters:
Le Rond Alembert, *Jean*

Meals

3 letters:	**8 letters:**	**11 letters:**
Tea	Barbecue	Smorgasbord
	Cream tea	
5 letters:	Deskfast	**12 letters:**
Feast	Luncheon	Afternoon tea
Lunch		Tousy tea
Snack	**9 letters:**	
Tapas	Beanfeast	
	Breakfast	
6 letters:	Elevenses	
Barbie		

Brunch	
Buffet	
Dinner	
Picnic	
Supper	
Tiffin	
7 letters:	
Banquet	
Fish fry	
High tea	

Meats

3 letters:		Chuck	Shank
Ham	Hogg	Chump	Skirt
Leg	Lamb	Devon	Steak
Rib	Loin	Gigot	T-bone
	Pork	Goose	Tripe
4 letters:	Rack	Hough	
Beef	Rump	Liver	**6 letters:**
Chop	Spam®	Mince	Breast
Duck	Veal	Offal	Collar
Game		Round	Cutlet
Hock	**5 letters:**	Scrag	Fillet
	Bacon		

Gammon
Haslet
Hogget
Kidney
Lights
Mutton
Oxtail
Pigeon
Polony
Saddle
Salami
Tongue
Turkey

7 letters:
Beef-ham
Brisket
Charqui
Chicken
Chorizo
Fatback
Gristle
Numbles
Sausage
Saveloy
Sirloin
Topside
Venison

8 letters:
Bath chap
Cervelat
Chitlins
Cold cuts

Escalope
Forehock
Lamb's fry
Medailon
Noisette
Oxtongue
Parma ham
Pastrami
Pemmican
Pheasant
Pope's eye
Salt pork
Shoulder
Sparerib
Undercut

9 letters:
Bockwurst
Boerewors
Bratwurst
Chipolata
Chitlings
Entrecôte
Foreshank
Medallion
Pepperoni
Short ribs
Tournedos

10 letters:
Chuck steak
Corned beef
Crown roast
Knackwurst

Knockwurst
Liverwurst
Médaillons
Mortadella
Prosciutto
Rolled lamb
Silverside
Sweetbread
Tenderloin

11 letters:
Baron of beef
Minute steak
Parson's nose
Square slice

12 letters:
Black pudding
Chitterlings
Liver sausage
Lorne sausage
Luncheon meat
Stewing steak

13 letters:
Chateaubriand
Colonial goose
Square sausage

16 letters:
Porterhouse steak

17 letters:
Cumberland sausage

Medals

9 letters:
Iron Cross

10 letters:
Bronze Star
Silver Star

11 letters:
George Cross
Purple Heart

13 letters:
Croix de Guerre
Legion of Merit
Royal Red Cross

Victoria Cross

14 letters:
Légion d'Honneur

20 letters:
Militaire Willemsorde

25 letters:
Congressional Medal of Honor

Distinguished Service Cross
Distinguished Service Order

Medicine

BRANCHES OF MEDICINE

5 letters:
Legal
Space

6 letters:
Sports

7 letters:
Anatomy
Myology
Nuclear
Otology
Surgery
Urology

8 letters:
Aviation
Etiology
Forensic
Internal
Nosology
Oncology
Physical
Posology
Serology
Tocology
Tokology
Virology

9 letters:
Aetiology
Anaplasty
Andrology
Angiology
Audiology
Chiropody
Dentistry
Dietetics
Midwifery

Neurology
Nostology
Nutrition
Optometry
Orthotics
Osteology
Pathology
Radiology
Rhinology

10 letters:
Balneology
Cardiology
Embryology
Exodontics
Geratology
Geriatrics
Gynecology
Hematology
Immunology
Industrial
Nephrology
Obstetrics
Odontology
Orthoptics
Palliative
Pediatrics
Preventive
Proctology
Psychiatry
Psychology
Toxicology
Trichology
Veterinary

11 letters:
Allergology
Biomedicine
Dermatology

Diagnostics
Eccrinology
Endodontics
Gene therapy
Gerontology
Gynaecology
Haematology
Laryngology
Naturopathy
Neonatology
Oral hygiene
Orthodontia
Orthopedics
Osteoplasty
Paediatrics
Physiatrics
Stomatology
Syphilology
Venereology

12 letters:
Anaesthetics
Bacteriology
Epidemiology
Nanomedicine
Neuroanatomy
Neurosurgery
Nosokinetics
Orthodontics
Orthopaedics
Periodontics
Pharyngology
Rheumatology
Therapeutics

13 letters:
Dental hygiene
Dental surgery
Endocrinology

Genitourinary
Materia medica
Morbid anatomy
Ophthalmology
Physiotherapy
Speech therapy

14 letters:
Neuropathology
Otolaryngology
Plastic surgery
Psychoanalysis
Symptomatology

15 letters:
Bioastronautics
Encephalography
Immunochemistry
Medical genetics
Neurophysiology
Neuropsychiatry

16 letters:
Gastroenterology
Spare-part surgery

17 letters:
Electrophysiology
Hydrotherapeutics
Veterinary science

18 letters:
Neuroendocrinology

19 letters:
Electrotherapeutics

MEDICAL PRACTITIONERS AND SPECIALISTS

2 letters:
GP

3 letters:
Vet

5 letters:
Nurse

6 letters:
Doctor
Extern
Intern
Matron
Physio

7 letters:
Dentist
Externe
Interne
Midwife
Orderly
Surgeon

8 letters:
Houseman
Optician
Resident

9 letters:
Anatomist
Dietitian
Internist
Myologist
Orthotist
Otologist
Paramedic
Registrar
Therapist
Urologist

10 letters:
Consultant
Etiologist
Exodontist
Geriatrist
Nosologist
Oncologist
Orthoptist
Serologist
Virologist

11 letters:
Aetiologist
Andrologist
Audiologist
Chiropodist
Endodontist
Neurologist

Optometrist
Orthopedist
Osteologist
Pathologist
Radiologist
Rhinologist

12 letters:
Anaesthetist
Balneologist
Cardiologist
Embryologist
Geriatrician
Gynecologist
Hematologist
Immunologist
Junior doctor
Nephrologist
Neurosurgeon
Nutritionist
Obstetrician
Odontologist
Orthodontist
Orthopaedist
Pediatrician
Proctologist
Psychiatrist
Psychologist
Radiographer
Toxicologist

Trichologist
Veterinarian

13 letters:
Allergologist
Dental surgeon
Dermatologist
Diagnostician
District nurse
Gene therapist
Gerontologist
Gynaecologist
Haematologist
Health visitor
Laryngologist
Neonatologist
Oral hygienist
Paediatrician
Psychoanalyst
Pulmonologist
Syphilologist
Venereologist

14 letters:
Bacteriologist
Barefoot doctor
Epidemiologist
House physician
Hydrotherapist
Neuroanatomist
Nursing officer
Pharyngologist
Plastic surgeon
Rheumatologist

15 letters:
Dental hygienist
Endocrinologist
Ophthalmologist
Physiotherapist
Speech therapist

16 letters:
Neuropathologist
Otolaryngologist

17 letters:
Forensic scientist
Neurophysiologist
Neuropsychiatrist
Veterinary surgeon

18 letters:
Gastroenterologist

19 letters:
Electrophysiologist
General practitioner

20 letters:
Laboratory technician

21 letters:
Occupational therapist

MEDICAL AND SURGICAL INSTRUMENTS AND EQUIPMENT

4 letters:
Drip
Swab

5 letters:
Clamp
Curet
Drain
Lance
Probe
Sling
Sound
Stent
Stupe

6 letters:
Bedpan
Canula
Lancet
Needle

Splint
Stylet
Suture
Trepan
Trocar

7 letters:
Bandage
Cannula
Catling
Curette
Forceps
Packing
Scalpel
Scanner
Syringe
Wet pack

8 letters:
Bistoury

Catheter
Heat lamp
Hemostat
Iron lung
Otoscope
Pulmotor®
Speculum
Trephine

9 letters:
Aspirator
CT scanner
Cymograph
Depressor
Endoscope
Fetoscope
Haemostat
Inhalator
Kymograph
Nebulizer

Pacemaker
Perimeter
Raspatory
Retractor
Rheometer
Skiascope
Stretcher

10 letters:
CAT scanner
Colposcope
Compressor
Cystoscope
Fiberscope
Fibrescope
Gonioscope
Hypodermic
Inspirator
Microscope
MRI scanner

Orthoscope
Oxygen mask
Oxygen tent
Respirator
Rhinoscope
Spirograph
Spirometer
Tourniquet
Urinometer
Ventilator

11 letters:
Arthroscope
Cardiograph
Colonoscope
Fluoroscope
Gamma camera
Gastroscope
Laparoscope
Nephroscope
Plaster cast
Pneumograph
Proctoscope
Retinoscope
Stethoscope
Stomach pump

Thermometer
X-ray machine

12 letters:
Bronchoscope
Laryngoscope
Resuscitator
Sphygmograph
Thoracoscope
Urethroscope

13 letters:
Defibrillator
Encephalogram
Esophagoscope
Kidney machine
Pharyngoscope
Pneumatometer
Röntgenoscope
Styptic pencil

14 letters:
Oesophagoscope
Ophthalmoscope
Roentgenoscope
Specimen bottle

15 letters:
Artificial heart
Dialysis machine
Electromyograph

16 letters:
Artificial kidney
Heart-lung machine
Hypodermic needle
Sphygmomanometer

17 letters:
Hypodermic syringe
Ultrasound scanner

18 letters:
Electrocardiograph
Life-support machine

19 letters:
Clinical thermometer

21 letters:
Electroencephalograph

BRANCHES OF ALTERNATIVE MEDICINE

5 letters:
Reiki
Unani

6 letters:
Siddha

7 letters:
Massage
Shiatsu

8 letters:
Ayurveda
Hypnosis

9 letters:
Herbalism

Iridology
Radionics

10 letters:
Homeopathy
Osteopathy

11 letters:
Acupressure
Acupuncture
Biofeedback
Homoeopathy
Kinesiology
Moxibustion
Naturopathy
Reflexology
Traditional

12 letters:
Aromatherapy
Chiropractic
Hydrotherapy
Hypnotherapy

14 letters:
Anthroposophic

16 letters:
Bach flower remedy

17 letters:
Autogenic training

18 letters:
Alexander technique

PEOPLE IN MEDICINE

4 letters:
Bell, *Sir Charles*
Best, *Charles*
Drew, *Charles*
Jung, *Carl*
Koch, *Robert*
Lind, *James*
Mayo, *Charles*
Reed, *Walter*
Ross, *Sir Ronald*
Salk, *Jonas E(dward)*

5 letters:
Black, *Sir James*
Broca, *Paul*
Bruce, *Sir David*
Cajal, *Santiago Ramon y*
Crick, *Francis*
Crohn, *Burrill B*
Curie, *Marie*
Freud, *Sigmund*
Galen
Henle, *Friedrich*
Kenny, *Elizabeth*
Krebs, *Sir Edwin*
Leach, *Penelope*
Lower, *Richard*
Osler, *Sir William*
Paget, *Sir James*
Remak, *Robert*
Sharp, *Phillip*
Spock, *Benjamin*
Steno, *Nicolaus*

6 letters:
Barton, *Clara*
Bichat, *Marie*
Bishop, *Michael*
Bright, *Richard*
Carrel, *Alexis*
Cavell, *Edith Louisa*
Cooper, *Sir Astley*
Cuvier, *Georges*

Fernel, *Jean*
Finsen, *Niels*
Garrod, *Sir Archibald*
Harvey, *William*
Hunter, *John*
Inglis, *Elsie*
Jenner, *Edward*
Lister, *Joseph*
Manson, *Sir Patrick*
Mesmer, *Franz Anton*
Mullis, *Kary*
Pavlov, *Ivan*
Sanger, *Margaret*
Treves, *Sir Frederick*
Varmus, *Harold*
Watson, *James*
Watson, *John*
Willis, *Thomas*

7 letters:
Addison, *Thomas*
Axelrod, *Julius*
Banting, *Sir Frederick*
Barnard, *Christiaan*
Bethune, *Henry Norman*
Burkitt, *Denis*
Cushing, *Harvey*
Ehrlich, *Paul*
Eijkman, *Christian*
Fleming, *Sir Alexander*
Gilbert, *William*
Hodgkin, *Dorothy*
Hodgkin, *Thomas*
Laennec, *Rene*
Laveran, *Charles*
Linacre, *Thomas*
MacEwen, *Sir William*
McIndoe, *Sir Archibald*
Medawar, *Sir Peter*
Nicolle, *Charles*
Pasteur, *Louis*
Röntgen, *Wilhelm Conrad*
Seacole, *Mary Jane*

Simpson, *Sir James Young*
Warburg, *Otto*
Winston, *Lord Robert*

8 letters:
Anderson, *Elizabeth Garrett*
Asperger, *Hans*
Avicenna
Beaumont, *William*
Billroth, *Theodor*
Charnley, *Sir John*
Delbruck, *Max*
Duchenne, *Guillaume*
Dulbecco, *Renato*
Geronimo
Jex-Blake, *Sophia*
Leishman, *Sir William*
Magendie, *Francois*
Malpighi, *Marcello*
Morgagni, *Giovanni*
Pattison, *Dorothy*
Stoppard, *Miriam*
Sydenham, *Thomas*
Tournier, *Paul*
Vesalius

9 letters:
Alzheimer, *Alois*
Bartholin, *Erasmus*
Blackwell, *Elizabeth*
Boerhaave, *Hermann*
Dupuytren, *Guillaume*
Dutrochet, *Henri*
Hahnemann, *Samuel*
Mackenzie, *Sir James*
Parkinson, *James*

10 letters:
Fracastoro, *Girolamo*
Greenfield, *Susan*
Langerhans, *Paul*
Paracelsus
Stephenson, *Elsie*

11 letters:
Hippocrates
Livingstone, *David*
Nightingale, *Florence*
Szent-Gyorgi, *Albert*

12 letters:
Erasistratus

Membranes

3 letters:
Haw

4 letters:
Dura
Kell

5 letters:
Exine
Mater

6 letters:
Amnion
Cornea
Extine
Foetal

Intima
Intine
Meninx
Mucosa
Mucous
Pleura
Sclera
Serosa
Serous
Tympan

7 letters:
Bilayer
Chorion
Choroid
Decidua

Hyaloid
Nuclear
Periost
Putamen

8 letters:
Axilemma
Ependyma
Frenulum
Indusium
Patagium
Pericarp
Pia mater
Synovial
Tympanic
Vacuolar

9 letters:	11 letters:	12 letters:
Arachnoid	Chromoplast	Schneiderian
Dura mater	Conjunctiva	
Endostium	Dissepiment	13 letters:
Involucre	Endocardium	Choroid plexus
Mesentery	Endometrium	Perichondrium
Tonoplast	Mediastinum	
Vitelline	Nictitating	15 letters:
	Pericardium	Chorioallantois
10 letters:	Pericranium	
Periosteum	Peritonaeum	
Peritoneum	Third eyelid	
Sarcolemma	Trophoblast	

Metals

Metal	Symbol
Actinium	Ac
Aluminium	Al
Americium	Am
Antimony	Sb
Barium	Ba
Berkelium	Bk
Beryllium	Be
Bismuth	Bi
Cadmium	Cd
Caesium *or* cesium	Cs
Calcium	Ca
Californium	Cf
Cerium	Ce
Chromium	Cr
Cobalt	Co
Copper	Cu
Curium	Cm
Dysprosium	Dy
Einsteinium	Es
Erbium	Er
Europium	Eu
Fermium	Fm
Francium	Fr
Gadolinium	Gd
Gallium	Ga
Germanium	Ge
Gold	Au
Hafnium	Hf

Metal	Symbol
Holmium	Ho
Indium	In
Iridium	Ir
Iron	Fe
Lanthanum	La
Lawrencium	Lr
Lead	Pb
Lithium	Li
Lutetium	Lu
Magnesium	Mg
Manganese	Mn
Mendelevium	Md
Mercury	Hg
Molybdenum	Mo
Neodymium	Nd
Neptunium	Np
Nickel	Ni
Niobium	Nb
Nobelium	No
Osmium	Os
Palladium	Pd
Platinum	Pt
Plutonium	Pu
Polonium	Po
Potassium	K
Praseodymium	Pr
Promethium	Pm
Protactinium	Pa
Radium	Ra
Rhenium	Re
Rhodium	Rh
Rubidium	Rb
Ruthenium	Ru
Samarium	Sm
Scandium	Sc
Silver	Ag
Sodium	Na
Strontium	Sr
Tantalum	Ta
Technetium	Tc
Terbium	Tb
Thallium	Tl
Thorium	Th
Thulium	Tm

Metal	Symbol
Tin	Sn
Titanium	Ti
Tungsten *or* wolfram	W
Uranium	U
Vanadium	V
Ytterbium	Yb
Yttrium	Y
Zinc	Zn
Zirconium	Zr
Zorgite	

Meteor showers

6 letters:
Boötes
Cetids
Lyrids
Ursids
Velids

7 letters:
Corvids
Cygnids
Hydrids
Leonids
Librids
Mensids
Normids
Piscids
Puppids
Scutids
Taurids

8 letters:
Aquilids
Arietids
Aurigids
Cancrids
Geminids
Orionids
Pavonids
Pegasids
Perseids

9 letters:
Aquariids
Craterids
Draconids
Eridanids
Herculids
Scorpiids
Virginids

10 letters:
Centaurids
Phoenicids
Sextantids

11 letters:
Andromedids
Quadrantids
Triangulids

12 letters:
Capricornids
Monocerotids
Sagittariids
Ursa Majorids

13 letters:
Canis Minorids

14 letters:
Coma Berenicids

Military ranks

2 letters:
AB
AC
AM
BO
CO
FM

FO
Lt
MO
OS
PO
QM
RA

SM
VA
WO

3 letters:
ACM
Adm

AVM
Cdr
Col
COS
Cpl
CPO
CSM
Gen
LAC
Maj
NCO
Pte
RSM
Sgt
SMO
Tpr

4 letters:
Brig
Capt
Cdre
C-in-C
Corp
Genl
L-Cpl
MRAF
Sub L

5 letters:
Flt Lt
G Capt
Lt-Col
Lt-Gen
Major
Sergt

6 letters:
Col Sgt
Flt Sgt
Lt-Comm
Maj-Gen
Marine
Sqn-Ldr

7 letters:
Admiral
Captain
Colonel
General
Marshal
Private

8 letters:
Corporal
Sergeant

9 letters:
Brigadier
Commander
Commodore
Drum major
Subaltern

10 letters:
Able rating
Able seaman
Air marshal
Air officer
Lieutenant
Midshipman

11 letters:
Aircraftmen
Rear admiral
Vice admiral

12 letters:
Air commodore
Chief of staff
Field marshal
Field officer
Fleet admiral
Group captain
Major general
Petty officer
Pilot officer

13 letters:
Branch officer

Flying officer
Lance corporal
Leading rating
Master aircrew
Quartermaster
Sergeant major
Staff sergeant
Sublieutenant
Wing commander

14 letters:
Air vice-marshal
Colour sergeant
Flight engineer
Flight mechanic
Flight sergeant
Medical officer
Ordinary rating
Ordinary seaman
Squadron leader
Warrant officer

15 letters:
Air chief marshal
Chief technician

16 letters:
Able-bodied seaman
Commander in chief
Flight lieutenant
Junior technician
Second lieutenant

17 letters:
Admiral of the fleet
Chief petty officer
Commanding officer
Lieutenant colonel
Lieutenant general
Senior aircraftman

18 letters:
Leading aircraftman

19 letters:
Acting sublieutenant
Commissioned officer
Lieutenant commander

20 letters:
Company sergeant major
Senior medical officer

22 letters:
Fleet chief petty officer
Noncommissioned officer

23 letters:
Regimental sergeant major

25 letters:
Marshal of the Royal Air Force

Minerals

4 letters:
Gang
Mica
Opal
Sard
Spar
Talc
Trap
Urao

5 letters:
Agate
Balas
Beryl
Borax
Chert
Emery
Flint
Fluor
Mafic
Nitre
Prase
Topaz
Trona
Umber

6 letters:
Acmite
Albite
Augite
Blende
Galena
Gangue

Garnet
Glance
Gypsum
Halite
Hauyne
Illite
Jargon
Jasper
Lithia
Norite
Nosean
Pinite
Pyrite
Quartz
Rutile
Schorl
Silica
Sphene
Spinel
Tincal
Zircon

7 letters:
Alunite
Amalgam
Anatase
Apatite
Axinite
Azurite
Barytes
Bauxite
Biotite

Bornite
Brucite
Calcite
Calomel
Catseye
Cuprite
Cyanite
Diamond
Dysodil
Epidote
Euclase
Eucrite
Fahlore
Felspar
Gahnite
Göthite
Gummite
Hessite
Ice spar
Jadeite
Jargoon
Kainite
Kernite
Kunzite
Kyanite
Leucite
Mellite
Mullite
Nacrite
Olivine
Pennine
Peridot

Pyrites
Realgar
Rosaker
Sylvine
Sylvite
Thorite
Thulite
Tripoli
Turgite
Ulexite
Uralite
Uranite
Uranium
Zeolite
Zincite
Zoisite
Zorgite

8 letters:
Adularia
Allanite
Analcime
Analcite
Andesine
Ankerite
Antimony
Aphanite
Asbestos
Autunite
Blue john
Boehmite
Boracite

Braunite
Brookite
Calamine
Cerusite
Chlorite
Chromite
Cinnabar
Cleveite
Corundum
Crocoite
Cryolite
Datolite
Dendrite
Diallage
Diaspore
Diopside
Dioptase
Disthene
Dolomite
Dysodile
Dysodyle
Enargite
Epsomite
Erionite
Euxenite
Fayalite
Feldspar
Flinkite
Fluorite
Galenite
Gibbsite
Goethite
Graphite
Gyrolite
Hematite
Hyacinth
Idocrase
Ilmenite
Iodyrite
Jarosite
Lazulite
Lazurite
Lewisite
Limonite
Massicot

Melilite
Metamict
Mimetite
Monazite
Nephrite
Noselite
Orpiment
Petuntse
Petuntze
Prehnite
Pyroxene
Resalgar
Rock-salt
Sanidine
Saponite
Siderite
Smaltite
Smectite
Sodalite
Stannite
Stibnite
Stilbite
Taconite
Tenorite
Titanite
Troilite
Xenotime
Zaratite

9 letters:
Alabaster
Allophane
Amazonite
Amphibole
Anglesite
Anhydrite
Anorthite
Aragonite
Argentite
Atacamite
Blackjack
Blacklead
Carnelian
Carnotite
Celestine

Celestite
Cerussite
Chabazite
Cheralite
Chondrule
Cobaltine
Cobaltite
Coccolite
Columbate
Columbite
Covellite
Elaeolite
Enhydrite
Enstatite
Erythrite
Fibrolite®
Fluorspar
Gehlenite
Germanite
Geyserite
Gmelinite
Goslarite
Haematite
Harmotome
Hercynite
Hiddenite
Kaolinite
Kermesite
Kieserite
Magnesite
Magnetite
Malachite
Manganite
Marcasite
Margarite
Marialite
Microlite
Microlith
Millerite
Mispickel
Mizzonite
Monzonite
Moonstone
Muscovite
Natrolite

Nepheline
Nephelite
Niccolite
Nitratine
Olivenite
Ottrelite
Ozocerite
Ozokerite
Pargasite
Pectolite
Penninite
Periclase
Pericline
Phenacite
Phenakite
Pigeonite
Pleonaste
Polianite
Pollucite
Powellite
Proustite
Rhodonite
Rubellite
Scapolite
Scheelite
Scolecite
Sepiolite
Spodumene
Sylvanite
Tantalite
Tremolite
Troostite
Tungstite
Turquoise
Uraninite
Uvarovite
Variscite
Vulpinite
Wavellite
Wernerite
Willemite
Witherite
Wulfenite
Zinkenite

10 letters:
Actinolite
Alabandine
Alabandite
Andalusite
Bastnasite
Calaverite
Carnallite
Chalcocite
Chessylite
Chrysolite
Chrysotile
Colemanite
Cordierite
Crocoisite
Dyscrasite
Forsterite
Gadolinite
Garnierite
Glauconite
Halloysite
Heulandite
Honey-stone
Hornblende
Indicolite
Indigolite
Jamesonite
Laurdalite
Meerschaum
Microcline
Oligoclase
Oomphacite
Orthoclase
Perovskite
Phosgenite
Polybasite
Polyhalite
Pyrolusite
Pyroxenite
Pyrrhotine
Pyrrhotite
Redruthite
Riebeckite
Ripidolite
Samarskite

Sapphirine
Serpentine
Smaragdite
Sperrylite
Sphalerite
Staurolite
Tennantite
Thaumasite
Thenardite
Thorianite
Tiemannite
Torbernite
Tourmaline
Triphylite
Vanadinite
Wolframite
Zinckenite

11 letters:
Alexandrite
Amblygonite
Annabergite
Apophyllite
Baddeleyite
Bastnaesite
Cassiterite
Cerargyrite
Chiastolite
Chloanthite
Chrysoberyl
Clay mineral
Clinochlore
Crocidolite
Dendrachate
Franklinite
Greenockite
Hypersthene
Josephinite
Labradorite
Lapis lazuli
Molybdenite
Pentlandite
Philogopite
Phosphorite
Piedmontite

Pitchblende
Psilomelane
Pyrargyrite
Sillimanite
Smithsonite
Tetradymite
Vermiculite
Vesuvianite
Ythro-cerite

12 letters:
Arfvedsonite
Arsenopyrite
Babingtonite
Bismuthinite
Chalcanthite
Chalcopyrite
Cristobalite
Dumortierite
Feldspathoid
Fluorapatite
Hemimorphite
Pyromorphite
Pyrophyllite
Senarmontite
Skutterudite
Strontianite
Synadelphite
Tetrahedrite
Wollastonite

13 letters:
Bismuth glance
Clinopyroxene
Cummingtonite
Rhodochrosite

15 letters:
Montmorillonite

Missiles

2 letters:
MX
V-2

3 letters:
AAM
ABM
AGM
ASM
ATM
SAM
SSM
UAM

4 letters:
Ammo
Ball
Bolt
Bomb
Dart
HEAT
ICBM
IRBM
LEAP
MIRV
Scud
Shot
SLBM
SLCM
Styx
Thor

5 letters:
Arrow
Atlas
Bolas
Kiley
Kyley
Kylie
Onion
Shell
Smart

Spear
Titan

6 letters:
AMRAAM
Bullet
Cruise
Dum-dum
Exocet
Guided
Pellet
Rocket
Topol M
Tracer

7 letters:
Dingbat
Grenade
Harpoon
Patriot
Polaris
Quarrel
Skybolt
Torpedo
Trident
Warhead

8 letters:
Air-to-air
Anti-ship
Anti-tank
Buzz bomb
Maverick
Pershing
Poseidon
Snowball
Standoff
Tomahawk

9 letters:
Ballistic
Boomerang
Doodlebug

Fléchette
Minuteman
Smart bomb

10 letters:
Blue streak
Flying bomb
Side-winder
Wire-guided

11 letters:
Heat-seeking
Interceptor
Thunderbird

12 letters:
Surface to air

13 letters:
Anti-ballistic

16 letters:
Surface to surface

17 letters:
Sea-launched cruise

25 letters:
Intercontinental ballistic

26 letters:
Submarine-launched
 ballistic

43 letters:
Multiple independently
 targeted re-entry vehicle

Molecules

3 letters:
DNA

5 letters:
Codon
Dimer
Kinin

6 letters:
Chiral
Hapten
Isomer
Ligand
Trimer

7 letters:
Achiral
Carbene
Monomer
Peptide
Polymer
Uridine

8 letters:
Acceptor
Cavitand
Coenzyme
Cofactor
Replicon

9 letters:
Buckyball
Cobalamin
Fullerene
Long-chain
Metameric
Semantide

10 letters:
Metabolite

11 letters:
Chromophore

Closed chain
Footballene

12 letters:
Enantiomorph
Stereoisomer

14 letters:
Polysaccharide

Monastic orders

6 letters:
Sangha

7 letters:
Cluniac
Saivite
Shaolin

8 letters:
Basilian
Trappist
Vaisnava

9 letters:
Capuchins
Carmelite
Celestine

Dominican
Mathurins
Red Friars

10 letters:
Bendictine
Carthusian
Cistercian
Feuillants
Franciscan

11 letters:
Augustinian
Bridgettine
Camaldolese
Gilbertines
Tironensian

White Canons

12 letters:
Redemptorist
Trinitarians

14 letters:
Knights Templar
Premonstratian

17 letters:
Christian Brothers
Premonstratensian
Visitation Sisters

20 letters:
Mendicant Augustinian

Monkeys, apes and other primates

3 letters:
Pug
Sai

4 letters:
Douc

Leaf
Mico
Mona
Nala
Saki
Tana

Titi
Zati

5 letters:
Cebus
Chimp

Diana
Drill
Green
Indri
Jocko
Lemur

Loris
Magot
Midas
Orang
Sajou
Silen
Toque

6 letters:
Aye-aye
Baboon
Bandar
Bonnet
Bonobo
Chacma
Coaita
Colugo
Galago
Gelada
Gibbon
Grison
Grivet
Guenon
Howler
Indris
Jackey
Langur
Macaco
Malmag
Monkey
Rhesus
Sagoin
Saguin
Sifaka
Simpai
Spider
Tee-tee

Uakari
Vervet
Wou-wou
Wow-wow

7 letters:
Cebidae
Colobus
Gorilla
Guereza
Hanuman
Hoolock
Jacchus
Kipunji
Macaque
Meerkat
Mycetes
Nasalis
Ouakari
Sagouin
Saimiri
Sapajou
Siamang
Silenus
Tamarin
Tarsier
Wistiti

8 letters:
Bushbaby
Capuchin
Durukuli
Entellus
Mandrill
Mangabey
Marmoset
Ouistiti

Squirrel
Talapoin
Wanderoo

9 letters:
Hylobates
Orang-utan
Phalanger
Proboscis

10 letters:
Barbary ape
Chimpanzee
Cynomolgus
Jackanapes
Silverback

11 letters:
Douroucouli
Flying lemur
Green monkey
Orang-outang
Platyrrhine

12 letters:
Bonnet monkey
Howler monkey
Rhesus monkey
Slender loris
Spider monkey

14 letters:
Squirrel monkey

15 letters:
Proboscis monkey

Monks

3 letters:
Dan
Dom

4 letters:
Bede
Lama

5 letters:
Abbot
Aidan
Arhat
Black

Bonze
Bruno
Friar
Prior

6 letters:
Austin
Bhikhu
Culdee
Jerome
Mendel
Oblate
Sangha

7 letters:
Beghard
Brother
Caedmon
Caloyer
Cluniac
Félibre
Hegumen
Jacobin
Maurist

8 letters:
Acoemeti
Basilian
Cenobite
Jacobite
Olivetan
Pelagian
Rasputin
Salesian
Talapoin
Theatine
Trappist

9 letters:
Celestine
Coenobite
Dominican
Gyrovague
Hesychast
Thelemite

10 letters:
Bernardine
Carthusian

Cistercian
Hildebrand
Norbertine
Savonarola
Thelonious

11 letters:
Abbey-lubber
Augustinian
Benedictine
Bodhidharma
Bonaventura
Ignorantine
Mekhitarist
Tironensian

12 letters:
Bethlehemite
Mechitharist

13 letters:
Archimandrite
Thomas à Kempis

Monsters

3 letters:
Orc

4 letters:
Eten
Ogre

5 letters:
Ettin
Giant
Harpy
Hydra
Lamia
Snark
Teras
Troll
Yowie

6 letters:
Alecto
Bunyip
Dragon
Erebus
Fafnir
Geryon
Gorgon
Kraken
Medusa
Moloch
Nessie
Scylla
Simorg
Simurg
Sphinx
Typhon
Wyvern

Zombie

7 letters:
Caliban
Chimera
Cyclops
Grendel
Simurgh
Taniwha
Vampire
Wendego
Wendigo
Werwolf
Ziffius

8 letters:
Asmodeus
Behemoth

Cerberus
Chimaera
Godzilla
Mastodon
Minotaur
Opinicus
Stegodon
Typhoeus
Werewolf

9 letters:
Dinoceras
Fire-drake
Leviathan
Stegosaur
Wasserman

10 letters:
Cockatrice
Hippogriff
Jabberwock

Sarsquatch

11 letters:
Chichevache
Hippocampus
Jörmungandr
Triceratops

12 letters:
Bandersnatch
Frankenstein

Mosses

3 letters:
Fog
Hag

4 letters:
Club
Hagg
Peat
Rose

5 letters:
Agate
Irish

Marsh
Usnea

6 letters:
Ceylon
Hypnum
Lichen
Litmus

7 letters:
Acrogen
Iceland
Lycopod

Muscoid
Parella
Spanish

8 letters:
Reindeer
Sphagnum
Staghorn

9 letters:
Carrageen
Lecanoram

Protonema
Wolf's claw

10 letters:
Carragheen
Fontinalis

11 letters:
Polytrichum
Selaginella

Motor sports

6 letters:
MotoGP

7 letters:
Karting

8 letters:
Rallying
Speedway

9 letters:
Autocross
Motocross

10 letters:
Drag racing
Formula One
Rallycross
Scrambling

11 letters:
Motor racing

12 letters:
Banger racing
Hillclimbing

13 letters:
Motor rallying

14 letters:
Stock car racing

15 letters:
Demolition derby
Sports car racing

16 letters:
Motor-cycle racing
Touring car racing

18 letters:
Monster truck racing

Mountaineers

5 letters:
Munro, *Sir HT*

6 letters:
Conway, *Sir Martin*
Harrer, *Heinrich*
Norgay, *Tenzing*
Willss, *Sir Alfred*

7 letters:
Corbett, *JR*
Hillary, *Sir Edmund*
Mallory, *George*
Messner, *Reinhold*

Shipman, *Eric*
Simpson, *Joe*
Whymper, *Edward*
Workman, *Fannie Bullock*

8 letters:
Petzoldt, *Paul*

9 letters:
Bonington, *Chris*

10 letters:
Freshfield, *DW*

Mountains

2 letters:
K2

3 letters:
Apo
Ida
Kaf
Ore

4 letters:
Alai
Blue
Bona
Cook
Etna
Fuji
Harz
Hoss
Isto
Jaya
Jura
Meru
Nebo
Oeta
Ossa
Rigi

Rosa
Viso
Zeil

5 letters:
Abora
Adams
Aldan
Altai
Amara
Andes
Aneto
Arber
Athos
Atlas
Badon
Black
Blanc
Coast
Corno
Djaja
Eiger
Ellis
Evans
Ghats
Green

Guyot
Hekla
Horeb
Idris
Kamet
Kenya
Leone
Logan
Marcy
Munro
Ozark
Rocky
Rydal
Sinai
Siple
Snowy
Table
Tabor
Tatra
Teide
Tyree
Urals
Welsh

6 letters:
Amhara

Anadyr
Arafat
Ararat
Averno
Balkan
Bogong
Carmel
Cho Oyu
Cradle
Dragon
Egmont
Elbert
Elberz
Elbrus
Erebus
Gilead
Gimbal
Hermon
Hoggar
Hoosac
Kunlun
Lhotse
Makalu
Mourne
Musala
Negoiu

Ortles
Pamirs
Pelion
Pisgah
Pocono
Robson
Scopus
Sorata
Steele
Tasman
Taunus
Taurus
Vernon
Vosges
Zagros

7 letters:
Aorangi
Aragats
Arcadia
Belukha
Bernina
Brocken
Buffalo
Calvary
Cariboo
Cascade
Chianti
Corbett
Dapsang
Everest
Helicon
Kaufman
Kennedy
Khingan
Kuenlun
Lebanon
Lucania
Manaslu
Markham
Nan Shan
Olympus
Orontes
Palomar
Perdido

Pilatus
Rainier
Rhodope
Scafell
Selkirk
Skiddaw
Snowdon
Sperrin
Stanley
Sudeten
Toubkal
Travers
Troglav
Whitney
Wicklow
Zard Kuh

8 letters:
Anai Mudi
Arcadian
Ben Nevis
Cambrian
Cevennes
Damavand
Demavend
Estrella
Fujiyama
Grampian
Hymettus
Illimani
Jungfrau
Katahdin
Kinabalu
King Peak
Klínovec
Leibnitz
McKinley
Mitchell
Mulhacén
Pennines
Pinatubo
Pyrenees
Rushmore
Skalitsy
Smólikas

St Helen's
Taraniki
Tien Shan
Vesuvius
Victoria
Waun Fach
Wrangell

9 letters:
Aconcagua
Allegheny
Annapurna
Apennines
Argentera
Ben Lomond
Blackburn
Blue Ridge
Cairngorm
Catskills
Caucasian
Connemara
Corcovado
Demavrand
Dhaulagir
Dolomites
El Capitan
Emi Koussi
Grampians
Guadalupe
Helvellyn
Highlands
Himalayas
Hindu Kush
Inselberg
Jebel Musa
Karakoram
Kings Peak
Lenin Peak
Longs Peak
Mansfield
Marmolada
Mont Blanc
Nanda Devi
Narodnaya
Parnassus

Pikes Peak
Puy de Dôme
Rock Creek
Sugarloaf
Tirich Mir
Tongariro
Vancouver
Venusberg
Weisshorn
Woodroffe
Zugspitze

10 letters:
Arakan Yoma
Ben Macdhui
Blanca Peak
Cantabrian
Carpathian
Delectable
Dhaulagiri
Erymanthus
Erzgebirge
Gannet Peak
Grand Teton
Great Gable
Harney Peak
Horselberg
Kongur Shan
Kosciuszko
Laurentian
Masharbrum
Matterhorn
Monte Corno
Montserrat
Pentelikon
Piz Bernina
Pobeda Peak
Puncak Jaya
Puy de Sancy
St Michael's
Tengri Khan
Timpanogos
Waddington
Washington
Wellington

11 letters:
Adirondacks
Alaska Range
Appalachian
Aran Fawddwy
Bartle Frere
Bimberi Peak
Brooks Range
Coast Ranges
Drakensberg
Fairweather
Gerlachovka
Kilimanjaro
Kolyma Range
Munku-Sardyk
Nanga Parbat
Picode Teide
Salmon River
Scafell Pike
Schneekoppe
Sierra Madre
Sir Sandford

12 letters:
Albert Edward
Cascade Range
Citlaltépetl
Godwin Austen
Gran Paradiso
Kanchenjunga
Ruahine Range

Sierra Nevada
Slieve Donard
Tararua Range
Ulugh Muztagh
Victoria Peak
Vinson Massif
Western Ghats

13 letters:
Carmarthen Van
Carrantuohill
Clingman's Dome
Croagh Patrick
Flinders Range
Frenchman's Cap
Grossglockner
Humphreys Peak
Kangchenjunga
Massif Central
Mount of Olives
Petermann Peak
San Bernardino
Slide Mountain
Table Mountain
White Mountain

14 letters:
Bohemian Forest
Carnarvon Range
Finsteraarhorn
Hamersley Range

Kaikoura Ranges
Kommunizma Peak
Liverpool Range
Musgrove Ranges
Rawenzori Range
Ruwenzori Range
Stirling Ranges
Stzelecki Range

15 letters:
Cerro de Mulhacén
Uncompahgre Peak

16 letters:
Blue Mountain Peak
Macdonnell Ranges
Thabana Ntlenyana

17 letters:
Continental Divide
Sir Wilfrid Laurier
Sugar Loaf Mountain
Transylvanian Alps
Warrumbungle Range

19 letters:
Macgillicuddy's Reeks

20 letters:
Salmon River Mountains

Murderers

4 letters:
Bird, *Derrick*
Cain
Gacy, *John*
Gein, *Ed*
Moat, *Raoul*
Ruby, *Jack*
Ryan, *Michael*
West, *Fred*
West, *Rosemary*

5 letters:
Booth, *John Wilkes*
Brady, *Ian*
Bundy, *Ted*
Ellis, *Ruth*

6 letters:
Bonney, *William*
Borden, *Lizzie*
Corday, *Charlotte*
Dahmer, *Jeffrey*

Graham, *Barbara*
Manson, *Charles*
Nilsen, *Dennis*
Oswald, *Lee Harvey*
Pearce, *Charlie*
Sirhan, *Sirhan*

7 letters:
Chapman, *Mark*
Crippen, *Hawley*
Gilmore, *Gary*

Hindley, *Myra*
Huntley, *Ian*
Macbeth
Panzram, *Carl*
Shipman, *Harold*
Wuornos, *Aileen*

8 letters:
Chessman, *Caryl*
Christie, *John*
Hamilton, *Thomas*
Son of Sam

9 letters:
Bible John
Hauptmann, *Bruno*
Sutcliffe, *Peter*

11 letters:
Billy the Kid

13 letters:
Jack the Ripper

14 letters:
Leopold and Loeb

17 letters:
The Moors Murderers

18 letters:
The Boston Strangler
The Yorkshire Ripper

Muscles

3 letters:
Abs
Lat
Pec

4 letters:
Pecs
Quad

5 letters:
Psoas
Teres
Tonus

6 letters:
Biceps
Flexor
Pathos
Rectus
Smooth
Soleus
Tensor
Thenar

7 letters:
Agonist
Azygous
Ciliary
Deltoid
Dilator

Erecter
Erector
Evertor
Gluteus
Iliacus
Laxator
Levator
Pylorus
Rotator
Sarcous
Scalene
Sthenic
Triceps

8 letters:
Abductor
Adductor
Effector
Elevator
Extensor
Glutaeus
Kreatine
Masseter
Myotonia
Occlusor
Omohyoid
Opponent
Pectoral
Peroneus
Platysma

Pronator
Risorius
Scalenus
Serratus
Splenial
Striated
Temporal

9 letters:
Arytenoid
Attollens
Cremaster
Depressor
Diaphragm
Digastric
Hamstring
Mylohyoid
Perforans
Quadratus
Retractor
Sartorius
Sphincter
Supinator
Suspensor
Tenaculum
Trapezius
Voluntary

10 letters:
Antagonist

Buccinator
Compressor
Contractor
Corrugator
Obicularis
Perforatus
Protractor
Quadriceps
Sarcolemma

Suspensory

11 letters:
Accelerator
Accessorius
Constrictor
Lumbricalis
Rhomboideus

13 letters:
Gastrocnemius

14 letters:
Gluteus maximus
Peroneal muscle

15 letters:
Latissimus dorsi

Muses

Name	Muse of
Calliope	Epic poetry
Clio	History
Erato	Love poetry
Euterpe	Lyric poetry and music
Melpomene	Tragedy
Polyhymnia	Singing, mime, and sacred dance
Terpsichore	Dance and choral song
Thalia	Comedy and pastoral poetry
Urania	Astronomy

Mushrooms and other edible fungi

3 letters:
Cep

5 letters:
Enoki
Horse
Hypha
Magic
Morel

6 letters:
Aedium
Agaric
Blewit
Button
Hyphal
Ink-cap
Meadow
Oyster
Shroom

Waxcap

7 letters:
Blewits
Parasol
Porcini
Porcino
Truffle

8 letters:
Aecidium
Penny-bun
Puffball
Shiitake

9 letters:
Fly agaric
Gyromitra
Shaggy cap

10 letters:
Champignon
Lawyer's wig
Liberty cap
Shaggymane

11 letters:
Ascomycetes
Chanterelle
Velvet shank

12 letters:
Black truffle
Horn of plenty
Scotch bonnet
Shaggy ink cap
White truffle

13 letters:
Straw mushroom

14 letters:
Button mushroom
Meadow mushroom
Oyster mushroom

15 letters:
Destroying angel
Wood ear mushroom

16 letters:
Shiitake mushroom

Music

CLASSICAL MUSIC GENRES

5 letters:
Early
Salon

6 letters:
Galant
Gothic
Rococo
Serial

7 letters:
Ars nova
Baroque

8 letters:
Romantic

9 letters:
Classical

10 letters:
Ars antiqua
Minimalist
Twelve-tone

11 letters:
Nationalist

Renaissance

12 letters:
Dodecaphonic
Late medieval
Neoclassical
Post-romantic

13 letters:
Early medieval
Expressionist
Impressionist
Music concrète

TYPES OF COMPOSITION

3 letters:
Air
Duo

4 letters:
Aria
Coda
Duet
Lied
Mass
Raga
Reel
Song
Trio

5 letters:
Canon
Dirge
Dumka
Elegy
Étude
Fugue

Galop
Gigue
March
Motet
Nonet
Octet
Opera
Polka
Psalm
Suite
Waltz

6 letters:
Anthem
Ballet
Bolero
Chorus
Lament
Medley
Minuet
Pavane
Septet

Sextet
Sonata

7 letters:
Ballade
Bourrée
Cantata
Canzona
Canzone
Chorale
Czardas
Fantasy
Gavotte
Ländler
Mazurka
Partita
Passion
Pibroch
Prelude
Quartet
Quintet
Requiem

Romance
Scherzo
Toccata

Serenade
Sonatina
Symphony
Tone poem

Humoresque
Opera buffa
Opera seria
Strathspey
Trio sonata

8 letters:
Barceuse
Canticle
Cavatina
Chaconne
Concerto
Fantasia
Galliard
Hornpipe
Madrigal
Nocturne
Notturno
Operetta
Oratorio
Overture
Part song
Pastiche
Phantasy
Rhapsody
Ricercar
Rigadoon
Rigadoun

9 letters:
Allemande
Bagatelle
Barcarole
Capriccio
Ecossaise
Farandole
Impromptu
Interlude
Passepied
Pastorale
Polonaise
Quadrille
Ricercare
Singspiel
Song cycle

10 letters:
Albumblatt
Canzonetta
Concertino
Grand opera

11 letters:
Concertante
Contradance
Contredanse
Passacaglia
Schottische
Sinfonietta

12 letters:
Concertstück
Divertimento

13 letters:
Symphonic poem

14 letters:
Concerto grosso
Divertissement

19 letters:
Sinfonia concertante

POPULAR MUSIC TYPES

3 letters:
AOR
Bop
Dub
Pop
Rag
Rai
Rap
Ska

4 letters:
Folk
Funk
Go-go
Goth
Jazz

Loco
Punk
Rave
Rock
Romo
Soca
Soul
Trad
Zouk

5 letters:
Bebop
Blues
Cajun
Crunk
Cu-bop

Disco
Dream
Early
Gabba
Grime
House
Indie
Kwela
Muzak®
Neume
P-funk
Piped
Ragga
Salon
Salsa
Samba

Sokah
Swing
Zoppo

6 letters:
Bebung
Doo-wop
Fusion
Gagaku
Garage
Gospel
Gothic
Grunge
Hip-hop
Jungle
Khayal

Marabi
Motown®
New Age
Reggae
Techno
Thrash
Trance
Zydeco

7 letters:
Afropop
Ambient
Bhangra
Britpop
Calypso
Ceilidh
Chamber
Country
Dubstep
Gangsta
Hardbag
Hardbop
Klezmer
New Wave
Pibroch
Qawwali
Ragtime
Skiffle
Soukous
Trip hop
Ziganka

8 letters:
Acid jazz
Acid rock
Bluebeat
Concrete
Cool jazz
Flamenco
Folk rock
Free jazz

Glam rock
Hardcore
Hard rock
High life
Jazz-funk
Jazz-rock
Karnatak
Lollipop
Mariachi
Mbaqanga
Punk rock
Trad jazz

9 letters:
Acid house
Bluegrass
Breakbeat
Bubblegum
Dixieland
Folk music
Hillbilly
Honky-tonk
Indie folk
Rock'n'roll
Spiritual
Surf music
Swingbeat
Technopop
Warehouse

10 letters:
Chopsticks
Death metal
Delta Blues
Gangsta rap
Gothic rock
Heavy metal
Hindustani
Industrial
Merseybeat
Modern jazz

New Country
Polyrhythm
Rockabilly
Rocksteady
Shoegazing
Urban blues
World music

11 letters:
Country rock
Harmolodics
Motor rhythm
New romantic
Psychobilly
Raggamuffin
Rock and roll
Stadium rock
Third stream
Thrash metal
Tin Pan Alley

12 letters:
Boogie-woogie
Country blues

13 letters:
Detroit techno
Happy Hardcore

14 letters:
Mainstream jazz
New Orleans jazz
Rhythm and blues

15 letters:
Musique concrete
Progressive rock

17 letters:
Country and western

MUSICAL EXPRESSIONS AND TEMPO INSTRUCTIONS

Instruction	Meaning
Accelerando	With increasing speed

Instruction	Meaning
Adagio	Slowly
Agitato	In an agitated manner
Allegretto	Fairly quickly or briskly
Allegro	Quickly, in a brisk, lively manner
Amoroso	Lovingly
Andante	At a moderately slow tempo
Andantino	Slightly faster than andante
Animato	In a lively manner
Appassionato	Impassioned
Assai	(in combination) very
Calando	With gradually decreasing tone and speed
Cantabile	In a singing style
Con	(in combination) with
Con affeto	With tender emotion
Con amore	Lovingly
Con anima	With spirit
Con brio	Vigorously
Con fuoco	With fire
Con moto	Quickly
Crescendo	Gradual increase in loudness
Diminuendo	Gradual decrease in loudness
Dolce	Gently and sweetly
Doloroso	In a sorrowful manner
Energico	Energetically
Espressivo	Expressively
Falsetto	high-pitched voice
Forte	Loud or loudly
Fortissimo	Very loud
Furioso	In a frantically rushing manner
Giocoso	Merry
Grave	Solemn and slow
Grazioso	Graceful
Lacrimoso	Sad and mournful
Larghetto	Slowly and broadly, but less so than largo
Largo	Slowly and broadly
Legato	Smoothly and connectedly
Leggiero	Light
Lento	Slowly
Maestoso	Majestically
Marziale	Martial
Mezzo	(in combination) moderately
Moderato	At a moderate tempo
Molto	(in combination) very
Non troppo or non tanto	(in combination) not too much

Instruction	Meaning
Pianissimo	Very quietly
Piano	Softly
Più	(in combination) more
Pizzicato	(in music for stringed instruments) to be plucked with the finger
Poco *or* un poco	(in combination) a little
Pomposo	In a pompous manner
Prestissimo	Faster than presto
Presto	Very fast
Quasi	(in combination) almost, as if
Rallentando	Becoming slower
Rubato	With a flexible tempo
Scherzando	In jocular style
Sciolto	Free and easy
Semplice	Simple and unforced
Sforzando	With strong initial attack
Smorzando	Dying away
Sospirando	'sighing', plaintive
Sostenuto	In a smooth and sustained manner
Sotto voce	Extremely quiet
Staccato	(of notes) short, clipped, and separate
Strascinando	Stretched out
Strepitoso	Noisy
Stringendo	With increasing speed
Tanto	(in combination) too much
Tardo	Slow
Troppo	(in combination) too much
Vivace	In a brisk lively manner
Volante	'flying', fast and light

MUSICAL MODES

Mode	Final note
I Dorian	D
II Hypodorian	A
III Phrygian	E
IV Hypophrygian	B
V Lydian	F
VI Hypolydian	C
VII Mixolydian	G
VIII Hypomixolydian	D
IX Aeolian	A
X Hypoaeolian	E
XI Ionian	C
XII Hypoionian	G

MUSICAL INSTRUMENTS

2 letters:
Ax
Gu

3 letters:
Axe
Gue
Jug
Kit
Lur
Oud
Saz
Uke
Zel

4 letters:
Bell
Crwd
Drum
Fife
Gong
Harp
Horn
Kora
Koto
Lure
Lute
Lyre
Moog®
Oboe
Pipa
Pipe
Rate
Reed
Rote
Sang
Tuba
Vina
Viol
Whip
Zeze

5 letters:
Aulos
Banjo
Bongo
Bugle
Cello
Chime
Clave
Cobza
Conga
Corno
Crowd
Crwth
Dobro®
Flute
Guiro
Gusla
Gusle
Gusli
Kazoo
Mbira
Naker
Nebel
Ngoma
Organ
Piano
Quena
Rebec
Regal
Sanko
Sansa
Sarod
Shalm
Shawm
Sitar
Tabla
Tabor
Tibia
Veena
Viola
Zanze
Zinke

6 letters:
Antara
Cither
Citole
Cornet
Cymbal
Euphon
Fiddle
Flugel
Guitar
Kanoon
Maraca
Poogye
Racket
Rebeck
Ribibe
Sancho
Santir
Santur
Shalme
Sittar
Spinet
Syrinx
Tabour
Tam-tam
Timbal
Tom-tom
Trigon
Tymbal
Vielle
Violin
Zither
Zufolo

7 letters:
Alphorn
Althorn
Bagpipe
Bandore
Bandura
Baryton
Bassoon
Bazooka

Bodhrán
Celesta
Celeste
Cembalo
Chikara
Cithara
Cithern
Cittern
Clarion
Clavier
Console
Cornett
Cowbell
Cymbalo
Dichord
Dulcian
Fagotto
Flutina
Gamelan
Gittern
Hautboy
Helicon
High-hat
Kalimba
Kantela
Kantele
Kithara
Klavier
Lyricon
Mandola
Marimba
Musette
Ocarina
Pandora
Pandore
Pandura
Pianola®
Piccolo
Poogyee
Posaune
Rackett
Sackbut
Sambuca

Samisen
Santour
Sarangi
Saxhorn
Saxtuba
Serpent
Sistrum
Tambour
Tambura
Theorbo
Timbrel
Timpani
Trumpet
Tympani
Tympany
Ukelele
Ukulele
Vihuela
Violone
Vocoder
Whistle
Zuffolo

8 letters:
Angklung
Archlute
Autoharp®
Bagpipes
Barytone
Bass drum
Bass viol
Bouzouki
Calliope
Canorous
Carillon
Charango
Cimbalom
Cimbalon
Clarinet
Clarsach
Clavecin
Cornetto
Cornpipe
Cromorna
Cromorne

Crumhorn
Cymbalon
Dulcimer
Gemshorn
Guarneri
Guimbard
Handbell
Hautbois
Hornpipe
Humstrum
Jew's-harp
Keyboard
Key-bugle
Langspel
Lyra viol
Mandolin
Manzello
Martenot
Melodeon
Melodica
Melodion
Mirliton
Ottavino
Panpipes
Phorminx
Polyphon
Psaltery
Recorder
Reco-reco
Reed pipe
Side drum
Slughorn
Spinette
Sticcado
Sticcato
Surbahar
Tamboura
Tamburin
Tenoroon
Theremin®
Triangle
Trombone
Virginal
Vocalion
Zambomba

Zampogna

9 letters:
Accordion
Alpenhorn
Baby grand
Balalaika
Bandoneon
Baryulele
Böhm flute
Bombardon
Castanets
Chalumeau
Cornemuse
Decachord
Euphonium
Flageolet
Flexatone
Gittarone
Gran cassa
Gutbucket
Harmonica
Harmonium
Idiophone
Kent-bugle
Krummhorn
Langspiel
Mandoline
Monochord
Mouth-harp
Nose flute
Octachord
Orpharion
Pantaleon
Pastorale
Polyphone
Reed organ
Saxophone
Seraphine
Slughorne
Snare drum
Sopranino
Stockhorn
Trompette
Washboard

Welsh harp
Wood block
Wurlitzer®
Xylophone
Xylorimba

10 letters:
Basset horn
Bass guitar
Bullroarer
Chitarrone
Clavichord
Concertina
Contrabass
Cor anglais
Didgeridoo
Double bass
Flugelhorn
French horn
Gramophone
Grand piano
Hurdy-gurdy
Kettledrum
Mellophone
Mouth organ
Oboe d'amore
Ophicleide
Orpheoreon
Pantachord
Shakuhachi
Sousaphone
Squeeze-box
Steam organ
Stylophone
Symphonium
Tambourine
Thumb piano
Vibraphone

11 letters:
Aeolian harp
Bach trumpet
Barrel organ
Chordophone
Clairschach

Contrabasso
Drum machine
English horn
Harmoniphon
Harpsichord
Heckelphone
Hunting horn
Nickelodeon
Orchestrina
Orchestrion
Phonofiddle
Player piano
Slide guitar
Square piano
Steel guitar
Straduarius
Synthesizer
Trump-marine
Viola d'amore
Violoncello

Chamber organ
Chapman stick®
Chinese block
Clavicembalo
Concert grand
Cottage piano
Glockenspiel
Hammond
  organ®
Harmoniphone
Metallophone
Oboe da caccia
Penny whistle
Sarrusophone
Stock and horn
Stradivarius
Tromba-marina
Tubular bells
Uillean pipes
Upright piano
Viola da gamba

13 letters:
Contrabassoon
Contrafagotto
Double bassoon
Ondes Martenot
Panharmonicon
Physharmonica
Spanish guitar

14 letters:
Electric guitar
Glass harmonica
Hawaiian guitar
Portative organ
Viola da braccio

15 letters:
Electronic organ

16 letters:
Pedal steel guitar

12 letters:
Boudoir grand

See also:
➤ **Composers** ➤ **Orchestral instruments** ➤ **Jazz: forms**
➤ **Jazz: terms** ➤ **Jazz: musicians** ➤ **Notes and rests** ➤ **Works of literature and music**

Musketeers

5 letters:
Athos

6 letters:
Aramis

7 letters:
Porthos

9 letters:
D'Artagnan

Muslim denominations and sects

4 letters:
Shia

5 letters:
Druse
Druze
Imami
Jafri

Malik
Shiah
Sunni
Zaidi

6 letters:
Hanafi
Nizari

Senusi
Shafi'i
Shiite
Sufism

7 letters:
Hanbali
Isma'ili

Senussi

8 letters:
Alawites

Wahabism
Zaidyyah

9 letters:
Alaouites
Isma'lilsm
Wahhabism

Mythology

CHARACTERS IN CLASSICAL MYTHOLOGY

2 letters:
Io

4 letters:
Ajax
Dido
Echo
Leda

5 letters:
Atlas
Circe
Helen
Ixion
Jason
Medea
Midas
Minos
Muses
Niobe
Orion
Paris
Priam
Remus
Sibyl

6 letters:
Adonis
Aeneas
Castor
Charon
Europa
Hector
Hecuba
Icarus
Medusa

Pollux
Psyche
Semele
Thisbe

7 letters:
Actaeon
Amazons
Arachne
Ariadne
Calypso
Electra
Galatea
Jocasta
Oedipus
Orestes
Orpheus
Pandora
Perseus
Pyramus
Romulus
Silenus
Theseus
Ulysses

8 letters:
Achilles
Antigone
Atalanta
Callisto
Daedalus
Eurydice
Ganymede
Heracles
Hercules
Menelaus

Odysseus
Penelope
Pleiades
Sisyphus
Tantalus
Tiresias

9 letters:
Agamemnon
Andromeda
Argonauts
Cassandra
Narcissus
Pygmalion

10 letters:
Andromache
Cassiopeia
Hippolytus
Hyacinthus
Persephone
Polydeuces
Polyphemus
Prometheus
Proserpina

12 letters:
Clytemnestra

14 letters:
Hermaphroditus

PLACES IN CLASSICAL MYTHOLOGY

4 letters:
Styx
Troy

5 letters:
Hades
Lethe

6 letters:
Erebus
Thebes

7 letters:
Acheron
Colchis
Elysium
Helicon
Olympus

8 letters:
Tartarus

9 letters:
Parnassus

10 letters:
Phlegethon

19 letters:
Islands of the Blessed

MYTHOLOGICAL CREATURES

3 letters:
Elf
Fay
Nix
Orc
Roc

4 letters:
Faun
Fury
Peri

5 letters:
Afrit
Dryad
Dwarf
Fairy
Genie
Giant
Harpy
Hydra
Jinni
Kylin
Lamia
Naiad
Nixie
Nymph
Oread
Pixie
Satyr

Siren
Sylph
Troll

6 letters:
Afreet
Bunyip
Djinni
Djinny
Dragon
Geryon
Goblin
Gorgon
Hobbit
Jinnee
Kelpie
Kraken
Merman
Nereid
Scylla
Sphinx

7 letters:
Banshee
Centaur
Chimera
Cyclops
Echidna
Erlking
Gremlin

Grendel
Griffin
Griffon
Gryphon
Mermaid
Oceanid
Phoenix
Tricorn
Unicorn

8 letters:
Basilisk
Behemoth
Cerberus
Chimaera
Minotaur

9 letters:
Charybdis
Hamadryad
Hobgoblin
Impundulu
Leviathan
Sasquatch
Tokoloshe
Wood nymph

10 letters:
Cockatrice
Hippogriff

Hippogryph
Leprechaun

Salamander
Water nymph

11 letters:
Androsphinx
Hippocampus

CHARACTERS IN NORSE MYTHOLOGY

3 letters:
Ask
Lif

4 letters:
Atli

5 letters:
Mimir
Regin

6 letters:
Fafnir
Gudrun
Gunnar
Sigurd

7 letters:
Andvari
Sigmund
Wayland

8 letters:
Brynhild
Gutthorn
Hreidmar

10 letters:
Lifthrasir

PLACES IN NORSE MYTHOLOGY

3 letters:
Hel

4 letters:
Hela

6 letters:
Asgard
Utgard

7 letters:
Asgarth
Bifrost
Midgard

8 letters:
Midgarth
Niflheim
Valhalla

9 letters:
Jotunheim

10 letters:
Jotunnheim

See also:
➤ **Actaeon's hounds** ➤ **Ancient cities** ➤ **Arthurian legend**
➤ **Fates** ➤ **Giants and giantesses** ➤ **Gods and Goddesses**
➤ **Gorgons** ➤ **Graces** ➤ **Greeks** ➤ **Harpies** ➤ **Hercules,
labours of** ➤ **Monsters** ➤ **Muses** ➤ **Rivers of Hell** ➤ **Seven
against Thebes** ➤ **Wonders of the ancient world**

Nn

Nerves

4 letters:
Axon

5 letters:
Cyton
Nidus
Optic
Ulnar
Vagus

6 letters:
Bouton
Facial

Myelon
Radial

7 letters:
Cranial
Dendron
Excitor
Sciatic
Somatic
Synapse

8 letters:
Acoustic

Ganglion

9 letters:
Autonomic
Depressor
Epicritic
Trochlear

10 letters:
Commissure
Perikaryon
Trigeminal
Vestibular

11 letters:
Octulomotor
Solar plexus

12 letters:
Baroreceptor
Electrotonus

13 letters:
Proprioceptor

Newspapers and magazines

2 letters:
GQ
OK

3 letters:
FHM
Red
She
Viz
Zoo

4 letters:
Best
Chat
Chic
Elle
Heat
Mind
Mojo

More
Nuts
Time
Word

5 letters:
Bella
Blick
Bliss
Hello
Metro
Prima
Punch
Ta Nea
Uncut
Vogue
Which
Wired
Woman

6 letters:
El Pais
Forbes
Granta
Loaded
Nature
Pepper
Pravda
Record
The Sun
War Cry

7 letters:
Company
Die Welt
Die Zeit
Esquire
Fortune
Hustler

Le Monde
Mayfair
Newsday
Options
Playboy
The Face
The Lady
The Star
Time Out
Tribune

8 letters:
Big Issue
Campaign
Gay Times
Il Giorno
La Stampa
Le Figaro
Navy News

Newsweek
New Woman
Observer
The Oldie
The Onion
The Times
USA Today

9 letters:
Classic FM
Dagbladet
Daily Mail
Daily Star
Expressen
Ideal Home
L'Humanité
New Yorker
Smash Hits
The Lancet
The Tablet
The Tatler
Total Film
Woman's Own

10 letters:
Asian Times
Daily Sport
Denver Post
Film Review
France-Soir
Il Giornale
Irish Times
La Lanterne
Libération
Private Eye
Racing Post
Radio Times
Sunday Mail
Sunday Post
Vanity Fair

11 letters:
Bild Zeitung
Boston Globe
Daily Mirror

De Telegraaf
El Periodico
Marie Claire
Melody Maker
Miami Herald
Morning Star
New York Post
Ouest France
Sunday Sport
Sunday World
The European
The Guardian
The Scotsman
The Universe
Woman's Realm

12 letters:
Angling Times
Boston Herald
Cosmopolitan
Daily Express
Family Circle
Fortean Times
History Today
Il Messaggero
La Repubblica
La Voix du Nord
New Scientist
New Statesman
New York Times
Nursing Times
People's Daily
Poetry Review
Seattle Times
Sunday Herald
Sunday Mirror
Sunday People
The Economist
The Spectator
Woman and Home
Woman's Weekly

13 letters:
Evening Herald
Horse and Hound

Just Seventeen
Mother and Baby
Reader's Digest
The Bookseller
The Watchtower
Wales on Sunday
Woman's Journal
Yorkshire Post

14 letters:
Chicago Tribune
Daily Telegraph
Financial Times
France-Dimanche
House and Garden
Kansas City Star
Literary Review
News of the World
Publishing News
The Independent
The Sunday Times
Washington Post

15 letters:
Algemeen Dagblad
Berliner Zeitung
Chicago Sun-Times
Evening Standard
Exchange and Mart
Express on Sunday
Harpers and Queen
Homes and Gardens
Los Angeles Times
The Mail on Sunday

16 letters:
Dazed and Confused
Detroit Free Press
Diario de Noticias
Houston Chronicle
Irish Independent
National Enquirer
New York Daily News
Scotland on Sunday
The People's Friend

The Scots Magazine

Philadelphia Enquirer

17 letters:
Corriere della Sera
Dallas Morning News
New Musical Express
Sunday Independent
Wall Street Journal

18 letters:
National Geographic
The Sunday Telegraph

20 letters:
Orange County Register

21 letters:
British Medical Journal
San Francisco Chronicle

22 letters:
The Independent on Sunday

26 letters:
International Herald Tribune
The Times Literary Supplement

28 letters:
Frankfurter Allgemeine Zeitung

Nobility

RANKS OF BRITISH NOBILITY (IN ORDER OF PRECEDENCE)

Royal duke	Marquis	Viscountess
Royal duchess	Marchioness	Baron
Duke	Earl	Baroness
Duchess	Countess	Baronet
Marquess	Viscount	

RANKS OF FOREIGN NOBILITY

5 letters:
Boyar
Count

6 letters:
Prince

7 letters:
Grandee

8 letters:
Archduke
Burgrave
Countess
Marchesa
Marchese

Marquis
Vicomte

Margrave
Marquise
Princess

9 letters:
Grand duke
Landgrave

10 letters:
Margravine

Vicomtesse

11 letters:
Archduchess
Landgravine

12 letters:
Grand duchess

Notes and rests

British name	American name
Breve	Double-whole note
Semibreve	Whole note
Minim	Half note
Crotchet	Quarter note
Quaver	Eighth note

British name	American name
Semiquaver	Sixteenth note
Demisemiquaver	Thirty-second note
Hemidemisemiquaver	Sixty-fourth note

Novelists

2 letters:
Mo, *Timothy*
Oë, *Kenzaburo*

3 letters:
Eco, *Umberto*
Kay, *Jackie*
Lee, *Harper*
Lee, *Laurie*
Nye, *Robert*
Rao, *Raja*

4 letters:
Amis, *Kingsley*
Amis, *Martin (Louis)*
Behn, *Aphra*
Bely, *Andrei*
Böll, *Heinrich*
Boyd, *William*
Buck, *Pearl*
Cela, *Camilo José*
Dunn, *Nell*
Fast, *Howard*
Ford, *Ford Madox*
Ford, *Richard*
Galt, *John*
Gide, *André (Paul Guillaume)*
Gold, *Herbert*
Gray, *Alasdair*
Hill, *Susan*
Hogg, *James*
Hope (Hawkins), *Sir Anthony*
Hugo, *Victor (Marie)*
Jong, *Erica*
King, *Francis*
King, *Stephen (Edwin)*
Levi, *Primo*
Mann, *Thomas*

Okri, *Ben*
Puzo, *Mario*
Read, *Piers Paul*
Rhys, *Jean*
Roth, *Henry*
Saki
Sand, *George*
Snow, *C(harles) P(ercy)*
Uris, *Leon*
Wain, *John*
West, *Morris*
West, *Rebecca*
Wouk, *Herman*
Zola, *Émile*

5 letters:
Adams, *Douglas*
Adams, *Richard*
Anand, *Mulk Raj*
Banks, *Iain*
Banks, *Lynne Reid*
Barth, *John*
Bates, *H(erbert) E(rnest)*
Bowen, *Elizabeth*
Bragg, *Melvin*
Brink, *André*
Brown, *George Douglas*
Brown, *George Mackay*
Bryne, *John*
Byatt, *A(ntonia) S(usan)*
Camus, *Albert*
Carey, *Peter*
Crane, *Stephen*
Defoe, *Daniel*
Desai, *Anita*
Doyle, *Arthur Conan*
Doyle, *Roddy*
Duffy, *Maureen*

Dumas, *Alexandre*
Eliot, *George*
Elkin, *Stanley*
Ellis, *Alice Thomas*
Elton, *Ben*
Faber, *Michel*
Figes, *Eva*
Frame, *Janet Paterson*
Frayn, *Michael*
Gogol, *Nikolai Vasilievich*
Gorky, *Maxim*
Gosse, *Sir Edmund (William)*
Grass, *Günter (Wilhelm)*
Hardy, *Thomas*
Hesse, *Hermann*
Heyer, *Georgette*
Hines, *Barry*
Hoban, *Russell*
Hulme, *Keri*
Innes, *(Ralph) Hammond*
James, *Henry*
James, *P(hyllis) D(orothy)*
Joyce, *James (Augustine Aloysius)*
Kafka, *Franz*
Keane, *Molly*
Kesey, *Ken*
Levin, *Adam*
Lewis, *(Harry) Sinclair*
Llosa, *Mario Vargos*
Lodge, *David (John)*
Lowry, *(Clarence) Malcolm*
Lurie, *Alison*
Marsh, *Ngaio*
Moore, *Brian*
Newby, *P(ercy) H(oward)*
Oates, *Joyce Carol*
O'Hara, *John*
Orczy, *Baroness Emmuska*
Ouida
Ozick, *Cynthia*
Paton, *Alan (Stewart)*
Peake, *Mervyn*
Powys, *John Cowper*
Queen, *Ellery*
Rolfe, *Frederick William*

Scott, *Sir Walter*
Selby, *Hubert Jr*
Shute, *Nevil*
Simon, *Claude*
Smith, *Iain Crichton*
Smith, *Zadie*
Spark, *Dame Muriel (Sarah)*
Stead, *C(hristian) K(arlson)*
Stein, *Gertrude*
Stone, *Robert*
Stowe, *Harriet Elizabeth Beecher*
Swift, *Graham*
Swift, *Jonathan*
Toole, *John Kennedy*
Tuohy, *Frank*
Twain, *Mark (Samuel L Clemens)*
Tyler, *Anne*
Verne, *Jules*
Vidal, *Gore*
Waugh, *Evelyn (Arthur St John)*
Wells, *H(erbert) G(eorge)*
Welsh, *Irvine*
Welsh, *Louise*
Welty, *Eudora*
White, *Antonia*
White, *Patrick*
White, *T(erence) H(anbury)*
Wilde, *Oscar (Fingal O'Flahertie Wills)*
Wolfe, *Thomas Clayton*
Wolfe, *Tom*
Wolff, *Tobias*
Woolf, *(Adeline) Virginia*
Yerby, *Frank*

6 letters:
Achebe, *Chinua*
Aldiss, *Brian*
Ambler, *Eric*
Archer, *Jeffrey*
Asimov, *Isaac*
Atwood, *Margaret*
Austen, *Jane*
Barker, *Elspeth*
Barker, *Pat*
Barnes, *Julian*

Bawden, *Nina*
Bellow, *Saul*
Berger, *John*
Berger, *Thomas*
Binchy, *Maeve*
Bowles, *Paul*
Braine, *John (Gerard)*
Brontë, *Anne*
Brontë, *Charlotte*
Brontë, *Emily (Jane)*
Brophy, *Brigid*
Buchan, *John*
Bunyan, *John*
Burney, *Fanny*
Butler, *Samuel*
Capote, *Truman*
Carter, *Angela*
Cather, *Willa*
Clarke, *Arthur C(harles)*
Cleary, *Jon*
Condon, *Richard*
Conrad, *Joseph*
Cooper, *James Fenimore*
Cooper, *Jilly*
Cooper, *William*
Davies, *(William) Robertson*
De Sade, *Marquis*
Didion, *Joan*
Farmer, *Philip José*
Fowles, *John (Robert)*
Fraser, *Antonia*
French, *Marilyn*
Fuller, *Roy*
Gaddis, *William*
Garner, *Helen*
Gibbon, *Lewis Grassic*
Godden, *(Margaret) Rumer*
Godwin, *William*
Goethe, *Johann Wolfgang von*
Graham, *Winston*
Graves, *Robert (Ranke)*
Greene, *(Henry) Graham*
Hailey, *Arthur*
Heller, *Joseph*
Hilton, *James*

Holtby, *Winifred*
Horgan, *Paul*
Howard, *Elizabeth Jane*
Hughes, *Thomas*
Hunter, *Evan*
Huxley, *Aldous (Leonard)*
Irving, *John*
Kaplan, *Johanna*
Kelman, *James*
Le Fanu, *(Joseph) Sheridan*
Le Guin, *Ursula*
Lively, *Penelope*
London, *Jack*
Mailer, *Norman (Kingsley)*
Malouf, *David*
Martel, *Yann*
Massie, *Allan*
McEwan, *Ian*
Miller, *Henry (Valentine)*
Mosley, *Nicholas*
O'Brien, *Edna*
O'Brien, *Flann*
Orwell, *George*
Passos, *John Roderigo Dos*
Porter, *Harold*
Porter, *Katherine Anne*
Powell, *Anthony*
Proulx, *E Annie*
Proust, *Marcel*
Rankin, *Ian*
Sartre, *Jean-Paul*
Sayers, *Dorothy L(eigh)*
Sharpe, *Tom*
Singer, *Isaac Bashevis*
Spring, *Howard*
Sterne, *Laurence*
Stoker, *Bram*
Storey, *David (Malcolm)*
Styron, *William*
Symons, *Julian*
Trevor, *William*
Updike, *John (Hoyer)*
Upward, *Edward (Falaise)*
Walker, *Alice*
Warner, *Marina*

Warren, *Robert Penn*
Weldon, *Fay*
Wesley, *Mary*
Wilder, *Thornton*
Wilson, *A(ndrew) N(orman)*
Wright, *Richard Nathaniel*

7 letters:
Ackroyd, *Peter*
Alvarez, *Al*
Angelou, *Maya*
Ballard, *J(ames) G(raham)*
Barstow, *Stan(ley)*
Bedford, *Sybille*
Bennett, *(Enoch) Arnold*
Burgess, *Anthony*
Burrows, *Edgar Rice*
Calvino, *Italo*
Canetti, *Elias*
Clavell, *James*
Coetzee, *J(ohn) M(ichael)*
Colette, *(Sidonie-Gabrielle)*
Collins, *Wilkie (William)*
Connell, *Evan*
Cookson, *Catherine*
DeLillo, *Don*
De Vries, *Peter*
Dickens, *Charles (John Huffam)*
Dickens, *Monica*
Dinesen, *Isak*
Drabble, *Margaret*
Durrell, *Gerald (Malcolm)*
Durrell, *Laurence*
Fleming, *Ian*
Forster, *E(dward) M(organ)*
Forsyth, *Frederick*
Francis, *Dick*
Gaskell, *Elizabeth*
Gibbons, *Stella*
Gilliat, *Penelope*
Gissing, *George (Robert)*
Glasgow, *Ellen*
Golding, *Sir William (Gerald)*
Goldman, *William*
Grisham, *John*

Haggard, *Sir H(enry) Rider*
Hartley, *L(eslie) P(oles)*
Hazzard, *Shirley*
Hurston, *Zora Neale*
Kennedy, *A(lison) L(ouise)*
Kennedy, *Margaret*
Kerouac, *Jack*
Kipling, *(Joseph) Rudyard*
Kundera, *Milan*
Lamming, *George*
Le Carré, *John*
Lehmann, *Rosamond*
Lessing, *Doris*
MacLean, *Alistair*
Mahfouz, *Naguib*
Malamud, *Bernard*
Manning, *Olivia*
Márquez, *Gabriel García*
Marryat, *(Captain) Frederick*
Maugham, *W(illiam) Somerset*
Mauriac, *François*
Mishima, *Yukio*
Mitford, *Nancy*
Murdoch, *Dame (Jean) Iris*
Nabokov, *Vladimir (Vladimirovich)*
Naipaul, *Sir V(idiadhar) S(urajprasad)*
Peacock, *Thomas Love*
Pynchon, *Thomas*
Raphael, *Frederic*
Renault, *Mary*
Rendell, *Ruth*
Richler, *Mordecai*
Robbins, *Harold*
Rushdie, *(Ahmed) Salman*
Saroyan, *William*
Shelley, *Mary (Wollstonecraft)*
Shields, *Carol*
Simenon, *Georges (Joseph Christian)*
Stewart, *J(ohn) I(nnes) M(ackintosh)*
Stewart, *Mary*
Süskind, *Patrick*
Tennant, *Emma*
Theroux, *Paul*
Tolkien, *J(ohn) R(onald) R(euel)*
Tolstoy, *Count Leo (Nikolayevich)*

Tranter, *Nigel*
Tremain, *Rose*
Tutuola, *Amos*
Walpole, *Horace*
Wharton, *Edith (Newbold)*
Wilding, *Michael*

8 letters:
Abrahams, *Peter*
Aldridge, *James*
Apuleius, *Lucius*
Beerbohm, *Max*
Bradbury, *Malcolm*
Bradford, *Barbara Taylor*
Brittain, *Vera*
Brookner, *Anita*
Bulgakov, *Mikhail Afanaseyev*
Cartland, *Barbara*
Chandler, *Raymond*
Christie, *Dame Agatha (Mary Clarissa)*
Correlli, *Maria*
Davidson, *Lionel*
De Balzac, *Honoré*
Deighton, *Len*
De Laclos, *Pierre Choderlos*
De Quincy, *Thomas*
Disraeli, *Benjamin*
Donleavy, *J(ames) P(atrick)*
Faulkner, *William*
Fielding, *Helen*
Fielding, *Henry*
Flaubert, *Gustave*
Forester, *C(ecil) S(cott)*
Freeling, *Nicholas*
Galloway, *Janice*
Gordimer, *Nadine*
Guterson, *David*
Heinlein, *Robert A(nson)*
Ishiguro, *Kazuo*
Jacobson, *Howard*
Jhabvala, *Ruth Prawer*
Keneally, *Thomas*
Kingsley, *Charles*
Lawrence, *D(avid) H(erbert)*
Macauley, *Rose*

MacInnes, *Colin*
McCarthy, *Tom*
Melville, *Herman*
Meredith, *George*
Michener, *James A(lbert)*
Mitchell, *Julian*
Mitchell, *Margaret*
Moorcock, *Michael*
Morrison, *Toni*
Mortimer, *John*
Mortimer, *Penelope*
Oliphant, *Margaret*
Ondaatje, *Michael*
Remarque, *Erich Maria*
Salinger, *J(erome) D(avid)*
Sillitoe, *Alan*
Smollett, *Tobias George*
Stendhal
Trollope, *Anthony*
Trollope, *Joanna*
Turgenev, *Ivan Sergeyevich*
Voltaire
Vonnegut, *Kurt*
Zamyatin, *Evgeny Ivanovich*

9 letters:
Blackmore, *R(ichard) D(oddridge)*
Bleasdale, *Alan*
Bromfield, *Louis*
Burroughs, *William*
Delafield, *E(dmée Elizabeth) M(onica)*
Du Maurier, *Dame Daphne*
Edgeworth, *Maria*
Feinstein, *Elaine*
Gerhardie, *William Alexander*
Goldsmith, *Oliver*
Goncharov, *Ivan Aleksandrovich*
Grossmith, *George*
Grossmith, *Weedon*
Hawthorne, *Nathaniel*
Hemingway, *Ernest (Millar)*
Highsmith, *Patricia*
Isherwood, *Christopher (William Bradshaw)*
Lermontov, *Mikhail Yurievich*

MacDonald, *George*
Mackenzie, *Sir (Edward Montague) Compton*
MacKenzie, *Henry*
Mankowitz, *(Cyril) Wolf*
McCullers, *Carson*
McLaverty, *Bernard*
Mitchison, *Naomi*
Monsarrat, *Nicholas*
O'Flaherty, *Liam*
Pasternak, *Boris Leonidovich*
Pratchett, *Terry*
Priestley, *J(ohn) B(oynton)*
Pritchett, *V(ictor) S(awdon)*
Radcliffe, *Ann*
Schreiner, *Olive*
Sholokhov, *Mikhail Aleksandrovich*
Steinbeck, *John (Ernest)*
Stevenson, *Robert Louis (Balfour)*
Thackeray, *William Makepeace*
Wa Thiong'o, *Ngugi*
Winterson, *Jeanette*
Wodehouse, *Sir P(elham) G(renville)*
Yourcenar, *Marguerite*

10 letters:
Bainbridge, *Beryl*
Ballantyne, *R(obert) M(ichael)*
Benedictus, *David*
Brooke-Rose, *Christina*
Chesterton, *G(ilbert) K(eith)*
De Beauvoir, *Simone*

Dostoevsky, *Fyodor Mikhailovich*
Fairbairns, *Zöe*
Fitzgerald, *F(rancis) Scott (Key)*
Fitzgerald, *Penelope*
Galsworthy, *John*
Markandaya, *Kamala*
McIlvanney, *William*
Richardson, *Dorothy*
Richardson, *Samuel*
Van der Post, *Laurens*
Vansittart, *Peter*
Waterhouse, *Keith*

11 letters:
Auchincloss, *Louis*
De Cervantes, *Miguel*
Di Lampedusa, *Guiseppe Tomasi*

12 letters:
De Maupassant, *(Henri René Albert) Guy*
Kazantazakis, *Nikos*
Solzhenitsyn, *Alexander Isayevich*

13 letters:
Alain-Fournier
Sackville-West, *Vita (Victoria Mary)*

14 letters:
Compton-Burnett, *Ivy*
De Saint-Exupéry, *Antoine*

Nuts

3 letters:
Cob

4 letters:
Cola
Kola
Mast
Pine
Rhus

5 letters:
Acorn
Areca
Arnut
Beech
Betel
Hazel
Lichi
Pecan

6 letters:
Acajou
Almond
Bauple
Brazil
Cashew
Cobnut
Illipe
Lichee
Litchi

Lychee
Marron
Monkey
Peanut
Pignut
Supari
Walnut

7 letters:
Arachis
Babassu
Coquina
Filberd
Filbert
Hickory
Praline
Prawlin

8 letters:
Chestnut
Earthnut
Hazelnut
Quandong
Sapucaia

9 letters:
Amygdalus
Barcelona
Beech-mast
Butternut
Chincapin
Chinkapin
Coco de mer
Goober pea
Groundnut

Macadamia
Mockernut
Pistachio
Sassafras

10 letters:
Chinquapin
Pine kernel
Queensland

12 letters:
Bertholletia

13 letters:
Dwarf chestnut

Oo

Occupations

2 letters:
AB
BA
CA
DD
GP
MA
MC
MD
MO
MP
Mr
PA
PM

3 letters:
BSc
CID
Deb
Doc
Don
Dux
Fan
Guy
Job
Kid
Lad
Man
Mrs
Nun
Pay
Rep
Sir
Spy

4 letters:
Aide
Babe
Baby
Bard
Beak
Bear
Beau
Boss
Bull
Chap
Char
Chef
Cook
Crew
Curé
Dean
Demy
Dick
Diva
Doxy
Dyer
Feed
Firm
Girl
G-man
Hack
Hand
Head
Hero
Hobo
Host
Lass
Lead
Magi

Maid
Miss
Monk
Page
Peer
Peon
Poet
Pope
Sage
Salt
Seer
Serf
Silk
Star
Tyro
Wage
Ward
Whip

5 letters:
Abbot
Actor
Ad-man
Adult
Agent
Baker
Belle
Boots
Bosun
Boxer
Buyer
Caddy
Cadet
Canon
Chief

Chips
Clerk
Coach
Crier
Crone
Crony
Crook
Decoy
Demon
Devil
Diver
Donor
Doyen
Dummy
Dutch
Elder
Envoy
Extra
Fakir
Felon
Fence
Fifer
Friar
Galen
Garbo
Ghost
Gipsy
Grass
Guard
Guest
Guide
Hewer
Issue
Judge
Juror

Laird
Limey
Local
Locum
Loser
Lover
Luter
Madam
Major
Maker
Maori
Mason
Mayor
Medic
Miner
Minor
Model
Nanny
Navvy
Nurse
Odist
Owner
Padre
Party
Pilot
Pin-up
Piper
Posse
Prior
Proxy
Pupil
Quack
Quill
Rabbi
Racer
Rider
Rishi
Rival
Rover
Saver
Sawer
Scout
Sewer
Slave
Smith

Sower
Staff
Tenor
Thief
Tiler
Tommy
Tramp
Tuner
Tutor
Uhlan
Usher
Valet
Vicar
Viner
Wench
Witch
Woman
Yokel
Youth

6 letters:
Abbess
Ad-mass
Air ace
Airman
Albino
Alumna
Archer
Artist
Au pair
Aurist
Author
Backer
Bandit
Banker
Barber
Bargee
Barker
Barman
Batman
Batter
Beadle
Bearer
Beater
Beggar

Beldam
Berber
Bishop
Boffin
Bookie
Bowman
Broker
Bugler
Bursar
Busker
Butler
Cabbie
Caddie
Caller
Camper
Cantor
Captor
Career
Carter
Carver
Casual
Censor
Cleric
Client
Codist
Co-heir
Consul
Coolie
Cooper
Copier
Copper
Co-star
Coster
Couper
Cowboy
Creole
Critic
Curate
Cutler
Cutter
Damsel
Dancer
Deacon
Dealer
Debtor

Deputy
Divine
Docker
Doctor
Double
Dowser
Draper
Drawer
Driver
Drudge
Duenna
Editor
Ensign
Escort
Eskimo
Etcher
Expert
Fabler
Factor
Feeder
Fellow
Fitter
Flunky
Flyman
Forger
Friend
Fuller
Gaffer
Gagman
Ganger
Gaoler
Garçon
Gaucho
German
Gigolo
Gillie
Glazer
Glover
Golfer
Graver
Grocer
Grower
Gunman
Gunner
Hatter

Hawker	Marine	Picket	Shadow
Healer	Marker	Pieman	Sheila
Helper	Master	Pirate	Shower
Herald	Matron	Pitman	Shrink
Hermit	Medico	Plater	Singer
Het-man	Medium	Player	Sister
High-up	Member	Pommie	Skater
Hippie	Menial	Porter	Skivvy
Hitman	Mentor	Potter	Skyman
Hosier	Mercer	Prater	Slater
Hunter	Mikado	Priest	Slavey
Hussar	Miller	Punter	Slayer
Hymner	Minion	Purser	Sleuth
Ice-man	Mister	Ragman	Smoker
Inmate	Moiler	Ranger	Sniper
Intern	Monger	Rating	Soutar
Jailer	Moppet	Reader	Souter
Jester	Mortal	Reaper	Sowter
Jet set	Mummer	Rector	Sparks
Jobber	Munshi	Regius	Squire
Jockey	Musico	Rhymer	Status
Joiner	Mystic	Rigger	Stoker
Jumper	Nannie	Ringer	Suitor
Junior	Native	Rioter	Sutler
Junker	Norman	Robber	Tailor
Keener	Notary	Rookie	Talent
Keeper	Novice	Runner	Tanner
Killer	Nudist	Sailor	Tartar
Lackey	Nuncio	Sapper	Tarvet
Lancer	Oboist	Sartor	Taster
Lascar	Odd job	Savage	Tatter
Lawyer	Office	Savant	Teller
Leader	Oilman	Sawyer	Tenant
Lector	Optime	Scorer	Teuton
Legate	Oracle	Scouse	Tiller
Lender	Orator	Scribe	Tinker
Lessee	Ostler	Sea-dog	Tinner
Levite	Outlaw	Sealer	Toiler
Limner	Packer	Seaman	Trader
Living	Parson	Second	Truant
Lodger	Pastor	Seller	Turner
Lutist	Patron	Senior	Tycoon
Lyrist	Pedlar	Sentry	Typist
Mahout	Penman	Server	Tyrant
Maiden	Pen-pal	Sexton	Umpire

Urchin	Ballboy	Collier	Esquire
Usurer	Bandman	Colonel	Farceur
Valuer	Barmaid	Commere	Farcist
Vanman	Baronet	Company	Farrier
Vendor	Bassist	Compere	Fiddler
Verger	Bedouin	Comrade	Fighter
Victor	Beldame	Convert	Fireman
Viking	Bellboy	Convict	Flagman
Waiter	Bellhop	Co-pilot	Flapper
Walk-on	Big name	Copyist	Flesher
Warden	Big shot	Copyman	Florist
Warder	Bit-part	Coroner	Footboy
Weaver	Blender	Corsair	Footman
Welder	Boarder	Cossack	Footpad
Whaler	Boatman	Counsel	Foreman
Winner	Bookman	Courier	Founder
Wizard	Bouncer	Cowherd	Frogman
Worker	Breeder	Cowpoke	Furrier
Wright	Brigand	Creator	Gambler
Writer	Builder	Crofter	Gate-man
Yeoman	Burglar	Crooner	General
	Bushman	Cropper	Ghillie
7 letters:	Butcher	Curator	Glazier
Abetter	Buttons	Custode	Gleaner
Abigail	Callboy	Cyclist	Grown-up
Acolyte	Calling	Danseur	Gun moll
Acrobat	Cambist	Daysman	Gymnast
Actress	Captain	Debater	Handler
Actuary	Captive	Denizen	Hangman
Admiral	Carrier	Dentist	Harpist
Adviser	Cashier	Diviner	Haulier
Almoner	Caulker	Dominie	Head boy
Alumnus	Caveman	Doorman	Headman
Amateur	Cellist	Dragoon	Heckler
Analyst	Chemist	Drayman	Heiress
Apostle	Chindit	Dresser	Heroine
Arbiter	Chorist	Driller	Hipster
Artisan	Citizen	Drummer	Histrio
Artiste	Cleaner	Dustman	Hostess
Assayer	Climber	Elogist	Hymnist
Athlete	Clippie	Embassy	Imagist
Attache	Coalman	Entrant	Invalid
Auditor	Cobbler	Equerry	Jack-tar
Aviator	Cockney	Escapee	Janitor
Bailiff	Colleen	Escaper	Jemedar

Juggler	Patient	Refugee	Starlet
Junkman	Patroon	Regular	Starman
Justice	Pearler	Remover	Starter
Knacker	Peasant	Rentier	Station
Knitter	Pianist	Rescuer	Steward
Learner	Picador	Reserve	Stipend
Lineman	Pierrot	Retinue	Student
Linkboy	Pilgrim	Rich man	Supremo
Linkman	Pioneer	Riveter	Surgeon
Lockman	Planner	Routine	Swagman
Look-out	Planter	Rustler	Tapster
Lorimer	Plumber	Saddler	Teacher
Maestro	Poacher	Sagaman	Tipster
Magnate	Poetess	Samurai	Tourist
Mailman	Pollman	Sandman	Trainee
Manager	Poloist	Scalper	Trainer
Mariner	Pontiff	Scenist	Trapper
Marshal	Poor man	Scholar	Trawler
Masseur	Pop idol	Scraper	Tripper
Matador	Pop star	Sea-cook	Trooper
Matelot	Post-boy	Sea-king	Trouper
Meatman	Postman	Sea-lord	Tumbler
Midwife	Prefect	Sea-wolf	Turfman
Milkman	Prelate	Seminar	Veteran
Mobsman	Premier	Senator	Viceroy
Mobster	Presser	Servant	Vintner
Modiste	Primate	Service	Visitor
Monitor	Printer	Settler	Warrior
Moulder	Privado	Sharper	Webster
Mourner	Private	Shearer	Whipper
Mudlark	Proctor	Sheriff	Wiseman
Navarch	Proofer	Shopman	Witness
Newsboy	Prophet	Shopper	Wolf cub
Newsman	Protégé	Showman	Woodman
Oarsman	Provost	Skinner	Woolman
Oculist	Prowler	Skipper	Workman
Officer	Puddler	Soldier	
Old salt	Punster	Soloist	**8 letters:**
Omnibus	Pursuer	Soprano	Abductor
Oratrix	Railman	Spartan	Adherent
Orderly	Rancher	Speaker	Adjutant
Page-boy	Rat race	Spinner	Advocate
Painter	Realtor	Sponsor	Aeronaut
Partner	Redskin	Spotter	Alderman
Passman	Referee	Stand-by	Alienist

Allopath	Chandler	Dragoman
Ambivert	Chaperon	Druggist
Anchoret	Chaplain	Duettist
Armorist	Choirboy	Educator
Armourer	Cicerone	Elegiast
Arranger	Cicisbeo	Embalmer
Assassin	Civilian	Emeritus
Assessor	Claimant	Emigrant
Attacker	Clansman	Emissary
Attorney	Classman	Employee
Axemaker	Clerkess	Engineer
Bagmaker	Clothier	Engraver
Banjoist	Co-author	Epic poet
Bankrupt	Comedian	Essayist
Banksman	Commando	Eulogist
Bargeman	Commoner	Examinee
Baritone	Compiler	Executor
Beadsman	Composer	Explorer
Bedesman	Conjurer	Exponent
Bedmaker	Convener	Fabulist
Beginner	Corporal	Factotum
Bigamist	Coryphee	Falconer
Blackleg	Cottager	Fanfaron
Blind man	Courtier	Fanmaker
Boardman	Coxswain	Farm hand
Bohemian	Creditor	Ferryman
Bondsman	Croupier	Figurant
Boniface	Cupmaker	Film idol
Borrower	Cutpurse	Filmstar
Botanist	Dairyman	Finalist
Bowmaker	Danseuse	Finisher
Boxmaker	Dead-head	Fishwife
Boy scout	Deck-hand	Flatfoot
Brakeman	Delegate	Flautist
Brunette	Deserter	Floorman
Bummaree	Designer	Forester
Cabin boy	Detainee	Forgeman
Call-girl	Dictator	Freshman
Canoness	Diet cook	Front-man
Cardinal	Diocesan	Fugitive
Castaway	Diplomat	Fusilier
Ceramist	Director	Gangsman
Chairman	Disciple	Gangster
Chambers	Dogsbody	Gaolbird
Champion	Domestic	Gardener

Garroter	Labourer	Muralist
Gendarme	Land-girl	Murderer
Goatherd	Landlady	Musician
Governor	Landlord	Narrator
Gownsman	Landsman	Naturist
Graduate	Lapidary	Neophyte
Guardian	Law agent	Netmaker
Gunsmith	Lawgiver	Newcomer
Ham actor	Lawmaker	News-hawk
Handmaid	Laywoman	Nightman
Handyman	Lecturer	Norseman
Hatmaker	Licensee	Novelist
Hawkshaw	Life-peer	Objector
Haymaker	Linesman	Occupant
Head cook	Linguist	Official
Head girl	Listener	Onlooker
Headship	Logician	Op artist
Hebraist	Loiterer	Operator
Helmsman	Looker-on	Opponent
Henchman	Lumberer	Optician
Herdsman	Luminary	Oratress
Hijacker	Lyricist	Ordinand
Hired gun	Magician	Organist
Hired man	Mandarin	Overlord
Hireling	Mapmaker	Overseer
Home help	Marauder	Pardoner
Horseman	Marksman	Parodist
Hotelier	Masseuse	Party man
Houseboy	Mechanic	Passer-by
Hula girl	Mediator	Patentee
Huntsman	Melodist	Penmaker
Idyllist	Mercator	Perfumer
Importer	Merchant	Perjurer
Inceptor	Milkmaid	Picaroon
Informer	Millgirl	Pilferer
Initiate	Millhand	Pillager
Inkmaker	Milliner	Plagiary
Inventor	Minister	Poetling
Islander	Ministry	Poisoner
Jailbird	Minstrel	Polisher
Jet pilot	Mistress	Pontifex
Jeweller	Modeller	Position
Jongleur	Moralist	Potmaker
Juvenile	Motorist	Practice
Knife-boy	Muleteer	Preacher

Pressman
Prioress
Prisoner
Prizeman
Producer
Promoter
Prompter
Psychist
Publican
Pugilist
Purveyor
Quarrier
Radar man
Rag trade
Ragwoman
Receiver
Recorder
Reformer
Reporter
Resident
Retailer
Retainer
Reveller
Revenant
Reviewer
Rewriter
Ridleman
Road-gang
Rotarian
Rugmaker
Saboteur
Salesman
Salvager
Satirist
Sawbones
Sawsmith
Sciolist
Scullion
Sculptor
Seafarer
Seedsman
Selector
Sentinel
Sergeant
Servitor

Shepherd
Shipmate
Shopgirl
Showgirl
Side-kick
Sidesman
Silk gown
Sketcher
Sky-scout
Small fry
Smuggler
Solitary
Songster
Sorcerer
Spaceman
Spearman
Speed cop
Sprinter
Stageman
Star turn
Stockman
Storeman
Stowaway
Stranger
Stripper
Stroller
Stunt man
Superior
Superman
Supplier
Surveyor
Survivor
Swagsman
Tallyman
Taxpayer
Teddy boy
Teenager
Thatcher
Thespian
Thurifer
Tin miner
Tinsmith
Tom Thumb
Tone post
Top brass

Toreador
Torturer
Townsman
Trainman
Trappist
Tripeman
Tunester
Unionist
Union man
Vagabond
Valuator
Vanguard
Virtuoso
Vocalist
Vocation
Waitress
Ward maid
Wardress
Watchman
Waterman
Wayfarer
Wet nurse
Wheelman
Whiphand
Whipjack
Whittler
Wig maker
Woodsman
Workfolk
Workgirl
Workhand
Wrangler
Wrestler
Yodeller

9 letters:
Aborigine
Absconder
Aerialist
Alchemist
Anatomist
Anchoress
Anchorite
Annotator
Announcer

Annuitant
Antiquary
Apologist
Applicant
Appraiser
Arch-enemy
Architect
Archivist
Art critic
Art dealer
Artificer
Assistant
Associate
Astronaut
Attendant
Authoress
Authority
Automaton
Axlesmith
Balladist
Ballerina
Bargainer
Barrister
Barrow-boy
Beefeater
Bee keeper
Beermaker
Beggarman
Bellmaker
Biologist
Bit player
Boatswain
Bodyguard
Bodymaker
Boilerman
Boltsmith
Bookmaker
Bootblack
Bootmaker
Bradmaker
Brass hats
Brigadier
Buccaneer
Bunny girl
Bus driver

Bush pilot
Byrewoman
Bystander
Cab driver
Cabin crew
Café owner
Cakemaker
Cameraman
Candidate
Canvasser
Cardsharp
Caretaker
Carpenter
Casemaker
Celebrity
Cellarman
Centurion
Chain gang
Charterer
Charwoman
Chauffeur
Choralist
Chorus boy
Clergyman
Clinician
Clogmaker
Coadjutor
Coal miner
Coenobite
Colleague
Collector
Columnist
Combatant
Commander
Commodore
Companion
Concierge
Concubine
Conductor
Confessor
Confidant
Conqueror
Conscript
Constable
Contender

Contralto
Cornerboy
Cosmonaut
Cost clerk
Costumier
Court fool
Couturier
Covergirl
Crackshot
Cracksman
Crayonist
Cricketer
Cupbearer
Custodian
Cutthroat
Cymbalist
Daily help
Day-labour
Deaconess
Dean of men
Debutante
Decorator
Defendant
Dependent
Designate
Desk clerk
Detective
Dialogist
Dietician
Dispenser
Dog walker
Dollmaker
Dramatist
Drum major
Drysalter
Ecologist
Economist
Embezzler
Emolument
Enamelist
Enchanter
Engrosser
Entourage
Errand boy
Espionage

Estimator
Exchanger
Exchequer
Exciseman
Executive
Eye doctor
Fieldwork
Figurante
Film actor
Film extra
Film maker
Financier
Fire guard
First mate
Fisherman
Foreigner
Foundling
Freelance
Freemason
Fruiterer
Furnisher
Garreteer
Garrotter
Gas fitter
Gazetteer
Gem cutter
Geologist
Girl guide
Gladiator
Gluemaker
Go-between
Goldsmith
Gondolier
Governess
Grapevine
Grenadier
Guarantor
Guardsman
Guerrilla
Guest star
Guitarist
Gunrunner
Handsewer
Harbinger
Harbourer

Harlequin
Harmonist
Harpooner
Harvester
Head clerk
Herbalist
Hillbilly
Hired hand
Hired help
Historian
Home maker
Homeopath
Hottentot
House dick
Housemaid
Husbandry
Hypnotist
Immigrant
Innkeeper
Inscriber
In service
Inside man
Inspector
Interview
Ironminer
Ironsmith
Jaywalker
Jitterbug
Jobholder
Key worker
Kidnapper
Lacemaker
Lady's maid
Lampmaker
Lampooner
Land agent
Land force
Landowner
Landreeve
Land shark
Larcenist
Launderer
Laundress
Lawmonger
Lay figure

Lay reader
Lay sister
Legionary
Lensmaker
Librarian
Life coach
Lifeguard
Linotyper
Liontamer
Lip-reader
Liveryman
Loan agent
Lockmaker
Locksmith
Log-roller
Lord Mayor
Lowlander
Lumberman
Machinist
Major domo
Major poet
Make-up man
Male model
Male nurse
Man-at-arms
Man Friday
Medallist
Mendicant
Mercenary
Mesmerist
Messenger
Middleman
Minor poet
Model girl
Monitress
Moonraker
Mortician
Muscleman
Musketeer
Mythmaker
Navigator
Neighbour
Newsagent
Newshound
Nursemaid

Occultist
Odd job man
Office boy
Old master
Old stager
Ombudsman
Operative
Osteopath
Otologist
Outfitter
Panellist
Pantomime
Paparazzo
Part-owner
Passenger
Patrolman
Patroness
Paymaster
Paysagist
Pedagogue
Pen friend
Pen pusher
Pensioner
Performer
Personnel
Phone girl
Physician
Physicist
Picksmith
Pierrette
Pistoleer
Pitwright
Plaintiff
Plasterer
Ploughboy
Ploughman
Plunderer
Poetaster
Policeman
Pop artist
Pop singer
Portrayer
Portreeve
Possessor
Postulant

Postwoman
Poulterer
Precentor
Precursor
Prelector
Presbyter
President
Priestess
Principal
Privateer
Professor
Profiteer
Prud'homme
Publicist
Publisher
Puppeteer
Raconteur
Rainmaker
Ransacker
Ranzelman
Ratefixer
Ratepayer
Recordist
Reference
Registrar
Residency
Rhymester
Ringsider
Roadmaker
Rocketeer
Rocket man
Ropemaker
Roundsman
Rum runner
Rural dean
Sackmaker
Sacristan
Safemaker
Sailmaker
Sales girl
Sales team
Sassenach
Scarecrow
Scavenger
Scenarist

Schoolma'm
Scientist
Scrapegut
Scribbler
Scrivener
Sea-lawyer
Secretary
Seneschal
Sentryman
Seraskier
Serenader
Sermonist
Servitude
Shoemaker
Signaller
Signalman
Situation
Skin diver
Solicitor
Songsmith
Sonneteer
Sophister
Sophomore
Sorceress
Soubrette
Space crew
Speedster
Spider man
Spokesman
Sportsman
Stagehand
Stage idol
Star gazer
Statesman
Stationer
Steersman
Stevedore
Strike pay
Subaltern
Sub-editor
Subsitute
Suffragan
Swineherd
Tablemaid
Tailoress

Tap dancer
Tax evader
Tentmaker
Test pilot
Therapist
Timberman
Toolsmith
Town clerk
Towncrier
Tradesman
Traveller
Tribesman
Trumpeter
Tympanist
Undergrad
Usherette
Vigilante
Violinist
Volunteer
Wassailer
Waxworker
Weekender
Wheelsman
Winemaker
Woodreeve
Workwoman
Yachtsman
Youngster
Zitherist
Zoologist

10 letters:
Able seaman
Accomplice
Accountant
Advertiser
Aeronomist
Agrologist
Agronomist
Aide-de-camp
Air hostess
Air steward
Amanuensis
Ambassador
Anglo-Saxon

Anvilsmith
Apothecary
Apprentice
Arbitrator
Archbishop
Archdeacon
Archpriest
Aristocrat
Astrologer
Astronomer
Auctioneer
Audit clerk
Au pair girl
Babe in arms
Babysitter
Ballet girl
Ballplayer
Bandmaster
Bank robber
Baseballer
Bassoonist
Bear leader
Beautician
Bellringer
Benefactor
Billbroker
Billposter
Biochemist
Biographer
Blacksmith
Bladesmith
Blockmaker
Bludgeoner
Bluebottle
Bluejacket
Boatwright
Bogtrotter
Bombardier
Bonesetter
Bonus clerk
Bookbinder
Book dealer
Bookfolder
Bookholder
Bookkeeper

Bookseller
Bookwright
Bootlegger
Brain drain
Brakemaker
Brass smith
Bricklayer
Brickmaker
Broom maker
Brushmaker
Bulb grower
Bumbailiff
Bureaucrat
Burlesquer
Camera team
Campaigner
Cartoonist
Cat breeder
Cat burglar
Catechumen
Cavalryman
Ceramicist
Chainmaker
Chairmaker
Chancellor
Changeling
Chargehand
Charity boy
Chauffeuse
Chorus girl
Chronicler
Cider maker
Cigar maker
Claim agent
Clapper boy
Cloakmaker
Clockmaker
Clocksmith
Clog dancer
Cloisterer
Cloistress
Clothmaker
Clubmaster
Coachmaker
Coastguard

Co-director
Collar-work
Coloratura
Colporteur
Comedienne
Commandant
Commission
Competitor
Compositor
Concertist
Consultant
Contestant
Contractor
Controller
Copyreader
Copywriter
Corn doctor
Cornettist
Coryphaeus
Councillor
Counsellor
Country boy
Countryman
Couturière
Cover agent
Crackbrain
Cultivator
Customs man
Cytologist
Day tripper
Demoiselle
Dilettante
Dirty nurse
Disc jockey
Discounter
Discoverer
Dishwasher
Dispatcher
Dog breeder
Donkey work
Doorkeeper
Dramatizer
Dramaturge
Dressmaker
Drug pusher

Drummer boy
Dry cleaner
Duty roster
Early riser
Empiricist
Equestrian
Evangelist
Eye witness
Fabricator
Faith curer
Farmer's boy
Fellmonger
Fictionist
Film editor
Firemaster
Fire raiser
Fishmonger
Flag bearer
Flight crew
Flower girl
Folk singer
Footballer
Foot doctor
Forecaster
Forerunner
Forty-niner
Frame maker
Freebooter
Fund raiser
Gamekeeper
Game warden
Garage hand
Gatekeeper
Gatewright
Geisha girl
Geneticist
Geochemist
Geographer
Glassmaker
Glossarist
Goalkeeper
Gold beater
Gold digger
Goldworker
Grammarian

Grand prior
Groceryman
Gubernator
Gunslinger
Hall porter
Handmaiden
Handshaker
Hatchetman
Headhunter
Headmaster
Head porter
Head waiter
Hedgesmith
Henchwoman
Highlander
High priest
Highwayman
Hitchhiker
Holy orders
Honorarium
Horn player
Horologist
House agent
Husbandman
Impresario
Incendiary
Inhabitant
Inquisitor
Instructor
Ironmaster
Ironmonger
Ironworker
Jewel thief
Job printer
Journalist
Junk dealer
Kennelmaid
Kitchenboy
Kitchenman
Knifesmith
Land holder
Land jobber
Landlubber
Land pirate
Land waiter

Lapidarist
Laundryman
Law officer
Lay brother
Leading man
Legislator
Liberty man
Librettist
Licentiate
Lieutenant
Lighterman
Lime burner
Linotypist
Lobsterman
Lock keeper
Loggerhead
Loomworker
Lumberjack
Machineman
Magistrate
Mail robber
Management
Manageress
Manicurist
Manservant
Medical man
Medicaster
Message boy
Midshipman
Militiaman
Millwright
Mind-curist
Mind healer
Mindreader
Ministress
Missionary
Model maker
Monopolist
Moonshiner
Motley fool
Mouthpiece
Naturalist
Nautch girl
Naval cadet
Negotiator

Neutralist
Newscaster
News editor
Newsvendor
Newswriter
Night float
Night nurse
Notability
Nurseryman
Obituarist
Oil painter
Pallbearer
Pantomimic
Pantry maid
Papermaker
Park keeper
Park ranger
Pastrycook
Pathfinder
Pawnbroker
Peacemaker
Pearl diver
Pearly king
Pedestrian
Pediatrist
Pedicurist
Penologist
Perruquier
Petitioner
Pharmacist
Piano tuner
Piccoloist
Pickpocket
Piermaster
Plagiarist
Platelayer
Playbroker
Playwright
Playwriter
Poet-artist
Poet-farmer
Poet-priest
Politician
Postmaster
Prebendary

Priesthood
Prima donna
Private eye
Procurator
Programmer
Prolocutor
Proprietor
Prospector
Proveditor
Questioner
Quizmaster
Railwayman
Raw recruit
Recitalist
Researcher
Retirement
Revenue man
Revivalist
Rhapsodist
Ringmaster
Roadmender
Ropedancer
Ropewalker
Safeblower
Sales clerk
Sales force
Saleswoman
Saltworker
Sand-dancer
Scrutineer
Sculptress
Sea-captain
Seamstress
Second mate
Seminarian
Sempstress
Serologist
Serviceman
Session man
Shanghaier
Shipwright
Shopfitter
Shopkeeper
Signwriter
Sinologist

Songstress
Sound mixer
Spacewoman
Specialist
Speculator
Spy catcher
Staff nurse
Starmonger
Steelmaker
Step dancer
Stewardess
Stick-up man
Stockrider
Stocktaker
Stonemason
Storesmith
Strategist
Submariner
Subscriber
Supercargo
Supervisor
Supplicant
Swordsmith
Symphonist
Syncopator
Tally clerk
Tallywoman
Taskmaster
Taxi driver
Technician
Technocrat
Televiewer
Tenderfoot
Third party
Tilewright
Timekeeper
Trafficker
Translator
Tripehound
Tripewoman
Trombonist
Troubadour
Tweedledee
Tweedledum
Typesetter

Typing pool
Underagent
Understudy
Undertaker
Vegetarian
Versemaker
Versesmith
Veterinary
Vice-consul
Vice-master
Victualler
Vine grower
Wage earner
Wage worker
Wainwright
Watchmaker
Water guard
Wharfinger
Wholesaler
Winebibber
Winewaiter
Wireworker
Woodcarver
Woodcutter
Woodworker
Wool carder
Wool comber
Wool sorter
Wool winder
Workfellow
Working man
Workmaster
Workpeople
Worshipper

11 letters:
Abecedarian
Academician
Accompanist
Actor's agent
Antiquarian
Appointment
Army officer
Astrologist
Astronomist

Audio typist
Backroom boy
Bag snatcher
Bank cashier
Bank manager
Bargemaster
Basketmaker
Beauty queen
Bell founder
Beneficiary
Billsticker
Bingo caller
Bird fancier
Bird watcher
Board member
Bodybuilder
Body servant
Boilermaker
Boilersmith
Breadwinner
Bridgemaker
Broadcaster
Bronzesmith
Bullfighter
Bushfighter
Businessman
Candlemaker
Car salesman
Chamberlain
Chambermaid
Charcoalist
Cheerleader
Cheesemaker
Chiropodist
Choirmaster
Clairvoyant
Clergywoman
Coachwright
Co-authoress
Coffinmaker
Cognoscenti
Commentator
Congressman
Conspirator
Contributor

Conveyancer
Co-ordinator
Coppersmith
Court jester
Crane driver
Crimewriter
Crown lawyer
Cub reporter
Cypher clerk
Day labourer
Dean of women
Delivery man
Demographer
Distributor
Double agent
Draughtsman
Drill master
Drug peddler
Duty officer
Electrician
Embroiderer
Enlisted man
Entertainer
Estate agent
Etymologist
Executioner
Extortioner
Factory hand
Faith healer
Field worker
Fifth column
Fighting man
Filing clerk
Fingersmith
Fire brigade
Fire watcher
Flag captain
Flag officer
Flat dweller
Flying squad
Foot soldier
Fruit picker
Funambulist
Functionary
Galley slave

Gamesmaster
Gentlewoman
Ghostwriter
Ginger group
Glass blower
Glass cutter
Grave digger
Greengrocer
Gunman's moll
Haberdasher
Hairdresser
Hair stylist
Hammersmith
Handservant
Hardwareman
Head teacher
Hedgepriest
High sheriff
High society
Home crofter
Horse doctor
Horse trader
Housekeeper
Housemaster
Housemother
Housewright
Ice-cream man
Illuminator
Illusionist
Illustrator
Infantryman
Interpreter
Interviewer
Iron founder
Kitchenmaid
Lamplighter
Landscapist
Land steward
Laundrymaid
Leading lady
Leaseholder
Leatherneck
Ledger clerk
Lifeboatman
Locum tenens

Lollipop man
Lord Provost
Lorry driver
Madrigalist
Maidservant
Mandolinist
Manipulator
Masquerader
Master baker
Matinée idol
Mechanician
Medicine man
Merchantman
Metalworker
Method actor
Military man
Millionaire
Mimographer
Miniaturist
Momorialist
Money lender
Moonlighter
Mother's help
Mountaineer
Music critic
Naval rating
Needlewoman
Neurologist
Night hunter
Night porter
Night sister
Night worker
Novelettist
Numismatist
Onion Johnny
Optometrist
Ornamentist
Orthopedist
Palaestrian
Pamphleteer
Panelbeater
Panel doctor
Papal nuncio
Paperhanger
Paragrapher

Parish clerk
Parlourmaid
Pathologist
Pearlfisher
Pearly queen
Penny-a-liner
Petrologist
Philatelist
Philologist
Philosopher
Phonologist
Piece worker
Police cadet
Policewoman
Portraitist
Predecessor
Prizewinner
Probationer
Proofreader
Protagonist
Purseholder
Questionist
Quill driver
Radiologist
Rag merchant
Rank and file
Rear admiral
Relic monger
Research man
Rhetorician
River keeper
Roadsweeper
Rocket pilot
Rugby player
Safebreaker
Safecracker
Sandwichman
Saxophonist
School nurse
Scorekeeper
Scoutmaster
Scrap dealer
Scythesmith
Search party
Secret agent

Semanticist
Semaphorist
Semi-skilled
Senior clerk
Sharebroker
Sheep farmer
Shepherdess
Shipbuilder
Ship's cooper
Ship's tailor
Ship's writer
Shop steward
Silversmith
Sister tutor
Slaughterer
Slave trader
Smallholder
Sociologist
Space doctor
Spacewriter
Speechmaker
Stage player
Stagewright
Stallholder
Steeplejack
Stenotypist
Stereotyper
Stipendiary
Stockbroker
Stockfarmer
Stockjobber
Stonecutter
Storekeeper
Storyteller
Straight man
Stripteaser
Subordinate
Surrebutter
Swordmaster
Talent scout
Taxidermist
Telegrapher
Telepathist
Telephonist
Terpsichore

Testimonial
Ticket agent
Toastmaster
Tobacconist
Tommy Atkins
Tooth doctor
Tooth drawer
Town planner
Toxophilite
Train bearer
Train robber
Transcriber
Travel agent
Tree surgeon
Truck farmer
Typographer
Upholsterer
Van salesman
Versemonger
Vice-admiral
Vine dresser
Viola player
War reporter
Washerwoman
Water doctor
Water finder
Welfare work
Whalefisher
Wheelwright
White-collar
White hunter
Witch doctor
Woodshopper
Wool stapler
Working girl
Xylophonist
Youth leader

12 letters:

Actor-manager
Advance party
Air commodore
Aircraftsman
Air-sea rescue
Ambulance man

Anaesthetist
Armour bearer
Artilleryman
Balladmonger
Ballad singer
Ballet dancer
Bibliologist
Bibliopegist
Body snatcher
Booking clerk
Bookstitcher
Border sentry
Bottlewasher
Boulevardier
Bridgemaster
Brigade major
Cabinet-maker
Calligrapher
Camp follower
Candlewright
Caricaturist
Carpetbagger
Carpet fetter
Cartographer
Casual labour
Cattle lifter
Cerographist
Check-weigher
Chicken thief
Chief cashier
Chief justice
Chief mourner
Chief of staff
Chimney sweep
Chirographer
Chiropractor
Churchwarden
Circuit rider
Civil servant
Civil service
Clarinettist
Clerk of works
Coachbuilder
Collaborator
Commissioner

Confectioner
Conquistador
Contemporary
Corn chandler
Costermonger
Customs clerk
Deep-sea diver
Demonstrator
Desk sergeant
Doctor's round
Dramaturgist
Ecclesiastic
Electrotyper
Elocutionist
Entomologist
Entrepreneur
Escapologist
Exhibitioner
Experimenter
Ex-serviceman
Exterminator
Family doctor
Father figure
Field-marshal
Figure dancer
Filed officer
Filibusterer
Film director
Film producer
First officer
First reserve
Flying column
Flying doctor
Footplateman
Garret master
General agent
Geriatrician
Globetrotter
Grandstander
Group captain
Guest speaker
Gynecologist
Headmistress
Headshrinker
Heir apparent

High official
Hockey player
Holidaymaker
Hotel manager
Housebreaker
Housepainter
Hydropathist
Immunologist
Impersonator
Improvisator
Instructress
Intermediary
Jazz musician
Junior rating
Juvenile lead
King's counsel
Kitchen staff
Knifegrinder
Knifethrower
Lady superior
Landed gentry
Land surveyor
Law stationer
Lay-out artist
Leader writer
Legal adviser
Letter writer
Lexicologist
Line sergeant
Literary hack
Literary lion
Lithographer
Longshoreman
Loss adjuster
Maid of honour
Maître d'hôtel
Major-general
Make-up artist
Man of letters
Man of science
Manual worker
Manufacturer
Mass-producer
Master-at-arms
Mastersinger

Metallurgist
Metropolitan
Mezzo-soprano
Mineralogist
Money-changer
Monographist
Motorcyclist
Musicologist
Naval officer
Newspaperman
Notary public
Nutritionist
Obstetrician
Office bearer
Office junior
Pastoral poet
Patent office
Pediatrician
Penitentiary
Petty officer
Photographer
Physiologist
Plant manager
Ploughwright
Plumber's mate
Poet laureate
Postgraduate
Postmistress
Practitioner
Press officer
Principal boy
Prison warder
Prison worker
Quarrymaster
Racing driver
Radiodontist
Radiographer
Receptionist
Restaurateur
Sales manager
Scene-painter
Scene-shifter
Schoolmaster
Screenwriter
Scriptwriter

Scullery maid
Sister german
Site engineer
Snake-charmer
Social worker
Soil mechanic
Sole occupant
Special agent
Speechwriter
Spiritualist
Sportscaster
Sports master
Sportswriter
Staff officer
Stage manager
Statistician
Steel erector
Stenographer
Stereotypist
Stonedresser
Stormtrooper
Street-trader
Tax-collector
Technologist
Telegraph boy
Telephone man
Tennis player
Test engineer
Theatre nurse
Ticket holder
Ticket writer
Top executive
Trained nurse
Trichologist
Trick-cyclist
Troutbreeder
Undermanager
Vaudevillist
Vice-director
Vice-governor
Warehouseman
Water-diviner
Wind musician
Wine merchant
Wood-engraver

Worker priest
Working party
Workmistress
Works manager

13 letters:
Alongshoreman
Antique dealer
Archaeologist
Articled clerk
Audio-engineer
Barber-surgeon
Campanologist
Church officer
Civil engineer
Common law wife
Contortionist
Contrabandist
Cook-housemaid
Cotton spinner
Counter-jumper
Craftsmanship
Cryptographer
Dancing master
Dental surgeon
District nurse
Feature editor
Fellow-servant
Fencing master
Fortune-teller
Guardian angel
Gynaecologist
Harbour master
Health visitor
Industrialist
Lady-in-waiting
Lexicographer
Lift attendant
Lighthouseman
Livery servant
Lollipop woman
Maid-of-all-work
Master builder
Master mariner
Nightwatchman

Office manager
Old-clothes man
Poultry farmer
Printer's devil
Prison visitor
Process server
Rag-and-
　bone-man
Rent collector
Reseach worker
Scrap merchant
Ship's chandler
Shop assistant
Shop detective
Skeleton staff
Skilled worker
Slave labourer
Still-room maid
Street sweeper
Toastmistress
Traffic warden
Universal aunt
Window cleaner
Window dresser

14 letters:
Accomplishment
Apprenticeship
Audiometrician
Black marketeer
Bus conductress
Casual labourer
Charcoal burner
Chimney sweeper
Clerical worker

Coastguardsman
Commissionaire
Common informer
Dramatic critic
Elder statesman
Hotel detective
House decorator
House detective
King's messenger
Labour exchange
Maintenance man
Market gardener
Marriage broker
Matron of honour
Mining engineer
Munition worker
Naval architect
Nursing officer
Opposite number
Opthalmologist
Prison governor
Reverend Mother
Ship's carpenter
Sports reporter
Stage carpenter
Stamp collector
Standard bearer
Station manager
Store detective
Street musician
Superintendent
Tobacco planter
Troubleshooter
Turf accountant
Valet de chambre

Wedding planner

15 letters:
Blastfurnaceman
Bow Street runner
Colliery manager
Commission agent
Crossing sweeper
Customs official
District visitor
Father Christmas
Funeral director
Gentleman farmer
Gentleman's usher
Gossip columnist
Jack-of-all-trades
Old-age pensioner
One-parent family
Personal trainer
Planning officer
Police constable
Programme seller
Queen's messenger
Research chemist
Shorthand typist
Shorthand writer
Slave trafficker
Stretcher bearer
Surrogate father
Surrogate parent
Ticket collector
Tight-rope walker
Under-cover agent
Youth club leader

Officials

2 letters:	GOC	Exon	Chair
MC		Imam	Ephor
SL	**4 letters:**	Prog	Imaum
	Agha	Suit	Jurat
3 letters:	Cigs	**5 letters:**	Mayor
Aga	Dean	Amban	Mirza

Sewer
Usher

6 letters:
Ataman
Beadle
Bursar
Censor
Consul
Datary
Deacon
Hazzan
Hetman
Keeper
Lictor
Master
Notary
Purser
Sexton
Syndic
Verger
Warden
Yeoman

7 letters:
Agistor
Attaché
Bailiff
Coroner
Darogha
Equerry
Filacer
Filazer
Hayward

Jamadar
Jemadar
Jemidar
Marshal
Mueddin
Muezzin
Pooh-Bah
Proctor
Provost
Sheriff
Speaker
Steward
Tribune

8 letters:
Bimbashi
Black rod
Chairman
Claviger
Cursitor
Decurion
Delegate
Mandarin
Palatine
Summoner
Surveyor
Tipstaff
Verderer
Whiffler

9 letters:
Apparitor
Catchpole
Catchpoll

Commissar
Constable
Ealdorman
Escheator
Exciseman
Gauleiter
Intendant
Jobsworth
Landdrost
Moderator
Ombudsman
Polemarch
Precentor
President
Principal
Tahsildar
Treasurer
Waldgrave

10 letters:
Ambassador
Bumbailiff
Bureaucrat
Chairwoman
Chancellor
Magistrate
Postmaster
Procurator
Proveditor
Pursuivant
Silentiary
Subchanter
Supercargo
Tidewaiter

Timekeeper

11 letters:
Chairperson
Chamberlain
Functionary
Infirmarian
Shop steward
Stadtholder

12 letters:
Borough reeve
Commissioner
Jack-in-office
Remembrancer

13 letters:
Quartermaster

14 letters:
Provost-marshal

15 letters:
Plenipotentiary

16 letters:
Procurator fiscal
Public prosecutor
Returning officer

17 letters:
Compliance officer

Oils

3 letters:
Gas
Nim
Nut

4 letters:
Bone
Coal

Corn
Fuel
Musk
Neem
Oleo
Palm
Poon
Soya

Tung
Yolk

5 letters:
Ajwan
Argan
Attar
Benne

Benni
Clove
Colza
Crude
Fixed
Fusel
Heavy
Maize

Olive
Pulza
Rosin
Savin
Shale
Sperm
Spike
Stand
Train
Whale

6 letters:
Ajowan
Banana
Canola
Carapa
Carron
Castor
Cloves
Croton
Diesel
Drying
Elaeis
Jojoba
Neroli
Peanut
Ramtil
Savine
Semsem

Seneca
Sesame
Virgin

7 letters:
Butyrin
Cajeput
Cajuput
Camphor
Coconut
Dittany
Gingili
Jinjili
Linalol
Linseed
Lumbang
Menthol
Mineral
Mustard
Myrrhol
Naphtha
Picamar
Retinol
Ricinus
Tea tree
Vitriol

8 letters:
Bergamot

Camphire
Cod-liver
Flaxseed
Gingelli
Gingelly
Hempseed
Lavender
Linalool
Macassar
Oiticica
Paraffin
Pristane
Rapeseed

9 letters:
Groundnut
Macaw-tree
Neat's foot
Parathion
Patchouli
Quinoline
Sassafras
Spikenard
Star-anise
Sunflower
Terpineol
Vegetable

10 letters:
Citronella

Cottonseed
Eucalyptus
Juniper tar
Peppermint
Sandalwood
Turpentine
Ylang-ylang

11 letters:
Camphorated
Chaulmoogra
Chinese wood
Wintergreen

12 letters:
Benzaldehyde
Benzonitrile

13 letters:
Pentyl acetate
Sunflower seed

14 letters:
Glutaraldehyde

15 letters:
Evening primrose

Orange, shades of

4 letters:
Gold

5 letters:
Amber

Ochre
Peach

9 letters:
Grenadine

Tangerine

10 letters:
Terracotta

11 letters:
Burnt sienna

Orchestral instruments

4 letters:
Gong
Harp
Oboe
Tuba

5 letters:
Cello
Flute
Piano
Viola

6 letters:
Violin

7 letters:
Bassoon

Celesta
Piccolo
Timpani
Trumpet

8 letters:
Bass-drum
Clarinet
Trombone

9 letters:
Snare drum
Xylophone

10 letters:
Cor anglais

Double bass
French horn

11 letters:
English horn
Violoncello

12 letters:
Tubular bells

13 letters:
Contra-bassoon

Ores

3 letters:
Tin
Wad

4 letters:
Alga
Wadd

6 letters:
Copper
Glance

7 letters:
Bauxite
Bornite
Dry-bone

Niobite
Oligist
Peacock
Realgar

8 letters:
Calamine
Cerusite
Crocoite
Galenite
Ilmenite
Limonite
Smaltite
Tenorite

9 letters:
Coffinite
Haematite
Hedyphane
Ironstone
Phacolite
Proustite
Stream-tin

10 letters:
Calaverite
Chalcocite
Horseflesh
Iridosmine
Melaconite
Sphalerite

Stephanite

11 letters:
Pitchblende
Psilomelane
Pyrargyrite

12 letters:
Babingtonite
Chalcopyrite
Pyromorphite
Tetrahedrite

15 letters:
Stilpnosiderite

Organizations and treaties

2 letters:
EU

3 letters:
CAP
CBI
ECO
EEA
EIB
EMS
EMU
ESC
IFC
ILO
IMF
MMC

OFT
TUC
WTO

4 letters:
ACAS
CACM
CCCM
CFTA
CMEA
ECSC
EFTA
EBRD
EMCF
ERDF
GATT

IBRD
NATO
NEDC
OECD
OPEC
SEMA

5 letters:
LAFTA
NAFTA
UNIDO

6 letters:
ECOSOC
ECOWAS
NZAFTA

UNCTAD
UNIDO

7 letters:
Amnesty
CARICOM
CARIFTA
COMECON

8 letters:
Red Cross

9 letters:
World Bank

12 letters:
Treaty of Rome

13 letters:
European Union

14 letters:
Lomé agreements

16 letters:
Maastricht Treaty

18 letters:
Bretton Woods System

19 letters:
Office of Fair Trading
Trades Union Congress

20 letters:
European Economic Area

21 letters:
European Monetary Union

22 letters:
Caribbean Free Trade Area
European Investment Bank
European Monetary System
World Trade Organization

23 letters:
Single European Market Act

24 letters:
Common Agricultural Policy
Economic and Social Council
European Coal Organization

25 letters:
International Monetary Fund

27 letters:
Central American Common Market

28 letters:
European Free Trade Association

29 letters:
European Coal and Steel Community

30 letters:
Confederation of British Industry
Monopolies and Mergers Commission

31 letters:
European Monetary Cooperation Fund
European Regional Development Fund
International Finance Corporation
International Labour Organization
North American Free Trade Agreement

33 letters:
Caribbean Community and
  Common Market
General Agreement on Tariffs and
  Trade
Latin American Free Trade
  Association

34 letters:
Council for Mutual Economic
  Assistance
National Economic Development
  Council

36 letters:
Economic Community
  Of West African States

40 letters:
New Zealand and Australia Free
  Trade Agreement

41 letters:
Advisory, Conciliation, and
  Arbitration Service
Organization of Petroleum
  Exporting Countries

43 letters:
European Bank for Reconstruction
and Development

44 letters:
United Nations Conference on Trade
And Development

46 letters:
United Nations Industrial
Development Organization

48 letters:
International Bank for Reconstruction
and Development
Organization for Economic Cooperation
and Development

Organs

3 letters:
Ear
Fin

4 letters:
Gill
Wing

5 letters:
Corti
Ctene
Gonad
Liver
Serra

6 letters:
Carpel
Feeler
Fundus
Kidney
Radula
Spleen
Stamen
Syrinx

Thymus
Tongue
Tonsil
Uterus
Viscus
Vitals

7 letters:
Isomere
Medulla
Nectary
Oogonia
Pudenda
Saprobe
Viscera

8 letters:
Hapteron
Pancreas
Placenta
Pulmones
Receptor
Tentacle
Tympanum

9 letters:
Sensillum
Spinneret

10 letters:
Nephridium
Ovipositor
Parapodium
Photophore
Sporangium
Sporophore

11 letters:
Archegonium

12 letters:
Exteroceptor

13 letters:
Chemoreceptor
Photoreceptor

Oxbridge colleges

3 letters:
New

5 letters:
Clare
Green

Jesus
Keble
King's
Oriel

6 letters:
Darwin
Exeter
Girton
Merton
Queen's

Selwyn
Wadham

7 letters:
Balliol
Christ's
Downing
Kellogg
Linacre
Lincoln
New Hall
Newnham
St Anne's
St Cross
St Hugh's
St John's
Trinity
Wolfson

8 letters:
All Souls
Emmanuel
Homerton
Magdalen
Nuffield
Pembroke

Robinson
St Hilda's
St Peter's

9 letters:
Brasenose
Churchill
Clare Hall
Magdalene
Mansfield
St Antony's
St Edmund's
Templeton
Worcester

10 letters:
Greyfriars
Hughes Hall
Peterhouse
Somerville
St Stephen's
University

11 letters:
Blackfriars
Campion Hall

Fitzwilliam
Regent's Park
Trinity Hall

12 letters:
Christ Church
Sidney Sussex
St Benet's Hall
St Catharine's
St Catherine's
St Edmund Hall
Wycliffe Hall

13 letters:
Corpus Christi
Lucy Cavendish

16 letters:
Gonville and Caius
Harris Manchester
Lady Margaret Hall

Pp

Palms

3 letters:
Ita

4 letters:
Atap
Coco
Date
Doum
Nipa

5 letters:
Areca
Assai
Betel
Bussu
Macaw
Nikau
Ratan

Sabal

6 letters:
Buriti
Corozo
Elaeis
Gomuti
Gomuto
Gru-gru
Jupati
Kentia
Macoya
Raffia
Raphia
Rattan
Trooly

7 letters:
Babassu
Calamus
Coquito
Corypha
Euterpe
Jipyapa
Moriche
Palmyra
Paxiuba
Pupunha
Talipat
Talipot
Troelie
Troolie

8 letters:
Carnauba
Date tree
Groo-groo
Jipi-japa
Macahuba

9 letters:
Burrawang
Carnahuba

10 letters:
Chamaerops
Jippi-jappa

12 letters:
Chiqui-chiqui
Washingtonia

Papers

3 letters:
Art
Rag
Wax

4 letters:
Bank
Bond
Chad
Demy
Exam
File
Laid

Note
Rice
Sand
Test
Wall
Wove

5 letters:
Bible
Brown
Crepe
Crown
Emery

Flock
Glass
Graph
Green
India
Kraft
Linen
Sheet
Sugar
Touch
Waste
Waxed
White

6 letters:
Ballot
Baryta
Carbon
Coated
Filter
Garnet
Litmus
Manila
Retree
Tissue
Toilet
Vellum

7 letters:
Bromide
Manilla
Papyrus
Torchon
Tracing
Whatman®
Writing

8 letters:
Document
Foolscap
Glassine
Turmeric
Wrapping

9 letters:
Cartridge

Chiyogami
Cigarette
Cream-laid
Cream-wove
Hieratica
Onion-skin
Papillote
Parchment
Willesden

10 letters:
Cellophane®
Deckle-edge
Electronic

11 letters:
Greaseproof

Parasites

3 letters:
Bot
Ked
Nit

4 letters:
Conk
Flea
Kade
Tick
Tryp
Worm

5 letters:
Leech
Louse

6 letters:
Coccus
Dodder
Isopod
Viscum

7 letters:
Ascarid
Bonamia
Candida
Copepod
Epizoon
Giardia
Hair-eel
Lamprey
Pinworm
Stylops

8 letters:
Entozoon
Epiphyte
Filarium
Hook-worm
Lungworm
Nematode
Phytosis
Puccinia
Sporozoa
Tapeworm
Trichina

9 letters:
Bilharzia
Ectophyte
Endamoeba
Endophyte
Entophyte
Heartworm
Ichneumon
Inquiline
Macdonald
Mistletoe
Orobanche
Rafflesia
Roundworm
Sporozoan
Strongyle
Trematode
Witchweed

10 letters:
Autoecious
Babesiasis
Liverfluke
Monogenean

Plasmodium
Rickettsia
Smut-fungus
Toxoplasma

11 letters:
Bladder-worm
Cryptozoite
Gregarinida
Haematozoon
Schistosoma
Strongyloid
Trypanosoma

12 letters:
Heteroecious
Licktrencher
Mallophagous
Rhipidoptera
Strepsiptera

15 letters:
Cryptosporidium

Parliaments

2 letters:
EP

4 letters:
Dail
Diet

Rump
Sejm

5 letters:
Lords
Thing

6 letters:
Cortes
Majlis
Seanad

7 letters:
Althing
Benelux
Commons
Knesset
Lagting

Riksdag
Tynwald

8 letters:
Congress
European

Holyrood	**9 letters:**	Stirthing	**11 letters:**
Lagthing	Barebones	Storthing	Volkskammer
Lok Sabha	Bundestag		Westminster
Mercosur	Eduskunta	**10 letters:**	
Stannary	Folketing	Landsthing	**13 letters:**
Stormont	Landsting	Odelsthing	European
Storting	Odelsting	Rajya Sabha	Parliament
	Reichstag	St Stephens	Seanad Eireann
	Sanhedrin		

Pasta

4 letters:	Gnocchi	**9 letters:**	Tortelloni
Pipe	Lasagne	Agnolotti	Vermicelli
Zita	Lumache	Fettucine	
Ziti	Noodles	Fettucini	**11 letters:**
	Ravioli	Spaghetti	Cappelletti
5 letters:	Spätzle		Maultaschen
Penne		**10 letters:**	Orecchiette
Ruote	**8 letters:**	Bombolotti	Pappardelle
	Bucatini	Cannelloni	Tagliatelle
6 letters:	Farfalle	Cellentani	Tortiglioni
Ditali	Linguine	Conchiglie	
	Macaroni	Fettuccine	**12 letters:**
7 letters:	Rigatoni	Gnocchetti	Paglia e fieno
Bavette	Spaetzle	Lasagnette	
Fusilli	Taglioni	Tortellini	

Pastry

4 letters:	**5 letters:**	**9 letters:**	Shortcrust
Filo	Choux	Rough puff	
Puff	Flaky		**14 letters:**
Suet		**10 letters:**	Pâte feuilletée
	8 letters:	Pâte brisée	
	Hot water	Pâte sucrée	

Peninsulas

4 letters:	**5 letters:**	Yorke	Bataan
Ards	Gaspé		Crimea
Cape	Gower	**6 letters:**	Deccan
Eyre	Lleyn	Alaska	Iberia
Kola	Malay	Avalon	Istria
	Sinai	Balkan	Palmer

Tasman
Wirral

7 letters:
Arabian
Boothia
Cape Cod
Chukchi
Florida
Iberian
Jutland
Kintyre
Kowloon
Leizhou

8 letters:
Cape York

Delmarva
East Cape
Labrador
Melville

9 letters:
Antarctic
Cape Verde
Gallipoli
Indo-China
Kamchatka
Kathiawar
The Lizard

10 letters:
Chalcidice
Chersonese

Dunnet Head
Mornington
Nova Scotia

11 letters:
Peloponnese

12 letters:
Scandinavian
South Jutland

14 letters:
Baja California

17 letters:
Wilson's Promontory

Peoples

AFRICAN PEOPLES

3 letters:
Edo
Ewe
Ibo
Luo
Rif
San
Tiv
Twi

4 letters:
Akan
Boer
Efik
Fang
Fula
Hutu
Igbo
Lozi
Luba
Moor
Munt
Mzee
Nama

Nuba
Nuer
Nupe
Pedi
Riff
Rifi
Susu
Tshi
Xosa
Zulu

5 letters:
Bantu
Bemba
Bintu
Chewa
Dinka
Duala
Dyula
Fanti
Fingo
Fulah
Galla
Ganda

Hausa
Ibibi
Kongo
Lango
Mande
Masai
Mende
Mossi
Muntu
Negro
Nguni
Nilot
Nyoro
Oromo
Pigmy
Pondo
Pygmy
Shluh
Shona
Sotho
Swazi
Temne
Tonga
Tutsi

Venda
Wolof
Xhosa

6 letters:
Basuto
Beento
Berber
Damara
Grikwa
Griqua
Hamite
Herero
Ibibio
Kabyle
Kenyan
Kikuyu
Libyan
Malawi
Malian
Nilote
Nubian
Nyanja
Ovambo

Somali
Tsonga
Tswana
Tuareg
Watusi
Yoruba

7 letters:
Angolan
Ashanti
Baganda
Bambara
Barbary
Barotse
Basotho
Biafran
Bushman
Cairene
Flytaal
Gambian

Ghanian
Gullash
Lesotho
Lowveld
Maghreb
Maghrib
Malinke
Maninke
Mashona
Mosotho
Namaqua
Ndebele
Shilluk
Songhai
Swahili
Voltaic
Watutsi
Yoruban
Zairean

8 letters:
Botswana
Cushitic
Eritrean
Gabonese
Ghanaian
Khoikhoi
Liberian
Mandingo
Matabele
Moroccan
Namibian
Negrillo
Shangaan
Sudanese
Transkei
Tunisian

9 letters:
Congolese

Ethiopian
Gazankulu
Hottentot
Rhodesian
Transvaal

10 letters:
Abyssinian
Mozambican

11 letters:
Rastafarian
Strandloper

12 letters:
Carthaginian

ASIAN PEOPLES

3 letters:
Hui
Hun
Jat
Lao
Mon

4 letters:
Ainu
Arab
Cham
Chin
Dani
Dard
Dyak
Gond
Jain
Kurd
Mede
Moro
Motu
Naga
Nair

Nuri
Shan
Sikh
Sind
Thai
Turk

5 letters:
Dayak
Hindu
Kafir
Karen
Kazak
Khmer
Kisan
Malay
Mogul
Munda
Nayar
Nogay
Oriya
Parsi
Sindh

Tajik
Tamil
Tatar
Uigur
Uzbek
Vedda
Yakut

6 letters:
Beduin
Bihari
Buryat
Cumans
Essene
Evenki
Fulani
Gurkha
Harsha
Igorot
Jewish
Kalmyk
Kazakh
Khalsa

Lepcha
Lycian
Lydian
Mazhbi
Mishmi
Mongol
Parsee
Pashto
Pathan
Pushto
Pushtu
Sabean
Semite
Sherpa
Sindhi
Tadjik
Tartar
Telegu
Tongan
Tungus
Uighur
Veddah

7 letters:
Adivasi
Adivisi
Amorite
Balochi
Baluchi
Bashkir
Bedouin
Bengali
Bisayan
Burmese
Chinese
Chukchi
Chuvash
Cossack
Elamite
Harijan
Hittite
Hurrian

Israeli
Kalmuck
Kassite
Maratha
Maratta
Negrito
Panjabi
Punjabi
Sabaean
Samoyed
Saracen
Sogdian
Tadzhik
Tagalog
Talaing
Turkmen
Visayan

8 letters:
Accadian
Akkadian
Canarese
Chaldean
Chukchee
Ephesian
Gujarati
Gujerati
Igorrote
Kanarese
Kashmiri
Mahratta
Sumerian
Turanian

9 letters:
Amalekite
Bakhtyari

Chaldaean
Dravidian
Kabardian
Sinhalese
Tocharian
Tokharian

10 letters:
Andamanese
Babylonian
Ephraimite
Kara-Kalpak
Kshatriyas
Montagnard
Phoenician

11 letters:
Palestinian

AUSTRALASIAN PEOPLES

5 letters:
Dayak
Māori

6 letters:
Aranda

7 letters:
Tagalog

8 letters:
Gurindji

9 letters:
Aborigine

10 letters:
Melanesian
Polynesian

CENTRAL AND SOUTH AMERICAN INDIAN PEOPLES

2 letters:
Ge

4 letters:
Cuna
Inca
Kuna
Maya
Tewa
Tupi

5 letters:
Aztec
Carib
Chimú

6 letters:
Aymara
Chibca
Kechua
Makuna

Mixtec
Toltec

7 letters:
Guarani
Nahuatl
Quechua
Quichua
Zapotec

8 letters:
Arawakan

9 letters:
Chichimac

10 letters:
Araucanian
Cashinahua

INUIT PEOPLES

5 letters:
Aleut
Inuit
Yupik

6 letters:
Innuit

8 letters:
Aleutian

13 letters:
Caribou Eskimo

EUROPEAN PEOPLES

4 letters:
Celt
Dane
Finn
Gaul
Goth
Jute
Komi
Lapp
Manx
Pict
Pole
Scot
Slav
Sorb
Turk
Wend

5 letters:
Angle
Aryan
Azeri
Croat
Cymry
Czech
Dutch
Frank
Gipsy
Greek
Gypsy
Iceni
Irish
Kymry
Latin
Norse
Saxon
Swede
Swiss
Vlach
Welsh

6 letters:
Basque

Belgae
Breton
Briton
Bulgar
Cimbri
Dorian
Eolian
French
Gaelic
Gascon
German
Goidel
Ingush
Ionian
Magyar
Norman
Ostyak
Sabine
Salain
Slovak
Teuton
Ugrian
Vandal
Viking
Volsci
Votyak
Walach

7 letters:
Achaean
Achaian
Aeolian
Azorean
Brython
Catalan
Chechen
Cornish
English
Fleming
Frisian
Iberian
Latvian
Lombard

Maltese
Mordvin
Russian
Samnite
Samoyed
Serbian
Silures
Slovene
Swabian
Walloon

8 letters:
Albanian
Alemanni
Armenian
Austrian
Bavarian
Cheremis
Corsican
Croatian
Ephesian
Estonian
Etrurian
Etruscan
Faeroese
Galician
Georgian
Hellenic
Illyrian
Karelian
Lusatian
Prussian
Romanian
Scythian
Sephardi
Sicilian
Thracian
Tyrolese
Visigoth

9 letters:
Aragonese
Ashkenazi

Bulgarian
Castilian
Celtiberi
Cheremiss
Esthonian
Icelandic
Langobard
Norwegian
Ostrogoth
Provençal
Sabellian
Sardinian
Ukrainian

10 letters:
Andalusian
Anglo-Saxon
Burgundian
Carinthian
Lithuanian
Macedonian
Portuguese

11 letters:
Anglo-Norman
Azerbaijani
Belorussian
Celtiberian
Montenegrin

12 letters:
Indo-European
Luxembourger

13 letters:
Bosnian Muslim

NATIVE AMERICAN TRIBES

3 letters:
Fox
Ute

4 letters:
Cree
Crow
Dene
Hopi
Hupa
Inca
Iowa
Maya
Moki
Pima
Pomo
Sauk
Tewa
Tico
Tiwa
Tupi
Yana
Yuma
Zuni

5 letters:
Aztec
Blood
Caddo
Cajun
Campa
Carib
Creek
Haida
Huron
Kansa
Kiowa
Lipan
Miami
Miwok
Moqui
Olmec
Omaha

Osage
Ponca
Sioux
Teton
Wappo
Yaqui
Yuchi
Yuman
Yunca

6 letters:
Abnaki
Apache
Aymara
Biloxi
Cayuga
Cocopa
Dakota
Dogrib
Kechua
Kichai
Lakota
Mandan
Micmac
Mistec
Mixtec
Mohave
Mohawk
Mojave
Navaho
Navajo
Nootka
Oglala
Ojibwa
Oneida
Ostiak
Ottawa
Paiute
Papago
Pawnee
Pequot
Pericu
Piegan

Plains
Pueblo
Quakaw
Quapaw
Salish
Santee
Sarcee
Seneca
Shasta
Siwash
Toltec
Warrau
Yanqui

7 letters:
Abenaki
Arapaho
Araucan
Arikara
Caddoan
Catawba
Chibcha
Chilcal
Chinook
Choctaw
Hidatsa
Kikapoo
Kutenai
Mahican
Mapuche
Mohegan
Mohican
Nahuatl
Natchez
Ojibway
Orejone
Palouse
Pontiac
Quechua
Quichua
Senecan
Serrano
Shawnee

Shuswap
Stonies
Tlingit
Tonkawa
Wichita
Wyandot
Yalkama

8 letters:
Aguaruna
Algonkin
Cahuilla
Cherokee
Cheyenne
Chippewa
Comanche
Delaware
Flathead
Illinois
Iroquois
Kickapoo
Kootenai
Kootenay
Kwakiutl
Malecite
Menomini
Mikasuki
Mogollon
Muskogee
Nez Percé
Okanagon
Onondaga
Powhatan
Seminole
Shoshone
Shoshoni
Shushwap

9 letters:
Algonkian
Algonquan
Algonquin
Apalachee

Ashochimi
Blackfoot
Chickasaw
Chipewyan
Chippeway
Karankawa
Manhattan
Melungeon
Menominee
Mescalero
Muskogean
Penobscot
Potawatom
Suquamash

Tsimshian
Tuscarora
Wampanoag
Winnebago
Wyandotte
Yawelmani

10 letters:
Algonquian
Athabascan
Bella Coola
Leni-Lenapé
Miniconjou
Minnetaree

Montagnais
Montagnard
Muskhogean
Root-digger
Tarahumara

11 letters:
Assiniboine
Kiowa Apache
Massachuset
Minneconjou
Narraganset
Susquehanna

12 letters:
Mound Builder
Pasamaquoddy

13 letters:
Massachusetts
Northern Piute
Southern Piute
Susquehannock

14 letters:
Northern Paiute
Southern Paiute

Philosophy

PHILOSOPHICAL SCHOOLS AND DOCTRINES

5 letters:
Deism

6 letters:
Monism
Taoism
Theism

7 letters:
Animism
Atomism
Dualism
Fideism
Marxism
Realism
Thomism

8 letters:
Cynicism
Fatalism
Hedonism
Humanism
Idealism
Nihilism
Stoicism

9 letters:
Platonism
Pluralism

10 letters:
Eleaticism
Empiricism
Kantianism
Nominalism
Positivism
Pragmatism
Pyrrhonism
Scepticism
Utopianism

11 letters:
Determinism
Hegelianism
Materialism
Rationalism

12 letters:
Behaviourism
Cartesianism
Confucianism
Epicureanism
Essentialism

Neo-Platonism

13 letters:
Conceptualism
Immaterialism
Phenomenalism
Scholasticism
Structuralism

14 letters:
Existentialism
Logical atomism
Pythagoreanism
Sensationalism
Utilitarianism

15 letters:
Aristotelianism
Conventionalism
Critical realism

16 letters:
Consequentialism

17 letters:
Logical positivism

PHILOSOPHERS

2 letters:
Xi, *Chu*
Zi, *Xun*
Zu, *Han Fei*

4 letters:
Ayer, *A(lfred) J(ules)*
Cato, *Marcus Porcius*
Hume, *David*
Kant, *Immanuel*
Mach, *Ernst*
Marx, *Karl*
Mill, *James*
Mill, *John Stuart*
More, *Henry*
Mo-zi
Reid, *Thomas*
Ryle, *Gilbert*
Vico, *Giovanni Battista*
Weil, *Simone*
Wolf, *Friedrich August*
Zeno *(of Elea)*
Zeno *(of Citium)*

5 letters:
Amiel, *Henri Frédéric*
Bacon, *Francis*
Bacon, *Roger*
Bayle, *Pierre*
Benda, *Julien*
Bruno, *Giordano*
Buber, *Martin*
Burke, *Edmund*
Comte, *Auguste*
Croce, *Benedetto*
Dewey, *John*
Frege, *Gottlob*
Fromm, *Erich*
Godel, *Kurt*
Green, *T(homas) H(ill)*
Hegel, *Georg Wilhelm
  Friedrich*
Iqbal, *Muhammad*

James, *William*
Lao, *Zi*
Locke, *John*
Lully, *Ramón*
Moore, *G(eorge) E(dward)*
Paine, *Thomas*
Paley, *William*
Pater, *Walter*
Plato
Rawls, *John*
Renan, *(Joseph) Ernest*
Royce, *Josiah*
Smith, *Adam*
Sorel, *Georges*
Taine, *Hippolyte Adolphe*

6 letters:
Adorno, *Theodor
  Wiesengrund*
Agnesi, *Maria Gaetana*
Arendt, *Hannah*
Austin, *J(ohn) L(angshaw)*
Berlin, *Isaiah*
Carnap, *Rudolf*
Cicero, *Marcus Tallius*
Cousin, *Victor*
Engels, *Friedrich*
Eucken, *Rudolph
  Christoph*
Fichte, *Johann Gottlieb*
Ficino, *Marsilio*
Gasset, *José Ortega y*
Godwin, *William*
Herder, *Johann Gottfried*
Herzen, *Aleksandr
  Ivanovich*
Hobbes, *Thomas*
Langer, *Suzanne*
Lao-Tzu
Lukács, *Georg*
Magnus, *Albertus*
Marcel, *Gabriel*
Newton, *Isaac*

Ortega (y Gasset), *José*
Pascal, *Blaise*
Peirce, *Charles Sanders*
Popper, *Karl*
Pyrrho
Sartre, *Jean-Paul*
Scotus, *John Duns*
Seneca, *Lucius Annaeus*
Tagore, *Rabindranath*
Tarski, *Alfred*
Thales

7 letters:
Abelard, *Peter*
Aquinas, *Thomas*
Barthes, *Roland*
Bentham, *Jeremy*
Bergson, *Henri Louis*
Bradley, *F(rancis)
  H(erbert)*
Buridan, *Jean*
Derrida, *Jacques*
Diderot, *Denis*
Eckhart, *Meister*
Emerson, *Ralph Waldo*
Erasmus, *Desiderius*
Erigena, *John Scotus*
Fechner, *Gustav Theodor*
Gentile, *Giovanni*
Gorgias
Haeckel, *Ernst Heinrich*
Hah-Levi, *Judah*
Haldane, *Richard*
Hartley, *David*
Herbart, *Johann Friedrich*
Herbert, *Edward*
Husserl, *Edmund*
Hypatia
Jaspers, *Karl*
Judaeus, *Philo*
Leibniz, *Gottfried
  Wilhelm*
Malthus, *Thomas Robert*

Marcuse, *Herbert*
Masaryk, *Tomáš Garrigue*
Mencius
Meng-tse
Murdoch, *Dame (Jean) Iris*
Proclus
Ricoeur, *Paul*
Russell, *Bertrand*
Sankara
Sankhya
Schlick, *Moritz*
Spencer, *Herbert*
Spinoza, *Baruch*
Steiner, *Rudolf*
Tillich, *Paul Johannes*
Tolstoy, *Count Leo (Nikolayevich)*
William *(of Ockham)*

8 letters:
Alembert, *Jean*
Al-Farabi, *Mohammed ibn Tarkhan*
Anderson, *John*
Averroës
Avicenna
Berkeley, *George*
Boethius, *Anicius Manlius Severinus*
Cassirer, *Ernst*
Cudworth, *Ralph*
Davidson, *Donald*
De Suárez, *Francisco*
Diogenes
Eberhard, *Johann August*
Epicurus
Foucault, *Michel*
Gassendi, *Pierre*
Hamilton, *William*
Harrison, *Frederic*
Leopardi, *Giacomo*
Maritain, *Jacques*
Menippus
Nicholas *(of Cusa)*
Passmore, *John*
Plotinus
Plutarch
Poincaré, *Jules Henri*

Porphyry
Ramanuja
Rousseau, *Jean Jacques*
Schiller, *Friedrich*
Shankara
Socrates
Spengler, *Oswald*
Strawson, *Peter*
Voltaire, *François-Marie Arouet de*
Von Hayek, *Friedrich August*
Williams, *Bernard*
Xenophon
Zhuangzi

9 letters:
Althusser, *Louis*
Aristotle
Berdyayev, *Nikolai Aleksandrovich*
Bosanquet, *Bernard*
Chuang-Tzu
Cleanthes
Confucius
Copleston, *Frederick (Charles)*
De Chardin, *Pierre Teilhard*
Descartes, *René*
De Unamuno, *Miguel*
Epictetus
Euhemerus
Feuerbach, *Ludwig Andreas*
Heidegger, *Martin*
Helvétius, *Claude Adrien*
Hutcheson, *Francis*
Leucippus
Lévy-Bruhl, *Lucien*
Lucretius
Marsilius *(of Padua)*
Nietzsche, *Friedrich Wilhelm*
Santayana, *George*
Schelling, *Friedrich Wilhelm Joseph Von*
Von Herder, *Johann Gottfried*
Whitehead, *A(lfred) N(orth)*

10 letters:
Anacharsis
Anaxagoras

Anaximenes
Apemanthus
Apollonius
Aristippus
Baumgarten, *Alexander Gottlieb*
Campanella, *Tommaso*
Chrysippus
Chrysostom, *Dio*
Churchland, *Paul*
Cumberland, *Richard*
De Beauvoir, *Simone*
Democritus
Empedocles
Heraclitus
Ibn-Gabirol, *Solomon*
Ibn-Khaldun
Maimonides
Parmenides
Protagoras
Pythagoras
Schweitzer, *Albert*
Swedenborg, *Emanuel*
Xenocrates
Xenophanes
Zeno of Elea

11 letters:
Anaximander
Antisthenes
Bonaventura
De Condillac, *Étienne Bonnot*
Heracleides
Kierkegaard, *Søren Aabye*
Machiavelli, *Niccolò*
Malebranche, *Nicolas*
Montesquieu, *Charles de Secondat*
  (*Baron de la Brède et de*)
Reichenbach, *Hans*

St Augustine (*of Hippo*)
Von Leibnitz, *Gottfried Wilhelm*
Von Schlegel, *Friedrich*

12 letters:
Callisthenes
De Fontenelle, *Bernard le Bovier*
De Saint-Simon, *Comte*
Merleau-Ponty, *Maurice*
Schopenhauer, *Arthur*
Theophrastus
Von Pufendorf, *Samuel*
Von Schelling, *Friedrich Wilhelm Joseph*
Wittgenstein, *Ludwig Josef Johann*
Zeno of Citium

13 letters:
De Montesquieu, *Baron de la Brède et*
Van Orman Quine, *Willard*

14 letters:
Della Mirandola, *Giovanni Pico*
Nicholas of Cusa
Rosmini-Serbati, *Antonio*
Schleiermacher, *Friedrich Ernst Daniel*
Shankaracharya

15 letters:
Le Rond d'Alembert, *Jean*
William of Ockham

16 letters:
Marsilius of Padua

18 letters:
De Caritat Condorcet, *Marie Jean*
  Antoine Nicholas
St Augustine of Hippo

Phobias

Phobia	Object
Acerophobia	Sourness
Achluophobia	Darkness
Acrophobia	Heights

Phobia	Object
Aerophobia	Air
Agoraphobia	Open spaces
Aichurophobia	Points
Ailurophobia	Cats
Akousticophobia	Sound
Algophobia	Pain
Amakaphobia	Carriages
Amathophobia	Dust
Androphobia	Men
Anemophobia	Wind
Anginophobia	Narrowness
Anthropophobia	Man
Antlophobia	Flood
Apeirophobia	Infinity
Aquaphobia	Water
Arachnophobia	Spiders
Asthenophobia	Weakness
Astraphobia	Lightning
Atephobia	Ruin
Aulophobia	Flutes
Bacilliphobia	Microbes
Barophobia	Gravity
Basophobia	Walking
Batrachophobia	Reptiles
Belonephobia	Needles
Bibliophobia	Books
Brontophobia	Thunder
Cancerophobia	Cancer
Cheimaphobia	Cold
Chionophobia	Snow
Chrematophobia	Money
Chronophobia	Duration
Chrystallophobia	Crystals
Claustrophobia	Closed spaces
Cnidophobia	Stings
Cometophobia	Comets
Cromophobia	Colour
Cyberphobia	Computers
Cynophobia	Dogs
Demonophobia	Demons
Demophobia	Crowds
Dermatophobia	Skin
Dikephobia	Justice
Doraphobia	Fur

Phobia	**Object**
Eisoptrophobia	Mirrors
Electrophobia	Electricity
Enetophobia	Pins
Entomophobia	Insects
Eosophobia	Dawn
Eremophobia	Solitude
Ereuthophobia	Blushing
Ergasiophobia	Work
Genophobia	Sex
Geumaphobia	Taste
Graphophobia	Writing
Gymnophobia	Nudity
Gynophobia	Women
Hadephobia	Hell
Haematophobia	Blood
Hamartiophobia	Sin
Haptophobia	Touch
Harpaxophobia	Robbers
Hedonophobia	Pleasure
Helminthophobia	Worms
Hodophobia	Travel
Homichlophobia	Fog
Homophobia	Homosexuals
Hormephobia	Shock
Hydrophobia	Water
Hypegiaphobia	Responsibility
Hypnophobia	Sleep
Ideophobia	Ideas
Kakorraphiaphobia	Failure
Katagelophobia	Ridicule
Kenophobia	Void
Kinesophobia	Motion
Kleptophobia	Stealing
Kopophobia	Fatigue
Kristallophobia	Ice
Laliophobia	Stuttering
Linonophobia	String
Logophobia	Words
Lyssophobia	Insanity
Maniaphobia	Insanity
Mastigophobia	Flogging
Mechanophobia	Machinery
Metallophobia	Metals
Meteorophobia	Meteors

Phobia	Object
Misophobia	Contamination
Monophobia	One thing
Musicophobia	Music
Musophobia	Mice
Necrophobia	Corpses
Nelophobia	Glass
Neophobia	Newness
Nephophobia	Clouds
Nosophobia	Disease
Nyctophobia	Night
Ochlophobia	Crowds
Ochophobia	Vehicles
Odontophobia	Teeth
Oikophobia	Home
Olfactophobia	Smell
Ommatophobia	Eyes
Oneirophobia	Dreams
Ophidiophobia	Snakes
Ornithophobia	Birds
Ouranophobia	Heaven
Panphobia	Everything
Pantophobia	Everything
Parthenophobia	Girls
Pathophobia	Disease
Peniaphobia	Poverty
Phasmophobia	Ghosts
Phobophobia	Fears
Photophobia	Light
Pnigerophobia	Smothering
Poinephobia	Punishment
Polyphobia	Many things
Potophobia	Drink
Pteronophobia	Feathers
Pyrophobia	Fire
Russophobia	Russia
Rypophobia	Soiling
Satanophobia	Satan
Selaphobia	Flesh
Siderophobia	Stars
Sitophobia	Food
Spermaphobia	Germs
Spermatophobia	Germs
Stasiphobia	Standing
Stygiophobia	Hell

Phobia	Object
Taphephobia	Being buried alive
Technophobia	Technology
Teratophobia	Giving birth to a monster
Thaasophobia	Sitting
Thalassophobia	Sea
Thanatophobia	Death
Theophobia	God
Thermophobia	Heat
Tonitrophobia	Thunder
Toxiphobia	Poison
Tremophobia	Trembling
Triskaidekaphobia	Thirteen
Xenophobia	Strangers *or* foreigners
Zelophobia	Jealousy
Zoophobia	Animals

Photography terms

3 letters:
Cam
Pan
TTL

4 letters:
Cock
Film
Gate
Gobo
Grip
JPEG
Load
Shot
Stop

5 letters:
Blimp
Crane
Dolly
F-stop
Set up
Track
T-stop

6 letters:
Mosaic
Screen
Target
Tripod
Unipod

7 letters:
Hot shoe
Key grip
Release
Saticon
Shutter
T-number
Vidicon

8 letters:
Cassette
Film pack
Lens hood
Long shot
Orthicon
Snapshot
Stop down
Zoom lens

9 letters:
Amplifier
Cameraman
Cartridge
Cokuloris
Ferrotype
Film speed
Macro lens
Objective
Paparazzo
Plumbicon
Time lapse

10 letters:
Autowinder
Camera tube
Focal plane
Iconoscope
Viewfinder
Vignetting

11 letters:
Caméra stylo
Fisheye lens
Focus puller
Large-format

12 letters:
Cable release
Depth of focus
Synchroflash
Tracking shot

13 letters:
Accessory shoe
Cinematograph

Delayed action
Extension ring
Image orthicon
Telephoto lens
Wide-angle lens

14 letters:
Automatic focus
Kinetheodolite

Pan and tilt head
Shooting script

18 letters:
Hyperfocal distance

19 letters:
Photoreconnaissance

Physicians

4 letters:
Salk, *Jonas*

6 letters:
Jenner, *Edward*
Wavell, *William*

7 letters:
Addison, *Thomas*
Russell, *Patrick*

Physics

BRANCHES OF PHYSICS

5 letters:
Solar

6 letters:
Atomic
Optics
Sonics

7 letters:
Applied
Nuclear
Quantum
Statics

8 letters:
Dynamics
Kinetics
Particle
Rheology

9 letters:
Acoustics
Cosmology
Harmonics
Magnetics
Magnetism

Mechanics

10 letters:
Biophysics
Cryogenics
Geophysics
High-energy
Nucleonics
Photometry
Pneumatics
Solid-state

11 letters:
Aerostatics
Electronics
Mesoscopics
Theoretical
Thermometry
Ultrasonics

12 letters:
Aerodynamics
Astrophysics
Macrophysics
Microphysics
Spectroscopy

13 letters:
Thermostatics

14 letters:
Electrostatics
Low-temperature
Magnetostatics
Thermodynamics

15 letters:
Condensed-matter

16 letters:
Electromagnetism
Quantum mechanics

17 letters:
Superaerodynamics

20 letters:
Statistical mechanics

PHYSICS TERMS

3 letters:
Ohm

4 letters:
Atom
Fuse
Lens
Mass
Muon
Volt
Watt
Wave
X-ray

5 letters:
Anion
Diode
Earth
Farad
Field
Force
Hertz
Joule
Laser
Meson

6 letters:
Ampere
Baryon
Cacion
Charge
Energy
Fusion
Kelvin
Lepton
Matter
Moment
Newton
Pascal
Proton
Vacuum

7 letters:
Calorie
Coulomb
Current
Decibel
Density
Fission
Gravity
Hyperon
Impetus
Inertia
Neutron
Nucleon
Nucleus
Ohm's law
Quantum
Tension

8 letters:
Angstrom
Electron
Friction
Gamma ray
Half-life
Infrared
Momentum
Neutrino
Particle
Red shift
Spectrum
Velocity

9 letters:
Amplifier
Becquerel
Boyle's law
Conductor
Cosmic ray
Cyclotron
Diffusion
Frequency
Generator
Microwave

Radiation
Radio wave
Viscosity

10 letters:
Antimatter
Cathode ray
Charles' law
Convection
Inductance
Reflection
Refraction
Relativity
Resistance
Rutherford
Thermostat
Transistor
Wavelength

11 letters:
Capacitance
Diffraction
Electricity
Tau particle
Transformer
Ultraviolet

12 letters:
Acceleration
Fluorescence
Luminescence

13 letters:
Direct current
Doppler effect
Kinetic energy
Radioactivity
Semiconductor
Superfluidity

14 letters:
Brownian motion
Planck constant

Surface tension

15 letters:
Centre of gravity
Planck's constant
Potential energy

16 letters:
Centrifugal force

Centripetal force
Terminal velocity

17 letters:
Static electricity
Subatomic particle
Superconductivity

18 letters:
Alternating current
Electromotive force

19 letters:
Potential difference

20 letters:
Simple harmonic motion

PHYSICISTS

3 letters:
Lee, *Tsung-Dao*
Ohm, *Georg Simon*

4 letters:
Abbe, *Ernst*
Bohr, *Aage Niels*
Bohr, *Niels (Henrik David)*
Born, *Max*
Bose, *Jagadis Chandra*
Bose, *Satyendra Nath*
Hahn, *Otto*
Hess, *Victor Francis*
Kerr, *John*
Lamb, *Willis Eugene*
Lawe, *William C*
Mach, *Ernst*
Néel, *Louis*
Rabi, *Isidor Isaac*
Snow, *C(harles) P(ercy)*
Swan, *Joseph Wilson*
Ting, *Samuel Chao Chung*
Vafa, *Cumrun*
Wien, *Wilhelm*
Yang, *Chen Ning*

5 letters:
Aston, *Francis William*
Auger, *Pierre*
Basov, *Nikolai*
Bethe, *Hans Albrecht*
Bloch, *Felix*
Bothe, *Walter*

Boyle, *Robert*
Bragg, *Sir William Henry*
Braun, *Karl Ferdinand*
Curie, *Marie*
Curie, *Pierre*
Debye, *Peter Joseph Wilhelm*
Dewar, *James*
Dirac, *Paul Adrien Maurice*
Fabry, *Charles*
Fermi, *Enrico*
Fuchs, *Klaus*
Gauss, *Carl Friedrich*
Gibbs, *Josiah Willard*
Henry, *Joseph*
Hertz, *Gustav*
Hertz, *Heinrich Rudolph*
Hooke, *Robert*
Jeans, *James Hopwood*
Joule, *James Prescott*
Lodge, *Oliver*
Nambu, *Yoshiro*
Pauli, *Wolfgang*
Popov, *Alexander Stepanovich*
Sègre, *Emilio*
Stark, *Johannes*
Volta, *Alessandro*
Weber, *Wilhelm Eduard*
Young, *Thomas*
Zener, *Clarence*

6 letters:
Alfvén, *Hannes Olaf Gösta*
Ampère, *André Marie*

Barkla, *Charles Glover*
Binnig, *Gerd*
Carnot, *Nicolas Leonard Sadi*
Cooper, *Leon*
Cronin, *James Watson*
Dalton, *John*
Davies, *Paul*
Franck, *James*
Frisch, *Otto*
Geiger, *Hans*
Giorgi, *Filippo*
Glaser, *Donald Arthur*
Graham, *Thomas*
Kelvin, *William Thomson*
Landau, *Lev Davidovich*
Newton, *Isaac*
Pascal, *Blaise*
Peirce, *Charles*
Penney, *William*
Perrin, *Jean Baptiste*
Picard, *Jean*
Planck, *Max (Karl Ernst Ludwig)*
Powell, *Celic*
Talbot, *William Henry Fox*
Teller, *Edward*
Townes, *Charles Hard*
Walton, *Ernest Thomas Sinton*
Wigner, *Eugene Paul*
Wilson, *Charles Thomson Rees*
Yukawa, *Hideki*
Zwicky, *Fritz*

7 letters:
Alvarez, *Luis Walter*
Babinet, *Jacques*
Bardeen, *John*
Bravais, *Auguste*
Broglie, *Maurice*
Charles, *Jacques*
Compton, *Arthur Holly*
Coulomb, *Charles Augustin De*
Crookes, *William*
Doppler, *C(hristian) J(ohann)*
Faraday, *Michael*

Fechner, *Gustav*
Feynman, *Richard*
Fresnel, *Augustin*
Galilei, *Galileo*
Galileo
Gell-Man, *Murray*
Gilbert, *William*
Goddard, *Robert Hutchings*
Hawking, *Stephen William*
Heitler, *Walter*
Huygens, *Christiaan*
Kapitza, *Piotr Leonidovich*
Langley, *Samuel Pierpont*
Laplace, *Pierre Simon*
Lippman, *Gabriel*
Lorentz, *Hendrik Antoon*
Marconi, *Guglielmo*
Maxwell, *James Clerk*
Meitner, *Lise*
Milikin, *Robert*
Moseley, *Henry Gwyn-Jeffreys*
Nielsen, *Holger*
Oersted, *Hans Christian*
Penrose, *Roger*
Piccard, *Auguste*
Prandtl, *Ludwig*
Purcell, *Edward Mill*
Réaumur, *René Antoine Ferchault De*
Richter, *Burton*
Röntgen, *Wilhelm Konrad Von*
Seaborg, *Glenn*
Szilard, *Leo*
Thomson, *Benjamin*
Thomson, *George Paget*
Thomson, *Joseph John*
Tyndall, *John*
Von Laue, *Max Theodor Felix*
Wheeler, *John Archibald*

8 letters:
Anderson, *Carl David*
Anderson, *Elizabeth Garrett*
Anderson, *Philip Warren*
Ångström, *Anders Jonas*

Appleton, *Edward*
Avogadro, *Amedeo*
Blackett, *Patrick Maynard Stuart*
Brattain, *Walter Houser*
Brewster, *David*
Bridgman, *Percy*
Chadwick, *James*
Cherwell, *Frederick Alexander Lindemann*
Clausius, *Rudolf*
Davisson, *Clinton Joseph*
Einstein, *Albert*
Foucault, *Jean Bernard Léon*
Gassendi, *Pierre*
Ipatieff, *Vladimir Nikolaievich*
Lawrence, *Ernest Orlando*
McMillan, *Edwin*
Millikan, *Robert*
Mullikin, *Robert Sanderson*
Oliphant, *Mark Laurence Elwin*
Poincaré, *Jules Henri*
Rayleigh, *John William Strutt*
Roentgen, *Wilhelm Konrad*
Sakharov, *Andrei*
Shockley, *William Bradfield*
Siegbahn, *Kai*
Susskind, *Leonard*
Van Allen, *James*
Von Mayer, *Julius Robert*
Weinberg, *Steven*
Zworykin, *Vladimir Kosma*

9 letters:
Arrhenius, *Svante August*
Becquerel, *Antoine Henri*
Bernoulli, *Daniel*
Boltzmann, *Ludwig*
Cavendish, *Henry*
Cherenkov, *Pavel Alekseyevich*
Cockcroft, *John Douglas*
De Coulomb, *Charles Augustin*
Eddington, *Arthur Stanley*

Gay-Lussac, *Joseph Louis*
Heaviside, *Oliver*
Josephson, *Brian David*
Kirchhoff, *Gustav*
Lindemann, *Frederick*
Michelson, *Albert*
Ovshinsky, *Stanford*
Von Békésy, *Georg*
Von Eötvös, *Roland*

10 letters:
Archimedes
Barkhausen, *Heinrich Georg*
Fahrenheit, *Gabriel Daniel*
Heisenburg, *Werner Karl*
Richardson, *Owen Willans*
Rutherford, *Ernest*
Torricelli, *Evangelista*
Watson-Watt, *Robert Alexander*

11 letters:
Chamberlain, *Owen*
Joliot-Curie, *Irène*
Oppenheimer, *J(ulius) Robert*
Schrödinger, *Erwin*
Van de Graaff, *R(obert) J(emison)*
Van der Waals, *Johannes Diderik*
Von Guericke, *Otto*

12 letters:
Von Helmholtz, *Hermann Ludwig Ferdinand*

13 letters:
Von Fraunhofer, *Joseph*

14 letters:
Le Rond Alembert, *Jean*

15 letters:
Kamerlingh-Onnes, *Heike*

See also:
➤ **Molecules** ➤ **Subatomic particles**

Physiologists

4 letters:
Dale, *Henry*
Loeb, *Jacques*

6 letters:
Bordet, *Jules*

Eccles, *John*

7 letters:
Bernard, *Claude*

8 letters:
Purkinje, *J(an)*
  E(vangelista)

9 letters:
Einthoven, *Willem*

Pigments

3 letters:
Hem

4 letters:
Haem
Heme

5 letters:
Ochre
Opsin
Sepia
Smalt
Umber

6 letters:
Bister
Bistre
Chrome
Cobalt
Flavin
Lutein
Madder
Naevus
Pterin

Sienna

7 letters:
Argyria
Carmine
Carotin
Etiolin
Flavine
Gamboge
Melanin
Sinopia
Tapetum
Tempera

8 letters:
Carotene
Gossypol
Iodopsin
Luteolin
Orpiment
Retinene
Verditer
Viridian

9 letters:
Anthocyan
Bilirubin
Chromogen
Colcothar
Lamp-black
Lithopone
Liverspot
Nigrosine
Porphyrin
Quercetin
Rhodopsin
Urochrome

10 letters:
Anthoclore
Betacyanin
Biliverdin
Carotenoid
Carotinoid
Hemocyanin
Hemoglobin
Lipochrome
Paris-green

Riboflavin
Terre-verte

11 letters:
Anthocyanin
Chlorophyll
Fucoxanthin
Haemocyanin
Haemoglobin
Phytochrome
Xanthophyll
Yellow ochre

12 letters:
Cappagh-brown
Phycoxanthin
Xanthopterin

13 letters:
Phycoerythrin
Xanthopterine

14 letters:
Phthalocyanine

Pigs

5 letters:
Duroc
Welsh

8 letters:
Cheshire
Landrace

Pietrain
Tamworth

9 letters:
Berkshire
Hampshire

10 letters:
Large Black
Large White
Saddleback
Small White

11 letters:
Middle White

12 letters:
Chester White

17 letters:
Gloucester Old Spot

20 letters:
Vietnamese pot-bellied

Pirates

4 letters:
Smee

7 letters:
Ben Gunn

8 letters:
Black Dog
Blind Pew
Mary Read
Redbeard

9 letters:
Anne Bonny

Thomas Tew

10 letters:
Barbarossa
Blackbeard
Calico Jack

11 letters:
Captain Hook
Edward Teach
Sir Henry Morgan
Jack Sparrow
Jean Laffite
John Rackham

12 letters:
Sir Francis Drake

13 letters:
Basil Ringrose

14 letters:
Captain Pugwash
Long John Silver
William Dampier

18 letters:
Bartholomew Roberts
William (Captain) Kidd

Places and their nicknames

Place	Nickname
Aberdeen	The Granite City
Adelaide	The City of Churches
Amsterdam	The Venice of the North
Birmingham	Brum *or* the Venice of the North
Boston	Bean Town
Bruges	The Venice of the North
California	The Golden State
Chicago	The Windy City
Dallas	The Big D
Detroit	The Motor City
Dresden	Florence on the Elbe
Dublin	The Fair City
Dumfries	Queen of the South
Edinburgh	Auld Reekie *or* the Athens of the North
Florida	The Sunshine State
Fraserburgh	The Broch
Fremantle	Freo
Glasgow	The Dear Green Place
Hamburg	The Venice of the North
Indiana	The Hoosier State
Iowa	The Hawkeye State
Ireland	The Emerald Isle

Place	Nickname
Jamaica	J.A. *or* the Yard
Jerusalem	The Holy City
Kentucky	The Bluegrass State
Kuala Lumpur	K.L.
London	The Big Smoke *or* the Great Wen
Los Angeles	L.A.
Newcastle	The Toon
New Jersey	The Garden State
New Orleans	The Crescent City *or* the Big Easy
New South Wales	The Ma State
New York (City)	The Big Apple
New York (State)	The Empire State
New Zealand	Pig Island
North Carolina	The Tarheel State
Nottingham	Queen of the Midlands
Oklahoma	The Sooner State
Oxford	The City of Dreaming Spires
Pennsylvania	The Keystone State
Philadelphia	Philly
Portsmouth	Pompey
Prince Edward Island	Spud Island
Queensland	Bananaland *or* the Deep North *(both derogatory)*
Rome	The Eternal City
San Francisco	Frisco
Southeastern U.S.A.	Dixie, Dixieland, *or* the Deep South
Tasmania	Tassie *or* the Apple Isle
Texas	The Lone Star State
Utah	The Beehive State
Venice	La Serenissima

Planets

4 letters:
Mars

5 letters:
Earth
Pluto (dwarf planet)

Venus

6 letters:
Saturn
Uranus

7 letters:
Jupiter
Mercury
Neptune

Plants

VARIETIES OF PLANT

3 letters:
Dal

Kex
Meu

Pia
Rue

Set
Til

Udo
Urd
Yam

4 letters:
Alga
Aloe
Anil
Deme
Fern
Forb
Herb
Ixia
Kali
Loco
More
Nard
Ombu
Poly
Rhus
Sego
Sola
Sunn
Taro
Thea
Vine
Yarr

5 letters:
Ajwan
Anise
Arnut
Aroid
Benni
Blite
Boree
Buchu
Bucku
Bugle
Calla
Canna
Clary
Clote
Cress
Fouat

Fouet
Gemma
Glaux
Gorse
Guaco
Hosta
Inula
Jalap
Kenaf
Knawe
Kudzu
Lathe
Lotus
Lurgi
Medic
Morel
Murva
Musci
Orpin
Orris
Oshac
Panax
Sedge
Sedum
Sotol
Spart
Spink
Tetra
Timbo
Urena

6 letters:
Acacia
Acorus
Ajowan
Alisma
Alpine
Arnica
Bablah
Betony
Burnet
Cactus
Cassia
Catnep
Catnip

Cnicus
Cosmea
Cosmos
Croton
Datura
Derris
Dodder
Erynga
Exogen
Gnetum
Hyssop
Iberis
Knawel
Madder
Mallow
Medick
Mimosa
Moorva
Nerium
Nettle
Nuphar
Orchis
Orpine
Pachak
Phloem
Protea
Rattle
Reseda
Retama
Rubber
Sesame
Silene
Smilax
Spider
Spurge
Spurry
Squill
Styrax
Teasel
Thrift
Tulipa
Tutsan
Yacona
Yarrow

7 letters:
Alkanet
All-good
Allseed
Alyssum
Brinjal
Burdock
Caltrop
Cardoon
Carduus
Carline
Cascara
Cat's ear
Chervil
Clivers
Dasheen
Dioecia
Dittany
Ephedra
Filaree
Fly-trap
Freesia
Frogbit
Gentian
Gerbera
Haemony
Henbane
Ipomoea
Isoetes
Lantana
Lucerne
Lychnis
Mahonia
Melilot
Mercury
Mullein
Nemesia
Nigella
Nonsuch
Opuntia
Palmiet
Pareira
Parella
Parelle
Petunia

Pinesap
Ragwort
Rhodora
Ribwort
Ruellia
Saffron
Salfern
Salsola
Sampire
Sanicle
Scandix
Setwall
Skirret
Spignel
Spiraea
Spurrey
Stapela
Syringa
Tagetes
Thallus
Triffid
Tritoma
Vanilla
Vervain
Vetiver
Zedoary

8 letters:
Acanthus
Agrimony
Angelica
Arenaria
Asphodel
Bindi-eye
Buckbean
Buplever
Camomile
Canaigre
Centaury
Costmary
Diandria
Dielytra
Dumbcane
Fluellin
Fumitory

Geophyte
Gesneria
Gnetales
Gromwell
Hag-taper
Henequen
Hepatica
Hibiscus
Khuskhus
Lad's love
Larkspur
Lavender
Locoweed
Mandrake
Monstera
Oleander
Opopanax
Plumbago
Psilotum
Putchock
Queencup
Ratsbane
Roly-poly
Samphire
Scammony
Self-heal
Shinleaf
Silphium
Sparaxis
Spergula
Stapelia
Staragen
Starwort
Suckling
Sunberry
Sundrops
Tamarisk
Tickseed
Tritonia
Tuberose
Tuckahoe
Wait-a-bit

9 letters:
Adderwort

Andromeda
Arrowroot
Artemisia
Aubrietia
Bald-money
Brooklime
Broom-rape
Browallia
Butterbur
Chamomile
Colocasia
Coltsfoot
Cordaites
Coreopsis
Coriander
Crosswort
Day nettle
Dittander
Erythrina
Euphorbia
Eyebright
Fatshedra
Fenugreek
Germander
Groundsel
Herb-paris
Horse-tail
Job's tears
Ladysmock
Lespedeza
Liver-wort
Lousewort
Mare's-tail
Moneywort
Moschatel
Patchouli
Pimpernel
Portulaca
Rocambole
Screwpine
Spearmint
Spearwort
Spikenard
Star grass
Stickseed

Stone-crop
Sweet-gale
Tomatillo
Tormentil
Wake-robin
Wincopipe
Wolf's bane

10 letters:
Alexanders
Angiosperm
Aspidistra
Astralagus
Dyer's-broom
Earth-smoke
Five-finger
Fraxinella
Fritillary
Goat-sallow
Goats-thorn
Goat-willow
Goldilocks
Icosandria
Joepyeweed
Maidenhair
Mignonette
Parkleaves
Rest-harrow
Salicornia
Sticktight
Touch-me-not
Tropophyte
Turtlehead
Yellowroot

11 letters:
Acidanthera
Bears-breech
Bristle-fern
Callitriche
Convolvulus
Dragon's head
Dusty-miller
Hurtleberry
Loosestrife

Meadowsweet
Nancy-pretty
Rupturewort
Schizophyte
Sempervivum
Shrimp plant
Sulphurwort
Thallophyte
White bryony

12 letters:
Adam's flannel
Epacridaceae
Midsummermen
Morning glory
Parsley-piert

Pasqueflower
Phytobenthos
Service berry
Southernwood
Spring beauty
Stone bramble
Water-soldier

13 letters:
Beggar's sticks
Flannelflower
Indian tobacco
Townhall clock

14 letters:
Chincherinchee

Lords and ladies
Shepherd's purse
Spanish bayonet
Vegetable sheep

16 letters:
Indian paintbrush

17 letters:
Queen of the prairie
Squarrose knapweed

20 letters:
Enchanter's nightshade

PARTS OF PLANTS

3 letters:
Bud
Lip
Pod

4 letters:
Cyme
Head
Leaf
Root
Seed
Spur
Stem

5 letters:
Bract
Calyx
Costa
Fruit
Glume
Joint
Lemma
Ovary
Ovule
Palea
Petal
Sepal

Spike
Stoma
Style
Tepal
Torus
Umbel
Xylem

6 letters:
Anther
Bulbil
Carpel
Catkin
Caulis
Corymb
Floret
Phloem
Pistil
Pollen
Raceme
Rachis
Sheath
Spadix
Spathe
Stamen
Stigma
Tassel

7 letters:
Blossom
Corolla
Foliage
Nectary
Panicle
Pedicel
Root cap
Seed pod
Taproot

8 letters:
Cyathium
Filament
Nucellus
Offshoot
Peduncle
Perianth
Placenta
Root hair
Spikelet
Thalamus

9 letters:
Capitulum
Dichasium
Epidermis

Guard cell
Gynoecium
Internode
Involucel
Involucre
Micropyle
Pollinium
Secundine

10 letters:
Androecium
Anthophore
Carpophore
Commissure
Hypanthium
Receptacle

11 letters:
Clinandrium
Gametophore
Monochasium
Pollen grain

12 letters:
Hibernaculum

Poetry

POETRY AND PROSODY TERMS

3 letters:
Bob

4 letters:
Foot
Iamb

5 letters:
Arsis
Canto
Envoi
Envoy
Epode
Ictus
Ionic
Metre
Octet
Paeon
Rhyme
Wheel

6 letters:
Adonic
Alcaic
Cesura
Cretic
Dactyl
Dipody
Iambic
Iambus
Octave
Rhythm
Septet

Sestet
Stanza
Tercet

7 letters:
Anapest
Cadence
Cadency
Caesura
Couplet
Distich
Elision
Paeonic
Pyhrric
Quintet
Refrain
Sapphic
Sestina
Sextain
Spondee
Stichic
Strophe
Triplet
Trochee

8 letters:
Amoebean
Anapaest
Bacchius
Choriamb
Dactylic
Dieresis
Eye rhyme

Pindaric
Quatrain
Quintain
Scansion
Spondaic
Trochaic

9 letters:
Amoebaean
Anacrusis
Anapestic
Assonance
Diaeresis
Free verse
Full rhyme
Half-rhyme
Hemistich
Hexameter
Long metre
Macaronic
Octameter
Pararhyme
Rime riche
Terza rima
Tetrapody
Unstopped
Vers libre

10 letters:
Amphibrach
Amphimacer
Anapaestic
Blank verse

Catalectic
Choriambus
Consonance
Consonancy
End-stopped
Heptameter
Heptastich
Hypermeter
Ottava rima
Pentameter
Pentastich
Rhyme royal
Short metre
Tetrabrach
Tetrameter
Tetrastich

11 letters:
Alexandrine
Antistrophe

Common metre
Enjambement
Jabberwocky
Rhyme scheme

12 letters:
Alliteration
Ballad stanza
Leonine rhyme
Onomatopoeia
Perfect rhyme
Sprung rhythm

13 letters:
Closed couplet
Common measure
Feminine rhyme
Heroic couplet
Internal rhyme
Syllabic metre

14 letters:
Accentual metre
Feminine ending
Masculine rhyme
Verse paragraph

15 letters:
Masculine ending

16 letters:
Spenserian stanza

17 letters:
Quantitative metre

19 letters:
Stress-syllabic metre

22 letters:
Accentual-syllabic metre

POETRY MOVEMENTS AND GROUPINGS

8 letters:
Imagists

9 letters:
Decadents
Lake Poets
Romantics

10 letters:
Symbolists

11 letters:
Petrarchans
The Movement

12 letters:
Alexandrians

13 letters:
Georgian Poets

14 letters:
Liverpool Poets

15 letters:
Russian Futurists

17 letters:
Metaphysical Poets

19 letters:
Scottish Chaucerians

POETS

2 letters:
AE
HD

3 letters:
Gay, *John*
Paz, *Octavio*
Poe, *Edgar Allan*

4 letters:
Abse, *Dannie*
Beer, *Patricia*
Blok, *Alexander
    Alexandrovich*
Cory, *William Johnson*
Dunn, *Douglas*
Dyer, *Sir Edward*
Gray, *Thomas*
Gunn, *Thom*

Hill, *Geoffrey*
Hogg, *James*
Hood, *Thomas*
Hope, *Alec*
Hugo, *Victor (Marie)*
Hunt, *(James Henry) Leigh*
Lang, *Andrew*
Muir, *Edwin*
Nash, *(Frederic) Ogden*
Ovid

Owen, *Wilfred*
Pope, *Alexander*
Rich, *Adrienne*
Rowe, *Nicholas*
Rumi, *Jelaluddin*
Tate, *(John Orley) Allen*
Vega, *(Garcilaso de la)*
Webb, *Francis Charles*

5 letters:
Aiken, *Conrad (Potter)*
Alley, *Rewi*
Arion
Auden, *W(ystan) H(ugh)*
Basho, *Braho*
Blair, *Robert*
Blake, *William*
Burns, *Robert*
Byron, *(George Gordon)*
Cadou, *René-Guy*
Carew, *Thomas*
Cinna, *Gaius Helvius*
Clare, *John*
Crane, *Hart*
Dante *(Alighieri)*
Donne, *John*
Duffy, *Carol Ann*
Eliot, *T(homas) S(tearns)*
Flint, *F(rank) S(tuart)*
Frost, *Robert (Lee)*
Gower, *John*
Heine, *Heinrich*
Henri, *Adrian*
Hesse, *Hermann*
Homer
Horne, *Richard Henry ('Hengist')*
Hulme, *Thomas Ernest*
Iqbal, *Sir Mohammed*
Jarry, *Alfred*
Keats, *John*
Keyes, *Sidney*
Lewis, *Cecil Day*
Logue, *Christopher*
Lorca, *Federico García*
Lucan *(Marcus Annaeus Lucanus)*

Marot, *Clément*
Meyer, *Conrad Ferdinand*
Moore, *Marianne*
Nashe, *Thomas*
Noyes, *Alfred*
O'Hara, *Frank*
Perse, *Saint-John*
Plath, *Sylvia*
Pound, *Ezra (Loomis)*
Prior, *Matthew*
Raine, *Kathleen*
Rilke, *Rainer Maria*
Sachs, *Hans*
Scott, *Sir Walter*
Smart, *Christopher*
Smith, *Stevie*
Tasso, *Torquato*
Theon
Wyatt, *Thomas*
Yeats, *W(illiam) B(utler)*
Young, *Edward*

6 letters:
Adamov, *Arthur*
Adcock, *(Karen) Fleur*
Arnold, *Matthew*
Austin, *Alfred*
Barham, *Richard Harris*
Barnes, *William*
Belloc, *(Joseph) Hilaire (Pierre)*
Binyon, *Laurence*
Bishop, *Elizabeth*
Brecht, *Bertolt (Eugen Friedrich)*
Brooke, *Rupert (Chawner)*
Brooks, *Gwendolyn*
Butler, *Samuel*
Carver, *Raymond*
Clarke, *Austin*
Clough, *Arthur Hugh*
Cowley, *Abraham*
Cowper, *William*
Crabbe, *George*
Curnow, *Allen*
Daniel, *Samuel*
Davies, *William*

Domett, *Alfred*
Dowson, *Ernest Christopher*
Dryden, *John*
Dunbar, *William*
Dutton, *Geoffrey*
Elliot, *Ebenezer*
Éluard, *Paul*
Empson, *William*
Ennius, *Quintus*
Fuller, *Roy*
George, *Stefan*
Glycon
Goethe, *Johann Wolfgang von*
Graves, *Robert (Ranke)*
Harpur, *Charles*
Heaney, *Seamus*
Hesiod
Horace
Hughes, *Ted*
Jonson, *Ben(jamin)*
Landor, *Walter Savage*
Larkin, *Philip*
Lawman
Lowell, *Amy*
Lowell, *Robert*
Millay, *Edna St Vincent*
Milton, *John*
Morgan, *Edwin (George)*
Morris, *Sir Lewis*
Motion, *Andrew*
Neruda, *Pablo*
Ossian
Patten, *Brian*
Pindar
Porter, *Peter*
Racine, *Jean (Baptiste)*
Riding, *Laura*
Sappho
Seaman, *Sir Owen*
Shanks, *Edward*
Sidney, *Sir Philip*
Tagore, *Sir Rabindranath*
Thomas, *Dylan (Marlais)*
Thomas, *Edward*
Thomas, *R(onald) S(tuart)*

Trench, *Frederick Herbert*
Villon, *François*
Virgil
Waller, *Edmund*
Wright, *Judith*

7 letters:
Addison, *Joseph*
Alcaeus
Alfieri, *Vittorio*
Angelou, *Maya*
Aretino, *Pietro*
Ariosto, *Ludovico*
Beddoes, *Thomas*
Belleau, *Rémy*
Blunden, *Edmund*
Bridges, *Robert Seymour*
Brodsky, *Joseph*
Caedmon
Campion, *Thomas*
Causley, *Charles*
Chapman, *George*
Chaucer, *Geoffrey*
Collins, *Wilkie (William)*
Corinna
Cynwulf
De Vigny, *Alfred Victor*
Doughty, *Charles*
Douglas, *Alfred*
Drayton, *Michael*
Emerson, *Ralph Waldo*
Enright, *Dennis*
Flaccus, *Horace (Quintus Horatius)*
Flecker, *James Elroy*
Herbert, *George*
Heredia, *José María*
Herrick, *Robert*
Hodgson, *Ralph*
Hopkins, *Gerard Manley*
Housman, *A(lfred) E(dward)*
Johnson, *Samuel*
Juvenal
Khayyam, *Omar*
Kipling, *(Joseph) Rudyard*
Layamon

Leonard, *Tom*
MacCaig, *Norman*
MacLean, *Sorley*
Martial
Marvell, *Andrew*
McGough, *Roger*
Meynell, *Alice*
Mistral, *Frédéric*
Newbolt, *Sir Henry John*
Orpheus
Pushkin, *Aleksander Sergeyevich*
Rimbaud, *Arthur*
Roethke, *Theodore Huebner*
Ronsard, *Pierre de*
Russell, *George William*
Sassoon, *Siegfried (Louvain)*
Schwarz, *Delmore*
Seifert, *Jaroslav*
Service, *Robert William*
Shelley, *Percy Bysshe*
Sitwell, *Edith*
Skelton, *John*
Southey, *Robert*
Spender, *Stephen*
Spenser, *Edmund*
Statius, *Publius Papinius*
Stevens, *Wallace*
Terence *(Publius Terentius Afer)*
Thomson, *James*
Vaughan, *Henry*
Vaughan, *William*
Walcott, *Derek*
Whitman, *Walt(er)*
Woolner, *Thomas*

8 letters:
Anacreon
Banville, *Theodore*
Beranger, *Pierre*
Berryman, *John*
Betjeman, *John*
Browning, *Elizabeth Barrett*
Browning, *Robert*
Campbell, *Thomas*

Catullus, *Gaius Valerius*
Clampitt, *Amy*
Cummings, *E(dward) E(stlin)*
Cynewulf
Davenant, *Sir William*
de la Mare, *Walter (John)*
Drummond, *William*
Ginsberg, *Allen*
Hamilton, *William*
Harrison, *Tony*
Hausmann, *Raoul*
Henryson, *Robert*
Jennings, *Elizabeth*
Kavanagh, *Patrick*
Kynewulf
Langland, *William*
Leopardi, *Giacomo*
Lovelace, *Richard*
Macauley, *Thomas*
MacNeice, *Louis*
Mallarmé, *Stéphane*
Menander
Petrarch
Rossetti, *Christina Georgina*
Rossetti, *Dante Gabriel*
Schiller, *(Johann Cristoph) Friedrich von*
Shadwell, *Thomas*
Stephens, *James*
Suckling, *John*
Taliesin
Tennyson, *Lord Alfred*
Thompson, *Francis*
Traherne, *Thomas*
Tyrtaeus
Verlaine, *Paul*
Voltaire, *Francois*
Whittier, *John Greenleaf*

9 letters:
Aeschylus
Akhmatova, *Anna*
Alexander, *William*
Bunthorne, *Reginald*
Coleridge, *Samuel Taylor*

De Camoëns, *Luis Vaz*
Deschamps, *Eustache*
Dickinson, *Emily*
Doolittle, *Hilda (H D)*
Euripides
Goldsmith, *Oliver*
Lamartine, *Alphonse Marie*
  Loius De
Lucretius
Marinetti, *Emilio Filippo*
  Tommaso
Masefield, *John*
Quasimodo, *Salvatore*
Rochester, *(John Wilmot)*
Rosenberg, *Isaac*
Shenstone, *William*
Simonides *(of Ceos)*
Sophocles
Stevenson, *Robert Louis (Balfour)*
Swinburne, *Algernon Charles*
Wergeland, *Henrik*

10 letters:
Baudelaire, *Charles Pierre*
Chatterton, *Thomas*
Cumberland, *Richard*
Drinkwater, *John*
Fitzgerald, *Edward*

Fitzgerald, *Robert*
Longfellow, *Henry Wadsworth*
MacDiarmid, *Hugh*
Propertius, *Sextus*
Szymborska, *Wislawa*
Tannhauser
Theocritus
Wordsworth, *William*

11 letters:
Apollinaire, *Guillaume*
Archilochus
Asclepiades
Callimachus
De Lamartine, *Alphonse Marie*
  Louis de Prat
Maeterlinck, *Count Maurice*
Shakespeare, *William*

12 letters:
Aristophanes
De La Fontaine, *Jean*

13 letters:
Corn Law Rhymers

15 letters:
Ettrick Shepherd

Poisons

POISONOUS SUBSTANCES AND GASES

4 letters:
Bane
Lead
Tutu
Upas

5 letters:
Aspic
Conin
Ergot
Sarin
Sassy
Soman

Timbo
Urali

6 letters:
Aldrin
Antiar
Arsine
Cicuta
Conine
Curare
Curari
Datura
Dioxin

Emetin
Endrin
Hebona
Ourali
Ourari
Phenol
Wabain

7 letters:
Aconite
Amanita
Aniline
Arsenic

Atropin
Benzene
Brucine
Cacodyl
Coniine
Cowbane
Cyanide
Emetine
Hebenon
Hemlock
Henbane
Lindane
Neurine
Ouabain
Phallin
Red lead
Safrole
Solpuga
Stibine
Stibium
Surinam
Tanghin
Tropine
Woorali
Woorara
Wourali

8 letters:
Acrolein
Adamsite
Apocynum
Atropine
Barbasco
Botulism
Cyanogen
Cyanuret
Daturine
Death cap
Dumbcane
Foxglove
Gossypol
Laburnum
Lewisite
Litharge
Lobeline

Locoweed
Mandrake
Methanol
Mezereon
Nerve gas
Oleander
Paraquat
Phosgene
Pokeroot
Pokeweed
Pulicide
Ratsbane
Rhodanic
Samnitis
Santonin
Sasswood
Solanine
Thallium
Thebaine
Urushiol
Veratrin
Warfarin

9 letters:
Aflatoxin
Afterdamp
Baneberry
Benzidine
Coyotillo
Digitalin
Echidnine
Fly agaric
Gelsemine
Monkshood
Muscarine
Nux vomica
Parathion
Poison gas
Poison ivy
Poison oak
Pokeberry
Sassy wood
Saxitoxin
Sparteine
Stonefish

Tanghinin
Toxaphene
Veratrine
Whitedamp
Wolf's-bane
Yohimbine

10 letters:
Aqua-tofana
Belladonna
Cadaverine
Colchicine
Cyanic acid
Death angel
Hydrastine
Liberty cap
Limberneck
Manchineel
Mandragora
Mustard gas
Oxalic acid
Paris green
Phalloidin
Phylotoxin
Picrotoxin
Stavesacre
Strychnine
Tetrotoxin
Thorn apple

11 letters:
Agent Orange
Black bryony
Calabar-bean
Death camass
Dog's mercury
Gelseminine
Hyoscyamine
Pilocarpine
Poison elder
Prussic acid
Scopolamine
Staggerbush
Sugar of lead
Veratridine

12 letters:
Allyl alcohol
Formaldehyde
Lead monoxide
Nitromethane
Noogoora burr
Poison sumach
Strophanthus
Tetrodotoxin
Water hemlock
Zinc chloride

13 letters:
Dieffenbachia
Mercuric oxide
Methyl bromide
Poison dogwood
Silver nitrate

Sodium cyanide

14 letters:
Carbon monoxide
Castor-oil plant
Hydrogen iodide
Mountain laurel

15 letters:
Arsenic trioxide
Barium hydroxide
Black nightshade
Destroying angel
Hydrogen cyanide
Indian liquorice
Nitrogen dioxide
Osmium tetroxide
Woody nightshade

16 letters:
Carbon disulphide
Deadly nightshade
Hydrogen fluoride
Hydrogen sulphide
Mercuric chloride
Potassium cyanide

19 letters:
Sodium fluoroacetate
Tetramethyldiarsine

21 letters:
Potassium permanganate

25 letters:
Antimony potassium
   tartrate

TYPES OF POISONING

4 letters:
Food
Lead

6 letters:
Iodism

7 letters:
Bromism

8 letters:
Botulism
Ergotism
Plumbism
Ptomaine

9 letters:
Fluorosis
Saturnism

10 letters:
Digitalism
Salmonella

11 letters:
Hydrargyria
Listeriosis
Phosphorism

12 letters:
Mercurialism
Strychninism

Political parties

AUSTRALIA

16 letters:
Australian Greens

20 letters:
Australian Labor Party

AUSTRIA

3 letters:
FPÖ
ÖVP
SPÖ

23 letters:
Liberal Party of Australia

24 letters:
National Party of Australia

12 letters:
Freedom Party
People's Party

21 letters:
Social Democratic Party

BELGIUM

2 letters:
PS
SP
VB

3 letters:
CVP
PRL
PSC
PVV

5 letters:
Ecolo

6 letters:
Agalev

11 letters:
Flemish Bloc

16 letters:
French Green Party

17 letters:
Flemish Green Party

19 letters:
Flemish Liberal Party

20 letters:
French Socialist Party

21 letters:
Flemish Socialist Party

24 letters:
French Liberal Reform Party

26 letters:
French Social Christian Party

27 letters:
Flemish Social Christian Party

CANADA

11 letters:
Reform Party

12 letters:
Liberal Party

13 letters:
Bloc Quebecois

17 letters:
Conservative Party
Social Credit Party

18 letters:
New Democratic Party

23 letters:
Progressive Conservative

DENMARK

1 letter:
V

2 letters:
CD
FP
KF
RV
SD

SF

3 letters:
KrF

8 letters:
Liberals

13 letters:
Progress Party

14 letters:
Left Socialists

15 letters:
Centre Democrats
Radical Liberals
Social Democrats

18 letters:
Danish People's Party

21 letters:
Christian People's Party

Socialist People's Party

24 letters:
Conservative People's Party

FINLAND

2 letters:
KD
KP
SD

3 letters:
KOK
SFP
SMP

4 letters:
SKDL

11 letters:
Centre Party
Green League

12 letters:
Left Alliance

17 letters:
Finnish Rural Party

18 letters:
Christian Democrats

19 letters:
Swedish People's Party

21 letters:
Democratic Alternative
Social Democratic Party

22 letters:
National Coalition Party

30 letters:
Finnish People's
   Democratic League

FRANCE

2 letters:
PC
PR
PS

3 letters:
RDR
UDF
UMP

9 letters:
New Centre

13 letters:
National Front

14 letters:
Communist Party
Socialist Party

15 letters:
Republican Party

19 letters:
Rally for the Republic

23 letters:
Union for French
   Democracy

24 letters:
Union for a Popular
   Movement

GERMANY

3 letters:
CDU
CSU
FDP
PDS
SPD

7 letters:
The Left

19 letters:
Alliance 90/The Greens
Free Democratic Party

20 letters:
Christian-Social Union

21 letters:
Social Democratic Party

24 letters:
Christian-Democratic
   Union

26 letters:
Party of Democratic
   Socialism

GREECE

2 letters:
ND

5 letters:
PASOK

12 letters:
New Democracy

14 letters:
Politiki Aniksi

15 letters:
Political Spring

19 letters:
Greek Communist Party

28 letters:
Pan-Hellenic Socialist
  Movement

INDIA

1 letter:
I

3 letters:
BJP
BSP
CPI
INC
NCP

4 letters:
CPI (M)

8 letters:
Congress

9 letters:
Janata Dal

17 letters:
Bahujan Samaj Party

20 letters:
Bharitiya Janata Party

21 letters:
Communist Party of India

24 letters:
Nationalist Congress
  Party

28 letters:
Communist Party of India
  (Marxist)

IRISH REPUBLIC

8 letters:
Fine Gael
Sinn Féin

10 letters:
Fianna Fáil

11 letters:
Labour Party

14 letters:
Democratic Left

20 letters:
Progressive Democrats

ISRAEL

4 letters:
Shas

5 letters:
Likud

6 letters:
Kadima

11 letters:
Labour Party

12 letters:
Independence

15 letters:
Yisrael Beiteinu

ITALY

3 letters:
PDS

11 letters:
Centre Union

Forza Italia

13 letters:
Italy of Values

14 letters:
Northern League

16 letters:
Future and Freedom

National Alliance

18 letters:
The People of Freedom

JAPAN
7 letters:
Komeito

21 letters:
Social Democratic Party

22 letters:
Christian Democrat Party

24 letters:
Democratic Party of the Left

22 letters:
Democratic Party of Japan
Liberal Democratic Party

24 letters:
Democratic Socialist Party

LUXEMBOURG
2 letters:
PD

3 letters:
PCS

4 letters:
POSL

14 letters:
Communist Party

15 letters:
Democratic Party

20 letters:
Christian Social Party

31 letters:
Luxembourg Socialist
  Workers' Party

MALTA
16 letters:
Malta Labour Party
Nationalist Party

MEXICO
3 letters:
PAN
PRD
PRI

19 letters:
National Action Party

25 letters:
Revolutionary Workers'
  Party

30 letters:
Party of the Democratic
  Revolution

31 letters:
Institutional
  Revolutionary Party

THE NETHERLANDS
3 letters:
CDA
PVV
VVD

4 letters:
PvdA

11 letters:
Labour Party

14 letters:
Socialist Party

15 letters:
Party for Freedom

25 letters:
Christian Democratic Appeal

34 letters:
People's Party for Freedom and
   Democracy

NEW ZEALAND

3 letters:
ACT

11 letters:
Green Party
Māori Party

11 letters:
Labour Party

13 letters:
National Party

NORTHERN IRELAND

4 letters:
SDLP

8 letters:
Sinn Féin

13 letters:
Alliance Party

23 letters:
Democratic Unionist
   Party

27 letters:
Official Ulster Unionist
   Party

30 letters:
Social Democratic and
   Labour Party

PORTUGAL

2 letters:
BE
PS

3 letters:
CDS
PCP
PRD
PSD

8 letters:
Left Bloc

14 letters:
Socialist Party

21 letters:
Social Democratic Party

22 letters:
Democratic Renewal
   Party

24 letters:
Portuguese Communist
   Party

27 letters:
Democratic Social Centre
   Party

SOUTH AFRICA

3 letters:
ANC
PAC

13 letters:
National Party

18 letters:
Democratic Alliance

19 letters:
Congress of the People
Inkatha Freedom Party

21 letters:
Pan-Africanist Congress

23 letters:
African National
   Congress

SPAIN

2 letters:
IU
PP

3 letters:
CiU
PNV

4 letters:
PSOE

10 letters:
United Left

12 letters:
People's Party

19 letters:
Convergence and Union

21 letters:
Socialist Workers' Party

22 letters:
Basque Nationalist Party

SWEDEN

3 letters:
SAP

9 letters:
Left Party

10 letters:
Green Party

11 letters:
Centre Party

13 letters:
Moderate Party

13 letters:
Sweden Democrats

19 letters:
Liberal People's Party

24 letters:
Christian Democratic Party

27 letters:
Social Democratic Labour Party

TURKEY

22 letters:
Peace and Democracy Party
Republican People's Party

24 letters:
Nationalist Movement Party

26 letters:
Justice and Development Party

UNITED KINGDOM (MAINLAND)

3 letters:
SNP

4 letters:
UKIP

10 letters:
Plaid Cymru

11 letters:
Labour Party

16 letters:
Liberal Democrats

21 letters:
Scottish National Party

28 letters:
Conservative and Unionist Party

UNITED STATES OF AMERICA

15 letters:
Democratic Party
Republican Party

Politicians

4 letters:
Benn, *Tony*
Eden, *Sir (Robert) Anthony*

Foot, *Michael*
Hume, *John*

5 letters:
Adams, *Gerry*
Astor, *Nancy*

Bevan, *Nye*
Ewing, *Winnie*
Laski, *Harold Joseph*

6 letters:
Aitken, *Jonathan*
Bright, *John*
Castle, *Barbara*
Delors, *Jacques*
Hardie, *Keir*
Healey, *Dennis*
Mosley, *Oswald*
Powell, *Enoch*

Thorpe, *Jeremy*

7 letters:
Paisley, *Ian*
Parnell, *Charles Stewart*
Trimble, *David*
Trotsky, *Leon*

8 letters:
Disraeli, *Benjamin*
Hamilton, *Neil*
Rumsfeld, *Donald*

9 letters:
Gaitskell, *Hugh*
Gladstone, *William*
Kissinger, *Henry*
Pankhurst, *Emmeline*
Stonehouse, *John*

11 letters:
Wilberforce, *William*

12 letters:
Chesterfield, *Philip Dormer Stanhope*

See also:
➤ **Presidents** ➤ **Prime Ministers**

Popes

Pope	Pontificate
Peter	Until c.64
Linus	c.64–c.76
Anacletus	c.76–c.90
Clement I	c.90–c.99
Evaristus	c.99–c.105
Alexander I	c.105–c.117
Sixtus I	c.117–c.127
Telesphorus	c.127–c.137
Hyginus	c.137–c.140
Pius I	c.140–c.154
Anicetus	c.154–c.166
Soter	c.166–c.175
Eleutherius	175–89
Victor I	189–98
Zephyrinus	198–217
Callistus I	217–22
Urban I	222–30
Pontian	230–35
Anterus	235–36
Fabian	236–50
Cornelius	251–53
Lucius I	253–54
Stephen I	254–57
Sixtus II	257–58

Pope	Pontificate
Dionysius	259–68
Felix I	269–74
Eutychianus	275–83
Caius	283–96
Marcellinus	296–304
Marcellus I	308–09
Eusebius	310
Miltiades	311–14
Sylvester I	314–35
Mark	336
Julius I	337–52
Liberius	352–66
Damasus I	366–84
Siricius	384–99
Anastasius I	399–401
Innocent I	402–17
Zosimus	417–18
Boniface I	418–22
Celestine I	422–32
Sixtus III	432–40
Leo I	440–61
Hilarus	461–68
Simplicius	468–83
Felix III (II)	483–92
Gelasius I	492–96
Anastasius II	496–98
Symmachus	498–514
Hormisdas	514–23
John I	523–26
Felix IV (III)	526–30
Boniface II	530–32
John II	533–35
Agapetus I	535–36
Silverius	536–37
Vigilius	537–55
Pelagius I	556–61
John III	561–74
Benedict I	575–79
Pelagius II	579–90
Gregory I	590–604
Sabinianus	604–06
Boniface III	607
Boniface IV	608–15
Deusdedit *or* Adeodatus I	615–18

Pope	Pontificate
Boniface V	619-25
Honorious I	625-38
Severinus	640
John IV	640-42
Theodore I	642-49
Martin I	649-54
Eugenius I	654-57
Vitalian	657-72
Adeodatus II	672-6
Donus	676-78
Agatho	678-81
Leo II	682-83
Benedict II	684-85
John V	685-86
Cono	686-87
Sergius I	687-701
John VI	701-05
John VII	705-07
Sisinnius	708
Constantine	708-15
Gregory II	715-31
Gregory III	731-41
Zacharias	741-52
Stephen II (not consecrated)	752
Stephen II (III)	752-7
Paul I	757-67
Stephen III (IV)	768-72
Hadrian I	772-95
Leo III	795-816
Stephen IV (V)	816-17
Paschal I	817-24
Eugenius II	824-27
Valentine	827
Gregory IV	827-44
Sergius II	844-47
Leo IV	847-55
Benedict III	855-58
Nicholas I	858-67
Hadrian II	867-72
John VIII	872-82
Marinus I	882-84
Hadrian III	884-85
Stephen V (VI)	885-91
Formosus	891-96

Pope	Pontificate
Boniface VI	896
Stephen VI (VII)	896–97
Romanus	897
Theodore II	897
John IX	898–900
Benedict IV	900–03
Leo V	903
Sergius III	904–11
Anastasius III	911–13
Lando	913–14
John X	914–28
Leo VI	928
Stephen VII (VIII)	928–31
John XI	931–35
Leo VII	936–39
Stephen IX	939–42
Marinus II	942–46
Agapetus II	946–55
John XII	955–64
Leo VIII	963–65
Benedict V	964–66
John XIII	965–72
Benedict VI	973–74
Benedict VII	974–83
John XIV	983–84
John XV	985–96
Gregory V	996–99
Sylvester II	999–1003
John XVII	1003
John XVIII	1004–09
Sergius IV	1009–12
Benedict VIII	1012–24
John XIX	1024–32
Benedict IX (first reign)	1032–44
Sylvester III	1045
Benedict IX (second reign)	1045
Gregory VI	1045–46
Clement II	1046–47
Benedict IX (third reign)	1047–48
Damasus II	1048
Leo IX	1048–54
Victor II	1055–57
Stephen IX (X)	1057–58
Nicholas II	1059–61

Pope	Pontificate
Alexander II	1061-73
Gregory VII	1073-85
Victor III	1086-87
Urban II	1088-99
Paschal II	1099-1118
Gelasius II	1118-19
Callistus II	1119-24
Honorious II	1124-30
Innocent II	1130-43
Celestine II	1143-44
Lucius II	1144-45
Eugenius III	1145-53
Anastasius IV	1153-54
Hadrian IV	1154-59
Alexander III	1159-81
Lucius III	1181-85
Urban III	1185-87
Gregory VIII	1187
Clement III	1187-91
Celestine III	1191-98
Innocent III	1198-1216
Honorious III	1216-27
Gregory IX	1227-41
Celestine IV	1241
Innocent IV	1243-54
Alexander IV	1254-61
Urban IV	1261-64
Clement IV	1265-68
Gregory X	1271-76
Innocent V	1276
Hadrian V	1276
John XXI	1276-77
Nicholas III	1277-80
Martin IV	1281-85
Honorious IV	1285-87
Nicholas IV	1288-92
Celestine V	1294
Boniface VIII	1294-1303
Benedict XI	1303-04
Clement V	1305-14
John XXII	1316-34
Benedict XII	1334-42
Clement VI	1342-52
Innocent VI	1352-62

Pope	Pontificate
Urban V	1362-70
Gregory XI	1370-78
Urban VI	1378-89
Boniface IX	1389-1404
Innocent VII	1404-06
Gregory XII	1406-15
Martin V	1417-41
Eugenius IV	1431-47
Nicholas V	1447-55
Callistus III	1455-58
Pius II	1458-64
Paul II	1464-71
Sixtus IV	1471-84
Innocent VIII	1484-92
Alexander VI	1492-1503
Pius III	1503
Julius II	1503-13
Leo X	1513-21
Hadrian VI	1522-23
Clement VII	1523-34
Paul III	1534-49
Julius III	1550-55
Marcellus II	1555
Paul IV	1555-59
Pius IV	1559-65
Pius V	1566-72
Gregory XIII	1572-85
Sixtus V	1585-90
Urban VII	1590
Gregory XIV	1590-91
Innocent IX	1591
Clement VIII	1592-1605
Leo XI	1605
Paul V	1605-21
Gregory XV	1621-23
Urban VIII	1623-44
Innocent X	1644-55
Alexander VII	1655-67
Clement IX	1667-69
Clement X	1670-76
Innocent XI	1676-89
Alexander VIII	1689-91
Innocent XII	1691-1700
Clement XI	1700-21

Pope	Pontificate
Innocent XIII	1721–24
Benedict XIII	1724–30
Clement XII	1730–40
Benedict XIV	1740–58
Clement XIII	1758–69
Clement XIV	1769–74
Pius VI	1775–99
Pius VII	1800–23
Leo XII	1823–29
Pius VIII	1829–30
Gregory XVI	1831–46
Pius IX	1846–78
Leo XIII	1878–1903
Pius X	1903–14
Benedict XV	1914–22
Pius XI	1922–39
Pius XII	1939–58
John XXIII	1958–63
Paul VI	1963–78
John Paul I	1978
John Paul II	1978–2005
Benedictus XVI	2005–

Ports

3 letters:
Abo
Ayr
Gao
Hué
Rio
Rye

4 letters:
Acre
Aden
Akko
Amoy
Apia
Baku
Bari
Cebu
Cóbh
Cork
Deal
Dill
Elat
Gaza
Gyor
Hilo
Hull
Icel
Kiel
Kobe
Lima
Lomé
Oban
Omsk
Oran
Oslo
Perm
Pula
Puri

Riga
Said
Suez
Suva
Tyre
Vigo
Wick

5 letters:
Accra
Aqaba
Arhus
Arica
Aulis
Banff
Barry
Basra
Batum
Beira

Belem
Brest
Cádiz
Cairo
Colón
Dakar
Derry
Dilli
Dover
Dubai
Eilat
Emden
Fowey
Galle
Genoa
Gijón
Haifa
Imari
Izmir

Jaffa
Jedda
Jidda
Kerch
Kochi
Lagos
Larne
Leith
Lulea
Macao
Malmo
Mocha
Newry
Osaka
Ostia
Palma
Pisco
Poole
Pusan

Rabat
Salto
Sidon
Sligo
Split
Surat
Tampa
Tokyo
Tunis
Turku
Visby
Yalta

6 letters:
Aarhus
Abadan
Agadir
Albany
Ancona
Ashdod
Bastia
Batumi
Beirut
Belize
Bergen
Bilbao
Bissau
Bombay
Bootle
Boston
Bremen
Burgas
Calais
Callao
Cannes
Canton
Cochin
Dalian
Danzig
Darwin
Dieppe
Duluth
Dundee
Durban
Elblag

Galata
Galway
Gdańsk
Gdynia
Harbin
Havana
Hobart
Iloilo
Inchon
Juneau
Khulna
Kisumu
Kuwait
Lisbon
Lobito
London
Luanda
Lübeck
Madras
Malaga
Manama
Manaus
Manila
Maputo
Melaka
Mobile
Muscat
Nagano
Nantes
Naples
Narvik
Nassau
Nelson
Oamaru
Odense
Odessa
Oporto
Ostend
Padang
Quincy
Ragusa
Recife
Rimini
Rostov
Santos

Sgezed
Smyrna
St Malo
Sydney
Tacoma
Tallin
Thurso
Venice
Whitby
Xiamen
Yangon

7 letters:
Abidjan
Ajaccio
Algiers
Antibes
Antwerp
Augusta
Bamberg
Bangkok
Belfast
Bristol
Buffalo
Bushehr
Cardiff
Catania
Chicago
Cologne
Colombo
Conakry
Corinth
Dunedin
Dunkirk
Ephesus
Esbjerg
Foochow
Funchal
Gauhati
Geelong
Glasgow
Gosport
Grimsby
Halifax
Hamburg

Hampton
Harwich
Incheon
Iquique
Iquitos
Karachi
Karumba
Kinsale
Kowloon
Latakia
Legaspi
Le Havre
Lerwick
Livorno
Lorient
Marsala
Melilla
Messina
Milazzo
Mitstwa
Mombasa
Munster
Newport
New York
Oakland
Okayama
Palermo
Piraeus
Qiqihar
Rangoon
Rapallo
Rosario
Rostock
Runcorn
Salerno
San Juan
Seattle
Seville
Stettin
Swansea
Tallinn
Tampico
Tangier
Taranto
Trieste

Tripoli
Ulan-Ude
Ushuaia
Wexford
Wicklow

8 letters:
Abeokuta
Aberdeen
Acapulco
Alicante
Arbroath
Auckland
Batangas
Bathurst
Benghazi
Bordeaux
Boulogne
Brindisi
Brisbane
Cagliari
Calcutta
Cape Town
Djibouti
Dortmund
Flushing
Freetown
Geropiga
Göteborg
Greenock
Hamilton
Harfleur
Helsinki
Holyhead
Honolulu
Istanbul
Kanazawa
Kawasaki
Keflavik
Kingston
La Coruña
La Guaira
Limassol
Limerick
Monrovia

Montreal
Murmansk
Nagasaki
Newhaven
Penzance
Pevensey
Plymouth
Portland
Port Said
Ramsgate
Rosslare
Salvador
San Diego
Sandwich
Savannah
Schiedam
Shanghai
St Helier
Syracuse
Szczecin
Takoradi
Valencia
Veracruz
Wakayama
Weymouth
Yokohama

9 letters:
Amsterdam
Anchorage
Angostura
Annapolis
Archangel
Baltimore
Barcelona
Cartagena
Cherbourg
Dartmouth
Dubrovnik
Dunkerque
Ellesmere
Esperance
Esquimatt
Europoort
Famagusta

Fishguard
Fleetwood
Fremantle
Gallipoli
Gateshead
Geraldton
Gravesend
Guayaquil
Immingham
Inhambane
Kao-hsiung
Kirkcaldy
Krasnodar
Las Palmas
Liverpool
Lowestoft
Marseille
Melbourne
Mogadishu
Morecambe
Newcastle
Peterhead
Phnom Penh
Port Louis
Port Sudan
Reykjavik
Rotterdam
Santander
Schleswig
Sheerness
Singapore
Stavanger
Stockholm
Stornoway
Stranraer
Tarragona
Trondheim
Tynemouth
Vancouver
Volgograd
Walvis Bay
Waterford
Zeebrugge

10 letters:
Alexandria
Balikpapan
Birkenhead
Bratislava
Bridgetown
Caernarfon
Cap-Haitien
Casablanca
Charleston
Chittagong
Copenhagen
East London
Folkestone
Fray Bentos
Georgetown
Gothenburg
Hammerfest
Launceston
Libreville
Los Angeles
Mogadiscio
Montego Bay
Montevideo
New Orleans
Paramaribo
Portsmouth
Port Talbot
Queenstown
Sevastopol
Sunderland
Townsville
Valparaíso
Wellington
Whitstable

11 letters:
Bahia-Blanca
Buenos Aires
Dar es Salaam
Grangemouth
Londonderry
Mar del Plata
Maryborough
Port Moresby

Punta Arenas
Scarborough
Southampton
Trincomalee
Vladivostok

12 letters:
Barranquilla
Buenaventura
Dún Laoghaire
Jacksonville
Milford Haven
Port Adelaide
Port au Prince

Rio de Janeiro
San Francisco
San Sebastian
Santo Domingo
South Shields

13 letters:
Ellesmere Port
Great Yarmouth
Ho Chi Minh City
Hook of Holland
Middlesbrough
Port Elizabeth
Tandjungpriok

14 letters:
Burnie-Somerset
Vishakhapatnam

15 letters:
Charlotte-Amalie
Forster-Tuncurry
Saint Petersburg

17 letters:
Newcastle upon Tyne

Potatoes

4 letters:
Cara

5 letters:
Wilja

6 letters:
Estima
Romano

7 letters:
Desiree
Marfona

Roseval

8 letters:
Catriona

9 letters:
Charlotte
Kerr's Pink
Maris Bard

10 letters:
Arran Comet
Arran Pilot

King Edward
Maris Piper

11 letters:
Jersey Royal

12 letters:
Arran Victory
Golden Wonder
Pentland Dell
Pink Fir Apple

13 letters:
Pentland Crown
Ulster Sceptre

14 letters:
Pentland Squire
Sharpe's Express

15 letters:
Belle de Fontenay
Pentland Javelin

Pottery

4 letters:
Delf
Ming
Raku
Sung
Ware

5 letters:
China
Delft
Spode

6 letters:
Bisque
Wemyss

7 letters:
Celadon
Ceramic
Etruria
Faience
Satsuma

8 letters:
Flatback
Gombroon
Majolica
Slipware
Wedgwood®
Whieldon

9 letters:
Agatewear
Creamware
Stoneware

10 letters:
Crouch-ware
Hollowware
Spongeware

11 letters:
Granitewear

Presidents

PRESIDENTS OF THE U.S.

President	Party	Term of office
1. George Washington	Federalist	1789-97
2. John Adams	Federalist	1797-1801
3. Thomas Jefferson	Democratic Republican	1801-1809
4. James Madison	Democratic Republican	1809-1817
5. James Monroe	Democratic Republican	1817-25
6. John Quincy Adams	Democratic Republican	1825-29
7. Andrew Jackson	Democrat	1829-37
8. Martin Van Buren	Democrat	1837-41
9. William Henry Harrison	Whig	1841
10. John Tyler	Whig	1841-45
11. James K. Polk	Democrat	1845-49
12. Zachary Taylor	Whig	1849-50
13. Millard Fillmore	Whig	1850-53
14. Franklin Pierce	Democrat	1853-57
15. James Buchanan	Democrat	1857-61
16. Abraham Lincoln	Republican	1861-65
17. Andrew Johnson	Republican	1865-69
18. Ulysses S. Grant	Republican	1869-77
19. Rutherford B. Hayes	Republican	1877-81
20. James A. Garfield	Republican	1881
21. Chester A. Arthur	Republican	1881-85
22. Grover Cleveland	Democrat	1885-89
23. Benjamin Harrison	Republican	1889-93
24. Grover Cleveland	Democrat	1893-97
25. William McKinley	Republican	1897-1901
26. Theodore Roosevelt	Republican	1901-1909
27. William Howard Taft	Republican	1909-13
28. Woodrow Wilson	Democrat	1913-21
29. Warren G. Harding	Republican	1921-23
30. Calvin Coolidge	Republican	1923-29
31. Herbert C. Hoover	Republican	1929-33
32. Franklin D. Roosevelt	Democrat	1933-45
33. Harry S. Truman	Democrat	1945-53
34. Dwight D. Eisenhower	Republican	1953-61
35. John F. Kennedy	Democrat	1961-63
36. Lyndon B. Johnson	Democrat	1963-69
37. Richard M. Nixon	Republican	1969-74
38. Gerald R. Ford	Republican	1974-77
39. James E. Carter, Jr	Democrat	1977-81
40. Ronald W. Reagan	Republican	1981-89
41. George H. W. Bush	Republican	1989-93

President	Party	Term of office
42. William J. Clinton	Democrat	1993–2001
43. George W. Bush	Republican	2001–2009
44. Barack Hussein Obama II	Democrat	2009–

PRESIDENTS (OTHER THAN USA)

5 letters:
Botha, *P(ieter) W(illem)*

6 letters:
Chirac, *Jacques*
Mugabe, *Robert*

Prey, birds of

3 letters:
Ern
Owl

4 letters:
Erne
Gled
Hawk
Kite
Ruru

5 letters:
Eagle
Glede
Hobby
Saker

6 letters:
Condor
Falcon
Lanner
Merlin
Mopoke
Osprey

7 letters:
Barn owl
Boobook
Buzzard
Goshawk
Harrier
Hawk owl
Hoot owl

Kestrel
Red kite
Vulture

8 letters:
Brown owl
Bush-hawk
Caracara
Duck hawk
Falconet
Karearea
Sea eagle
Snowy owl
Tawny owl

9 letters:
Accipiter
Bald eagle
Eagle-hawk
Fish eagle
Gerfalcon
Gier-eagle
Gyrfalcon
Horned owl
Little owl
Ossifraga
Ossifrage
Wind-hover

10 letters:
Hen harrier
Screech owl

11 letters:
Chicken hawk
Cooper's hawk
Golden eagle
Lammergeier
Lammergeyer
Sparrowhawk

12 letters:
Honey buzzard
Long-eared owl
Marsh harrier

13 letters:
Bateleur eagle
Secretary bird
Turkey buzzard

14 letters:
Bearded vulture

15 letters:
Montagu's harrier
Peregrine falcon

16 letters:
Wedge-tailed eagle

17 letters:
Australian goshawk

18 letters:
Rough-legged buzzard

Prime Ministers

BRITISH PRIME MINISTERS

Prime Minister	Party	Term of office
Robert Walpole	Whig	1721–42
Earl of Wilmington	Whig	1742–43
Henry Pelham	Whig	1743–54
Duke of Newcastle	Whig	1754–56
Duke of Devonshire	Whig	1756–57
Duke of Newcastle	Whig	1757–62
Earl of Bute	Tory	1762–63
George Grenville	Whig	1763–65
Marquess of Rockingham	Whig	1765–66
Duke of Grafton	Whig	1766–70
Lord North	Tory	1770–82
Marquess of Rockingham	Whig	1782
Earl of Shelburne	Whig	1782–83
Duke of Portland	Coalition	1783
William Pitt	Tory	1783–1801
Henry Addington	Tory	1801–04
William Pitt	Tory	1804–06
Lord Grenville	Whig	1806–7
Duke of Portland	Tory	1807–09
Spencer Perceval	Tory	1809–12
Earl of Liverpool	Tory	1812–27
George Canning	Tory	1827
Viscount Goderich	Tory	1827–28
Duke of Wellington	Tory	1828–30
Earl Grey	Whig	1830–34
Viscount Melbourne	Whig	1834
Robert Peel	Conservative	1834–35
Viscount Melbourne	Whig	1835–41
Robert Peel	Conservative	1841–46
Lord John Russell	Liberal	1846–52
Earl of Derby	Conservative	1852
Lord Aberdeen	Peelite	1852–55
Viscount Palmerston	Liberal	1855–58
Earl of Derby	Conservative	1858–59
Viscount Palmerston	Liberal	1859–65
Lord John Russell	Liberal	1865–66
Earl of Derby	Conservative	1866–68
Benjamin Disraeli	Conservative	1868
William Gladstone	Liberal	1868–74
Benjamin Disraeli	Conservative	1874–80
William Gladstone	Liberal	1880–85

Prime Minister	Party	Term of office
Marquess of Salisbury	Conservative	1885–86
William Gladstone	Liberal	1886
Marquess of Salisbury	Conservative	1886–92
William Gladstone	Liberal	1892–94
Earl of Rosebery	Liberal	1894–95
Marquess of Salisbury	Conservative	1895–1902
Arthur James Balfour	Conservative	1902–05
Henry Campbell-Bannerman	Liberal	1905–08
Herbert Henry Asquith	Liberal	1908–15
Herbert Henry Asquith	Coalition	1915–16
David Lloyd George	Coalition	1916–22
Andrew Bonar Law	Conservative	1922–23
Stanley Baldwin	Conservative	1923–24
James Ramsay MacDonald	Labour	1924
Stanley Baldwin	Conservative	1924–29
James Ramsay MacDonald	Labour	1929–31
James Ramsay MacDonald	Nationalist	1931–35
Stanley Baldwin	Nationalist	1935–37
Arthur Neville Chamberlain	Nationalist	1937–40
Winston Churchill	Coalition	1940–45
Clement Attlee	Labour	1945–51
Winston Churchill	Conservative	1951–55
Anthony Eden	Conservative	1955–57
Harold Macmillan	Conservative	1957–63
Alec Douglas-Home	Conservative	1963–64
Harold Wilson	Labour	1964–70
Edward Heath	Conservative	1970–74
Harold Wilson	Labour	1974–76
James Callaghan	Labour	1976–79
Margaret Thatcher	Conservative	1979–90
John Major	Conservative	1990–97
Tony Blair	Labour	1997–2007
Gordon Brown	Labour	2007–2010
David Cameron	Conservative	2010–

AUSTRALIAN PRIME MINISTERS

Prime minister	Party	Term of office
Edmund Barton	Protectionist	1901–03
Alfred Deakin	Protectionist	1903–04
John Christian Watson	Labor	1904
George Houston Reid	Free Trade	1904–05
Alfred Deakin	Protectionist	1905–08
Andrew Fisher	Labor	1908–09
Alfred Deakin	Fusion	1909–10

Prime Minister	Party	Term of office
Andrew Fisher	Labor	1910-13
Joseph Cook	Liberal	1913-14
Andrew Fisher	Labor	1914-15
William Morris Hughes	National Labor	1915-17
William Morris Hughes	Nationalist	1917-23
Stanley Melbourne Bruce	Nationalist	1923-29
James Henry Scullin	Labor	1929-31
Joseph Aloysius Lyons	United	1931-39
Earle Christmas Page	Country	1939
Robert Gordon Menzies	United	1939-41
Arthur William Fadden	Country	1941
John Joseph Curtin	Labor	1941-45
Joseph Benedict Chifley	Labor	1945-49
Robert Gordon Menzies	Liberal	1949-66
Harold Edward Holt	Liberal	1966-67
John McEwen	Country	1967-68
John Grey Gorton	Liberal	1968-71
William McMahon	Liberal	1971-72
Edward Gough Whitlam	Labor	1972-75
John Malcolm Fraser	Liberal	1975-83
Robert James Lee Hawke	Labor	1983-91
Paul Keating	Labor	1991-96
John Howard	Liberal	1996-2007
Kevin Rudd	Labor	2007-2010
Julia Gillard	Labor	2010-

CANADIAN PRIME MINISTERS

Prime Minister	Party	Term of office
John A. MacDonald	Conservative	1867-73
Alexander Mackenzie	Liberal	1873-78
John A. MacDonald	Conservative	1878-91
John J. C. Abbot	Conservative	1891-92
John S. D. Thompson	Conservative	1892-94
Mackenzie Bowell	Conservative	1894-96
Charles Tupper	Conservative	1896
Wilfrid Laurier	Liberal	1896-1911
Robert Borden	Conservative	1911-20
Arthur Meighen	Conservative	1920-21
William Lyon Mackenzie King	Liberal	1921-26
Arthur Meighen	Conservative	1926
William Lyon Mackenzie King	Liberal	1926-30
Richard Bedford Bennet	Conservative	1930-35
William Lyon Mackenzie King	Liberal	1935-48
Louis St Laurent	Liberal	1948-57

Prime Minister	Party	Term of office
John George Diefenbaker	Conservative	1957-63
Lester Bowles Pearson	Liberal	1963-68
Pierre Elliott Trudeau	Liberal	1968-79
Joseph Clark	Conservative	1979-80
Pierre Elliott Trudeau	Liberal	1980-84
John Turner	Liberal	1984
Brian Mulroney	Conservative	1984-93
Kim Campbell	Conservative	1993
Joseph Jacques Jean Chrétien	Liberal	1993-2003
Paul Martin	Liberal	2003-6
Stephen Joseph Harper	Conservative	2006-

NEW ZEALAND PRIME MINISTERS

Prime Minister	Party	Term of office
Henry Sewell	-	1856
William Fox	-	1856
Edward William Stafford	-	1856-61
William Fox	-	1861-62
Alfred Domett	-	1862-63
Frederick Whitaker	-	1863-64
Frederick Aloysius Weld	-	1864-65
Edward William Stafford	-	1865-69
William Fox	-	1869-72
Edward William Stafford	-	1872
William Fox	-	1873
Julius Vogel	-	1873-75
Daniel Pollen	-	1875-76
Julius Vogel	-	1876
Harry Albert Atkinson	-	1876-77
George Grey	-	1877-79
John Hall	-	1879-82
Frederick Whitaker	-	1882-83
Harry Albert Atkinson	-	1883-84
Robert Stout	-	1884
Harry Albert Atkinson	-	1884
Robert Stout	-	1884-87
Harry Albert Atkinson	-	1887-91
John Ballance	-	1891-93
Richard John Seddon	Liberal	1893-1906
William Hall-Jones	Liberal	1906
Joseph George Ward	Liberal/National	1906-12
Thomas Mackenzie	National	1912
William Ferguson Massey	Reform	1912-25
Francis Henry Dillon Bell	Reform	1925

Prime Minister	Party	Term of office
Joseph Gordon Coates	Reform	1925-28
Joseph George Ward	Liberal/National	1928-30
George William Forbes	United	1930-35
Michael Joseph Savage	Labour	1935-40
Peter Fraser	Labour	1940-49
Sidney George Holland	National	1949-57
Keith Jacka Holyoake	National	1957
Walter Nash	Labour	1957-60
Keith Jacka Holyoake	National	1960-72
John Ross Marshall	National	1972
Norman Eric Kirk	Labour	1972-74
Wallace Edward Rowling	Labour	1974-75
Robert David Muldoon	National	1975-84
David Russell Lange	Labour	1984-89
Geoffrey Palmer	Labour	1989-90
Mike Moore	Labour	1990
Jim Bolger	National	1990-97
Jenny Shipley	National	1997-99
Helen Clark	Labour	1999-2008
John Key	National	2008-

Programming languages

1 letter:
C

3 letters:
Ada
PHP
RPG
SQL

4 letters:
Java
LISP

LOGO
Perl
Ruby
XSLT

5 letters:
Algol
BASIC
Basic
COBOL
CORAL
FORTH

OCCAM

6 letters:
Pascal
PROLOG
Python
Simula
SNOBOL

7 letters:
FORTRAN
Haskell

9 letters:
Smalltalk

10 letters:
Javascript
Postscript

11 letters:
Visual Basic

Proteins

3 letters:
PSA
RNA

4 letters:
Zein

5 letters:
Abrin
Actin
Opsin
Pharm
Porin

Prion
Renin
Ricin

6 letters:
Avidin

Capsid
Enzyme
Fibrin
Globin
Gluten
Lectin

Leptin
Myosin
Ossein

7 letters:
Adipsin
Albumen
Albumin
Aleuron
Amyloid
Elastin
Fibroin
Gliadin
Hordein
Keratin
Legumin
Opsonin
Sarcode
Sericin
Spongin
Tubulin

8 letters:
Aleurone
Amandine
Collagen
Cytokine
Ferritin
Gliadine
Globulin
Permease
Prolamin
Spectrin
Troponin
Vitellin

9 letters:
Capsomere
Flagellin
Myoglobin
Ovalbumin
Phaseolin
Prolamine
Properdin

Protamine
Repressor
Sclerotin
Spirulina

10 letters:
Actomyosin
Apoprotein
Bradykinin
Calmodulin
Caseinogen
Conchiolin
Dystrophin
Factor VIII
Fibrinogen
Interferon
Lymphokine
Thrombogen
Toxalbumin

11 letters:
Angiotensin

Haploglobin
Interleukin
Lactalbumin
Transferrin
Tropomyosin

12 letters:
Lactoprotein
Serum albumin

13 letters:
Ceruloplasmin
Macroglobulin
Serum globulin

14 letters:
Immunoglobulin

16 letters:
Alpha-fetoprotein

Provinces

PROVINCES OF CANADA

Province	Abbreviation
Alberta	AB
British Columbia	BC
Manitoba	MB
New Brunswick	NB
Newfoundland	NF
Northwest Territories	NWT
Nova Scotia	NS
Nunavut	NU
Ontario	ON
Prince Edward Island	PE
Quebec	PQ
Saskatchewan	SK
Yukon Territory	YT

PROVINCES OF SOUTH AFRICA

Province	Capital
Eastern Cape	Bisho
Free State	Bloemfontein

Province	Capital
Gauteng	Johannesburg
KwaZulu-Natal	Pietermaritzburg
Limpopo	Pietersburg
Mpumalanga	Nelspruit
Northern Cape	Kimberley
North-West	Mafikeng *or* Mahikeng
Western Cape	Cape Town

PROVINCES - OTHER

4 letters:
Jaen

5 letters:
Hejaz
Skane

6 letters:
Anhwei

Gansul

7 letters:
Bohemia
Galilee
Tabasco
Tucuman

8 letters:
Nuristan

9 letters:
Bubalidar
Irian Jaya

10 letters:
Westphalia

Psychology

BRANCHES OF PSYCHOLOGY

5 letters:
Child

6 letters:
Social

8 letters:
Analytic
Clinical
Hedonics

10 letters:
Industrial

Psychiatry

11 letters:
Comparative
Educational

12 letters:
Experimental

13 letters:
Developmental
Psychometrics
Psychophysics

14 letters:
Organizational
Parapsychology

15 letters:
Neuropsychology

16 letters:
Psychophysiology

17 letters:
Psycholinguistics

PSYCHOLOGY TERMS

2 letters:
Id

3 letters:
Ego

4 letters:
Anal
Mind
Self

5 letters:
Angst

Mania

6 letters:
Phobia
Psyche
Stress
Trauma

7 letters:
Anxiety
Complex
Persona

8 letters:
Alter ego
Analysis
Delusion
Dementia
Fixation
Hypnosis
Hysteria
Neurosis
Paranoia
Superego
Syndrome

9 letters:
Death wish
Extrovert
Introvert

Obsession
Psychosis

10 letters:
Compulsion
Depression
Regression
Repression

11 letters:
Inkblot test
Personality
Sublimation
Unconscious

12 letters:
Conditioning
Freudian slip
Group therapy
Hypochondria
Subconscious

13 letters:
Consciousness
Primal therapy
Psychosomatic
Rorschach test
Schizophrenia

14 letters:
Electra complex
Gestalt therapy
Oedipus complex
Psychoanalysis

18 letters:
Inferiority complex
Persecution complex

19 letters:
Personality disorder
Primal scream therapy

PSYCHOLOGISTS

4 letters:
Coué, *Émile*
Jung, *Carl Gustav*

5 letters:
Adler, *Alfred*
Freud, *Sigmund*
Fromm, *Erich*
James, *William*
Janet, *Pierre Marie Félix*
Luria, *Alexander Romanovich*
Reich, *Wilhelm*
Wundt, *Wilhelm Max*

6 letters:
De Bono, *Edward*
Hering, *Ewald*
Horney, *Karen*
Köhler, *Wolfgang*
Müller, *Johannes Peter*

Pavlov, *Ivan Petrovich*
Piaget, *Jean*
Watson, *John*

7 letters:
Eysenck, *Hans Jürgen*
Fechner, *Gustav Theodor*
Skinner, *B(urrhus) F(rederic)*

9 letters:
Thorndike, *Edward Lee*

10 letters:
Ebbinghaus, *Hermann*

11 letters:
Münsterberg, *Hugo*

Purple, shades of

4 letters:
Plum
Puce
Wine

5 letters:
Lilac
Mauve
Pansy
Royal

6 letters:
Claret
Indigo

Tyrian
Violet

7 letters:
Carmine
Gentian
Heather
Magenta

8 letters:
Amethyst
Burgundy
Dubonnet
Lavender

Mulberry

9 letters:
Aubergine
Peach-blow

10 letters:
Heliotrope
Periwinkle

11 letters:
Amaranthine
Gentian blue

Qq

Queens

3 letters:
Mab
May

4 letters:
Anna
Anne
Bess
Dido
Juno
Leda
Mary
Noor

5 letters:
Helen
Maeve
Sheba

6 letters:
Atossa
Balkis
Esther
Hecuba
Isabel
Ishtar

Isolde

7 letters:
Beatrix
Camilla
Candace
Eleanor
Jocasta
Juliana
Matilda
Omphale
Phaedra
Titania

8 letters:
Adelaide
Alcestis
Boadicea
Boudicca
Brunhild
Caroline
Eleanora
Gertrude
Hermione
Margaret
Penelope

Victoria

9 letters:
Alexandra
Artemesia
Brunhilde
Cleopatra
Elizabeth
Guinevere
Hippolyta
Nefertiti
Semiramis

10 letters:
Hatshepset
Hatshepsut
Persephone
Proserpina

14 letters:
Henrietta Maria

15 letters:
Marie Antoinette

Rr

Rabbits and hares

4 letters:
Cony
Hare
Pika

5 letters:
Coney

6 letters:
Rabbit

10 letters:
Arctic hare
Cottontail
Jack rabbit

11 letters:
Belgian hare

12 letters:
Angora rabbit
Snowshoe hare

14 letters:
Snowshoe rabbit

Races

2 letters:
TT

4 letters:
Boat
Milk
Oaks

5 letters:
Derby
Palio

6 letters:
Le Mans

7 letters:
St Leger

8 letters:
Olympics
RAC Rally

10 letters:
Epsom Derby
Royal Ascot

11 letters:
Admiral's Cup
America's Cup

12 letters:
Melbourne Cup
National Hunt
Tour de France

13 letters:
Dubai World Cup
Grand National
Kentucky Derby
Manx Grand Prix

15 letters:
Monte Carlo Rally

17 letters:
Cheltenham Gold Cup

Red, shades of

3 letters:
Bay

4 letters:
Foxy
Pink

Plum
Puce
Rose

Rosy
Ruby
Rust

Wine

5 letters:
Coral
Flame
Flesh
Gules
Henna
Liver
Peach
Poppy
Sandy

6 letters:
Auburn
Cerise
Cherry
Claret
Copper
Damask
Ginger
Maroon
Russet

Titian
Turkey

7 letters:
Carmine
Carroty
Coppery
Crimson
Fuchsia
Magenta
Old rose
Oxblood
Roseate
Scarlet
Tea rose
Vermeil

8 letters:
Baby pink
Burgundy
Cardinal
Chestnut
Cinnabar

Cyclamen
Dubonnet
Mulberry
Safranin

9 letters:
Carnation
Grenadine
Peach-blow
Raspberry
Safranine
Shell pink
Vermilion

10 letters:
Oyster pink
Salmon pink
Strawberry
Terracotta

11 letters:
Burnt sienna

Regimental nicknames

Regiment	Nickname
Army Service Corps	Ally Sloper's Cavalry
21st SAS	Artist's Rifles
13th Hussars	Baker's Dozen
2nd Dragoon Guards	The Bays
Royal Leicestershire Regiment	Bengal Tigers
17th Lancers	Bingham's Dandies
Royal Dragoons	Birdcatchers
7th Dragoon Guards	Black Horse
North Staffordshire Regiment	Black Knots
50th Foot Regiment	Blind *or* Dirty Half Hundred
Manchester Regiment	Bloodsuckers
11th Foot	Bloody Eleventh
4th/7th Royal Dragoon Guards	Blue Horse
Royal Horse Guards	Blues
Royal Scots Greys	Bubbly Jocks
3rd Foot	Buffs, Nutcrackers *or* Resurrectionists
4th (Royal Irish) Dragoon Guards	Buttermilks

Regiment	Nickname
26th & 90th Foot	Cameronians or Scottish Rifles
3rd Prince of Wales's Dragoon Guards	Carabineers, Carbs or Tichborne's Own
55th Foot	Castle Reeves
Royal Army Medical Corps	Castor Oil Dragoons
11th Hussars (Prince Albert's Own)	Cherry Pickers or Cherubims
Coldstream Guards	Coldies
8th (King's Royal Irish) Hussars	Cross Belts
17th/21st Lancers	Death or Glory Boys
9th (Queen's Royal) Lancers	Delhi Spearmen
7th Armoured Division	Desert Rats
Inns of Court Regiment	Devil's Own
46th Foot (Duke of Cornwall's Light Infantry)	Docs or Red Feathers
18th (Queen Mary's Own) Hussars	Drogheda Light Horse
33rd Foot (Duke of Wellington's)	Duke's
Royal Scots Fusiliers	Earl of Mar's Grey Breeks
15th (The King's) Hussars	Eliott's Tailors
Territorial Army Emergency Reserve	Ever Readies
40th (XL) Foot	Excellers
68th Foot (Durham Light Infantry)	Faithful Durhams
Royal Berkshire Regiment	Farmers' Boys
87th Foot (Royal Irish Fusiliers)	Faugh-a-ballagh Boys or Old Fogs
15th (King's) Hussars	Fighting Fifteenth
5th Foot (Royal Northumberland Fusiliers)	Fighting Fifth
9th Foot (Royal Norfolk Regiment)	Fighting Ninth, Holy Boys or Norfolk Howards
Worcestershire Regiment	Firms
Welsh Regiment	1st Invalids, Old Agamemnons or Ups and Downs
Royal Scots (1st Foot)	First and Wurst or First Invalids
Queen's Royal Regiment (West Surrey)	First Tangerines
Royal Ulster Rifles	Fitch and Grenadiers
54th Foot (Dorset Regiment)	Flamers
Gloucestershire Regiment	Fore and Aft
42nd Foot (Black Watch)	Forty-Twas
Royal Highland Fusiliers	Fusil Jocks
Royal Horse Artillery	Galloping Gunners
3rd (King's Own) Hussars	Galloping Third
Gordon Highlanders	Gay Gordons
70th Foot (East Surrey)	Glasgow Greys
Highland Light Infantry	Glesca Keelies
5th (Princess Charlotte of Wales's) Dragoon Guards	Green Horse

Regiment	Nickname
Alexandra Princess of Wales's Own Yorkshire Regiment	Green Howards
King's Royal Rifle Corps	Green Jackets
21st (Empress of India's) Lancers	Grey Lancers
Royal Scots Greys	Greys
Royal Hampshire Regiment	Hampshire Tigers
33rd Foot (Duke of Wellington's Regiment)	Havercake Lads
Royal Army Veterinary Corps	Horse Doctors
17th (Duke of Cambridge's Own) Lancers	Horse Marines
South Wales Borderers	Howard's Greens
Royal Army Pay Corps	Ink Slingers
King's Royal Rifle Corps	Jaegers
Royal Marines	Jollies
Scots Guards	Kiddies
King's Own Scottish Borderers	Kokky-Olly Birds or Kosbies
King's Own Yorkshire Light Infantry	Kolis or Koylies
32nd Foot (Duke of Cornwall's Light Infantry)	Lacedaemonians
47th Foot Regiment	Lancashire Lads or The Loyal
8th Foot (King's Regiment)	Leather Hats
Oxfordshire & Buckinghamshire Light Infantry	Light Bobs
13th Hussars	Lily Whites
Irish Guards	Micks
Lancashire Fusiliers	Minden Boys
Royal Army Service Corps	Moke Train
Wiltshire Regiment	Moonrakers
4th (Royal Irish) Dragoon Guards	Mounted Micks
Royal Engineers	Mudlarks
Royal Marines	Neptune's Bodyguard
Welsh Regiment	Old Agamemnons
Gloucestershire Regiment	Old Braggs
53rd Foot (King's Shropshire Light Infantry)	Old Brickdusts or Old Five and Threepennies
3rd (Prince of Wales's) Dragoon Guards	Old Canaries
12th Foot (Suffolk Regiment)	Old Dozen
Grenadier Guards	Old Eyes
87th Foot (Royal Irish Fusiliers)	Old Fogs
7th (Queen's Own) Hussars	Old Saucy Seventh
Sherwood Foresters	Old Stubborns
35th Foot	Orange Lilies
4th (Queen's Own) Hussars	Paget's Irregular Horse

Regiment	Nickname
Bedfordshire & Hertfordshire Regiment	Peacemakers
90th Foot (Cameronians)	Perthshire Grey Breeks
Royal Lincolnshire Regiment	Poachers
56th Foot	Pompadours
77th Foot	Pot-Hooks
South Staffordshire Regiment	Pump and Tortoise
Royal Army Pay Corps	Quill Drivers
5th (Royal Irish) Lancers	Red Breasts
Royal Horse Artillery	Right of the Line
91st Foot (Argyll & Sutherland Highlanders)	Rorys
(1st) The Royal Dragoons	Royals
65th Foot (York & Lancaster Regiment)	Royal Tigers
2nd Dragoon Guards (Queen's Bays)	Rusty Buckles
Grenadier Guards	Sand Bags
39th Foot (Dorsetshire Regiment)	Sankey's Horse
Royal Engineers	Sappers
6th Foot (Royal Warwickshire Fusiliers)	Saucy Sixth
16th (Queen's Royal) Lancers	Scarlet Lancers
6th (Inniskilling) Dragoons	Skiffingers
5th Royal Inniskilling Dragoon Guards	Skins
17th (Duke of Cambridge's Own) Lancers	Skull and Crossbones
Gloucestershire Regiment	Slashers
15th Foot (East Yorkshire Regiment)	Snappers
Wiltshire Regiment	Springers
1st Northamptonshire Regiment	Steel Backs
7th (Princess of Wales's Royal) Lancers	Strawboots
12th (Prince of Wales's Royal) Lancers	Supple Twelfth
Rifle Brigade	Sweeps
Welsh Guards	Taffys
93rd Foot (2nd Battalion Argyll & Sutherland Highlanders)	Thin Red Line
30th Foot (East Lancashire Regiment)	Three Tens
Life Guards	Tin Bellies *or* The Tins
Yorkshire & Lancashire Regiment	Twin Roses
55th Foot (Border Regiment)	Two Fives
44th Foot (Essex Regiment)	Two Fours
20th Foot (Lancashire Fusiliers)	Two Tens
69th Foot	Ups and Downs
Royal Warwickshire Fusiliers	Warwickshire Lads
20th Hussars	The X's
31st Foot (East Surrey Regiment)	Young Buffs
7th (Queen's Own) Hussars	Young Eyes

Regions, administrative

FRENCH REGIONS

6 letters:
Alsace
Centre

7 letters:
Corsica

8 letters:
Auvergne
Brittany
Burgundy
Limousin
Lorraine
Picardie

9 letters:
Aquitaine

10 letters:
Rhône-Alpes

11 letters:
Île-de-France
Pays de Loire

12 letters:
Franche-Comté
Midi-Pyrénées

14 letters:
Basse-Normandie
Haute-Normandie

15 letters:
Nord-Pas-de-Calais
Poitou-Charentes

16 letters:
Champagne-Ardenne

19 letters:
Languedoc-Roussillon

22 letters:
Provence-Alpes-Côte
 d'Azur

FRENCH DÉPARTEMENTS

3 letters:
Ain
Lot
Var

4 letters:
Aube
Aude
Cher
Eure
Gard
Gers
Jura
Nord
Oise
Orne
Tarn

5 letters:
Aisne
Corse
Doubs
Drôme

Indre
Isère
Loire
Marne
Meuse
Paris
Rhône
Saône
Somme
Yonne

6 letters:
Allier
Ariège
Cantal
Creuse
Essone
Gayane
Landes
Loiret
Lozère
Manche
Sarthe

Savoie
Vendée
Vienne
Vosges

7 letters:
Ardèche
Aveyron
Bas Rhin
Corrèze
Cote d'Or
Gironde
Hérault
Mayenne
Moselle
Niveres
Réunion

8 letters:
Ardennes
Calvados
Charente
Dordogne

Haut Rhin
Morbihan
Val d'Oise
Vaucluse
Yvelines

9 letters:
Finistère
Provence
Puy de Dôme

10 letters:
Deux Sèvres
Eure et Loir
Guadeloupe
Haute Loire
Haute Marne
Loir et Cher
Martinique
Val de Marne

11 letters:
Côtes du Nord

Hautes Alpes
Haute Savoie
Haute Vienne
Pas de Calais

12 letters:
Haute Garonne
Hauts de Seine
Indre et Loire
Lot et Garonne
Maine et Loire
Saône et Loire
Seine et Marne

13 letters:
Ille et Vilaine
Seine Maritime
Tarn et Garonne

14 letters:
Alpes Maritimes
Bouches du Rhône
Hautes Pyrénées

15 letters:
Loire Atlantique
Seine Saint Denis

16 letters:
Charente Maritime
Meurthe et Moselle

18 letters:
Pyrénées Orientales

19 letters:
Pyrénées Atlantiques
Territoire de Belfort

20 letters:
Alpes de Haute Provence

GERMAN STATES

6 letters:
Berlin
Bremen
Hessen
Saxony

7 letters:
Bavaria
Hamburg

8 letters:
Saarland

9 letters:
Thuringia

11 letters:
Brandenburg
Lower Saxony

12 letters:
Saxony-Anhalt

16 letters:
Baden-Württemberg

17 letters:
Schleswig-Holstein

19 letters:
Rhineland-Palatinate

20 letters:
North Rhine-Westphalia

24 letters:
Mecklenburg-West
 Pomerania

ITALIAN REGIONS

5 letters:
Lazio

6 letters:
Marche
Molise

Puglia
Sicily
Umbria
Veneto

7 letters:
Abruzzo
Liguria
Tuscany

8 letters:
Calabria
Campania
Lombardy
Piedmont
Sardinia

10 letters:
Basilicata

11 letters:
Valle d'Aosta

13 letters:
Emilia-Romagna

17 letters:
Trentino-Alto Adige

19 letters:
Friuli-Venezia Giulia

ITALIAN PROVINCES

4 letters:
Asti
Bari
Como
Enna
Lodi
Pisa
Roma

5 letters:
Aosta
Cuneo
Forlì
Lecce
Lecco
Lucca
Nuoro
Parma
Pavia
Prato
Rieti
Siena
Terni
Udine

6 letters:
Ancona
Arezzo
Chieti
Foggia
Genova
Latina
Matera
Milano
Modena

Napoli
Novara
Padova
Pesaro
Ragusa
Rimini
Rovigo
Savona
Teramo
Torino
Trento
Varese
Verona

7 letters:
Belluno
Bergamo
Bologna
Bolzano
Brescia
Caserta
Catania
Cosenza
Cremona
Crotone
Ferrara
Firenze
Gorizia
Imperia
Isernia
L'Aquila
Livorno
Mantova
Messina
Palermo

Perugia
Pescara
Pistoia
Potenza
Ravenna
Salerno
Sassari
Sondrio
Taranto
Trapani
Treviso
Trieste
Venezia
Vicenza
Viterbo

8 letters:
Avellino
Brindisi
Cagliari
Grosseto
La Spezia
Macerata
Oristano
Piacenza
Siracusa
Verbania
Vercelli

9 letters:
Agrigento
Benevento
Catanzaro
Frosinone
Pordenone

10 letters:
Campobasso

11 letters:
Alessandria

12 letters:
Ascoli Piceno

Massa Carrara
Reggio Emilia
Vibo Valentia

13 letters:
Caltanissetta

16 letters:
Reggio di Calabria

21 letters:
Repubblica di San Marino

SPANISH REGIONS

5 letters:
Ceuta

6 letters:
Aragón
Madrid
Murcia

7 letters:
Galicia
La Rioja
Melilla
Navarra

8 letters:
Asturias
Castilla
La Mancha

9 letters:
Andalucía
Cantabria
Catalonia

11 letters:
Extremadura

12 letters:
Castilla-León

13 letters:
Basque Country
Canary Islands

15 letters:
Balearic Islands

16 letters:
Castilla-La Mancha

18 letters:
Valencian Community

SPANISH PROVINCES

4 letters:
Jaén
León
Lugo

5 letters:
Álava
Ávila
Cádiz
Ceuta
Soria

6 letters:
Burgos
Cuenca
Girona
Huelva
Huesca

Lleida
Madrid
Málaga
Murcia
Orense
Teruel
Toledo
Zamora

7 letters:
Almería
Badajoz
Cáceres
Córdoba
Granada
La Rioja
Melilla
Navarra

Segovia
Sevilla
Vizcaya

8 letters:
Albacete
Alicante
Asturias
La Coruna
Palencia
Valencia
Zaragoza

9 letters:
Alhucemas
Balearics
Barcelona
Cantabria

Castellón
Guipúzcoa
Las Palmas
Salamanca
Tarragona

10 letters:
Chafarinas

Ciudad Real
Pontevedra
Valladolid

11 letters:
Gualalajara

15 letters:
Vélez de la Gomera

19 letters:
Santa Cruz de Tenerife

See also:
> **Countries** > **Provinces** > **States and territories** > **Swiss cantons**

Religion

RELIGIONS

4 letters:
Babi
Druz
Jain

5 letters:
Baha'i
Druse
Druze
Hasid
Islam
Jaina
Jewry
Sunna

6 letters:
Babism
Culdee
Gueber
Guebre
Hadith
Hassid
Jesuit
Loyola
Sabian
Shaker
Shango
Shembe
Shinto

Taoism
Voodoo
Yezidi
Zabian

7 letters:
Aaronic
Animism
Baha'ism
Bogomil
Ismaili
Jainism
Judaism
Lamaism
Macumba
Mahatma
Orphism
Parsism
Piarist
Sikhism
Stundism
Tsabian
Yezidis

8 letters:
Buddhism
Druidism
Hinduism
Lutheran

Manichee
Mazdaism
Mazdeism
Paganism
Santeria
Satanism
Theatine

9 letters:
Celestine
Coenobite
Hindooism
Jansenism
Mithraism
Mormonism
Pantheist
Shamanism
Shintoism
Utraquist
Voodooism
Zoroaster

10 letters:
Albigenses
Carthusian
Cistercian
Gilbertine
Heliolatry
Hospitaler

Manicheism
Zend-avesta

Ryobu Shinto
Scientology®
Zoroastrism

Tractarianism

14 letters:
Rastafarianism
Zoroastrianism

11 letters:
Camaldolite
Hare Krishna
Hospitaller
Ignorantine
Manichaeism
Mithraicism
Rosicrucian

12 letters:
Christianity
Confucianism
Zarathustric

13 letters:
Sons of Freedom

15 letters:
Christadelphian
Jehovah's Witness

RELIGIOUS BOOKS

2 letters:
Lu

6 letters:
Granth
I Ching

Samaveda
Shi Ching
Tipitaka

11 letters:
Mahabharata

4 letters:
Veda

5 letters:
Bible
Koran
Li Chi
Quran
Torah

Talmud

7 letters:
Rigveda
Su Ching

8 letters:
Ayurveda
Ramayana

9 letters:
Adi Granth
Apocrypha
Atharveda
Siddhanta
Tripitaka
Yajurveda

12 letters:
Bhagavad-Gita
Book of Mormon
New Testament
Old Testament

15 letters:
Guru Granth Sahib

RELIGIOUS BUILDINGS

5 letters:
Abbey
Kaaba
Marae

Chapel
Church
Mosque
Temple

8 letters:
Gurdwara

9 letters:
Cathedral
Monastery
Synagogue

10 letters:
Tabernacle

6 letters:
Bethel

7 letters:
Convent

RELIGIOUS CLOTHING

3 letters:
Alb

5 letters:
Amice
Cotta
Habit
Mitre

Chimer
Cornet
Guimpe
Peplos
Peplus
Rochet
Tippet
Wimple

7 letters:
Biretta
Calotte
Capuche
Cassock
Chimere
Gremial
Infulae
Maniple

4 letters:
Coif
Cope
Cowl

6 letters:
Almuce
Chimar

Mozetta
Pallium
Soutane
Tunicle

Dalmatic
Mozzetta
Scapular
Surplice

Surcingle
Zucchetto

12 letters:
Superhumeral

8 letters:
Berretta
Capouche
Chasuble

9 letters:
Clericals
Dog collar
Shovel hat

10 letters:
Canonicals

11 letters:
Mantelletta
Pontificals

14 letters:
Clerical collar

RELIGIOUS FESTIVALS

4 letters:
Holi
Lent

Epiphany
Hanukkah
Id-ul-Adha
Id-ul-Fitr
Passover
Rogation

Janamashtami
Lailat ul-Qadr
Moon Festival
Quadragesima
Rosh Hashanah
Septuagesima

5 letters:
Hirja
Purim
Wesak

9 letters:
Candlemas
Ching Ming
Christmas
Eid ul-Adha
Eid ul-Fitr
Pentecost
Rama Naumi
Yom Kippur

13 letters:
Corpus Christi
Lailat ul-Barah
Passion Sunday
Quinquagesima
Raksha Bandhan
Shrove Tuesday

6 letters:
Advent
Diwali
Easter
Pesach

7 letters:
Ramadan
Shavuot
Succoth
Sukkoth
Trinity
Whitsun
Yuan Tan

10 letters:
Good Friday
Michaelmas
Palm Sunday
Sexagesima

14 letters:
Day of Atonement
Mahashivaratri
Maundy Thursday
Winter Festival

11 letters:
Dhammacakka
Hola Mohalla

18 letters:
Dragon Boat Festival
Feast of Tabernacles
Guru Nanak's Birthday

8 letters:
Al Hijrah
Baisakhi
Bodhi Day
Chanukah
Dussehra

12 letters:
Ascension Day
Ash Wednesday

20 letters:
Lailat ul-Isra Wal Mi'raj

See also:
➤ **Angels** ➤ **Apocalypse, Four Horsemen of** ➤ **Apostles**
➤ **Archbishops of Canterbury** ➤ **Bible** ➤ **Buddhism**

Religious movements

Adidam (The Way of the Heart)
African Methodist Episcopalian Church
AME Church
Amish
Ananda Church of Self Realization
Ananda Marga Yoga Society
Anglo-Israelism
Assemblies of God
Association for Research and
    Enlightenment
Atheism
Aetherius Society
Aum Shinrikyo
Baha'i Faith
Baptists, Primitive
Baptists, Southern
Bogomils
Boston Church of Christ
Branch Davidians
Branhamism
British-Israelism
Brownsville Revival
Bruderhof
Buddhism
Call to Renewal (Christians for a New
    Political Vision)
Calvary Chapel
Campus Crusade for Christ
Candomble
Cao Daism
Channeling
Charismatic Movement
Chen Tao (The Right Way)
Children of God
Christadelphians
Christian and Missionary Alliance
Christian Coalition
Christian Identity Movement
Christian Reconstructionism
Christian Reformed Church in America
Christian Science
Christianity in Japan
Church in Island Pond
Church of God International
Church of Satan
Church of Scientology International, Inc.
Church of Set
Church of the Nazarene
Church of the New Jerusalem
Church Universal and Triumphant
Concerned Christians
Course in Miracles
Deepak Chopra
Discordianism
Divine Light Mission
Druids
Druse
Druze
Eckankar
Elan Vital
Est
Falun Gong (Religious Freedom in
    China)
Father Divine
Feng Shui
First Church of Christ, Scientist
Foundation of Human Understanding
Foursquare Gospel Church
Freemasonry
Fundamentalism
Ghebers
Gnosticism

Guebres
Hare Krishnas
Hasidism
Healthy, Happy, Holy Organization
Heaven's Gate
Hinduism
Holy Order of MANS
Holy Spirit Association for the
  Unification of World Christianity
Huguenots
Hussites
Hutterian Brethern of New York, Inc.
I Am
Institute of Noetic Sciences
Integral Yoga
International Church of Scientology
International Church of the Foursquare
  Gospel
International Churches of Christ
International Peace Mission Movement
International Raelian Religion
International Society for Krishna
  Consciousness
ISKCON
Islam
Israeli School of Universal Practical
  Knowledge (The Twelve Tribes)
Jainism
Jehovah's Witnesses
Jesus Army
Jesus Fellowship Church
Jesus People USA
Jonestown
Kabbalah
Karaites
Knights of Columbus
Konkokyo
Lamaism
Landmark Education
Latter Day Saints
Latter Rain Movement
Lifespring
Local Church
Macumba Maitreya
Manichaeism

Masada
Masons
Mazdaism
Mazdeism
Meher Baba Groups
Mennonites
Messianic Jewish Alliance of America
Methodist Church
Millennium Prophecies
Mithraism
Moody Bible Institute
Moody Church
Moonies
Moral Rearmament
Moravian Church
Mormonism (LDS)
MOVE
Movement for the Restoration of the
  Ten Commandments of God
Movement of Spiritual Inner
  Awareness
MSIA
Nation of Islam
Nation of Yahweh
National Baptist Convention
Native American Religions
Nazarene
Neo-Paganism
Neturei Karta (Guardians of the City)
New Age
New Creation Christian Community
New Thought
Nichiren Shoshu
Northeast Kingdom Community
  Church
Nubian Islamic Hebrews
Old Catholicism
Oneida Movement
Opus Dei
Order of the Solar Temple
Osho
Oxford
Paramahansa Yogananda
Parseeism
Parsiism

Pentecostalism
Peoples Temple
Philadelphia Church of God
Primitive Baptists
Process Church of the Final Judgment
Promise Keepers
Puseyism
Quakers
Raelians
Rajneeshism
Ramakrishna Order of the Vendanta
   Society
Ramtha's School of Enlightenment
Rastafarianism
Rebirthing
Religious Science (United Church of)
Reorganized Church Of Jesus Christ of
   Latter Day Saints
Restoration Movement
Restoration of the Ten Commandments
   of God
Roman Catholicism
Rosicrucian Order (AMORC)
Sabbatarian
Sabians
Sacramentarians
Sahaja Yoga
Salvation Army
Santeria
Satanism
Scientific Pantheism
Scientology
Secular Humanism
Seicho No Ie
Self-Realization Fellowship
Seventh-Day Adventists
Shakers
Shamanism
Shambhala International
Shinreikyo
Shinto
Shirdi Sai Baba
Sikh Dharma
Sikhs
Silva Mind Control *or* Silva Method

Snake Handlers
Society of Friends
Soka Gakkai
Solar Temple
Southern Baptists
Southern Christian Leadership
   Conference (SCLC)
Spiritual Discovery (Suma Ching Hai)
Spiritualism
Sri Chinmoy
Sukyo Mahikari
Suma Ching Hai
Swedenborgianism
Synanon
Synchronicity Contemporary
   Meditation
Taoism
Tenrikyo
The Brethren
The Church of God (Seventh Day)
The Church of Jesus Christ of Latter
   Day Saints
The Family
The Forum
The Process
The Temple of Set
The Way International (The Way)
The Zarathushtrian Assembly
Theosophy
Toronto Blessing
Tractarianism
Transcendental Meditation
Twelve Tribes
Two X Twos
Unarius Academy of Science
Unification Church
Unitarian Universalist
United Church of Religious Science
United Methodist Church
United Pentecostal Church International
United Society of Believers
Unity School of Christianity
Universal Life Church
Universal Negro Improvement
   Association

Universal Peace Mission Movement
Urantia Brotherhood
Vendanta Society
Vineyard Churches
Voodooism
Watchtower and Bible Tract
  Society
Wicca

Willow Creek Community Church
Woman's Christian Temperance
  Union
Worldwide Church of God
Zen Buddhism
Zionism
Zoroastrianism

Religious orders

Assumptionist (A.A.)
Augustinian (O.S.A.)
Barnabite Fathers
Benedictine (O.S.B.)
Bridgitine (C.S.B.)
Brothers of St Gabriel
Brothers of St John of God
Brothers of the Christian Schools
  (F.S.C.)
Camaldolese Benedictines
Canossian Daughters of Charity
Carmelite (O.C., O.C.D., O.C.D.S.)
Carthusian (O. Cart.)
Celestine
Cenacle Sisters
Christian Brothers
Cistercian (O. Cist.)
Claretian Missionaries
Congregation Marians
Congregation of the Holy Cross (C.S.C.)
Cordeliers
Daughters of St Francis of Assisi
Daughters of St Mary of Providence
Daughters of St Paul
Dervish
Divine Word Missionaries (D.V.M.)
Dominican (O.P.)
Felician Sisters
Franciscan (O.F.M.)
Handmaids of the Precious Blood
Hare Krishna (International Society
  for Krishna Consciousness *or*
  I.S.K.C.O.N.)
Institute of Charity (Rosminians) (I.C.)

Jesuits (S.J.)
Lasallian Brothers
Little Brothers of the Good Shepherd
Little Sisters of the Poor
Loretto nuns
Marianists
Marist Fathers and Brothers
Maryknoll
Missionaries of Charity (M.C.)
Missionaries of the Sacred Heart
  (M.S.C.)
Norbertines (C.R.P.)
Oblates (O.M.I.)
Observants
Passionists (C.P.)
Piarists
Poor Clares
Poor Sisters of Nazareth
Redemptorists (C.S.S.R.)
Resurrectionists (C.R.)
Salesians
Salesians of Don Bosco (S.D.B.)
Salvatorians
Servites
Sisters of Charity
Sisters of Mercy (R.S.M.)
Sisters of Notre Dame de Namur
  (S.N.D., S.N.D. de N.)
St Joseph Sisters (C.S.J., S.S.J.)
Sulpicians (P.S.S.)
Trappists (O.C.R., O.C.S.O.)
Ursuline Sisters

Reptiles

2 letters:
Go

3 letters:
Asp
Boa

4 letters:
Habu

5 letters:
Adder
Agama
Anole
Cobra
Gecko
Krait
Mamba
Racer
Skink
Snake
Swift
Tokay
Viper

6 letters:
Agamid
Caiman
Cayman
Dugite
Dukite
Elapid
Freshy
Garial
Gavial
Goanna
Iguana
Leguan
Lizard
Moloch
Python
Saltie

Taipan
Turtle

7 letters:
Camoodi
Frillie
Gharial
Monitor
Ngarara
Perenty
Rattler
Tuatara

8 letters:
Anaconda
Bungarra
Cerastes
Hawkbill
Moccasin
Perentie
Pit viper
Rat snake
Ringhals
Sea snake
Slowworm
Terrapin
Tortoise

9 letters:
Alligator
Blindworm
Blue racer
Boomslang
Box turtle
Bull snake
Chameleon
Crocodile
Deaf adder
Galliwasp
Hamadryad
Hawksbill
Hoop snake
Jew lizard

King cobra
King snake
Milk snake
Mud turtle
Puff adder
Rock snake
Sand viper
Sphenodon
Tree snake
Whip snake

10 letters:
Bandy-bandy
Black snake
Blind snake
Blue tongue
Brown snake
Bushmaster
Chuckwalla
Copperhead
Coral snake
Death adder
Fer-de-lance
Glass snake
Grass snake
Horned toad
Kabaragoya
Loggerhead
Massasauga
Rock python
Sand lizard
Sidewinder
Tiger snake
Wall lizard
Water snake
Worm lizard

11 letters:
Amphisbaena
Carpet snake
Constrictor
Cottonmouth
Diamondback

Gaboon viper
Garter snake
Gila monster
Gopher snake
Green turtle
Horned viper
Indigo snake
Leatherback
Mallee snake
Rattlesnake
Smooth snake
Thorn lizard
Thorny devil

12 letters:
Diamond snake
Flying dragon
Flying lizard
Hognose snake
Komodo dragon
Komodo lizard

See also:
➤ **Dinosaurs** ➤ **Lizards** ➤ **Snakes**

13 letters:
Bearded dragon
Bearded lizard
Bicycle lizard
Cycling lizard
Diamond python
Frilled lizard
Giant tortoise
Mountain devil
Water moccasin

14 letters:
Boa constrictor
Cobra de capello
Harlequin snake
Leathery turtle
Malayan monitor
Snapping turtle

15 letters:
Hawksbill turtle

Schneider python

16 letters:
Loggerhead turtle

17 letters:
Amethystine python
Diamondback turtle
Frill-necked lizard
Soft-shelled turtle

18 letters:
Saltwater crocodile

19 letters:
Diamondback terrapin
Freshwater crocodile

20 letters:
Red-bellied black snake

Republics

3 letters:
UAR
USA

4 letters:
Chad
Cuba
Eire
Fiji
Iran
Komi
Laos
Mali
Peru
Togo

5 letters:
Belau

Benin
Chile
China
Czech

4 letters:
Egypt
Gabon
Ghana
Haiti
India
Italy
Khmer
Malta
Nauru
Nepal
Niger
Palau
Sudan
Syria

Yemen
Zaire

6 letters:
Angola
Bukavu
Cyprus
France
Gambia
Guinea
Guyana
Ingush
Israel
Kalmyk
Latvia
Malawi
Mexico
Myanma

Panama
Russia
Rwanda
Serbia
Turkey
Weimar
Zambia

7 letters:
Albania
Algeria
Andorra
Bashkir
Belarus
Bolivia
Burundi
Chechen
Comoros

Croatia
Ecuador
Estonia
Finland
Germany
Hungary
Iceland
Ireland
Kalmuck
Khakass
Lebanon
Liberia
Moldova
Myanmar
Namibia
Nigeria
Romania
Senegal
Somalia
Surinam
Tunisia
Ukraine
Uruguay
Vanuatu
Vietnam

8 letters:
Abkhazid
Botswana
Bulgaria
Cambodia
Cameroon
Chechnya
Colombia
Dagestan
Djibouti

Dominica
Esthonia
Honduras
Karelian
Kiribati
Malagasy
Maldives
Mongolia
Paraguay
Slovakia
Slovenia
Sri Lanka
Tanzania
Udmurtia
Zimbabwe

9 letters:
Argentina
Cape Verde
Costa Rica
Dominican
Guatemala
Indonesia
Kazakstan
Khakhassa
Lithuania
Macedonia
Mauritius
Nicaragua
San Marino
Tatarstan
Venezuela

10 letters:
Azerbaijan
Bangladesh

Belarussia
El Salvador
Kazakhstan
Kyrgyzstan
Madagascar
Mauritania
Montenegro
Mordvinian
Mozambique
Tajikistan
Ubang-Shari
United Arab
Yugoslavia

11 letters:
Afghanistan
Byelorussia
Philippines
Sierra Leone
South Africa
Switzerland

12 letters:
Guinea-Bissau
Turkmenistan

13 letters:
Bashkortostan

17 letters:
Bosnia-Herzegovina

21 letters:
United States of America

Resins

3 letters:
Gum
Lac

4 letters:
Arar

Hing
Kino
Urea

5 letters:
Amber

Amino
Copai
Copal
Damar
Elemi
Epoxy

Myrrh
Roset
Rosin
Rosit
Rozet
Rozit

Saran®

6 letters:
Balsam
Charas
Conima
Copalm
Dammar
Dammer
Gambir
Mastic
Storax
Styrax

7 letters:
Acaroid
Benzoin

Caranna
Carauna
Churrus
Copaiba
Copaiva
Galipot
Gambier
Gamboge
Glyptal
Hashish
Jalapin
Ladanum
Polymer
Shellac
Xylenol

8 letters:
Bakelite®
Benjamin
Cannabin
Galbanum
Guaiacum
Hasheesh
Labdanum
Melamine
Olibanum
Opopanax
Phenolic
Propolis
Retinite
Sandarac
Scammony
Takamaka

9 letters:
Asafetida
Courbaril
Polyester
Sagapenum
Sandarach

10 letters:
Asafoetida

11 letters:
Podophyllin

12 letters:
Dragon's blood
Frankincense

Rice and other cereals

4 letters:
Bran
Corn
Oats
Ragi
Sago

5 letters:
Maize
Wheat

6 letters:
Millet

7 letters:
Oatmeal
Tapioca

8 letters:
Couscous
Wild rice

9 letters:
Brown rice
Patna rice

10 letters:
Indian rice

11 letters:
Arborio rice
Basmati rice

Bulgur wheat

13 letters:
Long grain rice

14 letters:
Short grain rice

Rivers

2 letters:
Ob
Po
Si
Xi

3 letters:
Aar
Ain
Aln
Axe
Ayr

Bug
Cam
Dee
Don
Ems
Esk
Exe
Fal
Fly
Han
Hsi
Inn

Lee
Lot
Nar
Ord
Red
San
Tay
Tet
Ure
Usk
Var
Wye

4 letters:
Abus
Abzu
Acis
Adur
Aire
Alma
Alph
Amur
Aran
Aras
Arno

Aube
Aude
Avon
Back
Beni
Bomu
Cher
Dart
Deva
Doon
Dove
Drin

Earn
Ebbw
Ebro
Eden
Eder
Elbe
Erne
Esla
Eure
Gila
Göta
Huon
Idle
Isar
Iser
Isis
Juba
Kama
Kill
Kura
Kwai
Lahn
Lech
Lena
Liao
Lune
Maas
Main
Meta
Milk
Miño
Mole
Nene
Neva
Nile
Nith
Oder
Ohio
Oise
Ouse
Oxus
Prut
Ruhr
Saar
Sava

Save
Soar
Spey
Styx
Swan
Swat
Tadi
Taff
Tana
Tarn
Tees
Teme
Test
Tyne
Uele
Ural
Vaal
Waal
Wear
Xero
Yalu
Yare
Yate
Yser
Yüan
Yüen

5 letters:
Abana
Acton
Adige
Afton
Agate
Aisne
Aldan
Apure
Argun
Avoca
Benue
Boyne
Cauca
Chari
Clyde
Congo
Cross

Dasht
Desna
Doubs
Douro
Drava
Drave
Duero
Dvina
Eblis
Ebola
Firth
Fleet
Forth
Ganga
Gogra
Green
Havel
Indre
Indus
Isère
James
Jumna
Juruá
Kabul
Kaful
Kasai
Kenga
Kuban
Lethe
Liard
Lippe
Loire
Marne
Meuse
Minho
Mosel
Mulla
Namoi
Negro
Neman
Niger
Ogowe
Onega
Oreti
Peace

Pearl
Pecos
Pelly
Piave
Pison
Plate
Purús
Rance
Rhein
Rhine
Rhône
Rogue
Roper
Saône
Seine
Shari
Shiré
Siang
Siret
Skien
Slave
Snake
Snowy
Somme
Spree
Staff
Stour
Swale
Tagus
Tamar
Tapti
Tarim
Teign
Terek
Tiber
Tisza
Tobol
Trent
Tweed
Volga
Volta
Warta
Weser
Xiang
Xingú

Yaqui
Yarra
Yonne
Yssel
Yukon

6 letters:
Albany
Allier
Amazon
Anadyr
Angara
Arzina
Atbara
Barcoo
Barrow
Bío-Bío
Buller
Calder
Canton
Chenab
Clutha
Crouch
Cuiaba
Cydnus
Danube
Dawson
Donets
Duddon
Durack
Finlay
Fraser
Gambia
Ganges
Glomma
Granta
Hodder
Hsiang
Hudson
Humber
Iguaçú
IJssel
Irtish
Irwell
Itchen

Japurá
Javari
Javary
Jhelum
Jordan
Kagera
Kaveri
Kennet
Kolyma
Komati
Liffey
Loiret
Mamoré
Medway
Mekong
Mersey
Mohawk
Molopo
Morava
Moskva
Murray
Neckar
Neisse
Nelson
Nyeman
Ogooué
Orange
Orwell
Ottawa
Pahang
Paraná
Pripet
Rakaia
Ribble
Riffle
Rother
Sabine
Saluda
Sambre
Santee
Severn
Struma
Sutlej
Sutley
Swanee

Tanana
Tarsus
Teviot
Thames
Ticino
Tigris
Tugela
Tyburn
Ubangi
Ussuri
Vardar
Vienne
Vltava
Wabash
Wairau
Wensum
Wharfe
Yarrow
Yellow

7 letters:
Acheron
Alabama
Aruwimi
Bermejo
Caquetá
Cauvery
Chagres
Cocytus
Damodar
Darling
Derwent
Detroit
Dnieper
Dubglas
Durance
Ettrick
Fitzroy
Garonne
Genesee
Gironde
Guaporé
Helmand
Hooghly
Huang He

Hwangho
Iguassú
Irawadi
Kanawha
Klamath
Krishna
Lachlan
Limpopo
Lualaba
Madeira
Manning
Marañón
Maritsa
Mataura
Meander
Moselle
Narmada
Niagara
Orinoco
Orontes
Paraíba
Pechora
Pharpar
Potomac
Rubicon
Sabrina
Salinas
Salween
Salzach
Sanders
San Juan
Scheldt
Senegal
Shannon
Songhua
Spokane
St Johns
Swannee
Tapajós
Thomson
Ucayali
Uruguay
Vistula
Waikato
Waitiki

Washita
Welland
Xi Juang
Yangtse
Yangtze
Yenisei
Yenisey
Zambese
Zambezi

8 letters:
Amu Darya
Anderson
Apurimac
Araguaia
Arkansas
Berezina
Blue Nile
Burdekin
Canadian
Charente
Cherwell
Cheyenne
Chindwin
Clarence
Colorado
Columbia
Daintree
Delaware
Demerara
Dniester
Dordogne
Flinders
Franklin
Gascoyne
Godavari
Guadiana
Han Jiang
Illinois
Kennebec
Kentucky
Klondike
Kootenai
Kootenay
Maeander

Mahanadi	**9 letters:**	Salambria	Castlereagh
Menderes	Ashburton	Santa Cruz	Connecticut
Missouri	Athabaska	Tennessee	Cooper Creek
Mitchell	Billabong	Tocantins	Lesser Slave
Okanagan	Churchill	White Nile	Madre de Dios
Okavango	Crocodile	Wisconsin	Mississippi
Ouachita	Des Moines		Monongahela
Pactolus	Essequibo	**10 letters:**	Montmorency
Paraguay	Euphrates	Black Volta	Shatt-al-Arab
Parnaíba	Irrawaddy	Blackwater	Susquehanna
Putumayo	Kuskokwim	Chao Phraya	Yellowstone
Rio Negro	Mackenzie	Courantyne	
Safid Rud	Macquarie	Hawkesbury	**12 letters:**
Saguenay	Magdalena	Housatonic	Cooper's Creek
Savannah	Minnesota	Kizil Irmak	Guadalquivir
Suwannee	Murchison	Phlegethon	Murrumbidgee
Syr Darya	Ob'Irtyish	Rangitaiki	Saskatchewan
Thompson	Parnahiba	Rangitikei	Victoria Nile
Torridge	Pilcomayo	Sacramento	
Toulouse	Porcupine	Saint Croix	**13 letters:**
Tunguska	Qu'Appelle	St Lawrence	Little Bighorn
Victoria	Rangitata	White Volta	Saint Lawrence
Volturno	Richelieu		
Wanganui	Rio Branco	**11 letters:**	**14 letters:**
Windrush	Rio Grande	Assiniboine	Jacques Cartier
Zhu Jiang	Saint John	Brahmaputra	

Rivers of Hell

4 letters:
Styx (River of Oath)

5 letters:
Lethe (River of Forgetfulness)

7 letters:
Acheron (River of Woe)
Cocytus (River of Lament)

10 letters:
Phlegethon (River of Fire)

Rocks

2 letters:	Tor	Gang	Reef	**5 letters:**
Aa		Glam	Sill	Ayers
	4 letters:	Grit	Sima	Brash
3 letters:	Bell	Jura	Trap	Calpe
Gem	Clay	Lava	Tufa	Chair
Gib	Coal	Lias	Tuff	Chalk
Jow	Crag	Noup	Zoic	Chert

Cliff
Clint
Craig
Elvan
Flint
Geode
Glass
Krans
Loess
Mafic
Magma
Nappe
Olgas
Scalp
Scree
Shale
Skarn
Slate
Solid
Stone
Trass
Uluru
Wacke

6 letters:
Aplite
Arkose
Banket
Basalt
Dacite
Diapir
Dunite
Felsic
Flaser
Flysch
Fossil
Gabbro
Gangue
Gibber
Gneiss
Gossan
Gozzan
Gravel
Inlier
Kingle

Marble
Masada
Norite
Oolite
Pelite
Pluton
Pumice
Rognon
Sarsen
Schist
Sinter
Skerry
Sklate
Stonen
Synroc
Tephra

7 letters:
Aquifer
Boulder
Breccia
Clastic
Cuprite
Cyanean
Diamond
Diorite
Eucrite
Fastnet
Felsite
Granite
Greisen
Lignite
Lorelei
Marlite
Minette
Molasse
Moraine
Needles
Nunatak
Olivine
Ophites
Outcrop
Outlier
Peridot
Picrite

Remanie
Rhaetic
Sinking
Spilite
St Peter
Syenite
Thulite
Tripoli
Wenlock

8 letters:
Adularia
Aegirine
Andesite
Aphanite
Basanite
Brockram
Burstone
Calcrete
Calc-tufa
Calc-tuff
Ciminite
Diabasic
Dolerite
Dolomite
Eclogite
Eklogite
Elvanite
Eutaxite
Fahlband
Felstone
Ganister
Hepatite
Hornfels
Idocrase
Inchcape
Laterite
Lopolith
Mesolite
Mudstone
Mylonite
Obsidian
Oil shale
Peperino
Perknite

Petuntse
Phyllite
Pisolite
Plutonic
Plymouth
Porphyry
Psammite
Psephite
Ragstone
Regolith
Rhyolite
Rocaille
Roe-stone
Saxatile
Saxonite
Scorpion
Sunstone
Taconite
Tarpeian
Tephrite
The Olgas
Tonalite
Trachyte
Trappean
Whin sill
Xenolith

9 letters:
Anticline
Argillite
Batholite
Bentonite
Bluestone
Buhrstone
Caenstone
Claystone
Cockhorse
Colluvium
Cornstone
Dalradian
Eddystone
Edinburgh
Evaporite
Firestone
Flowstone

Gannister
Gibraltar
Goslarite
Granulite
Graywacke
Greensand
Greystone
Greywacke
Hornstone
Impactite
Intrusion
Ironstone
Laccolite
Laccolith
Limestone
Meteorite
Migmatite
Monadnock
Monocline
Monzonite
Mortstone
Mugearite
Natrolite
Neocomian
Nunatakkr
Ophiolite
Ottrelite
Pegmatite
Phonolite
Phosphate
Pleonaste

Protogine
Quartzite
Reservoir
Sandstone
Saprolite
Scablands
Schistose
Siltstone
Soapstone
Tachylyte
Theralite
Tinguaite
Toadstone
Travertin
Uriconian
Variolite
Vulcanite
Whinstone
Whunstane
Zechstein

10 letters:
Ailsa Craig
Amygdaloid
Anthracite
Camptonite
Epidiorite
Foundation
Granophyre
Greenstone
Hypabyssal

Ignimbrite
Kersantite
Kimberlite
Lherzolite
Limburgite
Novaculite
Palagonite
Peridotite
Permafrost
Phenocryst
Pitchstone
Pyroxenite
Rupestrian
Schalstein
Serpentine
Sparagmite
Stinkstone
Stonebrash
Stonehenge
Syntagmata
Teschenite
Touchstone
Travertine
Troctolite
Ultrabasic
Ultramafic

11 letters:
Agglomerate
Amphibolite
Annabergite

Anorthosite
Carbonatite
Geanticline
Halleflinta
Lamprophyre
Monchiquite
Napoleonite
Nephelinite
Phillipsite
Pyroclastic
Sedimentary
Symplegades

12 letters:
Babingtonite
Conglomerate
Granodiorite
Grossularite
Hornblendite
Slickenslide
Stromatolite
Syntagmatite
Thunderstone

13 letters:
Hypersthenite

14 letters:
Giant's Causeway
Rhombenporphyr
Roche moutonnée

See also:
➤ **Minerals** ➤ **Ores** ➤ **Stones**

Rodents

3 letters:
Mus
Rat

4 letters:
Cavy
Jird

Mara
Paca
Vole

5 letters:
Aguti
Bobac

Bobak
Civet
Coypu
Hutia
Hyrax
Kiore
Mouse

Murid
Ratel
Shrew
Taira

6 letters:
Agouti

Beaver
Boomer
Dassie
Gerbil
Glires
Gopher
Hog-rat
Jerbil
Jerboa
Marmot
Nutria
Ratton
Suslik
Taguan

7 letters:
Acouchi
Acouchy
Cane rat
Chincha
Glutton
Hamster
Lemming
Mole rat
Muskrat
Ondatra
Pack rat
Potoroo
Souslik

8 letters:
Banxring
Biscacha
Bizcacha

Black rat
Brown rat
Capybara
Chipmunk
Cricetus
Dormouse
Gerbille
Hedgehog
Māori rat
Musquash
Ochotona
Sciurine
Sewellel
Squirrel
Tucotuco
Tucu-tuco
Viscacha
Vizcacha
Water rat
White rat

9 letters:
Bandicoot
Bangsring
Chickaree
Deer mouse
Delundung
Desert rat
Groundhog
Guinea pig
Jerboa rat
Norway rat
Porcupine
Water vole

Woodchuck

10 letters:
Chinchilla
Dargawarra
Fieldmouse
House mouse
Springhaas
Springhase

11 letters:
Fox squirrel
Kangaroo rat
Pocket mouse
Red squirrel
Spermophile

12 letters:
Grey squirrel
Harvest mouse
Hopping mouse
Jumping mouse
Pocket gopher

14 letters:
Flying squirrel
Ground squirrel

16 letters:
White-footed mouse

20 letters:
Spinifex hopping mouse

Roman numerals

Numeral	Equivalent	Numeral	Equivalent
A	50	H	200
B	300	I	1
C	100	K	250
D	500	L	50
E	250	M	1000
F	40	N	90
G	400	O	11

Numeral	Equivalent	Numeral	Equivalent
P	400	V	5
Q	500	X	10
R	80	Y	150
S	7 or 70	Z	2000
T	160		

Rome, the seven hills of

7 letters:	8 letters:	9 letters:	10 letters:
Caelian	Aventine	Esquiline	Capitoline
Viminal	Palatine		
	Quirinal		

Roofing

3 letters:	5 letters:			9 letters:
Hip	Gable	Saddle	Mansard	Monopitch
	Skirt	Thatch	Shingle	
4 letters:		Thetch		10 letters:
Bell			8 letters:	Jerkin-head
Dome	6 letters:	7 letters:	Imperial	
	French	Belfast	Pavilion	12 letters:
	Hipped	Gambrel		Porte-cochère
	Pop-top	Hardtop		

Ropes

3 letters:			
Guy	Lasso	Marlin	Pastern
Tow	Longe	Prusik	Rawhide
	Lunge	Roband	Stirrup
	Riata	Robbin	Swifter
4 letters:	Sheet	Runner	Towline
Balk	Sugan	Shroud	Triatic
Cord	Trace	String	
Fall	Wanty	Tackle	8 letters:
Jeff	Widdy		Backstay
Line		7 letters:	Boltrope
Stay	6 letters:	Bobstay	Bunt-line
Vang	Cablet	Cringle	Downhaul
	Cordon	Halyard	Forestay
5 letters:	Earing	Lanyard	Gantline
Baulk	Halser	Marline	Halliard
Brail	Halter	Mooring	Headfast
Cable	Hawser	Outhaul	Jack-stay
Guide	Inhaul	Painter	Prolonge

Selvagee
Spun-yarn

9 letters:
Breeching

Foresheet
Mainbrace
Mainsheet
Reef point
Sternfast

Timenoguy

10 letters:
Hawser-laid
Kernmantel

11 letters:
Triatic stay

13 letters:
Futtock-shroud

Rugby terms

3 letters:
Try

4 letters:
Back
Ball
Mark
Maul
Pack
Pass
Punt
Ruck

5 letters:
Scrum

6 letters:
Centre
Hooker

Sevens
Tackle
Winger

7 letters:
Back row
Dropout
Flanker
Fly half
Forward
Knock on
Line-out
Penalty
Referee

8 letters:
Crossbar
Drop goal
Front row

Full back
Goalpost
Half back
Open side

9 letters:
Blind side
Garryowen
Loose head
Scrum half
Scrummage
Second row
Tight head

10 letters:
Conversion
Five-eighth
Touch judge
Up and under

11 letters:
Lock forward
Outside half
Prop forward
Wing forward

12 letters:
Loose forward
Stand-off half
Three-quarter
Video referee

18 letters:
Number eight
 forward

Rulers

TITLES OF RULERS

3 letters:
Ban
Bey
Dey
Mir
Oba
Raj
Rex

4 letters:
Amir
Cham
Czar
Doge

Duce
Duke
Emir
Imam
Inca
Khan
King
Pope
Raja
Rana
Rani
Ratu
Shah
Tsar

Vali
Wali

5 letters:
Ameer
Ardri
Calif
Chief
Dewan
Diwan
Imaum
Kalif
Mogul
Mpret

Mudir
Nabob
Nawab
Negus
Nizam
Pacha
Pasha
Queen
Rajah
Ranee
Shaka
Sheik
Sophi
Sophy

Tenno

6 letters:
Atabeg
Atabek
Caesar
Caliph
Chagan
Dergue
Despot
Dynast
Exarch
Führer
Kabaka
Kaiser
Khalif
Manchu
Mikado
Prince
Regent
Sachem
Satrap
Sharif
Sheikh
Sherif
Shogun

Sirdar
Squier
Squire
Sultan
Tycoon
Tyrant

7 letters:
Abbasid
Ardrigh
Autarch
Bajayet
Bajazet
Catapan
Chogyal
Elector
Emperor
Empress
Gaekwar
Gaikwar
Jamshid
Jamshyd
Khedive
Lesbian
Monarch
Pharaoh

Podesta
Shereef
Souldan
Toparch
Viceroy

8 letters:
Archduke
Autocrat
Burgrave
Caudillo
Dictator
Ethnarch
Heptarch
Hierarch
Hospodar
Maharaja
Maharani
Mameluke
Mistress
Oligarch
Padishah
Sagamore
Sassanid
Suzerain
Tetrarch

Theocrat

9 letters:
Bretwalda
Cosmocrat
Dalai Lama
Maharajah
Maharanee
Ochlocrat
Pendragon
Plutocrat
Potentate
Sovereign
Vicereine

10 letters:
Aristocrat
Great Mogul
Plantocrat
Rajpramukh
Stadholder
Stratocrat

11 letters:
Stadtholder

FAMOUS RULERS

4 letters:
Nero

5 letters:
Herod
Lenin
Louis

6 letters:
Castro
Cheops
Franco
Hitler
Nasser
Stalin

7 letters:
Idi Amin
Saladin

8 letters:
Augustus
Bismarck
Boadicea
Boudicca
Caligula
Cromwell
De Gaulle
Hirohito
Nicholas
Pericles
Victoria

9 letters:
Churchill
Cleopatra
Elizabeth
Mao Ze Dong
Montezuma
Mussolini
Tamerlane

10 letters:
Caractacus
Kublai Khan
Mao Tse-tung

11 letters:
Charlemagne
Genghis Khan

Prester John
Tamburlaine
Tutankhamen
Tutankhamun

12 letters:
Chandragupta
Julius Caesar

13 letters:
Haile Selassie
Peter the Great

14 letters:
Alfred the Great

15 letters:
Ivan the Terrible

17 letters:
Alexander the Great
Catherine the Great
Napoleon Bonaparte

18 letters:
Edward the Confessor

19 letters:
Richard the Lionheart
William the Conqueror

22 letters:
Suleiman the Magnificent

ENGLISH RULERS (IN CHRONOLOGICAL ORDER)

Saxons
Egbert
Ethelwulf
Ethelbald
Ethelbert
Ethel(d)red I
Alfred the Great
Edward the Elder
Athelstan
Edmund (I)
Edred
Edwy
Edgar
Edward the Martyr
Ethel(d)red II the Unready
Edmund II (Ironside)

Danes
Canute
Harold I
Hardecanute

Saxons
Edward the Confessor
Harold II

Normans
William (I) the Conqueror
William II Rufus
Henry I
Stephen

Plantagenets
Henry II
Richard I The Lionheart
John
Henry III
Edward I
Edward II
Edward III
Richard II

Lancasters
Henry IV
Henry V
Henry VI

Yorks
Edward IV
Edward V
Richard III

Tudors
Henry VII
Henry VIII
Edward VI
Lady Jane Grey
Mary (I)
Elizabeth (I)

Stuarts
James I (VI of Scotland)
Charles I (Stuart)

Commonwealth Protectors
Oliver Cromwell
Richard Cromwell

Stuarts
Charles II
James II (interregnum)
William III and Mary II
Anne

Hanovers
George I
George II

George III
George IV
William IV
Victoria
Edward VII (Saxe-Coburg-Gotha)

Windsors
George V
Edward VIII (abdicated)
George VI
Elizabeth II

SCOTTISH RULERS (IN CHRONOLOGICAL ORDER)

Kenneth (I) M(a)cAlpin
Donald
Constantine I
Aedh
Eocha
Donald
Constantine II
Malcolm I
Indulph
Dubh
Cuilean
Kenneth II
Constantine III

Malcolm II
Duncan I
Macbeth
Lulach
Malcolm III
Donald Bane
Duncan II
Donald Bane
Edmund
Edgar
Alexander I
David I
John Baliol

Robert (the) Bruce
David II
Robert II
Robert III
James I
James II
James III
James IV
James V
Mary (Queen of Scots)
James VI

Russian federal republics

VOLGA DISTRICT

6 letters:	**8 letters:**	**9 letters:**	**10 letters:**
Mari El	Mordovia	Chuvashia	Tartarstan
	Taymyria	Mordvinia	
7 letters:	Udmurtia		**13 letters:**
Mariy El			Bashkortostan

NORTHERN CAUCASUS

7 letters:	Dagestan	**15 letters:**	**18 letters:**
Adygeya	Kalmykia	Northern Ossetia	Karachay-Cherkessia
			North Ossetia-Alania
8 letters:	**10 letters:**	**17 letters:**	
Chechnia	Ingushetia	Kabardino-Balkaria	
Chechnya			

NORTHWESTERN RUSSIA

4 letters:
Komi

7 letters:
Karelia

SIBERIA

4 letters:
Tuva

8 letters:
Buryatia

5 letters:
Altay

9 letters:
Khakassia

RUSSIAN FAR EAST

5 letters:
Sakha

Ss

Saints

Saint	Feast day
Agatha	5 February
Agnes	31 January
Aidan	31 August
Alban	22 June
Albertus Magnus	15 November
Aloysius (patron saint of youth)	21 June
Alphege	19 April
Ambrose	7 December
Andrew (Scotland)	30 November
Anne	26 July
Anselm	21 April
Anthony *or* Antony	17 January
Anthony *or* Antony of Padua	13 June
Athanasius	2 May
Augustine of Hippo	28 August
Barnabas	11 June
Bartholomew	24 August
Basil	2 January
Bede	25 May
Benedict	11 July
Bernadette of Lourdes	16 April
Bernard of Clairvaux	20 August
Bernard of Menthon	28 May
Birinus	3 December
Bonaventura *or* Bonaventure	15 July
Boniface	5 June
Brendan	16 May
Bridget, Bride *or* Brigid (Ireland)	1 February
Bridget *or* Birgitta (Sweden)	23 July
Catherine of Alexandria	25 November
Catherine of Siena (the Dominican Order)	29 April
Cecilia (music)	22 November
Charles Borromeo	4 November
Christopher (travellers)	25 July

Saint	Feast day
Clare of Assisi	11 August
Clement I	23 November
Clement of Alexandria	5 December
Columba *or* Colmcille	9 June
Crispin (shoemakers)	25 October
Crispinian (shoemakers)	25 October
Cuthbert	20 March
Cyprian	16 September
Cyril	14 February
Cyril of Alexandria	27 June
David (Wales)	1 March
Denis (France)	9 October
Dominic	7 August
Dorothy	6 February
Dunstan	19 May
Edmund	20 November
Edward the Confessor	13 October
Edward the Martyr	18 March
Elizabeth	5 November
Elizabeth of Hungary	17 November
Elmo	2 June
Ethelbert *or* Æthelbert	25 February
Francis of Assisi	4 October
Francis of Sales	24 January
Francis Xavier	3 December
Geneviève (Paris)	3 January
George (England)	23 April
Gertrude	16 November
Gilbert of Sempringham	4 February
Giles (cripples, beggars, and lepers)	1 September
Gregory I (the Great)	3 September
Gregory VII *or* Hildebrand	25 May
Gregory of Nazianzus	2 January
Gregory of Nyssa	9 March
Gregory of Tours	17 November
Hilary of Poitiers	13 January
Hildegard of Bingen	17 September
Helen *or* Helena	18 August
Helier	16 July
Hilarion	21 October
Ignatius	17 October
Ignatius of Loyola	31 July
Isidore of Seville	4 April
James	23 October

Saint	Feast day
James the Less	3 May
Jane Frances de Chantal	12 December
Jerome	30 September
Joachim	26 July
Joan of Arc	30 May
John	27 December
John Bosco	31 January
John Chrysostom	13 September
John Ogilvie	10 March
John of Damascus	4 December
John of the Cross	14 December
John the Baptist	24 June
Joseph	19 March
Joseph of Arimathaea	17 March
Joseph of Copertino	18 September
Jude	28 October
Justin	1 June
Kentigern *or* Mungo	14 January
Kevin	3 June
Lawrence	10 August
Lawrence O'Toole	14 November
Leger	2 October
Leo I (the Great)	10 November
Leo II	3 July
Leo III	12 June
Leo IV	17 July
Leonard	6 November
Lucy	13 December
Luke	18 October
Malachy	3 November
Margaret	20 July
Margaret of Scotland	10 June (16 November in Scotland)
Maria Goretti	6 July
Mark	25 April
Martha	29 July
Martin de Porres	3 November
Martin of Tours (France)	11 November
Mary	15 August
Mary Magdalene	22 July
Matthew *or* Levi	21 September
Matthias	14 May
Methodius	14 February
Michael	29 September
Neot	31 July

Saint	Feast day
Nicholas (Russia, children, sailors, merchants, and pawnbrokers)	6 December
Nicholas I (the Great)	13 November
Ninian	16 September
Olaf *or* Olav (Norway)	29 July
Oliver Plunket *or* Plunkett	1 July
Oswald	28 February
Pachomius	14 May
Patrick (Ireland)	17 March
Paul	29 June
Paulinus	10 October
Paulinus of Nola	22 June
Peter *or* Simon Peter	29 June
Philip	3 May
Philip Neri	26 May
Pius V	30 April
Pius X	21 August
Polycarp	26 January *or* 23 February
Rose of Lima	23 August
Sebastian	20 January
Silas	13 July
Simon Zelotes	28 October
Stanislaw *or* Stanislaus (Poland)	11 April
Stanislaus Kostka	13 November
Stephen	26 *or* 27 December
Stephen of Hungary	16 *or* 20 August
Swithin *or* Swithun	15 July
Teresa *or* Theresa of Avila	15 October
Thérèse de Lisieux	1 October
Thomas	3 July
Thomas à Becket	29 December
Thomas Aquinas	28 January
Thomas More	22 June
Timothy	26 January
Titus	26 January
Ursula	21 October
Valentine	14 February
Veronica	12 July
Vincent de Paul	27 September
Vitus	15 June
Vladimir	15 July
Wenceslaus *or* Wenceslas	28 September
Wilfrid	12 October
Xavier	3 December

Salts

2 letters:
AB

4 letters:
Corn
NaCl
Rock
Soap
Urao

5 letters:
Azide
Borax
Urate

6 letters:
Aurate
Borate
Halite
Iodide
Malate
Mucate
Oleate
Osmate
Sebate
Sodium
Uranin

7 letters:
Bromate
Bromide

Caprate
Citrate
Cyanate
Formate
Glauber
Ioduret
Lactate
Lithate
Muriate
Niobate
Nitrate
Nitrite
Osmiate
Oxalate
Picrate
Sorbate
Sulfite
Tannate

8 letters:
Alginate
Caproate
Cerusite
Chlorate
Chlorite
Chromate
Datolite
Malonate
Mersalyl
Plumbite
Pyruvate

Resinate
Rochelle
Selenate
Stannate
Stearate
Suberate
Sulphate
Sulphite
Tartrate
Titanate
Vanadate
Xanthate

9 letters:
Aluminate
Aspartite
Caprylate
Carbamate
Carbonate
Cyclamate
Glutamate
Linoleate
Magnesium
Manganate
Palmitate
Periodate
Phosphate
Phthalate
Potassium
Succinate
Tellurate

Tungstate

10 letters:
Andalusite
Bichromate
Dithionate
Isocyanide
Pandermite
Propionate
Salicylate
Sulphonate

11 letters:
Bicarbonate
Carboxylate
Microcosmic
Monohydrate
Perchlorate
Sal ammoniac
Sal volatile
Thiocyanate

12 letters:
Ferricyanide
Thiosulphate

13 letters:
Hydrochloride

Satellites

EARTH

4 letters:
Moon

5 letters:
Astra (artificial)
Tiros (artificial)

JUPITER

2 letters:
Io

4 letters:
Leda
Teba

5 letters:
Carme
Elara

Karme
Metis
Thebe

6 letters:
Ananke
Europa
Metida
Pacife
Sinope

7 letters:
Amaltea
Gimalia
Himalia
Lisitea

8 letters:
Adrastea
Amalthea
Callisto
Galilean
Ganymede

Lysithia
Pasiphaë

SATURN

3 letters:
Pan

4 letters:
Rhea

5 letters:
Atlas
Dione

Janus
Mimas
Titan

6 letters:
Helene
Phoebe
Tethys

7 letters:
Calypso
Iapetus
Pandora
Telesto

8 letters:
Hyperion

9 letters:
Enceladus

10 letters:
Epimetheus
Prometheus

URANUS

4 letters:
Puck

5 letters:
Ariel

6 letters:
Bianca

Juliet
Oberon
Portia

7 letters:
Belinda
Caliban
Miranda

Ophelia
Sycorax
Titania
Umbriel

8 letters:
Cordelia
Cressida

Rosalind

9 letters:
Desdemona

NEPTUNE

5 letters:
Naian

6 letters:
Nereid
Triton

7 letters:
Despina
Galatea
Larissa
Proteus

8 letters:
Thalassa

MARS

6 letters:
Deimos
Phobos

PLUTO

6 letters:
Charon

Sauces

2 letters:
HP®

3 letters:
Soy

4 letters:
Fish
Hard
Mint
Mole
Ragu
Soja
Soya
Sugo
Wine

5 letters:
Apple
Bread
Brown
Caper
Cream
Curry
Fudge
Garum
Gravy
Melba
Pesto
Salsa
Satay
Shoyu
White

6 letters:
Cheese
Chilli
Coulis
Creole
Fondue
Fu yong
Fu yung
Hoisin
Mornay
Nam pla
Orange
Oxymal
Oyster
Panada
Pistou
Relish
Sambal
Tamari
Tartar
Tomato

7 letters:
À la king
Alfredo
Custard
Harissa
Ketchup
Newburg
Nuoc mam
Parsley
Passata
Rouille
Sabayon
Soubise

Suprême
Tabasco®
Tartare
Velouté

8 letters:
Barbecue
Béchamel
Chasseur
Chow-chow
Fenberry
Marinara
Matelote
Meunière
Mirepoix
Piri-piri
Ravigote
Red pesto
Salpicon
Verjuice
Vindaloo
Yakitori

9 letters:
Allemande
Béarnaise
Black bean
Bolognese
Carbonara
Chocolate
Cranberry
Enchilada
Espagnole
Rémoulade
Worcester

10 letters:
Bolognaise
Bordelaise
Chaudfroid
Cumberland
Mayonnaise
Mousseline
Piccalilli
Puttanesca
Salad cream
Salsa verde
Stroganoff

11 letters:
Hollandaise
Horseradish
Vinaigrette

12 letters:
Brandy butter
Sweet-and-sour

13 letters:
Bourguignonne
Salad dressing

14 letters:
French dressing
Worcestershire

15 letters:
Russian dressing

Sausages

3 letters:
Sav

4 letters:
Lola

Snag

5 letters:
Black
Blood

Devon
Kiska
Kiske
Liver
Lorne

Lyons
Metts
Sujuk
Wurst

6 letters:
Banger
Boudin
Garlic
Haggis
Hot dog
Kishka
Kishke
Lolita
Mirkas
Polony
Salami
Square
Summer
Tuscan
Vienna
Wiener
Wienie

7 letters:
Abruzzo
Bologna
Cheerio
Chorizo
Frizzes
Kolbasa
Merguez
Saveloy
Soujouk
Yershig

Zampone

8 letters:
Cervelat
Chaurice
Chourico
Drisheen
Kielbasa
Lap chong
Lap chung
Linguica
Linguisa
Lop chong
Morcilla
Peperoni
Rohwurst
Teewurst
Toulouse

9 letters:
Andouille
Blutwurst
Bockwurst
Boerewors
Bratwurst
Chipolata
Cotechino
Glamorgan
Jagdwurst
Knoblauch

Kochwurst
Landjager
Lap cheong
Longanisa
Longaniza
Loukanika
Mettwurst
Pepperoni
Red boudin
Rookworst
Saucisson
Sulzwurst

10 letters:
Bauerwurst
Boerewurst
Bruehwurst
Cumberland
Knackwurst
Knockwurst
Landjaeger
Liverwurst
Mortadella
Potato korv
Weisswurst

11 letters:
Bauernwurst
Boudin blanc
Boudin rouge

Frankfurter
Genoa salami
Grutzewurst
Knublewurst
Pinkelwurst
White boudin
Wienerwurst
Zungenwurst

12 letters:
Andouillette
Bierschinken
Black pudding
Fleischwurst
Lincolnshire
White pudding

13 letters:
Schinkenwurst

14 letters:
Braunschweiger
Lebanon bologna
Medisterpoelse

15 letters:
Katenrauchwurst

Scarves

4 letters:
Doek
Haik
Hyke

5 letters:
Curch
Fichu
Haick
Pagri
Patka
Shash

Stole

6 letters:
Cravat
Haique
Madras
Rebozo
Tippet

7 letters:
Belcher
Dupatta

Muffler
Orarium
Tallith

8 letters:
Babushka
Cataract
Mantilla
Neckatee
Palatine
Trot-cosy
Trot-cozy

Vexillum

9 letters:
Comforter
Muffettee

10 letters:
Lambrequin

11 letters:
Nightingale

Schools

NAMES OF SCHOOLS

3 letters:
RAM

4 letters:
Dada
Eton
RADA

5 letters:
Perse
Slade
Stowe

6 letters:
Fettes
Harrow
Oundle
Repton

7 letters:
Bauhaus
Chicago
Flemish
Lancing
Loretto
Roedean
Rossall

8 letters:
Austrian
Barbizon
Benenden
Downside
Mannheim

9 letters:
Chartreux
Darmstadt

Frankfurt
Notre Dame
Tonbridge

10 letters:
Ampleforth
Manchester
Stonyhurst
Wellington
Winchester

11 letters:
Giggleswick
Gordonstoun
Marlborough
Westminster

12 letters:
Charterhouse

TYPES OF SCHOOL

3 letters:
CAT
CTC
GPS
LSE
Uni

4 letters:
Co-ed
Poly
Prep
Tech

5 letters:
Kindy
Lycée

6 letters:
Feeder
Hostel

Kindie

7 letters:
Academe
Academy
College
Convent
Crammer
Madrasa
Nursery
Varsity
Yeshiva

8 letters:
Business
Seminary

9 letters:
Alma mater
Day school

Gymnasien
Gymnasium
Institute
Ivy League
Madrassah
Palaestra

10 letters:
Chautauqua
Dame school
High school
Pensionnat
Prep school
University

11 letters:
Charm school
Choir school
Drama school
First school

Grade school
Hedge-school
List D school
Lower school
Mixed school
Night school
Open College
Peripatetic
Polytechnic
Reformatory
State school
Trade school
Upper school

12 letters:
Church school
Conservatory
Infant school
Junior school
Kindergarten

Magnet school
Middle school
Multiversity
Normal school
Progymnasium
Public school
Ragged school
Reform school
Summer school
Sunday school

13 letters:
Community home
Comprehensive
Conservatoire
Convent school
Council school
Grammar school
Junior college
Nursery school
Primary school
Private school
Sabbath school
Special school

14 letters:
Approved school
Bluecoat school
Boarding school

Hospital school
National School
Open University
Schola cantorum
Separate school
Village college

15 letters:
Civic university
Community school
Composite school
Finishing school
Parochial school
Secondary school
Single-sex school
Tertiary college

16 letters:
Classical college
Community college
Elementary school
Grant-aided school
Integrated school
Maintained school
Sixth-form college
Technical college

17 letters:
Direct-grant school

Independent school
Preparatory school
Residential school
Technology college

18 letters:
College of education
District high school
Great Public Schools
Intermediate school

19 letters:
Collegiate institute
Comprehensive school
Land grant university

20 letters:
Correspondence school

21 letters:
City technology college
Grant-maintained school
Secondary modern school

27 letters:
College of advanced
  technology

See also:
➤ **Colleges** ➤ **Degrees** ➤ **Education terms** ➤ **Ivy League**
universities ➤ **Oxbridge colleges**

Sea birds

3 letters:
Auk
Cob
Ern
Mew

4 letters:
Cobb
Coot

Erne
Gull
Shag
Skua
Tara
Titi

5 letters:
Booby

Kawau
Prion

6 letters:
Auklet
Fulmar
Gannet
Korora
Petrel

Scoter
Sea-cob
Sea-mew
Seapie
Takapu

7 letters:
Oldwife
Sea duck
Seagull
Taranui

8 letters:
Black cap
Blue shag
Fish hawk
Murrelet
Old squaw
Skua-gull
Surf duck

9 letters:
Albatross
Black shag
Cormorant
Guillemot
Ivory gull

Kittiwake
Razorbill

10 letters:
Gooney bird
Mutton bird
Sea swallow
Shearwater
Surf scoter

11 letters:
Blue penguin
Caspian tern
Frigate bird
Herring gull
Kahawai bird
Storm petrel

12 letters:
Fairy penguin
Glaucous gull
Man-of-war bird
Stormy petrel
Velvet scoter

13 letters:
Little penguin

Oystercatcher
Wilson's petrel

14 letters:
Black guillemot
Razor-billed auk

15 letters:
Black-backed gull

16 letters:
White-fronted tern

17 letters:
Little blue penguin

18 letters:
Wandering albatross

19 letters:
Mother Carey's chicken
Tasmanian mutton bird

21 letters:
Short-tailed shearwater

Seafood

3 letters:
Cod
Dab
Eel

4 letters:
Bass
Carp
Clam
Crab
Hake
Huss
Ling
Pike
Pipi

Pout
Shad
Sild
Sole
Tuna

5 letters:
Bream
Brill
Koura
Perch
Prawn
Roach
Shark
Skate

Snoek
Snook
Sprat
Squid
Trout
Tunny
Wahoo
Whelk
Witch
Yabby

6 letters:
Bonito
Callop
Cockle

Dorado
Kipper
Marron
Megrim
Mullet
Mussel
Oyster
Pillie
Plaice
Saithe
Salmon
Shrimp
Turbot
Winkle
Yabbie

Zander

7 letters:
Abalone
Anchovy
Bloater
Blue cod
Catfish
Codling
Crawbob
Craybob
Craydab
Dogfish
Gemfish
Haddock
Halibut
Herring
Jewfish
Kahawai
Lobster
Morwong
Mud crab
Octopus
Pollack
Pomfret
Queenie
Redfish

Sardine
Scallop
Scollop
Sea bass
Snapper
Sockeye
Whiting

8 letters:
Clawchie
Coalfish
Crawfish
Crayfish
Flounder
Grayling
John Dory
Kingfish
Lumpfish
Mackerel
Monkfish
Mulloway
Nannygai
Pilchard
Rockfish
Sand crab
Tarakihi
Teraglin

Terakihi
Tilefish
Trevally
Wolffish

9 letters:
Blackfish
Blue manna
Clabby-doo
Clappy-doo
Dover sole
King prawn
Lemon sole
Red salmon
Swordfish
Whitebait

10 letters:
Balmain bug
Barramundi
Butterfish
Parrotfish
Red snapper
Tiger prawn

11 letters:
Banana prawn

Blue swimmer
Langoustine
School prawn
Sea cucumber
Yellow belly

12 letters:
Queen scallop
Rainbow trout
Skipjack tuna

13 letters:
Moreton Bay bug
Norway lobster

14 letters:
Cornish sardine
Dublin Bay prawn

16 letters:
Australian salmon
Greenland halibut

18 letters:
Shovel-nosed
  lobster

Seals

4 letters:
Harp
Monk

5 letters:
Eared
Great
Otary
Phoca

Silky

6 letters:
Hooded
Hudson
Ringed
Sealch
Sealgh
Selkie

Silkie

7 letters:
Earless
Harbour
Sea-bear
Weddell

8 letters:
Elephant
Seecatch
Zalophus

9 letters:
Crab-eater
Greenland
Pintadera

10 letters:
Pinnipedia
Seecatchie

11 letters:
Bladdernose
Leopard seal

Sea mammals

4 letters:
Seal

6 letters:
Dugong
Sea cow

Walrus

7 letters:
Manatee
Sea lion

8 letters:
Harp seal
Sea horse

9 letters:
Eared seal

10 letters:
Hooded seal

11 letters:
Earless seal

12 letters:
Elephant seal

Seas and oceans

3 letters:
Ler
Med
Red

4 letters:
Aral
Azov
Dead
Java
Kara
Ross
Sulu

5 letters:
Banda
Black
Ceram
China
Coral
Hadal
Irish
Japan
North
South
Timor
White

6 letters:
Abssal
Aegean
Arctic
Baltic
Bering
Biscay
Celtic
Euxine
Flores
Indian
Inland
Ionian
Laptev
Scotia
Tasman
Tethys
Yellow

7 letters:
Andaman
Arabian
Arafura
Barents
Caspian
Celebes
Channel
Chukchi
Euripus

Galilee
Icarian
Lincoln
Marmara
Marmora
Okhotsk
Pacific
Pelagic
Polynya
Solomon
Weddell

8 letters:
Adriatic
Amundsen
Atlantic
Beaufort
Bismarck
Bosporus
Hwang Hai
Labrador
Ligurian
Sargasso
Southern
Tiberias

9 letters:
Antarctic
Bosphorus

Caribbean
East China
Greenland
Hudson Bay
Melanesia
Norwegian
Polynesia
Skagerrak
Thalassic

10 letters:
Philippine
South China
Tyrrhenian

11 letters:
Herring-pond
Spanish main

12 letters:
East Siberian
Nordenskjöld

13 letters:
Mediterranean

14 letters:
Bellingshausen

Seasons

Season	Related adjective
Spring	Vernal
Summer	Aestival *or* estival
Autumn	Autumnal
Winter	Hibernal *or* hiemal

Seats

3 letters:
Box
Pew
Pit

4 letters:
Banc
Love
Sofa
Sunk

5 letters:
Bench
Chair
Couch
Dicky
Divan
Perch
Sedes

Siege
Squab
Stool

6 letters:
Bucket
Canapé
Dickey
Houdah
Howdah
Humpty
Pouffe
Rumble
Saddle
Settee
Settle
Sunkie
Throne

7 letters:
Ejector
Hassock
Ottoman
Palfrey
Pillion
Taboret
Tonneau

8 letters:
Sedilium
Tabouret
Woolsack

9 letters:
Banquette
Bleachers
Davenport

Deckchair
Faldstool
Palanquin
Passenger

10 letters:
Faldistory
Knifeboard
Sidesaddle
Strapontin
Subsellium
Sunlounger
Synthronus

12 letters:
Chaise longue
Rumble-tumble

Seaweeds

3 letters:
Ore

4 letters:
Agar
Alga
Kelp
Kilp
Nori
Tang
Ulva
Ware

5 letters:
Algae
Arame
Dulse
Fucus
Kombu
Laver

Varec
Vraic
Wrack

6 letters:
Desmid
Diatom
Hijiki
Sea-mat
Varech
Wakame
Wakane

7 letters:
Oarweed
Redware
Sea-lace
Sea-moss
Seaware

8 letters:
Chondrus
Conferva
Gulfweed
Porphyra
Rockweed
Sargasso
Sea-wrack

9 letters:
Carrageen
Coralline
Cystocarp
Laminaria
Nullipore
Seabottle
Sea-tangle

10 letters:
Badderlock

Carragheen
Ceylon moss
Sea-lettuce
Sea-whistle

11 letters:
Bladderwort
Devil's apron
Purple laver
Sea-furbelow

12 letters:
Bladderwrack
Enteromorpha
Heterocontae
Peacock's tail

Seven against Thebes

6 letters:
Tydeus

8 letters:
Adrasyus
Capaneus

9 letters:
Polynices

10 letters:
Amphiaraüs
Hippomedon

13 letters:
Parthenopaeus

Seven deadly sins

4 letters:
Envy
Lust

5 letters:
Anger
Pride
Sloth

7 letters:
Avarice

8 letters:
Gluttony

12 letters:
Covetousness

Shakespeare

CHARACTERS IN SHAKESPEARE

Character	Play
Sir Andrew Aguecheek	Twelfth Night
Antonio	The Merchant of Venice
Antony	Antony and Cleopatra, Julius Caesar
Ariel	The Tempest
Aufidius	Coriolanus
Autolycus	The Winter's Tale
Banquo	Macbeth
Bassanio	The Merchant of Venice
Beatrice	Much Ado About Nothing
Sir Toby Belch	Twelfth Night
Benedick	Much Ado About Nothing
Bolingbroke	Richard II
Bottom	A Midsummer Night's Dream
Brutus	Julius Caesar
Caliban	The Tempest
Casca	Julius Caesar
Cassio	Othello
Cassius	Julius Caesar
Claudio	Much Ado About Nothing, Measure for Measure
Claudius	Hamlet
Cleopatra	Antony and Cleopatra
Cordelia	King Lear
Coriolanus	Coriolanus

Character	Play
Cressida	Troilus and Cressida
Cymbeline	Cymbeline
Demetrius	A Midsummer Night's Dream
Desdemona	Othello
Dogberry	Much Ado About Nothing
Edmund	King Lear
Enobarbus	Antony and Cleopatra
Falstaff	Henry IV Parts I and II, The Merry Wives of Windsor
Ferdinand	The Tempest
Feste	Twelfth Night
Fluellen	Henry V
Fool	King Lear
Gertrude	Hamlet
Gloucester	King Lear
Goneril	King Lear
Guildenstern	Hamlet
Hamlet	Hamlet
Helena	All's Well that Ends Well, A Midsummer Night's Dream
Henry	Henry IV, V, VI, VII
Hermia	A Midsummer Night's Dream
Hero	Much Ado About Nothing
Hotspur	Henry IV Part I
Iago	Othello
Jaques	As You Like It
John	King John
John of Gaunt	Richard II
Juliet	Romeo and Juliet
Julius Caesar	Julius Caesar
Katharina *or* Kate	The Taming of the Shrew
Kent	King Lear
Laertes	Hamlet
Lear	King Lear
Lysander	A Midsummer Night's Dream
Macbeth	Macbeth
Lady Macbeth	Macbeth
Macduff	Macbeth
Malcolm	Macbeth
Malvolio	Twelfth Night
Mercutio	Romeo and Juliet
Miranda	The Tempest
Oberon	A Midsummer Night's Dream
Octavius	Antony and Cleopatra
Olivia	Twelfth Night
Ophelia	Hamlet

Character	Play
Orlando	As You Like It
Orsino	Twelfth Night
Othello	Othello
Pandarus	Troilus and Cressida
Perdita	The Winter's Tale
Pericles	Pericles, Prince of Tyre
Petruchio	The Taming of the Shrew
Pistol	Henry IV Part II, Henry V, The Merry Wives of Windsor
Polonius	Hamlet
Portia	The Merchant of Venice
Prospero	The Tempest
Puck	A Midsummer Night's Dream
Mistress Quickly	The Merry Wives of Windsor
Regan	King Lear
Richard	Richard II, Richard III
Romeo	Romeo and Juliet
Rosalind	As You Like It
Rosencrantz	Hamlet
Sebastian	The Tempest, Twelfth Night
Shylock	The Merchant of Venice
Thersites	Troilus and Cressida
Timon	Timon of Athens
Titania	A Midsummer Night's Dream
Titus Andronicus	Titus Andronicus
Touchstone	As You Like It
Troilus	Troilus and Cressida
Tybalt	Romeo and Juliet
Viola	Twelfth Night

PLAYS OF SHAKESPEARE

6 letters:
Hamlet
Henry V

7 letters:
Macbeth
Othello

8 letters:
King John
King Lear

9 letters:
Cymbeline

Henry VIII
Richard II

10 letters:
Coriolanus
Richard III
The Tempest

11 letters:
As You Like It

12 letters:
Henry IV Part I
Henry VI Part I

Julius Caesar
Twelfth Night

13 letters:
Henry IV Part II
Henry VI Part II
Timon of Athens

14 letters:
Henry VI Part III
Romeo and Juliet
The Winter's Tale

15 letters:
Titus Andronicus

The Merchant of Venice
The Taming of the Shrew

16 letters:
Love's Labour's Lost

20 letters:
All's Well that Ends Well
Pericles, Prince of Tyre

17 letters:
Measure for Measure
The Comedy of Errors

21 letters:
A Midsummer Night's Dream

18 letters:
Antony and Cleopatra
Troilus and Cressida

22 letters:
The Merry Wives of Windsor

19 letters:
Much Ado About Nothing

23 letters:
The Two Gentlemen of Verona

POEMS OF SHAKESPEARE

7 letters:
Sonnets

16 letters:
The Rape of Lucrece

22 letters:
The Phoenix and the
   Turtle

14 letters:
Venus and Adonis

20 letters:
The Passionate Pilgrim

Sharks

3 letters:
Cow
Dog

4 letters:
Blue
Huss
Mako
Noah
Rigg
Sand
Tope

5 letters:
Angel
Gummy
Nurse
Tiger
Whale

6 letters:
Beagle
Carpet
School
Sea-ape
Whaler

7 letters:
Basking
Dogfish
Requiem
Reremai
Soupfin
Zygaena

8 letters:
Mackerel
Monkfish

Penny-dog
Rhinodon
Sailfish
Thrasher
Thresher

9 letters:
Angelfish
Grey nurse
Houndfish
Lemonfish
Porbeagle
Rhineodon
Seven-gill
Six-gilled
Wobbegong

10 letters:
Blue whaler

Bonnethead
Cestracion
Demoiselle
Great white
Hammerhead
Nursehound
Shovelhead

11 letters:
Blue pointer
Plagiostomi
Smoothhound

12 letters:
Bronze whaler

Sheep

4 letters:
Down
Kent
Lonk
Mule
Soay
Udad

5 letters:
Ammon
Ancon
Dall's
Jacob
Lleyn
Texel
Urial

6 letters:
Aoudad
Argali
Bharal
Bident
Burhel
Burrel
Exmoor
Masham
Merino
Muflon
Musmon
Oorial
Orkney
Oxford

7 letters:
Ancones
Bighorn
Boreray
Burrell
Caracul
Cheviot
Colbred
Dinmont
Karakul

Lincoln
Loghtan
Loghtyn
Mouflon
Musimon
Ryeland
St Kilda
Suffolk

8 letters:
Cheviots
Cotswold
Dartmoor
Drysdale
Herdwick
Loaghtan
Moufflon
Mountain
Polwarth
Portland
Shetland

9 letters:
Blackface
Blue-faced
Broadtail
Cambridge
Coopworth
Dalesbred
Fat-tailed
Hampshire
Hebridean
Kerry Hill
Leicester
Llanwenog
Marco Polo
Perendale
Romeldale
Rough Fell
Shorthorn
Southdown
Swaledale
Teeswater

Welsh Mule

10 letters:
Clun Forest
Corriedale
Dorset Down
Dorset Horn
Exmoor Horn
Hill Radnor
Shropshire

11 letters:
Île de France
Manx Loghtan
Norfolk Horn
Rambouillet
Romney Marsh
Wensleydale

12 letters:
British Texel

13 letters:
East Friesland
Hampshire Down
Mountain sheep
Rouge de l'Ouest
Welsh Halfbred
Welsh Mountain
Wiltshire Horn

14 letters:
British Vendéen
Devon Closewool
North Ronaldsay

15 letters:
Border Leicester
English Halfbred
Hexham Leicester
Lincoln Longwool
Oxfordshire Down

16 letters:
British Friesland
British Milksheep
British Oldenburg
Scottish Halfbred

17 letters:
British Charollais
Leicester Longwool
Scottish Blackface
Welsh Hill Speckled

White Face Dartmoor

18 letters:
Beulah Speckled-face
Black Welsh Mountain
British Bleu du Maine
South Wales Mountain
Whitefaced Woodland

19 letters:
Derbyshire Gritstone

North Country Cheviot
Wensleydale Longwool

20 letters:
Brecknock Hill Cheviot

24 letters:
Devon and Cornwall
   Longwool
Welsh Mountain Badger
   Faced

Shellfish

3 letters:
Mya
Top

4 letters:
Arca
Boat
Clam
Clio
Crab
Lamp
Paua
Pawa
Pipi
Spat
Tusk
Unio

5 letters:
Bulla
Capiz
Chank
Cohog
Conch
Cowry
Doris
Drill
Gaper
Helix
Koura
Murex

Olive
Ormer
Pinna
Polyp
Prawn
Razor
Sepia
Solen
Spoot
Squid
Turbo
Venus
Whelk
Yabby
Zimbi

6 letters:
Buckie
Chiton
Cockle
Cowrie
Cuttle
Limpet
Marron
Mussel
Ostrea
Oyster
Pecten
Pereia
Pholas
Poulpe

Purple
Quahog
Sea-ear
Sea-pen
Stromb
Tellen
Tellin
Teredo
Triton
Wakiki
Winkle
Yabbie

7 letters:
Abalone
Balanus
Bivalve
Crawbob
Craybob
Craydab
Isopoda
Lobster
Mud crab
Octopod
Octopus
Piddock
Quahaug
Scallop
Scollop
Sea-hare
Sea-slug

Toheroa
Torpedo
Trochus
Vitrina

8 letters:
Ammonite
Argonaut
Ark-shell
Chelonia
Clawchie
Copepoda
Crawfish
Crayfish
Deerhorn
Escallop
Haliotis
Nautilus
Ostracod
Pteropod
Sand crab
Saxicava
Sea-lemon
Shipworm
Strombus
Trivalve
Univalve
Xenophya

9 letters:
Belemnite

Blue manna
Clabby-doo
Clappy-doo
Cone-shell
Crustacea
Dentalium
Gastropod
King prawn
Langouste
Monocoque
Neopilina
Scalarium
Thermidor
Tusk-shell
Wing-shell

10 letters:
Acorn-shell
Amphineura
Cuttlefish

Gasteropod
Periwinkle
Razorshell
Scaphopoda
Stomatopod
Swan-mussel
Turritella
Wentletrap

11 letters:
Banana prawn
Blue swimmer
Foraminifer
Globigerina
Langoustine
Paper-sailor
School prawn
Soldier crab
Tectibranch
Trochophore

12 letters:
Malacostraca
Pelican's-foot

13 letters:
Lamellibranch
Moreton Bay bug
Norway lobster
Opisthobranch
Paper nautilus

14 letters:
Dublin Bay prawn
Pearly nautilus

16 letters:
Freshwater shrimp

18 letters:
Shovel-nosed lobster

Ships, parts of

3 letters:
Bow
Gyn
Jib
Rig

4 letters:
Amas
Beam
Bung
Bunk
Deck
Foil
Foot
Gaff
Hank
Head
Helm
Hull
Keel
Line

Loof
Luff
Mast
Peak
Prow
Rode
Rope
Sail
Skin
Slot
Spar
Yard

5 letters:
Berth
Bilge
Bitts
Blade
Block
Cabin
Chine

Chock
Cleat
Flare
Genoa
Hatch
Hoist
Kedge
Leech
Lines
Loofe
Oakum
Screw
Sheet
Slide
Staff
Stern
Wheel
Winch

6 letters:
Anchor

Bridge
Burgee
Davite
Dinghy
Dorade
Drogue
Fender
Fiddle
Fo'c'sle
Frames
Galley
Gunnel
Jigger
Rudder
Sheave
Shroud

7 letters:
Ballast
Bearers
Bobstay

Boomkin
Buoyage
Capstan
Channel
Coaming
Colours
Cordage
Dunnage
Fardage
Fin keel
Gallows
Gudgeon
Gunwale
Halyard
Iron-jib
Jibboom
Jib stay
Nippers
Outhaul
Quarter
Raffees

Rigging
Sea cock
Snubber
Toe rail
Topmast
Trysail
Yard arm

8 letters:
Backstay
Boom-vang
Bowsprit
Bulkhead
Bulwarks
Ditty box
Fife rail
Foredeck
Foremast
Forepeak
Foresail
Forestay
Full keel
Headsail
Headstay
Jib sheet
Leeboard
Life boat
Lifeline
Life raft
Mainmast
Mainsail
Masthead
Moonsail
Poop deck

Porthole
Scuppers
Shear pin
Staysail
Storm jib
Telltale
Trip line

9 letters:
Bilge keel
Bilge pump
Bitter end
Cabin sole
Crow's nest
Deck plate
Gang plank
Hard chine
Hawse hole
King spoke
Lazarette
Lazyjacks
Lazysheet
Mainbrace
Main sheet
Moonraker
Outrigger
Preventer
Royal mast
Sea-anchor
Sheathing
Spinnaker
Stanchion
Traveller

10 letters:
Anchor ball
Canoe stern
Figurehead
Forecastle
Jib netting
Jib topsail
Jigger-mast
Martingale
Mizzen mast
Mizzen sail
Riding sail
Rudder post
Sailing-rig
Sidelights
Turnbuckle

11 letters:
Anchor chain
Anchor light
Bosun's chair
Carline wood
Chafing gear
Foretopmast
Heaving line
Holding tank
Main topsail
Mooring line
Planing-hull
Sampson post
Spring lines
Towing light

12 letters:
Anchor locker
Bosun's locker
Charley noble
Companionway
Forestaysail
Hatch coaming
Kicking-strap
Reefing lines

13 letters:
Flame arrester
Iron-spinnaker
Running lights
Spinnaker boom
Spinnaker lift
Spinnaker pole
Stability sail

14 letters:
Anchor windlass
Courtesy ensign
Mizzen staysail
Running rigging

15 letters:
Running backstay

16 letters:
Painted waterline

17 letters:
Spinnaker pole lift

Shirts

3 letters:
Tee

4 letters:
Bush
Hair
Polo
Sark

5 letters:
Dress
Kurta
Rugby
Tunic

6 letters:
Banyan

Blouse
Boiled
Camise
Guimpe
Khurta
Skivvy
Sports
T-shirt

7 letters:
Chemise
Dashiki
Grandad
Kerbaya

8 letters:
Lava-lava

Swanndri®

9 letters:
Garibaldi
Halter top
Jacky Howe

10 letters:
Overblouse

11 letters:
Middy blouse

13 letters:
Cover-shoulder

Shoes and boots

3 letters:
Dap
Tie

4 letters:
Boot
Clog
Flat
Geta
Muil
Mule
Pump
Sock
Soft
Spat
Vamp
Vibs
Zori

5 letters:
Court
Gatty
Plate
Sabot
Scuff
Spike
Stoga
Stogy
Suede
Track
Wader
Wedge
Welly

6 letters:
Arctic

Ballet
Bootee
Brogan
Brogue
Buskin
Casual
Chopin
Flatty
Gaiter
Galosh
Golosh
Jandal®
Lace-up
Loafer
Mukluk
Oxford
Panton
Patten
Racket
Rivlin
Rubber
Saddle
Safety
Sandal
Sannie
Slip-on
T-strap
Vamper
Vibram®
Wedgie

7 letters:
Blucher
Bottine
Chopine
Cothurn

Creeper
Flattie
Galoche
Ghillie
Gumboot
Gumshoe
Gym shoe
High-low
Open-toe
Oxonian
Peeptoe
Racquet
Rullion
Sabaton
Slipper
Sneaker
Top boot
Trainer

8 letters:
Athletic
Balmoral
Crowboot
Deck shoe
Flip-flop
Golf shoe
Half boot
High heel
Jackboot
Larrigan
Mary-Jane®
Mocassin
Moccasin
Moonboot
Overshoe
Pantofle

Platform
Plimsole
Plimsoll
Poulaine
Rock boot
Sandshoe
Snowshoe
Solleret
Stiletto
Velskoen

9 letters:
Ankle boot
Biker boot
Cothurnus
Court shoe
Doc Marten®
Field boot
Pantoffle
Pantoufle
Rope-soled
Scarpetto
Slingback
Thigh boot
Track shoe
Veldskoen
Wedge heel

10 letters:
Bovver boot
Chukka boot
Cowboy boot
Espadrille
Kitten heel
Kurdaitcha
Orthopedic

Tennis shoe
Veld-schoen

11 letters:
Birkenstock®
FiveFingers

Hessian boot
Hobnail boot
Hush-puppies®
Running shoe

12 letters:
Co-respondent
Football boot
Kletterschue
Surgical boot
Training shoe

Winkle-picker

14 letters:
Brothel creeper
Wellington boot

Shrews and other insectivores

4 letters:
Mole

5 letters:
Shrew

6 letters:
Desman

Tenrec

7 letters:
Moon rat

9 letters:
Shrew mole
Solenodon

Tree shrew

10 letters:
Shrewmouse
Water shrew

12 letters:
Star-nose mole

13 letters:
Elephant shrew
Star-nosed mole

Shrubs

3 letters:
Box
Kat
Qat
Rue
Tea
Wax

4 letters:
Coca
Cola
Hebe
Nabk
Olea
Rhus
Rose
Ruta
Titi
Tutu

5 letters:
Aalii
Brere
Briar
Brier

Broom
Brush
Buaze
Buazi
Caper
Gorse
Hakea
Heath
Henna
Lilac
Maqui
Monte
Pyxie
Salal
Savin
Senna
Thyme
Toyon
Wahoo
Yacca
Yacka
Yapon
Yupon
Zamia

6 letters:
Acacia
Alhagi
Aucuba
Azalea
Bauera
Correa
Cotton
Crowea
Daphne
Fatsia
Feijoa
Frutex
Fynbos
Garrya
Jojoba
Laurel
Lignum
Manoao
Maquis
Matico
Mimosa
Myrica
Myrtle
Pituri

Privet
Protea
Savine
Sumach
Tawine
Tutsan
Wandoo
Yaupon

7 letters:
Arboret
Arbutus
Banksia
Boronia
Bramble
Bullace
Cascara
Cytisus
Dogwood
Emu bush
Epacris
Fuchsia
Geebong
Geebung
Heather

Hop-tree
Jasmine
Jibbong
Juniper
Lantana
Mesquit
Oleacea
Olearia
Rhatany
Romneya
Shallon
Skimmia
Tarwine
Tauhinu
Tea-tree
Waratah

8 letters:
Acanthus
Balisier
Barberry
Bilberry
Black boy
Bluebush
Buddleia
Camellia
Clematis
Coprosma
Gardenia
Hardhack

Hawthorn
Hibiscus
Inkberry
Jetbread
Laburnum
Lavender
Magnolia
Ninebark
Ocotillo
Oleander
Rock rose
Rosemary
Saltbush
Shadbush
Spekboom
Sweetsop
Tamarisk

9 letters:
Andromeda
Blueberry
Buckthorn
Clianthus
Coyotillo
Cranberry
Daisy bush
Firethorn
Forsythia
Grevillea
Hydrangea

Jaborandi
Jessamine
Kerrawang
Liquorice
Melaleuca
Mistletoe
Patchouli
Poison ivy
Poison oak
Raspberry
Screw bean
Spicebush
Twinberry
Waxflower
Yacca bush

10 letters:
Blackthorn
Coralberry
Cottonbush
Cottonwood
Crossandra
Eriostemon
Frangipani
Gooseberry
Horizontal
Joshua tree
Laurustine
Mock orange
Parkleaves

Poinsettia
Potentilla
Pyracantha
Redcurrant
Strawberry
Supplejack

11 letters:
Beautybrush
Blanket bush
Bottlebrush
Farkleberry
Honeysuckle
Pittosporum
Sheep laurel
Silverberry
Steeplebush

12 letters:
Blackcurrant
Rhododendron
Southernwood

13 letters:
Christmas bush
Crown-of-thorns

18 letters:
Geraldton
  waxflower

Silicas and silicates

4 letters:
Opal
Sard

5 letters:
Chert
Silex

6 letters:
Albite
Humite
Iolite

Pinite
Quartz

7 letters:
Kyanite
Olivine
Tripoli
Zeolite

8 letters:
Analcite
Datolite

Diopside
Dioptase
Saponite

9 letters:
Chabazite
Hiddenite
Natrolite
Penninite
Rhodonite
Scapolite
Tridymite

10 letters:
Andalusite
Float-stone
Kieselguhr
Staurolite
Ultrabasic

11 letters:
Vermiculite

12 letters:
Cristobalite
Monticellite

15 letters:
Montmorillonite

Silks

4 letters:
Corn
Flox
Pulu
Tram

5 letters:
Atlas
Crape
Crepe
Flosh
Floss
Gazar
Honan
Ninon
Satin
Seric
Surah
Tabby
Tasar
Tulle

6 letters:
Dupion
Faille
Kincob
Madras
Pongee
Samite
Sendal
Shalli
Sleave
Tussah
Tusseh
Tusser
Velvet

7 letters:
Alamode
Brocade
Chiffon
Foulard
Marabou
Organza

Ottoman
Sarsnet
Schappe
Tabaret
Taffeta
Tiffany
Tussore

8 letters:
Barathea
Chenille
Duchesse
Florence
Lustrine
Lustring
Makimono
Marabout
Milanese
Paduasoy
Prunella
Prunelle
Prunello

Sarsenet
Shantung
Sien-tsan

9 letters:
Charmeuse®
Filoselle
Georgette
Matelasse
Parachute
Sericeous
Serigraph

10 letters:
Florentine
Lutestring
Peau de soie

11 letters:
Thistledown

Skin, afflictions of

4 letters:
Boba
Buba
Rash
Yaws

5 letters:
Favus
Hives
Mange
Pinta
Tinea

6 letters:
Cowpox
Dartre
Eczema
Herpes
Livedo
Morula
Sapego
Scurvy
Tetter

7 letters:
Ecthyma
Prurigo

Rosacea
Scabies
Serpigo
Verruca
Verruga

8 letters:
Chloasma
Cyanosis
Dyschroa
Exanthem
Impetigo
Miliaria
Pyoderma

Ringworm
Rose-rash
Vaccinia
Vitiligo
Xanthoma

9 letters:
Chloracne
Exanthema
Pemphigus
Psoriasis

10 letters:
Dermatitis

Dermatosis
Erysipelas
Framboesia
Ichthyosis
Pityriasis
Seborrhoea

Strophulus

11 letters:
Mal del pinto

12 letters:
Sclerodermia

13 letters:
Leishmaniasis
Lupus vulgaris

Skirts

4 letters:
Bell
Full
Hoop
Hula
Kilt
Mini
Ra-ra
Tace
Tutu

5 letters:
A-line
Cargo
Grass
Harem

Pareo
Pareu
Tasse

6 letters:
Circle
Dirndl
Hobble
Pencil
Peplum
Piu-piu
Riding
Sarong
Taslet
Tasset
Tonlet

7 letters:
Culotte
Divided
Filibeg
Lamboys
Pleated

8 letters:
Bouffant
Culottes
Fillibeg
Half-slip
Lava-lava
Philibeg
Puffball
Wrapover

9 letters:
Cheongsam
Crinoline
Gabardine
Gaberdine
Maxiskirt
Midiskirt
Miniskirt
Overskirt
Petticoat
Waist-slip
Wrapround

10 letters:
Fustanella
Fustanelle

Microskirt
Underskirt
Wraparound

11 letters:
Drop-waisted

13 letters:
Button-
  through

Snails, slugs and other gastropods

4 letters:
Slug

5 letters:
Conch
Cowry
Murex
Ormer
Snail

Whelk

6 letters:
Cowrie
Limpet
Sea-ear
Triton
Winkle

7 letters:
Abalone
Sea hare
Sea slug

8 letters:
Ear shell
Top-shell

10 letters:
Nudibranch
Periwinkle
Roman snail
Wentletrap

13 letters:
Ramshorn snail

Snakes

3 letters:
Asp
Boa
Rat

4 letters:
Boma
Bull
Corn
Habu

Hoop
King
Milk
Naga
Naia

Naja
Pine
Pipe
Rock
Seps

Tree
Whip

5 letters:
Adder

Blind
Brown
Cobra
Congo
Coral
Cribo
Elaps
Glass
Grass
Krait
Mamba
Mulga
Racer
Tiger
Viper
Water

6 letters:
Carpet
Clotho
Daboia
Dipsas
Dugite
Ellops

Garter
Indigo
Karait
Python
Ribbon
Smooth
Taipan
Thirst
Uraeus
Vasuki

7 letters:
Camoodi
Coluber
Diamond
Hognose
Langaha
Rattler

8 letters:
Anaconda
Cerastes
Jararaca
Jararaka

Lachesis
Mocassin
Moccasin
Pit-viper
Ringhals
Ringneck
Rinkhals
Slowworm
Spitting
Sucuruju
Surucucu
Takshaka

9 letters:
Blue-racer
Boomslang
Coachwhip
Hamadryad
Horsewhip
King cobra
Kingsnake
Puff-adder
River jack
Sand viper

10 letters:
Bandy-bandy
Blacksnake
Bush-master
Copperhead
Death-adder
Dendrophis
Fer-de-lance
Homorelaps
Massasauga
Sidewinder

11 letters:
Amphisbaena
Cottonmouth
Diamond-back
Horned viper

13 letters:
Russell's viper
Water moccasin

17 letters:
Timber rattlesnake

Snooker and billiards terms

1 letter:
D

3 letters:
Lag
Pot
Red
Top

4 letters:
Ball
Blue
Draw
Foul
Kick
Kiss
Pink
Rack

Rail
Rest
Side
Spot
Stun

5 letters:
Baize
Baulk
Black
Break
Brown
Carom
Chalk
Fluke
Frame
Green
In-off

Jenny
Massé
Nurse
Plant
Screw
White

6 letters:
Bridge
Cannon
Cueman
Cue tip
Double
Hazard
Miscue
Pocket
Safety
Spider

Yellow

7 letters:
Bouclée
Bricole
Cue ball
Cushion
English
Maximum
Scratch
Snooker

8 letters:
Backspin
Free ball
Half-butt
Headrail

Spot ball
Triangle

9 letters:
Baulkline
Clearance
Long jenny
Plain ball

Trick shot

10 letters:
Drop cannon
Foul stroke
Object ball
Short jenny

11 letters:
Whitechapel

12 letters:
Cue extension
Maximum break

13 letters:
Follow through
Nursery cannon

14 letters:
Respotted black

Socks and tights

3 letters:
Toe

4 letters:
Hose
Sock

5 letters:
Putty
Stock

6 letters:
Anklet

Argyle
Hold-up
Nylons
Puttee
Seamed
Sports
Stay-up
Tights

7 letters:
Bed sock
Maillot
Pop sock

8 letters:
Fishnets
Half-hose
Stocking

9 letters:
Ankle sock
Bobby sock
Legwarmer
Pantihose
Pantyhose

10 letters:
Slouch sock

12 letters:
Knee-high sock

13 letters:
Lisle stocking

Sofas

5 letters:
Couch
Divan
Futon
Squab

6 letters:
Canapé

Chaise
Day bed
Lounge
Settee
Settle

7 letters:
Bergère

Sofa bed
Vis-à-vis

8 letters:
Love seat

9 letters:
Davenport

Tête-à-tête

11 letters:
Studio couch

12 letters:
Chaise longue
Chesterfield

Sounds

4 letters:
Jura

5 letters:
Puget
Smith

6 letters:
Achill
Nootka
Tromsø

7 letters:
Mcmurdo

Milford
Pamlico

8 letters:
Plymouth
Scoresby
The Sound

9 letters:
Lancaster

10 letters:
Kilbrennan
King George

12 letters:
Sound of Sleat

14 letters:
Queen Charlotte

Spiders and other arachnids

3 letters:
Red

4 letters:
Bird
Mite
Tick
Wolf

5 letters:
Money
Water

6 letters:
Aranea
Chigoe
Diadem
Epeira
Jigger
Katipo
Lycosa

Mygale
Redbug
Violin

7 letters:
Chigger
Hunting
Jumping
Red-back
Solpuga
Spinner

8 letters:
Arachnid
Araneida
Attercop
Cardinal
Ethercap
Ettercap
Huntsman
Itch mite

Podogona
Sand flea
Trapdoor

9 letters:
Bobbejaan
Funnel-web
Harvester
Orb-weaver
Phalangid
Ricinulei
Tarantula

10 letters:
Bird spider
Black widow
Cheese mite
Harvestman
Pycnogonid
Spider mite
Wolf spider

11 letters:
House spider
Money spider
Vinegarroon
Water spider

12 letters:
Book scorpion
Jockey spider
Whip scorpion

13 letters:
Daddy-longlegs
False scorpion
Hunting spider
Jumping spider
Red-back spider

14 letters:
Cardinal spider
Trap-door spider

Sports

2 letters:
RU

3 letters:
BMX

4 letters:
Golf
Polo
Pool
Sumo

5 letters:
Bandy
Bowls
Darts

Fives
Rugby
Sambo
Skeet

6 letters:
Aikido
Boules
Boxing
Hockey
Hurley
Karate
Pelota
Quoits
Savate
Shinty

Soccer
Squash
Tennis

7 letters:
Angling
Archery
Camogie
Cricket
Croquet
Curling
Cycling
Fencing
Fishing
Gliding
Hurling

Jai alai
Kabbadi
Netball
Parkour
Putting
Rackets
Shotput
Snooker

8 letters:
Aquatics
Baseball
Climbing
Coursing
Falconry
Football

Goalball
Handball
Kayaking
Korfball
Lacrosse
Octopush
Pétanque
Rounders
Shooting
Skipping
Skittles
Softball
Speedway
Tug-of-war

9 letters:
Athletics
Autocross
Badminton
Billiards
Decathlon
Ice hockey
Potholing
Skijoring
Skydiving
Stool ball
Triathlon
Water polo
Wrestling

10 letters:
Ballooning
Basketball
Candlepins
Cyclo-cross
Drag-racing
Fly-fishing
Fox-hunting
Freediving
Gymnastics
Kickboxing
Lawn tennis
Paddleball
Paraskiing
Real tennis
Rugby union
Volleyball

11 letters:
Free running
Hang gliding
Parachuting
Paragliding
Parasailing
Rugby league
Scuba diving
Showjumping
Table tennis
Tent-pegging
Windsurfing

12 letters:
Bullfighting
Cockfighting
Orienteering
Parascending
Pigeon racing
Rock climbing
Roller hockey
Snowboarding
Speed-skating
Steeplechase
Trampolining
Trapshooting
Wakeboarding

13 letters:
Roller skating
Rugby football
Skateboarding
Skeet-shooting

Squash rackets
Tenpin bowling
Weightlifting

14 letters:
Gaelic football
Mountain biking
Mountaineering
Sambo wrestling

15 letters:
Australian Rules
Greyhound racing

16 letters:
American football
Bicycle motorcross
Canadian football
Modern pentathlon

17 letters:
Five-a-side football

18 letters:
Clay pigeon shooting
Rhythmic gymnastics

19 letters:
Association football

23 letters:
Australian Rules football

See also:
➤ **American football teams** ➤ **Athletic events** ➤ **Ball games**
➤ **Baseball teams** ➤ **Boxing weights** ➤ **Cricketers**
➤ **Equestrianism** ➤ **Fencing terms** ➤ **Football** ➤ **Football clubs** ➤ **Footballers** ➤ **Golfers** ➤ **Golf terms**
➤ **Grand Prix circuits** ➤ **Gymnastic events** ➤ **Martial arts**
➤ **Motor sports** ➤ **Rugby terms** ➤ **Snooker and billiards terms** ➤ **Sportspeople** ➤ **Swimming strokes**
➤ **Tennis players** ➤ **Tennis terms** ➤ **Water sports** ➤ **Winter sports**

Sportspeople

3 letters:
Coe, *Sebastian*
Hoy, *Sir Chris*

4 letters:
Anne, *Princess*
Bolt, *Usain*
Dean, *Christopher*
Leng, *Virginia*
Lowe, *John*
Rose, *Sir Alec*
Ruth, *Babe*
Witt, *Katarina*

5 letters:
Blyth, *Sir Chay*
Curry, *John*
Davis, *Steve*
Ebdon, *Peter*
Lewis, *Carl*
Lewis, *Denise*
McCoy, *A(nthony) P(eter)*
Meade, *Richard*
Orser, *Brian*
Ovett, *Steve*
Owens, *Jesse*
Smith, *Harvey*
Spitz, *Mark*
Stark, *Ian*
Viren, *Lasse*
Wells, *Allan*

White, *Jimmy*

6 letters:
Broome, *David*
Davies, *Sharron*
Foster, *Brendan*
Foster, *Tim*
Gunnel, *Sally*
Hendry, *Stephen*
Holmes, *Dame Kelly*
Joiner, *Florence Griffith*
Jordan, *Michael*
Korbut, *Olga*
Martin, *Rhona*
Palmer, *Lucinda Prior*
Schenk, *Christian*
Taylor, *Phil 'The Power'*
Wilson, *Jockey*

7 letters:
Bristow, *Eric*
Cousins, *Robin*
Edwards, *Eddie 'The Eagle'*
Edwards, *Jonathan*
Fosbury, *Dick*
Francis, *Claire*
Freeman, *Cathy*
Higgins, *Alex 'Hurricane'*
Johnson, *Ben*
Pinsent, *Matthew*

Reardon, *Ray*
Simpson, *O(renthal) J(ames)*
Torvill, *Jayne*
Zvereva, *Ellina*

8 letters:
Boardman, *Chris*
Brabants, *Tim*
Chataway, *Christopher*
Christie, *Linford*
Comaneci, *Nadia*
Hamilton, *Scott*
Petrenko, *Viktor*
Redgrave, *Steve*
Thompson, *Daley*
Thorburn, *Cliff*

9 letters:
Bannister, *Roger*
Bullimore, *Tony*
Cracknell, *James*
O'Sullivan, *Ronnie*
Schumaker, *Michael*

10 letters:
Chichester, *Sir Francis*

11 letters:
Weissmuller, *Johnny*

Stars and constellations

STARS

3 letters:		**5 letters:**	
Sol	Lyra	Acrux	Hyads
	Mira	Agena	Indus
	Pavo	Algol	Lupus
	Pole	Ceres	Mensa
4 letters:	Ursa	Deneb	Merak
Argo	Vega	Draco	Mizar
Grus	Vela	Dubhe	Norma
Idol			North

Polar
Rigel
Rigil
Venus
Virgo
Wagon
Whale

6 letters:
Alioth
Alkaid
Altair
Aquila
Auriga
Boötes
Carina
Castor
Cygnus
Dorado
Esther
Fornax
Hyades
Megrez
Merope
Octans
Phecda

Plough
Pollux
Psyche
Puppis
Saturn
Sirius
Sothis
The Sun
Uranus
Vesper
Volans

7 letters:
Antares
Calaeno
Canopus
Capella
Cepheus
Columba
Dolphin
Lucifer
Phoenix
Polaris
Procyon
Proxima
Regulus

Serpens
Triones
Wagoner

8 letters:
Achernar
Arcturus
Barnard's
Canicula
Circinus
Denebola
Equuleus
Hesperus
Pegasean
Pleiades
Pointers
Praesepe
Scorpius
Waggoner

9 letters:
Aldebaran
Andromeda
Bellatrix
Betelgeux
Big Dipper

Centaurus
Delphinus
Fomalhaut
Ophiuchus
Wolf-Rayet

10 letters:
Betelgeuse
Betelgeuze
Cassiopeia
Mogen David
Orion's belt
The Dog Star

11 letters:
The Pointers
The Pole Star

12 letters:
Little Dipper
Solomon's seal
The North Star

15 letters:
Proxima centauri

CONSTELLATIONS

Latin name	**English name**
Andromeda	Andromeda
Antlia	Air Pump
Apus	Bird of Paradise
Aquarius	Water Bearer
Aquila	Eagle
Ara	Altar
Argo	Ship of the Argonauts
Aries	Ram
Auriga	Charioteer
Boötes	Herdsman
Caelum	Chisel
Camelopardalis	Giraffe
Cancer	Crab
Canes Venatici	Hunting Dogs
Canis Major	Great Dog
Canis Minor	Little Dog

Latin name	English name
Capricornus	Sea Goat
Carina	Keel
Cassiopeia	Cassiopeia
Centaurus	Centaur
Cepheus	Cepheus
Cetus	Whale
Chamaeleon	Chameleon
Circinus	Compasses
Columba	Dove
Coma Berenices	Bernice's Hair
Corona Australis	Southern Crown
Corona Borealis	Northern Crown
Corvus	Crow
Crater	Cup
Crux	Southern Cross
Cygnus	Swan
Cynosure	Dog's Tail
Delphinus	Dolphin
Dorado	Swordfish
Draco	Dragon
Equuleus	Little Horse
Eridanus	River Eridanus
Fornax	Furnace
Gemini	Twins
Grus	Crane
Hercules	Hercules
Horologium	Clock
Hydra	Sea Serpent
Hydrus	Water Snake
Indus	Indian
Lacerta	Lizard
Leo	Lion
Leo Minor	Little Lion
Lepus	Hare
Libra	Scales
Lupus	Wolf
Lynx	Lynx
Lyra	Harp
Mensa	Table
Microscopium	Microscope
Monoceros	Unicorn
Musca	Fly
Norma	Level
Octans	Octant

Latin name	English name
Ophiuchus	Serpent Bearer
Orion	Orion
Pavo	Peacock
Pegasus	Winged Horse
Perseus	Perseus
Phoenix	Phoenix
Pictor	Easel
Pisces	Fishes
Piscis Austrinus	Southern Fish
Puppis	Ship's Stern
Pyxis	Mariner's Compass
Reticulum	Net
Sagitta	Arrow
Sagittarius	Archer
Scorpius	Scorpion
Sculptor	Sculptor
Scutum	Shield
Serpens	Serpent
Sextans	Sextant
Taurus	Bull
Telescopium	Telescope
Triangulum	Triangle
Triangulum Australe	Southern Triangle
Tucana	Toucan
Ursa Major	Great Bear (contains the Plough or (U.S.) Big Dipper)
Ursa Minor	Little Bear or (U.S.) Little Dipper
Vela	Sails
Virgo	Virgin
Volans	Flying Fish
Vulpecula	Fox

States and territories

AUSTRALIAN STATES AND TERRITORIES

8 letters:
Tasmania
Victoria

10 letters:
Queensland

13 letters:
New South Wales

14 letters:
South Australia

16 letters:
Western Australia

17 letters:
Northern Territory

26 letters:
Australian Capital
  Territory

INDIAN STATES

3 letters:	7 letters:	Meghalaya	13 letters:
Goa	Gujarat	Rajasthan	Andhra Pradesh
	Haryana	Tamil Nadu	Madhya Pradesh
5 letters:	Manipur		
Assam	Mizoram	10 letters:	15 letters:
Bihar	Tripura	West Bengal	Himachal Pradesh
			Jammu and
6 letters:	8 letters:	11 letters:	Kashmir
Indore	Jharkand	Maharashtra	
Kerala	Nagaland	Uttaranchal	16 letters:
Orissa			Arunachal Pradesh
Punjab	9 letters:	12 letters:	
Sikkim	Hyderabad	Chhattisgarh	
	Karnataka	Uttar Pradesh	

INDIAN UNION TERRITORIES

5 letters:	11 letters:	19 letters:
Delhi	Daman and Diu	Dadra and Nagar Haveli
	Lakshadweep	
10 letters:	Pondicherry	24 letters:
Chandigarh		Andaman and Nicobar
		Islands

TERRITORIES OF NEW ZEALAND

4 letters:	11 letters:	14 letters:
Niue	Cook Islands	Ross Dependency
7 letters:	12 letters:	
Tokelau	Union Islands	

US STATES

State	Abbreviation	Zip code	Nickname	Capital
Alabama	Ala.	AL	Cotton	Montgomery
Alaska	Alas.	AK	Last Frontier	Juneau
Arizona	Ariz.	AZ	Apache	Phoenix
Arkansas	Ark.	AR	Wonder	Little Rock
California	Cal.	CA	Golden	Sacramento
Colorado	Colo.	CO	Centennial	Denver
Connecticut	Conn.	CT	Nutmeg	Hartford
Delaware	Del.	DE	Diamond	Dover
District of Columbia	D.C.	DC	-	-
Florida	Fla.	FL	Sunshine	Tallahassee

State	Abbreviation	Zip code	Nickname	Capital
Georgia	Ga.	GA	Peach	Atlanta
Hawaii	Haw.	HI	Aloha	Honolulu
Idaho	Id. *or* Ida.	ID	Gem	Boise
Illinois	Ill.	IL	Prairie	Springfield
Indiana	Ind.	IN	Hoosier	Indianapolis
Iowa	Ia. *or* Io.	IA	Hawkeye	Des Moines
Kansas	Kan. *or* Kans.	KS	Sunflower	Topeka
Kentucky	Ken.	KY	Bluegrass	Frankfort
Louisiana	La.	LA	Pelican	Baton Rouge
Maine	Me.	ME	Pine Tree	Augusta
Maryland	Md.	MD	Free	Annapolis
Massachusetts	Mass.	MA	Bay	Boston
Michigan	Mich.	MI	Wolverine	Lansing
Minnesota	Minn.	MN	Gopher	St Paul
Mississippi	Miss.	MS	Magnolia	Jackson
Missouri	Mo.	MO	Show-me	Jefferson City
Montana	Mont.	MT	Treasure	Helena
Nebraska	Neb.	NE	Cornhusker	Lincoln
Nevada	Nev.	NV	Sagebrush	Carson City
New Hampshire	N.H.	NH	Granite	Concord
New Jersey	N.J.	NJ	Garden	Trenton
New Mexico	N.M. *or* N.Mex.	NM	Sunshine	Santa Fe
New York	N.Y.	NY	Empire	Albany
North Carolina	N.C.	NC	Tar Heel	Raleigh
North Dakota	N.D. *or* N.Dak.	ND	Sioux	Bismarck
Ohio	O.	OH	Buckeye	Columbus
Oklahoma	Okla.	OK	Sooner	Oklahoma City
Oregon	Oreg.	OR	Beaver	Salem
Pennsylvania	Pa., Penn., *or* Penna.	PA	Keystone	Harrisburg
Rhode Island	R.I.	RI	Little Rhody	Providence
South Carolina	S.C.	SC	Palmetto	Columbia
South Dakota	S.Dak.	SD	Coyote	Pierre
Tennessee	Tenn.	TN	Volunteer	Nashville
Texas	Tex.	TX	Lone Star	Austin
Utah	Ut.	UT	Beehive	Salt Lake City
Vermont	Vt.	VT	Green Mountain	Montpelier
Virginia	Va.	VA	Old Dominion	Richmond
Washington	Wash.	WA	Evergreen	Olympia
West Virginia	W.Va.	WV	Panhandle	Charleston
Wisconsin	Wis.	WI	Badger	Madison
Wyoming	Wyo.	WY	Equality	Cheyenne

US STATES: YEAR OF ACCESSION TO THE UNION

State	Year of Accession	State	Year of Accession
Alabama	1819	Missouri	1821
Alaska	1959	Montana	1889
Arizona	1912	Nebraska	1867
Arkansas	1836	Nevada	1864
California	1850	New Hampshire	1788
Colorado	1876	New Jersey	1787
Connecticut	1788	New Mexico	1912
Delaware	1787	New York	1788
District of Columbia	1889	North Carolina	1789
		North Dakota	1889
Florida	1845	Ohio	1803
Georgia	1788	Oklahoma	1907
Hawaii	1959	Oregon	1859
Idaho	1890	Pennsylvania	1787
Illinois	1818	Rhode Island	1790
Indiana	1816	South Carolina	1788
Iowa	1846	South Dakota	1889
Kansas	1861	Tennessee	1796
Kentucky	1792	Texas	1845
Louisiana	1812	Utah	1896
Maine	1820	Vermont	1791
Maryland	1788	Virginia	1788
Massachusetts	1788	Washington	1889
Michigan	1837	West Virginia	1863
Minnesota	1858	Wisconsin	1848
Mississippi	1817	Wyoming	1890

Stones

3 letters:
Gem, Hog, Pip, Pit, Rag, Tin

Flag, Hone, Horn, Iron, Jasp, Kerb, Lias, Lime, Lode, Onyx, Opal, Plum, Ragg

Sard, Skew, Slab, Soap, Tile

Chert, Coade, Culch, Drupe, Flint, Gooly, Grape, Jewel, Kenne, Lapis, Logan, Menah, Metal

4 letters:
Bath, Blue, Celt, Door

5 letters:
Agate, Amber, Balas, Beryl, Black, Chalk

Mocha
Niobe
Paste
Prase
Pumie
Quern
Quoin
Quoit
Rubin
Rufus
Rybat
Scone
Scree
Slate
Sneck
Stela
Stele
Topaz
Wacke
Wyman

6 letters:
Amazon
Ashlar
Ashler
Baetyl
Bezoar
Brinny
Cobble
Coping
Cultch
Dolmen
Flusch
Fossil
Gibber
Gooley
Goolie
Gravel
Humite
Jargon
Jasper
Kernel
Kidney
Kingle
Ligure

Lithic
Menhir
Metate
Muller
Nutlet
Oamaru
Paving
Pebble
Pot-lid
Pumice
Pyrene
Rip-rap
Sarsen
Scarab
Summer
Tanist

7 letters:
Asteria
Avebury
Azurite
Blarney
Bologna
Boulder
Breccia
Callais
Chuckie
Curling
Girasol
Granite
Hyacine
Hyalite
Jargoon
Lia-fail
Lithoid
Moabite
Niobean
Olivine
Parpane
Parpend
Parpent
Peridot
Perpend
Perpent
Petrous

Pudding
Purbeck
Putamen
Rocking
Rosetta
Sardine
Sarsden
Scaglia
Schanse
Schanze
Smaragd
Tektite
Telamon
Tripoli
Urolith
Zauxite

8 letters:
Aerolite
Aerolith
Amethyst
Asteroid
Baguette
Cabochon
Calculus
Cinnamon
Corundum
Cromlech
Ebenezer
Elf-arrow
Endocarp
Essonite
Ganister
Girasole
Keystone
Lapidate
Megalith
Menamber
Monolith
Nephrite
Omphalos
Onychite
Parpoint
Petrosal
Phengite

Portland
Rollrich
Sapphire
Sardonyx
Scalpins
Schantze
Tonalite
Voussoir

9 letters:
Alabaster
Almandine
Asparagus
Cairngorm
Carnelian
Cholelith
Chondrite
Cornelian
Crossette
Dichroite
Firestone
Gannister
Greensand
Hessonite
Hoarstone
Lithiasis
Paleolith
Pipestone
Rubicelle
Scagliola
Trilithon
Turquoise
Ventifact

10 letters:
Adamantine
Alectorian
Aragonites
Chalcedony
Draconites
Enhydritic
Fieldstone
Foundation
Gastrolith
Grey-wether

Kimberlite
Lherzolite
Lithophyte

Rhinestone

11 letters:
Peristalith

12 letters:
Carton-pierre
Philosopher's

See also:
➤ **Minerals**   ➤ **Ores**   ➤ **Rocks**

Straits

4 letters:
Bass
Cook
Mena
Palk

5 letters:
Cabot
Davis
Dover
Kerch
Korea
Sumba

6 letters:
Bangka
Barrow
Bering
Hainan
Hecate
Hudson
Lombok
Madura
Taiwan
Tartar
Torres

7 letters:
Denmark
Dolphin
Euripus
Evripos
Florida
Formosa
Foveaux
Le Maire
Malacca
Molucca
Øresund

8 letters:
Bosporus
Makassar
Minch, The
Sound, The

9 letters:
Bosphorus
East River
Great Belt
La Pérouse
Small Belt
Solent, The

10 letters:
Gut of Canso
Juan de Fuca
Limfjorden
Little Belt
North Minch

11 letters:
Bab-el-Mandeb
Dardanelles
Kattegat, The
Little Minch
Mona Passage

12 letters:
Skagerrak, The

13 letters:
Strait of Canso
Strait of Sunda

14 letters:
Northumberland
Strait of Hormuz
Straits of Johor

15 letters:
Strait of Georgia
Strait of Malacca
Strait of Messina
Strait of Otranto
Straits of Harris
Windward
  Passage

16 letters:
Strait of Magellan

17 letters:
Passage of
  Colonsay
Strait of Belle Isle
Strait of Bonifacio
Straits of
  Mackinac

18 letters:
Strait of Juan de
  Fuca
Straits of Gibraltar

Subatomic particles

1 letter:
J
W
Z

3 letters:
Chi

Eta
Psi
Tau

4 letters:
Kaon
Muon

Pion

5 letters:
Axion
Boson
Gluon
Meson

Omega
Quark
Sigma
Tauon

6 letters:
Baryon

Hadron	**7 letters:**	**8 letters:**	**9 letters:**
Lambda	Fermion	Electron	Resonance
Lepton	Neutron	Monopole	
Parton	Tachyon	Neutrino	**10 letters:**
Photon	Upsilon		Higgs boson
Proton			

Sugars

3 letters:	**6 letters:**	Pentose	Granulose
Goo	Aldose	Penuche	Laevulose
Gur	Barley	Refined	Muscovado
	Caster	Sorbose	Raffinose
4 letters:	Fucose	Sorghum	Trehalose
Beet	Hexose	Tetrose	
Cane	Inulin	Trehala	**10 letters:**
Cube	Invert		Aldohexose
Goor	Ribose	**8 letters:**	Cellobiose
Loaf	Sorgho	Demerara	Glucosoric
Lump	Triose	Dextrose	Granulated
Milk	Xylose	Fructose	Saccharine
Palm		Furanose	Saccharoid
Wood	**7 letters:**	Honeydew	
	Caramel	Jagghery	**11 letters:**
5 letters:	Cellose	Powdered	Deoxyribose
Brown	Glucose	Pyranose	
Candy	Heptose	Rhamnose	**12 letters:**
Grape	Jaggary		Crystallized
Icing	Jaggery	**9 letters:**	Disaccharide
Maple	Lactose	Amygdalin	
Sorgo	Maltose	Arabinose	**14 letters:**
White	Mannose	Cassonade	Monosaccharide
	Panocha	Galactose	

Suits

1 letter:	**4 letters:**	Shell	Safari
G	Jump	Slack	Sailor
	Pant	Sweat	Sweats
3 letters:	Zoot		
Dry		**6 letters:**	**7 letters:**
Mao	**5 letters:**	Boiler	Catsuit
Ski	Anti-G	Judogi	Pajamas
Wet	Dress	Lounge	Penguin
	G-suit	Romper	Pyjamas

Sunsuit
Trouser

8 letters:
Birthday
Playsuit
Skeleton

Swimsuit

9 letters:
Buckskins
Spacesuit
Tracksuit

10 letters:
Three-piece

12 letters:
Evening dress
Morning dress

14 letters:
Double-breasted
Single-breasted

Supernatural

PEOPLE WITH SUPERNATURAL POWERS

3 letters:
Hag
Hex

4 letters:
Mage
Seer

5 letters:
Magus
Siren
Witch

6 letters:
Dowser

Medium
Shaman
Wizard

7 letters:
Diviner
Warlock

8 letters:
Conjurer
Exorcist
Magician
Sorcerer
Spaewife

9 letters:
Archimage
Enchanter
Rainmaker
Sorceress
Superhero

10 letters:
Channeller
Water witch
White witch

11 letters:
Clairvoyant
Enchantress

Necromancer
Thaumaturge
Witch doctor
Witch master

12 letters:
Clairaudient
Water diviner

13 letters:
Clairsentient
Fortune-teller

SUPERNATURAL CREATURES

3 letters:
Elf
Fay
God
Imp

4 letters:
Ogre
Peri

5 letters:
Angel
Demon
Devil
Dwarf
Fairy
Genie

Ghost
Ghoul
Giant
Gnome
Golem
Jinni
Lamia
Pixie
Sylph
Troll
Zombi

6 letters:
Djinni
Djinny
Dybbuk
Goblin

Jinnee
Kelpie
Manito
Selkie
Silkie
Sprite
Wraith
Zombie

7 letters:
Banshee
Brownie
Endemon
Goddess
Gremlin
Incubus
Kachina

Manitou
Monster
Phantom
Sandman
Spectre
Vampire

8 letters:
Familiar
Succubus
Werewolf

9 letters:
Hobgoblin
Tokoloshe

10 letters:
Leprechaun
Little folk

11 letters:
Lycanthrope

Poltergeist

12 letters:
Little people

13 letters:
Guardian angel

14 letters:
Fairy godmother

SUPERNATURAL TERMS

3 letters:
ESP
Hex
Obi

4 letters:
Aura
Fate
Jinx
Juju
Mojo
Rune
Wand

5 letters:
Charm
Curse
Obeah
Ouija®
Sigil
Spell

6 letters:
Amulet

Apport
Fetish
Grigri
Hoodoo
Kismet
Séance
Voodoo

7 letters:
Evil eye
Philtre
Portent

8 letters:
Exorcism
Greegree
Grimoire
Gris-gris
Talisman

9 letters:
Ectoplasm
Magic wand
Pentagram

Telepathy

10 letters:
Black magic
Divination
Indian sign
Levitation
Magic spell
Necromancy
Possession
Sixth sense
Telegnosis
White magic
Xenoglossy

11 letters:
Abracadabra
Incantation
Magic circle
Premonition
Second sight
Telekinesis
The Black Art
Xenoglossia

12 letters:
Clairvoyance
Invultuation
Telaesthesia
Witching hour

13 letters:
Clairaudience
Psychokinesis
Reincarnation

14 letters:
Clairsentience
Cryptaesthesia
Parapsychology

17 letters:
Speaking in
tongues

22 letters:
Extrasensory
perception

Surgical operations

5 letters:
Graft
Taxis

6 letters:
Bypass

7 letters:
Section

8 letters:
Ablation
Avulsion
Cesarean
Colotomy
Face-lift
Liposuck
Lobotomy
Tenotomy
Vagotomy

9 letters:
Anaplasty
Autograft
Caesarean
Colectomy
Colostomy
Colpotomy
Cordotomy
Costotomy
Curettage

Cystotomy
Ileostomy
Iridotomy
Leucotomy
Lithotomy
Lobectomy
Necrotomy
Neoplasty
Neurotomy
Osteotomy

Plication
Resection
Rhizotomy
Skin graft
Tummy tuck
Vasectomy
Zooplasty

10 letters:
Adenectomy
Amputation
Autoplasty
Biosurgery
Craniotomy
Cystectomy
Enterotomy
Episiotomy
Frenectomy
Gastrotomy
Iridectomy
Keratotomy
Laparotomy
Lithotrity
Lumpectomy
Mastectomy
Myomectomy
Nephrotomy
Neurectomy
Ovariotomy
Phlebotomy
Pleurotomy
Rachiotomy
Sclerotomy
Strabotomy
Thymectomy
Transplant
Varicotomy

11 letters:
Anastomosis
Angioplasty
Arthrectomy
Arthrodesis
Cryosurgery

Débridement
Embolectomy
Embryectomy
Enterectomy
Enterostomy
Gastrectomy
Gastrostomy
Glossectomy
Hysterotomy
Laminectomy
Laryngotomy
Liposuction
Mammoplasty
Nephrectomy
Osteoclasis
Osteoplasty
Ovariectomy
Phlebectomy
Pneumectomy
Pylorectomy
Rhinoplasty
Splenectomy
Tenorrhaphy
Thoracotomy
Tracheotomy
Vaginectomy
Venesection

12 letters:
Arthroplasty
Circumcision
Dermabrasion
Fenestration
Heteroplasty
Hysterectomy
Keratoplasty
Microsurgery
Neurosurgery
Oophorectomy
Orichiectomy
Paracentesis
Pharyngotomy
Replantation
Tonsillotomy

Tracheostomy

13 letters:
Adenoidectomy
Dermatoplasty
Mastoidectomy
Pneumonectomy
Prostatectomy
Psychosurgery
Salpingectomy
Stomatoplasty
Sympathectomy
Thoracoplasty
Thyroidectomy
Tonsillectomy
Tubal ligation

14 letters:
Abdominoplasty
Appendicectomy
Blepharoplasty
Cardiocentesis
Clitoridectomy
Coronary bypass
Electrosurgery
Keyhole surgery
Plastic surgery
Staphyloplasty
Xenotransplant

15 letters:
Cholecystectomy
Cosmetic surgery
Staphylorrhaphy

16 letters:
Abdominal surgery
Caesarean section
Open-heart surgery
Radial keratotomy
Spare-part surgery

17 letters:
Commando operation

Spurtle
Whinger
Yatagan

8 letters:
Cemitare
Claymore
Curtal-ax
Falchion
Faulchin
Partisan
Schlager
Scimitar
Semitaur
Sgian-dhu
Skene-dhu
Spadroon
Spontoon
Stiletto
Stone axe

Tomahawk
Whiniard
Whinyard
White-arm
Yataghan

9 letters:
Arondight
Backsword
Balisarda
Battle-axe
Damascene
Excalibur
Faulchion
Glamdring
Jackknife
Schiavone

10 letters:
Angurvadel

Bowie knife
Broadsword
Smallsword
Swordstick

11 letters:
Sheath knife
Snickersnee
Trench knife

12 letters:
Spurtleblade
Sword bayonet

13 letters:
Andrew Ferrara

14 letters:
Swiss Army Knife

Tt

Tables and desks

3 letters:
Bar

4 letters:
Desk

6 letters:
Buffet
Bureau
Carrel
Lowboy
Teapoy

7 letters:
Counter

8 letters:
Lapboard
Tea table

9 letters:
Card table
Davenport
Drum table
Side table
Wool table
Workbench
Worktable

10 letters:
Escritoire
Secretaire
Tea trolley
Traymobile

11 letters:
Coffee table
Dining table
Reading desk
Roll-top desk
Writing desk

12 letters:
Bedside table
Breakfast bar
Console table
Folding table
Gate-leg table
Kitchen table
Nest of tables
Pedestal desk
Snooker table
Trestle table

Writing table

13 letters:
Billiard table
Dressing table
Drop-leaf table
Pembroke table
Piecrust table

14 letters:
Breakfast table
Refectory table

15 letters:
Gate-legged table
Occasional table

Teeth

5 letters:
Molar

6 letters:
Canine

7 letters:
Incisor

8 letters:
Premolar

9 letters:
Foretooth

11 letters:
Wisdom tooth

Tennis players

MALE

4 letters:
Ashe, *Arthur*
Borg, *Bjorn*
Cash, *Pat*
Moya, *Carlos*

Rios, *Marcelo*

5 letters:
Blake, *James*
Canas, *Guillermo*

Costa, *Albert*
Laver, *Rod*
Lendl, *Ivan*
Lloyd, *John*
Nadal, *Rafael*

Novak, *Jiri*
Perry, *Fred*
Roche, *Tony*
Safin, *Marat*
Vilas, *Guillermo*

6 letters:
Agassi, *Andre*
Becker, *Boris*
Edberg, *Stefan*
Henman, *Tim*
Hewitt, *Lleyton*
Murray, *Andy*
Rafter, *Pat*

FEMALE

4 letters:
Graf, *Steffi*
King, *Billie-Jean*
Wade, *Virginia*

5 letters:
Bueno, *Maria*
Court, *Margaret*
Dokic, *Jelena*
Evert, *Chris*
Jones, *Ann*
Rubin, *Chanda*
Seles, *Monica*
Stove, *Betty*

6 letters:
Barker, *Sue*
Casals, *Rosie*
Cawley, *Evonne*

7 letters:
Amitraj, *Vijay*
Connors, *Jimmy*
Emerson, *Roy*
Federer, *Roger*
Ferrero, *Juan Carlos*
Gambill, *Jan-Michael*
Maskell, *Dan*
McEnroe, *John*
Nastase, *Ilie*
Roddick, *Andy*
Sampras, *Pete*

8 letters:
Corretja, *Alex*
Djokovic, *Novak*

Farina, *Silvia*
Hingis, *Martina*

7 letters:
Lenglen, *Suzanne*
Maleeva, *Magdalena*
Myskina, *Anastasia*
Novotna, *Jana*

8 letters:
Capriati, *Jennifer*
Connolly, *Maureen*
Mauresmo, *Amelie*
Sabatini, *Gabriela*
Williams, *Serena*
Williams, *Venus*

9 letters:
Clijsters, *Kim*

Gonzalez, *Fernando*
Grosjean, *Sebastien*
Newcombe, *John*
Rosewall, *Ken*
Rusedski, *Greg*
Schalken, *Sjeng*

10 letters:
Ivanisevic, *Goran*
Kafelnikov, *Yevgeny*
Nalbandian, *David*
Srichaphan, *Paradorn*

13 letters:
Philippoussis, *Mark*

Davenport, *Lindsay*
Goolagong, *Evonne*
Pistolesi, *Anna*
Sharapova, *Maria*
Stevenson, *Alexandra*

10 letters:
Hantuchova, *Daniela*
Kournikova, *Anna*
Wills Moody, *Helen*

11 letters:
Navratilova, *Martina*

13 letters:
Henin-Hardenne, *Justine*

14 letters:
Sanchez-Vicario, *Arantxa*

Tennis terms

3 letters:	Set	Game	Deuce
Ace	Love	Love	Fault
Let	**4 letters:**		Match
Lob	Ball	**5 letters:**	Rally
Net	Chip	Court	Slice

Smash

Topspin

Undercut

Half-volley
Lawn tennis
Tiebreaker

6 letters:
Racket
Return
Server
Umpire
Volley

8 letters:
Backhand
Baseline
Drop shot
Forehand
Line call
Linesman
Love game
Receiver
Set point
Sideline
Tie-break
Tramline

9 letters:
Advantage
Clay court
Foot fault
Forecourt
Hard court

11 letters:
Double fault
Passing shot
Service line

7 letters:
Doubles
Net cord
Racquet
Service
Singles

10 letters:
Break point
Cannonball
Centre line
Centre mark
Grass court

12 letters:
Approach shot
Break of serve
Ground stroke
Mixed doubles

Theatre terms

3 letters:
Act
Cue
Ham

Speech
Stalls

7 letters:
Curtain
Gallery
Overact
Resting
Scenery
Unities
Upstage

Monologue
Noises off
Orchestra
Scene dock
Soliloquy
Soubrette
Stage door
Stagehand
Stage left

4 letters:
Exit
Flat
Gods
Prop
Role

10 letters:
Auditorium
First night
Leading man
Opera house
Stage right
Understudy

5 letters:
Flies
Fluff
House
Lines
Scene
Stage
Wings

8 letters:
Broadway
Crush bar
Entr'acte
Entrance
Juvenile
Offstage
Prompter
Scene bay
Thespian

11 letters:
Catastrophe
Curtain call
Greasepaint
Leading lady
Off-Broadway
Stage fright
Stage-struck

6 letters:
Chorus
Circle
Corpse
Prompt
Script

9 letters:
Backstage
Downstage
Greenroom

12 letters:
Front of house
Orchestra pit
Stage manager
Stage whisper

13 letters:
Coup de théâtre

Curtain-raiser
Curtain speech

14 letters:
Off-off-Broadway
Proscenium arch
Stage direction

16 letters:
Comédie Française
Dramatis personae
First-night nerves

17 letters:
Theatre-in-the-round

Ties and cravats

3 letters:
Boa
Tie

5 letters:
Ascot
Dicky
Fichu
Scarf
Stock
Stole

6 letters:
Bertha
Bow tie
Clip-on
Cravat
Madras
Rebozo

7 letters:
Foulard
Muffler

Necktie

8 letters:
Black tie
Carcanet
Dicky bow
Kerchief
White tie

9 letters:
Comforter

Neckcloth
School tie

10 letters:
Windsor tie

11 letters:
Falling band
Neckerchief

Time

RELATED VOCABULARY

2 letters:
AD
Am
BC
Mo
Pm

3 letters:
Age
Ago
Aye
Day
Due
E'en
E'er
Eld
Eos
Era

Ere
Eve
May
Oft
Old
Sec
Ult
Yet

4 letters:
Aeon
Ages
Anon
Ante
Date
Dawn
Dial
Dusk

Even
Ever
Fall
Fast
Fore
Ides
Inst
Jiff
July
June
Late
Lent
Moon
Morn
Next
Noel
Noon
Once

Over
Past
Post
Prox
Slow
Soon
Span
Term
Then
Tick
Tide
Till
Time
Unto
Week
When
Xmas
Year

Yore
Yule

5 letters:
Again
Annum
April
As yet
Brief
Clock
Cycle
Daily
Dekad
Delay
Diary
Early
Epact
Epoch
Fasti
Flash
Jiffy
Later
March
Matin
Month
Never
Night
Nonce
Nones
Often
Passé
Pause
Point
Prime
Prior
Purim
Ready
Shake
Sharp
Short
Since
So far
Space
Spell
Still

Style
Sunup
Tempo
Today
Trice
Until
Watch
While
Years
Young
Youth

6 letters:
Actual
Advent
Always
Annual
At once
August
Aurora
Autumn
Bairam
Brumal
Coeval
Coming
Crisis
Curfew
Decade
Dotage
During
Easter
Elapse
Ere now
Extant
Ferial
Friday
Future
Gnomon
Heyday
Hiemal
Hourly
Ice Age
In time
Jet Age
Julian

Lammas
Lapsed
Lately
Latest
Latish
Lustre
Mañana
Man-day
May Day
Midday
Minute
Modern
Moment
Monday
Morrow
New day
O'clock
Off-day
Of late
Old age
One day
On time
Period
Presto
Pre-war
Prompt
Pronto
Pro tem
Rarely
Recent
Season
Second
Seldom
Sooner
Spring
Sudden
Summer
Sunday
Sunset
Timely
To date
Update
Vernal
Vesper
Weekly

Whilst
Winter
Yearly
Yester

7 letters:
Abiding
Ack emma
Ageless
Ages ago
All over
Almanac
Already
Ancient
Anytime
Archaic
At night
Bedtime
Belated
Betimes
Boyhood
By-and-by
Calends
Century
Chiliad
Current
Dawning
Daylong
Day-peep
Daytime
Diurnal
Dog days
Earlier
Elapsed
Endless
Epochal
Equinox
Estival
Evening
Exactly
Expired
Extinct
Fast day
Flag day
Forever

For good
For life
Harvest
High day
History
Holiday
Holy day
Infancy
Instant
Interim
Iron Age
January
Journal
Jubilee
Just now
Kalends
Lady Day
Long ago
Long run
Lustrum
Manhood
Man-hour
Matinal
Mid-week
Monthly
Morning
Newborn
New Year
Nightly
Noonday
October
One-time
Overdue
Pending
Pip emma
Postwar
Present
Proximo
Quarter
Quondam
Ramadan
Ripe age
Sabbath
Secular
Shortly

Sine die
Some day
Stretch
Sukkoth
Sundial
Sundown
Sunrise
Teenage
Tertian
This day
Time-lag
Time was
Tonight
Too late
Too soon
Tuesday
Twinkle
Two two's
Unready
Up to now
Usually
Weekday
Weekend
Whereon
Whitsun

8 letters:
Abruptly
A long day
Antedate
As soon as
Biannual
Biennial
Birthday
Biweekly
Blue moon
Brumaire
Calendar
Civil day
Darkling
Date line
Daybreak
Daylight
Deadline
December

Derby Day
Directly
Dogwatch
Doomsday
Duration
Eggtimer
Enduring
Entr'acte
Epiphany
Eternity
Eventide
Evermore
Every day
Evil hour
Fast time
Feast day
February
Fleeting
Foredawn
Forenoon
Formerly
Frequent
Gain time
Gloaming
Half hour
Half past
Hanukkah
Hereunto
Hibernal
High time
Hitherto
Hogmanay
Holy days
Holy Week
Horology
Ill-timed
In a flash
In a trice
Infinity
In future
In no time
In season
Interval
Juncture
Keep time

Kill time
Lang syne
Last time
Last week
Lateness
Latterly
Leap year
Lifelong
Life-span
Lifetime
Livelong
Long time
Lord's Day
Lose time
Lunation
Mark time
Mean time
Medieval
Menology
Meridian
Meteoric
Midnight
Momently
Natal day
New Style
Next week
Noontide
Noontime
Not often
November
Nowadays
Obsolete
Occasion
Ofttimes
Old times
On the dot
Our times
Passover
Pass time
Postdate
Postpone
Previous
Promptly
Punctual
Recently

Right now	Boxing Day	Immediacy	Opportune
Ringtime	Bronze Age	Immediate	Out of date
Saturday	Candlemas	In a second	Overnight
Seasonal	Canicular	In due time	Pentecost
Seedtime	Centenary	Instanter	Perennial
Semester	Childhood	Instantly	Permanent
Solar day	Christmas	Interlude	Postcenal
Solstice	Chronicle	In the past	Preceding
Some time	Civil time	Julian Day	Precisely
Space Age	Civil year	Lammas Day	Premature
Sporadic	Clepsydra	Later date	Presently
Steel Age	Continual	Latter day	Quarterly
Stone Age	Crepuscle	Light year	Quarter to
Suddenly	Days of old	Local time	Quotidian
Take time	Dayspring	Longevity	Recurrent
Temporal	Decennary	Long-lived	Regularly
This week	Decennial	Long since	Remote age
Thursday	Decennium	Long spell	Right time
Timeless	Due season	Long while	Saint's day
Time-worn	Earliness	Lunar year	Salad days
Tomorrow	Early bird	Many a time	Sandglass
Too early	Ember days	Many times	Semestral
Twilight	Empire Day	Mardi Gras	September
Ultimate	Ephemeral	Martinmas	Short term
Until now	Ephemeris	Mature age	Short time
Untimely	Epochally	Matutinal	Solar time
Up-to-date	Erstwhile	Meanwhile	Solar year
Weeklong	Ever since	Mediaeval	Sometimes
Whenever	Every hour	Menstrual	Space time
Year-book	Far future	Metronome	Spare time
Yearlong	First time	Midday sun	Spend time
Years ago	Foregoing	Middle age	Stop watch
Yoretime	Forthwith	Midsummer	Swiss plan
Yuletide	Fortnight	Midwinter	Temporary
	From now on	Mistiming	Temporize
9 letters:	Gnomonics	Momentary	Therewith
Adulthood	Golden Age	Monthlong	Till death
Afternoon	Great year	Nevermore	Time being
After that	Gregorian	Nightfall	Time check
After time	Hallowe'en	Nightlong	Time clock
All at once	Hallowmas	Nighttide	Time flies
Antiquity	Happy days	Night time	Time limit
Atomic Age	Hereafter	Nocturnal	Time of day
At present	Honeymoon	Octennial	Timepiece
Bimonthly	Hourglass	Oftentime	Times past

Timetable
To this day
Transient
Triennial
Twinkling
Two shakes
Upon which
Vicennial
Waste time
Wednesday
Well-timed
Wherefore
Whereunto
Whereupon
Wrong time
Yesterday

10 letters:

Afterwards
After which
Alarm clock
Allhallows
All the time
Anno Domini
At all times
At that time
At this time
Beforehand
Before long
Beforetime
Behindhand
Behind time
Better days
Break of day
Bygone days
By the clock
Centennial
Childermas
Chronogram
Chronology
Close of day
Common time
Consequent
Constantly
Continuous

Cosmic time
Crepuscule
Days gone by
Days of yore
Eastertide
Easter time
Evanescent
Eventually
Father's Day
Father Time
Fiscal year
Fleetingly
Frequently
Futuristic
Generation
Good Friday
Half a jiffy
Half an hour
Half a shake
Hardly ever
Hebdomadal
Hebrew year
Henceforth
Here and now
Heretofore
Historical
Immemorial
Incidental
In good time
Invariably
Isochronon
Julian year
Just in time
Lammastide
Last chance
Last minute
Lententide
Lunar month
Methuselah
Michaelmas
Middle-aged
Middle Ages
Midmorning
Millennium
Moratorium

Mother's Day
Near future
Nick of time
Now or never
Occasional
Of the clock
Olden times
One fine day
On occasion
On the eve of
Palm Sunday
Posthumous
Prehistory
Present day
Previously
Proper time
Repeatedly
Retrospect
Ripe old age
Sabbath day
Seasonable
Semiweekly
Septennial
Sextennial
Short spell
Small hours
Soon enough
Springtide
Springtime
Subsequent
Summertide
Summertime
Thereafter
This minute
Time-keeper
Timeliness
Time signal
Time to come
Time to kill
Transitory
Tricennial
Triple time
Ultimately
Very seldom
Vespertime

Water clock
Wedding day
Whensoever
Whitmonday
Whitsunday
Wintertide
Wintertime
With the sun
Wristwatch
Years on end
Yesteryear

11 letters:

Adjournment
Adolescence
After-dinner
Against time
Ahead of time
All Fools' Day
All Souls' Day
Anachronism
Anniversary
At intervals
Bicentenary
Bygone times
Ceaselessly
Chronograph
Chronometer
Chronoscope
Coincidence
Concurrence
Continually
Crack of dawn
Crepuscular
Cuckoo clock
Day after day
Day and night
Day in day out
Dead of night
Endless time
Ever and a day
Ever and anon
Everlasting
Every moment
Fin de siècle

Flower of age
For evermore
Former times
Fortnightly
Gay Nineties
Golden hours
Good old days
Halcyon days
Half a second
Hebdomadary
Hereinafter
Ides of March
Immediately
In an instant
Incessantly
In due course
Inopportune
Intercalary
Interregnum
Judgment Day
Lapse of time
Leisure time
Little while
Livelong day
Long-lasting
Long overdue
March of time
Microsecond
Middle years
Millisecond
Modern times
Momentarily
Morningtide
Morningtime
Never-ending
New Year's Day
New Year's Eve
Night and day
Once or twice
On the morrow
Opportunely
Opportunity
Out of season
Passion Week
Penultimate

Perennially
Perfect year
Perpetually
Play for time
Point of time
Present time
Prime of life
Promptitude
Punctuality
Quadrennial
Quarter past
Rogation Day
Sands of time
Semi-monthly
Shining hour
Short notice
Some time ago
Split second
Straightway
Synchronism
Synchronize
Tempus fugit
Thenceforth
The other day
This morning
This very day
Time and tide
Time drags by
Time machine
Time to spare
Turret clock
Twelvemonth
Ultramodern
Waiting time
Whitsuntide
With the lark
Year of Grace

12 letters:

All of a sudden
All Saints' Day
A long time ago
Ancient times
Annunciation
Antediluvian

Ante meridiem
Antemeridien
Armistice Day
Ascension Day
Ash Wednesday
Auld lang syne
Before Christ
Bide one's time
Calendar year
Christmas Day
Christmas Eve
Consequently
Contemporary
Course of time
Decisive hour
Decline of day
Donkey's years
Eleventh hour
Feast of Weeks
Following day
Fourth of July
From that time
Greek calends
Holy Thursday
In days of yore
Indian summer
Innocents' Day
In olden times
Intermission
Late in the day
Long-standing
Many a long day
Metachronism
Nychthemeron
Occasionally
Old-fashioned
Once in a while
On the instant
Parachronism
Periodically
Postdiluvian
Post meridiem
Postponement
Postprandial
Quadrigesima

Quinquennial
Quinquennium
Rare occasion
Red letter day
Sempiternity
Sidereal time
Simultaneous
Stall for time
Standard time
Still of night
Stitch in time
Synodic month
Tercentenary
The dawn of day
Then and there
The year round
Time and again
Time-honoured
Timelessness
Time will tell
Turning point
Twelfth Night
Twelve o'clock
Unseasonable
Witching hour
Without delay

13 letters:
Again and again
All Hallows Eve
April Fools' Day
Ascensiontide
At short notice
Broad daylight
Calendar month
Christmas-tide
Christmas-time
Chronographer
Chronological
Days of the week
Every few hours
Every few years
Every other day
Financial year
For the present

From the outset
From the word go
Generation gap
Getting on a bit
Golden jubilee
Golden wedding
Greenwich time
Michaelmas Day
Old as the hills
Once upon a time
Passion Sunday
Quincentenary
Quinquagesima
Retrospective
Right up to date
Roman calendar
Round the clock
Shrove Tuesday
Silver jubilee
Silver wedding
Some of the time
Some other time
Sooner or later
Speaking clock
St Crispin's Day
St Luke's summer
St Swithin's Day
Summer holiday
Synchronology
The time is ripe
Time after time
Time marches on
Time of arrival
Time out of mind
Tomorrow night
Trinity Sunday
Tropical month
Turn of the year
Up-to-the-minute
Up with the lark
Vernal equinox
Week in, week out
Year in, year out

14 letters:
Advancing years
Before and after
Behind schedule
Breathing space
Chronometrical
Day in and day out
Daylight saving
Declining years
Diamond jubilee
Diamond wedding
During the night
Easter holidays
For ever and a day
For ever and ever
For the duration
From time to time
Fullness of time
Geological time
In ancient times
In course of time
Interval of time
In the afternoon
In the beginning
In the meanwhile
Julian calendar
Keep early hours
Maundy Thursday
Midsummer night
Month of Sundays
Pancake Tuesday
Past and present
Remembrance Day
Sabbatical year
Septuagenarian
Walpurgis Night
Witches' Sabbath

15 letters:
Against the clock
Ahead of schedule
Chronologically
Contemporaneity
Contemporaneous
Continental time

Continuation day
Dominical letter
Equinoctial year
Every now and then
For a year and a day
Fourth dimension
How goes the enemy
In the nick of time
Month after month
Months and months

Months of the year
Mothering Sunday
Night after night
Once in a blue moon
Once in a lifetime
Put back the clock
Put the clock back
Quatercentenary
Retrospectively
Spur of the moment

St Valentine's Day
Thanksgiving Day
The morning after
This year of grace
Tomorrow evening
Tomorrow morning
World without end

17 letters:
Gregorian calendar

GREGORIAN CALENDAR

January	April	July	October
February	May	August	November
March	June	September	December

JEWISH CALENDAR

Tishri	Tevet	Nisan	Tammuz
Cheshvan	Shevat	Iyar	Av
Heshvan	Shebat	Iyyar	Ab
Kislev	Adar	Sivan	Elul

MUSLIM CALENDAR

Muharram	Rabia II	Shaaban	Dhu'l-Qa'dah
Moharram	Jumada I	Ramadan	Dhu'l-Hijjah
Safar	Jumada II	Rhamadhan	
Saphar	Rajab	Ramazan	
Rabia I	Shaban	Shawwal	

FRENCH REVOLUTIONARY CALENDAR

Vendémiaire	Pluviôse	Prairial	Fructidor
Brumaire	Ventôse	Messidor	
Frimaire	Germinal	Thermidor	
Nivôse	Floréal	Fervidor	

TIME ZONES

17 letters:
British Summer Time
Greenwich Mean Time
Yukon Daylight Time
Yukon Standard Time

Central Standard Time
Eastern Daylight Time
Eastern Standard Time
Pacific Daylight Time
Pacific Standard Time

19 letters:
Central Daylight Time
Central European Time

20 letters:
Atlantic Daylight Time
Atlantic Standard Time

Mountain Daylight Time
Mountain Standard Time

Newfoundland Daylight Time
Newfoundland Standard Time

Tobacco

TYPES OF TOBACCO

4 letters:
Shag

5 letters:
Snout
Snuff

6 letters:
Burley
Filler
Rappee

7 letters:
Caporal

Perique
Sumatra
Turkish

8 letters:
Canaster
Makhorka
Maryland
Virginia

9 letters:
Broadleaf
Fire-cured
Flue-cured

11 letters:
Cigar binder
Cigar filler

12 letters:
Cigar wrapper
Dark air-cured

14 letters:
Chewing tobacco
Cuban cigar leaf

TYPES OF CIGAR AND CIGARETTE

5 letters:
Breva
Claro
Stogy

6 letters:
Concha
Corona
Havana
Maduro

Manila
Roll-up
Stogey

7 letters:
Cheroot

8 letters:
Perfecto
Puritano

9 letters:
Cigarillo
Imperiale
Panatella

10 letters:
Tailor-made

11 letters:
Roll-your-own

PIPES

4 letters:
Clay

5 letters:
Briar
Peace

6 letters:
Hookah

7 letters:
Corncob

8 letters:
Calabash

10 letters:
Meerschaum

12 letters:
Churchwarden
Hubble-bubble

GENERAL SMOKING TERMS

3 letters:
Ash

4 letters:
Bowl
Butt
Pipe
Plug
Stem

5 letters:
Flint

6 letters:
Dottle
Smoker
Splint

7 letters:
Ashtray

Humidor
Lighter
Makings
Matches
Pigtail

8 letters:
Calabash
Pipe rack
Rollings
Snuffbox

9 letters:
Filter tip
Smoke room

11 letters:
Pipe cleaner
Smoking room
Tobacconist

12 letters:
Tobacco pouch

13 letters:
Cigarette case
Smoking jacket

14 letters:
Cigarette paper

15 letters:
Cigarette holder

18 letters:
Smoking compartment

Tools

3 letters:
Awl
Axe
Bit
Gab
Gad
Hob
Hoe
Saw
Sax

4 letters:
Bosh
Comb
File
Fork
Froe
Frow
Hack
Hone

Maul
Pick
Rake
Rurp
Spud

5 letters:
Auger
Borer
Broad
Burin
Clink
Croze
Drift
Drill
Drove
Facer
Float
Gavel
Graip

Kevel
Plane
Punch
Shave
Slick
Snake
Spade
Swage

6 letters:
Beetle
Bodkin
Broach
Chaser
Chisel
Comber
Cradle
Dibble
Fillet
Flange

Former
Fraise
Fuller
Gimlet
Gouger
Graver
Gympie
Hammer
Jumper
Mallet
Padsaw
Pestle
Pliers
Rabble
Rammer
Ripple
Rocker
Router
Sander
Scutch

Scythe
Shears
Sickle
Spider
Stylus
Trepan
Trowel
Wimble
Wrench

7 letters:
Bolster
Dresser
Flatter
Ice pick
Jointer
Mattock
Nibbler
Nippers
Rabbler
Rounder
Scalper
Scauper
Scorper
Scriber
Slasher
Spanner
Spudder

8 letters:
Allen key
Billhook

Bitstock
Chainsaw
Clippers
Driftpin
Edge tool
Screw tap
Scutcher
Stiletto

9 letters:
Alligator
Drawknife
Drawshave
Eyeleteer

10 letters:
Bushhammer
Claw hammer
Cold chisel
Drill press
Hack hammer
Icebreaker
Jackhammer
Piledriver
Power drill
Tack hammer
Tilt hammer
Triphammer

11 letters:
Brace and bit
Centre punch

Countersink
Drove chisel
Hammer drill
Mitre square
Ploughstaff
Pruning hook
Screwdriver
Spitsticker
Steam-hammer

12 letters:
Diamond point
Firmer chisel
Floatcut file
Monkey wrench
Pitching tool
Sledgehammer

13 letters:
Rawhide hammer
Soldering iron

14 letters:
Ball-peen hammer
Knapping hammer
Percussion tool

15 letters:
Half-round chisel
Pneumatic hammer

Torture

INSTRUMENTS OF TORTURE

4 letters:
Boot
Rack

5 letters:
Brake
Wheel

7 letters:
Scourge

8 letters:
Triphook

9 letters:
Treadmill

10 letters:
Iron maiden
Pilliwinks

Thumbscrew

13 letters:
Cat-o'-nine-tails

14 letters:
Procrustean bed

TYPES OF TORTURE

5 letters:
Water

8 letters:
Gauntlet

9 letters:
Bastinado
Strappado
Water cure

12 letters:
Chinese water

Towns

3 letters:
Ems
Gao
Ife
Lod
Niš
Spa
Zug

4 letters:
Agen
Albi
Asti
Biel
Bury
Bute
Cheb
Cork
Deal
Edam
Eton
Genk
Györ
Hamm
Hove
Hyde
Kent
Lens
León
Lodi
Mayo
Melk
Mons
Mull
Niue

Oahu
Sale
Sfax
Skye
Thun
Toul
Trim
Tyre
Wick

5 letters:
Aarau
Aduwa
Ahwaz
Aksum
Alloa
Alost
Aosta
Arlon
Arras
Aruba
Ascot
Aswan
Aulis
Aydin
Balkh
Banff
Bohol
Capua
Cavan
Clare
Cluny
Conwy
Copán
Corby

Cowes
Crewe
Daman
Delft
Dinan
Doorn
Dubna
Egham
Elche
Elgin
Emmen
Ennis
Epsom
Esher
Faial
Flint
Gotha
Gouda
Hilla
Hotan
Ikeja
Ipsus
Irbid
Issus
Izmit
Jerez
Jinja
Kauai
Kells
Kerry
Korçë
Krems
Lahti
Laois
Leigh

Lewes
Leyte
Lorca
Louth
Luton
Luxor
Lydia
Maraş
Massa
Meath
Namur
Negev
Nikko
Niort
Noyon
Öland
Omagh
Ostia
Otago
Pavia
Pelée
Pemba
Płock
Ponce
Pydna
Qeshm
Rugby
Sedan
Sibiu
Sitka
Skien
Sligo
Stans
Ta'izz
Tomsk

Tours
Trier
Truro
Ujiji
Upolu
Vaduz
Vichy
Wigan
Youth
Ypres
Zarqa

6 letters:
Abydos
Actium
Aegina
Agadir
Almada
Al Marj
Amalfi
Anadyr
Antrim
Anyang
Armagh
Arnold
Ashdod
Assisi
Atbara
Aveiro
Ayodha
Bangor
Bastia
Batley
Battle
Bauchi
Bayeux
Bethel
Bingen
Biskra
Bodmin
Bolton
Bouaké
Brecon
Butung
Buxton

Can Tho
Carlow
Celaya
Cognac
Crosby
Cuenca
Dachau
Dawson
Denton
Deurne
Dinant
Dodona
Dudley
Dunoon
Eccles
Edessa
Edirne
Epping
Évreux
Flores
Forfar
Galway
Gibeon
Glarus
Guyana
Hameln
Harlow
Havant
Hawick
Huambo
Huesca
Hwange
Ilesha
Ilkley
Irvine
Kalisz
Kendal
Kirkby
Kiruna
Kokura
Kumasi
Labuan
Lashio
Latina
Lemnos

Lesbos
Lombok
Ludlow
Lugano
Lützen
Macapá
Maldon
Medway
Megara
Menton
Merano
Mérida
Miseno
Morley
Nablus
Nakuru
Nelson
Newark
Oakham
Offaly
Oldham
Örebro
Osijek
Ottawa
Owerri
Pernik
Phuket
Pleven
Poitou
Pudsey
Ragusa
Rashid
Rijeka
Sarnen
Schwyz
Sennar
Sestos
Seveso
Shache
Shiloh
Sintra
Slough
Sokoto
Soweto
Tarbes

Tivoli
Tralee
Tyumen
Verdun
Vienne
Warley
Welkom
Widnes
Woking
Zabrze
Zwolle

7 letters:
Airdrie
Alençon
Ålesund
Al Hufuf
Almadén
Altdorf
Amboise
Antibes
Appleby
Armenia
Arundel
Ashford
Augusta
Auxerre
Baalbek
Bacolod
Bamberg
Banbury
Bedford
Belfort
Bien Hoa
Blaydon
Bonaire
Burnley
Cabimas
Cambrai
Cannock
Carlton
Carrara
Caserta
Cassino
Chatham

Cholula	Kutaisi	Setúbal	Ballarat
Chorley	La Línea	Seville	Banstead
Clacton	La Palma	Shakhty	Barbados
Clonmel	Legnica	Sheppey	Barnsley
Colditz	Leitrim	Shkodër	Basildon
Concord	Lerwick	Skipton	Bastogne
Consett	Leuctra	Sovetsk	Beauvais
Corinth	Lifford	Staines	Bedworth
Cortona	Lisieux	Stanley	Benfleet
Crawley	Locarno	Swindon	Beverley
Crotone	Lourdes	Tampere	Biarritz
Cwmbran	Louvain	Tanagra	Billiton
Cythera	Malvern	Taunton	Boa Vista
Devizes	Margate	Telford	Bornholm
Dhahran	Matlock	Thapsus	Budapest
Donegal	Megiddo	Tobolsk	Buraydah
Donetsk	Meissen	Torquay	Caerleon
Dongola	Melilla	Tripoli	Calabria
Douglas	Minorca	Tutuila	Campania
Dundalk	Morpeth	Urmston	Chamonix
Eleusis	Moulins	Üsküdar	Chartres
Entebbe	Newbury	Valence	Chepstow
Evesham	Newport	Vellore	Chertsey
Exmouth	Newtown	Walsall	Cheshunt
Falkirk	Numidia	Warwick	Chigwell
Falster	Okinawa	Watford	Courtrai
Fareham	Olsztyn	Wexford	Damietta
Farnham	Orvieto	Wicklow	Dartford
Fashoda	Otranto	Windsor	Daventry
Felling	Paisley	Wisbech	Demerara
Fiesole	Papeete	Woomera	Dewsbury
Görlitz	Peebles	Worksop	Dumfries
Gosport	Penrith	Wrexham	Ebbw Vale
Halifax	Pereira	Zaandam	El Faiyûm
Harlech	Plovdiv	Zealand	Erlangen
Hasselt	Punakha		Fribourg
Herisau	Pushkin	**8 letters:**	Galloway
Heywood	Reading	Abeokuta	Golconda
Hoylake	Red Deer	Aberdare	Grantham
Ipswich	Reigate	Abingdon	Guernica
Iqaluit	Renfrew	Amravati	Hamilton
Karbala	Runcorn	Aquileia	Hastings
Keswick	Sagunto	Armidale	Hatfield
Khojent	Saint-Lô	Aubusson	Hertford
Kildare	Segovia	Aycliffe	Hinckley

Holyhead	Rothesay	Chiengmai	New Romney
Ilkeston	Sabadell	Chinatown	Northwich
Jemappes	Sarajevo	Clydebank	Ogbomosho
Junagadh	Seremban	Coleraine	Paderborn
Keighley	Solihull	Colwyn Bay	Palm Beach
Kerkrade	Spalding	Deauville	Périgueux
Kilkenny	Stafford	Dodge City	Perpignan
Kirkwall	Subotica	Dolgellau	Pharsalus
Le Cateau	Tamworth	Doncaster	Pontypool
Limerick	Ternopol	Dumbarton	Portadown
Llandaff	Timbuktu	Dunstable	Port Royal
Llanelli	Touraine	Eastleigh	Prestwich
Longford	Tübingen	Elizabeth	Prestwick
Lüneburg	Uxbridge	Esslingen	Princeton
Lyonnais	Viti Levu	Five Towns	Roscommon
Mafikeng	Wallasey	Gällivare	Rotherham
Mainland	Wallsend	Galwegian	Saint Gall
Maitland	Waterloo	Gelligaer	Saint-Ouen
Manassas	Zlatoust	Godesberg	Salamanca
Maubeuge	Zululand	Gold Coast	Santa Cruz
Mézières		Gütersloh	Sherborne
Mindanao	**9 letters:**	Halesowen	Solothurn
Monaghan	Abbeville	Harrogate	Sosnowiec
Monmouth	Agrigento	Inveraray	Southport
Montreux	Alcántara	Jamestown	Stevenage
Mufulira	Aldershot	Kettering	Stockport
Murmansk	Ambleside	Killarney	Stralsund
Nanterre	Apeldoorn	King's Lynn	Stranraer
Nazareth	Appenzell	Kitchener	Stretford
Nijmegen	Auschwitz	Kitzbühel	Surakarta
Nishapur	Aylesbury	Lambaréné	Tipperary
Normandy	Bebington	Lancaster	Tombstone
Nuneaton	Beersheba	Le Creusot	Tonbridge
Omdurman	Bethlehem	Llandudno	Tourcoing
Paignton	Bethsaida	Lockerbie	Tullamore
Pembroke	Blackpool	Long Eaton	Vancouver
Penzance	Bracknell	Los Alamos	Viareggio
Peterlee	Brentwood	Lower Hutt	Wadi Halfa
Piacenza	Brighouse	Lymington	Wad Medani
Piedmont	Capernaum	Maidstone	Waterford
Portland	Castlebar	Mansfield	Westmeath
Redditch	Chaeronea	Middleton	Woodstock
Richmond	Chantilly	Mullingar	Worcester
Rijswijk	Charleroi	Neuchâtel	Wuppertal
Rochdale	Chernobyl	Newmarket	

10 letters:
Accrington
Altrincham
Amersfoort
Anderlecht
Austerlitz
Barnstaple
Bellinzona
Bennington
Bridgwater
Bromsgrove
Buckingham
Caerphilly
Canterbury
Carmarthen
Castleford
Chadderton
Cheltenham
Ciudad Real
Coatbridge
Colchester
Coldstream
Darjeeling
Darlington
Dorchester
Eisenstadt
Ffestiniog
Frauenfeld
Galashiels
Gettysburg
Gillingham
Glenrothes
Hammerfest
Huntingdon
Interlaken
Kalgoorlie
Kapfenberg
Kenilworth
Kilmarnock
Kragujevac
Letchworth
Leverkusen
Linlithgow
Livingston
Llangollen

Longbenton
Los Angeles
Maidenhead
Middelburg
Monte Carlo
Montego Bay
Motherwell
Neumünster
New Castile
Paramaribo
Pontefract
Pontypridd
Portlaoise
Regensburg
Ruda Śląska
Sacramento
Saint Croix
Saint-Denis
San Antonio
Scunthorpe
Shrewsbury
Simferopol
Tewkesbury
Trowbridge
Twickenham
Vijayawada
Warrington
Washington
Whitehorse
Winchester
Winterthur
Xochimilco

11 letters:
Aberystwyth
Aix-les-Bains
Alessandria
Armentières
Basingstoke
Cirencester
Clackmannan
Cumbernauld
Dawson Creek
Downpatrick
Enniskillen

Farnborough
Fort William
Glastonbury
Halberstadt
High Wycombe
Kanchipuram
Kigoma-Ujiji
Leatherhead
Marlborough
Mississauga
Missolonghi
Montbéliard
Montpellier
Nakhichevan
Northampton
Novosibirsk
Nyíregyháza
Prestonpans
Rambouillet
Saint-Brieuc
Saint David's
Saint Helena
Saint Helens
Saint Helier
Saint Pierre
San Fernando
Sharpeville
Sierra Leone
Stourbridge
Wanne-Eickel

12 letters:
Alice Springs
Anuradhapura
Ascoli Piceno
Beaconsfield
Bielsko-Biała
Bougainville
Cerro de Pasco
Chesterfield
Chilpancingo
Christchurch
East Kilbride
Huddersfield
Kristianstad

Loughborough
Luang Prabang
Macclesfield
Milton Keynes
Newtownabbey
Peterborough
Saint Austell
Saint-Étienne
Saint-Quentin
San Ildefonso
Schaffhausen
Secunderabad
Seringapatam
Skelmersdale
Valenciennes
Villahermosa
Villeurbanne
Wattenscheid
West Bromwich

13 letters:
Berchtesgaden
Blantyre-Limbe
Bury St Edmunds
Carrickfergus
Évian-les-Bains
Fontainebleau
Hradec Králové
Kidderminster

Leamington Spa
Lons-le-Saunier
Melton Mowbray
Merthyr Tydfil
Middlesbrough
New Providence
Northallerton
Southend-on-Sea

14 letters:
Annapolis Royal
Ashby-de-la-Zouch
Bishop Auckland
Château-Thierry
Griqualand East
Griqualand West
Hemel Hempstead
Henley-on-Thames
Mariánské Lázně
Saint Augustine
Tunbridge Wells
Wellingborough

15 letters:
Ashton-under-Lyne
Barrow-in-Furness
Burton-upon-Trent
Camborne-Redruth
Neuilly-sur-Seine

Stratford-on-Avon
Sunbury-on-Thames
Sutton Coldfield
Weston-super-Mare

16 letters:
Alcazar de San Juan
Berwick-upon-Tweed
Eastern Townships
Houghton-le-Spring
Sutton-in-Ashfield
Welwyn Garden City

17 letters:
Talavera de la Reina

18 letters:
Aldridge-Brownhills
Newcastle-under-Lyme
Saint-Maur-des-Fossés

19 letters:
Charleville-Mézières

21 letters:
Queenborough in
  Sheppey

Trade terms

2 letters:
CA
Co
HP
Rd

3 letters:
Bag
Bar
Bid
Bob
BOT
Buy

Cap
COD
Con
Dot
Due
Dun
EEC
Fee
IOU
Job
Lot
Ltd
Net

Oof
Owe
Par
Pay
Pit
Pro
Put
Rig
Sag
SET
Sum
Tag
Tax

Tin
Tip
VAT
Wad

4 letters:
Agio
Back
Bank
Bear
Body
Bond
Boom

Buck
Bulk
Bull
Bury
Call
Cant
Cash
Cess
Char
Chip
Coin
Co-op
Corn

Cost	List	Tout	Clerk	Prize
Crop	Loan	Vend	Costs	Purse
Curb	Long	Visa	Craft	Queer
Deal	Loss	Wage	Crash	Quota
Dear	Make	Ware	Cycle	Quote
Debt	Mart	Work	Debit	Rails
Desk	Meed		Depot	Rally
Dibs	Milk	**5 letters:**	Dives	Rebuy
Dole	Mill	Agent	Dough	Remit
Drug	Mint	Amass	Dowry	Repay
Dues	Nail	Angel	Draft	Rhino
Dump	Note	Assay	Entry	Rocks
Dust	Paid	Asset	Ernie	Salve
Duty	Pawn	At par	Exact	Scalp
Earn	PAYE	Audit	Files	Scoop
EFTA	Peag	Baron	Float	Score
Fair	Perk	Batch	Forge	Scrip
Fees	Pool	Beans	Funds	Set up
Fine	Post	Bears	Gilts	Share
Fire	Rags	Bid up	Gnome	Shark
Firm	Raid	Block	Goods	Shift
Fisc	Rate	Blunt	Gross	Short
Free	Reap	Board	Guild	Skill
Fund	Rent	Bogus	Hoard	Slash
Gain	Risk	Bones	House	Slump
Game	Roll	Bonus	Index	Smash
Gift	Roup	Boost	Ingot	Smith
Gild	Ruin	Booth	Issue	Snide
Gilt	Sack	Brand	Lease	Spend
Giro	Safe	Brass	Lucre	Spiel
Glut	Sale	Broke	Maker	Spots
Gold	Salt	Bucks	Means	Stake
Good	Save	Bulls	Midas	Stall
Haul	Scab	Bunce	Money	Stand
Hawk	Sell	Buyer	Ochre	Stint
Heap	Shop	Buy up	Offer	Stock
Hire	Sink	By-bid	Order	Store
Hive	Slug	Cadge	Owing	Strop
Hold	Sold	Cargo	Panic	Tally
Hype	Stag	Cheap	Paper	Taxes
Idle	Swap	Check	Piece	Terms
Item	Tare	Chink	Pitch	Tithe
Lend	Task	Chips	Plant	Token
Levy	Tick	Chore	Pound	Trade
Line	Till	Clear	Price	Treat

Trend
Truck
Trust
Usury
Utter
Value
Venal
Wages
Wares
Welsh
Works
Worth
Yield

6 letters:
Abacus
Accept
Accrue
Admass
Afford
Agency
Agenda
Amount
Appeal
Arrear
Assets
At cost
Avails
Backer
Banker
Barker
Barter
Bazaar
Bearer
Boodle
Borrow
Bought
Bounce
Bounty
Bourse
Branch
Broker
Budget
Bureau
Bursar

Button
Buying
Buy out
Cambio
Career
Cartel
Cash in
Change
Charge
Cheque
Client
Coffer
Consol
Copper
Corner
Costly
Coupon
Cowrie
Credit
Crisis
Custom
Dealer
Deal in
Debtee
Debtor
Defray
Demand
Dicker
Drawer
Dunner
Emptio
Enrich
Equity
Errand
Estate
Excise
Expend
Export
Figure
Fiscal
Fold up
Freeze
Future
Garage
Gazump

Godown
Go slow
Gratis
Grease
Growth
Guinea
Haggle
Hammer
Hard up
Hawker
Import
Impose
Impost
In bulk
In cash
Income
In debt
In-tray
Jobber
Job lot
Labour
Leader
Ledger
Lender
Liable
Living
Luxury
Mammon
Merger
Minute
Moneys
Monger
Monies
Notice
Nugget
Octroi
Odd job
Odd lot
Office
On call
Oncost
On tick
Option
Outbid
Outcry

Outlay
Outlet
Output
Packet
Parity
Patron
Pauper
Pay day
Pay for
Paying
Pay-off
Payola
Pay out
Peddle
Pedlar
Picket
Pirate
Pledge
Plunge
Plutus
Pocket
Policy
Profit
Public
Purvey
Racket
Raffle
Rating
Ration
Realty
Rebate
Recoup
Redeem
Refund
Reject
Remedy
Render
Rental
Resale
Resell
Resign
Retail
Retire
Return
Reward

Rialto
Riches
Ruined
Salary
Save up
Saving
Sell up
Settle
Shares
Shorts
Silver
Simony
Smithy
Specie
Spiral
Sponge
Spread
Stable
Staker
Stocks
Strike
Sundry
Supply
Surtax
Swings
Tariff
Taxman
Teller
Tender
Tenths
Ticker
Ticket
Towage
Trader
Treaty
Tycoon
Unload
Unpaid
Usurer
Valuta
Vendor
Vendue
Wallet
Wampum
Wealth

Worker
Wright

7 letters:
Abscond
Account
Actuary
Allonge
Annuity
Arrears
Article
Atelier
Auction
Auditor
Automat
Average
Backing
Bad debt
Balance
Ballast
Banking
Bargain
Berries
Bidding
Bonanza
Bondage
Boycott
Bullets
Bullion
Bursary
Buy back
Cabbage
Calling
Cambist
Capital
Cash box
Cashier
Ceiling
Chapman
Charity
Chinker
Clinker
Coinage
Coining
Company

Concern
Consols
Contact
Convert
Coppers
Corn pit
Cottons
Counter
Croesus
Cumshaw
Customs
Cut-rate
Damages
Daybook
Dealing
Declare
Default
Deficit
Deflate
Deposit
Deviser
Dockage
Draw out
Due bill
Dumping
Economy
Effects
Embargo
Emption
Endorse
Engross
Entrust
Expense
Exploit
Exports
Factory
Failure
Fall due
Finance
Flutter
Foot lot
Foreman
Forgery
For sale
Fortune

Foundry
Freebie
Freight
Full lot
Futures
Gabelle
Gas bill
Gift box
Go broke
Good buy
Good sum
Go under
Guerdon
Half-day
Harvest
Haulage
Head tax
Holding
Imports
Inflate
In funds
Intrust
Invoice
Iron men
Jingler
Jobbers
Jobbing
Jobless
Journal
Killing
Land tax
Leading
Lending
Lettuce
Limited
Lockout
Lombard
Long-run
Lottery
Lump sum
Manager
Man-made
Mintage
Mission
Moneyed

Nest egg
Net gain
Notions
Nummary
Oddment
On offer
On terms
On trust
Opening
Opulent
Out-tray
Package
Parlour
Parvenu
Payable
Pay cash
Payment
Pay rise
Payroll
Payslip
Peddlar
Pending
Pension
Pet bank
Plunger
Poll tax
Poor man
Portage
Pre-empt
Premium
Prepaid
Pricing
Produce
Profits
Promote
Pro rata
Prosper
Provide
Pursuit
Pyramid
Realize
Realtor
Refusal
Regrate
Reissue

Release
Requite
Reserve
Retiral
Returns
Revenue
Rich man
Rigging
Rollers
Room man
Rouleau
Royalty
Sacking
Salable
Salt tax
Salvage
Savings
Seconds
Selling
Sell out
Service
Shekels
Shopman
Shopper
Skilled
Smelter
Solvent
Sponger
Squeeze
Stipend
Storage
Striker
Subsidy
Surplus
Swindle
Takings
Taxable
Tax-free
Terrier
The city
Tidy sum
Trade in
Trading
Traffic
Tranche

Trustee
Utility
Vacancy
Vending
Venture
Voucher
Walkout
War bond
Warrant
Wealthy
Welfare
Well off
Welsher
Wildcat
Workday

8 letters:
Above par
Accredit
Affluent
After tax
Agiotage
Agronomy
Amortize
Appraise
At a price
Auditing
Automate
Badly off
Bad money
Ballyhoo
Bankbook
Bank loan
Bank note
Bank roll
Bankrupt
Base coin
Basic pay
Bear pool
Bear raid
Beat down
Below par
Blackleg
Blue chip
Board lot

Boardman
Bondager
Boom town
Borrower
Boutique
Breakage
Brochure
Bull pool
Bull raid
Business
Buying in
Campaign
Carriage
Cashbook
Cash down
Cash sale
Circular
Clientry
Close out
Cold cash
Commands
Commerce
Consumer
Contango
Contract
Converts
Counting
Creditor
Credit to
Currency
Customer
Cut-price
Day shift
Dealings
Defrayal
Director
Disburse
Discount
Disposal
Dividend
Dry goods
Earnings
Embezzle
Employee
Employer

Emporium
Entrepot
Estimate
Evaluate
Exchange
Expended
Expenses
Exporter
Face ruin
Finances
Fire sale
Flat rate
Floorman
For a song
Free gift
Free port
Function
Gasworks
Gazetted
Gazumper
Gift shop
Gilt edge
Giveaway
Gold mine
Gold rush
Good will
Gratuity
Grow rich
Hallmark
Hard cash
Hard sell
Hardware
Hoarding
Homework
Hot money
Huckster
Importer
In arrear
Increase
Indebted
Industry
In pocket
Interest
In the red
Investor

Issuance
Issue par
Jeweller
Junkshop
Keep shop
Kitemark
Knitwork
Labourer
Lame duck
Largesse
Large sum
Legation
Levanter
Lifework
Live high
Live well
Long side
Low price
Low water
Make a bid
Make good
Manifest
Manpower
Mark down
Material
Maturity
Merchant
Mint drop
Monetary
Moneybag
Moneybox
Monopoly
Mortgage
Net price
Net worth
No charge
Notation
Notecase
Oddments
Off price
On credit
On demand
On strike
Operator
Opulence

Ordinary
Overhaul
Overhead
Overseer
Overtime
Par value
Passbook
Pawn shop
Pay talks
Pin money
Pipeline
Pittance
Position
Post paid
Poundage
Practice
Premises
Price cut
Price war
Proceeds
Producer
Property
Prospect
Purchase
Put price
Quit rent
Rack rent
Rag trade
Rainy day
Receipts
Reckoner
Recorder
Recovery
Refinery
Register
Regrater
Rent-free
Rent roll
Requital
Reserves
Retailer
Retainer
Richesse
Richling
Round lot

Round sum
Rush hour
Salaried
Saleroom
Salesman
Salt down
Sanction
Scalping
Scarcity
Schedule
Security
Self-made
Shipment
Shipyard
Shopping
Short-run
Showcase
Showroom
Sideline
Sinecure
Small sum
Soft cell
Solatium
Solidity
Solvency
Spending
Spot cash
Spot sale
Square up
Sterling
Sundries
Supertax
Supplies
Swapping
Takeover
Take stop
Tallyman
Taxation
Tax dodge
Taxpayer
Time bill
Tolbooth
Tool shop
Toolwork
Top price

Trade gap
Trade off
Treasure
Treasury
Turnover
Underbid
Undercut
Usufruct
Valorize
Valuable
Venality
Vendible
Vocation
Wash sale
Watchdog
Well-to-do
Wharfage
Workaday
Work late
Workroom
Workshop
Write off

9 letters:
Absconder
Ad valorem
Affiliate
Affluence
Aggregate
Allowance
Amount due
Appraisal
Arbitrage
Arrearage
Assigment
Avocation
Back shift
Bad cheque
Bank clerk
Bank stock
Barrow boy
Bartering
Bear panic
Blind pool
Board room

Bond issue	Dollar gap	Heavy cost	Night safe
Bon marché	Draw wages	High price	Officiate
Bonus bond	Drug store	High value	Off market
Borrowing	Easy money	Holy stone	On account
Box office	Easy terms	Hot market	On the nail
Brand name	Economics	Hush money	Operative
Breadline	Economies	Import tax	Order book
Brokerage	Economise	In arrears	Outgoings
Bucketing	Emolument	Incentive	Out of debt
Bull panic	Establish	Income tax	Out of work
Buy in bulk	Exchequer	In deficit	Outworker
By auction	Exciseman	Indemnity	Overdraft
By-bidding	Excise tax	Inflation	Overdrawn
By-product	Executive	Insolvent	Overheads
Cable code	Expansion	Insurance	Overspend
Cable rate	Expensive	In the city	Patronage
Call price	Exploiter	Invention	Patronize
Cash grain	Export tax	Inventory	Pay dearly
Catalogue	Extortion	Job of work	Pay in kind
Cellarage	Face value	Joint bank	Paymaster
Chain bank	Fair price	Keep books	Pecuniary
Cheapjack	Fair trade	Knock down	Pecunious
Check rate	Fat profit	Late shift	Penniless
Clearance	Fiat money	Legal bond	Penny wise
Clientage	Financial	Liability	Petty cash
Clientele	Financier	Life's work	Piecework
Co-emption	Firm offer	Liquidate	Piggy bank
Coin money	Firm price	List price	Plutocrat
Commodity	Flash note	Long purse	Poorly off
Costerman	Flat broke	Lossmaker	Portfolio
Cost price	Flotation	Low-priced	Pound note
Craftsman	Free trade	Luxury tax	Pourboire
Death duty	Full purse	Mail order	Practical
Debenture	Gilt-edged	Make a sale	Priceless
Deduction	Going rate	Market day	Price list
Defaulter	Gold piece	Marketing	Price ring
Deflation	Good price	Means test	Price rise
Depositor	Greenback	Middleman	Prime cost
Dime store	Guarantee	Moneybags	Principal
Directors	Guarantor	Money belt	Profiteer
Direct tax	Half-price	Mortgagee	Promotion
Dirt-cheap	Handiwork	Mortgager	Purchaser
Discharge	Hard goods	Neat price	Qualified
Dishonour	Hard money	Negotiate	Quittance
Dismissal	Head buyer	Net income	Quotation

Ratepayer
Ready cash
Real wages
Recession
Reckoning
Reduction
Redundant
Reference
Refinance
Reflation
Registrar
Reimburse
Repayment
Resources
Restraint
Sacrifice
Sale block
Salesgirl
Sales talk
Secretary
Sell short
Shift work
Shop floor
Short sale
Short side
Sight bill
Single tax
Situation
Soft goods
Sole agent
Soundness
Speculate
Spendings
Spot grain
Spot price
Stability
Stamp duty
Statement
Stock list
Stockpile
Stock rate
Strike pay
Strongbox
Subsidize
Substance

Sumptuary
Surcharge
Sweatshop
Sweet shop
Syndicate
Synthetic
Tax return
Technical
The actual
The market
The street
Tie-in sale
Timocracy
Tollbooth
Trade fair
Trademark
Trade name
Trade sale
Tradesman
Traffic in
Treadmill
Treasurer
Undersell
Union card
Unit trust
Unsalable
Unskilled
Up for sale
Utilities
Utterance
Valuation
Vendition
Wage claim
Wage scale
Warehouse
Wealth tax
Well-lined
Whitewash
Wholesale
Work force
Workhouse
Work study
World Bank

10 letters:
Acceptance
Accountant
Accounting
Accumulate
Adjustment
Advertiser
Appreciate
Apprentice
Assessment
At a bargain
At a premium
At the spear
Auctioneer
Auction off
Automation
Average out
Bank credit
Bankruptcy
Bearer bond
Bear market
Best seller
Bill broker
Bill of sale
Blood money
Bondholder
Bonus stock
Bookkeeper
Bucket shop
Bulk buying
Buy and sell
Buy futures
Calculator
Capitalism
Capitalist
Capitalize
Chain store
Chancellor
Chargeable
Chargehand
Cheapening
Cheap skate
Cheque book
Chrematist
Chrysology

Closed shop
Closing bid
Collateral
Colporteur
Commercial
Commission
Compensate
Conference
Consortium
Contraband
Cost centre
Coupon bond
Credit card
Credit slip
Curb broker
Curb market
Daily bread
Dead market
Deep in debt
Defalcator
Defrayment
Del credere
Deliquence
Demand bill
Department
Depository
Depreciate
Depression
Direct cost
Dirty money
Dividend on
Dollar bill
Dummy share
Dutch treat
Easy market
Economizer
Efficiency
Employment
Encumbered
End product
Enterprise
Estate duty
Eurodollar
Evaluation
Ex-dividend

Exorbitant	Insolvency	Occupation	Remittance
Exposition	Instalment	Off licence	Remunerate
False money	In the black	Oil of palms	Repair shop
Fancy goods	In the money	On the block	Reparation
Fancy price	Investment	On the cheap	Repository
Fancy stock	Job-hunting	On the rocks	Repurchase
Filthy rich	Joint bonds	On the shelf	Retail shop
First offer	Joint stock	Opening bid	Retirement
Fiscal year	Jumble sale	Open market	Rock bottom
Fixed price	Laboratory	Out of funds	Round trade
Fixed trust	Lighterage	Overcharge	Run up a bill
Flat market	Liquidator	Paper money	Salability
Floor price	Livelihood	Pawnbroker	Sales force
Floor trade	Living wage	Peppercorn	Saving bank
Forced sale	Loan market	Percentage	Saving game
Free gratis	Long market	Picket duty	Scrip issue
Free market	Long seller	Pig in a poke	Second-hand
Free sample	Loss leader	Pilot plant	Securities
Free trader	Management	Plutocracy	Serial bond
Freightage	Man of means	Pocket book	Settlement
Full stocks	Marked down	Power plant	Settle with
Funded debt	Marketable	Pre-emption	Share index
Give credit	Market hall	Preference	Shoestring
Gold nugget	Mass market	Prepayment	Shopkeeper
Go on strike	Meal ticket	Price index	Shop window
Go shopping	Member bank	Price level	Short bonds
Government	Mercantile	Printworks	Sick market
Green pound	Merchantry	Prix unique	Skilled man
Grindstone	Midas touch	Production	Slave trade
Half stocks	Monetarism	Profession	Slow market
Handicraft	Monetarist	Profitable	Smart money
Hand market	Moneyed man	Prospector	Soft market
Have in hand	Money order	Prospectus	Sole agency
Head office	Monopolise	Prosperity	Speciality
Heavy purse	Monopolist	Provide for	Speculator
High-priced	Moratorium	Purchasing	Split shift
Hold office	Negotiable	Pure profit	Statistics
Honorarium	Never never	Put and call	Steelworks
Import duty	Nightshift	Ration book	Steep price
Imposition	Nominal fee	Ready money	Stock issue
In business	Nominal par	Real estate	Stony broke
Income bond	Nonpayment	Recompense	Straitened
Incumbered	Note of hand	Recoupment	Stronghold
Incur a debt	Numismatic	Redeemable	Strongroom
Industrial	Obligation	Redundancy	Sum of money

Swap horses
Take a flier
Taskmaster
Tax evasion
Technician
Technocrat
The needful
Thin margin
Third World
Ticker tape
Tour of duty
Trade board
Trade cycle
Trade guild
Trade price
Trade route
Trade union
Treaty port
Typewriter
Typing pool
Underwrite
Unemployed
Upset price
Wad of notes
Wage freeze
Wage policy
Walk of life
Wall Street
Waterworks
Wealthy man
Well afford
Well-heeled
Wholesaler
Window-shop
Working day
Work to rule
Written off

11 letters:
Accountancy
Account book
Acquittance
Advertising
Agriculture
Antique shop

Appointment
Asking price
Assemby line
Association
At face value
Auction ring
Bank account
Bank balance
Bank holiday
Bank manager
Bank of issue
Barclaycard®
Bargain sale
Bear account
Bear the cost
Betting shop
Big business
Billionaire
Bill of costs
Black market
Blank cheque
Bonus scheme
Book-keeping
Bottom price
Bread winner
Brisk market
Budget price
Bull account
Businessman
Capital gain
Carbon paper
Cash account
Catallactic
Caught short
Central bank
Certificate
Chamberlain
Chancellery
Chemist shop
Chrysocracy
Circulation
Closing down
Come to terms
Commodities
Common stock

Company rule
Competition
Competitive
Comptometer
Consumption
Cool million
Co-operative
Copperworks
Corn in Egypt
Corporation
Cost-benefit
Counterfeit
Cover charge
Cum dividend
Custom house
Customs duty
Danger money
Defence bond
Demand curve
Demarcation
Deposit slip
Devaluation
Direct debit
Display case
Distributor
Dividend off
Double entry
Down payment
Drive a trade
Dutch aution
Earn a living
Economic law
Economic man
Economy size
Embarrassed
Endorsement
Established
Estate agent
Expenditure
Fabrication
Fetch a price
Filthy lucre
Fixed assets
Fixed income
Floor broker

Fluctuation
Foot the bill
Foreclosure
Free harbour
Future grain
Future price
Gingerbread
Gross income
Hard bargain
High finance
Horse market
Hypermarket
Impecunious
Indirect tax
Industrials
Inexpensive
Institution
Intercourse
Ironmongery
Joint return
Key industry
King's ransom
Lap of luxury
Legal tender
Liberty bond
Life savings
Line of goods
Liquidation
Local branch
Local office
Long account
Long service
Loose change
Machine-made
Machine shop
Made of money
Manufactory
Manufacture
Market place
Market price
Mass-produce
Merchandise
Millionaire
Minimum wage
Mint of money

Money broker
Money dealer
Money lender
Money's worth
Money to burn
Negotiation
Nest factory
Net interest
Net receipts
Nuisance tax
Numismatics
On easy terms
On good terms
On the market
Open account
Open-end bond
Out of pocket
Outstanding
Overpayment
Package deal
Paper credit
Partnership
Pay cash down
Pay on demand
Pay spot cash
Pay the piper
Piece of work
Pilot scheme
Place of work
Pocket money
Polytechnic
Possessions
Postal order
Pots of money
Poverty line
Poverty trap
Premium bond
Pretty penny
Price-fixing
Price freeze
Price spiral
Price ticket
Property tax
Proposition
Purchase tax

Put-up market
Queer Street
Quoted price
Raw material
Reserve bank
Resignation
Restriction
Retiring age
Risk capital
Rummage sale
Run into debt
Safe deposit
Sales ledger
Salesperson
Savings bank
Self-service
Sell at a loss
Sell forward
Sell futures
Sharebroker
Shareholder
Share ledger
Shopping bag
Short change
Short seller
Single entry
Sinking fund
Slot machine
Small change
Small trader
Sole emption
Speculation
Sponsorship
Spondulicks
Stagflation
Stockbroker
Stock dealer
Stockholder
Stockjobber
Stock ledger
Stock market
Stockpiling
Stocktaking
Storekeeper
Subsistence

Supermarket
Take-home pay
Take-over bid
Tattersall's
Tax assessor
Tax gatherer
Technocracy
The have-nots
Tight budget
Tight market
Time bargain
Tired market
To the tune of
Trade school
Trading post
Transaction
Travel agent
Truck system
Undercharge
Underwriter
Vendibility
Wherewithal
Working life
Workmanlike
Workmanship
Works outing
World market

12 letters:
Active market
Ad valorem tax
Amalgamation
Amortization
Amortizement
Arithmometer
Auction stand
Balance sheet
Bank examiner
Bargain offer
Bargain price
Barter system
Be in business
Bill of lading
Board meeting
Board of Trade

Bond to bearer
Bottom dollar
Bottomry bond
Branch office
Broker's agent
Brokers board
Business deal
Business life
Businesslike
Buyers' market
Buying public
Callable bond
Capital gains
Capital goods
Capital stock
Cash and carry
Cash register
Casual labour
Catallactics
Circular note
Clearing bank
Closing price
Common market
Compensation
Cook the books
Costermonger
Cost of living
Counting-room
Credit rating
Critical path
Currency note
Current price
Customs union
Denomination
Depreciation
Direct labour
Disbursement
Discount rate
Distribution
Dollar crisis
Durable goods
Early closing
Earned income
Econometrics
Economy drive

Entrepreneur
Exchange rate
Exhaust price
Extend credit
Extravagance
Fair exchange
Fill an office
First refusal
Fiscal policy
Fixed capital
Floating debt
Folding money
Foreign trade
Gate receipts
General store
Get rich quick
Going concern
Gold standard
Goods for sale
Great expense
Haberdashery
Hard currency
High pressure
Hire purchase
Hungry market
Impulse buyer
In conference
Indebtedness
Interest rate
Internal bond
In the gazette
Joint account
Keep accounts
Labour of love
Laissez-faire
Leather goods
Line of credit
Live in clover
Lively market
Long interest
Make a bargain
Make a fortune
Make delivery
Make one's pile
Manipulation

Manufacturer
Marginal cost
Mass-produced
Mercantilism
Monetization
Money changer
Money matters
Mortgage bond
National bank
Nearest offer
Nine till five
Nominal price
Nominal value
Nouveau riche
Odd-lot dealer
Offered price
Offer for sale
Office junior
Open-end trust
Opening price
Organization
Packing house
Pay as you earn
Pay in advance
Pegged market
Peg the market
Ply one's trade
Porte-monnaie
Pressure belt
Price ceiling
Price control
Price current
Price of money
Price rigging
Productivity
Professional
Profiteering
Profit margin
Profit motive
Purse strings
Rags to riches
Rate of growth
Redeployment
Regional bank
Remuneration

Remunerative
Reserve price
Retaining fee
Retrenchment
Rigged market
Rig the market
Rising prices
Rolling stock
Rubber cheque
Sale by outcry
Sale or return
Sales gimmick
Sales manager
Salesmanship
Satisfaction
Sell on credit
Severance pay
Share company
Shareholding
Short account
Show business
Slender means
Sliding scale
State lottery
Steady market
Sterling area
Stock company
Stock dealing
Stockholding
Stock in trade
Stockjobbery
Street market
Strike action
Strike it rich
Strong market
Superannuate
Sustain a loss
Tax collector
Tax exemption
Ten-cent store
The long green
Ticker market
Trade balance
Trade mission
Trading stamp

Travel agency
Treasury bill
Treasury note
Trial balance
Trustee stock
Unemployment
Variety store
Watered stock
Welfare State
Without a bean
Working class
Working order

13 letters:
Advertisement
Asset stripper
Bank messenger
Bank of England
Bank overdraft
Bank statement
Budget account
Budget surplus
Bulls and bears
Burial society
Business hours
Cash dispenser
Cash in advance
Cash on the nail
Clearance sale
Clearing-house
Commercialism
Commercialist
Company report
Concessionary
Confetti money
Confidence man
Consumer goods
Copartnership
Cost-effective
Counting-house
Credit account
Credit balance
Credit company
Credit squeeze
Crossed cheque

Current assets
Depressed area
Discount house
Discount store
Excess profits
Eye to business
Falling prices
Filing cabinet
Financial year
Fire insurance
Free-trade area
Fringe benefit
Going for a song
Impulse buying
Incorporation
Industrialism
In Queer Street
Life assurance
Life insurance
Lombard Street
Man of business
Millionairess
Modernisation
Money no object
Multinational
Multiple store
Parkinson's Law
Payment in kind
Payment in lieu
Penalty clause
Petticoat Lane
Price increase
Private income
Private sector
Profitability
Profit and loss
Profit sharing
Protectionism
Protectionist
Public company
Purchase price
Raise the money
Rate for the job
Rates and taxes
Regular income

Sellers' market
Service charge
Small business
Small investor
Spending spree
Stock exchange
Strike breaker
Subcontractor
Tax-deductible
Trade discount
Trade unionism
Trade unionist
Trading estate
Value added tax
White elephant
Wild-cat strike

14 letters:

Accident policy
Asset stripping
Balance of trade
Bargain counter
Bill discounter
Capitalisation
Cash on delivery
Certain annuity
Clearance house
Company meeting
Concessionaire
Consumer demand
Corporation tax
Cost accountant
Cost accounting
Cost efficiency
Current account
Deposit account
Direct-debiting
Discount broker
Distressed area
Expense account
Eye for business
Family business
Finance company
Free enterprise
Free of interest

Full employment
Gnomes of Zurich
Holding company
Imprest account
Inertia selling
Letter of credit
Lighting-up time
Limited company
Lloyd's Register
Market research
Mass production
Merchant banker
Monthly payment
National income
National wealth
Ordinary shares
Overproduction
Over the counter
Penny-in-the-slot
Peppercorn rent
Peter Principle
Private company
Production line
Pyramid selling
Quality control
Rate of exchange
Rate of interest
Second-hand shop
Shopping centre
Simple interest
Superannuation
Surrender value
Tariff reformer
Three mile limit
Under the hammer
Unearned income
Vending machine
Vested interest
Visible exports
Window shopping
Working capital

15 letters:

American Express®
Bargain basement

Building society
Business as usual
Business circles
Business contact
Business manager
Business studies
Business venture
Capital gains tax
Carriage forward
Cash transaction
Closing-down sale
Commission agent
Company director
Company promoter
Complete annuity
Cottage industry
Deferred annuity
Deferred payment
Department store
Development area
Distress warrant

Dividend warrant
Do a roaring trade
Electricity bill
Endowment policy
Entrepreneurial
Exchange control
Family allowance
Floating capital
Foreign exchange
Franking machine
Friendly society
Golden handshake
Income-tax demand
Income-tax rebate
Income-tax relief
Income-tax return
Insurance broker
Insurance policy
Investment trust
Invisible import
Labour-intensive

Lightning strike
Marine insurance
Money for old rope
National Savings
No-claim discount
Non-profit-making
Preference stock
Public ownership
Purchasing power
Registration fee
Regular customer
Reserve currency
Rock-bottom price
Service industry
Settle an account
Sleeping partner
Supply and demand
Suspense account
Under the counter
Unemployment pay
World of commerce

Trees

2 letters:	Sal	Cola	Mowa
Bo	Tea	Cork	Nipa
Ti	Til	Dali	Ombu
	Ule	Deal	Palm
3 letters:	Wax	Dhak	Pear
Ash	Yew	Dika	Pine
Asp		Dita	Plum
Bay	**4 letters:**	Eugh	Poon
Bel	Acer	Gean	Rata
Ben	Akee	Hule	Rhus
Box	Aloe	Ilex	Rimu
Elm	Amla	Jack	Shea
Fig	Arar	Kaki	Silk
Fir	Atap	Kiri	Sloe
Gum	Bael	Kola	Sorb
Ita	Bhel	Lime	Tawa
Jak	Bito	Lind	Teak
Koa	Boab	Lote	Teil
Mot	Bosk	Mako	Titi
Nim	Cade	Ming	Toon
Oak	Coco	Mott	Tung

Tutu
Upas
Yang

5 letters:
Abele
Abies
Ackee
Afara
Alamo
Alder
Alnus
Anona
Apple
Areca
Argan
Aspen
Balsa
Beech
Belah
Belar
Birch
Bodhi
Boree
Bunya
Butea
Cacao
Carap
Carob
Cedar
Ceiba
China
Cocoa
Cocus
Coral
Ebony
Elder
Fagus
Fever
Flame
Guava
Hakea
Hazel
Hevea
Holly

Iroko
Jambu
Jarul
Judas
Karri
Kauri
Khaya
Kiaat
Kokum
Larch
Lemon
Lilac
Lotus
Mahoe
Mahua
Mahwa
Mamey
Mango
Maple
Marri
Matai
Melia
Motte
Mugga
Mulga
Mvule
Myall
Ngaio
Nyssa
Olive
Opepe
Osier
Palas
Palay
Panax
Papaw
Peach
Pecan
Pinon
Pipal
Pipul
Plane
Quina
Ramin
Roble

Rowan
Sabal
Saman
Sassy
Scrog
Silva
Smoke
Sumac
Taxus
Thorn
Thuja
Thuya
Tilia
Tsuga
Tuart
Tulip
Vitex
Wahoo
Wilga
Witch
Xylem
Yacca
Yucca
Yulan
Zaman
Zamia

6 letters:
Abroma
Acacia
Alerce
Almond
Angico
Annona
Antiar
Arbute
Arolla
Balsam
Banana
Banyan
Baobab
Bilian
Billar
Bombax
Bonsai

Bo-tree
Bottle
Brazil
Buriti
Cadaga
Cadagi
Carapa
Carica
Cashew
Cassia
Cembra
Cerris
Chaste
Chenar
Cherry
Chinar
Citron
Citrus
Coffee
Cordon
Cornel
Cornus
Deodar
Diana's
Dragon
Durian
Durion
Emblic
Eumong
Eumung
Feijoa
Fustet
Fustic
Gallus
Garjan
Gidgee
Gidjee
Gingko
Ginkgo
Glinap
Gnetum
Gopher
Guango
Gurjun
Gympie

Illipe	Quince	Arbutus	Kumquat
Illipi	Raffia	Avodire	Lacquer
Jarool	Red-bud	Bebeeru	Lagetto
Jarrah	Ricker	Bilimbi	Lentisk
Joshua	Roucou	Bilsted	Logwood
Jujube	Rubber	Bubinga	Lumbang
Jupati	Sabicu	Buck-eye	Madrono
Kamala	Sallow	Bursera	Mahaleb
Kamela	Samaan	Cabbage	Manjack
Kanuka	Sapele	Cajeput	Marasca
Karaka	Sapium	Cajuput	Margosa
Karite	Sapota	Calamus	Mazzard
Kentia	Saxaul	Camphor	Meranti
Kowhai	She-oak	Camwood	Mesquit
Laurel	Sinder	Canella	Moringa
Lebbek	Sissoo	Carbean	Morrell
Linden	Souari	Carbeen	Pereira
Locust	Spruce	Catalpa	Pimento
Longan	Stemma	Cedrela	Platane
Loquat	Styrax	Champac	Pollard
Lucuma	Sumach	Champak	Populus
Macoya	Sunder	Chayote	Quassia
Mallee	Sundra	Coconut	Quicken
Manuka	Sundri	Conifer	Quillai
Mastic	Tamanu	Coquito	Quinain
Mimosa	Tewart	Cork oak	Radiata
Mopane	Titoki	Corylus	Rampike
Mopani	Tooart	Corypha	Redwood
Myrtle	Totara	Cumquat	Rock elm
Nutmeg	Tupelo	Cypress	Saksaul
Obeche	Waboom	Dagwood	Sandbox
Orange	Walnut	Dogwood	Saouari
Padauk	Wandoo	Dryades	Sapling
Padouk	Wattle	Durmast	Sausage
Pagoda	Wicken	Geebung	Sequoia
Papaya	Willow	Genipap	Seringa
Pawpaw	Witgat	Gluinap	Service
Peepul	Yarran	Grey gum	Shittah
Pepper	Zamang	Hemlock	Snow gum
Platan		Hickory	Sourgum
Pomelo	**7 letters:**	Holm-oak	Soursop
Poplar	Ailanto	Iron gum	Spindle
Popple	Amboina	Jipyapa	Sundari
Protea	Apricot	Juniper	Tea-tree
Puriri	Araroba	Karbeen	Varnish

Wallaba
Wirilda
Witchen
Wych-elm
Xylopia
Zelkova

8 letters:
Aguacate
Algaroba
Aquillia
Bangalay
Bangalow
Banyalla
Basswood
Beefwood
Benjamin
Berrigan
Black boy
Black oak
Blimbing
Bountree
Bourtree
Breadnut
Brigalow
Bulwaddy
Calabash
Chestnut
Cinchona
Cinnamon
Cocoplum
Coolabah
Coolibah
Corkwood
Date palm
Dendroid
Dracaena
Espalier
Eucalypt
Flittern
Fraxinus
Garcinia
Ghost gum
Gnetales
Guaiacum

Hagberry
Hawthorn
Hoop pine
Hornbeam
Huon pine
Igdrasil
Ironbark
Ironwood
Jelutong
Kingwood
Laburnum
Lacebark
Lecythis
Loblolly
Magnolia
Mahogany
Makomako
Mangrove
Manna-ash
Mesquite
Mulberry
Ocotillo
Oiticica
Oleaceae
Oleaster
Palmetto
Pichurim
Pinaster
Pyinkado
Quandang
Quandong
Quantong
Quillaia
Quillaja
Quondong
Raintree
Rambutan
Rangiora
Rewa-rewa
Rivergum
Rosewood
Sago-palm
Sandarac
Santalum
Sapindus

Sapucaia
Scots fir
Sea grape
Silky oak
Simaruba
Soapbark
Sourwood
Stinging
Sugar gum
Sweet gum
Sweetsop
Sycamine
Sycamore
Sycomore
Tamarack
Tamarind
Tamarisk
Taxodium
Umbrella
White ash
Whitegum
Witch elm
Ygdrasil

9 letters:
Agila-wood
Ailantous
Albespine
Angophora
Azedarach
Bauple nut
Bilimbing
Bimble box
Bitternut
Black bean
Blackbutt
Black pine
Blackwood
Bloodwood
Boobialla
Bulletrie
Bullwaddy
Bully-tree
Bulwaddee
Burrawang

Burrawary
Butternut
Caliatour
Caliature
Candlenut
Carambola
Casuarina
Cherimoya
Chile pine
Chincapin
Chinkapin
Coachwood
Coco-de-mer
Cordyline
Courbaril
Crab apple
Cupressus
Currajong
Evergreen
Firewheel
Flame-leaf
Grasstree
Greengage
Greenwood
Ground ash
Ground oak
Hackberry
Ivory palm
Jacaranda
Jackfruit
Kahikatea
Kahikatoa
Krummholz
Kurrajong
Lancewood
Lemonwood
Macadamia
Melaleuca
Mockernut
Monkeypot
Naseberry
Native oak
Nux vomica
Paloverde
Paperbark

Paulownia
Persimmon
Piccabean
Pistachio
Pitch-pine
Poinciana
Ponderosa
Pontianac
Primavera
Quebracho
Rauwolfia
Rose-apple
Sapodilla
Sassafras
Satinwood
Scots pine
Star-anise
Stinkwood
Stonepine
Tacamahac
Terebinth
Toothache
Torchwood
Wagenboom
Whitebeam
Whitewood
Yellow box
Yggdrasil
Zebrawood

10 letters:
Arbor vitae
Bitterbark
Bitterbush
Blackbully
Bulletwood
Bullwaddie
Bunya-bunya
Calamondin
Calliature
Candle-wood
Cannonball
Celery pine
Chamaerops
Chaulmugra

Cheesewood
Chinaberry
Chinquapin
Cottonwood
Cowrie-pine
Douglas fir
Eucalyptus
Fiddlewood
Flamboyant
Flindersia
Flooded gum
Frangipani
Grapefruit
Green-heart
Hackmatack
Ilang-ilang
Jaboticaba
Jippi-jappa
Kentia palm
Letter-wood
Lilli pilli
Lilly pilly
Macrocarpa
Manchineel
Mangabeira
Mangosteen
Marblewood
Mudgerabah
Palisander
Paper birch
Pohutukawa
Prickly ash
Quercitron
Ribbonwood
Sandalwood
Sappanwood
Schefflera
Silverbell
Sneezewood
Spotted gum
Strawberry
Tallowwood
Turpentine
Witch-hazel
Witgatboom

Woollybutt
Yellowwood
Ylang-ylang

11 letters:
Appleringie
Black wattle
Blanket-leaf
Cabbage-palm
Chaulmoogra
Chokecherry
Cryptomeria
Dipterocarp
Eriodendron
Flamboyante
Fothergilla
Gutta-percha
Leatherwood
Lignum vitae
Liquidambar
Loblolly bay
Maceranduba
Mountain ash
Osage orange
Pomegranate
Purpleheart
Pussy willow
Radiata pine
River red gum
Scribbly gum
Shittimwood
Silver birch
Sitka spruce
Stringy-bark

12 letters:
Bangalow palm
Golden wattle
Gympie nettle
Hercules' club
Insignis pine
Liriodendron
Mammee-sapota
Masseranduba
Monkey puzzle

Monterey pine
Washingtonia

13 letters:
Camphor laurel
Celery-top pine
Horse chestnut
Moreton Bay ash
Moreton Bay fig
Paper-mulberry
Peppermint gum
Queensland nut

Weeping willow

14 letters:
Antarctic beech
Bunya-bunya pine
Cedar of Lebanon
Illawarra flame
Stinking wattle

15 letters:
Bastard mahogany
Cabbage tree palm

16 letters:
Tasmanian blue gum

17 letters:
Bat's wing coral-tree
Norfolk Island pine

18 letters:
Moreton Bay chestnut

Trousers and shorts

5 letters:
Cords
Jeans
Levis®
Loons
Slops
Trews

6 letters:
Breeks
Capris
Chinos
Denims
Flares
Slacks
Trouse

7 letters:
Combats
Joggers
Kachera
Pyjamas
Rammies
Shalwar

8 letters:
Bloomers
Breeches
Britches
Culottes

Flannels
Hipsters
Hot pants
Jodhpurs
Knickers
Leggings
Overalls
Ski pants

9 letters:
Buckskins
Churidars
Corduroys
Dungarees
Loon pants
Plus fours
Trunk hose
Wranglers®

10 letters:
Capri pants
Cargo pants
Drainpipes
Hip-huggers
Lederhosen
Oxford bags
Pantaloons
Salopettes
Stovepipes

11 letters:
Bell-bottoms

12 letters:
Galligaskins
Gallygaskins
Palazzo pants
Pedal pushers
Smallclothes

13 letters:
Bermuda shorts
Cycling shorts
Spatterdashes
Toreador pants

14 letters:
Indescribables
Knickerbockers
Riding breeches
Swimming trunks

15 letters:
Jogging trousers

17 letters:
Sweat-suit trousers
Tracksuit trousers

Tumours

3 letters:
Wen
Yaw

4 letters:
Crab
Mole
Wart

5 letters:
Grape
Gumma
Myoma
Talpa
Wilm's

6 letters:
Anbury
Cancer
Epulis
Glioma
Lipoma
Myxoma
Struma

7 letters:
Adenoma
Angioma
Dermoid
Fibroid
Fibroma
Myeloma

Neuroma
Osteoma
Polypus
Sarcoma
Thymoma

8 letters:
Crab-yaws
Ganglion
Hepatoma
Lymphoma
Melanoma
Seminoma
Steatoma
Teratoma
Windgall
Xanthoma

9 letters:
Carcinoid
Carcinoma
Chondroma
Condyloma
Encanthis
Exostosis
Granuloma
Haematoma
Papilloma

10 letters:
Meningioma

11 letters:
Astrocytoma
Encephaloma
Gioblastoma
Haemangioma
Liposarcoma
Oncogenesis
Rous sarcoma

12 letters:
Angiosarcoma
Endothelioma
Fibrosarcoma
Mesothelioma
Neurofibroma
Osteosarcoma

13 letters:
Neuroblastoma
Osteoclastoma

14 letters:
Carcinosarcoma
Retinoblastoma

15 letters:
Burkitt lymphoma
Medullablastoma
Teratocarcinoma

16 letters:
Burkitt's lymphoma

Typefaces

3 letters:
Gem

4 letters:
Pica
Quad
Ruby

5 letters:
Agate
Arial
Canon
Elite
Pearl
Roman
Ronde

Serif
Times

6 letters:
Aldine
Caslon
Cicero
Futura

Gothic
Minion
Primer
Tahoma

7 letters:
Braille
Brevier
Calibri
Cambria
Courier
Elzevir
Emerald
Fraktur
Old-face
Paragon

Plantin
Quadrat
Univers
Verdana

8 letters:
Bold face
Egyptian
Frutiger
Garamond
Motorway
Old style
Sanserif
Semibold

9 letters:
Bourgeois
Brilliant
Clarendon
Columbian
Non-pareil

10 letters:
Longprimer

11 letters:
Baskerville
Black-letter
Great primer

Uu

Underwear

3 letters:
Bra

4 letters:
Body
Vest

5 letters:
Pants
Shift
Teddy

6 letters:
Basque
Boxers
Briefs
Bustle
Corset
Garter
Girdle
Kaccha
Shorts
Trunks
T-shirt

7 letters:
Drawers
G-string
Pannier
Panties

Singlet
Stammel
Step-ins
Y-fronts

8 letters:
Balmoral
Bloomers
Broekies
Camisole
Corselet
Half-slip
Knickers
Lingerie
Thermals

9 letters:
Brassiere
Crinoline
Jockstrap
Long johns
Petticoat
Suspender
Undervest
Union suit
Waist-slip

10 letters:
Bodyshaper
Chemisette

Garter belt
String vest
Underpants
Undershirt
Underskirt

11 letters:
Boxer shorts
Panty girdle
Tallit katan
Undershorts

12 letters:
Body stocking
Camiknickers
Combinations
Underdrawers

13 letters:
Liberty bodice
Suspender belt

14 letters:
French knickers

15 letters:
Athletic support

17 letters:
Foundation garment

Units

1 letter:
K

2 letters:
SI

3 letters:
Amp

Bar
Bel
Bit
Erg
Gal
GeV
Lux
Mho
Mil
Mol
Nit
Ohm
Rad
Rem
Rep
Tod
Tog

4 letters:
Baud
Byte
Dyne
Foot
Gill
Gram
Gray
Hour
Inch
Mile
Mole
Octa
Okta
Phot
Pint
Slug
Sone
Torr
Volt
Watt
Yard

5 letters:
Cable
Chain

Crith
Cusec
Daraf
Darcy
Debye
Ephah
Farad
Fermi
Gauss
Henry
Hertz
Joule
Litre
Lumen
Metre
Neper
Nepit
Ounce
Pixel
Pound
Quart
Remen
Sabin
Stilb
Stoke
Stone
Tesla
Therm
Voxel
Weber
Yrneh

6 letters:
Ampere
Dalton
Degree
Denier
Dobson
Emdash
Fathom
Gallon
Jansky
Kelvin
Kilerg
League

Lexeme
Micron
Morgan
Morgen
Newton
Pascal
Probit
Radian
Second
Sememe
Stokes

7 letters:
Candela
Congius
Coulomb
Dioptre
Energid
Exabyte
Fresnel
Furlong
Gigabit
Gilbert
Lambert
Man-hour
Maxwell
Megaton
Micella
Micelle
Milline
Minute
Nephron
Oersted
Phoneme
Poundal
Röntgen
Semeion
Siemens
Sievert
Syntagm
Tagmeme

8 letters:
Abampere
Angstrom

Chaldron
Electron
Glosseme
Kilowatt
Magneton
Megabyte
Megaflop
Megawatt
Morpheme
Petabyte
Roentgen
Syntagma
Terabyte
Therblig

9 letters:
Becquerel

Degree-day
Kilderkin
Kilometre
Light-year
Megahertz
Microinch
Microvolt
Steradian
Yottabyte
Zettabyte

10 letters:
Centimetre
Centipoise
Dessiatine
Microcurie
Millilitre

Millimetre
Nanosecond
Person-hour
Picosecond
Ploughgate
Rutherford

11 letters:
Centimorgan
Pennyweight

13 letters:
Hundredweight

Vv

Vegetables

3 letters:
Cos
Oca
Pea
Udo
Yam

4 letters:
Beet
Cole
Corn
Guar
Kail
Kale
Leek
Neep
Okra
Okro
Puha
Sium
Spud
Taro

5 letters:
Ackee
Beans
Chard
Chive
Choko
Chufa
Cress
Ingan
Mooli
Navew
Onion

Orach
Pease
Puwha
Savoy
Swede
Syboe

6 letters:
Adjigo
Allium
Batata
Bhindi
Calalu
Carrot
Celery
Daikon
Endive
Fennel
Frisee
Greens
Jicama
Kumara
Kumera
Lablab
Mangel
Marrow
Mizuna
Orache
Pepper
Potato
Pratie
Quinoa
Radish
Rapini
Rocket

Sorrel
Sprout
Squash
Tomato
Turnip
Warran

7 letters:
Arugula
Bok choy
Brinjal
Cabbage
Calaloo
Cardoon
Chayote
Chicory
Cocoyam
Collard
Gherkin
Lettuce
Mangold
Pak-choi
Parsnip
Pimento
Pumpkin
Rauriki
Romaine
Salsify
Shallot
Skirret
Spinach
Spinage
Sprouts
Succory

8 letters:
Baby corn
Beetroot
Brassica
Broccoli
Capsicum
Celeriac
Cucumber
Eggplant
Escarole
Eschalot
Hastings
Kohlrabi
Leaf-beet
Pimiento
Rutabaga
Samphire
Scallion
Zucchini

9 letters:
Artichoke
Asparagus
Aubergine
Broad bean
Calabrese
Corn salad
Courgette
Finocchio

See also:
➤ **Potatoes**

Mangetout
Radicchio
Rocambole
Succotash
Sweet corn
Tonka-bean
Turnip-top

10 letters:
Alexanders
Bean sprout
Beef tomato
Bell pepper
Cos lettuce
Lollo rosso
Salad onion
Scorzonera
Silver beet
Swiss chard

11 letters:
Cauliflower
Chinese leaf
Horseradish
Lady's finger
Oyster plant
Spinach-beet
Spring onion
Sweet potato

12 letters:
Cherry tomato
Corn on the cob
Lamb's lettuce
Mangel-wurzel
Marrow squash
Savoy cabbage
Spanish onion
Spring greens

13 letters:
Pe-tsai cabbage

14 letters:
Brussels sprout
Chinese cabbage
Globe artichoke
Iceberg lettuce

15 letters:
Vegetable marrow

16 letters:
Butternut pumpkin

18 letters:
Jerusalem artichoke

Vehicles

3 letters:
ATV
Bus
Cab
Car
Hog
JCB®
LEM
SUV

Ute
Van

4 letters:
Bike
Boat
Cart
Dray
Jeep®

Kago
Kart
Limo
Luge
MIRV
Pram
Quad
Rego
Scow

Shay
Ship
Sled
Tank
Taxi
Tram
Trap

5 letters:
Artic
Brake
Buggy
Coach
Coupé
Crate
Cycle
Float
Hatch
Lorry
Moped
Ratha
Reggo
Soyuz
Sulky
Tip-up
Tonga
Towie
Train
Truck
Turbo
Vespa
Wagon
Yacht

6 letters:
Barrow
Boxcar
Camion
Camper
Chaise
Dennet
Fiacre
Gharri
Gharry
Go-cart
Go-kart
Hansom
Hearse
Jet ski
Jingle
Jinker
Jitney
Koneke

Launch
Limber
Litter
Maglev
Pick-up
Put-put
Rocket
Samlor
Skibob
Skidoo®
Sledge
Sleigh
Sno-Cat®
Spider
Surrey
Tandem
Tanker
Telega
Tourer
Tricar
Troika
Tuk tuk
Vahana
Waggon

7 letters:
Air taxi
Amtrack
Bicycle
Caravan
Chariot
Dog-cart
Gritter
Growler
Jeepney
Kibitka
Komatik
Minibus
Minicab
Minivan
Norimon
Omnibus
Pedicab
Phaeton
Postbus

Railcar
Ricksha
Scooter
Sidecar
Tempera
Tipcart
Tracked
Tractor
Trailer
Tramcar
Travois
Trishaw
Trolley
Tumbrel
Tumbril
Utility
Volante
Wildcat

8 letters:
Aircraft
Brancard
Carriage
Carry-all
Curricle
Dustcart
Electric
Motorbus
Motorcar
Panda car
Rickshaw
Runabout
Scout car
Sport ute
Stanhope
Steam-car
Tarantas
Toboggan
Tow truck
Tricycle
Trimotor
Unicycle

9 letters:
Ambulance

Autocycle
Battlebus
Bulldozer
Cabriolet
Camper van
Charabanc
Dormobile®
Dump truck
Dune buggy
Estate car
Gladstone
Half-track
Hansom cab
Hatchback
Hydrofoil
Jaunty car
Jinriksha
Landaulet
Land Rover
Land yacht
Limousine
Low-loader
Milk float
Motorbike
Police car
Racing car
Road train
Sand-yacht
Spaceship
Sports car
Streetcar
Tarantass
Trail bike
Tumble-car
Wagonette
Winnebago®

10 letters:
All-terrain
Amphibious
Black Maria
Earthmover
Fire engine
Gas-guzzler
Hovercraft

Jinricksha
Jinrikisha
Juggernaut
Locomotive
Motorcycle
Panel truck
Post chaise
Roadroller
Shandrydan
Skateboard
Snowmobile
Snow plough
Spacecraft
Space probe
Stagecoach
Tank engine
Touring car
Trolleybus
Trolley car
Tumble-cart
Two-wheeler
Velocipede
Velomobile
Waggonette

11 letters:
Articulated
Caterpillar®
Delivery van
Dumper-truck
Jaunting car
Jinrickshaw
Landaulette
Light engine
Semitrailer
Steamroller
Tipper lorry
Tipper truck
Wheelbarrow

12 letters:
Autorickshaw
Breakdown van
Double-decker
Garbage truck
Motorbicycle
Motor caravan
Motor scooter
Motor vehicle

Pantechnicon
Perambulator
Single-decker
Space capsule
Space shuttle
Station wagon
Three-wheeler
Troop carrier
Utility truck

13 letters:
Fork-lift truck
Paddock-basher
Penny-farthing
People carrier

14 letters:
Conestoga wagon
Off-road vehicle
Traction engine

16 letters:
Articulated lorry
Combine harvester

See also:
➤ **Aircraft** ➤ **Bicycles** ➤ **Boats and ships** ➤ **Carriages and carts** ➤ **Cars** ➤ **Locomotives**

Veins

4 letters:	**7 letters:**	**8 letters:**	Sectorial
Spur	Basilic	Terminal	
	Femoral	Vena cava	**10 letters:**
6 letters:	Jugular		Subclavian
Portal	Saphena	**9 letters:**	
Radius		Arteriole	**11 letters:**
		Pulmonary	Subscapular

Verse forms

3 letters:	**4 letters:**	Song	**5 letters:**
Lay	Epic		Ditty
Ode	Sijo		Elegy

Epode
Haiku
Idyll
Lyric
Rhyme
Tanka
Verse

6 letters:
Ballad
Epopee
Ghazal
Monody
Senary
Sonnet
Tenson
Tenzon

7 letters:
Bucolic

Couplet
Eclogue
Epigram
Georgic
Pantoum
Rondeau
Sestina
Triolet
Virelay

8 letters:
Acrostic
Cinquain
Clerihew
Jintishi
Limerick
Lipogram
Madrigal
Palinode
Pastoral

Thin poem
Verselet
Versicle

9 letters:
Free verse
Roundelay
Shape poem

10 letters:
Villanelle

12 letters:
Concrete poem
Epithalamium
Nursery rhyme
Prothalamion

15 letters:
Poulter's measure

Volcanoes

3 letters:
Apo
Aso
Puy
Usu

4 letters:
Etna
Fuji
Maui
Pelé
Taal

5 letters:
Askja
Elgon
Hekla
Kauai
Kenya
Mayon
Misti
Pelée

Teide
Teyde
Thira

6 letters:
Ararat
Asosan
Egmont
Erebus
Ischia
Katmai
Kazbek
Llaima
Merapi
Semeru
Tolima

7 letters:
Aragats
El Misti
Hornito
Huascán

Iliamna
Iwo Jima
Kilauea
Redoubt
Ruapehu
Semeroe
Tambora

8 letters:
Antisana
Cameroon
Cotopaxi
Krakatau
Krakatoa
Mauna Kea
Mauna Loa
St Helens
Taranaki
Vesuvius

9 letters:
Aniakchak

Corcovado
Haleakala
Helgafell
Huascarán
Paricutín
Pozzolana
Puzzolana
Soufrière
Stromboli
Suribachi
Tangariro

10 letters:
Chimborazo
Lassen Peak
Montserrat
Nyiragongo
Pozzuolana

Santa Maria
Tungurahua

11 letters:
Erciyas Dagi
Kilimanjaro
Mount Egmont
Mount Erebus
Mount Katmai
Mount Shasta
Nyamuragira
Olympus Mons

12 letters:
Citlaltépetl
Ixtaccihuatl
Iztaccihuatl
National Park

Popocatépetl

13 letters:
Mount Demavend
Mount Pinatubo
Mount St Helens

14 letters:
Nevado de Colima
Nevado de Toluca
Soufrière Hills
Tristan da Cunha

16 letters:
Eyjafjallajökull

17 letters:
Warrumbungle Range

Warfare terms

2 letters:
AB
GI
MP
RA
RE
RN

3 letters:
Arm
Axe
Bow
Cap
Cut
Dud
Foe
Gat
Gun
Hun
NCO
POW
RAF
Ram
Rat
Rod
Row
Sap
Spy
Sub
TNT
Tyr
Van
Vet
War

4 letters:
Ally
Ammo
Ares
Arms
Army
A-war
AWOL
Ball
Band
Barb
Bard
Bill
Bird
Bola
Bolt
Bomb
Bone
Bout
Bren
Butt
Camp
Club
Cock
Coif
Colt
Cosh
Dart
D-day
Dike
Dirk
Dove
Duck
Duel
Dump

Duty
Épée
Exon
Feud
File
Fire
Fish
Flak
Foil
Fort
Fray
Guns
Hate
Hawk
Helm
Hero
Hilt
Hold
Host
H-war
ICBM
Impi
Jack
Jamb
Jeep
Jock
Keep
Kill
Kris
Levy
Load
Lock
Mail
Mars
Mere

Mine
MIRV
Moat
Mole
Navy
Odin
Peel
Peon
Pike
Post
Rack
Rank
Rath
Riot
Rock
Rout
Rush
Shot
Slug
Spit
Spur
Stab
Tank
Tuck
Unit
WACS
Wage
Wall
Ward
WAVE
Wing
WRNS
Yomp
Zone
Zulu

5 letters:
AA gun
A-bomb
Aegis
Arena
Armed
Armet
Array
Arrow
At bay
At war
Baton
Beset
Blade
Blank
Blast
Blitz
Boche
Bolas
Brave
Broch
Buffs
Burst
Cadre
Chute
Clash
Corps
Cover
Ditch
Draft
Drive
Enemy
Feint
Fence
Field
Fight
Flail
Flank
Fleet
Foray
Fosse
Front
Fusee
Fusil
Grape

Guard
Harry
H-bomb
H-hour
Jerid
Jerry
Jihad
Jingo
Knife
Kukri
Lager
Lance
Leave
Luger
Melee
Mound
Muket
Onset
Orgue
Parry
Pavis
Plate
Poilu
Posse
Power
Provo
Rally
Range
Ranks
Rebel
Recce
Redan
Repel
Rifle
Rowel
Sally
Salvo
Scarp
Scene
Scout
Sepoy
Serve
Shaft
Shako
Shell

Shoot
Siege
Skean
Sling
Snake
Sowar
Spahi
Spear
Spike
Spray
Spurs
Squad
Staff
Steel
Stick
Stone
Storm
Sword
Targe
Tasse
Tommy
Train
Troop
Truce
U-boat
Uhlan
Visor
WAACS
WAAFS
Waddy
Woden
Wound
WRACS
Wrens

6 letters:
Abatis
Ack-ack
Action
Air arm
Air gun
Alpeen
Amazon
Ambush
Animus

Anzacs
Archer
Archie
Argosy
Armada
Armour
Askari
Assail
Attack
Barbel
Barrel
Batman
Battle
Beaver
Bellum
Big gun
Billet
Bomber
Breech
Bugler
Bullet
Bunker
Camail
Cannon
Casque
Castle
Casual
Charge
Cohort
Column
Combat
Convoy
Cordon
Corium
Creese
Cudgel
Cuisse
Curfew
Curtal
Dagger
Defeat
Defend
Detail
Donjon
Dry run

Duello
Dugout
Dumdum
Enlist
Ensign
Escarp
Escort
Exocet
Fewter
Flight
Foeman
Forage
Forces
Gabion
Galoot
Glacis
Glaive
Gorget
Greave
Gunner
Gun shy
Gurkha
Gusset
Hagbut
Hammer
Hanger
Hanjar
Harass
Heaume
Helmet
Hot war
Hussar
Impact
Impale
In arms
Inroad
Jereed
Jingal
Laager
Labrys
Lancer
Legion
Lorica
Mailed
Maquis

Marine
Mauser
Merlon
Minnie
Morion
Mortar
Muster
Muzzle
Oilcan
Outfit
Panzer
Parade
Parole
Patrol
Pavise
Pellet
Pepper
Petard
Picket
Pierce
Pistol
Pogrom
Pompom
Powder
Pow-pow
Quiver
Rafale
Rajput
Ramrod
Rapier
Rappel
Ray gun
Razzia
Rebuff
Reduit
Report
Revolt
Rioter
Rocket
Rookie
Salade
Sallet
Salute
Sangar
Sapper

Sconce
Scutum
Sentry
Set gun
Shield
Slogan
Sniper
Sortie
Sparth
Spying
Strafe
Strike
Swivel
Talion
Target
Tenail
Thrust
To arms
Tocsin
Toledo
Tom-tom
Trench
Troops
Tulwar
Turret
Vallum
Valour
Vandal
Victor
Volley
War cry
War god
Weapon
Womera
Yeoman
Zouave

7 letters:
Abattis
Advance
Air raid
Amnesty
Archery
Armoury
Arsenal

Assault
Assegai
Atom gun
Atom war
Baldric
Barrack
Barrage
Barrier
Bar shot
Basinet
Bastion
Battery
Bayonet
Bazooka
Beat off
Bellona
Big guns
Big shot
Blowgun
Boer War
Bombard
Bombing
Booster
Bravado
Bren gun
Bricole
Brigade
Buckler
Bulldog
Bulwark
Caisson
Caitiff
Calibre
Caliver
Caltrop
Canonry
Cap-a-pie
Carbine
Carcass
Carrier
Cashier
Cavalry
Chamade
Chamber
Charger

Chicken	Grapnel	Maniple	Sandbag
Citadel	Grenade	Mantlet	Seabees
Cold war	Gunboat	Marines	Section
Command	Gundeck	Martial	Self bow
Company	Gunfire	Matross	Service
Conchie	Gunlock	Megaton	Shoot at
Conquer	Gunnage	Militia	Shooter
Cordite	Gunnery	Missile	Shotgun
Corslet	Gunning	Mission	Soldier
Cossack	Gun park	Neutral	Spartan
Coupure	Gunplay	Offence	Sparthe
Courage	Gun port	On guard	Spinner
Courser	Gunroom	Open war	Sten gun
Crusade	Gunshot	Outpost	Supremo
Cudgels	Hackbut	Outwork	Tactics
Cuirass	Halberd	Paladin	Tear-gas
Curtain	Handjar	Panoply	Tenable
Curtana	Harness	Parados	Testudo
Cutlass	Hatchet	Parapet	Theatre
Dastard	Hauberk	Patriot	The fray
Defence	Heroism	Pedrero	Torpedo
Disband	Hessian	Petrary	Traitor
Distaff	Heyduck	Phalanx	Trigger
Dragoon	Hold off	Pikeman	Trooper
Draught	Holster	Pillbox	Tumbril
Dry fire	Holy war	Platoon	Uniform
Dudgeon	Hostage	Poleaxe	Veteran
Dueller	Invader	Poniard	Victory
Dungeon	Jackman	Private	Wage war
Echelon	Jambeau	Quarrel	War club
Enomoty	Jankers	Rampage	Ward off
Fall-out	Javelin	Rampart	War drum
Fend off	Jollies	Ravelin	War game
Fighter	Jump jet	Recruit	Warhead
Firearm	Knifing	Red army	Warlike
Fortify	Kremlin	Redcoat	Warlord
Fortlet	Lambast	Redoubt	Warpath
Foxhole	Lamboys	Regular	Warring
Gallant	Longbow	Repulse	Warrior
Gallery	Long Tom	Retreat	Warship
Gas bomb	Lookout	Riposte	War song
Gas mask	Lunette	Sabaoth	Weapons
Germ war	Lyddite	Sabaton	Wind gun
Gisarme	Machete	Salient	Woomera
Go to war	Make war	Samurai	Wounded

Yatagan
Yomping

8 letters:
Aceldama
Activate
Air force
Air rifle
Air-to-air
All-clear
Alliance
Ammo dump
Anabasis
Anti-mine
Arbalest
Armament
Armature
Armoured
Arms race
Arquebus
Art of war
Atom bomb
Attacker
Aventail
Ballista
Banderol
Barbette
Barbican
Barracks
Bartisan
Baselard
Battalia
Battling
Bear arms
Besieger
Betrayer
Blockade
Blowpipe
Bludgeon
Bomb rack
Bomb site
Brattice
Brickbat
Broadaxe
Browning

Buckshot
Buttress
Buzzbomb
Campaign
Casemate
Catapult
Cavalier
Chaffron
Chamfron
Champion
Chasseur
Chivalry
Civil war
Claymore
Cold feet
Commando
Conflict
Corselet
Crossbow
Cry havoc
Culverin
Cylinder
Defender
Demilune
Deserter
Destrier
Division
Doughboy
Drum call
Drumfire
Drumhead
Duellist
Dynamite
Embattle
Enfilade
Enlistee
Entrench
Envelope
Errantry
Escalade
Exercise
Falchion
Falconet
Fasthold
Fastness

Fencible
Field gun
Fighting
File fire
Fireball
Fire bomb
Firelock
Fire upon
Flotilla
Fortress
Fugleman
Furlough
Fusilier
Gambeson
Garrison
Gauntlet
Great War
Guerilla
Gunflint
Gunmetal
Gunpoint
Gunsmith
Gunstick
Gunstock
Hang fire
Heavy gun
Hedgehog
Herisson
Hill fort
Hireling
Hornwork
Howitzer
Infantry
Informer
Invading
Invasion
Ironclad
Janizary
Jazerant
Jingoism
Jump area
Killadar
Knuckles
Lancegay
Land-army

Land-mine
Langrage
Last post
Launcher
Leon mine
Lewis gun
Loophole
Magazine
Mailclad
Man-of-war
Mantelet
Marksman
Martello
Massacre
Maxim gun
Melinite
Militant
Military
Mobilize
Morrison
Muniment
Munition
Mushroom
Musketry
Nerve gas
Open fire
Ordnance
Orillion
Outguard
Overkill
Pacifist
Palisade
Palstaff
Palstave
Partisan
Password
Pauldron
Petronel
Pikehead
Poltroon
Puncheon
Quisling
Quo vadis
Recreant
Regiment

Renegade
Repulsor
Reserves
Reveille
Revolver
Ricochet
Rifleman
Risalder
Runagate
Safehold
Scabbard
Scimitar
Sentinel
Shrapnel
Side arms
Siege cap
Skean dhu
Skirmish
Soldiery
Solleret
Space gun
Spadroon
Spearman
Spontoon
Squadron
Stabbing
Stalwart
Star Wars
Stave off
Stiletto
Stockade
Strafing
Strategy
Struggle
Surprise
Surround
Take arms
Tenaille
The front
The sword
Time bomb
Tomahawk
Tommy gun
Total war
Transfix

Trenches
Turnback
Turncoat
Turntail
Up in arms
Uprising
Vambrace
Vamplate
Vanguard
Vanquish
Vendetta
War cloud
Warcraft
War dance
Warfarer
War horse
War hound
War paint
War whoop
Waterloo
Wayfarer
Weaponry
World War
Yeomanry
Zero hour

9 letters:
Accoutred
Aggressor
Air-to-ship
Ambuscade
Arch enemy
Army corps
Army issue
Army lists
Arrowhead
Artillery
Assailant
Atomic gun
Atomic war
Attacking
Attrition
Automatic
Auto-rifle
Backplate

Ballistic
Banderole
Bandolier
Bastinado
Battalion
Battleaxe
Battlecry
Beachhead
Beefeater
Beleaguer
Bellicism
Bellicose
Big Bertha
Blackjack
Bloodshed
Bomb-happy
Bombs away
Bombshell
Bombsight
Booby trap
Boomerang
Broadside
Brown Bess
Brown bill
Camouflet
Cannonade
Cannoneer
Caparison
Carronade
Carry arms
Cartouche
Cartridge
Casemated
Castellan
Cease fire
Chain mail
Chain shot
Challenge
Chamfrain
Chassepot
Cold steel
Combatant
Combative
Conqueror
Conscript

Crackshot
Cross fire
Defensive
Derringer
Desert rat
Deterrent
Detonator
Discharge
Doodlebug
Double sap
Drop a bomb
Earthwork
Embattled
Encompass
Enemy camp
Enemy fire
Escopette
Espionage
Explosive
Face guard
Fence wall
Field army
Fieldwork
Fire a shot
Firepower
Fireworks
First line
Flintlock
Flying sap
Fortalice
Fortified
Fourth arm
Free-lance
Front line
Fulgurite
Fusillade
Gas attack
Gelignite
Gladiator
Grapeshot
Grenadier
Guardsman
Guerrilla
Gun battle
Guncotton

Gunpowder
Gun turret
Habergeon
Harquebus
Headpiece
Heavy fire
Heroic act
Home Guard
Hostility
Hydrobomb
Incursion
Incursive
In defence
Ironbound
Irregular
Irruption
Janissary
Jesserant
Katabasis
Keep guard
Keep vigil
Lance-jack
Langridge
Last ditch
Legionary
Levy war on
Lie in wait
Lionheart
Logistics
Long-range
Luftwaffe
Make war on
Man-at-arms
Manoeuvre
March past
Matchlock
Mercenary
Militancy
Minefield
Minuteman
Monomachy
Munitions
Musketeer
Musketoon
Needle gun

Nose guard
Nosepiece
Offensive
Onslaught
Open order
Operation
Other side
Overthrow
Panoplied
Parachute
Peel-house
Peel-tower
Pikestaff
Prick-spur
Projector
Pugnacity
Pyroxylin
Ram rocket
Rearguard
Rebel call
Rebellion
Rerebrace
Ressalder
Rifle ball
Rocket gun
Rocket man
Roundhead
Round shot
Rowel spur
Royal Navy
Sally port
Saltpetre
Sea battle
Seat of war
Sentry box
Shellfire
Signalman
Single sap
Ski troops
Skyrocket
Sky troops
Slaughter
Slingshot
Slungshot
Small arms

Small bore
Small-shot
Smoke bomb
Soldierly
Soldier on
Sonic mine
Son of a gun
Spearhead
Spring gun
Stand fire
Stink bomb
Strategic
Subaltern
Submarine
Super bomb
Surprisal
Surrender
Swivel gun
Sword-play
Take sides
Tank corps
Target day
Task force
Tit for tat
Torpedoed
Torpedoer
Trainband
Trench gun
Troopship
Truncheon
Under arms
Under fire
Vigilante
Volunteer
Warmonger
War Office
War rocket
Watchword
White flag
Woomerang
Zumbooruk

10 letters:
Activation
Active army

Active duty
Active list
Adventurer
Aerial bomb
Aerial mine
Aggression
Aggressive
Air Command
Air service
Ambushment
Ammunition
Antagonism
Armageddon
Armed force
Armed guard
Armed truce
Armigerous
Armipotent
Arm's length
Atomic bomb
Atomic pile
Atom-rocket
Ballistics
Barbed-wire
Battle flag
Battle hymn
Battle line
Battlement
Battleship
Blitzkrieg
Blockhouse
Bold stroke
Bombardier
Bowie knife
Box barrage
Breastwork
Bridgehead
Brigandine
Broadsword
Bugle corps
Call to arms
Camel corps
Camouflage
Campaigner
Cannon ball

Cannon shot
Cantonment
Carabineer
Carry on war
Cavalryman
Coastguard
Coat of mail
Combat area
Combat team
Commandant
Contingent
Cross-staff
Cuirassier
Declare war
Defendable
Defensible
Demobilize
Detachment
Direct fire
Dragonnade
Dragoonade
Drawbridge
Drummer boy
Embankment
Encampment
Engarrison
Eprouvette
Escalation
Expedition
Faint heart
Fieldpiece
Field train
Fiery cross
Fire trench
Firing area
Flying bomb
Flying tank
Foot Guards
Foot Rifles
Gatling gun ·
Ground fire
Ground mine
Ground zero
Halberdier
Heavy-armed

Impalement
Incendiary
Investment
Jingoistic
Knighthood
Knobkerrie
Kriegspiel
Lambrequin
Lay siege to
Life Guards
Light-armed
Line of fire
Loaded cane
Long knives
Lookout man
Machine gun
Martiality
Militarism
Militarize
Militiaman
Missile man
Mob tactics
Mount guard
Mural crown
Musket shot
Mustard gas
Napalm bomb
No man's land
Nuclear war
Obsidional
Occupation
Old soldier
On the march
Operations
Other ranks
Over the top
Oyster mine
Paratroops
Percussion
Petrol bomb
Picket duty
Point blank
Portcullis
Private war
Projectile

Raking fire
Rally round
Raw recruit
Resistance
Revolution
Rifle range
Rocket bomb
Rocket fire
Rules of war
Run-through
Second line
Sentry duty
Serviceman
Shellshock
Shillelagh
Short-range
Siegecraft
Siege train
Six-shooter
Slit trench
Smallsword
Smooth bore
Spill blood
Stand guard
State of war
Strategist
Stronghold
Submachine
Sure as a gun
Sword fight
Swordstick
Sworn enemy
Take to arms
Tenderfoot
Ten-pounder
Test rocket
Touch paper
Trajectile
Trajectory
Under siege
Vanquisher
Volunteers
War goddess
Winchester

11 letters:

Air-to-ground
Anti-missile
Anti-tank gun
Area bombing
Armed combat
Armed forces
Armoured car
Auxiliaries
Barnstormer
Battle array
Battledress
Battlefield
Battle order
Battle plane
Battle royal
Beach master
Bersaglieri
Besiegement
Blockbuster
Bloody shirt
Blunderbuss
Bombardment
Bomber pilot
Bomb-release
Bow and arrow
Breastplate
British Army
British Navy
Buck private
Bulletproof
Buoyant mine
Bushwhacker
Camaraderie
Castellated
Castle guard
Caterpillar
Change sides
Combat train
Contentious
Countermine
Crack troops
Declaration
Demibastion
Depth charge

Dive-bombing
Emplacement
Enemy action
Engine of war
Enlisted man
Envelopment
Fighting man
Fire a volley
Fire tactics
Firing party
Firing squad
Firing table
First strike
Fission bomb
Flare rocket
Flying corps
Footed arrow
Footslogger
Foot soldier
Forced march
Force of arms
Friend or foe
Full harness
Full of fight
Gang warfare
Generalship
Germ warfare
Giant powder
Ground-to-air
Guerrillero
Guncarriage
Hair trigger
Hand grenade
Heavy armour
Heavy bomber
High dudgeon
Hill station
Horse Guards
Horse pistol
Hostilities
Infantrymen
Irish Guards
Iron rations
Land warfare
Light bomber

Lionhearted
Lochaber axe
Loggerheads
Look daggers
Magazine gun
Maginot line
Marine Corps
Might of arms
Military man
Mine thrower
Moral defeat
Mountain gun
Naval bomber
Naval forces
Nitre powder
Nitrocotton
Nuclear bomb
Open warfare
Pattern bomb
Peace treaty
Picket guard
Plate armour
Platoon fire
Postern gate
Powder grain
Provisional
Put to flight
Rallying cry
Rank and file
Rebel action
Reconnoitre
Recruitment
Regular army
Retro-rocket
Rolling fire
Safe-conduct
Safety catch
Scots Guards
Service call
Ship-to-shore
Shock troops
Shooting war
Shoot to kill
Shuttle raid
Signal Corps

Smell powder
Smoke screen
Sneak attack
Soldatesque
Soldierlike
Soldiership
Spent bullet
Stand at ease
Stand of arms
Step rockets
Stormtroops
Stray bullet
Subdivision
Swiss Guards
Sword in hand
Take by storm
Thin red line
Tommy Atkins
Torpedo boat
Trench knife
Trigger talk
True colours
Trusty sword
Under attack
Underground
Up and at them
Warlikeness
War of nerves
Warriorlike
War to end war
Water cannon
Wooden horse
Wooden walls

12 letters:

Acoustic mine
Anti-aircraft
Appeal to arms
Armour-plated
Army reserves
Artilleryman
Atomic cannon
Awkward squad
Banzai charge
Battering ram

Battleground
Beat a retreat
Belligerence
Breakthrough
Breechloader
Buccaneering
Bushfighting
Cannon fodder
Cannon's mouth
Civil defence
Council of war
Counter march
Court martial
Cut-and-thrust
Daggers drawn
Deadly weapon
Demi-culverin
Dumdum bullet
Dutch courage
Electron bomb
Encirclement
Engines of war
Entrenchment
Escaramouche
False colours
Field of blood
Flame-thrower
Floating mine
Flying column
Forward march
Fowling piece
Gladiatorial
Go over the top
Grand tactics
Ground forces
Guerrilla war
Guided weapon
Heavy dragoon
Home reserves
Homing rocket
Horse and foot
Horse marines
Hydrogen bomb
Lady from hell
Launching pad

Leathernecks
Light Brigade
Light dragoon
Line of action
Line of battle
Machicolated
Magnetic mine
March against
Marching song
Medical Corps
Medium bomber
Military zone
Mine detector
Mobilization
Moral courage
Moral support
Moral victory
Muzzle-loader
Naval militia
Naval reserve
Naval warfare
On the warpath
Parthian shot
Pearl Harbour
Picked troops
Pioneer corps
Plunging fire
Powder charge
Pyrotechnics
Quarterstaff
Reactivation
Religious war
Rifled cannon
Rifle grenade
Rocket attack
Second strike
Sharpshooter
Shock tactics
Shoulder a gun
Shoulder arms
Siege warfare
Signal rocket
Single combat
Smoker rocket
Standing army

Stormtrooper
Stouthearted
Sudden attack
Supply troops
Sword bayonet
Tactical unit
Take the field
Theatre of war
Tooth and nail
Trench mortar
Trigger happy
Under the flag
Vertical fire
Virus warfare
Warmongering
White feather
Who goes there
Yellow streak

13 letters:
Active service
Andrew Ferrara
Armaments race
Armed conflict
Arms and the man
Army exercises
Articles of war
Assault course
Baptism of fire
Battle cruiser
Battle honours
Battle-scarred
Bayonet charge
Beleaguerment
Bomber command
Breechloading
British Legion
Cartridge belt
Cavalry charge
Cheval-de-frise
Churchill tank
Cobelligerent
Combat fatigue
Comrade in arms
Counter-attack

Desert warfare
Disengagement
Dispatch rider
Drill sergeant
Evasive action
Exocet missile
Field hospital
Field of battle
Fighter patrol
First World War
Flammenwerfer
Flying colours
Flying officer
Force de frappe
Foreign legion
Fortification
Generalissimo
Guard of honour
Guided missile
Gunnery school
High-explosive
Lance-corporal
Light infantry
Line of defence
Listening post
Machine gunner
Messerschmitt
Military Cross
Military Medal
Mine detection
Mini-submarine
Muzzle loading
Non-resistance
Nuclear weapon
Order of battle
Order of the day
Passage of arms
Peninsular War
Pitched battle
Prisoner of war
Put to the sword
Quarter-gunner
Quartermaster
Reinforcement
Royal Air Force

Running battle
Sabre-rattling
Scorched earth
Senior service
Sergeant-major
Siegfried line
Staff-sergeant
Striking force
Sublieutenant
Sub-machine gun
Trench warfare
Two-edged sword
Unarmed combat
Victoria Cross
War department
War to the death
Wing commander
Yeoman service

14 letters:
Action stations
Airborne forces
Airborne troops
Aircraftswoman
Air vice-marshal
Ammunition dump
Army cadet force
Army manoeuvres
Barrage balloon
Battle stations
Blank cartridge
Blockade runner
Captain-general
Cavalry officer
Chevaux-de-frise
Cloak-and-dagger
Coastal battery
Coastal command
Colonel-in-chief
Colour-sergeant
Comrades in arms
Conquering hero
Demobilisation
Field ambulance
Field artillery

Fifth columnist
Fighter command
Fight to a finish
Flag-lieutenant
Freedom fighter
Guerrilla chief
Guerrilla force
Heavy artillery
Horse artillery
Incendiary bomb
Liaison officer
Light artillery
Marching orders
Militarisation
Military police
Military tattoo
Muzzle velocity
Non-operational
Nuclear warfare
Nuclear warhead
Operations room
Orderly officer
Ordinary seaman
Pincer movement
Powder magazine
Pyrrhic victory
Reconnaissance
Regimental band

Royal Artillery
Royal Engineers
Royal Fusiliers
Royal Tank Corps
Squadron-leader
Street fighting
Supreme command
Unknown soldier
Unknown warrior
Urban guerrilla
Warrant officer
Wars of the Roses
Winter quarters

15 letters:
Adjutant general
Air chief marshal
Aircraft carrier
Anderson shelter
Armed to the teeth
Armoured cruiser
Brigade of Guards
Chemical warfare
Displaced person
First lieutenant
Gentleman-at-arms
Grenadier Guards
Light machine-gun

Military mission
Military service
Molotov cocktail
Morrison shelter
Mulberry harbour
National defence
National service
Naval engagement
Naval operations
Non-commissioned
Observation post
Officer of the day
On active service
Orderly corporal
Orderly sergeant
Parachute troops
Rearguard action
Recruiting drive
Regimental march
Second-in-command
Spoils of victory
Sword-and-buckler
Telescopic sight
Territorial Army

17 letters:
Up guards and at them

Waterfalls

5 letters:
Angel
Pilao
Tysse

6 letters:
Iguaçú
Kahiwa
Mardel
Ormeli
Ribbon
Tugela

7 letters:
Mtarazi
Niagara
Roraima

8 letters:
Cuquenan
Itatinga
Kaieteur
Takakkaw
Victoria
Yosemite

9 letters:
Churchill

10 letters:
Cleve-Garth
Sutherland

11 letters:
Montmorency
Yellowstone

13 letters:
Vestre Mardola

Water sports

6 letters:
Diving
Rowing

7 letters:
Sailing
Surfing

8 letters:
Canoeing
Swimming
Yachting

9 letters:
Canoe polo
Water polo

10 letters:
Skin diving

11 letters:
Aquabobbing
Parasailing
Water-skiing
Windsurfing

12 letters:
Powerboating

15 letters:
Powerboat racing

20 letters:
Synchronized swimming

Weapons

2 letters:
V1

3 letters:
Dag
Gad
Gun

4 letters:
Bill
Bolo
Bomb
Club
Cosh
Dart
Gade
Gaid
Kris
Mace®
Nuke
Spat
Sten

5 letters:
Arrow
Baton
Estoc
Flail

Maxim
Orgue
Pilum
Rifle
Sabre
Saker
Sling
Sting
Sword
Taser®
Vouge

6 letters:
Airgun
Binary
Cestus
Cohorn
Cudgel
Dagger
Gingal
Glaive
Jingal
Mauser®
Mortar
Musket
Napalm
Onager
Pistol

Sparke
Sparth
Sumpit
Taiaha
Tomboc
Voulge

7 letters:
Arblast
Assegai
Ataghan
Bayonet
Bazooka
Bondook
Caliver
Caltrap
Caltrop
Carbine
Coehorn
Cutlass
Dragoon
Enfield
Fougade
Gingall
Gisarme
Grenade
Halberd
Halbert

Harpoon
Javelin
Longbow
Machete
Matchet
Quarrel
Sandbag
Shotgun
Sticker
Swatter
Torpedo
Trident

8 letters:
Arbalest
Armalite®
Arquebus
Ballista
Blowpipe
Bludgeon
Calthrop
Catapult
Crossbow
Culverin
Death ray
Elf-arrow
Fougasse
Howitzer
Mangonel
Nunchaku
Partisan
Petronel

Repeater
Revolver
Shuriken
Skean-dhu
Skene-dhu
Spontoon
Stiletto
Stinkpot
Whirl-bat
Whorl-bat

9 letters:
Arquebuse
Backsword
Battleaxe
Derringer
Doodlebug
Excalibur
Fléchette
Flintlock
Forty-five
Grapeshot
Greek fire
Harquebus
Poison gas
Sarbacane
Slingshot
Slungshot
Trebuchet
Trebucket
Truncheon

10 letters:
Broadsword
Mustard gas

11 letters:
Germ warfare
Morgenstern
Singlestick
Snickersnee

12 letters:
Flame-thrower
Quarterstaff
Rifle grenade

13 letters:
Knuckle-duster
Life-preserver
Manrikigusari

14 letters:
Nunchaku sticks

15 letters:
Chemical warfare

17 letters:
Biological warfare

22 letters:
Bacteriological warfare

Weather

WEATHER DESCRIPTIONS

3 letters:
Dry
Hot
Icy
Raw
Wet

4 letters:
Cold

Dull
Fine
Foul
Hazy
Mild

5 letters:
Balmy
Bland

Clear
Close
Dirty
Foggy
Fresh
Humid
Misty
Muggy
Nippy

Parky
Rainy
Snowy
Sunny
Windy

Filthy
Sticky
Stormy
Sultry
Wintry

Freezing
Overcast
Thundery
Tropical

6 letters:
Arctic
Baking
Breezy
Clammy
Cloudy
Dreich

7 letters:
Clement
Drizzly
Showery

8 letters:
Blustery

9 letters:
Inclement
Perishing
Scorching

10 letters:
Blistering

WEATHER PHENOMENA

3 letters:
Fog
Ice

4 letters:
Gale
Gust
Haar
Hail
Mist
Rain
Snow
Thaw
Wind

5 letters:
Cloud
Sleet
Smirr
Storm

6 letters:
Breeze
Freeze
Shower
Squall
Zephyr

7 letters:
Cyclone
Drizzle
Tempest
Thunder
Tornado
Tsunami
Typhoon

8 letters:
Acid rain
Cold snap
Heatwave
Pressure
Sunshine

9 letters:
Dust devil
Dust storm
Hurricane
Lightning
Peasouper
Sandstorm
Tidal wave
Whirlwind

10 letters:
Waterspout
Willy-willy

13 letters:
Ball lightning
Precipitation

14 letters:
Sheet lightning

METEOROLOGICAL TERMS

4 letters:
Scud

5 letters:
Front
Ridge

Virga

6 letters:
Isobar
Trough

7 letters:
Cyclone
Lee wave
Thermal

9 letters:
Cold front
Isallobar
Warm front

10 letters:
Depression
Heat-island

11 letters:
Anticyclone

13 letters:
Occluded front
Synoptic chart

GATHERERS OF WEATHER DATA

9 letters:
Dropsonde
Met. Office

10 letters:
Radiosonde
Weatherman

11 letters:
Weather ship

12 letters:
Meteorograph
Pilot balloon
Weatherwoman

14 letters:
Weather station

20 letters:
Meteorological Office

WEATHER MEASURING INSTRUMENTS

Instrument	Phenomenon measured
Anemometer	Wind velocity
Anemoscope	Wind direction
Atmometer	Rate of water evaporation into atmosphere
Barograph	Atmospheric pressure
Barometer	Atmospheric pressure
Baroscope	Atmospheric pressure
Hygrometer	Humidity
Maximum-minimum thermometer	Temperature variation
Nephoscope	Cloud velocity, altitude, and direction of movement
Psychrometer	Humidity
Rain gauge	Rainfall and snowfall
Rawinsonde	Atmospheric wind velocity
Stevenson's screen	Temperature
Sunshine recorder	Hours of sunshine
Thermometer	Temperature
Weathercock	Wind direction
Weather vane	Wind direction
Wet-and-dry-bulb thermometer	Humidity
Wind gauge	Wind velocity
Wind tee	Wind direction

See also:
➤ **Atmosphere, layers of**   ➤ **Clouds**   ➤ **Winds**

Weeds

3 letters:
Ers

4 letters:
Alga

Dock
Nard

Ragi
Sudd
Tare
Tine
Ulva
Yarr

5 letters:
Couch
Daisy
Dulse
Lemna
Reate
Runch
Tansy
Vetch

6 letters:
Blinks
Clover
Cockle
Dallop
Darnel
Dollop
Elodea
Fat hen
Fucoid
Indian
Joe-pye
Knawel
Nettle
Nostoc

Oxygen
Sorrel
Spurge
Twitch
Widow's
Winnow

7 letters:
Allseed
Burdock
Femitar
Fenitar
Helodea
Mayweed
Ragwort
Ruderal
Senecio
Spurrey
Thistle

8 letters:
Arenaria
Bedstraw
Bell-bind
Charlock
Fumitory
Knapweed
Matfelon
Pilewort
Piri-piri
Plantain
Purslane

Sargasso

9 letters:
Adderwort
Anacharis
Chickweed
Chlorella
Coltsfoot
Groundsel
Knot-grass
Mare's-tail
Pearlwort
Sun-spurge
Tormentil
Wartcress

10 letters:
Carpetweed
Corncockle
Nipplewort
Rest-harrow
Sagittaria

11 letters:
Potamogeton
Swine's-cress
Ulotrichale

Weights and measures

IMPERIAL SYSTEM

Linear	**Square**	**Weight**
Mile	Square mile	Ton
Furlong	Acre	Hundredweight
Rod	Square rod	Stone
Yard	Square yard	Pound
Foot	Square foot	Ounce
Inch	Square inch	-
Mil	-	-

Land	**Volume**	**Liquid volume**
Square mile	Cubic yard	Gallon
Acre	Cubic foot	Quart
Square rod	Cubic inch	Pint
Square yard	-	Fluid ounce

METRIC SYSTEM

Linear	**Square**	**Weight**
Kilometre	Square kilometre	Tonne
Metre	Square metre	Kilogram
Centimetre	Square centimetre	Gram
Millimetre	Square millimetre	-

Land	**Volume**	**Liquid volume**
Square kilometre	Cubic metre	Litre
Hectare	Cubic decimetre	Millilitre
Are	Cubic centimetre	-
-	Cubic millimetre	-

Whales and dolphins

4 letters:
Orca

6 letters:
Beluga
Dorado

7 letters:
Bowhead
Grampus
Narwhal
Rorqual
Ziphius

8 letters:
Bay whale
Cachalot

Greyback
Porpoise
Sei whale

9 letters:
Blackfish
Blue whale
Grey whale

10 letters:
Black whale
Minke whale
Pilot whale
Right whale
Sperm whale
White whale

11 letters:
Baleen whale
Killer whale

12 letters:
Toothed whale

13 letters:
Humpback whale
Sulphur-bottom

14 letters:
Greenland whale
Whalebone whale

17 letters:
Bottlenose dolphin

Windows

3 letters:
Bay
Bow

4 letters:
Rose
Sash

5 letters:
Gable
Jesse
Judas

Ogive
Oriel
Ox-eye
Storm

6 letters:
Dormer
French
Garret
Lancet
Monial
Oculus
Rosace
Wicket

7 letters:
Compass
Guichet
Lattice
Lucarne
Lunette
Luthern
Mullion

Picture
Transom
Trellis
Ventana
Weather
Windock
Windore
Winnock

8 letters:
Casement
Fanlight
Fenestra
Porthole

9 letters:
Companion
Deadlight

Dream-hole
Loop-light
Mezzanine

10 letters:
Double-hung
Fenestella
Shed dormer

11 letters:
Lychnoscope
Oeil-de-boeuf

12 letters:
Quarterlight

14 letters:
Catherine-wheel

Winds

4 letters:
Berg
Bise
Bora
Bura
Föhn
Gale
Gust
Puna

5 letters:
Blore
Buran
Eurus
Foehn
Gibli
Noser
Notus
Trade
Zonda

6 letters:
Aquilo
Auster

Baguio
Boreas
Ghibli
Haboob
Kamsin
Levant
Samiel
Sciroc
Simoom
Simoon
Solano
Squall
Wester
Zephyr

7 letters:
Aeolian
Aquilon
Bluster
Chinook
Cyclone
Draught
Etesian
Gregale

Kamseen
Khamsin
Meltemi
Mistral
Monsoon
Nor'east
Norther
Pampero
Shimaal
Sirocco
Snifter
Snorter
Souther
Sumatra
Tornado
Twister
Typhoon

8 letters:
Argestes
Easterly
Favonian
Favonius
Levanter

Libeccio
Scirocco
Williwaw
Zephyrus

9 letters:
Anti-trade
Dust devil
Euraquilo
Harmattan
Hurricane
Hurricano

Libecchio
Nor'wester
Volturnus

10 letters:
Cape doctor
Euroclydon
Rip-snorter
Tourbillon
Tramontana
Tramontane
Whirlblast

Willy-willy

11 letters:
White squall

13 letters:
Northwesterly

Wines

WINE-PRODUCING AREAS

Area	Country
Ahr	Germany
Alentejo	Portugal
Alsace	France
Alto Adige *or* Südtirol	Italy
Anjou	France
Baden	Germany
Barossa Valley	Australia
Black Sea	Bulgaria
Bordeaux	France
Burgundy	France
California	U.S.A.
Central Valley	Chile
Chablis	France
Champagne	France
Chianti	Italy
Clare Valley	Australia
Coonawarra	Australia
Côte d'Or	France
Douro	Portugal
Finger Lakes	U.S.A.
Franken	Germany
Friuli	Italy
Gisborne	New Zealand
Goulburn Valley	Australia
Hawkes Bay	New Zealand
Hessiches Bergstrasse	Germany
Hunter Valley	Australia

Area	Country
Languedoc	France
Loire	France
Margaret River	Australia
Marlborough	New Zealand
Martinborough	New Zealand
McLaren Vale	Australia
Mendocino	U.S.A.
Mendoza	Argentina
Mittelrhein	Germany
Mornington Peninsula	Australia
Mosel-Saar-Ruwer	Germany
Nahe	Germany
Napa Valley	U.S.A.
Navarra	Spain
New York State	U.S.A.
Nistreana	Moldova
Oregon	U.S.A.
Padthaway	Australia
Penedès	Spain
Piedmont	Italy
Provence	France
Rheingau	Germany
Rheinhessen	Germany
Rheinpfalz	Germany
Rhône	France
Ribera del Duro	Spain
Rioja	Spain
Robertson	South Africa
Sicily	Italy
Sonoma	U.S.A.
Stellenbosch	South Africa
Târnave	Romania
Ticino	Switzerland
Tokaj-Hegyalja	Hungary
Touraine	France
Tuscany	Italy
Umbria	Italy
Valdepeñas	Spain
Veneto	Italy
Washington State	U.S.A.
Weinviertel	Austria
Württemberg	Germany
Yarra Valley	Australia

WINE TERMS

2 letters:
AC
NV
PX

3 letters:
AOC
DOC
Dry
IGT
LBV
QbA
QmP
Sec
TBA

4 letters:
Aszú
Brix
Brut
DOCG
Fino
Flor
Rosé
Sekt
VDQS

5 letters:
Baumé
Cream
Cuvée
Dolce
Maqui
Plonk
Secco
Sweet
Tinto

6 letters:
Malbec
Medium
Solera

Sur lie
Tannin

7 letters:
Amabile
Auslese
Crianza
Demi-sec
Eiswein
Malmsey
Oechsle
Oloroso
Organic
Passito
Recioto
Récolte
Reserva
Riserva
Semi-dry
Terroir
Trocken
Unoaked
Vin gris
Vintage
Weingut

8 letters:
Ausbruch
Botrytis
Grand cru
Kabinett
Moelleux
Mousseux
Noble rot
Prädikat
Prosecco
Ruby Port
Spätlese
Spumante
Varietal
Vigneron
Vignoble

Vinsanto

9 letters:
Abbocatto
Cru classé
Frizzante
Grosslage
Medium-dry
Pale cream
Pétillant
Puttonyos
Table wine
Tafelwein
Tawny Port
Vin de pays

10 letters:
Biodynamic
Botrytized
Einzellage
Garrafeira
Manzanilla
Non-vintage
Premier cru
Second wine
Sin crianza
Vin de table

11 letters:
Amontillado
Dessert wine
Gran reserva
Halbtrocken
Late harvest
Medium-sweet
Palo cortado
Weissherbst

12 letters:
Cru bourgeois
Disgorgement
Vino da tavola

13 letters:
Beerenauslese
Estate bottled
Fortified wine
Qualitätswein
Sparkling wine

14 letters:
Vendage tardive
Vieilles vignes
Vin doux naturel

15 letters:
Pourriture noble

16 letters:
Single Quinta Port

17 letters:
Erzeugerabfüllung

18 letters:
Late-Bottled Vintage
Méthode champenoise

20 letters:
Appellation contrôlée
Trockenbeerenauslese
Winzergenossenschaft

22 letters:
Late-Bottled Vintage Port
Malolactic fermentation

24 letters:
Qualitätswein mit Prädikat

28 letters:
Appellation d'origine contrôlée

30 letters:
Vin Délimité de Qualité Supérieure

33 letters:
Denominazione di origine controllata

34 letters:
Qualitätswein bestimmter Anbaugebiet

43 letters:
Denominazione di origine controllata e
    garantita

See also:
➤ **Drinks**

Winter sports

4 letters:
Luge

6 letters:
Skiing
Slalom
Super-G

7 letters:
Curling
Skating

8 letters:
Biathlon
Skeleton

9 letters:
Bobsleigh
Ice hockey
Skijoring

10 letters:
Ice dancing

Ice skating
Skibobbing
Ski jumping

11 letters:
Tobogganing
Skeleton bob

12 letters:
Alpine skiing
Nordic skiing

Snowboarding
Speed skating

13 letters:
Figure skating

14 letters:
Downhill racing

15 letters:
Freestyle skiing

Wonders of the ancient world

Colossus of Rhodes
Hanging Gardens of Babylon
Mausoleum of Halicarnassus
Pharos of Alexandria

Phidias' statue of Zeus at Olympia
Pyramids of Egypt
Temple of Artemis at Ephesus

Wood, types of

3 letters:
Ash
Box
Elm
Fir
Koa
Oak
Red
Yew

4 letters:
Beef
Cade
Eugh
Iron
Lana
Lime
Pear
Pine
Poon
Rata
Teak
Toon
Yang

5 letters:
Agila
Algum
Almug
Apple
Balsa
Beech
Birch
Cedar
Ebony

Hazel
Heben
Iroko
Jarul
Kauri
Kiaat
Kokra
Larch
Maple
Myall
Olive
Opepe
Plane
Ramin
Rowan
Sapan
Sassy
Stink
Sumac
Thorn
Tulip
Zante

6 letters:
Alerce
Bamboo
Bog oak
Brasil
Brazil
Canary
Carapa
Cherry
Citron
Fustet
Fustic

Fustoc
Gaboon
Gopher
Jarool
Jarrah
Lignum
Locust
Obeche
Orache
Orange
Padauk
Padouk
Poplar
Red fir
Red gum
Red oak
Sabele
Sabicu
Sandal
Sapele
Sappan
Sissoo
Sponge
Spruce
Sumach
Tupelo
Waboom
Walnut
Willow

7 letters:
Amboina
Amboyna
Assagai
Assegai

Barwood
Boxwood
Camwood
Cypress
Durmast
Gumtree
Gumwood
Hemlock
Hickory
Meranti
Mesquit
Nutwood
Palmyra
Pimento
Quassia
Sanders
Sapwood
Shawnee
Shittim
Wallaba

8 letters:
Agalloch
Alburnum
Basswood
Beefwood
Chestnut
Corkwood
Crabwood
Guaiacum
Guaiocum
Hardwood
Harewood
Hornbeam
Ironwood
Jelutong
Kingwood
Laburnum
Mahogany

Mesquite
Pulpwood
Pyengadu
Pyinkado
Red cedar
Rosewood
Sandarac
Sapucaia
Sasswood
Shagbark
Softwood
Southern
Sycamore
Tamarack
Tamarind

9 letters:
Briarwood
Butternut
Caliature
Campeachy
Coachwood
Eaglewood
Hackberry
Jacaranda
Lancewood
Partridge
Persimmon
Pitch pine
Primavera
Quebracho
Satinwood
Scots pine
Shellbark
Stinkwood
Torchwood
Tulipwood
White pine
Whitewood

Zebrawood

10 letters:
Afrormosia
Bulletwood
Calamander
Candlewood
Coromandel
Durmast oak
Fiddlewood
Greenheart
Hackmatack
Marblewood
Nettle-tree
Orangewood
Palisander
Paraná pine
Ribbonwood
Sandalwood
Sappanwood
Sneezewood
Spotted gum
Summerwood
White cedar
Yellowwood

11 letters:
Black walnut
Lignum-vitae
Sanderswood
Slippery elm

13 letters:
Partridge-wood
Savanna-wattle

15 letters:
African mahogany
Western red cedar

Works of literature and music

3 letters:		**4 letters:**	
Job	She	Aida	Howl
Kim		Emma	Lulu
			Maud

5 letters:
Brand
Comus
Faust
Fetes
Kipps
La Mer
Manon
Medea
Money
Norma
Scoop
Tosca

6 letters:
Alcina
Amelia
Becket
Ben Hur
Carmen
Egmont
En Saga
Ghosts
Hassan
Helena
Iberia
Jenufa
Lolita
Martha
Mignon
Nuages
Oberon
Otello
Rienzi
Rob Roy
Rokeby
Salome
Semele
Sylvia
Trilby
Utopia
Walden

7 letters:
Adonais

Aladdin
Amadeus
Babbitt
Beowulf
Camilla
Candida
Don Juan
Dracula
Electra
Erewhon
Euphues
Fidelio
Giselle
Ivanhoe
Lord Jim
Lycidas
Macbeth
Manfred
Marmion
Ma Vlast
Mazeppa
Messiah
Nabucco
Othello
Rebecca
Ring, The
Shirley
Sirenes
Tapiola
Ulysses
Volpone
Werther
Wozzeck

8 letters:
Adam Bede
Adam Zero
Alcestis
Anabasis
Antigone
Arabella
Bells, The
Born Free
Carnaval
Carnival

Catriona
Cenci, The
Coppelia
Cranford
Endymion
Everyman
Falstaff
Gloriana
Hay Fever
Hiawatha
Hudibras
Hyperion
Idiot, The
Idomeneo
Iliad, The
In the Wet
Iolanthe
Jane Eyre
King Lear
La Bohème
L'Allegro
Lavengro
Les Noces
Lucky Jim
Moby Dick
Parsifal
Patience
Peer Gynt
Pericles
Rasselas
Sea Drift
Swan Lake
Tom Jones
Trial, The
Turandot
Villette
Waves, The

9 letters:
Aeneid, The
Agamemnon
Beau Geste
Billy Budd
Brigg Fair
Capriccio

Cavalcade
Checkmate
Choephori
Coningsby
Cox and Box
Critic, The
Cymbeline
Dandy Dick
Don Carlos
Dr Zhivago
Dubliners
East Lynne
Egoist, The
Eumenides
Euryanthe
Hard Times
Hobbit, The
I, Claudius
I Puritani
Kidnapped
Kubla Khan
Les Biches
Lohengrin
Mein Kampf
Men at Arms
Mikado, The
No Highway
On Liberty
On the Road
Papillon
Prince, The
Pygmalion
Rigoletto
Rivals, The
Ruddigore
Saint Joan
Siegfried
Tom Sawyer
Venusberg
Vice Versa
Warden, The

10 letters:
All for Love
Animal Farm

Appalachia
Bleak House
Borough, The
Cannery Row
Casablanca
Cinderella
Citadel, The
Coriolanus
Das Kapital
Die Walküre
Don Quixote
Dunciad, The
Dynasts, The
Howards End
Il Seraglio
Inferno, The
In Memoriam
Intermezzo
I Pagliacci
Jamaica Inn
John Gilpin
Kenilworth
Kingdom, The
La Gioconda
La Traviata
Les Troyens
Lorna Doone
Lysistrata
My Fair Lady
My Son, My Son
Nelson Mass
Odyssey, The
Oedipus Rex
Only Way, The
On the Beach
Our Village
Pantagruel
Persuasion
Petroushka
Planets, The
Prelude, The
Prince Igor
Relapse, The
Rural Rides
Seagull, The

Seasons, The
Semiramide
Tannhauser
Tempest, The
Tono-Bungay
Trojans, The
Uncle Remus
Uncle Vanya
Vanity Fair
Vile Bodies
War Requiem
Water Music
Westward Ho

11 letters:
American, The
Apostles, The
As You Like It
Big Sleep, The
Black Beauty
Blue Bird, The
Boule de Suif
Cakes and Ale
Creation, The
Cruel Sea, The
Doll's House, A
Don Giovanni
Don Pasquale
Firebird, The
Georgics, The
Greenmantle
Harp Quartet
Hedda Gabler
High Windows
HMS Pinafore
Hymn of Jesus
I Like It Here
Il Penseroso
Il Trovatore
Jack and Jill
Journey's End
Judith Paris
Little Eyolf
Little Women
Loved One, The

Love for Love
Luisa Miller
Mary Poppins
Middlemarch
Minute Waltz
Mrs Dalloway
Mr Standfast
Newcomes, The
Now We Are Six
Noye's Fludde
Ode to Autumn
Oliver Twist
Peter Grimes
Peter Simple
Pippa Passes
Princess Ida
Princess, The
Puss in Boots
Redgauntlet
Rosmersholm
Salut d'Amour
Sea Symphony
Silas Marner
Sorcerer, The
South Riding
Stalky and Co
Stenka Razin
Tale of a Tub, A
Talisman, The
Tam o'Shanter
Trial by Jury
What Katy Did
Wild Duck, The
William Tell
Women in Love
Wrong Box, The

12 letters:
Alchemist, The
Anna Karenina
Antiquary, The
Apple Cart, The
Archduke Trio
Areopagitica
Ash Wednesday

Barnaby Rudge
Blithe Spirit
Boris Godunov
Brighton Rock
Buddenbrooks
Caretaker, The
Charley's Aunt
Childe Harold
Cosi fan Tutte
Danse Macabre
Decameron, The
Dogs of War, The
Dombey and Son
Epithalamion
Eugene Onegin
Excursion, The
Four Quartets
Frankenstein
Golden Ass, The
Grand Duke, The
Guy Mannering
Handley Cross
Julius Caesar
Karelia Suite
Khovanschina
Kinderscenen
Kreisleriana
La Sonnambula
Le Père Goriot
Les Huguenots
Les Sylphides
Linz Symphony
Little Dorrit
Locksley Hall
Lost Chord, The
Madame Bovary
Major Barbara
Manon Lescaut
Moll Flanders
Moonstone, The
Nixon in China
Old Mortality
Owen Wingrave
Paradise Lost
Piers Plowman

Porgy and Bess
Precious Bane
Private Lives
Prothalamion
Rheingold, Das
Rip Van Winkle
Rogue Herries
Romany Rye, The
Sardanapalus
Spring Sonata
Trout Quintet
Twelfth Night
Valkyries, The
Whisky Galore

13 letters:
Albert Herring
Almayer's Folly
Andrea Chenier
Angel Pavement
Arms and the Man
Art of Fugue, The
Bab Ballads, The
Black Arrow, The
Black Mischief
Blue Danube, The
Boris Godounov
Brave New World
Cancer Ward, The
Carmina Burana
Chanson de Nuit
Clock Symphony
Crown Imperial
Death in Venice
Der Freischutz
Dido and Aeneas
Doctor Faustus
Doctor Zhivago
Fame is the Spur
Finnegan's Wake
Ghost Train, The
Gondoliers, The
Harold in Italy
Hatter's Castle
Jungle Book, The

Just So Stories
La Cenerentola
L'Elisir d'Amore
Mabinogion, The
Magic Flute, The
Magistrate, The
Mansfield Park
Metamorphosen
Missa Solemnis
Nutcracker, The
Odessa File, The
Orb and Sceptre
Path to Rome, The
Peg Woffington
Private Angelo
Religio Medici
Schindler's Ark
Sketches by Boz
Songs of Travel
Sons and Lovers
Stamboul Train
Tarka the Otter
Timon of Athens
Under Milk Wood
Utopia Limited
Virginians, The
White Devil, The
Winnie-the-Pooh
Winslow Boy, The
Zuleika Dobson

14 letters:
Ambassadors, The
Andrea del Sarto
Battle Symphony
Bee's Wedding, The
Book of Snobs, The
Brief Encounter
Chanson de Matin
Choral Symphony
Cider with Rosie
Claudius the God
Coral Island, The
Country Wife, The
Crotchet Castle

Darkness at Noon
Decline and Fall
Deep Blue Sea, The
Die Zauberflöte
Ein Heldenleben
Emperor Quartet
Entertainer, The
Eroica Symphony
Forsyte Saga, The
Four Just Men, The
Gay Lord Quex, The
Golden Bough, The
Goodbye Mr Chips
Goodbye to Berlin
Great Gatsby, The
Handful of Dust, A
Horse's Mouth, The
Jude the Obscure
Kreutzer Sonata
Le Morte d'Arthur
London Symphony
Loom of Youth, The
Lord of the Flies
Lord of the Rings
Lost Horizon, The
Lyrical Ballads
Madam Butterfly
Man and Superman
Masterman Ready
National Velvet
Nightmare Abbey
Nine Tailors, The
Of Human Bondage
Our Man in Havana
Passage to India
Pickwick Papers
Plain Dealer, The
Prague Symphony
Quentin Durward
Rhapsody in Blue
Rights of Man, The
Robinson Crusoe
Roderick Random
Romeo and Juliet
Separate Tables

Shropshire Lad, A
Siegfried Idyll
Sinister Street
Sins of my Old Age
Slavonic Dances
Spring Symphony
Stones of Venice
Time Machine, The
Town Like Alice, A
Tragic Symphony
Treasure Island
Tristram Shandy
Uncle Tom's Cabin
Venus and Adonis
Vicar of Bray, The
Voices of Spring
Water Babies, The
Widowers' Houses
Winter's Tale, The
Woodlanders, The

15 letters:
African Queen, The
Allan Quatermain
Ariadne auf Naxos
Bartholomew Fair
Beggar's Opera, The
Child of our Time, A
Christmas Carol, A
Clarissa Harlowe
Dangerous Corner
Daphnis and Chloe
Divine Comedy, The
Emperor Concerto
Emperor Waltz, The
Essays of Elia, The
Faerie Queene, The
Fanny by Gaslight
Farewell to Arms, A
Frenchman's Creek
From the New World
Golden Legend, The
Gone with the Wind
Götterdämmerung
Haffner Symphony

Hansel and Gretel
Heartbreak House
Huckleberry Finn
Iceman Cometh, The
Invisible Man, The
Italian Symphony
Jupiter Symphony
Le Nozze di Figaro
Letters of Junius
Life for the Tsar, A
Look Back in Anger
Moonlight Sonata
Northanger Abbey
Old Wives Tale, The
Our Mutual Friend
Pearl Fishers, The
Peregrine Pickle
Peter and the Wolf
Puck of Pook's Hill
Put out More Flags

Raindrop Prelude
Rite of Spring, The
Rupert of Hentzau
Samson Agonistes
Samson and Delilah
Scholar Gipsy, The
Serenade to Music
Simon Boccanegra
Soldier's Tale, The
Tanglewood Tales
Three Men in a Boat
Titus Andronicus
To the Lighthouse
Waiting for Godot
Waldstein Sonata
Weir of Hermiston
Woman in White, The
Yarrow Revisited
You Never Can Tell

Worms

3 letters:
Bob
Dew
Fan
Lob

4 letters:
Tube

5 letters:
Acorn
Arrow
Fluke
Leech
Lytta
Piper

6 letters:
Caddis
Guinea
Nereid
Paddle

Palmer
Palolo
Ribbon
Scolex
Taenia
Teredo
Tongue

7 letters:
Ascarid
Bladder
Bristle
Catworm
Cestode
Cestoid
Filaria
Gordius
Hair-eel
Ragworm
Sabella
Serpula
Stomach

Tag-tail
Tenioid
Triclad
Tubifex
Vinegar

8 letters:
Bootlace
Capeworm
Caseworm
Clamworm
Filander
Gilt-tail
Hairworm
Hookworm
Inchworm
Nematoda
Nematode
Nemertea
Paste-eel
Seamouse
Strongyl

Toxocara
Trichina
Wheat-eel
Whipworm

9 letters:
Bilharzia
Brandling
Diplozoon
Heartworm
Horsehair
Lumbricus
Peripatus
Planarian
Strawworm

Strongyle
Tiger tail
Trematode
Wheatworm

10 letters:
Anguillula
Liver-fluke
Polychaete
Threadworm

11 letters:
Oligochaete
Schistosome
Scoleciform

Trichinella
Trichinosis
Turbellaria

12 letters:
Enteropneust
Hemichordata
Night-crawler
Sipunculacea

13 letters:
Platyhelminth
Sipunculoidea

Writers

3 letters:
APH *(Sir Alan Patrick Herbert)*
Eco, *Umberto*
Lee, *Sophia*
Paz, *Octavio*
Poe, *Edgar Allan*
RLS
Roy, *Arundhati*

4 letters:
Amis, *Martin (Louis)*
Asch, *Sholem*
Aymé, *Marcel*
Bede, *the Venerable*
Bolt, *Robert (Oxton)*
Buck, *Pearl*
Cary, *(Arthur) Joyce Lunel*
Cole, *Babette*
Dahl, *Roald*
Dyer, *Geoff*
Fine, *Ann*
Galt, *John*
Gide, *André (Paul Guillaume)*
Hogg, *James*
Hope (Hawkins), *Sir Anthony*
Hugo, *Victor (Marie)*
Hunt, *E(verette) Howard*

King, *Stephen (Edwin)*
Lamb, *Charles*
Lear, *Edward*
Loos, *Anita*
Loti, *Pierre*
Lyly, *John*
Mahy, *Margar*
Mann, *Thomas*
More, *Henry*
Nash, *(Frederic) Ogden*
Opie, *Iona*
Ovid
Pope, *Alexander*
Rudd, *Steele*
Saki *(Hector Hugh Munro)*
Sand, *George*
Shaw, *George Bernard*
Snow, *C(harles) P(ercy)*
Ward, *Mary Augusta*
West, *Nathanael*
Zola, *Émile*

5 letters:
Acton, *Sir Harold Mario*
Aesop
Albee, *Edward (Franklin)*
Alger, *Horatio*

Auden, *W(ystan) H(ugh)*
Ayres, *Noreen*
Banks, *Lynne Reid*
Bates, *H(erbert) E(rnest)*
Benet, *Stephen*
Blake, *William*
Blume, *Judy*
Burke, *Edmund*
Byatt, *A(ntonia) S(usan)*
Caine, *Sir (Thomas Henry) Hall*
Camus, *Albert*
Capek, *Karel*
Corvo, *Baron*
Crane, *Stephen*
Crump, *Barry*
Defoe, *Daniel*
Digby, *Anne*
Doyle, *Arthur Conan*
Dumas, *Alexandre*
Duras, *Marguerite*
Eliot, *T(homas) S(tearns)*
Ellis, *(Henry) Havelock*
Genet, *Jean*
Gogol, *Nikolai Vasilievich*
Gorky, *Maxim*
Gosse, *Sir Edmund (William)*
Greer, *Germaine*
Grimm, *Wilhelm Carl*
Hardy, *Thomas*
Henry, *O (William Sydney Porter)*
Henty, *G(eorge) A(lfred)*
Hesse, *Hermann*
Heyer, *Georgette*
Homer
Ibsen, *Henrik*
Innes, *(Ralph) Hammond*
James, *Henry*
Jones, *Diana Wynne*
Joyce, *James (Augustine Aloysius)*
Kafka, *Franz*
Kempe, *Margery*
Lewis, *C(live) S(taples)*
Lodge, *David (John)*
Lorca, *Federico García*
Marsh, *Ngaio*

Mason, *Alfred Edward Woodley*
Milne, *A(lan) A(lexander)*
Munro, *H(ector) H(ugh)*
Musil, *Robert*
Nashe, *Thomas*
Ouida
Paine, *Tom*
Pater, *Walter Horatio*
Paton, *Alan (Stewart)*
Pepys, *Samuel*
Pliny
Pound, *Ezra (Loomis)*
Powys, *John Cowper*
Reade, *Charles*
Renan, *(Joseph) Ernest*
Rilke, *Rainer Maria*
Sagan, *Françoise*
Scott, *Sir Walter*
Seuss, *Dr (Theodor Seuss Geisel)*
Shute, *Nevil*
Smith, *Dick King*
Spark, *Dame Muriel (Sarah)*
Stark, *Dame Freya Madeline*
Stead, *C(hristian) K(arison)*
Stein, *Gertrude*
Stowe, *Harriet Beecher*
Swift, *Jonathan*
Synge, *(Edmund) J(ohn) M(illington)*
Twain, *Mark (Samuel L(anghome) Clemens)*
Verne, *Jules*
Waugh, *Evelyn (Arthur St John)*
Wells, *H(erbert) G(eorge)*
Wilde, *Oscar (Fingal O'Flahertie Wills)*
Woolf, *(Adeline) Virginia*
Yates, *Dornford*
Yonge, *Charlotte Mary*

6 letters:
Alcott, *Louisa May*
Ambler, *Eric*
Arnold, *Matthew*
Artaud, *Antonin Marie Joseph*
Ascham, *Roger*
Asimov, *Isaac*

Austen, *Jane*
Balzac, *Honoré de*
Baring, *Maurice*
Barrie, *J(ames) M(atthew)*
Belloc, *(Joseph) Hilaire (Pierre)*
Bellow, *Saul*
Blyton, *Enid (Mary)*
Borges, *Jorge Luis*
Borrow, *George Henry*
Braine, *John (Gerard)*
Brecht, *Bertolt (Eugen Friedrich)*
Bronte, *Emily Jane (Ellis Bell)*
Buchan, *John*
Bunyan, *John*
Butler, *Samuel*
Capote, *Truman*
Cardus, *Neville*
Cather, *Willa*
Cicero, *Marcus Tullius*
Colfer, *Eoin*
Conrad, *Joseph*
Cooper, *James*
Cowper, *William*
Cronin, *A(rchibald) J(oseph)*
Daudet, *Alphonse*
De Sade, *Marquis*
Dryden, *John*
Duggan, *Maurice*
Durrel, *Laurence George*
Engels, *Friedrich*
Ennius
Fowles, *John (Robert)*
France, *Anatole*
Gibbon, *Edward*
Godwin, *William*
Goethe, *Johann Wolfgang von*
Graves, *Robert (Ranke)*
Greene, *(Henry) Graham*
Harris, *Joel Chandler*
Heller, *Joseph*
Hobbes, *Thomas*
Hughes, *Thomas*
Hutton, *R(ichard) H(olt)*
Huxley, *Aldous (Leonard)*
Inkpen, *Mike*

Irving, *Washington*
Jarvis, *Robin*
Jekyll, *Gertrude*
Jerome, *Jerome K(lapka)*
Jonson, *Ben(jamin)*
Le Fanu, *(Joseph) Sheridan*
London, *Jack*
Lucian
Lytton, *Bulwer*
Mailer, *Norman (Kingsley)*
Malory, *Thomas*
Mannin, *Ethel*
Miller, *Henry (Valentine)*
Milton, *John*
Morgan, *Edwin (George)*
Murphy, *Jill*
Nerval, *Gérard de*
Nesbit, *E(dith)*
Onions, *Charles Talbut*
Orwell, *George*
Parker, *Dorothy*
Powell, *Anthony*
Proust, *Marcel*
Racine, *Jean (Baptiste)*
Runyon, *Damon*
Ruskin, *John*
Sachar, *Louis*
Sapper *(H(erman) C(yril) McNeile)*
Sartre, *Jean-Paul*
Sayers, *Dorothy L(eigh)*
Sewell, *Anna*
Singer, *Isaac Bashevis*
Smiles, *Samuel*
Sontag, *Susan*
Spring, *Howard*
Steele, *Richard*
Sterne, *Laurence*
Storey, *David (Malcolm)*
Tagore, *Rabindranath*
Thiele, *Colin*
Thomas, *Dylan (Marlais)*
Updike, *John (Hoyer)*
Virgil
Walker, *Alice*
Walton, *Izaac*

Wilder, *Laura Ingalls*
Wilson, *Jacqueline*

7 letters:
Addison, *Joseph*
Aldrich, *Thomas Bailey*
Allston, *Washington*
Angelou, *Maya*
Aretino, *Pietro*
Baldwin, *James*
Beckett, *Samuel (Barclay)*
Bennett, *(Enoch) Arnold*
Bentley, *Edmund Clerihew*
Boileau, *Nicholas (Despréaux)*
Boswell, *James*
Burgess, *Anthony*
Carlyle, *Thomas*
Carroll, *Lewis (Charles Lutwidge Dodgson)*
Chaucer, *Geoffrey*
Chekhov, *Anton Pavlovich*
Claudel, *Paul*
Cobbett, *William*
Coetzee, *J(ohn) M(axwell)*
Colette, *(Sidonie-Gabrielle)*
Collins, *Wilkie (William)*
Coppard, *A(lfred) E(dgar)*
Corelli, *Marie*
Cranmer, *Thomas*
Cushman, *Karen*
Deeping, *(George) Warwick*
Dickens, *Charles (John Huffam)*
Dineson, *Isak*
Douglas, *Norman*
Drabble, *Margaret*
Dreiser, *Theodore Herman Albert*
Duhamel, *Georges*
Durrell, *Gerald (Malcolm)*
Emerson, *Ralph Waldo*
Erasmus, *Desiderius*
Fénelon, *François de Salignac de la Mothe*
Fleming, *Ian*
Forster, *Margaret*
Gardner, *Eric*

Gaskell, *Elizabeth*
Gissing, *George (Robert)*
Golding, *Sir William (Gerald)*
Grahame, *Kenneth*
Haggard, *Sir H(enry) Rider*
Hazlitt, *William*
Herbert, *George*
Herriot, *James*
Hichens, *Robert Smythe*
Johnson, *Samuel*
Kerouac, *Jack*
Kipling, *(Joseph) Rudyard*
Lardner, *Ring(gold Wilmer)*
Leacock, *Stephen*
Le Carre, *John*
Lessing, *Doris*
Malamud, *Bernard*
Marryat, *(Captain) Frederick*
Maugham, *W(illiam) Somerset*
Mauriac, *François*
Mérimée, *Prosper*
Mitford, *Jessica Lucy*
Moravia, *Alberto*
Murdoch, *Dame (Jean) Iris*
Nabokov, *Vladimir (Vladimirovich)*
Naipaul, *Sir V(idiadhar) S(urajprasad)*
Narayan, *Jayaprakesh*
Peacock, *Thomas Love*
Pullman, *Philip*
Pushkin, *Aleksander Sergeyevich*
Ransome, *Arthur Mitchell*
Rendell, *Ruth*
Richter, *Johann*
Riddell, *Chris*
Rostand, *Edmond*
Rowling, *J(oanne) K(athleen)*
Saroyan, *William*
Sassoon, *Siegfried (Louvain)*
Shelley, *Mary (Wollstonecraft)*
Simenon, *Georges (Joseph Christian)*
Sitwell, *Sir (Francis) Osbert*
Spender, *Stephen*
Stephen, *Leslie*
Stewart, *Paul*
Surtees, *Robert Smith*

Tennant, *Kylie*
Terence
Theroux, *Paul*
Thoreau, *Henry David*
Tolkien, *J(ohn) R(onald) R(euel)*
Tolstoy, *Count Leo (Nikolayevich)*
Travers, *Ben(jamin)*
Ustinov, *Peter*
Wallace, *(Richard Horatio) Edgar*
Walpole, *Sir Hugh Seymour*
Wharton, *Edith (Newbold)*
Whitman, *Walt(er)*

8 letters:
Andersen, *Hans Christian*
Beaumont, *Sir John*
Beerbohm, *Max*
Brittain, *Vera*
Brookner, *Anita*
Browning, *Robert*
Caldwell, *Erskine*
Chandler, *Raymond*
Childers, *(Robert) Erskine*
Christie, *Dame Agatha (Mary Clarissa)*
Constant, *Benjamin*
Coolidge, *Susan*
Crompton, *Richmal*
Deighton, *Len*
De la Mare, *Walter (John)*
Disraeli, *Benjamin*
Donleavy, *Brian*
Faulkner, *William*
Fielding, *Henry*
Flaubert, *Gustave*
Forester, *C(ecil) S(cott)*
Goncourt, *Jules*
Gordimer, *Nadine*
Ishiguro, *Kazuo*
Kingsley, *Mary St Leger*
Koestler, *Arthur*
Lawrence, *T(homas) E(dward)*
Mannheim, *Baron Carl Gustav Emil*
McCarthy, *Mary*
Melville, *Herman*
Meredith, *George*

Mitchell, *Margaret*
Morpurgo, *Michael*
Ondaatje, *Michael*
Perrault, *Charles*
Plutarch
Rabelais, *François*
Rattigan, *Sir Terence (Mervyn)*
Remarque, *Erich Maria*
Rousseau, *Jean-Jacques*
Salinger, *J(erome) D(avid)*
Schiller, *(Johann Christoph) Friedrich von*
Shadbolt, *Maurice*
Sheridan, *Richard*
Smollett, *Tobias George*
Spillane, *Mickey*
Stendhal *(Marie-Henri Beyle)*
Strachey, *Lytton*
Taffrail *(Henry Taprell Dorling)*
Traherne, *Thomas*
Trollope, *Anthony*
Trollope, *Joanna*
Turgenev, *Ivan Sergeyevich*
Voltaire *(François Marie Arouet)*
Vonnegut, *Kurt*
Williams, *Tennessee*

9 letters:
Aeschylus
Ainsworth, *William Harrison*
Aldington, *Richard*
Allingham, *Margery*
Blackmore, *R(ichard) D(oddridge)*
Boccaccio, *Giovanni*
Brent-Dyer, *Elinor M(ary)*
Burroughs, *Edgar Rice*
Charteris, *Leslie*
Courtenay, *Bryce*
De Quincey, *Thomas*
Dos Passos, *John Roderigo*
Du Maurier, *Dame Daphne*
Edgeworth, *Maria*
Goldsmith, *Oliver*
Hawthorne, *Nathaniel*
Hemingway, *Ernest (Millar)*

Isherwood, *Christopher (William Bradshaw)*
Jefferson, *Thomas*
Lermontov, *Mikhail Yurievich*
Linklater, *Eric*
Mackenzie, *Sir (Edward Montague) Compton*
Madariaga, *Salvador de*
Mansfield, *Katherine*
McCullers, *Carson*
O'Flaherty, *Liam*
Oppenheim, *Edward Phillips*
Pasternak, *Boris Leonidovich*
Pratchett, *Terry*
Priestley, *J(ohn) B(oynton)*
Santayana, *George*
Sholokhov, *Mikhail Aleksandrovich*
Steinbeck, *John (Ernest)*
Stevenson, *Robert Louis (Balfour)*
Thackeray, *William Makepeace*
Wodehouse, *Sir P(elham) G(renville)*

10 letters:
Ballantyne, *R(obert) M(ichael)*
Chesterton, *G(ilbert) K(eith)*
Dostoevsky, *Fyodor Mikhailovich*
Fitzgerald, *F(rancis) Scott (Key)*
Galsworthy, *John*
Richardson, *H(enry) H(andel)*

11 letters:
De Cervantes (Saavedra), *Miguel*
De Montaigne, *Michel Eyquem*
Dostoyevsky, *Fyodor*
Machiavelli, *Niccolò*
Maeterlinck, *Count Maurice*
Shakespeare, *William*
Streatfield, *Noel*

12 letters:
Aristophanes
Chesterfield, *Lord*
De Mandeville, *Sir Jehan* (or *John*)
De Maupassant, *(Henri René Albert) Guy*
Robbe-Grillet, *Alain*
Saint-Exupery, *Antoine*
Solzhenitsyn, *Alexander Isayevich*

13 letters:
Sackville-West, *Vita (Victoria Mary)*

14 letters:
Compton-Burnett, *Ivy*
Wollstonecraft, *Mary*

15 letters:
De Chateaubriand, *Vicomte (François René)*

See also:
➤ **Diarists**   ➤ **Dramatists**   ➤ **Novelists**   ➤ **Poets**
➤ **Shakespeare**

Yy

Yellow, shades of

4 letters:
Buff
Ecru
Gold

5 letters:
Amber
Beige
Lemon
Maize
Ochre
Straw
Topaz

6 letters:
Almond
Bisque
Bistre
Citron
Golden
Sulfur

7 letters:
Gamboge
Jasmine

Mustard
Nankeen
Oatmeal
Old gold
Saffron
Sulphur
Tea rose

8 letters:
Cinnamon
Daffodil
Eau de nil
Eggshell
Magnolia
Primrose

9 letters:
Butternut
Champagne

12 letters:
Canary yellow

13 letters:
Tortoiseshell

Zz

Zodiac

Name	Symbol	Name	Symbol
Aquarius	the Water Carrier	Libra	the Scales
Aries	the Ram	Pisces	the Fishes
Cancer	the Crab	Sagittarius	the Archer
Capricorn	the Goat	Scorpio	the Scorpion
Gemini	the Twins	Taurus	the Bull
Leo	the Lion	Virgo	the Virgin

CHINESE ANIMAL YEARS

Chinese	English	Years				
Shu	Rat	1960	1972	1984	1996	2008
Niu	Ox	1961	1973	1985	1997	2009
Hu	Tiger	1962	1974	1986	1998	2010
Tu	Hare	1963	1975	1987	1999	2011
Long	Dragon	1964	1976	1988	2000	2012
She	Serpent	1965	1977	1989	2001	2013
Ma	Horse	1966	1978	1990	2002	2014
Yang	Sheep	1967	1979	1991	2003	2015
Hou	Monkey	1968	1980	1992	2004	2016
Ji	Cock	1969	1981	1993	2005	2017
Gou	Dog	1970	1982	1994	2006	2018
Zhu	Boar	1971	1983	1995	2007	2019

Zoology

BRANCHES OF ZOOLOGY

3 letters:
Shu

7 letters:
Zootomy

8 letters:
Cetology
Ethology

Zoometry

9 letters:
Mammalogy
Ophiology
Zoography

10 letters:
Entomology

Malacology

11 letters:
Arachnology
Herpetology
Ichthyology
Myrmecology
Ornithology
Primatology

12 letters:
Protozoology
Zoogeography

13 letters:
Palaeozoology

14 letters:
Archaeozoology

ZOOLOGY TERMS

3 letters:
Fin

4 letters:
Gill
Prey
Pupa

5 letters:
Biped
Imago
Larva
Spawn
Spine

6 letters:
Caudal
Cocoon
Coelom
Colony
Dorsal

Raptor
Rodent
Sucker
Thorax

7 letters:
Abdomen
Antenna
Bivalve
Decapod
Primate
Reptile
Segment
Ventral

8 letters:
Anterior
Arachnid
Chordate
Dipteran
Edentate

Omnivore
Pectoral
Placenta
Predator
Ruminant
Skeleton

9 letters:
Amphibian
Appendage
Arthropod
Carnivore
Chrysalis
Gastropod
Herbivore
Marsupial
Migration
Passerine
Posterior
Protozoan
Quadruped

10 letters:
Crustacean
Echinoderm
Gasteropod
Parenchyma
Vertebrate

11 letters:
Aestivation
Hibernation
Insectivore

12 letters:
Coelenterate
Invertebrate
Lepidopteran

13 letters:
Metamorphosis

ZOOLOGISTS

5 letters:
Elton, *Charles Sutherland*

6 letters:
Cuvier, *Georges*
Darwin, *Charles (Robert)*
Kinsey, *Alfred Charles*
Lorenz, *Konrad Zacharias*
Morgan, *Thomas Hunt*

7 letters:
Dawkins, *Richard*
Driesch, *Hans Adolf Eduard*
Durrell, *Gerald (Malcolm)*

Lamarck, *Jean Baptiste Pierre Antoine De Monet*
Medawar, *Peter Brian*
Wallace, *Alfred Russel*

8 letters:
Kammerer, *Paul*

9 letters:
Lankester, *Edwin Ray*
Tinbergen, *Nikolaas*
Von Frisch, *Karl*
Zuckerman, *Solly*